THE AUTOMOBILE UNDER THE BLUE EAGLE

THE AUTOMOBILE UNDER THE BLUE EAGLE

*Labor, Management, and the
Automobile Manufacturing Code*

BY SIDNEY FINE

Ann Arbor : The University of Michigan Press

To Jean

PREFACE

Although President Franklin D. Roosevelt stated in approving the National Industrial Recovery Act that history would probably record the measure as "the most important and far-reaching legislation ever enacted by the American Congress," historians have actually paid relatively little attention to the impact of the law on the nation's industries. The best over-all analysis of the statute remains Leverett S. Lyon *et al., The National Recovery Administration* (Washington, 1935), which was completed even before the N.I.R.A. was declared unconstitutional by the United States Supreme Court; and despite the availability of an abundance of documentary material, the major N.R.A. codes remain largely unstudied.

The code of the automobile manufacturing industry, although the most important of the automotive codes, was only one of 557 basic codes approved during the N.R.A. era; but because of the vital relationship of automobile manufacturing to the process of economic recovery, no other code was so favored by President Roosevelt or Administrator for Industrial Recovery General Hugh S. Johnson or received so much of their attention. The history of the code was obviously unique in many respects, but it nevertheless reveals in microcosm something of the nature of the N.I.R.A. experiment as a whole and suggests how widespread were the effects of this overly ambitious effort to codify the industries of the nation.

Since the automobile code was essentially a labor code and was distinguished by the absence among its provisions of any trade practice regulations, the history of the code is largely a history of labor-management relations in the automobile industry. An account of the drafting and the implementation of the code would not be complete, however, were not some consideration given to the relationship of the automobile manufacturers to the automotive parts and equipment manufacturing industry, the special tool, die, and machine shop industry, the wholesale automotive trade, and the automobile dealers.

It is a pleasure to acknowledge here the assistance that I received while working on this book. My research was facilitated by a Guggenheim Fellowship and by two Summer Faculty Fellowships and several research grants provided by the Horace H. Rackham School of Graduate Studies of The University of Michigan. Professor Harold M. Levinson of the department of economics of The University of Michigan and Professor Dallas L. Jones of the School of Business Administration of The University of Michigan both gave the entire manuscript a detailed reading and made many suggestions for its improvement. My research in the extensive manuscript collections on which this study is so largely based was aided and made more pleasurable by Meyer H. Fishbein, Morris Rieger, Walter Weinstein, Jerome Finster, and Joseph D. Howerton of the National Archives and Records Service; Herman Kahn, formerly the director of the Franklin D. Roosevelt Library, and his staff; F. Clever Bald, Robert M. Warner, Richard M. Doolen, Ruth B. Bordin, and Ida C. Brown of the Michigan Historical Collections; Philip P. Mason and Stanley D. Solvick of the Wayne State University Archives; Henry E. Edmunds, Archivist of the Ford Motor Company; E. Logan Kimmel, Chief, General Files, A.F. of L. and C.I.O.; Lawrence E. Eady and Lester J. McGee of the Federal Mediation and Conciliation Service; and David C. Mearns, Chief, Manuscripts Division, Library of Congress, and his staff. Oscar P. Pearson, Mrs. Edwin A. Wieck, Anthony Lucheck, Richard Frankensteen, Tracy M. Doll, and Stephen M. DuBrul kindly supplied me with documentary material in their possession. The persons who graciously permitted me to interview them and who responded to my letters requesting information are listed in the bibliography. My wife, Jean Fine, was so intimately associated with my work on the book from beginning to end that it is difficult to express the extent of my obligation to her.

The editors of the *Mississippi Valley Historical Review,* the *Journal of Economic History,* the *Business History Review,* the *Industrial and Labor Relations Review,* the *Ohio Historical Quarterly, Michigan History,* the *Michigan Alumnus Quarterly,* and *Current History* have permitted me to use material from my articles in these journals. I have been granted permission by the Viking Press to quote from Clayton W. Fountain, *Union Guy* (New York, 1949).

February 18, 1963   Sidney Fine

CONTENTS

ABBREVIATIONS

A.F. of L.	American Federation of Labor
A.I.A.	American Industrial Association
A.A.W.A.	Associated Automobile Workers of America
A.L.A.M.	Association of Licensed Automobile Manufacturers
A.W.U.	Auto Workers Union
A.L.B.	Automobile Labor Board
A.M.A.	Automobile Manufacturers Association
A.I.W.A.	Automotive Industrial Workers' Association
A.P.E.M.	Automotive Parts and Equipment Manufacturers, Inc.
A.T. and D.M.A.	Automotive Tool and Die Manufacturers Association
B.L.S.	Bureau of Labor Statistics
C.W.W.	Carriage and Wagon Workers' International Union
C.W.A.W.	Carriage, Wagon and Automobile Workers' International Union
C.L.U.	Central Labor Union
C.I.O.	Committee for Industrial Organization
C.A.B.	Consumers' Advisory Board
D.F. of L.	Detroit Federation of Labor
E.V.C.	Electric Vehicle Company
F.L.U.	Federal Labor Union
F.T.C.	Federal Trade Commission
F.A.W. of A.	Federated Automobile Workers of America
F.A.A.	Federated Automotive Association
F.A.W.	Federation of Automotive Workers
G.M.	General Motors Corporation
I.W.A.	Independent Workers Association
I.A.B.	Industrial Advisory Board
I.W.W.	Industrial Workers of the World
I.A.M.	International Association of Machinists
L.A.B.	Labor Advisory Board
M.E.S.A.	Mechanics Educational Society of America
N.A.M.	National Association of Manufacturers
N.A.C.C.	National Automobile Chamber of Commerce
N.A.D.A.	National Automobile Dealers' Association
N.I.R.A.	National Industrial Recovery Act
N.I.R.B.	National Industrial Recovery Board
N.L.B.	National Labor Board
N.L.R.B.	National Labor Relations Board
N.R.A.	National Recovery Administration
P.R.A.	President's Reemployment Agreement
P.R.	Public Resolution
R.L.B.	Regional Labor Board
S.D.E.	Society of Designing Engineers
T.U.U.L.	Trade Union Unity League
U.A.A.V.W.	United Automobile, Aircraft and Vehicle Workers of America
U.A.W.	United Automobile Workers

I

BEFORE THE BLUE EAGLE

I

IN NOVEMBER 1895, at a time when only four automobiles were registered in the United States, the editors of the newly founded *Horseless Age* presciently observed that "those who have taken the pains to search beneath the surface for the great tendencies of the age see what a giant industry is struggling into being there." By the end of the 1920's the automobile industry, which had not even been listed in the census of 1900, was the leading manufacturing industry in the United States in terms of the value of its product; and in the last year of prosperity before the great depression an industry that in 1900 had turned out 4192 passenger cars with a wholesale value of $4,899,000 produced 5,337,087 passenger cars, motor trucks, and buses with a wholesale value of $3,413,148,000. The combined motor vehicle industries (motor vehicle manufacturing and motor vehicle bodies and parts) employed an average of 12,049 wage earners in 1904, but this number had increased to an average of 447,448 in 1929. Of this total, 226,116 were employed in the motor vehicle branch of the industry and 221,332 in the bodies and parts branch.[1]

During the first decade of the twentieth century automobile manufacturing, which, as John B. Rae has pointed out, had previously been primarily "a sideline to other industrial operations," emerged as an independent industry. The automobile manufacturers of that era were largely engaged in the assembling of parts into finished vehicles. They purchased their parts on thirty to ninety days' credit from the established foundries and machine shops, some of which soon began to specialize in the production of automobile parts, and sold their completed vehicles to franchised distributors and dealers for cash. The fabrication of parts was already a highly developed business during the early days of the automobile industry, and the parts manufacturer was therefore able to extend credit to the capital-poor vehicle assembler. At the same time, the rapid growth of the industry and the increasing demand for automobiles made the business prospects for the automobile distributor and dealer sufficiently attractive to reduce their resistance to the idea of paying cash for the vehicles that they received.[2]

In the second and third decades of the twentieth century the automobile manufacturers were able to extend the market for their product to the masses. The application of the technique of mass production to the manufacture of automobiles and the subsequent reduction in the price of passenger cars, the invention of the self-starter, the advent of the closed car, and the use of the installment plan in the purchase of automobiles all helped to make the motor car a possession of "the great multitude"[3] rather than a luxury vehicle of the rich. Automobile production continued to mount after World War I and the recession of 1920–21, but the competition among the automobile manufacturers in the 1920's was increasingly for the replacement market, and the used car for the first time became a major problem for the industry and particularly for the automobile dealer.[4]

The automobile industry on the eve of the great depression was dominated by three great producers, the Ford Motor Company, the General Motors Corporation, and Chrysler Corporation. The first of the Big Three to gain prominence and still the leading producer of motor vehicles in 1929 was the Ford Motor Company. Capitalized originally at a nominal figure of $150,000 but with only $28,000 of this sum in the form of cash, the company, without drawing on any outside source for additional funds, had become one of the nation's greatest business concerns, with total assets in 1929 of $925,612,419.[5]

It was the Ford Motor Company which in introducing the moving assembly line in its Highland Park plant in 1913 first realized the full potentialities of the system of mass production in the manufacture of automobiles and found the key to large-volume, low-cost production. Between 1908 and May 1927, when their manufacture was discontinued, more than fifteen million Model T's rolled off the Ford assembly lines and were offered to the public at prices which moved steadily downward.[6] The famous Tin Lizzie enabled Ford to hold first place among all passenger car producers from 1911 to 1926, but the increasing concern of an affluent society with the style and comfort of its passenger vehicles, and the competition provided the Model T by used cars of the more expensive lines led Ford to a reluctant and belated recognition that "the first log cabin of the Motor Age," to use Charles Merz's phrase, would have to be replaced by a more stylish model. The new Model A made its appearance late in 1927, and with it Ford in 1929 once again forged ahead of his competitors.[7]

Ford's principal rival from the time it was formed in 1908 by William C. Durant was the General Motors Company. Whereas the Ford Motor Company exemplified the process of unitary growth, General Motors grew initially by merger. The Buick was the principal passenger car of General Motors when the company was formed, but to it were added within the next two years the Oldsmobile, the Cadillac, and the Oakland, several other makes soon to be forgotten, and a variety of parts plants. Durant, however, overreached himself in the process of putting together his first automobile empire, and he was forced to withdraw from active management of the concern in 1910 when Eastern banking interests had to step in to rescue the company from insolvency.

Durant's career with General Motors had not, however, come to an end. Following his departure from the company, he built up the Chevrolet Motor Company and used its stock to purchase General Motors stock and to gain control of the firm once again in 1916. Two years later the General Motors Corporation (G.M.) was formed, and it took over the Chevrolet Motor Company, which owned the old General Motors Company. Still committed to expansion, Durant was soon to add the Fisher Body Company to the G.M. complex and was to take the corporation into the refrigerator and tractor business as well. Durant, however, ran into serious difficulties in the stock market in 1920, and to avoid financial ruin was forced to sell his 2,500,000 shares of G.M. stock to the DuPont Company and to resign his position as G.M. president.[8] G.M. was the leading producer of passenger vehicles in 1909 and 1910 and in 1927 and 1928. It recaptured first place from Ford in 1931 and has maintained its position of leadership in the industry ever since.[9]

The third of the Big Three to make its appearance in the automotive field was the Chrysler Corporation, which was formed in 1925 with the Chrysler car as its principal product. The DeSoto and the Plymouth were added to the corporation's line in 1928, and in the same year Chrysler bought out the Dodge Brothers Manufacturing Company. In 1928 Chrysler Corporation accounted for 10.6 per cent of new passenger car and truck registrations in the United States. By 1932 it had increased this figure to 15.7 per cent.[10]

Although the automobile manufacturing industry was dominated by three great companies on the eve of the great depression, it had once been an industry of many small firms and of easy entry. As assemblers who bought on credit and sold for cash, the early automobile manufacturers had been able to launch their concerns with a minimum of paid-in capital. The successful among them grew by reinvesting the profits made possible by the increasing demand for their product. The economies to be realized from volume production, however, and the increasing necessity of having a diversified product line, an adequate dealer organization, and the capital resources for integration, research, and development, to withstand financial losses and to finance the construction of new annual models all militated against the success of most of the concerns which hopefully entered the industry.[11]   Of the 181 companies which were actually engaged in the manufacture of passenger cars at some time between 1903 and 1926, only forty-four were still in business in the latter year, and this number had been still further reduced to fifteen by 1929. In that year only 24.2 per cent of new passenger car registrations were accounted for by firms other than the Big Three.   Among these so-called independent producers, the Hudson Motor Car Company and the Nash Motors Company were the most important concerns.[12]

Not only was the automobile industry concentrated in the hands of a few producers, but it was also concentrated geographically in the Detroit industrial area and the state of Michigan.   Of the 447,-448 wage earners in the combined motor vehicle industries in 1929, approximately 48 per cent were located in Michigan, and approximately 73 per cent of these Michigan workers were to be found in the Detroit industrial area.   About 13 per cent of the automobile workers were located in Ohio, 7 per cent in Indiana, 6.7 per cent in New York, 5 per cent in Wisconsin, and 4.3 per cent in Pennsylvania. Michigan accounted for about 40 per cent of the value of the motor vehicles produced in 1929 and about 48 per cent of the value of automobile bodies and parts. The residence in Michigan of some of the important pioneers in the development of automobile manufacturing appears to have been the major initial reason for the state's ascendancy in the industry.[13]

The increasing reliance of the automobile manufacturers on new annual models as a means of stimulating the demand for their passenger cars tended to make the irregularity of production and employment one of the distinguishing characteristics of the industry. The automobile manufacturers found that a "model changeover period" was the most effective method of installing the new tools and dies and integrating the various parts for a new model and of securing volume production for the remainder of the model year. The first step in the bringing out of a new model was the approval of its design and styling.   The manufacturing division of the company then had to arrange for the tools and dies, patterns, and other equipment required for the vehicle. The production of the new model would proceed slowly at first so that machine operations could be perfected and the production employees could become accustomed to their work. Before the model was offered for sale sufficient units would have to be produced to supply the dealers with an adequate number of vehicles to display and to begin making deliveries to the public. From that point forward production was scheduled in accordance with sales forecasts and the demand for the product.

As the time approached for the introduction of a new model, additional production of the old model would have to be carefully scheduled in an effort to turn out no more cars than could be sold before the appearance of the new design. When the line was stopped at the end of the model run, the bulk of the production force would be laid off, new machinery would be installed, new dies moved into place, and the assembly line rearranged for the production of the new model. The drop in sales just before a new model was introduced and the stimulus to sales which followed its appearance, coupled with the tendency of consumers in the populous northern states to purchase their cars in the spring and early summer rather than in the fall and winter, further contributed to the irregularity of automobile sales and automobile production.[14] More regular production could have been obtained had the automobile manufacturers or their distributors and dealers been able to store a significant number of vehicles in anticipation of sales, but the automobile, unfortunately, is not a commodity that can be easily and economically stored.

As more and more automobile manufacturers sought to have their new models ready to display at the annual New York and Chicago automobile shows in January, production and sales tended to be concentrated in the first six months of the year, and particularly during the spring, with the period of sluggish production and layoffs coming during the last quarter of the year. The production of cars and trucks during the second quarter of the year from 1926 to 1929 constituted about 32 per cent of total production and was double the level of production during the last quarter of the year. The Bureau of Labor Statistics reported in February 1929 that not only did the automobile industry as a whole make "a very bad showing" in so far as stability of employment was concerned but that "irregularity and uncertainty of employment conditions" were characteristic of all the plants covered in the Bureau's study of the industry. Average employment per month between 1923 and 1928 in plants manufacturing automobiles, trucks, buses, bodies, or "some substantial part" of an automobile did not exceed 83.3 per cent of the maximum monthly employment for the year and in 1924 was only 78.7 per cent of the maximum monthly employment.[15]

The automobile industry was comprised not only of manufacturers and assemblers of motor vehicles of various types but also of concerns that produced automotive parts, tools and dies, and bodies. According to an estimate made in 1935 in a federal government report on the industry, about 50 to 60 per cent of the labor on automobiles at that time was accounted for by labor on parts.[16] The first automobile parts makers specialized in the production of original equipment, but the widespread increase in the use of motor vehicles created an additional demand for replacement parts and automobile accessories with the result that some parts manufacturers began to specialize in this branch of the parts business.

Although the early automobile manufacturers were actually little more than assemblers of motor vehicles, the larger firms in the industry soon began to fabricate some of their own parts. As this practice became more common, the parts manufacturer had to be concerned not only about the competition of other parts manufacturers but also the competition of the car manufacturers as well. He could remain in business only if he could turn out his parts more efficiently and more economically than they could be fabricated in the main plants. This placed the independent parts manufacturer, and similarly the job shops manufacturing tools and dies and, to a much lesser degree, the independent body manufacturer, in a highly precarious position. Although there were numerous parts manufacturers—the census of manufacturers listed 1188 separate parts establishments in 1929—they competed for the trade of a few large customers who could manufacture the same parts themselves or purchase them from their own subsidiaries or from concerns that were closely tied to them through ownership or contractual obligations. It is not surprising, therefore, that wage rates in the parts plants tended to be lower than the wages paid in the main plants. The failure of the automobile manufacturer to specify a definite quantity when he first placed a purchase order with a parts manufacturer and the restriction of purchase commitments to a short-term basis further complicated the production problems of the parts maker and helped to make his employment curve as irregular as that of the automobile manufacturer.[17]

Although the automobile manufacturers originally sold their product through factory branches and a variety of other agencies, the practice of the trade, increasingly, was to entrust the retail sale of automobiles to independent dealers.[18] Because, as already noted, a dealership in the years when the industry was expanding represented a good business opportunity—the problem of the industry at the outset was production and not sales—franchises were "awarded on terms favorable to the manufacturers." Its provisions determined by the manufacturer alone, the dealer franchise could be terminated by the factory without notice for certain specified causes and without indicated cause provided fifteen to thirty days' notice was given. The Ford Motor Company reserved the right to terminate its dealer franchises at any time without the necessity of showing cause.

The manufacturers initially exercised only a limited degree of supervision over their dealers, but the greater concern with the distribution of passenger cars in the 1920's led to increasing factory control of the dealer's business. The manufacturer generally forbade the dealer to handle competing makes. He largely determined the number of cars the dealer was to sell and the retail price at which he was to sell them, the way he was to keep his books, the appearance of his place of business, the manner in which he was to service the cars he was franchised to sell, and, in some instances, the nature of his advertising. He placed rigid restrictions on dealer use of parts and accessories which were neither manufactured nor distributed by the factory, designated the minimum stock of "genuine parts" the dealer was to maintain, and set the retail price at which these parts were to be sold. "In no other industry," Ralph Epstein found in 1928, "does the tendency towards dealer control . . . appear to have developed quite so extensively as in automobiles." The manufacturer, *Fortune* declared in 1931, "*sells* the car. His dealer, free and independent capitalist though he may be, has been reduced to taking orders and making repairs." [19]

Whatever the automobile manufacturer may have thought about his relationship to his parts suppliers and his dealers, he was convinced, to paraphrase Henry Ford, that he was doing all that he could for his workers.[20] As evidence of this, he was most likely to point to the high hourly wages that he paid his employees. The high-wage era in the industry was initiated by Henry Ford, who startled the nation when he announced on January 5, 1914, that the Ford Motor Company would "inaugurate the greatest revolution in the matter of rewards for its workers ever known to the industrial world" by paying its factory employees a basic wage of $5 for an eight-hour day, almost double the minimum then prevailing in the industry for common labor.[21] During the next few years Ford's competitors raised the wages in their plants to the Ford level, and the industry became famous for its high hourly wages.

Throughout the 1920's the automobile industry, enjoying high profits and faced with an "almost chronic condition of labor scarcity," continued its high-wage policy. The average hourly wage for workers in the combined motor vehicle industries was 65.7 cents in 1922 as compared to 48.7 cents for production workers in manufacturing as a whole. By 1928 the average hourly wage of automobile workers had risen to 75 cents as compared to 56.2 cents for production workers in manufacturing as a whole.[22]

The institution of the $5 day by Ford was part of a broad new program in employer-employee relations that gave the Ford Motor Company in 1914 and for a few years thereafter what Allan Nevins and Frank Ernest Hill have characterized as "the most advanced labor policy in the world." Along with the high basic wage came the eight-hour day, sick-leave allowances, an employee savings and loan association, an English school for immigrants, removal from foremen of the power to discharge workers, and the establishment of a Sociological Department to ensure that the new high wage was put to good use by Ford employees. The policy of the company, and particularly of the Sociological Department, was one of benevolent paternalism until 1921, but after an interval of especially harsh working conditions and the "scrapping of old procedures," the Ford factory became by 1923 "just like any other factory." Toward the end of the decade the emergence of Harry Bennett and the Ford Service Department injected an element of "arbitrary brutality" into employer-employee relations in the Ford Motor Company that distinguished it to some degree at least from its competitors.[23]

None of the other automobile manufacturers sought to imitate the paternalism of the Ford Sociological Department, but many of them, in an effort "to stabilize a floating labor supply," did introduce schemes of welfare capitalism during World War I which they, like so many other employers, maintained throughout the 1920's. A study by the Bureau of Labor Statistics in 1926 of nineteen automobile companies, with approximately 250,000 employees, revealed that all of them had lunchrooms in their plants and maintained hospital or emergency rooms; four companies had indoor recreational facilities and fourteen sponsored outdoor recreational facilities; thirteen sponsored dances or other social affairs; seven had company bands, five had company orchestras, and two had company glee clubs; six companies maintained benefit associations of one sort or another; and the same number made group insurance available to their employees. In addition, several of the G.M. divisions provided for employee-stock ownership and helped to maintain clubhouses for company employees. Only the White Motor Company among the automobile manufacturers, however, felt it necessary to introduce a "full-fledged" company union into its plant.[24]

The automobile manufacturers were unanimous in their view that employer-employee relations in the industry should be determined without benefit of outside unionism. To Henry Ford, labor unions were simply "predatory" organizations and were "part of the exploitation scheme," and to the automobile manufacturers as a whole, they were a threat to production, employment, and profits. Through membership in the Employers' Association of Detroit and the National Metal Trades Association, the automobile companies supported organizations which became identified, like the automobile manufacturers themselves, with the open shop. The Employers' Association of Detroit, which had eliminated unionism in the metal trades of the city by the end of the first decade of the century, proudly proclaimed that "the open shop exists in Detroit as it exists nowhere else." The Association and the automobile manufacturers were agreed that the open shop was a key factor in the growth of the automobile industry.[25]

The National Automobile Chamber of Commerce (N.A.C.C.), the trade association of the automobile manufacturers, did not, prior to 1933, concern itself with the problems of unionism. It was the Selden patent rather than any worry about employer-employee relations that originally impelled the bulk of the automobile manufacturers to draw together into a formal organization. George B. Selden, a Rochester, New York, patent attorney, had submitted a patent application for a gasoline-powered "road carriage" in 1879 but had succeeded in delaying the actual granting of the patent until 1895. Four years later, Selden, for $10,000 and a percentage of the royalties that could be collected, virtually assigned his patent to the Columbia and Electric Vehicle Company, soon to be reorganized as the Electric Vehicle Company (E.V.C.).

In 1900 the E.V.C. brought suit against the Winton Motor Company, then the leading producer of automobiles, for infringement of the Selden patent. Before the suit was closed, Winton and seventeen other automobile manufacturers conferred with the E.V.C. and agreed to establish the Association of Licensed Automobile Manufacturers (A.L.A.M.) and in return for a license to manufacture automobiles to pay to the E.V.C. a royalty of 1¼ per cent on the retail price of each car that was sold. The E.V.C. was to retain 40 per cent of the royalty payment for itself, to send 20 per cent to Selden, and to return the other 40 per cent to the A.L.A.M. The A.L.A.M., which was formed in 1903, was to determine who should or should not be

licensed under the patent.   After these arrangements had been concluded, the Winton suit was settled, with the defendants accepting
the validity of the Selden patent.

When the fledgling Ford Motor Company refused to seek a license
to manufacture its cars, the A.L.A.M. brought suit against the firm.
The validity of the patent was upheld by the Circuit Court of the
Southern District of New York in 1909, but Ford appealed the decision and in effect won the case when the Circuit Court of Appeals,
Second Circuit, ruled on January 9, 1911, that the patent applied only
to vehicles using engines of the Brayton two-cycle type.   Since Ford,
like nearly all of the other automobile manufacturers, was using the
Otto four-cycle engine, he had not infringed the patent.[26]   Ford's
victory led to the dissolution of the A.L.A.M. and the formation in the
same year of the Automobile Board of Trade.   In 1913 the Automobile Board of Trade merged with the Association of Automobile Manufacturers, which had been organized in 1900, to form the National
Automobile Chamber of Commerce.   As of 1933 member companies
of the N.A.C.C. produced twenty-eight makes of passenger cars,
twenty-eight makes of trucks, nine makes of buses, four makes of taxi-
cabs, and five makes of special vehicles such as fire engines, ambulances, and funeral vehicles.   Forty-four vehicle manufacturers (parts
manufacturers and the body firms were not included) were listed
as members, with the Ford Motor Company the only important nonmember.   Ford did, however, maintain a connection with the N.A.C.C.
through the Lincoln Motor Company, which Ford had acquired in
January 1922 and which was a member concern.[27]

One of the best publicized activities of the N.A.C.C. and a heritage of the controversy over the Selden patent was the Association's
cross-licensing of automotive patents.   The member companies agreed
in 1915 to the mutual cross-licensing without charge of all patents
that they held as of the first of that year.   Patents acquired during
the next ten years were also to be cross-licensed, but excluded from
this arrangement were "revolutionary" patents, patents on body
shapes and designs, and patents on trucks, motorcycles, and special
vehicles.   When the agreement was renewed in 1925 and then again
in 1930, only existing patents were covered.   The Ford Motor Company did not join the patent pool although it took out patents only
for legal protection and licensed them without charge.   The Packard
Motor Car Company, which was also a nonparticipant, exchanged licenses only on a royalty basis.[28]

Through the N.A.C.C. the automobile manufacturers had what was
later described as "a complete coverage of Fair Trade Practices."   As

of 1933 the Association provided its members with a variety of statistics relative to the production, sale, and use of motor vehicles. It managed the annual New York and Chicago automobile shows, and member concerns more or less adhered to its recommendation of January 7, 1931, that they concentrate the introduction of their new models in the two-month period preceding these shows. The N.A.C.C. conducted research on matters related to the industry, studied transportation rates and services, acted as the contact for the industry with insurance rate makers, advocated improved highways and "sound and equitable" legislative principles, conducted a Motor Truck Educational Bureau and fostered state organizations of truck owners, acted as the clearing house for activities designed to encourage the world-wide use of motor transportation, promoted the salvaging of old vehicles, and conducted advertising conventions for the exchange of views on improved practices and desirable standards.[29]

The Sales Managers Committee of the N.A.C.C. provided a convenient mechanism for the automobile manufacturers to exchange price information and to discuss such price issues as the items that should be included in the advertised list price for automobiles and the "pack" that should be allowed the dealers, but there is no evidence that the automobile companies engaged in any price fixing among themselves. The Federal Trade Commission, after an exhaustive investigation of the industry, concluded in 1939 that it had found no evidence of "price agreements or other cooperative activities that appear to be contrary to the antitrust acts." [30]

Had the individualistically inclined automobile manufacturers been tempted to come to an agreement on the prices that they would charge for their vehicles, they would have been discouraged from doing so because Ford remained outside the N.A.C.C. and because the product they had to sell was, as the general manager of the Association put it, "a proprietary article which depends in large measure upon individualistic treatment and an element of style." On the other hand, the oligopolistic nature of the industry, the ease with which one make could be substituted for another, and the belief of the manufacturers that the demand for automobiles was influenced less by their price than by the condition of the economy discouraged any real price competition among the automobile concerns. Although the prices of cars in the same class were rarely identical, the industry's prices were administered prices, with Ford more than any other producer, at least until the middle 1930's, serving as the price leader. As R. H. Grant of G.M. declared at a Sales Managers Committee meeting of December 9, 1932, "Mr. Ford, who won't play, is pretty much the price setter in this industry. I'll bet if Mr. Ford's cars were $50 higher ours would be $50 higher. We care about Ford. We have been struggling with him for years." [31]

Although the automobile manufacturers did not fix prices among themselves, they did, individually, set the retail price at which their vehicles were to be sold. The dealers were required to maintain these prices, but, depending on the demand for a particular car, they could, in effect, deviate from list price by allowing either more or less than its market value for the used car that was traded in by the new-car purchaser. It was the dealer, therefore, who bore the brunt of such price competition as existed in the automobile industry, and it was at the dealer level that the disturbing trade practices in the industry were to be found.[32]

The absence of real price competition among the automobile manufacturers did not mean that competition itself had disappeared from the industry. In the areas of product differentiation, innovations in design and style, and improvement in quality, and in advertising and sales campaigns, the automobile manufacturers competed vigorously. The Federal Trade Commission concluded in 1939 that "Consumer benefits from competition in the automobile-manufacturing industry have probably been more substantial than in any other large industry studied by the Commission." [33]

The difficulty of storing automobiles and the necessity of stocking dealers with the varieties in color and design of a particular model that their customers desired tended to result in a rather close correlation of automobile output and automobile sales and to mitigate the likelihood of the overproduction of motor vehicles.[34] The meshing of production and sales was far from perfect, however, and the dealers on occasion found themselves with cars that were difficult to dispose of at list prices.

II

The workers who manned the new automobile factories that began to appear in the cities of Michigan and particularly in Detroit after the turn of the century were drawn from Michigan's declining lumber industry and from her farms, from the South, from Canada, and from Europe. The foreign-born—the Poles and the Italians—and the Negroes were particularly conspicuous among the wage earners in the Detroit automobile plants. Of 99,861 Detroit automobile workers classified by the census of 1930 as "operatives" or "laborers," approximately 42 per cent were foreign-born and approximately 13 per cent were Negroes, the combined total of Negroes and foreign-born thus exceeding the number of native-born whites in these two major job classifications. Women and children were not particularly numerous among the employees in the industry as of 1930. Of the 640,474 persons categorized by the census of 1930 as having automotive occupations of any kind, only about 7 per cent were women, and only 1 per cent were children under eighteen years of age.[35] Whether native- or foreign-born, white or black, male or female, the workers in the industry in the pre-New Deal era had at least one characteristic in common: they were, in the vast majority, almost entirely innocent of trade unionism in so far as their personal work experience was concerned.[36]

The skilled workers originally drawn to the automobile industry from the metal, machine, and woodworking trades were soon swamped by workers of lesser skill. Henry Ford estimated in 1922 that 85 per cent of his workers required less than two weeks of training and that 43 per cent of them were able to work proficiently within one day. A study by the United States Employment Service in 1935 revealed that 26.9 per cent of the workers in the industry required no training at all and that only 9.8 per cent required more than one year of training.[37] The bulk of the automobile workers were obviously not the stuff out of which craft unions are formed.

With hourly wages high and jobs plentiful in the industry prior to 1929, the automobile factory worker appears to have been reasonably content with his economic lot; but depression and the opportunity provided by the National Industrial Recovery Act for unionism and the airing of employee complaints revealed that working conditions were far from perfect in the automobile plants in the opinion of many automobile workers and that there were employee grievances upon which union organizers could seek to capitalize.

To a marked degree, such dissatisfaction as existed among the automobile workers derived from the content of their jobs. Contrary to the popular image of the nature of work in an automobile plant, only about 10–20 per cent of the employees in the automobile industry were engaged in assembly-line operations, but the work of the remainder was "no less specialized or less carefully planned." The "close coordination of jobs" required the "centralized determination of production standards," [38] and herein lay the source of employee complaints.

To the worker on the assembly line in particular, it was the "coerced rhythms" of the line, the "externally controlled compulsion to maintain a steady work tempo," that determined his attitude toward his job. He was not free, as he perhaps had been on some previous job, to set the pace of his work or to determine the manner in which it was to be performed. The tempo of his work was now determined for him, and the line kept moving, inexorably. It was natural for him under the circumstances to complain of a speed-up, to believe that he was constantly under pressure to turn out more and more work. He was later to protest to President Roosevelt and the National Recovery Administration that "no human on earth can keep up with the lines" and that "the way they are using these moving lines sure is slavery." The conveyor line, one automobile worker wrote to the President, "means that human flesh and blood with souls and ideals is [*sic*] placed in competition with and paced by a mechanical robot which never tires; that can be speeded up at the whim or caprice of some minor foreman. . . . If Simon Legree were to come back to life and see a modern conveyor line in operation, when it is really strutting it's [*sic*] stuff, he would dig Uncle Tom up and kick Hell out of him because of not doing anywhere near his possibilities. In the . . . [automobile] factories, men are driven to the last extreme of mental, physical and nerve endurance." [39]

Output per man hour rose dramatically in the motor vehicle industry in the 1920's, increasing a total of 63 per cent between 1922 and 1929, as compared to a 27 per cent increase for manufacturing as a whole, but undoubtedly these figures primarily reflect sheer mechanical improvement rather than an accelerated pace of work. It must be remembered, however, that assembly-line workers were not mechanical men stamped from a single mold, and a tempo of work that was entirely satisfactory for the average worker might be too fast for some workers.[40] The assembly line did not allow for individual differences.

Whether he was an assembler, a machine tender, a helper, or a laborer, the automobile factory employee was apt to find his work repetitious, monotonous, and, perhaps, physically tiring. One union official, a paint sprayman at the Plymouth plant, later observed that he was not so much bothered by the speed of the work as by its "unfailing regularity: a monotony of motion, repetitious and unchanging." This coupled with the concentration the job required sent him home not physically exhausted but "in a state of nervous tension." The wife of an employee at the Fisher Body plant in Oakland, California, complained to Eleanor Roosevelt that her husband came home "wringing wet every night with sweat and so tired he can't eat or sleep." [41]

Despite the high level of employment in the automobile industry in the 1920's, the work, as we have seen, tended to be relatively irregular. One catches a glimpse of what the seasonality of automobile production meant for at least some of the automobile workers in the service records of a few of the employees who later became the subject of Automobile Labor Board decisions. Archie Kling, we learn from one of these decisions, was hired by the Fisher Body plant in Cleveland on November 20, 1922. He was laid off on January 8, 1924, was rehired September 25, 1924, laid off November 4, 1924, rehired January 19, 1925, laid off September 28, 1927, rehired March 1, 1928, laid off August 29, 1928, rehired December 5, 1928, and then laid off on July 2, 1929. Glenn Harmon was hired on at the Pontiac plant on March 28, 1927, as an assembler. He was laid off on July 29, 1927, in a reduction of force, was recalled on August 2, 1927, and placed on cam shaft work until October 19, 1927, when he was once again laid off. He returned to work on November 18, 1927, as a machine operator and this time worked until May 26, 1930.[42] It was possible for at least some of the automobile workers during the prosperous 1920's to find other jobs during the period of their layoff, but it could hardly have been pleasant to be seeking work as frequently as Kling and Harmon had to do.

Undoubtedly contributing to the automobile worker's sense of insecurity was the fact that he had no guaranteed tenure on the job and could therefore be laid off or discharged arbitrarily. Some plants did, more or less, follow the principle of seniority in determining the order of layoff and rehiring,[43] but even in these plants there was no union contract to reassure the worker that his seniority would be recognized when the working force was reduced or when production resumed its upward curve. The resulting situation as it appeared to the worker was later described, undoubtedly in exaggerated terms, by Clayton W. Fountain:

> The annual layoff during the model change was always a menace to the security of the workers. Along about June or July it started. The bosses would pick the men off a few at a time, telling them to stay home until they were notified to come back. There was no rhyme or reason in the selection of the fortunate ones chosen to continue working. The foreman had the say. If he happened to like you, or if you sucked around him and did him favors—or if you were one of the bastards who worked like hell and turned out more than production—you might be picked to work a few weeks longer than the next guy....
>
> In October and November we began to trickle back into the plants. Again, the bosses had the full say as to who was rehired first. Years of service with the company meant nothing.... generally speaking, the laid-off worker had no assurance of any kind that he would be called back at any specific time.[44]

It was not only uncertainty and favoritism in layoff and rehiring about which the automobile worker had to be concerned in an era when the control of jobs was entirely the prerogative of management. In the Ford plants at least, employees who were laid off were commonly re-engaged at the hiring-in rate even though they had been receiving a higher rate before their work had ceased.[45]

The irregularity of automobile employment meant that the high hourly wages of automobile workers were not necessarily translated into equally high annual wages. Thus a motor vehicle worker who in 1925 earned the average hourly rate of 72.3 cents and worked the industry full-time average of 50.3 hours per week would have earned an annual wage of $1891. The average annual wage of workers in the combined motor vehicle industries in 1925 was, however, $1675, which indicates that the average automobile worker in that prosperous year for the industry worked about forty-six weeks.[46] Many workers, obviously, worked fewer than forty-six weeks.

The methods of wage payment prevalent in the industry in the 1920's were also to come in for a good deal of criticism at a later time. With the conspicuous exception of the Ford plants, piece rates were more common than hourly rates, and there were the usual protests that management reduced the rates as the worker boosted his output. A few plants in the 1920's employed a so-called premium system of wage payment whereby a standard time was set for the completion of a particular operation and the worker would be paid an hourly rate for the hours that he actually worked and the same rate or a lesser rate for each hour that he saved from the estimated time.[47]

A common method of wage payment in the 1920's and the object of a great deal of later criticism was the production bonus plan, which was used in thirty-eight of ninety-four plants studied by the Bureau of Labor Statistics in 1928. In some plants the bonus was based on the work of the individual, in others on the work of a group, with the bonus divided among group members in accordance with the basic wage rates of the individuals who made up the group. The size of the groups ranged from just a few workers to as many as fifty. Where the plan was in effect, a set standard of production would be established on the basis of time study, and the workers would receive a bonus payment for production in excess of the standard or in excess of a specified percentage of the standard (the bonus, for example, might be paid for production in excess of 75 per cent of the standard). The greater the production in excess of standard production or of the specified percentage of standard, the greater the percentage of his base rate the worker received as his bonus. In some plants the bonus plans applied to all workers, including even final assemblers; in other plants only some departments were included. Although not necessarily an inequitable method of wage payment, the group bonus was criticized by the workers as a "cock-eyed method of pay that few understand" and that was "not meant to be understood." It was "highway robbery in kid gloves," "a deliberate steal," and could be and was being used by employers as a means of speeding up production.[48]

The automobile worker was also to complain that he was paid only for time actually spent on production and not for any "dead" time, that is, for time consumed in preparing for work before the line was started and for delays occasioned by interruptions of production that were beyond the worker's control. The employees were also displeased that they received no call-in pay when they were requested to appear at the plant and then had to wait around to learn whether there would be any work for them. "I remember very distinctly," a former Briggs employee recalled, "that many of the workers who reported to work with their lunches were told, 'You will have to wait on the sidewalk or in the cafes across the street and if we need you, the foreman will go over and bring you over....' they would often go home after eating their lunch ... without obtaining one minute of work." Finally, some of the workers objected to the deductions from their wages to help defray the costs of group insurance or company welfare plans, particularly when these plans were exclusively controlled by the management.[49]

III

Since its product is one of the consumer durable goods whose purchase in most instances is readily postponable, the automobile industry is peculiarly sensitive to the ups and downs of the business cycle. This had been demonstrated during the recession of 1920–21,[50] but it was even more apparent during the depression of 1929 and following, by which time, as already noted, the automobile market had become largely a replacement market. Factory sales of cars and trucks fell from a total of 5,337,087 units in 1929 to 1,331,860 units in 1932, a decrease of approximately 75 per cent. The number of wage earners in the combined motor vehicle industries declined from an average of 447,448 in 1929 to an average of 243,614 in 1933, a drop of about 45 per cent; total payrolls during the same years decreased about 62 per cent; and according to the Bureau of Internal Revenue, the net income after taxes available for dividends of fifty-six automobile companies shrank from $451 million in 1929 to a minus figure of $186 million in 1932. The average car price during these years of depression, however, declined only 14.2 per cent (from $743 to $637), which indicates the extent to which the pricing of automobiles departed from the natural laws of economics so confidently described by the classical economists. A more substantial price reduction, the manufacturers contended, would simply have resulted in still lower wages and profits rather than in increased sales.[51]

The depression, "a powerful winnowing agency," reduced the number of establishments in the combined motor vehicle industries and increased the share of the passenger car and truck market held by the Big Three. Between 1929 and 1933 the number of establishments in the motor vehicle branch of the industry decreased from 210 to 122, and the number of parts and body plants from 1188 to 701. The independent passenger car and truck producers were especially hard hit by the downturn in the economy and the spectacular drop in the demand for motor vehicles. Without the financial reserves to weather so many bad years and less able than the large producers to reduce costs and to adjust to changed market conditions, they either went out of business altogether or were threatened with insolvency. Whereas the eight major independents showed a total profit of $74,-218,000 in 1929, they suffered a loss of $30,257,000 in 1932; and their working capital plummeted from $179,572,000 to $106,044,000 during the same years. The independents' share of new car and truck registrations declined from 23.5 per cent in 1929 to 17.7 per cent in 1932.[52]

Of the Big Three, Chrysler during the Hoover years made the largest relative gain in so far as share of the market is concerned, raising its percentage of new car and truck registrations from 8.8 in 1929 to 15.7 in 1932. Chrysler, however, lost money on its motor vehicle sales in both 1930 (more than $3 million) and 1932 (almost $10.9 million) and made a net profit after taxes of only $2.888 million in 1931. The Ford Motor Company (including Lincoln), which had made money in 1929 and 1930 with its Model A but which was beginning to suffer from "organizational dry rot," lost almost $87 million in 1931 and 1932 on its domestic motor vehicle business. Its percentage of new car and truck registrations dwindled from 34.9 in 1929 to 25.7 in 1932. G.M., the strongest of the Big Three, showed a net profit after income taxes on its consolidated operations during each of the Hoover years, but on its motor vehicle division alone (including Fisher Body), although it earned over $200 million before income taxes in 1930 and 1931 combined, it lost just under $7 million in 1932. Its share of new passenger car and truck registrations rose from 32.8 per cent in 1929 to 40.9 per cent in 1932. The low-priced makes of the Big Three fared the best during the depression: Chevrolet, Ford, and Plymouth accounted for 56.1 per cent of new car sales in 1929 and 63.2 per cent in 1932, as the percentage of new cars whole-saling for less than $500 during these years increased from 53.9 per cent to 67 per cent.[53]

With automobile sales falling precipitously, the automobile dealers during the depression were finding it hard to remain in business or to show a profit if they did. The number of car and truck dealers was reduced from 53,091 in January 1929 to 39,871 as of April 1, 1933, and 53 per cent of the dealers suffered losses in 1930, before the full impact of the depression had really hit the automobile industry. In order to sell the vehicles in their inventory, dealers found it necessary to overvalue trade-ins, which, of course, cut their profit margin on the shrinking volume of new cars that they were able to sell. The dealers complained that the factories were overloading them with cars, that the manufacturers failed to observe representative sales areas in granting new franchises, and that dealers were given insufficient protection on their existing stock of cars when new models were introduced or when their contracts were cancelled.[54] Whether justified in their criticism of the manufacturers or not, the dealers were ready and eager to adopt a code of fair trade practices when the National Industrial Recovery Act provided them with the opportunity to do so.

The automobile workers, a government investigator reported in 1934, had been "completely deflated" by the depression and some of them had been "crushed physically as well as mentally by their experience." "The depression began," one automobile worker informed President Roosevelt, "and things went down and down until now they are about as bad as they could be. I used to have money in the bank, a car and some decent clothes to wear and now I have nothing." The city of Detroit during the early years of the depression had the worst relief crisis of any major American metropolis and the highest jobless rate in the United States. "I have never confronted such misery as on the zero day of my arrival in Detroit," a social worker reported in the spring of 1930. The average monthly case load of Detroit's Department of Public Welfare increased from 5,029 during the last six months of 1929 to 49,314 during the first six months of 1933.[55]

Not only did automobile employment decline sharply between 1929 and 1932, but workers who remained on the payroll found themselves working many fewer hours than they formerly had as automobile manufacturers co-operated in the national share-the-work movement. Average full-time hours per week for wage earners in the combined motor vehicle industries dropped only from 49.4 in

1928 to 48.4 in 1932, but automotive workers actually worked only an average of 31.9 hours per week in the latter year. For employees of N.A.C.C. members, the average weekly hours actually worked fell from 45.6 in 1929 to 30.8 in 1932. An increase of 84.5 per cent between 1929 and 1932 in the number of employees in the industry per car produced is another indication of the extent to which employers sought to spread the available work among as many employees as possible.[56]

The automobile worker not only worked a shorter work week during the depression than he had in the 1920's but he also worked far more irregularly. The annual layoff rate per one hundred employees in automobile and body plants, which corresponds closely to the automobile manufacturing industry as codified under the N.I.R.A., increased from 49.73 in 1930 to 86.16 in 1932, a jump of about 75 per cent, and the total annual separation rate during the same years increased from 70.15 to 98.87 or about 40 per cent. This compares with an increase in all manufacturing of about 16 per cent in the layoff rate and a *decrease* of about 13 per cent in the total separation rate.[57] These figures indicate how extensive was the labor turnover in automobile employment during the early depression years and how insecure in his job the automobile worker was.

Henry Ford's initial reaction to the downward swing of the business cycle had been to raise minimum wages in his plants to $7 a day and to declare that "If every one will attend to his own work, the future is secure"; but in the end Ford was no more able than his competitors to hold the wage line: the minimum wage of Ford laborers was slashed to $4 a day in 1932.[58] The average hourly wage of factory workers in the combined motor vehicle industries dropped from 75 cents in 1928 to 72.4 cents in 1930, and 62.8 cents in 1932, an overall decline of only 16 per cent; but because of reduced hours of labor and increased irregularity of employment, weekly and yearly wages fell far more than the drop in hourly rates would indicate. The average actual weekly earnings of wage earners in automobile, body, and parts plants declined from $35.14 in 1928 to $20.00 in 1932, a drop of 43 per cent as compared to a 32 per cent drop for production workers in manufacturing and a 20 per cent decline in the consumer price index. According to the Federal Trade Commission, the average annual wage of workers in the combined motor vehicle industries declined from $1638 in 1929 to $1035 in 1933, a drop of about 37 per cent as compared to a decline of 24 per cent in the consumer price index.[59]

The automobile workers and the American Federation of Labor

complained that the employers took advantage of the oversupply of labor in the depression years and the insecurity of those who remained at work to accelerate the pace of automobile production, and Nevins and Hill in their study of Ford contend that the "superintendents in most factories during the depression years showed a disposition to speed up the working forces" in an effort to cut costs. A Chrysler employee complained to the National Recovery Administration on July 28, 1933, that the speed-up had become "the worst weed in our wheat field." During the previous two years, he insisted, there had been a demand for "more and more production" to be achieved by "less and less men" with the result that the plant had become "a race track."

Actually, however, the efforts of employers to spread the work and the increase in labor turnover in the industry militated against any increase in man-hour productivity. The Research and Planning Division of the National Recovery Administration later found that there had been a greater drop in labor productivity between 1930 and 1932 in the automobile manufacturing industry than in any of the other industries that it had studied. The index number of output per man hour in the combined motor vehicle industries increased from 84.2 in 1929 to 89.1 in 1930 (1939 = 100), but it declined to 79.6 in 1931 and 69.4 in 1932, an over-all drop for the four years of over 17 per cent as compared to virtually no decline at all in output per man hour in manufacturing as a whole.[60]

In one respect, though, there was no change in the automobile industry during the early years of the depression: management remained free, as it had been before 1929, to formulate its employment policies without significant challenge from organized labor. The labor unions of the country had all been unable to organize a sufficient number of automobile workers in the pre-New Deal era to have any direct impact on employer-employee relations in the nation's greatest industry.

IV

The nation's largest labor federation, the American Federation of Labor (A.F. of L.), had succeeded by 1933 in organizing a few craftsmen in the automobile industry—principally pattern makers, molders, and metal polishers—but despite a sporadic display of concern it had failed altogether to unionize the unskilled and semiskilled production workers who constituted the bulk of the labor force in the automobile and parts plants. Detroit, the motor capital of the nation, had attained a reputation as "the graveyard of organizers." [61]

Organizational interest in the automobile workers had been evidenced during the early years of the twentieth century by the Carriage and Wagon Workers' International Union (C.W.W.), which had been established in 1891 and had affiliated with the A.F. of L., but, significantly, its ambitions had foundered on the rock of craft-union jurisdictional claims. In conflict with various craft unions regarding the organization of skilled workers in the automobile industry, the C.W.W. in 1910, at a time when its membership was a meager eleven hundred, petitioned the A.F. of L. for permission to include the word "automobile" in its name and, presumably, for a grant of jurisdiction over all workers in the automobile industry. Two of the A.F. of L. affiliates, the International Brotherhood of Blacksmiths and Helpers and the Upholsterers' International Union, agreed in 1911 to allow the automobile workers over whom they claimed jurisdiction to choose between membership in the two craft unions or in the Carriage, Wagon and Automobile Workers' International Union (C.W.A.W.), as the Carriage and Wagon Workers had now become known, but the Blacksmiths repudiated this arrangement the next year on the grounds that the C.W.A.W. had violated the agreement.

At the 1913 convention of the A.F. of L. the representatives of nine craft unions introduced a resolution which called upon the C.W.A.W. to cease efforts to organize workers falling within the jurisdiction of the nine unions and to surrender to them all workers whom it had unlawfully organized. The charter of the C.W.A.W. was to be revoked unless it complied with these conditions. The resolution was approved by the convention after the threat of expulsion had been removed from it.

During the first half of the following year the nine craft unions, working through the Metal Trades Department, launched a joint organizing campaign in the automobile industry. Although the campaign proved unsuccessful, the A.F. of L. at its convention of November 1914 ordered the C.W.A.W. to abandon efforts to organize automobile workers falling within the jurisdiction of other national and international unions and to strike the word "automobile" from its name. Since its membership was now made up largely of automobile workers and since the carriage and wagon industry was in decline, the union refused to comply with this order and was consequently suspended from the Federation on April 1, 1918. It was then reorganized as the United Automobile, Aircraft and Vehicle Workers of America (U.A.A.V.W.). It was "dedicated," it announced, to "the principle of Industrial Unionism," and it charged that the craft form of organization made it possible for employers "to pit one group of workers against other groups of workers in the same industry" and by so doing to defeat them in "wage wars."

Prospering as the result of World War I, the U.A.A.V.W. attained a claimed membership of 45,000 in 1920, concentrated mainly among the painters, trimmers, and woodworkers in the small custom body plants in the East and in the body factories in Detroit. The recession of 1920–21, an "ill-advised" strike against Fisher Body in Detroit in 1921, the introduction of lacquer in automobile paint shops, and the resistance of the employers contributed, however, to the disintegration of the union in the 1920's, and it became "a pauper organization with only a few members" and an easy target for communist penetration.[62]

Following the expulsion of the C.W.A.W. and prior to 1933 the A.F. of L. on two occasions projected an organizing campaign in the automobile industry, but its efforts proved to be little more than rhetorical. In August 1920 the Executive Council asked each of eight international unions claiming jurisdiction over some of the automobile workers to assign an organizer to the automobile industry, and offered to supply an organizer of its own; but nothing came of this proposal.[63]

Six years later the A.F. of L. convention, on the recommendation of the Metal Trades Department, voted to initiate an organizing campaign in the automobile industry. In March 1927, President William Green of the Federation secured the unenthusiastic approval of most of the internationals concerned for a plan of organization that called for the assignment to the appropriate national union of automobile workers engaged in "the construction and maintenance of plants, equipment, parts or tools" and the placement of all other workers in the industry in directly affiliated federal labor unions. The national unions involved temporarily waived their jurisdiction over these production workers, but they were to be transferred to craft unions "as speedily as possible." Paul Smith of the A.F. of L. staff was designated to head the campaign, and organizers were assigned by several of the internationals.

A few weeks after arriving in Detroit to launch the organizing drive, Smith complained to Green of the lack of response from the automobile workers, which he attributed to fear and the unemployment resulting from the discontinuance of production of Ford's Model T. Smith advised that an effort should be made to organize Nash and Studebaker plants in Wisconsin and Chicago and to persuade the employers, and particularly Henry Ford, "to try collective bargaining," but he thought the Federation should "keep quiet in Michigan." Green endorsed Smith's proposals, but nothing came of the A.F. of L.'s organizing efforts or of attempts to persuade the employers "to try collective bargaining." [64]   Green on March 19, 1928, expressed the hope to Smith "that at some future time, when conditions seem to be more favorable, we may be permitted to take up again this work of organizing automobile workers," but the half-hearted manner in which the A.F. of L. and its affiliates had tackled the problem in the 1920's and their reluctance to face up boldly to the jurisdictional questions involved did not augur well for the future success of the Federation in the automobile industry even under "more favorable" conditions.[65]

The Industrial Workers of the World (I.W.W.) and the communists were ready to rush in where the A.F. of L. had been reluctant to tread, but they too failed to develop any real strength among the automobile workers.   Preaching its gospel of industrial unionism, the I.W.W. had sought to win converts among the auto workers in Detroit in the years shortly before World War I broke out in Europe. Its major effort in the motor city was mounted in May and June 1913, and it did cause some apprehension among the automobile manufacturers; but at the end of May the I.W.W. claimed but two hundred members among the auto workers, and although it brought six thousand Studebaker employees out on strike in June, the strike failed and the Wobbly campaign collapsed.

The depression of 1929 and following persuaded the I.W.W. to revive efforts to organize Detroit automobile workers, with the result that a Detroit branch of the organization's General Recruiting Union was established on January 31, 1932. "Never before," optimistically proclaimed the I.W.W., "has there been such a fertile field for a strong industrial unionism movement in the automobile industry," but in the next four months fewer than eighty auto workers were initiated into Metal and Machinery Workers Industrial Union No. 440, which had been assigned jurisdiction over the metal and machinery industries in the greater Detroit area.   Throughout the remainder of the year the I.W.W. continued to preach its message in Detroit but without evident success.[66]

The communists were destined to play a more important role in the automobile industry than the I.W.W., but only a handful of auto workers joined the Communist party or its controlled labor union in the industry.   The Communist party began work in the Detroit auto factories in 1925.   By the end of the next year seven shop nuclei had been established, but the total party membership was only 316.   At the same time the communists began to infiltrate the moribund and virtually memberless U.A.A.V.W. They gained control of the key Detroit local of the organization in the late 1920's, secured the election of Phil Raymond as secretary, converted the national organization into the Auto Workers Union (A.W.U.), and affiliated it in 1929 with the Trade Union Unity League (T.U.U.L.), which had just been established by the communists as a center for dual unionism. Its membership probably not in excess of one hundred, the A.W.U. was little more than a paper union at the time it joined the T.U.U.L.[67]

The A.W.U. proclaimed itself to be founded on "the principles of the class struggle" and to be aiming at the "abolition of the capitalist system" and the building up of "a workers and farmers government." It stood, it declared, for the "united front" of all auto workers, and it announced itself as ready to participate in "common action with the rank and file in the reformist trade unions against the common enemy, the automobile companies, the labor bureaucrats and their government."[68] The "labor bureaucrats" referred to were, of course, the officials of the A.F. of L.

From the very beginning the communists concentrated on the Detroit area's most important business concern and the symbol of the free-enterprise system itself, the Ford Motor Company. When depression struck and employment at Ford's great Rouge plant was drastically reduced,[69] it was a small group of communists who organized and led a "hunger march" on Ford's Dearborn citadel. The objective of the march, staged on March 7, 1932, was to present a petition to the Ford management at the Rouge calling for jobs or relief for unemployed Ford workers and improved working conditions for the employed Ford workers. The several hundred marchers, who are said to have "represented a cross-section of Ford workers, former Ford employes, and, above all, the miscellaneous unemployed," were halted at the Dearborn line by the city's police; and when they crossed into the city in defiance of a police warning, they were subjected to a tear-gas attack. A pitched battle ensued which continued up to the gates of the Rouge plant, where Harry Bennett's plant watchmen and private police joined in the fray, and Bennett himself was injured. Four of the hunger marchers were killed in the fight, a lamentable consequence of the affair that the communists naturally sought to exploit.[70]

More than a year later, on June 5, 1933, the A.W.U. and the communist-controlled Unemployed Councils staged a second hunger march on the Rouge. Ford workers inside the plant were asked to join in a one-hour strike in support of the petitioners. The communists hailed the march as "a shining example of working-class power and organization," but the results seem to have been entirely negative. The more than three thousand marchers were not permitted to cross into Dearborn to make a formal presentation of their demands to Ford officials, and there was no strike within the plant itself. The A.W.U. conceded that the major weakness of the effort was the ineffectiveness of its organization within the Rouge.[71]   In the Ford plant as in several other automobile factories, the A.W.U. had been able to enlist a very small nucleus of supporters prior to the enactment of the National Industrial Recovery Act, but it had failed altogether to make any significant impact on the mass of the automobile workers.

Whereas the I.W.W. and the A.W.U. directed their appeal principally to the mass of production workers in the automobile plants, the Society of Designing Engineers (S.D.E.), created in Detroit in December 1932 by William Foster and some of his friends, spoke for an elite minority of automotive employees who designed tools, dies, special machines, motors, bodies, and chassis.   Troubled by the decline in wages and earnings of the designing engineers after 1929 and the seasonality of their employment, the founders of the society concluded that economic organization along trade-union lines was the answer for these skilled white-collar employees.   By the spring of 1933 some two hundred designing engineers had cast their lot with the S.D.E.[72]

After the enactment of the National Industrial Recovery Act, the S.D.E. spread its organization beyond Detroit, and by September 1934 had established chapters in Flint, Pontiac, Jackson, and Auburn, Indiana.   Its membership by March 1935 was two thousand, and it claimed to include in its ranks the bulk of the automotive designers in Michigan.   Although in part at least a professional organization, the S.D.E. during the early New Deal years behaved like a trade union and aggressively sought to improve the economic conditions under which its members worked.[73]

About the same time the S.D.E. was founded a new organization of skilled workers, the Dingmen's Welfare Club, was formed in Detroit, primarily among dingmen employed by the Chrysler Corporation.   Composed of highly skilled and well-paid workers who removed imperfections from finished car bodies, the Dingmen's Welfare Club severely controlled the available number of dingmen by limiting its membership to those who could probably find work at their trade and by itself assuming the responsibility of training dingmen as they were needed.   Little was heard of the Club until April 30, 1935, when 260 dingmen in the Chrysler and Briggs plants went on strike to combat an attempt by the employers to end their dependence on the Club by assigning metal finishers and blacksmiths to the tasks normally performed by dingmen. The strikers returned to work after six weeks without a formal strike settlement having been concluded but on the understanding that there would be no discrimination against Club members.[74]

Since only a tiny minority of the automobile workers were organized when the full impact of the depression hit the automobile industry, it is not surprising that the first important automobile strikes in Detroit during the depression years owed nothing in their origin to union inspiration but were rather "spontaneous movements among unorganized automobile workers." Coming at so unlikely a time, the strikes, to use the phrasing of Josephine Gomon, who was then on the staff of Detroit Mayor Frank Murphy, "just burst like lightning" on the Detroit scene and served as "a kind of an outlet for all of the frustration and the difficulties that they [the workers] were having." [75]

The strike movement was initiated by 450 workers of the Briggs Manufacturing Company's Waterloo plant who quit their jobs on January 11, 1933, in protest against a wage cut. The company, caught by surprise, rescinded its action in a couple of days, and the workers returned to their jobs. A few days later a spontaneous walkout of Motor Products employees also led to the revocation of a recently imposed reduction in wages. The flurry of strikes reached its peak on January 23 and 24 when six thousand Briggs workers struck the four Briggs plants in Detroit, and four thousand Murray Body workers converted a plant shutdown into a strike. A strike of three thousand Hudson workers on February 7 necessitated the closing down of the Hudson plant and the consequent idling of six thousand additional workers. Adjustment of wages and working conditions soon brought the Murray Body and Hudson disputes to a close, but the Briggs strike defied settlement.[76]

The principal grievances of the Briggs workers were the excessively low wages that they had been receiving, the result, at least in part, of management's recent abandonment of a guaranteed hourly base rate for employees on piece work, and also the substantial amount of dead time for which the workers received no compensation. The strikers also complained of a speed-up of production, unhealthful, unsanitary, and dangerous working conditions, irregular employment, extremely long hours of work on occasion, and the company practice of charging the workers for tools that they damaged. The strikers were unquestionably guilty of some exaggeration in their description of the terms of their employment, but working conditions in the Briggs plants were notoriously poor (the workers called Briggs the "butcher shop"); and the Fact-Finding Committee appointed by Mayor Murphy to investigate the circumstances that produced the strike concluded that the strikers' complaints about low wages, dead time, and the speed-up were "in many respects well founded." Conciliator Robert H. Pilkington similarly found "the greater percentage" of the strikers to be "decent law-abiding men and women" who had "good and sufficient reason to rebel against the conditions imposed upon them." [77]

Totally without organization when the walkout began, the Briggs strikers turned for assistance to the A.W.U.'s Phil Raymond, who had been the communist candidate for mayor of Detroit in 1930. Seeing their opportunity, the A.W.U. and the communists moved into the strike picture and made the "first effective efforts" to organize the strikers. The strikers tolerated the communists for a while because of the organizing ability that they provided, but when the "outsiders" began to subordinate assistance to the strikers to the promotion of communist objectives and the enrollment of the strikers in the A.W.U., the strikers made a "sincere effort," to quote the Fact-Finding Committee, to rid themselves of communist domination. Communist strike leaders were "publicly repudiated and ousted," and only Briggs employees were permitted to serve on the Committee of Twenty-Five, which had been set up to represent the strikers in negotiations for a settlement. Whether the strikers were successful in completely dislodging the communists is a moot point, but it is clear that the strike was the product of intolerable conditions rather than of communistic influence and that the A.W.U. began playing a conspicuous part in the affair only after the walkout had occurred.[78]

The Briggs management in the very early stages of the strike promised to eliminate dead time,[79] and it reinstituted a guaranteed minimum hourly rate for piece workers, but the strikers were not satisfied with these concessions. They advised the Fact-Finding Committee that they were also seeking a nine-hour day, a five-day week, the elimination of overtime except in emergency situations, the furnishing of tools and gloves by the employer, no further deductions from employees' pay for health and accident insurance, and management recognition of an employee-elected shop committee.

The company's response to these demands was that in restoring a guaranteed minimum rate and in dealing with the problem of dead time, it had already corrected all "just grievances" of the workers. It declared the strike to be entirely communistic in origin and made it clear that it would not meet with the strikers "for any purpose whatsoever." It advised the Fact-Finding Committee that it would "never" alter its "position that all grievances must be heard individually through the foremen or through designated company officials when the men had returned to work. No opportunity for workmen's representation would ever be given." In the end the company did meet with a committee of strikers, but it remained adamant on the matter of recognition. It disclaimed any knowledge of the principle of collective bargaining and asserted that the question of the open shop was not negotiable. "The automobile industry," it informed the Fact-Finding Committee, "has been developed around the existing system of industrial relations," and Briggs would permit no change in the status quo. In taking this position, the Briggs management was undoubtedly reflecting the point of view of the automobile manufacturers as a whole on the eve of the inauguration of Franklin D. Roosevelt as President of the United States. As a matter of fact, the Department of Labor conciliator assigned to the strike believed that orders from the larger auto manufacturers were "contingent upon the Briggs Company's successful resistance to any plan of settlement that might involve union recognition in any form." [80]

Confronted by an unyielding management, without real organization, and without funds, the strikers began drifting back to work, in so far as it was possible to do so, or sought employment elsewhere. Although the strike was never officially terminated, it had for all practical purposes come to an end by the beginning of March. The strikers had failed to gain most of their demands, and they had been completely rebuffed in their effort to attain some kind of recognition, but they had nevertheless demonstrated by their "blind revolt" that not all of the automobile workers were as content with their lot as their employers liked to believe, and they had revealed to the labor leadership of the nation that at least some automobile workers were capable of militant action even at a time of severe unemployment.

The A.W.U. and the I.W.W. to a more limited extent had injected themselves into the strike picture; but the A.F. of L., whose "energies" at that time, as John P. Frey remembered, "were devoted more to trying to hold what we had than to getting into any new fields," does not appear to have made any real effort to organize the strikers. Some strikers were won over by the A.W.U. and a few by the I.W.W., but the principal result of the strike in an organizational sense was the creation in the spring of 1933 of the American Industrial Association (A.I.A.). The new organization was founded by Briggs strikers who looked for leadership to A. J. Muste, the former chairman of the faculty of Brookwood Labor College, and who were receptive to the approach of the Conference for Progressive Labor Action, which

Muste had founded in 1929 "to rally the elements in the American labor movement that could accept neither the leadership of the A.F. of L. nor that of the Communists." When the hearings on the automobile code were held on August 18, 1933, Muste appeared on behalf of the A.I.A., but the organization passed into oblivion soon after that date.[81]

V

The first major legislative weapon employed by the Roosevelt administration in its effort to arrest the downward swing of the business cycle and to initiate the process of recovery was the National Industrial Recovery Act (N.I.R.A.). "History," President Roosevelt declared when he affixed his signature to the statute on June 16, 1933, "probably will record the . . . Act as the most important and far-reaching legislation ever enacted by the American Congress. It represents a supreme effort to stabilize for all time the many factors which make for the prosperity of the Nation, and the preservation of American standards." [82]

The N.I.R.A. drew its inspiration from a variety of sources. It was, as Frederick Lewis Allen later remarked, "a whole plum pudding of contrasting elements." The statute reflected the depression-inspired thinking of some businessmen and the United States Chamber of Commerce that trade associations should be permitted to control prices, production, and possibly labor standards free from the restraints of the antitrust laws; the idea "long held" by business-cycle theorists that public works could be used to stimulate employment; the theory of some New Dealers that recovery could be achieved if the destructive spiral of wage and price cutting were halted and if purchasing power were increased as the result of greater employment and higher wages; and the view of organized labor that shorter hours of work were necessary to combat unemployment and that the stabilization of production by business organizations should be accompanied by a legislative guarantee to workers of the right to organize and bargain collectively through representatives of their own choosing. President Roosevelt and Secretary of Labor Frances Perkins were less interested in promoting unionism than in lifting labor standards, but they were not opposed to the inclusion of a guarantee of collective bargaining in the recovery legislation if only to gain support for the measure from organized labor. It was Senator Robert F. Wagner of New York who was "the principal link between the unions and the New Deal" and who believed that the right of collective bargaining was "the bottom of social justice for the worker" and that in the denial of this right lay "the difference between despotism and democracy." [83]

The process of framing recovery legislation was initiated by the advocates of shorter hours. On December 21, 1932, Senator Hugo Black of Alabama introduced a bill which barred from interstate commerce the products of any establishment "in which any person was employed or permitted to work more than five days in any week or more than six hours in any day." In a historic reversal of its policy of voluntarism, the A.F. of L. threw its support behind the Black Bill. The measure was favorably reported by the Senate Judiciary Committee on March 30, 1933, and it passed the Senate on April 6.

President Roosevelt regarded the Black Bill as "economically unworkable" and probably unconstitutional, but rather than attack the measure frontally he decided to support the proposals addressed to the House Labor Committee on April 25 by Secretary Perkins which called for amending the bill to provide greater flexibility. The Secretary of Labor recommended that both hours and minimum wages should be established industry by industry by tripartite boards, with the hours to range from a minimum of thirty to a maximum of forty per week. President Green of the A.F. of L. opposed the inclusion in the Black Bill of a minimum-wage provision for other than women and children and proposed instead that the measure should stipulate that workers should "not be denied by their employer the free exercise of the right to belong to a *bona fide* labor organization and to collectively bargain for their wages through their own chosen representatives."

The House Labor Committee on May 10 issued a unanimous report on the bill which accepted the A.F. of L. proposal with regard to collective bargaining but which also made some concessions to the Secretary of Labor. The measure now provided for a tripartite Federal Trade Regulation Board which was to license firms to engage in interstate and foreign commerce provided that they were affiliated with national trade associations that had entered into agreements with unions regarding wages, working conditions, and production, or if unaffiliated with trade associations nevertheless complied with the terms of such agreements, or were willing to comply with the regulations of the board pertaining to these matters. Licensed firms were to observe a thirty-hour week unless exempted from this requirement by the board and were to pay weekly wages sufficient to enable their workers to maintain "standards of living of decency and comfort." Licenses were to be denied to firms that used yellow-dog contracts or refused their employees the right to organize and to bargain collectively through representatives of their own choosing. The products of unlicensed firms were to be barred from interstate and foreign commerce.[84]

The Black Bill, however, was to be sidetracked in favor of an administration substitute. President Roosevelt had requested Senator Wagner in March to undertake the task of framing a recovery program. Wagner was initially aided in this assignment by business and labor representatives, and somewhat later his group joined forces with an administration team composed of John Dickinson, the Assistant Secretary of Commerce, Jerome Frank, the General Counsel of the Agricultural Adjustment Administration, and Rexford Guy Tugwell, the Assistant Secretary of Agriculture.[85]

Without informing him of the existence of the Wagner group— "the whole thing was a pretty bad mix-up," Tugwell later recalled— the President on April 11 asked brain-truster Raymond Moley to try his hand at shaping a recovery bill. The busy Moley soon delegated the task to General Hugh S. Johnson. The fifty-one year old Johnson had lived as a boy among the Indians of Oklahoma Territory, had been a West Point classmate of Douglas MacArthur, had helped frame and administer the Selective Service Act of 1917, had served as the War Department's representative on the War Industries Board, and had become the youngest brigadier general in the United States since the Civil War. After resigning from the Army in 1919 and working briefly for Bernard Baruch, he had joined forces with George Peek at the Moline Plow Company, and with Peek he had authored the celebrated pamphlet, *Equality for Agriculture*. He had later broken with Peek and again become associated with Baruch. A man of "red face, thick neck, hulking shoulders and barrel-chest," Johnson was soon to gain a reputation as Roosevelt's "noisiest"—and hardest-drinking—lieutenant.[86]

Ever since World War I Johnson had had little faith in the antitrust laws and had believed in the necessity of business-government partnership in the management of the economy. Realizing, however, that any major recovery program would have to include some concession to organized labor and not being particularly knowledgeable in this area, Johnson enlisted the aid of Donald Richberg, then probably "the best-known labor lawyer in the country." Richberg, who was described by one observer as looking like "an amiable woodchuck," had been a devoted follower of Theodore Roosevelt, had served as chairman of the resolutions committee at the Progressive national convention of 1924, had helped wage the legal battle against Samuel Insull's utilities empire, and as counsel for the Railway Labor Executives Association had been the chief draftsman of the Railway

Labor Act of 1926 and had aided in the drafting of the Norris-LaGuardia Act of 1932.[87]

Early in May Roosevelt brought together the two principal groups that were working on recovery legislation and told them to compose their differences and to prepare a bill that he could submit to Congress. A drafting committee of Lewis W. Douglas, the Director of the Budget, Wagner, Johnson, Richberg, Dickinson, Tugwell, and Perkins undertook the task of drawing up an acceptable measure, with the final draft being the work of Douglas, Wagner, Richberg, and Johnson. The National Industrial Recovery Bill was submitted to Congress on May 17 and by June 13 had received the approval of both houses of Congress. The President signed the measure into law three days later.[88]

Title I [89] of the N.I.R.A. permitted trade or industrial associations to draw up codes of fair competition whose provisions were to become "the standards of fair competition" for the trade or industry concerned when the codes had been approved by the President. On his own initiative or on complaint, the President could himself prescribe a code for a trade or industry for which a code had not already been approved. The President was also authorized to enter into agreements with, or to approve voluntary agreements between and among, persons engaged in a trade or industry, trade or industrial associations, or labor organizations. Moreover, when the President found that "destructive wage or price cutting" or other practices contrary to the purposes of the act were being carried on in any trade or industry, he could license the business enterprises concerned in order to make a code or agreement effective, and no person in that line of endeavor could then operate without a license. The President was permitted to suspend or revoke a license for violation of its terms. The licensing provision of the statute gave the President "the power of life or death over business enterprises."

The most hotly debated portion of the new statute and the one that was to have the greatest impact on the automobile manufacturing industry was its labor clause, the famous Section 7(a). It provided that every code, agreement, or license approved or issued under Title I had to stipulate that employees were to have "the right to organize and bargain collectively through representatives of their own choosing" and were to be free from employer "interference, restraint, or coercion" in designating such representatives, in self-organization, or in "other concerted activities for the purpose of collective bargaining or other mutual aid or protection"; that no employee and no one seeking work was to be required as a condition of employment to join a company union or to refrain from joining, organizing, or assisting a labor organization of his own choice; and, finally, that employers were to comply with the maximum hours of labor, minimum rates of pay, and other conditions of employment which the President might approve or prescribe.[90]

As originally submitted to the Congress Section 7(a) had not included any language forbidding employers from interfering with the right of employees to organize and to bargain collectively. William Green, however, had proposed to the House Ways and Means Committee the addition to the section of language taken directly from the policy statement of the Norris-LaGuardia Act which prohibited employer interference with the rights guaranteed to employees, and it was with Section 7(a) in the form Green had recommended that the recovery bill had passed the House.

The language which Green had successfully urged the House to adopt provided for an important change in the labor law of the United States. The existing law of labor relations recognized the right of workers to organize and to bargain collectively, but employers outside the railroad field [91] were equally free to interfere with this right. Under the circumstances, employers used their obviously superior power to discourage organization and to limit its effectiveness where it existed. The language added to Section 7(a) was thus designed to convert a theoretical right into an actual one.

When the recovery bill was before the Senate Finance Committee, the National Association of Manufacturers (N.A.M.) proposed that Section 7(a) be amended "to make it clear that there is neither the intention nor the power to reorganize present mutually satisfactory employment relations, nor to establish any rule which will deny the right of employers and employees to bargain individually or collectively." The Senate Finance Committee was sympathetic to the manufacturers' position, and when it reported the bill it included an amendment to the labor section which stated that nothing in Title I was to "be construed to compel a change in existing satisfactory relationships between the employees and employers of any particular plant, firm, or corporation" other than that the employees had "the right to organize for the purpose of collective bargaining." The amendment, which, to quote Irving Bernstein, "not only sanctioned company unions but might have been construed to negate Sec. 7(a) entirely," was endorsed by both Johnson and Richberg but was beaten on the Senate floor.[92] The A.F. of L. thus won a major victory over the N.A.M. and the many employers who supported its stand, but in view of the important positions to which Johnson and Richberg were soon to be appointed, the Federation's victory was less significant than it momentarily appeared to be.

On the same day that he signed the N.I.R.A. into law, the President selected General Johnson as Administrator for Industrial Recovery and also provided for the creation of a Labor Advisory Board (L.A.B.), to be appointed by the Secretary of Labor, an Industrial Advisory Board (I.A.B.), to be appointed by the Secretary of Commerce, and a Consumers' Advisory Board (C.A.B.), later appointed by the Administrator for Industrial Recovery, to represent labor, industry, and the consumer in matters affecting their interests that might arise under the N.I.R.A. It was also made clear on the same day that of the several alternative lines of action provided for in the N.I.R.A., the administration intended to rely on the initiative of trade and industrial associations in the formulation of codes. Johnson selected the voluntary method of code initiation because he feared that the N.I.R.A., which so enormously expanded the concept of interstate commerce and which permitted the federal government to play a more prominent role than it previously had in peacetime in the allocation of resources, the organization of production, the determination of wages and hours, and the working out of relations between labor and management, might be unconstitutional. Industrial self-government, with some government supervision, was thus to be the rule, and the more drastic alternatives authorized by the statute were relegated to the background.[93]

Quoting President Roosevelt, the National Recovery Administration (N.R.A.)—the name given to the administrative agency headed by Johnson which was to implement Title I of the N.I.R.A.—informed the nation at the outset that the immediate purpose of the statute was *"to put people back to work"* and that the next step was "to plan for a better future for the longer pull." The trade associations were invited to submit "basic" codes dealing with wages, hours, and the methods deemed necessary to prevent destructive competition by a minority. At a later time they could draw up more comprehensive documents dealing with trade practices in general and "competitive methods and relations."

The average work week stipulated in the basic codes, the N.R.A. advised, should be designed to provide jobs "so far as practical" for the employees normally attached to a particular industry. Minimum wages were to be set with a view to furnishing "a decent standard of living" for employees, and the conditions of work specified were to provide for the stabilization of employment in the industry. Businessmen were told that, despite the wage increases that they were being requested to grant, the President wished them to take into account the increased volume of sales resulting from the expected boost in consumer purchasing power and to defer price increases as long as it was possible to do so. The N.R.A. reminded the trade associations that Section 7(a) had to be included in the codes, but at the same time it stated that codes dealing with wages, hours, and other conditions of employment would be subject to approval even if their provisions had not been arrived at through the process of collective bargaining.[94]

Believing that "speed and mass action" were required to spur re-employment and recovery, the N.R.A. urged the ten basic industries of the country which accounted for the bulk of the industrial employment—the automobile industry was among them—to submit basic codes "at once" so that the month of July would mark the beginning of the re-employment effort. Six weeks after the N.I.R.A. had gone into effect, however, only one code, that of the cotton textile industry, had received final approval. The failure of the business community to submit codes as rapidly as the N.R.A. desired was explained in part by the improved business conditions of the early months of the New Deal. The increased production resulting from the expectation of many businessmen that the N.R.A. codes would increase costs and that New Deal policies were likely to lead to inflation had stimulated a business boomlet that diminished the ardor of some industries for codification. Other trades and industries were not as yet sufficiently well organized to submit codes with any great dispatch.

Disturbed at the slow pace of code making and convinced that it was necessary to rouse public opinion as an aid to code enforcement and to provide the confidence needed for a full-fledged business revival, Johnson decided to invoke the section of the N.I.R.A. which authorized the President to enter into voluntary agreements with persons engaged in trade and industry in order to further the purposes of the statute. On July 20 the N.R.A. accordingly announced an "emergency reemployment drive" for the period August 1 to December 31, 1933, and set forth the terms of a President's Reemployment Agreement (P.R.A.) which it invited employers to sign and abide by pending the adoption of their codes.[95]

Employers who signed either a voluntary agreement or their industry's code were permitted to display the seal of the N.R.A., a blue eagle, on their goods and premises, and the public was urged to patronize only those employers who thus indicated their compliance with the purposes of the statute. "There is no force here except conscience and opinion," the N.R.A. announced. "This is a test of patriotism." [96]

General Johnson, described by Matthew Josephson as "one of the greatest masters of hullabaloo since Barnum," mounted a vast publicity campaign to arouse public support for the Blue Eagle and the recovery program. Employers with sixteen million employees eventually accepted the P.R.A., although they were commonly permitted to deviate to some degree from the recommended wages and hours. The P.R.A. also served as a stimulus to code formulation and code submission. Since employers, in the absence of a code for their industry, felt obliged to sign the P.R.A. and hence, in all probability, to incur higher labor costs, they concluded that it was preferable to secure approval for a code which although it would probably have to include labor standards similar to those in the P.R.A. could also make provision for trade practices which might mean greater security and greater profits for the members of the industry.[97]

When an employer signed the P.R.A. or when the code for his trade or industry became effective, he was obligated by the N.I.R.A. to observe the requirements of Section 7(a). Just what this entailed, however, was by no means self-evident. The particular employer tactics that constituted "interference, restraint, or coercion" were not defined in the section, nor were employers specifically obligated to recognize and to deal with the representatives of the workers. Section 7(a) gave no indication of how employee representatives were to be selected, did not appear to have prohibited individual bargaining or company unions per se, and it was silent on the question of the closed shop. Above all, no administrative machinery was provided for the enforcement of the section.

Organized labor, naturally enough, contended that Section 7(a) was designed to promote trade unionism and that workers were most likely to benefit from the statute if they joined an outside labor organization. Management, however, insisted with equal vigor that the act was permissive in character and that neither the company union nor individual bargaining was proscribed by its terms. The A.F. of L. sought to give substance to its views by attempting to spread its organization to the unorganized, but the employers in many industries responded by establishing company unions in their plants. When the steel industry submitted its code on July 15, 1933, it stipulated that employees in the industry were to be hired without regard to their membership or nonmembership in a union, and specific provision was made for an employee-representation plan. The

N.A.M. shortly thereafter advised employers before signing the P.R.A. to secure approval for additional language which made clear their "constitutional right" to deal with their employees in "such form" as was "mutually agreeable." [98]

General Johnson reacted to this controversy between organized labor and management as to the meaning of Section 7(a) by pursuing what he defined to be a policy of "perfect neutrality." "I am not shading either way," he told a meeting of the Special Industrial Recovery Board [99] on August 14. Again and again, he stated that the language of Section 7(a) would have to be written into every code but that the statute was not intended to force the organization of either labor or industry. "We are not trying to unionize labor by federal command," declared Donald Richberg, who as General Counsel occupied the second most important position in the N.R.A.'s administrative hierarchy.[100]

The rash of strikes resulting from labor's efforts to organize the unorganized, the resistance of the employers, and the improvement in business conditions in the summer of 1933 persuaded the President on August 5 to create the National Labor Board (N.L.B.) to "consider, adjust, and settle differences and controversies" arising under the P.R.A. Although it was not specifically authorized to do so until December 16, 1933, the N.L.B., which consisted of three employer representatives, three labor representatives, and Senator Wagner as impartial chairman, began adjusting labor disputes arising under the codes as well as under the P.R.A. It attempted, moreover, not only to forestall and to mediate strikes but also to interpret Section 7(a) and to conduct elections among the workers to determine whom they wished to represent them in collective bargaining.[101] Located entirely outside the N.R.A. administrative structure the N.L.B. was destined to become involved in a jurisdictional conflict with the recovery agency regarding the adjustment of labor disputes.

VI

When it became clear that the N.I.R.A. would be passed, President Green called the presidents of the Federation's national and international unions to a conference in Washington on June 6 and 7 to formulate plans for the organization of the unorganized. It was at this conference that the decision was made to launch an organization campaign in the automobile industry. To head the drive, which was to be centered in Detroit, Green selected William Collins, an A.F. of L. organizer who had previously served the Federation in the motor city and who had been consulted by the organization's leadership in preparation for the ill-fated automobile organizing campaign of 1927. Collins was aptly described by one columnist as having the appearance of "a middle-aged Sunday School teacher." [102]

When Collins arrived in Detroit on June 21, he discovered that an organization campaign had already been launched in the automobile industry by the Detroit Federation of Labor (D.F. of L.). Frank Martel, the president of the D.F. of L., promised to co-operate with Collins in his efforts to unionize the city's automobile workers, but as it turned out, the D.F. of L. was probably more a hindrance than a help to Collins in the Detroit campaign.[103]

In directing the A.F. of L's campaign in the auto industry, Collins was aided by organizers assigned directly to him, who operated principally but not exclusively in Michigan's automobile centers, and by organizers in such places as South Bend, Cleveland, and the Wisconsin auto towns, who devoted only part of their time to the automobile industry. Where A.F. of L. organizers were not available, the local city federation of labor or central labor union was expected to aid in the job of recruiting union members.[104]

Efforts were made to reach workers through general meetings and plant meetings, and the union message was also spread by handbills, radio, and, in Detroit at least, by sound truck. The workers were told that the higher wages and shorter hours intended by the N.I.R.A. would come to them only through organization and that employers were now forbidden to interfere with the right of their employees to join a union. "The door of opportunity to organization," Collins proclaimed in his first campaign circular, "is open to the worker for the first time in the history of the country." The workers who heeded the A.F. of L.'s message were placed in federal labor unions chartered directly by the Federation. One federal labor union was generally provided for each automobile plant, but in Toledo, for no logical reason, a single local served all of the city's numerous auto plants.[105]

Green and Collins had hoped that there would be sufficient organization in the automobile industry by the time that public hearings were held on the automobile code to permit the auto unionists to send their own spokesmen to Washington to argue the case of the automobile workers. Progress in the early weeks of the campaign was far from impressive, however. Although six charters had been issued in Detroit by the end of July, Collins complained that unemployment, fear, and the "determined underground opposition" of the employers were making it difficult to enlist union members. He informed A.F. of L. secretary Frank Morrison on August 5 that he had taken in but $1300 in initiation fees—which represented perhaps one thousand members—and that he would not issue membership cards or books until the automobile code had been approved because it was too dangerous as yet to establish unions that could function openly. The result was that, when hearings were held on the code on August 18, it was Green himself who spoke for the automobile workers, and not a single representative from the ranks of the new federal labor unions was present to testify.[106]

Whereas the A.F. of L. welcomed the N.I.R.A. as providing an opportunity for it, at long last, to organize the automobile workers, the communists, then in the midst of their so-called "social-fascist" period, heaped scorn upon the measure as upon the evolving New Deal as a whole. The *Michigan Worker* castigated "the semi-Fascist Roosevelt" N.I.R.A. and warned that the A.F. of L. would use the statute "to smash the struggles of the workers." At the A.W.U. convention of June 24–25, 1933, Phil Raymond, in dutiful conformity with the party line, attacked the N.I.R.A. as designed to reduce working standards and to place laborers in organizations designated by the employers.

Although it chose to treat the N.I.R.A. as a "vicious sugar-coated attack against the workers," the A.W.U. nevertheless drew up a code for presentation at the automobile code hearings. Because of the "murderous speed-up system" in the industry, the A.W.U. insisted on the need for a "drastic" reduction in hours and a substantial increase in wages. Its code, as finally presented, called for a minimum wage of 75 cents an hour, a thirty-hour week, a guaranteed annual wage of $900, employee-elected committees in all departments of the auto plants to regulate production schedules and the speed of the line, a policy of no discrimination against women, Negro, and young workers, a social insurance system financed by the federal government and the employers to cover unemployment, sickness and disability, and old age, the right of the workers to elect shop and departmental committees, and the right to strike and to engage in mass picketing. A special code was also proposed by the A.W.U. for the Ford Motor Company on the grounds that the speed-up at Ford and the company's interference in the private lives of its employees required special attention.[107]

The provisions of the A.W.U. code, as the organization was aware, were totally unrealistic in terms of what was likely to be included in an automobile code, but the A.W.U. framed its code not in the expectation of having it adopted or even for bargaining purposes but only for its propaganda effect on the automobile workers. It offered itself to them as an industrial union run by the rank and file and, with its customary disregard for the facts, as the victor in the automobile strikes of early 1933.[108]

The I.W.W., perhaps because of its anarcho-syndicalist tendencies, perhaps because it was hardly visible as an organization in the automobile industry, did not even bother to formulate a code for presentation in Washington. "Political morons," it declared, "trust in codes. Industrial workers build unions." It attacked the N.I.R.A. as "Fascist" and as a "deadly menace" to the labor movement and asserted that industrial recovery would come about only when the workers "organize as a class, take possession of the earth and machinery of production, and abolish the wage system." The I.W.W. had always been strong on rhetoric, and despite a flurry of activity in the fall of 1933, it was destined to be more a commentator on, than a participant in, the automobile labor scene of the New Deal era.[109]

By the time the code hearings were held in Washington two new organizations, the Federation of Automotive Workers (F.A.W.) and the Mechanics Educational Society of America (M.E.S.A.), had emerged to take their place among the several labor groups competing for the favor of the auto workers. The existence of both of these organizations reflected the impotence of the A.F. of L. in the automobile industry at the beginning of the New Deal. The F.A.W. developed in the early months of the New Deal out of the desire of some automobile workers in Lansing, Michigan, site of several automobile plants, to join the A.F. of L. They approached the Lansing Trades and Labor Council for a charter, but President John Reid, not quite knowing if workers of this sort had a place in the Federation, referred them to Socialist headquarters in the city, where attorney Peter Fagan took them under his wing and helped them to form an organization. No one in the A.F. of L. seemed to know whether the F.A.W. was "purely a political move" or a dual union, although Collins originally inclined to the former view. Since he could not himself devote time to Lansing, Collins referred the matter to the city's Trades and Labor Council and designated Reid as special organizer for the area.

At the automobile code hearings Fagan indicated that his organization, which by that time had also taken root in Pontiac, was not in disagreement with the A.F. of L. and would probably merge with it. Events were not destined to take this course, however, possibly because of the Socialist and anti-A.F. of L. tone which Fagan and his wife imparted to the F.A.W., possibly because the A.F. of L. came to view the organization as dual in character. Following the code hearings, the F.A.W. reorganized as the Chamber of Labor. It continued to be active for a time in Pontiac in particular, but it soon faded from the automobile scene, although it seems to have lingered on for a while in other areas of the economy.[110]

The M.E.S.A. was formed during the early months of 1933 by a small number of Detroit tool and die makers. Although it was later claimed that the name of the organization was selected to "confuse" the employers, the expressed purpose of the organization at the outset was social and educational, and early meetings appear to have been given over to the consideration of some of the technical problems of the trade. Whatever the character of the M.E.S.A. as initially formed, the enactment of the N.I.R.A. persuaded the leaders of the organization to seek support for the M.E.S.A. among the workers as a full-fledged trade union. Tool and die makers in the automobile plants and in the job shops that served the automobile and other industries were informed that President Roosevelt had given them "the right to organize under his protection" and that they should take advantage of the opportunity. Through an organization like the M.E.S.A., they were told, they might be able to do something about the seasonality of their employment, the reduced wages the depression had brought, and the contract system.[111] By late August the M.E.S.A. claimed five thousand members in Detroit, a local in Flint, and some membership in Pontiac.[112]

In seeking to organize the highly skilled workers who made or repaired tools, dies, jigs, fixtures, and machinery, the M.E.S.A. was invading the jurisdiction of the A.F. of L.'s International Association of Machinists (I.A.M.). Despite its jurisdictional claims, however, the I.A.M. had precious few members in the automobile manufacturing industry, and the organization's reputation among the auto workers, particularly in Detroit, was not high. The M.E.S.A. not only capitalized on this fact, but it also initially offered membership to tool and die makers without an initiation fee and for monthly dues of twenty-five cents, whereas the I.A.M. at the time imposed a $5–$20 initiation fee and charged monthly dues of $1.75.[113]

Just beginning to gather strength in the automobile industry, the M.E.S.A. did not send a representative to the automobile code hearings, although it did transmit a written brief requesting a thirty-hour week and a minimum hourly wage of $1.50 for tool and die makers.[114] Its willingness to fight for its demands was soon to be made evident, for in September 1933 it was to wage the most widespread strike in the history of the automobile industry up to that time.

By the time the M.E.S.A. initiated its strike, the code of the automobile manufacturing industry had passed through the various stages of the code-making process and had received the approval of the President. The A.F. of L. had hoped that the terms of the code would serve to enhance the Federation's appeal to the automobile workers, but the document that emerged from the code negotiations primarily reflected the preponderant power in the industry of the automobile manufacturers rather than the aspirations of the small number of automobile unionists.

II

DRAFTING OF THE AUTOMOBILE CODE

THE AUTOMOBILE MANUFACTURING INDUSTRY first made its views known with respect to the impending recovery legislation early in April 1933, when the Black Bill was before the Senate. In response to a request from Michigan's Senator Arthur Vandenberg for an expression of opinion regarding the measure, several auto manufacturers indicated their opposition to any rigid limitation of hours should it become necessary to enact legislation of the sort being contemplated. B. E. Hutchinson, vice-president and treasurer of Chrysler, who obviously did not believe that the nation's economic ills required a "New Deal" for their solution, regarded the whole scheme as "unsound and impractical." "We feel," he declared, "that our economic salvation can be worked out along lines proved by experience if the government will continue and make effective its determination to balance the budget and give us a sound fiscal structure...." [1]

The official view of the National Automobile Chamber of Commerce on the Thirty-Hour Bill was presented to the House Committee on Labor on May 5, 1933, by Alfred P. Sloan, Jr., the president of G.M. There was so much unemployment, Sloan observed, that "most anything is justified that appears to offer a reasonable chance of relief." The industry, he indicated, approved the share-the-work principle but found the Black Bill too rigid in this regard. Greater flexibility would have to be permitted to a seasonal business such as automobile manufacturing because otherwise the automobile companies would have to employ additional workers during the rush season who would have to be taken care of somehow during the period of slack production, and also because the additional work provided when output was at its peak was required to offset the reduced hours of employment and the meager earnings of the slack season. Sloan consequently proposed that employees be permitted to work up to forty-eight hours per week provided that they did not exceed thirty-two (rather than thirty) hours per week averaged on an annual basis. He also recommended that supervisory personnel and employees engaged in maintenance, repair, and construction be exempted from the hours requirements of the statute and that the Secretary of Labor be authorized to make additional exceptions. He further indicated that he would like to see the bill apply to intrastate as well as interstate commerce lest interstate employers be placed at a competitive disadvantage.

Because he feared the deflationary effect of a program of reduced hours unaccompanied by an increase in wage rates, Sloan accepted the concept of the minimum wage as a desirable corollary of shorter hours "if universally applicable and scientifically developed." The rate, he advised, should be set by the Secretary of Labor, should be adjusted according to the cost of living in different sections of the country or in different communities, and should be sufficient provided the prescribed number of hours was worked to cover the "necessities of life." Sloan made it clear that he was thinking of a minimum wage below that which prevailed in the high-wage automobile industry, and he expressed his opposition to any regulation of wages above the minimum.

As for proposals being bruited about to provide for the regulation of production, Sloan noted that the automobile industry already exercised control over its production by limiting stocks of cars to the "minimum amount essential to [the] current movement of business." He observed that other businesses, however, might find it necessary to regulate production through their trade associations and indicated that he objected neither to this nor to the use of the power of government to restrain the minority in a particular trade who engaged in cutthroat competition.[2]

Although the Black Bill was to be sidetracked in favor of the more comprehensive recovery legislation recommended by the administration, the views expressed by Sloan foreshadowed the stand the automobile manufacturers were likely to take on an automobile code. The industry, it seemed clear, would insist on flexibility in the hours provision of its code and on minimum wages below prevailing minima in the industry, and it would be unlikely to seek controls over production or competitive practices. Sloan had not discussed the views of the N.A.C.C. on the subject of labor organization and collective bargaining, but it was not difficult to predict that the open-shop automobile industry would resist with all its power any pressures designed to cause it to alter its traditional labor policies. It might also have been predicted that should the upswing in automobile production and automobile sales that had become evident in April continue during the next few months, as indeed it did,[3] the industry would retreat from the official position taken by Sloan and the N.A.C.C. in the direction of the less accommodating views expressed by Hutchinson.

While the National Industrial Recovery Bill was before Congress, the automobile manufacturers expressed public concern only about the new three-fourths of a cent tax on gasoline imposed by the measure;[4] but behind the scenes their Washington representative, Pyke Johnson, was asking the bill's draftsmen questions that indicated the industry's awareness of the broader implications of the measure, and Johnson was warning the manufacturers that the proposed legislation was "far more drastic than anything this country has faced in the past." A few days after the bill was reported out by the House Ways and Means Committee, President Alvan Macauley of the N.A.C.C., obviously aware that more was at stake for the industry than a new gasoline tax, appointed a special committee consisting of Sloan as chairman, Walter P. Chrysler, president and chairman of the board of Chrysler Corporation, Charles W. Nash, chairman of the board of Nash Motors, Roy D. Chapin, president of the Hudson Motor Car Company, Edsel Ford, and Macauley himself to consider the bill in relation to the auto industry and to report its views to the annual meeting of the N.A.C.C. on June 15.[5]

Before the Senate Committee on Finance on May 31 the only objection the automobile industry raised to the recovery bill once again concerned the tax on gasoline,[6] but by that time, as Chapin and Sloan were to advise Pyke Johnson, the manufacturers were more disturbed by the labor clause of the bill than by any of its other sections. "I have been here through every year that the motor industry has existed in the state," Chapin wrote Johnson on June 1, "and realize that its prosperity is partly due to lack of restrictions on the handling of our labor." He was "very skeptical" of the effect of unionism on automobile prices and on the ability of the auto manufacturers "to handle our plants efficiently." Sloan stated flatly that G.M. would "not subscribe to the Industrial Recovery Act as long as the possibility remains for the American Federation of Labor to organize ... [its] plants." On the strength of these two letters, Pyke Johnson "felt safe" in advising administration representatives and Senator Vandenberg of the industry's opposition to any statute permitting the A.F. of L. "to go into its plants and organize workers."[7]

General Johnson, soon to be appointed Administrator for Industrial Recovery, was in the meantime urging the industry to submit a code promptly and was seeking to allay its fears concerning some of the implications of the recovery bill. In an interview on June 2 with Alfred Reeves, N.A.C.C. vice-president and general manager, and Pyke Johnson, the general warned that the economic situation would deteriorate further unless the large industries co-operated in the recovery program. He advised Pyke and Reeves, as the N.R.A. was soon to advise industry in general, that the automobile manufacturers could submit a code dealing with working conditions without previously consulting labor representatives. Above all, the general made it clear that it was "emphatically not the intention that the administration shall be used as an instrument for promoting the interest of organized labor." As for the N.A.C.C.'s fear that Ford would refuse to join with fellow automobile manufacturers in the acceptance of a code, Johnson noted that all units of an industry would have to abide by the provisions of a code once it had received Presidential approval.[8]

The general unquestionably made a good impression on Pyke and Reeves, and his views on the subject of organized labor were particularly encouraging, but the N.A.C.C. continued to have its doubts about the implications of the recovery bill. The law itself, after all, might encourage unionization no matter what Johnson's personal views were. Also, the presence among the statute's drafters of Donald Richberg and the likelihood that he would play some part in the administration of the measure caused fear that labor would have "a decided voice in the procedure." [9] This fear seems ironic in view of the role the erstwhile labor lawyer was ultimately to play in the implementation of the recovery program.

Although an N.A.C.C. bulletin of June 8 described the recovery bill as "the most revolutionary proposal of our generation," Sloan, on behalf of his committee, made an "interesting and sympathetic report" on the measure to the N.A.C.C. meeting of June 15. Following this report, Macauley was authorized to name a new committee to study the subject and to report back on the desirability of a code, and he was also instructed to inform Roosevelt and Johnson of the unanimous wish of the industry to co-operate "in getting men back to work." Within a few days Macauley had named a Committee on the National Industrial Recovery Act consisting of Donaldson Brown, a G.M. vice-president, Robert Graham of Graham-Paige, A. E. McKinstry, an International Harvester vice-president, Walter Chrysler, and Herman L. Moekle, who was in charge of Ford's auditing department. Reeves had informed Henry Ford of the N.A.C.C.'s desire to have the entire industry represented on the committee and had suggested Moekle, who had attended the June 15 meeting, as a committee member. Edsel Ford replied that he was "glad" to have Moekle serve.[10]

As the auto manufacturers turned to the task of code making, they were aware that the administration was particularly anxious that the automobile industry, as the pacesetter of the economy, should be included among the early code adopters. Because of the nature of the N.I.R.A., however, the administration was not in a strong bargaining position in seeking to enlist the industry's support. In return for the agreement of industrial and trade associations to incorporate in their codes the terms of Section 7(a) and to adopt wage and hour provisions designed to spur re-employment and to increase purchasing power, the administration was prepared to sanction the inclusion in the codes of trade practices that might otherwise have been regarded as in violation of the antitrust laws. Although this seemed like a fair exchange to many businessmen, it had little appeal for the automobile manufacturers. Unlike so many other industries, the automobile industry, as we have seen, was not faced in 1933 with the problem of overproduction or of destructive price cutting, and the manufacturers, through the N.A.C.C., had already standardized their trade practices to the extent they thought necessary. If the Pandora's box of trade practices were opened, there was always the danger that pressure would be put on the automobile manufacturers by the administration or others to accept an unsatisfactory definition of their relationship with their dealers and their suppliers. Consequently, although the industry did not altogether rule out the possibility that it might be interested in "improved trade practices" that would lead to reduced costs, it was unique among the major businesses of the nation in its lack of interest in the opportunity for cartelization that the N.I.R.A. provided.[11]

As for the N.I.R.A. objectives of shorter hours and higher wages, the industry was able to point to the share-the-work program it had already put into effect and the fact that its hourly wage rates were well above those of other manufacturing industries. N.A.C.C. members, moreover, were soon to boost the wage rates of their workers by an additional 10–20 per cent and thus to lend added support to the argument that it did not require an N.R.A. code to bring the automobile industry into line with the administration's recovery program. In announcing a 10 per cent wage increase on July 21 Chrysler Corporation specifically declared that it was putting into effect "the most important part" of the N.I.R.A.[12]

The adoption of a code, furthermore, meant the mandatory inclusion of the terms of Section 7(a), which the industry viewed as irrelevant to the recovery program [13] and as a threat to its traditional open-shop policy. Believing that it had little if anything to gain from a code, the industry thus feared that it actually had much to lose. Unless appropriate code language could be devised that specifically permitted them to operate their plants on an open-shop basis, the automobile manufacturers, who saw no compensatory advantages to be derived in the form of legalized trade practices, were prepared to do without a code.

If the N.R.A., in a sense, needed the automobile industry more than the industry needed the N.R.A., the automobile companies, nevertheless, could not afford to ignore the fact that the N.I.R.A. had the support of a very popular President and that in the crisis atmosphere of the early months of the New Deal, General Johnson was able to identify support of the statute with patriotism itself. From a public-relations standpoint, certainly, it was preferable for the industry to submit a code voluntarily than to have the President impose a code on it, as he was authorized to do, or even to let it appear that the industry was acting only because of administration pressure. Considerations of this sort undoubtedly explain the stance of the automobile manufacturers with regard to the codification of the industry.[14]

At its first meeting on June 22 the N.A.C.C. code committee elected Donaldson Brown as its chairman and decided that its principal function should be to submit to the N.A.C.C. recommendations concerning the terms of a code rather than to decide whether or not it was desirable for the industry to formulate a code altogether. Although, as Moekle noted, there was "a strong sentiment in the committee that no code at all should be filed, if such a thing is possible," the prevailing view was that the only real choice available to the industry was to submit a code or to accept one prescribed by the federal government. It was agreed that the basic code should be a simple one, covering only hours and wages.[15]

The committee met again on at least three occasions, and by July 25 it had prepared a code for submission to the board of directors of the N.A.C.C. and to the general membership. The committee was assisted in its labors by the attorney Gilbert H. Montague, an authority on antitrust law who had once numbered Franklin D. Roosevelt among his economics students at Harvard and who had been engaged by Brown in a "consulting and advisory capacity"; by attorneys for the companies represented by the committee's membership; by Alfred Reeves; and by an N.A.C.C. labor relations committee, of which William S. Knudsen, then president of the Chevrolet division, was the chairman. The code had gone through at least eight different drafts by the time it was finally submitted to Johnson on July 28.[16]

One of the basic questions that the Brown committee had to decide was to whom the automobile code should apply. Should it cover only the manufacturers and assemblers of motor vehicles, or should it also embrace the manufacturers of parts and accessories, the wholesale automotive trade, and the automobile dealers? Little if any attention was actually given to the inclusion of the automotive wholesalers and the dealers, but since the vehicle manufacturers and the parts manufacturers competed in the fabrication of a large number of parts, there was some feeling that a common code for these two groups of manufacturers—or at least an agreement regarding "mutual standards of labor"—might be desirable. The Motor and Equipment Manufacturers Association and the National Standard Parts Association, the two principal trade associations of the parts manufacturers, were invited to join with the automobile manufacturers in the submission of a code, but the drafting of the auto code reached its final stages before the parts organizations had been able to ascertain the wishes of their membership regarding the desirability of a common code. General Johnson, anxious for speed, indicated his preference for a code applying to automobile manufacturing alone rather than that the N.A.C.C. delay matters in an effort to secure "more comprehensive coverage." The result was that the automobile code as submitted applied only to the "manufacturing and assembling within the United States of motor vehicles and bodies therefor, and of component and repair parts and accessories by manufacturers or assemblers of motor vehicles." [17]

It is unlikely that the automobile manufacturers were in the end distressed by the failure of their code to encompass the automobile parts industry since this meant that they would not have to answer for working conditions in the parts plants, which were generally inferior to those in the main plants, and because of the difficulty there would have been in administering a code that included not only the relatively small number of vehicle manufacturers but also the hundreds of parts plants as well. Many of the parts manufacturers were undoubtedly also pleased that they were to have a separate code since they believed that this enhanced the status of parts making as a separate industry. [18]

In addition to the question of coverage, the code committee had to decide whether the expiration date of the code should be December 31, 1933, or June 16, 1935, the date the N.I.R.A. itself was scheduled to come to an end. The committee eventually chose the December date since this would leave the industry free after a relatively short time to decide whether the terms of the code were suitable or, indeed, whether it wished to continue under a code at all. [19]

The committee considered but paid relatively little attention to the subject of trade practices. Before the first meeting of the group, Reeves circulated among the membership a list of passenger-car trade practices that had been discussed in the industry from time to time,[20] and the following week Brown suggested that each member of the committee should submit to Reeves the specific practices that he believed deserved consideration for possible inclusion in a supplementary code. Moekle, at least, prepared such a list, but the available minutes of code meetings do not indicate that the subject was even discussed, and none of the various code drafts emanating from the committee contains any reference to trade practices.[21]

The subjects to which the code committee gave greatest attention were hours, wages, and management-labor relations. In its treatment of the hours question, the committee was agreed from the start that some sort of averaging principle would have to be adopted to give the employers sufficient flexibility in the handling of their labor force to cope with the irregularity of automobile production, and also that some employees vital to the production process would have to be exempted from the hours limitations imposed upon other workers.

After examining the employment records of N.A.C.C. plants in the Detroit area and seeking the views of member firms outside the motor city, the committee decided to set the maximum weekly hours for covered factory employees at forty-eight and to stipulate that working hours averaged on an annual basis should not exceed forty per week. When it was determined, however, that the code should run only until December 31 and thus apply to a period of the year when production tended to be low, it was agreed that the average hours should be set at thirty-five per week from the effective date to the expiration date. The "supervisory staff and employees engaged in the preparation, care, and maintenance of plant machinery and facilities of and for production" were exempted from all hourly limitations. The maximum weekly hours specified for factory employees were also applied to office and salaried employees receiving less than $35 per week, but the white-collar workers were permitted to average forty hours per week from the effective date to the expiration date.[22]

The proposed hours provisions of the auto code differed in some respects from the standards set forth in the P.R.A., which was announced on July 20, before the auto code was submitted to the N.R.A. The P.R.A. also provided a basic thirty-five hour week for factory employees until December 31, 1933, but whereas the proposed auto code permitted a forty-eight hour week during this period as long as the thirty-five hour average was observed, the deviation from the standard permitted by the P.R.A. was a more modest forty-hour week for six weeks. The P.R.A. exempted from the hours limitations applying to other workers approximately the same categories of employees as were exempted by the auto code, but the President's agreement provided a time-and-one-third-overtime rate for at least some of the nonmanagerial exempted employees, whereas there was no overtime provision in the auto code. White-collar workers were limited to forty hours per week by the P.R.A. but could work up to forty-eight hours during some weeks under the auto code.[23]

Although the hours provisions of the draft auto code were less stringent than the standards set forth in the P.R.A., they nevertheless called for a substantial change in the predepression practice of the industry with regard to hours of employment. In 1929, for example, slightly more than 70 per cent of the employees engaged in the manufacture of motor vehicles normally worked more than forty-eight hours per week, and work weeks of sixty or more hours were not uncommon in the 1920's during periods of peak production. The average hours of employment of N.A.C.C. employees fell from 45.6 per week in 1929 to 30.8 in 1932, but the improvement in business conditions in the spring and summer of 1933 led to an increase in the working hours in the automobile plants, and the average work week of N.A.C.C. employees rose to forty-five hours in June.[24]

The code committee initially decided that the country should be zoned for wage purposes, but it abandoned this idea after General Johnson advised that code minimum wages should vary according to the size of the community in which a plant was located. In its early drafts of the code, the Brown committee specified a minimum wage of thirty-five cents for adult males and thirty cents for women and employees under twenty-one years of age; but possibly because it erroneously thought that this was what the P.R.A. required, the committee eventually decided that the minimum wage of adult male factory employees should be 40 cents per hour in cities of less than 250,000 population, 41½ cents in cities with populations of 250,000 to 500,000, and 43 cents in cities of over 500,000 population. A five-cent differential was specified for female employees and for male factory employees under twenty-one; and the labor of children under sixteen years of age was entirely prohibited, which accorded with the practice of the industry and the terms of the P.R.A. The minimum wage of office and salaried employees was set at $14.00, $14.50, or $15.00 per week depending on the size of the community in which they worked. No provision was made for the adjustment of wages above the minimum.[25]

The minimum hourly wage of forty to forty-three cents proposed in the auto code was above the thirty- to forty-cent minimum specified for factory workers by the P.R.A., but it should be noted that 90 per cent of N.A.C.C. male employees were receiving more than 43 cents per hour at the end of June 1933, and the pay increases put into effect in July and August, before the code was approved, increased this number to 95 per cent. The auto code also made no provision for the adjustment of rates above the minimum whereas the P.R.A. stated that such wages were not to be reduced because of the reduction in hours and called for the "equitable readjustment of all pay schedules." Unlike the proposed auto code, the P.R.A. did not permit a wage differential for women and for male employees between the ages of sixteen and twenty-one. The pay provided for white-collar workers was similar in both documents.[26]

The question which most concerned the Brown committee was the manner in which the relations of labor and management should be defined in the code. Section 7(a), of course, had to be included, but since the meaning of the section was by no means clear, the code committee was determined to add explanatory language which would permit the industry to continue its open-shop policy. The auto manufacturers contended that it was not the intention of the statute to coerce the workers into joining labor unions but only to protect employees against "the unscrupulous—whoever they may be." Since the manufacturers were convinced that their employees were satisfied with the prevailing character of labor relations in the industry, the "unscrupulous," as the N.A.C.C. saw it, were not the employers but rather the labor "agitators or organizers," who, the automobile manufacturers insisted, had no interest in the welfare of the industry but were simply anxious to collect dues from the automobile workers. It had to be made clear in the code that this sort of "outside" interference simply would not be tolerated.[27]

In an effort to secure official recognition of its understanding of the meaning of Section 7(a), the Brown committee decided to incorporate in the automobile code a somewhat abridged version of language interpreting the section that had originally been suggested for inclusion in the various codes by the National Industrial Conference, a meeting of businessmen convened in Chicago on June 20 by the N.A.M. "In accordance with the foregoing provisions [Section 7(a)]," the automobile code as submitted to the N.R.A. stated, "the employers in the automobile industry propose to continue the open shop policy heretofore followed and under which unusually satisfactory and harmonious relations with employees have been maintained. The selection, retention and advancement of employees will be on the basis of individual merit without regard to their affiliation or non-affiliation with any labor or other organization." [28]

One final question that the code committee had to determine was the composition of the agency that would administer the code. Provision was orginally made for the administration of the code by representatives of both the N.A.C.C. and the Ford Motor Company, but when it began to appear that Ford would not join in the submission of the code, it was decided to vest governing responsibilities in the N.A.C.C. alone. The principal duties, which were to be exercised for the Chamber by its board of directors, were to collect the statistics required by the code or the President and to represent the industry in conferences with the N.R.A. Each employer was to furnish the N.A.C.C. approximately every four weeks reports showing the hours worked by the various occupational groups and the wages that they received.[29]

The code agreed on by the Brown committee was submitted to the N.A.C.C.'s board of directors on July 25 and to the Chamber's membership the next day. Although the directors and a "substantial majority" of the membership [30] approved the document, no final action was immediately taken on the code by the automobile manufacturers. Before the N.A.C.C. leaders would submit their code they wanted unequivocal assurances from the N.R.A. on two crucial matters—the status of the Ford Motor Company under the N.I.R.A. should it refuse to sign the code and also the meaning of Section 7(a). By July 26 it was beginning to appear that Henry Ford might not sign, and N.A.C.C. members were concerned lest Ford enjoy some advantage over them if they agreed to the code and he did not. The N.A.C.C. was also alarmed at reports that the A.F. of L. was telling auto workers that they had to join the Federation to enjoy the full benefits of the N.I.R.A. and by the news that six federal labor unions had already been established in the automobile plants in Detroit. Under the circumstances, the manufacturers believed that an advance endorsement by the N.R.A. of the industry's interpretation of the controversial Section 7(a) was required.[31]

Never one to make a virtue of patience and convinced that the success of the N.R.A. and of the recovery program depended on the speedy codification of the nation's major industries, General Johnson decided that personal diplomacy was the way to hasten action by the automobile manufacturers. Leaving Washington, he flew to Detroit on July 27 to talk with N.A.C.C. leaders and to give them a "clearer understanding" of the meaning and purposes of the N.I.R.A. He would not leave Detroit, he declared upon his arrival, until the code was "buttoned up." [32]

Whatever final doubts the auto manufacturers had about the N.I.R.A. must have been resolved in their conversations with Johnson. In direct fashion and with occasional injections of the profanity for which he was famous, Johnson succeeded in "clarifying a lot of things" for the manufacturers and in convincing them that he was not only "damn serious" [33] but that he was on the whole sympathetic with the industry's point of view.

The most significant discussion between Johnson and the N.A.C.C. leadership took place on July 28 in the General Motors Building. [34] The twelve industrialists present made clear to the general their concern about Ford's apparent reluctance to associate himself with the code. "We want every advantage and every disadvantage equal," Chrysler told Johnson. The N.A.C.C. leaders were troubled by the cost advantage the Ford Motor Company enjoyed because of the lower wages it was then paying, [35] and at the same time they were apprehensive that Henry Ford, with his penchant for the dramatic, would take some action that would embarrass them. "If that baby," Chrysler remarked, "should go to 30 hours a week and $1.00 an hour and he signs that clause VII it will put us in a hell of a position." Johnson sought to allay the fears of the manufacturers by telling them that if Ford did not sign the industry's code, his cars could not display the Blue Eagle. "I wouldn't like to go out and sell any product in the United States that didn't have that bird on it," Johnson declared. He also assured the auto executives that he would not permit Ford to "upset" the industry's price structure.

Most of the discussion at the July 28 conference revolved about Section 7(a). As Chapin plaintively told Johnson, "We have been sitting here and cooperating to the limit. The thing that sticks is this Section 7-A." To reassure the executives Johnson, as he was to do publicly before he left Detroit and on other occasions as well, explained that it was not the "function" of the N.I.R.A. to organize either industry or labor and that it was not necessary for a worker to join either a trade union or a company union in order to receive the benefits of the act. Employers might bargain individually with their men, but they could not refuse to bargain with the chosen representatives of the workers, nor could they require a worker as a condition of employment to join or not to join a particular organization. Johnson explained, however, that "The fact that you bargain with the men doesn't mean you have to agree." In an obiter dictum that must have been comforting to the automobile manufacturers, he declared that labor was better treated in the automobile industry than in any other industry.

Knudsen, curiously enough in view of the events that were to follow, remarked that the auto executives had no objection to the formation of a single automobile union for the whole country, but that they were opposed to separate plant unions and to separate craft unions within a plant. None of Knudsen's fellow executives took exception to this startling statement although it could hardly have been in accord with their views. Johnson endorsed the idea with some enthusiasm and talked vaguely about industry-wide bargaining that would take place in Washington, presumably with the federal government also involved in the negotiations. Sloan cut short any further discussion along these lines by bluntly declaring that he "would rather be in the hands of the Labor Unions than ... in the hands of the politicians."

Macauley read to Johnson the explanatory statements regarding Section 7(a) that the code committee had agreed upon, and Johnson unhesitatingly remarked, "I am glad you put it just that way." He asked to have the two propositions read again, and when this was done, his comment was simply, "100%." Later, after he came to regret the approval that he had given these statements, Johnson, in explaining his action, declared that he had read the language "hastily" and had then agreed to it. "I made such a slip as I suppose might be expected of anybody in such stress." [36] That Johnson, who was devoting all of his fabulous energies to the N.R.A., was under stress goes without saying. But the rest of his statement is more fiction than fact. The language had been read to him not once but twice, and the approval that he gave was entirely consistent with the statements regarding Section 7(a) that he had made to the manufacturers. As a matter of fact, Johnson, as he later informed the Special Industrial Recovery Board, thought that it was one of the purposes of the statute to "bring about open shops," by which he meant shops in which a man's employment did not depend on whether or not he belonged to a union.[37] Johnson was well aware from his own business experience, however, that to many employers the so-called open shop really meant a shop closed to union men. "The way we used to run [an] open shop," he told the N.A.C.C. executives, "is that if we found a man with a union card we'd fire him." When Chrysler indicated that his company had "fired a fellow who was going around agitating" and would continue to dismiss such employees, Johnson raised no objection and asked no questions.

The other problems that came up at the private N.A.C.C.–Johnson

conference were disposed of quickly. The general did not object to
the averaging of hours provided for in the proposed code. The minimum wage rates set by the code committee were acceptable to him,
and he indicated that he was not really much interested in rates above
the minimum (at least if they were above 60 cents per hour), although he did inquire as to whether the existing wages for skilled
labor were above the minimum in about the same proportion as they
had been in the past. When Macauley observed that although the
title of the code was "Code of Fair Competition" there was nothing in
the document concerning competition (trade practices), Johnson
simply remarked, "You may need it."

Reassured by Johnson, the executives, while the general stepped
out of the room, agreed unanimously to submit the code for approval. Johnson himself took the document to Washington, the first
code to receive this personal treatment. Asked by reporters before
he left Detroit what the code provided, Johnson replied, "Hell, I
don't know—haven't read it." [38] The N.A.C.C. executives, presumably, did not take this remark too seriously.

In preparation for the prehearing conferences and the public hearing on the automobile code, the N.R.A. announced the appointment
on August 1 of Robert W. Lea as deputy administrator for the code.
Lea, described as "a shrewd, suave and diplomatic man," had served
in the Purchase, Storage, and Traffic Division of the General Staff
during World War I, had been general manager of the Stephen Motor
Car Company of Freeport, Illinois, from 1919 to 1924, and had been
president of the Moline Plow Company from 1924 to 1929, during
part of which time Johnson had also been associated with the firm.
Like his friend Johnson, Lea tended to view economic problems
through the eyes of the employer—he was inclined, in the words of
one of the aides of the Labor Advisory Board, "to weep copious tears
on behalf of the industrialists." [39] William Green was designated as
the representative of the L.A.B. for the auto code, and Professor
Lawrence H. Seltzer of Detroit City College (now Wayne State University), an expert on the automobile industry, was selected as the
L.A.B. technical advisor for the code. Addes E. McKinstry, vice-
president of International Harvester and, as noted, a member of the
committee that had drafted the code, was named the representative
of the Industrial Advisory Board after Charles W. Nash had been
obliged to turn down the post because of illness. [40]

In the prehearing discussions of the code, the L.A.B., which was
supposed to develop the labor point of view in code negotiations and
which became "the spokesman within the NRA of the organized labor

movement in the United States," voiced its opposition to virtually all provisions of the document. The open-shop clause of the code came under especially heavy criticism within the N.R.A. The Legal Division advised Lea on August 14 that the language in question either qualified Section 7(a) or was superfluous and was for either or both of these reasons improperly in the code. The L.A.B., not surprisingly, also objected to the clause as not in keeping with the "spirit" of the N.I.R.A. The iron and steel industry, under L.A.B. pressure, had already agreed to eliminate the open-shop clause originally included in its code, and the L.A.B. could see no reason why the automobile industry should be permitted to retain a similar clause. The most the industry would agree to, however, was a slight modification of the original statement to make it read: "Employers may continue the open-shop policy under which the selection, retention and advancement of employees will be on the basis of individual merit without regard to their affiliation or non-affiliation with any labor or other organization." [41]

The public hearings on the automobile code were held in Washington on August 18, 1933, with Lea presiding. [42] The opening remarks were made by General Johnson, who declared that it was proper for the automobile industry to participate in the N.R.A. program "with a fervor of cooperation" since it would be the first to benefit from recovery. He regretted, however, that not all of the manufacturers were joining in the submission of the code, an obvious reference to Ford's failure to align himself with his fellow manufacturers.

The code itself was presented and defended by Donaldson Brown. The subject to which he devoted his major attention was the need for flexibility of hours in the automobile industry. Following pretty much the reasoning advanced by Sloan in the House hearings on the Thirty-Hour Bill, Brown explained how the nature of consumer demand, the difficulty of forecasting automobile sales and of storing finished vehicles, and the annual introduction of new models all contributed to the irregularity of automobile production and to variation in the total man hours of employment from week to week and from month to month. During periods of peak production the employer either had to work his regular employees overtime or add new workers to his labor force. Not only was it inefficient from an operating standpoint to add temporary workers for a short period but it was also unwise from a social standpoint since this would attract workers to the industry who would burden the relief resources of the community during the greater portion of the year. If the regular employees were actually to average the thirty-five hours per week stipulated in the code, they would have to be permitted to exceed this figure during weeks of peak production in order to compensate for the reduced hours of employment during the time of restricted output. Also, if the industry was to retain its highly skilled employees, it would have to provide them with sufficient employment to enable them to earn a satisfactory annual income; and this could not be done if the weekly hours of employment were set at too low a figure. As it was, Brown contended, the implementation of the forty-eight hour weekly maximum would itself involve a "drastic readjustment of past operating practices," and the industry was undertaking this experiment "with grave misgivings."

Although irregularity of employment was from a labor and a community point of view one of the most serious problems confronting the automobile industry, Brown's defense of the hours provisions of the auto code was based on the assumption that there was little if anything the employers could do to stabilize automobile production and employment. This was the vulnerable point in Brown's argument, and it was one which labor representatives sought to exploit.

Brown estimated that the employees exempted from all hourly limitations by the proposed code constituted about 10–12 per cent of the factory labor force. This, as it turned out, was an underestimate of the number involved. These workers supposedly required special treatment since it was on their efforts that the employment of other workers depended. They were the employees who kept the plant "going," who dealt with emergencies caused by the breakdown of machinery, and who made the necessary preparations for work on the new model. Brown did not satisfactorily explain why it was necessary to exempt these employees from all hourly limitations, and Lea did not press him on this point. The N.A.C.C. had previously indicated that employees in this category were in short supply,[43] but William Green was to point out in rebuttal that twice as many of these workers had been employed in 1929 as in June 1933 and that it could therefore be assumed that they were available in sufficient number.

Brown conceded that the minimum wages specified in the code would not "directly affect" many employees, but he contended that the adjustment of rates above the minimum which would be required "properly to reflect the necessary wage differential" could well have "a very considerable effect." The proposed minima, he asserted, were equal to or exceeded the minimum wages paid for similar labor in other manufacturing industries and were not out of line with above-minimum rates in the auto industry. Also, since average hourly earnings in the industry for male employees were already sixty-seven cents, as compared to seventy-two cents in June 1929, an increase in the minimum might cause average hourly wages in the industry to exceed those paid when the automobile companies were in a much stronger financial position.

On the whole, Brown's defense of the minimum wages proposed in the N.A.C.C. code was less well worked out than his argument for a flexible hours policy, and it was based on altogether inadequate statistical data. He did not indicate whether the probable earnings of the auto workers under the code would be sufficient to enable them to maintain a decent standard of living; he made no attempt to justify the territorial differentials on the basis of industry practice; and he ignored the argument that higher wages were required in the auto industry because of its greater irregularity of employment as compared to other manufacturing industries.

Regarding the controversial open-shop clause in the proposed code, Brown stated that the industry was not trying to limit "the language or application of Section 7," but that since there had been so much confusion concerning the meaning of the section, the N.A.C.C. had added a statement that it thought would be "reassuring" to employers and employees. At this point Lea called on Richberg, who as the N.R.A.'s General Counsel had been asked by Johnson to comment on the subject. Richberg declared that Johnson wished it to be understood that the statement concerning the selection and retention of employees on the basis of merit was "a proper construction of the law," but the General Counsel raised objections to the words "may continue the open-shop policy." The words, "may continue," he pointed out, sanctioned the retention by the industry of labor policies that might now be in violation of the N.I.R.A. Richberg also advised the dropping of the phrase "open shop" from the code since it was subject to various interpretations and was understood by organized labor to describe a shop that was closed to union members or at least to their organizations.

The attack on the code was spearheaded by William Green, who was appearing in the dual role of L.A.B. representative and A.F. of L. president. With convenient vagueness, Green declared that he was authorized to speak for "many thousands of automobile workers." If by this Green meant to imply that the A.F. of L. had several thousand members in the automobile industry at that time, he was guilty of an exaggeration. On the other hand, the N.R.A. had announced that the L.A.B. would look after the interests of workers in code negotiations whether they were organized or not.[44] It was therefore in his capacity as L.A.B. representative rather than as A.F. of L. president that Green, with some justice, could be looked upon as the spokesman for the automobile workers.

Green, in effect, proposed an A.F. of L. code as a substitute for the N.A.C.C. code submitted by Brown. He buttressed his recommendation with a more impressive array of statistics than Brown had marshaled in support of the N.A.C.C. code, but since they applied to the combined motor vehicle industries (bodies and parts as well as vehicles) rather than to the particular segment of the automobile industry covered by the proposed code, Green's figures were not entirely relevant.

To assist the N.R.A. in executing his code and also "to facilitate long-range planning of equitable industrial relationships" in the automobile manufacturing industry, Green proposed the establishment of a Planning and Coordinating Committee consisting of nine members, three each to represent the employers, the A.F. of L., and the N.R.A. The committee was to consider complaints regarding labor provisions of the code and was to ensure that its collective-bargaining provisions were observed.

Green proposed a basic work week of thirty hours for all automobile production workers. He would permit a thirty-five hour week in emergencies and in periods of high seasonal demand provided that the hours above thirty were compensated at a time-and-a-half rate. Maintenance and repair crews might work beyond the thirty-five hour limit in the event of emergencies and breakdowns which would otherwise occasion the layoff of production workers, but with this exception the thirty-five hour limit could be exceeded only if the permission of the Planning and Coordinating Committee had been obtained in advance. Office and salaried employees receiving less than $35 per week were not to exceed forty hours per week nor more than thirty-five hours averaged over a three-month period.

Green argued that the hours provisions of an N.I.R.A. code were supposed to increase employment but that the proposed N.A.C.C. code was unlikely to have this effect. Ignoring the experience of the industry in more prosperous times, he pointed out that the forty-eight hour week permitted in the N.A.C.C. code was 20 per cent more than the weekly hours worked in the combined motor vehicle industries in June 1933 and that the thirty-five hour average permitted compared with an industry average of 32.7 per worker reported by the B.L.S. for the previous eighteen months. Green estimated that as of June 1933 the motor-vehicle division of the automobile industry would have had to reabsorb 125,000 workers to attain the average employment levels of 1929. He predicted that even the thirty-hour week that he was proposing would result in the re-employment of only about 35,000 workers, assuming that production remained constant, and that if production were doubled, a work week of 29.2 hours would still be required to secure the desired amount of re-employment. The overtime rate specified, he contended, would provide "a powerful economic incentive'" to employers to spread employment among a large number of wage earners.

Green's wage proposals like his hours proposals were drastically different from those set forth in the N.A.C.C. code. He suggested that the minimum wage of factory employees be sixty cents per hour, that existing wage differentials between common labor and the various classes of skilled workers be "substantially maintained," that the minimum wage for office and salaried employees be $15 per week, that no employee be paid for less than six hours of work on any day that he was called to his job, and that any employee who was discharged or laid off before he had had an opportunity to complete 480 hours of employment within a period of four months or less immediately preceding his discharge or layoff was to receive a "discharge or lay-off compensation" of ten cents for each hour completed in the preceding period of employment.

In defense of his wage proposals, Green argued that the N.A.C.C. wage provisions were inadequate to build up purchasing power in the industry and thus did not conform to N.I.R.A. objectives. The differentials according to size of city that the N.A.C.C. was proposing had "no solid basis in existing wage conditions" in the industry: a Bureau of Labor Statistics study of 1932 of representative classes of auto workers in sixteen cities showed no relationship whatsoever between the population of a community and the wages received. Green attacked the differential for female labor in the auto code as neither "morally [n]or economically right" and also opposed the differential for employees under the age of twenty-one.

The sixty-cent minimum he was proposing, Green contended, was the lowest that could restore purchasing power among auto workers and was only one or two cents per hour above the average hourly rate paid common labor in the combined motor vehicle industries in the years 1928 to 1930, when factory employees were working longer hours. He conceded that the rates he was recommending were above those suggested in the P.R.A.—he did not point out that the sixty-cent minimum was actually above the *average* earned rate per hour of N.A.C.C. employees during the first six months of 1933—but he argued that the irregularity of employment in the industry [45] made a high hourly rate imperative if the automobile workers were to receive annual wages "sufficient to maintain tolerable standards of living."

Not only did Green contend that the irregularity of employment in the auto industry justified a higher minimum wage than was paid by more stable industries, but he also advanced his dismissal-pay suggestion to meet this problem. He claimed that the implementation of this proposal would tend to reduce the industry's high layoff and turnover rates by penalizing employers who provided workers with less than four months of steady employment. The dismissal-wage plan had undoubtedly been worked out by Lawrence Seltzer, who, interestingly enough, had reported to the L.A.B. that he had received "the strongest personal assurances" from Donaldson Brown that he would urge the idea on his code committee and that Lea had promised to give the suggestion "a sympathetic consideration." Green's brief treatment of the subject would seem to indicate that neither he nor Seltzer had really thought through the implications of their proposal. Whereas dismissal pay had normally been regarded as a means of compensating workers whose employment with a particular concern was being permanently terminated, Green and Seltzer were suggesting that the idea also had validity as a means of coping with the problem of seasonality. Some of the automobile companies had experimented with severance pay plans, but none of them had attempted to protect the temporarily laid-off worker, and all but the White Motor Company had limited the coverage to salaried employees.[46]

Since the total wages bill of the motor-vehicle division of the industry constituted only 10 per cent of the wholesale value of the product in 1931, Green claimed that his wage proposals, which he estimated would amount to a 22.1 per cent increase over the average hourly wage in the industry in 1932, would result in an increase of only 4.8 per cent in the total wholesale value of vehicles even if productivity per worker remained static and all wage increases attributable to the code were added to the wholesale value of the product. Comparing total payrolls of the combined motor vehicle industries and motor vehicle output for June 1933 with the corresponding monthly averages for 1929, he concluded that the wages of automobile workers were lagging behind their output and that this justified a wage increase.[47]

In addition to his wage and hour recommendations, Green also proposed that the individual and group bonus systems employed in the industry be simplified so that the ordinary worker could understand them and also that these methods of wage payment not be used to compel a speed-up injurious to health and safety. No changes in the wage payment plans in effect on August 1, 1933, were to be made without the consent of the Planning and Coordinating Committee. The highest speed of all conveyors in the month ending July 31, 1933, was to be registered with the committee, and there was to be no increase in speed without its approval. No person under sixteen was to be employed in the industry, and no one under eighteen was to be employed in factory or yard operations. Finally, Green recommended that Section 7(a) be included in the code without the qualifying language proposed by the N.A.C.C.

In discussing Section 7(a) and collective bargaining, Green revealed how wide the difference was between the A.F. of L. and the N.A.C.C. in the interpretation of the meaning of the N.I.R.A. For true collective bargaining to exist, Green declared, labor as well as management had to have bargaining power. The individual worker would have to organize with his fellows in a group that was independent of the employer and was self-governing in internal affairs; the employee organization would have to be industry-wide in scope and would have to be affiliated with the A.F. of L.; and the final result would have to be a labor contract that both management and labor were willing and able to enforce. Such an industry-wide employee organization was also required if the labor provisions of the code were to be satisfactorily enforced. Since the conditions of true collective bargaining did not, however, exist in the auto industry, Green argued that it was the duty of the federal government to promote their development. He therefore looked to the Planning and Coordinating Committee to put the code into operation, to be responsible for "the careful planning of industrial relations" and "the development of agencies for collective bargaining," and to co-operate with code members in attacking the problem of irregular employment by "the creation of an employment insurance fund." [48]

On the whole, Green was rather successful in pointing up the weaknesses of the N.A.C.C. code in so far as the objectives of the N.I.R.A. were concerned, but he was less successful in arguing the reasonableness of his own proposals in terms of the industry's ability to pay for their cost. He was asking the automobile manufacturers to assume heavy obligations before the volume of consumer demand for automobiles justified such action by the industry as a whole. As Macauley had pointed out at the beginning of the code hearings, only three of the fifteen auto companies whose financial reports for the first six months of 1933 had been made public showed any profit, whereas the other twelve had lost over $11 million. Green also made no effort to reconcile proposals such as the dismissal wage and unemployment insurance that were designed to provide for more regular employment for automobile workers with ideas such as an overtime rate and shorter hours which might have increased the number of employees in the industry but at the expense of more regular jobs.

As he was well aware, Green was looking to the federal government to accomplish objectives which the A.F. of L. traditionally believed should be realized through the collective-bargaining process. As the A.F. of L.'s endorsement of unemployment insurance in 1932 and its later support of the Black Bill indicated, however, the depression had begun to erode the Federation's faith in voluntarism, and Green saw in the N.I.R.A. and its vision of the partnership of government, management, and labor the possibility of government support for A.F. of L. efforts to spread its organization to areas of the economy that it had hitherto been unable to penetrate by its own exertions. Green, however, was attempting to thrust on the N.R.A. a role which it had no intention of playing. General Johnson, as he had already made evident, had no desire to use the N.R.A. to promote labor organization or to alter in any fundamental way the wage and hour policies of such powerful employer groups as the automobile manufacturers.

Following the code hearings,[49] N.A.C.C. representatives conferred with Johnson, Richberg, and Lea, and then on August 23 submitted a revised code and a supplementary statement designed to satisfy some of the criticisms voiced at the code hearings and to clarify further the industry's position. In order to meet Richberg's objection to the language originally used in explanation of Section 7(a), the code committee now proposed that the statement following Section 7(a) in the code should read: "Under the foregoing provisions, any employer in the industry may operate under [rather than may continue] an open shop policy which is hereby defined to mean [rather than under which] the selection, retention, and advancement of employees on the basis of individual merit, without regard to their affiliation or non-affiliation with any labor or other organization." The new language still fell short of satisfying either the A.F. of L. or the L.A.B.

On the wage issue, the N.A.C.C. made two concessions. In accordance with the P.R.A., it now defined "city" so as to include the "immediate trade area" (Highland Park, Michigan, would thus receive the Detroit rate); and, in addition, it specifically stated in the code that in accordance with the prevailing practice in the industry, Pontiac and Flint would be regarded as in the Detroit area. This, as the L.A.B. pointed out in its rebuttal of the N.A.C.C. statement, still left places such as Lansing, Michigan, and Syracuse, New York, in the forty-cent area although the hourly earnings of common labor in the automobile industry in these cities were higher than the earnings of similar labor in most of the cities in the forty-three cent category. The N.A.C.C. declared that population differentials were justified because the cost of living was generally related to the size of a city, but it failed to explain why it proposed to follow the P.R.A. pattern in this matter rather than the actual practice of the industry.[50]

The N.A.C.C. further agreed that the wage differential should apply to "apprentices and learners and females not doing the same work as adult males," [51] which meant the addition of apprentices and learners to this category but the exclusion of male factory employees between the ages of sixteen and twenty-one. The employees to whom the differential applied, it was ultimately provided, were to receive not less than 87½ per cent of the specified minima, which was an insignificant change from the five-cent differential originally permitted, and their number was not to exceed 5 per cent of the total number of factory employees of any employer. The A.F. of L. and the L.A.B. were opposed to any differential, but the amended code at least limited the extent to which workers in these categories might be employed and eliminated the wage differential originally stipulated for male factory employees under twenty-one. No mention was made in the supplementary brief of the adjustment of pay rates above the minimum, but the N.R.A., before the code was approved, secured the insertion of a provision requiring the "equitable adjustment in all pay schedules of factory employees" by September 15, 1933, unless the employer had already made such adjustments. The minimum wage levels originally proposed by the N.A.C.C., however, remained intact.

On the question of hours, the N.A.C.C. now agreed that "employees engaged in the preparation, care, and maintenance of plant machinery and facilities of and for production," who had previously been exempted from all hourly limitations, should not work more than forty-two hours per week averaged on an annual basis. It retained the noncontroversial total exemption for employees receiving more than $35 per week and for "executives and managerial and supervisory staffs." It further provided that the hours of individual employees in the thirty-five hour group were to conform as closely as possible to the required thirty-five hour average for the group as a whole and were in no case to exceed this figure by more than 3 per cent. This, it was contended, allowed the employer somewhat greater flexibility in the treatment of individual workers.

As before, the N.A.C.C. maintained in its supplementary brief that the irregularity of employment in the industry was beyond the manufacturers' control. It rejected as unfair the comparison of labor turnover in the youthful automobile industry with turnover rates in old, established industries and complained without adequate basis that the B.L.S. figures cited by Green to demonstrate the high annual labor turnover in the industry were "irrelevant and meaningless."

The N.A.C.C. represented the overtime rate proposed by Green as a "penal measure" designed to make employers do something "beyond their control," that is, to spread employment more evenly over the year. It insisted, inconsistently, that an overtime rate would attract "floating workers" to the industry and yet would, at the same time, increase rather than reduce the amount of overtime. It also rejected the proposal of a dismissal wage on the grounds that it would be difficult to administer and that inability to forecast the business outlook four months in advance would, if the plan were put into effect, make employers reluctant to take on new workers at all. The N.A.C.C. did agree, however, to include in its code a promise to make a study of the problem of irregular employment "in an effort," as the code stated, "to develop any further practical measures which can be taken to provide more stable and continuous employment and to reduce to a minimum the portion of employees temporarily employed." It committed itself to submit a report on this question to the Administrator by December 1, 1933. This, at least, was a step in the right direction, and it was, in the end, to have important consequences for the industry and its workers.

In conclusion, the N.A.C.C. pointed out that during the depression the industry, "in the interest of humanity and fairness to employees," had adopted a work-sharing program and had maintained wages above those of other industries, and it urged the administration not to use its record during these years "as indicative of a permanent system likely to prevail" nor to view the industry's code "from this background." It reminded the administration of the "remarkably satisfactory labor relations" that had prevailed in the industry and of how much of a contribution the automobile manufacturers had already made to business recovery.[52]

Although the N.A.C.C. code revision of August 23 was opposed in almost all of its particulars by the L.A.B.,[53] only the continued reference in the document to the open shop aroused concern in the higher echelons of the N.R.A.[54] Prompted by the refusal of the automobile manufacturers to yield on this point, Johnson and Richberg on August 23 issued a joint statement declaring that the "plain meaning" of Section 7(a) could not be changed by interpretation. The words "open shop" and "closed shop," which had no "agreed meaning" and were not used in the N.I.R.A., could not be written into a code and would be "erased from the dictionary of the N.R.A." The two officials reaffirmed what Johnson had previously said regarding the meaning of Section 7(a) but pointed out at the same time that "cooperation in all industrial relations depends largely on the making and maintenance of agreements," and they declared that the N.R.A. would "promote and aid such cooperation." [55]

Johnson repeated the statement over the air that evening and at the same time administered "a public spanking" to the automobile industry. He appealed to the nation against those who "in this time of national stress are willing to risk the very success of this great movement to maintain some stubborn point." "If harm comes to the public," he warned, "we shall know exactly where to place ... [the] responsibility." [56]

The next day an auto manufacturers' delegation that included Donaldson Brown and William Knudsen called on Johnson and apparently accused him of having run out on the promise regarding 7(a) that he had made to the N.A.C.C. leaders in Detroit on July 28. Throughout the day the code committee conferred with Johnson, Richberg, and Lea, and finally a compromise was arranged. Reference to the open shop was dropped from the code, but the auto manufacturers were permitted to retain a so-called merit clause in the document. "Without in any way attempting to qualify or modify, by interpretation, the foregoing requirements of the National Industrial Recovery Act [Section 7(a)]," the pertinent code provision now read, "employers in this Industry may exercise their right to select, retain, or advance employees on the basis of individual merit, without regard to their membership or nonmembership in any organization." [57] Johnson and Richberg had won their point on the open shop, but after the commitments he had made in Detroit Johnson was in no position to insist that the N.A.C.C. make any additional concessions. For their part, the auto manufacturers had reached their last line of defense—there would be no further retreat.

As far as Johnson was concerned, the agreement of August 24 regarding Section 7(a) removed the last obstacle to the approval of the code, although Green insisted that the issue of the merit clause required further airing by the L.A.B.[58] On August 25 Deputy Administrator Lea submitted his report recommending approval of the code. By this time he had been informed that the code had the approval of the Consumers' Advisory Board and the Industrial Advisory Board, and he had a letter from L.A.B. chairman Leo Wolman which was interpreted as indicating approval by that agency. The official report of the Division of Economic Research and Planning was not submitted until the next day.

The Consumers' Advisory Board pointed out that the code was of little interest to consumers, but it did raise questions concerning the absence from the document of provisions concerning the manufacturer-dealer relationship, consumer representation on the code authority, and the seasonal character of automobile production. It noted that the highly competitive character of the industry protected the consumer in so far as price was concerned.[59]

That the industrial adviser, A. E. McKinstry, approved the code is hardly surprising since he was himself a member of the N.A.C.C. drafting committee. McKinstry's report, which carried the endorsement of the I.A.B., simply echoed the opinions of the automobile manufacturers on the various code problems and noted that the inclusion of an open-shop clause in the code "would bring enthusiastic support to the Recovery Program in many places where it is now lacking." [60]

Wolman did not specifically endorse the code but merely informed Johnson that he had considered the document, regretted that it had not been possible to establish higher minimum rates, and was pleased that the industry was to undertake a study of the problem of irregular employment. It is entirely possible that Wolman had not consulted with members of the L.A.B. before dispatching this brief message. His failure to make any mention of the various code provisions that troubled other L.A.B. members and particularly the omission of any reference to the merit clause tend to strengthen this possibility.[61]

The slightly tardy report of the Division of Economic Research and Planning, whose director was Alexander Sachs, formerly of Lehman Brothers, endorsed some of the proposals of both the N.A.C.C. and the L.A.B. On the basis of the probable maximum automobile production for the remainder of the year (the period the code was to be in effect) and the man hours of labor required per car, the division concluded that the average work week of thirty-five hours specified in the code was reasonable; but to attain this average it was estimated that a maximum work week of approximately forty-five hours rather than the forty-eight hours specified in the code was adequate. The division also advocated a modest overtime rate of time-and-one-fifth. It sided with the L.A.B. in opposing the exemption from the hourly limitations of the employees placed in the forty-two hour category since in the view of the division the industry had failed to prove that these employees were in short supply.

Although pointing out that hourly wage rates in the automobile industry in July 1933 were substantially above those in most other industries, the division contended that the minimum rates specified in the auto code would not result in average annual earnings sufficient to provide "a minimum standard of health and decency" unless the automobile worker enjoyed steady employment or received some compensation for irregular employment. The division consequently defended the A.F. of L.'s proposal for dismissal pay as a means of helping to bring average weekly, monthly, and annual earnings in the automobile industry in line with earnings in more stable industries. The division also approved Green's idea of call-in pay—it set the figure at $1—in order to discourage the "sheer wantoness" [*sic*] in the employment practices of some factory managers.[62]

In his report recommending approval of the code, Lea stated that in forming his conclusions he had "kept in mind the fact that the success of the operations under the Code depends upon keeping everything reasonable and in balance. If the existing work is spread too thinly, average weekly wages, and hence purchasing power, will not be satisfactory; if wage rates are increased too much in order to offset the broader distribution of work, manufacturers ... [who] have practically exhausted their financial resources in struggling through the depression, may fail and further unemployment result." Since this statement was taken virtually verbatim from McKinstry's report, it is not surprising that Lea in his report largely endorsed the N.A.C.C. position with regard to the code.

Lea conceded that there was some truth in the L.A.B. argument that the minimum wages and the maximum hours provided in the code would not result in the re-employment at satisfactory wages of a substantial portion of the workers engaged in the industry during its peak years and now jobless; but he argued that the question was not whether an industry as depressed as the automobile industry could immediately rehire all of its former workers but rather whether the wage and hour schedules of the code were such that if a high level of activity were restored, the industry could employ more men at "reasonable wages" than it had previously employed when operating at the same volume. The automobile code, he believed, satisfied this criterion since the industry, because of the required reduction of hours, would actually be employing the same average number of factory workers as it had in 1929 when it reached an operating rate equal to 74 per cent of its 1929 volume. Lea accepted the decision of the automobile industry to study the problem of irregular employment as a satisfactory answer to the L.A.B. demand for a dismissal wage, and he found the code entirely consistent with the requirements of Section 7(a).[63]

The automobile code was taken to President Roosevelt in Hyde Park on August 26 by Johnson's private secretary, Frances Robinson. The same day the L.A.B. met to consider the merit clause, with Wolman absent and with Johnson, Richberg, and Edward McGrady, Assistant Secretary of Labor and Assistant Administrator of the N.R.A., sitting in with board members Green, John L. Lewis, John P. Frey, head of the Metal Trades Department of the A.F. of L., Rose Schneiderman, president of the Women's Trade Union League, and the Rev. Francis J. Haas of the National Catholic Welfare Conference. The L.A.B. decided to accept the code "with the understanding that no section or sentence contained therein modifies, qualifies or changes Section 7(a)" and that the merit clause did "not establish a precedent to be followed in the preparation or acceptance of any other code." Green had been persuaded to agree to this statement in part because of a promise by Johnson that a board on which labor would be represented would be appointed for the auto industry to deal with code violations.[64]

The L.A.B. decision was wired to Roosevelt on the same day that he received the code, but the President in approving the document made no mention of the L.A.B. statement. Anxious to have the automobile manufacturers covered by a code, aware of their strong bargaining position and of their unwillingness to retreat any further on the issue of collective bargaining, and undoubtedly apprised by Johnson that he had give prior consent to an even stronger affirmation of the industry's open-shop policy than was contained in the merit clause, the President was willing to accept the code as it stood without further qualifications.

Although the automobile manufacturers estimated that the code would raise their costs by about $20 to $30 per car,[65] the N.A.C.C. on the whole had been able to win for the automobile manufacturers the sort of code that would affect their operations as little as possible. The minimum wage stipulated would not in itself compel them to raise the wages of more than a few of their workers. They could no longer work their employees as many hours as they previously had, but the averaging principle which they had succeeded in keeping in the code gave them a considerable measure of flexibility in the handling of their factory labor force. They had not been able to retain a reference to the open shop in the code, but the merit clause seemed to carry the implication that despite Section 7(a), industrial relations in the open-shop automobile industry were to remain unchanged. The manufacturers had been able to resist the inclusion in the code of provisions requiring a dismissal wage, an overtime rate, call-in pay, changes in the incentive pay methods employed in the industry, and labor representation on the code authority. They had succeeded in deferring for another day any consideration of the potentially troublesome question of trade practices. The auto code, declared *Business Week,* "stands as a model of knowing what you want, putting it all within the law, and sticking to your guns." [66]

The code, understandably, was hailed in circles friendly to the automobile manufacturers as a victory for the employers. John Lovett, general manager of the Michigan Manufacturers' Association, announced that the code "substantially represents the views the automobile manufacturers have contended for from the beginning"; and *Automotive Industries* viewed the code as "the first victory of industry over organized labor under the Industrial Recovery Act." Left-wing labor groups agreed with this analysis, and they were unsparing in their criticism of code provisions.[67]

The A.F. of L., defeated in its efforts to modify the code in any substantial manner, tried at first to place as favorable a construction upon the document as was possible under the circumstances. Green informed Collins that nothing in the code modified or altered Section 7(a) "in any way" and that the discharge of employees because of their union activity violated the code. "Let no one deceive automobile workers by misrepresentation or false statements," Green declared. "Their right to organize has been clearly established." The *American Federationist* argued that the maximum hours provided in the code would help stabilize employment in the industry and that the minimum wages specified would result in wage increases for many workers.[68]

Green was aware that it was the weakness of organized labor in the industry that had prevented the A.F. of L. from making its suggestions prevail. The lack of organization, he told Collins, had "greatly interfered with a forceful and influential presentation" of labor's case. Seltzer of the L.A.B. thought that another factor had aided the employers in winning most of their points: "We were forced to accept," he lamented, "because the automobile manufacturers asked nothing from the Government in their Code." [69]

There seemed to be a general recognition that although the merit clause could be viewed as simply "a statement of rights the employers undeniably would have had in any event," it was something more than "harmless surplusage," to use Donald Richberg's phrase. If the employer was to be the sole judge of efficiency, organized labor asked, would not union members find it difficult to hold jobs in the industry? The merit clause, an irate employee wrote to Johnson, was inserted in the code to provide the employers with "an excuse to fire any one caught organizing or affiliating with a labor union." [70] Symbolically, perhaps more than in substance, the inclusion of the merit clause in the automobile code loomed as an important victory for the N.A.C.C.

The success of the automobile manufacturing industry in inserting a merit clause in its code persuaded other industries to seek the inclusion of a similar clause in their codes. By the end of August merit clauses had appeared in twenty-nine proposed codes, and early the next month Henry Harriman, the president of the United States Chamber of Commerce, recommended the incorporation of such provisions in all codes so as to safeguard the open shop. [71] Following a discussion of the subject by the L.A.B. on August 31, Green announced that the N.R.A. would "court disaster" if it accepted a merit clause in any more codes. At his press conference a few days later General Johnson agreed that the clause had become a source of trouble and that the wisest course henceforth would be to forbid the inclusion of interpretive language in any other code. [72]

President Roosevelt also concluded that the efforts to interpret Section 7(a) in the various codes led only to "confusion and misunderstanding." He vetoed an interpretation of the section agreed upon by the L.A.B. and the I.A.B., and then on October 19 he instructed Johnson by letter that no interpretations of Section 7(a) were henceforth to be embodied in any code. There was nothing in Section 7(a), he declared, to interfere with the "bona fide exercise of the right of an employer to select, retain, or advance employees on the basis of individual merit," but the section did prohibit "the pretended exercise" of this right by an employer as a means of denying to his employees the rights guaranteed to them by the law. [73] The President did not indicate how one was to distinguish between the "bona fide exercise" of the right to hire and fire and its "pretended exercise," nor did he suggest that the merit clause be eliminated from the automobile code when it came up for renewal. As a matter of fact, despite the determined opposition of organized labor and the L.A.B. and despite the fact that the inclusion of similar language was permitted in no other code, [74] the merit clause remained in the automobile code throughout the life of the N.I.R.A.

Unique in its inclusion of a merit clause, the automobile code remained unique among the codes of the major industries in its failure to specify any trade practices. President Macauley on August 10, 1933, did appoint a committee to consider passenger-car trade practices and a separate committee to consider truck trade practices; but despite some prodding from the N.R.A., the industry did not submit a supplementary code of trade practices.   Lea felt that he had "practically had a definite promise from Mr. Donaldson Brown that this [supplementary] code would be forthcoming in the near future," and he talked about insisting on "action."   The N.A.C.C., however, undoubtedly anxious to avoid the inclusion in its code of provisions defining the relationship of the manufacturer to his dealers and suppliers, responded evasively to Lea's inquiries concerning the matter, and in the end "action" was neither insisted on nor taken.[75]   On this issue as on so many others that arose under the N.I.R.A. the automobile manufacturers, in the final analysis, had their way.

III

HENRY FORD VERSUS THE N.R.A.

I

FOR ALL PRACTICAL PURPOSES the Ford Motor Company,[1] as far as the general public was concerned, was indistinguishable from the man who had given the concern his name. For almost two decades before 1933, no other business figure had loomed so large in the public view as Henry Ford. It was Ford who had successfully fought the A.L.A.M. in the Selden patent suit, Ford who had become the world symbol of mass production, Ford who had proclaimed the five-dollar day.

The depression persuaded many businessmen that measures such as the N.I.R.A. were necessary to revive the economy, but there was little reason to have expected that Henry Ford would view with favor legislation that called for the stabilization of the economy through the co-operation of government, business, and labor. Ford, it had already been demonstrated, was simply not the sort of person who could work well in harness. As he later remarked, he had decided at the beginning of the century, after serving as superintendent of the Detroit Automobile Company, "never again to put myself under orders." He realized his ambitions in this regard to the full when in 1919 he bought out the minority stockholders of the Ford Motor Company and thus gained complete control of the concern.[2]

A believer in self-help and self-reliance, Ford did not look to government to solve the economic problems of the nation even in a depression and at a time when his company was losing ground to its major competitors. It was unlikely, moreover, that one who had stood out against the A.L.A.M. and who had refused to join his fellow automobile manufacturers in the N.A.C.C. would look with approbation on legislation that encouraged trade associations. Above all, it was safe to assume that Ford would oppose legislation and administrative actions that might lead to the establishment of unionism in his plants.

As noted, Macauley had appointed Edsel Ford to the committee he established late in May 1933 to consider the impending recovery bill in its relationship to the auto industry; and Herman L. Moekle had served on the N.A.C.C. committee that drafted the automobile code. As Moekle later recalled, his objective on the committee had been to keep the industry "as free as possible of controls," [3] which, of course, coincided with the purpose of the other committee members.

The participation of the Ford Motor Company in the code-making process ceased when the Brown committee submitted its draft to the N.A.C.C. Ford did not join with the N.A.C.C. in presenting the code to General Johnson and did not take part in the conferences on the code that preceded the public hearing, in the public hearing itself, or in the posthearing conferences that led to the President's approval of the document. The obstacle to any further Ford co-operation was clearly Henry Ford himself. Moekle and Louis Colombo, a Ford attorney who had assisted Moekle on the code committee, recommended acceptance of the code as "the best kind of agreement that could come out of that law," and according to Ernest G. Liebold, Ford's business secretary, "Everyone around, including Edsel," thought that the company should sign. Fear of the possible adverse effect on sales if the company refused to sign undoubtedly motivated Ford executives to take this position.[4]

Anxious to enlist Henry Ford's support for the N.I.R.A., Johnson, whose admiration for the Detroit industrialist was "unstinted," had decided shortly after the passage of the act to discuss the subject with Ford in person. "I want to talk to you about the whole show," he told Henry on the telephone on June 22. Two days later, Johnson secretly flew to Dearborn and explained to Henry and Edsel the purposes and character of the N.I.R.A. Johnson came away from the conference thinking that Henry Ford would support the N.I.R.A. "to the limit and even beyond." The reason for Johnson's erroneous estimate of the situation is clear. In explaining the act to Henry, he had apparently emphasized its immediate objectives, the re-employment of labor through the reduction of working hours and the stimulation of purchasing power through the fixing of minimum-wage levels. Ford could easily endorse these objectives since he thought of himself as a pioneer in this area. "It was only what I had been practicing all my life," he later wrote to Charles Edison. It was thus possible for Ford on July 15 to praise General Johnson and to state that "what he [Johnson] wants is not Government control of business; he wants the best business principles of the best business men to become the rules of all business."

Johnson obviously did not stress in his conversation with Ford the possible implications of Section 7(a) and the likelihood that the codes of fair competition that the act contemplated would include price and production controls. It is no doubt for this reason that Liebold later remarked, "I don't think at that time Mr. Ford knew what the NRA was," and that William J. Cameron, Ford's spokesman, doubted that Ford "understood the full drift of it." [5]

As the time for the final approval of the auto code approached, Ford began to have second thoughts about the N.I.R.A. He undoubtedly learned through Moekle of the N.A.C.C. fears concerning the threat which Section 7(a) posed to the open shop, and perhaps he also became aware of the restraints on competition included in the codes that the various industries of the nation were submitting. When Josephus Daniels, then ambassador to Mexico, urged Ford to sign the code, Cameron replied: "There can be no doubt . . . that proposals are being made in the name of recovery that have nothing to do with recovery, and that seriously affect the fundamental American idea. We doubt that it is necessary to scrap America in order to achieve recovery." [6]

In particular, Ford, like the other auto manufacturers, was not anxious to "scrap" the open shop that prevailed in his plants, and he feared that Section 7(a) would have precisely this effect. The N.I.R.A., his secretary replied to a complaint about Ford's refusal to sign the code, "contains a section which in effect makes obligatory the unionization of industry." From Ford's point of view, collective bargaining, in Cameron's phrasing, was simply "a smooth sounding name for the labor racketeer." Ford comforted himself with the thought that he made better bargains for his men than any labor organizer could. "We have bargained for our men; we have never been compelled to bargain *against* them nor they against us." [7]

The result was that when Johnson, on his visit to Detroit late in July to talk with N.A.C.C. leaders, telephoned Edsel to find out "what the hell was the matter," Ford's son replied that the company did not like Section 7(a). Johnson sought to de-emphasize the importance of this portion of the statute and informed Edsel, as he informed the N.A.C.C. leadership, that Section 7(a) was not inconsistent with the maintenance of the open shop. Edsel apparently pressed Johnson for a written promise that Section 7(a) would not be applied to the Ford Motor Company, but this far Johnson would not go. [8]

Even more important than the threat of unionization, Ford later stated in explaining his refusal to sign the code, was the extensive government control of business that he saw implicit in the N.I.R.A.

The Ford Motor Company, he informed the public on June 25, had achieved "industrial decencies" without "regulation or compulsion" or "'gentlemen's agreements.'" Under the N.I.R.A., however, Ford insisted a few months later, "every detail of our operation can be placed under control of a committee one-third of whom are politicians and one-third of whom are labor leaders." If he signed the code, Moekle recalled, Ford "felt it would be giving away the control of his own business. . . ."⁹ •

Ford, as a matter of fact, was too much alarmed at the threat the N.I.R.A. posed to his business. Although the statute had drastic implications and although many of the codes included provisions that were obnoxious to Ford, it was possible, as the N.A.C.C. demonstrated, to have a code which ignored price and production matters entirely and which even mitigated the threat posed to the open shop by Section 7(a). Also, as Ford must have known, he could not escape the terms of his industry's code by refusing to sign the document. Once the President approved the code, Ford was obligated by the N.I.R.A. to observe its provisions whether he liked them or not. By refusing to sign, Ford merely indicated his displeasure with the statute and placed himself in a more advantageous position to challenge it in court or in the press. He also made it impossible for Ford products to display the Blue Eagle, but apparently this fact did not trouble the motor king. "Hell," Liebold remembers him saying, "that Roosevelt buzzard! I wouldn't put it on the car." ¹⁰

Ford's failure to sign the code, plus the refusal of the federal government, for a time, to purchase Ford cars, stimulated a flood of letters to the N.R.A. and a lesser number to the company in criticism or in praise of Ford's action. One of Ford's critics thought him nothing less than a "traitor"; another referred to him as "mentally twisted, unbalanced and prejudiced"; and still another described him to the President as "the only Snake in the Grass of your whole N.R.A. Program." The president of the Ford Owners Alliance, who claimed two hundred thousand members, wrote on September 1, 1933, that all members would soon display windshield stickers stating "My last Ford supports NRA." But Ford also had his defenders, one of whom denounced this "Jewish-Johnson-Baruch-Wall Street persecution," and another of whom deplored the government's attack on "the nation's greatest benefactor." Ford drew praise, in particular, from businessmen who saw him as a symbol of opposition to government regulation and collectivism and to the New Deal. One of Ford's defenders, who congratulated him on his stand against "the present damned rotten Administration," even composed a bit of doggerel for the occasion:

NRA me down to sleep
I pray Johnson my code to keep;
If I should bust before I wake
AF of L my plant will take.

Many of Ford's critics wanted the federal government to demonstrate that it was bigger than Henry Ford and, in the words of one of them, to "Turn the hose on Henry." [11] Actually though, as long as Ford complied with the automobile code, there was little the federal government could do to chastise him for his recalcitrance other than to refuse to award government contracts to the Ford Motor Company or to Ford dealers and, similarly, to urge the public not to purchase Ford products. At his press conference of August 29, Johnson, when asked if he intended to "'crack down'" on Ford, replied: "I think maybe the American people will crack down on him when the Blue Eagle is on other cars and he does not have one." Public authorities in various jurisdictions and some individuals promptly responded to Johnson's suggestion by announcing their refusal to purchase Ford products.[12]

Obviously antagonized by Ford's unwillingness to sign the auto code, Johnson was anxious to have the federal government proclaim its refusal to purchase Ford products. He found sanction for a boycott policy in Executive Order 6246 of August 10, 1933, which stated that the recipients of government contracts were to comply with the applicable provisions of the code of their industry or trade or, if their trade was uncodified, with the terms of the President's Reemployment Agreement.[13] In so far as the federal government's purchase of Ford products was concerned, two questions were posed by this executive order: would the Ford Motor Company be eligible for government contracts if it complied with the automobile code but did not sign it; and, second, could a Ford dealer who had signed the P.R.A. or the motor vehicle retailing code (approved October 3, 1933) be denied a government contract even if the Ford Motor Company itself fell under the order's ban? The Ford Motor Company answered the first question by ceasing to bid on federal government contracts, but the problem of the government and the Ford dealer was not so easily resolved.

When he learned that the Ford Motor Company was no longer seeking government business, independent Ford dealer R. P. Sabine, the proprietor of the Northwest Motor Company of Bethesda, Maryland, sought permission from Ford to start bidding on government contracts. Not only did Sabine receive the requested permission, but E. C. Simons of Ford's Washington District Sales Office was instructed to render Sabine "every assistance possible," although Simons was "cautioned to avoid any action that could be construed as participation by the Ford Motor Company in . . . direct sales." With credit supplied through Ford's Universal Credit Corporation and with Simons "doing most of the work of preparing the bids and processing the orders," Sabine was soon submitting bids for government business.[14]

At the September 6, 1933, meeting of the Special Industrial Recovery Board, Secretary of Commerce Daniel Roper noted that Sabine had been the low bidder on some trucks for the United States Coast and Geodetic Survey and raised the question as to whether the government should purchase Ford products. "This," Assistant Attorney General Harold M. Stephens correctly predicted, "is going to be very embarrassing." Turner Battle, Assistant Secretary of Labor, reported that President Roosevelt had declared the previous day that the federal government would not "do any boycotting," but General Johnson had other ideas and was soon taking the position that the federal government should not purchase vehicles from Ford dealers even though they certified their compliance with the P.R.A. or the dealers' code. "To let Mr. Ford escape the consequences of this Act because his dealer has a Blue Eagle," Johnson wrote to Roper on September 22, "would be to allow a billion dollar corporation hide behind the skirts of a thirty thousand dollar company." Reversing himself and now concurring in Johnson's view of the matter, President Roosevelt remarked at his press conference on October 27 that the federal government should buy goods manufactured not only in accord with N.R.A. standards but "by people who have gone along with the general agreement." "It is the article rather than the person you buy it through," the President declared. ". . . we have got to eliminate the purchase of Ford cars."[15]

On October 28 Sabine protested to Comptroller General J. R. McCarl that his firm had been denied a government contract for several hundred trucks for the Civilian Conservation Corps (C.C.C.) although it was the low bidder and had certified that it was complying with the dealers' code. In submitting his bid, Sabine had insisted that the Ford Motor Company was not a party to the bid and that therefore its status under the N.I.R.A. was not at issue. The Comptroller General on November 10 rejected Sabine's contention that the federal government, in effect, could not go behind dealer compliance to require compliance by the manufacturer, but at the same time he ruled that there was nothing in the N.I.R.A. or the auto code that required a company actually to sign a code or to signify its intent to comply. The fact that Ford had failed to take such action was "not controlling here," and unless the contrary was proved, and it had not been, it had to be assumed that Ford was complying.[16]

The crucial question thus was not whether Ford had signed the code but whether he was complying with it. The answer was not long in coming. Five days after the Comptroller General's ruling, Deputy Administrator Karl Ammerman reported that "To the extent of our information, the Ford Motor Co. has, save in respect of certain technical particulars which we consider immaterial, complied satisfactorily with the Code. . . ." Ammerman's conclusion was based on a study of the wages and hours reports that Ford had submitted to the N.R.A., and there is, indeed, no question that Ford scrupulously observed the wages and hours provisions of the code throughout the life of the N.I.R.A.[17] Whether he similarly observed the requirements of Section 7(a), which were embodied in Section VII of the code, is, however, another matter. Publicly, the N.R.A. never charged Ford with failure to comply with Section 7(a), but, as we shall see, the Compliance Board of the N.R.A. eventually concluded that Ford had violated the section's requirements.

At all events, the Comptroller General's ruling of November 10 opened the way to the award of government contracts to Ford dealers. Rexford Guy Tugwell declared at the November 3 meeting of the Special Industrial Recovery Board: "As I intrepret the Comptroller General's opinion we would be in awfully hot water if we bought Chevrolets [when a Ford dealer was the low bidder]."[18] On December 1, 1933, the Secretary of Agriculture awarded Sabine a contract for over eight hundred trucks for the C.C.C., and by March 1, 1934, approximately $1 million in government contracts had been granted to Ford dealers. The contest between Ford and the N.R.A. was by no means over, however. On March 14, the day after the Ford Motor Company had announced its return to the five-dollar day, the President issued a new executive order (6646), which specified, with obvious reference to the Ford case, that the federal government would not contract for materials "in whole or in part, produced or furnished by any person who shall not have certified that he is complying with each code of fair competition that relates to such articles, materials, or supplies. . . ."[19] A signed certificate of compliance by Ford was thus essential if Ford dealers were to receive government contracts.

In submitting a bid to the Department of Commerce on March 30, 1934, the Northwest Motor Company certified its compliance with the dealers' code but stated that it could not make representations concerning the various manufacturers who had a part in fabricating the product it was attempting to sell, and to require it to do so was "unfair and unjust." The Comptroller General, however, ruled against Sabine on May 17. Sabine thereupon secured a court order temporarily restraining the government departments concerned from rejecting his bids, but on May 24 Justice Daniel W. O'Donoghue of the Supreme Court of the District of Columbia denied the company a temporary injunction. "It would seem unreasonable," O'Donoghue declared, "that the President should be compelled to contract with any company, no matter how wealthy or how powerful, if that company is thwarting the Recovery Act and defying the government to enforce it." [20]

Despite this ruling, which Sabine did not appeal, Ford stubbornly refused to sign a certificate of compliance, and for several months Chevrolet virtually monopolized the federal government's purchase of small cars and trucks. However, although Executive Order 6646 remained in effect, the federal government eventually relaxed its ban on the purchase of Ford products. It first deviated from the requirements of the executive order by permitting the purchase of repair and replacement parts for Fords already in the government service, an obvious necessity unless the federal government was prepared to replace all of its Fords. Lest it "would look as though we were backing down," the N.R.A. for a time authorized the purchase of such parts only on the basis of emergency exceptions to 6646; no general exception to the order was made for this purpose until January 16, 1935. [21]

The Compliance Division of the N.R.A. became aware in October 1934 that government departments were beginning to purchase new Fords on the strength of certificates of compliance furnished by dealers, but Johnson advised the division "not to make an issue of this" because of negotiations then under way which it was hoped would result in Ford's certification of his compliance. Whatever the nature of these negotiations, they did not result in Ford's altering his stand in any way, although Sabine late in October tried to persuade the N.R.A. to accept as the equivalent of a certificate of compliance a telegram dated January 5, 1934, from Ford's sales manager, W. C. Cowling, to the Secretary of the Interior which stated that Ford had complied with the code and would continue to do so. Sabine did not explain how a wire dated January 5, 1934, could contain a reference to Executive Order 6646, dated March 14, 1934. [22]

Despite Ford's refusal to compromise and in the face of objections from Chrysler, the purchase of Fords by the federal government continued. It was announced on February 19, 1935, that the Department of the Interior had purchased thirty-five Fords and the Department of Agriculture about four hundred, and a few days later the War Department, anxious to widen the competition in the bidding for its contracts, requested Ford to bid on a $4 million order for the C.C.C.[23]

All in all, Ford's refusal to sign a certificate of compliance did not seriously affect the sale of Ford cars and trucks. It is true that Ford lost out on the possibility of gaining his share of several million dollars of government business, particularly between March and October 1934, but the civilian purchase of Ford products suffered not at all. It would appear that the nation's motorists agreed with Will Rogers when he remarked, "You can take the rouge from female lips, the cigarettes from the raised hands, the hot dogs from the tourists' greasy paw, but when you start jacking the Fords out from under the traveling public you are monkeying with the very fundamentals of American life." Indeed, whereas the Ford Motor Company (including Lincoln) had suffered a net loss of $7,888,718 after taxes and accounted for only 21.59 per cent of the total new passenger car and truck registrations in the United States in 1933, in 1934 it made a profit of $21,362,118 after taxes and increased its percentage of total new car and truck registrations to 28.8. Ford triumphantly announced on November 1, 1934, that the depression was over for him and that this would be true of the nation as a whole "if American industrialists would just forget these alphabet schemes and take hold of their industries and run them with good, sound American business sense." [24]

II

Particularly during the early months of the Ford–N.R.A. controversy, there was speculation in the press concerning the possibilities of a meeting between President Roosevelt and Henry Ford to discuss N.R.A. problems. Roosevelt certainly desired such a meeting, but the various attempts to bring the two men together all came to naught.

When George J. Atwell wrote the President late in September 1933 that Ford was anxious to visit with him, the Chief Executive instructed his secretary, Marvin H. McIntyre, to reply that the President would be glad to talk with Ford, "but that he has never even suggested that he would like to see the President." [25] Not wishing to leave this important matter to chance, Charles Edison, son of Ford's long-time friend Thomas A. Edison and active in N.R.A. work in New Jersey, tried his hand at about this time at arranging a meeting between the President and the industrialist. Edison's effort elicited a long letter from Ford on October 6 in which the auto magnate indicated that he had "deep respect" for Roosevelt "personally and as President" and that he credited him "with an earnest and religious desire to do everything possible to ease the situation of this country...." Ford remarked that he had "to make a sharp distinction . . . between the President and the NIRA" because he could not believe that Roosevelt had conceived that "complicated and impractical plan."

Upon reading this letter, the President, Edison informed Dearborn by phone, commented, "Oh, he doesn't get it at all. I wish he would let me talk this over with him." The next day, in a letter which he had drafted with McIntyre's aid and which the President had edited, Edison wrote Ford that it appeared to him that the two men were willing to meet but that each thought the other should request the meeting. Edison felt it necessary to remind Ford that Roosevelt "is, after all, the President of the United States." The feeling of the President for Ford, Edison thought, was "a very friendly one. I noted no note of antagonism, beyond his statement made with a smile that 'If Henry will quit being a damn fool about this matter and call me on the telephone I would be glad to talk with him.'" Ford, however, did not make the call, and Edison had to concede, "As a Clearing House, I guess I'm something of a flop." [26]

A few weeks after Edison's unsuccessful effort, Ford's former business associate, Senator James Couzens, informed the President that Ford would like to visit with him. Roosevelt, therefore, on November 7, 1933, invited Henry to the White House "as an old friend whom I used to know in my Navy days." Ford declined the invitation, however, allegedly because he feared that his visit would be construed as an effort on his part to persuade the government to buy Ford cars.[27]

Roosevelt renewed the invitation in a general way in responding to birthday greetings which Ford wired him on January 30, 1934. "We all admire the directness with which you are attacking the nation's problems," Ford wrote, "and we are all the grateful beneficiaries of your immeasurable services in maintaining a courageous spirit amongst all the people." In reply, Roosevelt said that he would "like very much" to have Ford visit him any time he was in Washington.[28]

Assuming the initiative once again, Roosevelt, late in October 1934, decided to invite Henry and Edsel Ford and their wives to the White House to talk about plans to relocate urban dwellers in "country communities" and to locate smaller industries in small towns. This time Mrs. Roosevelt intervened and informed Presidential Press Secretary Steve Early that she thought "it would be a 'stupid political mistake' to have them here, invited by you." It was her view, Early informed the President, that "Ford did more than any other man to wreck NRA; to have him here would be to encourage NRA opposition and discourage the friends of NRA."

Undoubtedly because of Mrs. Roosevelt's objections, the President decided to delay the invitation to Ford until after the Congressional elections. The letter was sent on November 8, and the Fords were asked not to the White House but to Warm Springs. Henry and his wife were unable to come because of the state of Mrs. Ford's health, but Mr. and Mrs. Edsel Ford visited with the President on November 24. [29] Whether Edsel and the President discussed N.R.A. problems is not known, but what does appear clear is that Edsel's father not only refused to sign the code for his industry but was unwilling even to discuss the matter with the President of the United States.

III

The answer as to whether or not the Ford Motor Company complied with Section 7(a) is to be found in the events growing out of the labor disturbances that occurred in late September 1933 at the Ford assembly plants in Chester, Pennsylvania, and Edgewater, New Jersey. The trouble at Chester began on the morning of September 26. The principal grievance of the men appears to have been the recently announced decision of the company that the work week would be reduced from five to four days without any increase in the base pay of $4 a day. There was no union in the plant, and there had been no effort on the part of the men to present any demands to the local management. At about 10:00 A.M. on the twenty-sixth there was a commotion at the rear end of the chassis line occasioned by a few men who threw down their tools and shouted to the other workers to follow them out of the plant. This sudden action caused a shutdown of the chassis line. Superintendent A. M. Harris then appeared and, when he failed to persuade the employees congregated about the line to return to their jobs, ordered the workers out of the plant. Approximately twenty-five hundred persons were employed in the plant at that time.

Outside the plant, the workers formed a committee to present demands to the plant management. The committee informed Harris that the men wanted a seven-hour day, a five-day week, and a minimum wage of $5 per day. Harris replied that the matter would have to be referred to company headquarters in Dearborn, and he advised the committee to have the workers back at their jobs by 7:30 the next morning. Harris then called Dearborn and was instructed to post a sign that the plant was closed indefinitely.[30] This decision was made without any knowledge as to whether the workers would return to their jobs the next morning.

When the committee reported the results of its meeting with Harris to the workers outside, the decision was made to organize an A.F. of L. federal labor union. An A.F. of L. representative was called in, and an application for a charter was made. The National Labor Board on the same day instructed James F. Dewey, a Department of Labor conciliator and a Chester resident, to proceed to Chester to arrange a settlement.[31]

When the workers arrived at the plant on the morning of the twenty-seventh, prepared to return if their demands were met or, perhaps, pending mediation by the N.L.B.,[32] they learned for the first time that the plant was closed indefinitely. Dewey arrived on the scene within a few hours and informed plant manager F. A. Atcheson that if the company would meet with the committee and with him, the dispute could be settled in five minutes. The men could return to work, and any unresolved issues could be taken up with Dearborn. Atcheson called his superiors in Dearborn and then informed Dewey that the plant was closed and that he could not discuss the situation with either Dewey or the employees' committee. Dewey, who regarded the company's attitude as "very arbitrary and unfair," presented the situation to the N.L.B. the next day and recommended "drastic action." Senator Wagner then tried his hand at persuading the company to negotiate with the employees and a representative of the N.L.B., but he was no more successful than Dewey had been.[33]

The company decided to reopen the plant on October 16, and approximately eight hundred workers were summoned by invitation to report on that date. The union insisted that many of these men had not been on the company payroll on September 26, but apparently only seven of those summoned were new employees. It should be noted that in the view of the Ford Motor Company, the workers who remained away from their jobs at Chester, and also at Edgewater, thereby severed their connection with the company and had to apply for re-employment if they wished to return to work, whereas the. N.L.B., taking a position most employers were not prepared to accept, regarded strikers (and certainly workers who had been locked out) as continuing in the status of employees.[34]

The N.L.B. failed to persuade the Ford Motor Company to attend a hearing on charges that it had discriminated against some of its employees in the reopening of the Chester plant and that it had refused to engage in collective bargaining, but Dewey was able to arrange a conference between the employees' committee and the plant management on October 25. The conference, however, involved no real discussion of issues since Atcheson was utterly without authority to make any decisions. He even had to consult with Dearborn before rejecting the committee's request to engage a stenographer. Worried about the re-employment of strikers not yet called back to work and advised to concentrate on this subject by Dewey, the committee requested that those not working be returned without discrimination; that those who could not be reinstated at once because of lack of work should be re-employed before new employees were engaged; that men on the payroll who were not working on September 26 should be discharged to make room for those who had been "locked out"; and that after full operations had resumed or as soon as any of the committeemen had been re-employed, a conference should be held to discuss wages and other grievances, with regular meetings to follow.[35]

The reply to these demands was worked out in Dearborn and was handed by Atcheson to the employees' committee on November 10 without comment and without discussion. The company stated that it always judged applications for work on the basis of merit alone and without discrimination and that its policy was also to rehire "former" employees on this basis. No one then working, the company declared, would be discharged for reasons other than lack of work or incompetence. Finally, a system of regularly scheduled meetings was "unnecessary to the continuance of just relations between the Company and the employees" since the management was "ready at all reasonable times to hear individual employees or their representatives on matters that properly pertain to the relations between them." Instructed to report to Dearborn on the effect of this communication on the workers, Atcheson was able to state in a few days that he had learned through an "agent" that most of the active union men now realized that they had been defeated and were prepared to return to work.[36]

Anxious for the assistance of the federal government, the employees' committee presented its case to the N.L.B. in a conference conducted by Milton Handler, the N.L.B.'s General Counsel, on December 4 and 5.[37] A few days later, Handler, in response to a phone call from the acting secretary of the union, who appears to have been a Ford labor spy, indicated that the employees had been in error in walking out before any demands had been submitted, that the evidence they had presented did not indicate any violation of the N.I.R.A. by Ford, and that the N.L.B. would take no further action in the case.[38] Discouraged by this report and by their inability to secure any material aid from the A.F. of L., the workers voted to disband their union and to return its charter. Their case was eventually turned over to the

Compliance Division of the N.R.A., and a hearing, which the Ford Motor Company refused to attend, was held by the Compliance Board on March 3.[39]   The conclusions of the board will be noted below.

The facts in the Chester case make it clear that what had begun as an unorganized strike soon developed into a lockout.   There also seems little doubt that the company practiced discrimination in its re-employment of the workers who had walked out on September 26.   As late as the first of March, 477 employees had not been rehired even though the total number at work on that date exceeded the number employed on September 26.   Since those denied employment were persons whose merit had already presumably been tested by their former service for the company—some of them were employees of long standing—there is reason to believe that factors such as hostility to the self-organization of the workers played a larger part in the company's decision than the efficiency of the employees concerned. The fact that active union leaders were not rehired strengthens this inference.[40]   The N.L.B., it should be noted, did not regard the displacement in a strike of unionists by nonunionists as in itself discrimination within the meaning of Section 7(a), but it did consider such action by the employer as discriminatory if its purpose was to interfere with the self-organization of the workers.[41]

Above all, the company's conduct raises the question as to whether anything that can be described as collective bargaining actually took place at Chester.   Atcheson's authority was limited to transmitting the workers' demands to Dearborn and the company's replies to the workers.   At no time was there any real discussion between labor and management, any of the higgling and haggling one associates with bargaining, nor was there any effort on the company's part to reach a collective agreement.   Collective bargaining, to be sure, was undefined in Section 7(a), and it remained for a succession of government labor boards to clothe it with meaning;[42] nevertheless, it is difficult to regard what went on at Chester as collective bargaining even if the term is defined in the loosest possible sense.   Of course, it must also be noted that the employees considerably weakened their case against the company by walking out before they had made any effort to discuss their grievances with the management.   In the eyes of the N.L.B., the strike was a weapon of last resort, and its precipitate use was "incompatible with the process of collective bargaining."[43]

The labor trouble that had developed at Chester on September 26 spilled over to the Ford assembly plant at Edgewater two days later. Unlike the situation at Chester, an A.F. of L. federal labor union had been formed at Edgewater prior to the strike.   The first organizational meeting had been held on August 22, 1933, and the Ford management had a full report of what transpired. Indeed, throughout the strike, Ford was kept unusually well-informed by its labor spies of the union's activities.[44]

In the weeks following the August 22 meeting, Neill S. Brown, the plant superintendent, called in several of the men prominent in the new union and questioned them as to whether the formation of an A.F. of L. local was in the best interests of the employees, although Brown later claimed that he had made it clear that the existence of the union was of no consequence to Ford. The secretary of the local, however, stated that Brown had hinted that the presence of the union might cause Ford to close the Edgewater plant.[45]

On the morning of September 28 approximately twelve hundred Chester workers appeared at the gates of the Edgewater plant, having made the 125-mile trip from Chester by auto, and began picketing aggressively. They had decided on this action because of unconfirmed reports that as the result of the labor disturbance at Chester, Ford planned to transfer Chester export contracts to Edgewater. As a consequence of this picketing, approximately five hundred Edgewater employees did not enter the Edgewater plant that morning. They were joined by other employees during the course of the day, and within a few days the number of workers in the plant had been reduced from 2044 to 395. The union later claimed that sixteen hundred of the strikers were union members.[46]

As at Chester, the workers quit their jobs at Edgewater without any prompting from the union and without having presented any formal demands to the plant management. The men did have their grievances against the company, however, and some of them were troubled by reports that Chester work would be transferred to Edgewater. Some of the employees were thus predisposed to respond favorably to the Chester picketing, which triggered the Edgewater strike.[47]

The day after the strike began the strike committee requested the New Jersey N.R.A. to mediate the dispute and informed that agency that the strike demands were a seven-hour day, a five-day week, a minimum wage of $5 a day, recognition of collective bargaining through representatives of the workers' choice, permission to leave the plant during the thirty-minute lunch period, and the return of all the workers without discrimination when the other demands had been adjusted. The Ford Motor Company refused to accept the offer of the New Jersey N.R.A. to mediate the dispute.[48]

On October 4 three Bergen County clergymen carried the strike demands to the Edgewater management. They learned that the demand concerning lunch would be met, that the matter of recognition would have to be decided in Dearborn, and that the strike leaders "would be forever banned." A few days later plant manager E. A. Esslinger stated in a phone conversation with Edsel Ford, "When we hire we will take men from other parts of N[ew] Jersey and not local men." He also informed Edsel that he had refused to meet the strike committee, which led Edsel to say, "Be careful—Section 7A of code." [49]

The strikers formally presented their demands to the plant management in a meeting on October 19 that had been arranged by the N.L.B. and the New Jersey N.R.A. Brown advised the strike committee that all policy issues would have to be referred to Dearborn but that he was able to state that the workers could have forty-five minutes for lunch, during which time they could leave the plant. He pointed out that despite the fact that letters had been sent out terminating the service of the strikers, three hundred of them had already been re-employed. He insisted that no employee had been "blackballed," but he noted at the same time that he did not regard all strikers as employees. The reaction of the workers to the conference, to quote an A.F. of L. official, was that Brown was "asking the fellows to buy a yellow brick." [50]

The reply to the strikers' demands was worked out in Dearborn, and Brown was instructed on October 31 to transmit the company's answer to the strike committee "without any formal meeting for the purpose of discussing same." Brown presented the company's unsigned statement to the committee the next day. The statement claimed that three of the four demands were already company practice. The lunch demand had previously been more than met, recognition of collective bargaining was required by Section 7(a), and the workers would be re-employed without discrimination, each applicant for employment being considered "strictly on the basis of merit." In regard to the wage-and-hour issue, the company stated that its wage rates were the highest in the area for the same class of work, that wages would be increased as business conditions permitted, and that the forty-hour week would be maintained when the law and business conditions permitted. [51] The workers regarded the Ford reply as a "delayed ambiguous statement" that met unequivocally only their demand concerning the lunch hour. There was no guarantee that the idle strikers would be re-employed or that meaningful collective bargaining would take place. [52]

Since the Ford statement had noted that recognition of the right to bargain was company practice, the strike committee informed Edsel Ford by letter on November 9 that it was prepared to meet with any duly authorized Ford representative to discuss the strikers' demands. Edsel replied on November 21 that Brown was authorized to meet with the committee and that "proper consideration" would be given to whatever committee members had to say. The kind of "consideration" the strikers could expect was indicated the same day in a letter Brown sent to his superiors in Dearborn. Brown noted that of the fourteen hundred men working in the plant at the time, only twenty-five were union members. "We checked the men very carefully," he declared, "and do not intend to take back all the men that are out on strike [approximately six hundred]. However, if any of these men can prove their sincerity and loyalty to the Company, we will be glad to consider their case. Frankly speaking, we do not believe there will be over 50 more men now out on strike that we will again use in the plant." The strike, Brown thought, had been "a blessing in disguise" because it had helped to "break up the cliques" in the plant.[53]

Following the receipt of Edsel's letter, the strike committee arranged a meeting with Brown, which was held on November 27. In reply to questions, Brown indicated that he would take back individuals as needed, according to merit, but that he would not re-employ the strikers as a group, would not lay off anyone then at work to make room for the strikers, and would not set a date by which time the strikers would be re-employed. Claiming in characteristic Ford fashion that he rather than the committee represented the men back at work, Brown made it clear that the company had no interest in an election among its employees to determine whom they wished to represent them in collective bargaining. The strike committee, with some justice, complained to the New Jersey N.R.A. two days later that it was Ford's purpose "to carry on with gestures as long as possible in order to defeat the ultimate purpose for which the men are striking, namely, to bargain collectively with the Ford Motor Co., through their chosen representatives."[54]

The failure of direct negotiations to satisfy the striking Edgewater workers caused the N.L.B. to take a hand in the matter once again. "Why don't you take these poor fellows that are still out on strike back to work?" Senator Wagner asked Brown on December 11. Brown assured Wagner that he had not refused to deal with anyone applying for re-employment and that the active unionists who had approached the company had been taken back in every case. Brown informed Dearborn that he had tried to be "very careful" in talking with Wagner so that "no undesirable publicity might be given in connection with the showing of the new cars."[55]

When the N.L.B. failed to follow up Wagner's call to Brown with any positive action, President William Green of the A.F. of L. stepped into the dispute and on December 21 presented a statement on the case to Johnson in which he charged that Ford had violated Section 7(a). Johnson referred the matter to the N.R.A.'s Compliance Division for investigation. A few weeks later both Green and William Davis, the National Compliance Director, advised the men to return to work pending the N.R.A.'s disposition of the case. The strikers, their ranks depleted and the attendance at their meetings dwindling, as Ford's labor spies had reported, called off the strike on January 8.[56]

On January 17 Davis advised the Ford Motor Company of the complaint that had been filed with the N.R.A. alleging violation of Section VII of the automobile code. Replying for Ford on February 2, B. J. Craig, the company secretary, informed Davis that the company had not violated Section 7(a) of the N.I.R.A. or Section VII of the code, that it had engaged in collective bargaining whenever requested by its employees to do so, that the men on strike had left Ford's employ voluntarily, and that those who applied for re-employment would be re-engaged when production warranted in accordance with the company's rights as guaranteed by the code's merit clause.[57]

Davis, who regarded Edgewater as "a border line case well handled by the company and badly handled by the men," decided that the conflicting versions of the strike events presented by the company and the strikers required further examination. The Compliance Board accordingly scheduled a hearing for February 23, but the Ford Motor Company, regarding its answer of February 2 as sufficient, refused to attend. Thus, no Ford representative was present at the hearing to challenge the workers' account of their grievances against the company. As in the Chester affair, however, one may well question whether anything more than the form of collective bargaining had been observed by the Ford Motor Company at Edgewater and whether it had not practiced discrimination in the re-employment of the strikers. As late as February 2, for example, although there were several hundred more persons employed at Edgewater than at the time the strike began, 350 of the strikers had still not been returned to their jobs despite the fact that over two hundred of them had applied for reinstatement.[58]

After studying such evidence as was available to it regarding both the Chester and Edgewater labor disturbances, the National Compliance Board informed Johnson on March 15, 1934, that the Chester affair had been a lockout designed to break up the self-organization of the employees and to stop collective bargaining and that it had been followed up at Chester and Edgewater by the company's refusal to bargain and by discrimination in re-employment "with the result that all organization of employees within these plants and all collective bargaining has [sic] been eliminated." The board recommended that the case be referred to the Attorney General with the request that he institute proceedings against Ford in order to compel him to abide by the law.[59]

From a public-relations standpoint, it was thought within the N.R.A. that it would be unwise to give the case any publicity unless the government was sure of victory. Charles Michelson, director of the N.R.A.'s Public Relations Division, advised against any publicity until the Attorney General was prepared to proceed "with speed and vigor." He contended that the effect on the N.R.A. would be "inestimably bad" if it became known that the case had been referred to the Attorney General and that nothing had come of it or if a grand jury, after hearing the evidence, refused an indictment. Johnson agreed that "absolutely no publicity is to be given this case," [60] and, as a matter of fact, the public was never made aware of the fact that the Compliance Board had recommended prosecution and that the possibility of implementing this recommendation had been the subject of considerable controversy within the government.

The Justice Department, like the N.R.A. Public Relations Division, was unwilling to prosecute unless it was certain of victory, and it did not think that the available evidence (the Justice Department, of course, had no record of the exchange of communications noted above between the Ford Motor Company and the branch plants) was likely to produce this result. "You will appreciate," Assistant Attorney General Harold Stephens wrote Davis on March 16, "that a suit against the Ford Motor Company would be of such national importance and would be so ably and vigorously defended that it should be based only upon the clearest and highest proof of violations of the section involved. The proof referred to must necessarily be of such evidentiary value as to render the Government's position on the facts impregnable." In subsequent communications Stephens pointed out that the auto code's merit clause would make it difficult to prove that discrimination had been practiced and that the behavior of the workers at both plants would weaken the charge that the company had refused to bargain with its employees.[61]

Despite objections from the Justice Department, J. C. Randal, a Compliance Division attorney, strongly urged that the case be pressed to a decision. He was convinced that the evidence added up to a prima facie case of conspiracy on the part of the Ford Motor Company to violate Section 7(a). "No person," he wrote, "can read the records in these cases without being convinced beyond any doubt, reasonable or otherwise, that the Ford employees were *restrained, coerced,* and *interfered* with in their efforts to organize for their mutual benefit and protection." Unless demurrer were sustained, he believed that "barring jury fixing, it is impossible to lose the case on the facts, even given only mediocre trial talent." He pointed to the procedural advantages and the heavier penalty that could be imposed if the government proceeded by indictment for conspiracy rather than for the substantive offense alone.[62]

No doubt Randal was influenced, at least in part, to take the position he did because of his strong bias against Ford. "High pressure publicity and pious professions to the contrary notwithstanding," he stated in a memorandum on the case, "Ford is, and has been as ruthless an exploiter of labor and small business as this country has ever known." It is not surprising that Blackwell Smith, the Compliance Division's Associate Counsel, thought Randal's conclusions "intemperate." Like Stephens, he did not think the evidence strong enough for the government to proceed. He welcomed the prospect of having "a really tough, big fellow to go after," and if it could have been done without publicity, he would have been willing "to proceed against him [Ford] on a complaint and develop our case in court," but he thought this would be "a bit foolhardy" under the existing circumstances.[63]

In a final effort to convince his superiors and the Justice Department, Randal prepared a detailed summary of the case, which he presented to Franklin S. Pollak, the Compliance Division's Counsel, on or about April 23, 1934, but the Justice Department was not swayed by this brief.[64] It continued to believe that the government's "position on the facts" was not sufficiently strong to warrant the prosecution of Ford for alleged violation of Section 7(a) of the N.I.R.A. It is entirely possible that a different decision would have been reached had the department had in its possession the evidence now available in the Ford Archives and had a statute been involved that depended more for its success on compulsion and less on voluntary compliance by businessmen.

Thus, to the end, Ford was able to pursue without successful challenge his policy of minimum accommodation to the principles and purposes of the N.I.R.A. At no significant cost to himself, he had once again provided evidence of the independent character of his judgment and of his unwillingness to allow himself to be governed by the actions of his fellow automobile manufacturers or, for that matter, the wishes of government functionaries.

IV

THE AUTOMOBILE CODE AND ITS NEIGHBORS

I

THE PERIOD DURING which the automobile code was in effect was a time of economic improvement for the automobile manufacturing industry. As far as the Big Three, at least, were concerned, the worst of the depression was over. Total car and truck production in the United States for the last quarter of 1933 was 275,931 units, as compared to 215,612 units during the last quarter of 1932. G.M. converted a 1932 loss of almost $7 million on its motor vehicle investment into a 1933 profit before income taxes of more than $53 million, with the vast bulk of this gain coming in the last nine months of the year; Chrysler registered a net profit on the sale of new motor vehicles of more than $15 million in 1933, as compared to a loss of almost $11 million in 1932; and Ford (including Lincoln), although still using red ink, reduced the deficit on its domestic motor vehicle business from over $50 million in 1932 to a little over $8 million in 1933. The major independents—Hudson, Nash, Packard, and Studebaker—did not, however, fare as well as the Big Three: of the group, only Packard showed a profit in 1933, and a small one at that.

The upward march of production continued in 1934. Total car and truck output for the year was 2,753,111 units, as compared to 1,920,057 units in 1933, an increase of more than 43 per cent. The greatest gain in the industry was registered by the Ford Motor Company, which showed a net profit for the year of almost $14 million on its domestic motor vehicle business, the first black-ink year for the company since 1930. G.M.'s profit on its motor vehicle investment of $50 million before income taxes was slightly below the corporation's 1933 record. Chrysler's net profit on motor vehicle sales dropped to a little over $9 million, although the corporation's retail sales were the greatest in its history up to that time. All of the major independents registered losses for the year.

The five months that the code was in effect in 1935 were, as far as production was concerned, the best five months that the industry had enjoyed since 1930. Passenger car and truck output for this period totaled 1,861,915 units, which almost equaled the production for all of 1933 and substantially exceeded the figures for the same months of 1934. For the year as a whole, G.M. showed a net profit before income taxes on its motor vehicle investment of more than $116.6 million, Chrysler a net profit of almost $43 million on its sales of new motor vehicles, and Ford a net profit of only $262,142 on its domestic motor vehicle business but a total net profit after taxes of $18.5 million. Hudson and Packard converted 1934 losses into 1935 profits, but Nash and Studebaker remained in the red.[1]

II

Although never officially recognized as such by the N.R.A., the N.A.C.C.'s board of directors, to which the administration of the automobile manufacturing code was entrusted, served as the industry's code authority. Because of its very limited functions as a code authority, the board of directors met in that capacity only rarely, but there was nothing to prevent the directors from discussing code matters at their regular meetings. The day-to-day problems arising under the code were handled as a part of his trade-association duties by the amiable Alfred Reeves, vice-president and general manager of the N.A.C.C. The monthly statistical reports required by the code were processed by Oscar P. Pearson, the manager of the N.A.C.C.'s statistical department; and many of the labor problems were dealt with by the Chamber's Manufacturers Committee.[2]

The N.A.C.C. board of directors spoke for only 70–75 per cent of the automobile manufacturing industry as far as volume of production was concerned since the Ford Motor Company did not seek representation on the board. As was true of most code authorities,[3] only employer interests were represented on the code authority of the automobile manufacturing industry. Organized labor sought but failed to gain representation, and since the code affected consumer interests only tangentially, the Consumers' Advisory Board did not press for consumer representation.

The theory of the N.R.A. was that the administration member of the code authority would protect the public interest. The procedure at the outset was for the deputy administrator for an industry to serve as the administration member of its code authority. Karl J. Ammerman, who succeeded Lea in October 1933 as deputy administrator for automotive codes and who had previously served as assistant to the president of the American Car and Foundry Company and as sales manager of the Newark branch of the Packard Motor Car Company, was accordingly appointed administration member of the automobile code authority on December 11, 1933. He filled this post until March 22, 1934, when he resigned so as to conform with the recently devised N.R.A. policy of bringing in persons from outside the N.R.A. to serve on a per diem basis as administration members of the code authorities. Ammerman was succeeded by Frederick J. Haynes, who had previously been president of both Dodge Brothers Corporation and Durant Motors and had served several terms as an N.A.C.C. director but was now no longer active in the automobile business. Most of the administration members of code authorities appointed in accord with the new N.R.A. policy were drawn from businesses other than those covered by the codes to which they were assigned, but Haynes was an exception to this rule. Although he signed a statement indicating that he had no personal economic interest in the operation of the automobile code, he could hardly be considered a "neutral" person.[4]

Given the nature of the automobile code, few problems of earth-shaking significance came before the code-authority administration member for approval or disapproval; but in so far as Ammerman and Haynes had to express opinions on code problems, they generally supported the position of the employers. The N.R.A. goal of industrial self-government was thus fully realized in the automobile manufacturing industry, for neither labor, the consumer, nor the N.R.A. to any appreciable extent shared in the decision-making process of the code authority. This is not to say, however, that there was no challenge to N.A.C.C. decisions once made; organized labor and the Labor Advisory Board attempted as best they could with their limited power to influence N.A.C.C. policy in a prolabor direction, but the struggle was from the first an unequal one.

It was the responsibility of Oscar Pearson in processing the hours and wages reports required by the code to analyze the statistical information provided, to bring any violations to the attention of the company concerned, and then to forward the reports and the relevant correspondence thereon to the N.R.A. for review by the deputy administrator and for checking and filing by the Research and Planning Division. At the outset, Pearson assumed that strict compliance with the provisions of the code was not anticipated. He thus informed one auto manufacturer that as long as a company provided evidence that it was "trying to comply" with the general purposes of the code, "minor infractions" would be overlooked. Ammerman, when he saw this letter, felt it necessary to advise Pearson that the law had to be upheld exactly "as written in a Code." [5]

Strictly speaking, the code authority issued neither official explanations nor official interpretations of the code. Members of the N.A.C.C. staff like Reeves and Pearson aided manufacturers in interpreting the code, but the opinions rendered were not regarded as authoritative. The usual procedure of the code authority was to refer requests of individual manufacturers for interpretations or explanations to the N.R.A. with a recommendation based on the "generally accepted practice or interpretation in the industry." Pyke Johnson specifically advised against permitting the deputy administrator to interpret the code without the benefit of an advisory opinion submitted by the code authority. "Every time government is brought in," he warned, "government is given a new part in the conduct of business. It is in the accumulation of these minor decisions finally that self-government is destroyed." [6]

It was the opinion of the code authority that the code should be strictly observed without requests by individual manufacturers for exemption from its provisions.[7] Not a single request for an exemption was made directly by one of the Big Three, and relatively few were made by the other companies. Requests for exemption were passed on in the first instance by the code authority, and its recommendation and that of the administration member were then submitted to the deputy administrator within whose bailiwick the auto code fell. After he or one of his assistants had consulted with representatives of the various N.R.A. advisory boards, the deputy administrator recommended approval or disapproval to the head of the N.R.A. division to which the code had been assigned.[8]

Although industrial disputes and labor relations in general were the concern primarily of the individual automobile manufacturers, the N.A.C.C., for the first time in its history, established formal machinery during the N.R.A. period to facilitate the exchange of information among its members on at least some aspects of labor policy. Following a report to its October 11, 1933, meeting by William S. Knudsen, chairman of the Detroit labor committee that had aided in the drafting of the code, the N.A.C.C. board of directors decided to continue the committee on a regular basis as a Committee on Labor Relations and to provide it with a full-time secretary. The job was assigned to William J. Cronin, who had previously served as executive secretary of the National Metal Trades Association and the Tri-City Manufacturers' Association and who was later to become the managing director of the Automobile Manufacturers Association (the name the N.A.C.C. took in August 1934). The functions of the Committee on Labor Relations were to aid N.A.C.C. members in the interpretation of labor sections of the code and to make surveys and distribute reports to members on such matters as wage rates, hours of labor, and working conditions. The name of the committee was changed to "Manufacturers Committee" at the end of January 1934 so as to distinguish the group from the bipartisan code-authority committees the N.R.A. was advising codified industries to establish to handle labor complaints (wages and hours) and labor disputes.[9]

The disposition of labor complaints, which was outside the jurisdiction of the N.A.C.C.'s labor committee, was the subject of discussion at the January 10, 1934, meeting of the code authority, which was attended by both Lea and Ammerman. Lea observed that a "considerable number" of alleged violations of the labor provisions of the code had been reported to the Department of Labor and the National Labor Board and that some provision should therefore be made by the code authority for their disposition. It was agreed that for the time being the complaints would be sent to Reeves, who would refer them to the company involved.[10]

The establishment of more formal machinery to deal with labor complaints was considered at a special meeting of the Committee on Labor Relations late in January 1934. The discussion centered on a memorandum prepared by K. T. Keller, vice-president and general manager of Chrysler Corporation, and Nicholas Kelley, Chrysler Corporation's counsel. Keller declared his opposition to a tripartite complaints board that would include government and labor representatives as well as industry members. He did not, however, object to the establishment on a trial basis of a labor complaints agency if three "outstanding and impartial men" could be found to serve as members and if it was clearly understood that the N.R.A. would give the agency "firm support" and would not scuttle it "merely because the labor people attack it." The committee agreed to recommend to the N.A.C.C. that a labor complaints agency be established under the code authority, that the members of the agency be selected from a list of six impartial persons, of whom three would be designated as principals and three as alternates, and that Cronin be made the executive secretary of the agency. The precise functions of the agency were not spelled out by the committee, and it may be that the committee members themselves were somewhat confused on this point.[11]

The N.A.C.C. board of directors accepted the recommendation of its labor committee, although it reduced the list of suggested names from six to five.[12] In submitting the plan for N.R.A. approval, Reeves noted that the N.A.C.C. wished to have complaints against the industry which were before the N.L.B. transferred to the contemplated agency, which might indicate that the automobile manufacturers intended that not only wage and hour complaints but also cases involving labor disputes or the alleged violation of Section 7(a) should fall within the agency's jurisdiction, although Reeves was no clearer on this point than the N.A.C.C. labor committee had been.[13] What is perfectly evident, however, is that the N.A.C.C. did not wish to have either labor or government representatives serve on any labor complaints agency that might be established for the industry, regardless of the functions of that agency.

Although Deputy Administrator Ammerman was aware that the composition of the agency was not consistent with the N.R.A. policy that the complaints boards should have both labor and employer representation, he recommended approval of the plan on the grounds that it was a step in the right direction and, if approved, would aid efforts to persuade the heavy industries to establish machinery for the adjustment of labor complaints. The L.A.B. did not, however, relish the idea of having the agency made up entirely of code-authority nominees and, in accord with N.R.A. policy, indicated its readiness to nominate representatives for a bipartisan board. Whether because of L.A.B. objections or because the proposal was simply not consonant with N.R.A. thinking at that time, the N.A.C.C. plan was not adopted.[14] When a labor board was finally established for the automobile manufacturing industry late in March 1934, following a series of dramatic labor developments in the industry, it was to have a character quite different from the agency proposed by the N.A.C.C. in January.

The automobile code authority ran into no particular difficulties in raising the small funds necessary to cover its expenses. The initial budget it drew up near the end of 1933 called for a contribution of $30,000 from members and "a comparable additional budget" of $18,661 from nonmembers, of which Ford was asked to contribute about one-half. Members and nonmembers alike were assessed on the basis of 20.6 cents per employee, as of September 1933. The total expenses incurred by the code authority during the life of the code were $48,441.45, which was more than matched by the voluntary contributions of $51,705.37 by members and nonmembers. The Ford Motor Company made no contribution to this sum, although it may have met its share of the costs after the N.I.R.A. was declared unconstitutional. A considerable proportion of the total budgeted expenditures was incurred in the drafting of the code—$14,000 went to Montague alone for his services. Once the code was adopted, the expenses were minimal since most of the duties related to code administration were assumed by the N.A.C.C. staff as part of its regular work load.[15]

The automobile code applied not only to the forty-one member companies of the N.A.C.C. (this total included five Chrysler plants and six G.M. divisions) but also to the single nonmember passenger-car manufacturer (Ford); twenty-nine nonmember truck manufacturers, of which seven did not sign the code; eleven nonmember body manufacturers, of which two failed to sign the code; and twelve nonmember ambulance and hearse manufacturers, of which six were nonsigners.[16] Independent body manufacturers such as Briggs, Murray, and Budd were deemed subject to the code, despite some N.R.A. confusion on this point. Considering the "constant and intimate relation between car and body builders," it would have been illogical and unwise to subject independent body manufacturers to the code of the automotive parts and equipment manufacturing industry while body manufacturers such as Fisher and Seaman, which were subsidiaries of vehicle makers, were governed by the automobile manufacturing code.[17]

The automobile manufacturers insisted throughout the life of the N.I.R.A. that all of their operations should be included under the automobile code alone regardless of the definitions contained in other codes.[18] They had no intention of allowing any of their collateral activities such as the production of gray iron and malleable iron to be subject to a code authority they themselves did not control and which might "write the rules of the game" in a manner unsatisfactory to them. Unquestionably, the automobile manufacturers were prompted to retain their code beyond the initial expiration date partly because of the fear that otherwise their various operations would "come under a multiplicity of codes with a confusion of standards, accounting, administration and what not." [19]

The auto manufacturers successfully resisted all attempts to subject any of their manufacturing operations to the provisions of any code but their own. When, for example, the commercial body manufacturers late in 1934 sought to amend their code so as to include the previously exempted vehicle manufacturers, the A.M.A. blocked the move. Reeves informed Jo G. Roberts, a former Nash distributor who succeeded Ammerman in July 1934 as deputy administrator for auto codes, that it was impossible for a company that manufactured both passenger car and commercial vehicle bodies to operate under conflicting wage and hour provisions since the bodies were produced on the same assembly line. Moreover, Reeves pointed out, if the amendment were allowed, the automobile manufacturers would be subject to assessments determined by the commercial vehicle body code authority even though it would no longer be fully representative of the industry. Faced with the opposition of the A.M.A., the commercial vehicle body industry was forced to retreat.[20]

Not only did the automobile manufacturers succeed in preventing their factory operations from being governed by any code other than their own, but, as we shall see, they were also successful in resisting efforts to subject their relations with their suppliers and their dealers to the provisions of other codes. Knowing precisely what they wanted and having far greater bargaining power than the trade groups with which they contended, the automobile manufacturers were always able to make their view regarding matters of code coverage prevail.

III

With the exception of the crucial issue of the relationship of the automobile manufacturers to organized labor, no problem arising under the automobile code created as much difficulty or was the subject of so much concern within the industry and the N.R.A. as the question of the hours of employment of automobile workers. Whereas the wage provisions of the code did not require any major change in the prevailing practices of the industry, the hours provisions set limits on management prerogatives which the industry was not accustomed to observe.

Anxious to gain industry support for the N.R.A. at a time when the N.A.C.C. seemed to be holding back, Johnson had apparently promised the automobile manufacturers before they submitted their code that if the code were extended for a year, he would approve an increase of the permitted hours to forty per week averaged on an annual basis.[21] When the automobile code was amended on December 18, 1933, to change its expiration date to September 4, 1934, the N.A.C.C. did not request a change in the hours provisions, but a little more than a week later, the industry asked Johnson to cash his promise, and the N.R.A. administrator felt that he had no alternative but to comply.

Both Johnson and Ammerman justified an upward revision in the authorized code hours on the grounds that skilled automobile workers were already in short supply in Detroit and that the expected production increase of the spring would otherwise attract laborers to the motor city who would be without jobs when the spring peak came to an end. The only authority cited for the alleged shortage of skilled workers in Detroit was the auto manufacturers themselves. No effort was made to check their judgment with employment officials in Detroit, nor was any attempt made to ascertain whether the employees claimed to be in short supply were in the thirty-five or forty-two hour category specified by the code.[22]

Despite the inadequacy of the data presented, a characteristic shortcoming of N.R.A. decision-making, and despite the fact that the L.A.B. had not even been consulted, an amendment to the auto code was approved on January 8, 1934, that authorized employers to operate their plants so that the average employment of each factory employee did not exceed forty hours per week from the effective date of the code to the scheduled expiration date. The 3 per cent tolerance for individual employees, a totally unenforceable provision, was dropped from the code, but the forty-eight hour weekly limit remained intact, and no change was made regarding employees in the forty-two hour category.[23]

Since no other industry had been permitted to revise its code hours upward, it is not surprising that advocates of shorter hours were critical of the change in the auto code, even though the forty-hour week was the standard specified by most codes.[24] Chairman William P. Connery of the House Labor Committee denounced the amendment as an "outrage" and asserted that the action taken proved the need for labor representation on the code authority. Connery's opinion was seconded by two hundred officers of the federal labor unions in the industry who wired President Roosevelt that the change was "not in accord with the real conditions" in the industry and that the automobile manufacturers simply wished to operate their plants with "a large pool of unemployed workers."

In order to quiet the criticism, Johnson, undoubtedly to the surprise of the automobile manufacturers, stated that the change was "only experimental" and that hours would be reduced in the spring if the results proved unsatisfactory.[25] Little was made of the fact that the industry had not sought the hours amendment when the code had been extended three weeks earlier. One suspects that the N.A.C.C. thought it wise not to request the change at a time when the code as a whole was subject to consideration lest this provide organized labor and the L.A.B. with the opportunity to demand the amendment of other provisions of the code, such as the merit clause. With the code safely renewed for nine months without change, the industry had less to fear in bringing forward its proposal.

Although total factory employment in the automobile industry increased from 218,981 in December 1933 to 368,565 in April 1934, and the number of factory workers of N.A.C.C. members in April 1934 was only about 5 per cent below the number these firms had employed during the same month in 1929,[26] labor representatives in the automobile industry remained dissatisfied with the hours provisions of the auto code. Speaking on February 27, 1934, at one of the group sessions of the conference called by the N.R.A. to provide the public with an opportunity to criticize N.R.A. policies ("squawkers convention" was the term applied to these meetings), Collins complained about the recent increase in hours and charged that there were 128,-000 persons unemployed in Detroit as of February 15. President Roosevelt spoke to the code authorities' conference on March 5 and stressed the immediate need for a reduction in hours and an increase in pay; and two days later General Johnson made this request specific by requesting industries that found it possible to do so to reduce hours by 10 per cent and to increase hourly wages by the same amount.[27]

Faced at the time by a serious strike threat and seeking to win both administration and public support for their position, the automobile manufacturers decided to comply with the administration's request. On March 13, on the eve of scheduled N.L.B. hearings on a threatened automobile strike, the board of directors of the N.A.C.C. recommended to Chamber members that they reduce the average weekly hours of employment of their workers from forty to thirty-six effective March 31, 1934, and that they increase hourly wages by an equivalent 10 per cent. Johnson promptly announced that he was "deeply gratified" at this action by the N.A.C.C., which was the "first really big industry to come forward" in response to the President's request.[28]

The N.A.C.C. recommendation of a wage increase was implemented by the automobile manufacturers without difficulty, but the hours recommendation was, in the end, ignored. Following conferences with the N.R.A. concerning the best procedure for giving effect to the recommendation, the N.A.C.C. board of directors formally requested on April 6 that the code be amended to provide that the weekly hours of most factory employees in the industry should average thirty-six from April 1, 1934, to the expiration date of the code. With production booming in April and average weekly hours running beyond thirty-six, however, the automobile manufacturers began having second thoughts about the wisdom of the proposed amendment. On April 17, 1934, Reeves had to explain to Johnson that the industry regarded the recommended change as "undesirable at this time." If the amendment were put into effect, he declared, the manufacturers would have to lay off a considerable number of employees since they had been scheduling factory operations with a view to having their workers average forty hours per week during the twelve-month period ending September 4, 1934, and they would now have only twenty weeks to make the necessary adjustments.   It would also be necessary were the amendment approved to import workers from outside the Detroit area since all the available skilled workers in some categories in the motor city were already being employed.   (Of course, in so far as these skilled workers were in the forty-two hour category, the proposed amendment would not have affected them anyhow.)   Finally, Reeves contended, a reduction in hours would be difficult to explain to the workers and might cause labor unrest.[29]

Although the N.R.A. had hoped that the industry would agree to an amendment reducing average hours, there is no indication that the administration placed any pressure on the automobile manufacturers to honor in full a promise that they had used for public-relations purposes when it had been expedient to do so.   As a matter of fact, had the amendment been adopted, the industry would have had no difficulty in observing it.   Only in April during the period the amendment would have been in effect did the average weekly working hours of employees in the forty-hour group exceed thirty-six,[30] and these excess hours could easily have been absorbed in the over-all average for the period.

When the code was renewed at the end of August 1934 and again in November, no change was made in the hours provisions, but on January 31, 1935, when the code was extended for the final time, an amendment was inserted providing that employees were to be paid time-and-a-half for work above forty-eight hours per week.   This provision affected only the employees in the forty-two hour category —about 17 per cent of the industry's 344,128 employees as of January 1935—since only workers in this group were permitted to exceed forty-eight hours per week.   The statistics the automobile manufacturers supplied the N.R.A. give no indication of the number of employees who received the overtime rate during the few months the code remained in effect.[31]

The most troublesome question raised by the hours provisions of the automobile code was the interpretation and implementation of the averaging clause.   The automobile code was by no means unique in its provision for the averaging of the hours of labor: averaging clauses were included in approximately 16 per cent of the codes, supplements, and divisions and applied to 21.3 per cent of the employees covered by codes.   The eight hours per week above forty permitted by the auto code for the bulk of the industry's employees was typical of the amount of elasticity provided in averaging clauses, but the lack of any limit on the weekly hours of auto employees in the forty-two hour category was not so usual. Also, whereas 42.6 per cent of the codes with averaging provisions, applying to 46.6 per cent of the employees covered by codes of this type, provided for an overtime rate and even though this practice was not uncommon in the automobile industry before the depression, the auto code did not stipulate an overtime rate for basic employees and made provision for such a rate for the forty-two hour group only after January 31, 1935.[32]

Following the renewal of their code on December 18, 1933, the automobile manufacturers took the position that averaging should be applied on an annual basis for all automobile factory employees. The code had already made this provision for employees in the forty-two hour group, but the stated averaging period for other employees was from the effective date to the expiration date. Now the industry contended that the period of averaging should be from September 5, 1933, to September 4, 1934, when a new annual averaging period would begin. The code authority insisted that any other basis for averaging hours was "impractical" because of the industry's production cycle.

Despite the complaints of the L.A.B., Deputy Administrator Ammerman and his successors accepted the industry's interpretation regarding the length of the averaging period,[33] although language to this effect applying to employees outside of the forty-two hour category was never placed in the code. The L.A.B. argued that the period of averaging must perforce be the time from the effective date to the expiration date as provided by the code at any particular moment. Since it could not be assumed in advance that the code would be renewed when a particular expiration date was reached and since it was questionable procedure to have amendments extending the life of the code applied retroactively for averaging purposes, which is what in effect happened to the amendment of December 18, 1933, logic at least was on the L.A.B.'s side even though its view did not prevail. The auto code thus must be included among the minority of codes with averaging provisions that had an averaging period for as long as one year.[34]

The automobile industry not only had its way regarding the proper length of the averaging period, but it also won support for its contention that an employee's hours of labor should be averaged for the entire period September 5–September 4 even though he had been newly engaged at some point after September 5. This meant that the employee who was taken on for only the final six months of the period could work forty-eight hours per week every week during these months and still be well within the permitted forty-hour average for the twelve-month period.

Early in June 1934, Reeves, on behalf of the code authority, requested that the automobile code be officially interpreted to permit temporary employees to work as many hours in the departments in which they were employed as the regular employees. In a letter to Ammerman, Reeves explained that if the period of averaging for each worker was to be reckoned only from the time of his initial employment to the expiration date, newly hired employees would not be able to work up to forty-eight hours per week for as many weeks as employees whose averaging period extended over the whole year. As a practical matter, however, he argued, it was impossible under a system of line production to employ newly engaged workers for fewer hours than were being worked by the other employees. If the requested interpretation were not approved, Cronin was soon to contend, the working schedules of several manufacturers would be disrupted, and both new and old employees in various departments would have to be laid off. Similarly, Stephen DuBrul of G.M. warned that "If we get into a mess of arbitrary regulations, we cannot run our business any more."

The industry's views on this subject were endorsed by the administration member of the code authority and won general approval within the N.R.A. An interpretation was drafted late in July which called for the averaging of the hours of employment from the period September 5, 1933, to September 4, 1934, regardless of whether an employee had worked all or part of that period and provided that no employee was to work more than 2080 hours during the period (52×40) or more than forty-eight hours or six days in any one week. Before the proposed interpretation could be officially issued by the division administrator, however, the automobile manufacturers on August 8 withdrew their request. In a letter to Assistant Deputy Administrator Isaac D. Everitt, Cronin explained that since only about three weeks remained until the code expired, it would be necessary for a large section of the industry to shut down altogether were the manufacturers required to give effect to any interpretation regarding averaging contrary to the one that they had advanced.[35] There the matter rested. Since the statistics the industry supplied the N.R.A. give no indication of the hours worked by individual employees, it is impossible to determine how many hours newly engaged employees actually worked between June and September, but in view of the fact that these were months of declining production and declining total man hours of labor, it is unlikely that any great number of employees in the forty-hour group worked even forty hours per week during many weeks of the period.[36]

The basic objection to the averaging provision of the automobile code, as to averaging provisions in general, was the difficulty of enforcement. No question of compliance could be raised, for example, if employees in the forty-hour group averaged as high as forty-eight hours per week for some months since layoffs or reduced hours in succeeding months could bring the total hours worked during the twelve months within the permitted average for the year. Also, since the monthly statistics supplied by the industry gave only the total and average hours worked by all employees of each company in the forty and forty-two hour categories, the N.R.A. had no way of ascertaining precisely how many hours an individual employee had worked during the averaging period.

The difficulties presented by averaging provisions in the codes led the N.R.A. to issue a statement of policy late in July 1934 attacking the use of the averaging of hours as a means of providing flexibility and suggesting that industries which could not agree to an inflexible maximum of hours might provide for a maximum with a definite tolerance on a daily and weekly basis and for the payment of an overtime rate for hours within the permitted tolerance but above the maximum. If it was necessary for an industry to have unlimited hours of labor, the N.R.A. advised that an overtime rate be specified for hours above the indicated maximum. Despite the announcement of this new policy, the automobile manufacturers were able to maintain intact the averaging clause in their code and to resist the payment of an overtime rate to employees other than those in the forty-two hour group who, after January 31, 1935, worked more than forty-eight hours per week.[37]

Like other codes,[38] the automobile code excepted certain categories of workers from the hourly limitations applying to other workers. Although the ambiguous language of the code led to some uncertainty within the industry and the N.R.A. as to whether supervisory employees receiving less than $35 per week and nonsupervisory workers receiving more than $35 per week were exempted from the code's hourly limitations,[39] this was of minor importance as compared to the determination of which of the factory workers could be placed in the forty-two hour group as "employees engaged in the preparation, care, and maintenance of plant machinery and facilities of and for production." In November 1933 the deputy administrator issued an informal interpretation of the code which placed twenty-nine separate types of workers in this category, included among whom were blacksmiths, tool and die makers of various sorts, template makers, draftsmen, pattern makers, welders, foundry maintenance men, millwrights, and machine repair men. Employees placed in this category constituted as high as 25 per cent of the total labor force during model-change-over time, when their services were in demand for retooling and other employees were apt to be laid off, and as low as 17 per cent of the total labor force when production was at its peak. The average hours per week of employees in this group, throughout the code period, were considerably above the average hours worked by the forty-hour group. During no single month that the N.R.A. was in effect did the employees in the forty-two hour category average fewer than thirty-five hours per week, and during seven months of the period, their hours of labor averaged out at more than forty per week.[40]

Confusion existed from the very beginning as to whether watchmen and firemen should be placed in the forty-two hour category. It was orginally agreed that firemen belonged in this group but not watchmen; but when complaints came in from watchmen that this interpretation reduced their earnings, Ammerman ruled that they too should be placed in the forty-two hour category. The auto industry followed this interpretation to the end, although the N.R.A. staff decided unofficially in May 1935, when it was too late to do anything about the matter, that watchmen belonged in the forty-hour group.[41] Although a very minor matter, the uncertainty regarding the proper classification of firemen and watchmen illustrates the range of problems with which N.R.A. officials had to deal and the confusion that frequently attended the formulation of N.R.A. policy.

It is not surprising that unions representing the skilled workers who were placed in the forty-two hour category regularly objected that some workmen in this group were kept at the job for excessively long hours while others of the trade remained unemployed. Thus the business manager of the Pattern Makers' Association of Detroit and Vicinity complained late in January 1934 that some pattern makers in the area were working sixty hours or more per week at a time when half of the Detroit pattern makers were unemployed. Could not the work be done on a shift basis so that more pattern makers could be employed? At the request of Ammerman, the code authority checked into the situation, but Cronin reported after contacting the companies against whom the complaint had been directed that management believed it inadvisable for efficiency reasons to divide up among several pattern makers the work on a single pattern. Complaints similar to that of the pattern makers were registered by the Mechanics Educational Society of America and the Society of Designing Engineers, but as long as the industry observed the forty-two hour average for the affected employees—and this could not be determined until after a twelve-month period—there was little the N.R.A. could do about the matter other than to advise the complainants that if the hours of employees in this category were limited, there might be less work for production employees.[42]

Requests for temporary exemptions from the hours provisions of the auto code were made by only five companies or their employees. The most complex of these exemption cases [43] stemmed from a request on April 9, 1934, by 202 skilled mechanics employed at Chrysler's New Castle, Indiana, plant that the 120–150 excess hours above the forty-two hour average that they had already worked be ignored so that the company would not have to lay them off during the remainder of the averaging period. What followed indicates how difficult it was for busy officials dealing with a variety of complex code problems to arrive at sensible conclusions based on adequate evidence. After a hearing on the matter, the request was denied by the N.R.A. on the grounds that no evidence had been presented to indicate that other men were unavailable to do the work of those requesting the exemption and that an exemption could be granted on this basis only. The men involved thereupon sent in information from the mayor of New Castle, the chairman of the N.R.A. compliance board of the county, and the director of the Indiana State Employment Service to the effect that there were no unemployed drop forge sinkers or tool makers in New Castle and that it was difficult to bring workers into the city from outside the area because of a housing shortage.

Following a hearing at which the L.A.B. presented data that contradicted the information submitted in support of the petitioners, the N.R.A. decided to refer the matter for investigation to the code authority. The code authority, in turn, delegated the task to the Manufacturers Committee. After journeying to New Castle and conferring with the parties concerned, William Cronin, the secretary of the committee, reported to Assistant Deputy Administrator Everitt that the evidence justified the granting of the exemption to the petitioners, whose number had now been reduced to 167.

A third N.R.A. hearing on the matter was held on June 15 at which evidence was presented to indicate that at least die sinkers and tool makers were in short supply in the New Castle area. The L.A.B. representative present, however, stated that the International Association of Machinists had asserted that it could furnish workers for the plant and that the real issue was not hours but wages; if the wages paid by Chrysler were high enough, workers would become available. No one present knew what the wage rates were at the New Castle plant, nor was any information available from the Chrysler Corporation regarding the need for the exemption, although, technically, such evidence was required. It was nevertheless decided to permit forty-four die sinkers and twenty-five tool makers to work not more than forty-two hours per week for a three-week period beginning June 15 provided that the average hours of these employees for the life of the code did not exceed thirty-five per week. During the three-week period it was presumed that Everitt would gather the information necessary to determine whether the exemption should be continued. No one present seemed to realize how ridiculous this decision actually was. The employees in question were in the forty-two hour group and so were permitted by the code to work unlimited weekly hours as long as they did not exceed the forty-two hour average over the year. The N.R.A. officials concerned not only appeared to be unaware that these employees were in the forty-two hour category but also seemed ignorant of the fact that the bulk of the automobile factory employees had been permitted since January 8 to average forty rather than thirty-five hours per week. To add a further appropriate touch of lunacy to this bizarre episode, the order granting the exemption was not officially approved until July 23, 1934, by which time the three-week period had expired. The Chrysler Corporation, which had been informed that if it desired a further exemption it would have to apply for it itself, brought the episode to a merciful close when it reported on August 11, 1934, that its records indicated that the men involved would not exceed forty-two hours per week averaged on an annual basis.[44]

In so far as it is possible to judge from the inadequate statistics the automobile companies supplied the N.R.A., the industry complied rather well with the hours requirements of its code. To be sure, because of the averaging provision and the unlimited weekly hours permitted workers in the forty-two hour category, the only violation that could readily be detected by a check of the monthly statistical reports was the employment of workers in the forty-hour group for more than forty-eight hours per week or for more than six days per week. The greatest violation of the forty-eight hour limitation—the Fisher Body No. 1 plant in Flint appears to have been the chief offender—occurred in January 1934 when 101,728 excess hours were worked by employees in the forty-hour group, which was .34 of 1 per cent of the total hours worked by employees in this category. During the same month, 1.29 per cent of the industry's production employees worked more than six days per week. The record of compliance was improved after January, however, and by July 1934 the total number of excess hours was only 488, which was .001 of 1 per cent of the total hours worked by the forty-hour group.[45]

When the forty-eight hour limit was exceeded, employers generally attributed the violation to the errors of foremen, emergency conditions, or the necessity of meeting production schedules. Nash Motors paid little attention to the forty-eight hour limitation during the first few months the code was in effect since President Eugene H. McCarty did not regard it as good business practice nor a proper interpretation of the law to keep a few men from working extra hours if this aided in putting other men back to work "quickly." The smaller companies doing a custom business complained that it was difficult for them to comply because skilled labor was scarce in the small towns in which they were, for the most part, located and when they received an order, they had to turn out the work quickly lest the order be cancelled. The Big Three, on the other hand, particularly after January 1934, complied quite faithfully with the hours requirements of the code, but, as a Chrysler Corporation official lamented, despite efforts to avoid violations, "we do find them creeping in and it is usually too late to do anything about it." [46]

It was the hours provisions of the automobile code more than any of its other clauses that led to conflicting relationships between the code of the automobile manufacturing industry and the codes of the automotive parts and equipment manufacturing industry and the special tool, die, and machine shop industry. At the hearing on the parts code on October 3, 1933, the parts manufacturers contended that their industry, which provided original equipment and replacement parts and accessories for automobiles, was "a separate and distinct industry" and was therefore entitled to code terms different from those of the automobile manufacturing industry. In presenting the proposed code, C. C. Carlton, the executive vice-president of the newly formed Automotive Parts and Equipment Manufacturers, Inc. (A.P.E.M.), claimed that the parts manufacturers would be able to re-employ all the workers normally attached to the industry if the bulk of the production employees were permitted to average forty hours per week over a six-month period. He justified minimum-wage levels below those specified in the auto code on the grounds that average hourly wages in the parts plants were normally below those in the main plants—the average hourly wage in the parts plants was 45.29 cents during the first six months of 1933 as compared to 59.3 cents in the plants of N.A.C.C. members—and contended that if the costs of the parts manufacturers were now increased relative to those of the vehicle manufacturers, the latter would simply fabricate a larger share of their parts. Carlton made no effort to reconcile this argument with his claim that parts making was "a separate and distinct industry."

Speaking for the workers in the industry, William Green and Lawrence Seltzer sought to have included in the parts code roughly the same labor provisions that the A.F. of L. and the L.A.B. had proposed for the automobile code. The "balanced competitive situation" as between the parts plants and the main plants, Seltzer advised, should not be disturbed by the inclusion of different hour and wage provisions in the two codes.[47]

Shortly after the hearing on the code, Seltzer quit the L.A.B. and returned to Detroit. The L.A.B.—and how typical this was of the turbulent N.R.A. days—"forgot" to keep in touch with the code after Seltzer's departure with the result that its final terms were hammered out without the board's participation. The code, which was approved by the President on November 8, 1933, excepted parts fabricated by the automobile manufacturers exclusively for use in their own products. It set a minimum wage of forty cents per hour for most male factory employees and thirty-five cents for most female factory employees, which was below the comparable figures of the auto code. The bulk of the factory employees were permitted to work forty-eight hours per week provided that their hours did not exceed forty hours per week averaged over a six-month period. Provision was also made for a forty-two hour category identical with that specified in the automobile code. The code did not contain a merit clause, despite Carlton's contention that this placed the administration "in the position of having recognized a special privilege." There were some general provisions in the code regarding fair practices, and these were much elaborated upon when the various product groups in the industry subsequently adopted their own supplementary codes.[48]

The chief point of friction between the auto code and the parts code was their different provisions for the averaging of hours. When the automobile code was amended on January 8, 1934, to permit the automobile manufacturers to work their factory employees forty hours per week, averaged, in effect, on an annual basis, the parts manufacturers insisted that their code must be similarly altered. No longer pleading their uniqueness as an industry, they now claimed that their code must have hours provisions at least as favorable as those of the auto code since "in no small sense we are strictly a part of the automobile production set-up." With the industry booming in February and March 1934 and with employees working long hours, the parts manufacturers, whose averaging period ended on May 18, feared that they would have to lay off workers or drastically reduce hours toward the end of the period in order to stay within the forty-hour average prescribed by their code. This, they contended, would make it difficult for the auto manufacturers to maintain their production schedules and would also encourage workers in the parts plants to shift to the main plants, something that the A.P.E.M. alleged was already occurring. The representatives of organized labor in the industry and the L.A.B. did not like the idea of "making a bad code worse," but Collins, at least, recognized that the request of the parts manufacturers was reasonable considering the provisions of the automobile code. The parts code was accordingly amended on March 29, 1934, to permit the averaging of hours on an annual basis.[49]

On the whole, the parts industry fared rather well during the N.R.A. period. Thirty-one major parts makers who had lost a total of over $21 million in 1932 earned $7.6 million after income taxes in 1933; twenty-seven major parts makers increased their net income after taxes from $8.54 million in 1933 to $27.3 million in 1934; and twenty-three of the larger companies realized a profit of $20.36 million during the first six months of 1935 as compared to a profit of $12.1 million during the first six months of 1934. The index number of shipments of parts and accessories, which stood at 59 (January 1925 = 100) in October 1933, before the code was adopted, was 78 in January 1934; 141 in March 1934; 113 in January 1935; and 132 in May 1935, the last month the code was in effect. Not surprisingly in view of the increase in motor vehicle production as compared to the two years previous to 1933, shipments of original equipment increased relatively more than shipments of replacement parts. The parts industry also supplied a greater percentage of parts used in new motor vehicles than it had during the Hoover years. The ratio of cost of materials to value of the product for the motor vehicle industry, which reflects the extent to which parts are purchased by the automobile manufacturers from outside suppliers, rose from 67 in 1931 to 70 in 1933 and 75 in 1935.[50]

Employees in the parts industry also improved their economic position under the code. Average factory employment increased 55.7 per cent in 1934 as compared to 1933 and stood at 179.3 in May 1935 (1933 = 100) as compared to 104.1 in November 1933. The average hours of work per week of factory employees declined from 37.9 in 1933 to 33.3 in 1934 and then rose to 36.8 in May 1935, but average hourly pay for these workers rose from 56.4 cents in November 1933 to 62.2 cents in May 1935, and average weekly pay from $19.92 to $22.87 during the same months.[51]

Like the automobile parts manufacturers, the special tool, die, and machine shop industry eventually concluded that its competitive relationship with the automobile manufacturing industry required it to have hours provisions in its code as favorable as those contained in the automobile code. The special tool, die, and machine shop industry produced tools, dies, moulds, jigs, gauging fixtures, and custom-built machinery for the automobile, automobile parts, and other industries and also furnished repair services to a variety of industrial plants. In the Detroit area the chief customer, and at the same time the chief competitor, of the tool and die job shops was the automobile manufacturing industry. The tool and die departments of the main plants were primarily equipped to perform the ordinary maintenance and repair jobs required during the production season but not all of the great variety and amount of work that had to be completed during the period of tooling-up prior to the introduction of the new models. During these months the job shops carried a great part of the load, but there was always the possibility that the main plants would do more of the work themselves. Approximately 80–90 per cent of the production of the fifty-nine member shops of the Special Tool, Die, and Machine Shop Institute in Detroit was for the automobile industry, and approximately 70 per cent of this work was concentrated into the peak months of the model-changeover period. Frequently, a job shop had to be able to turn out work on short notice, and its ability to provide service under these conditions was an important factor in its business success.[52]

The job shops prior to 1933 did not have a national organization to represent them, but the need to formulate a code persuaded the larger establishments to form the Special Tool, Die, and Machine Shop Institute late in August 1933. At the time the industry's code was adopted, the Institute represented approximately 750 job shops, and these firms were responsible for about 80 per cent of the industry's business. The number of wage earners in the industry in 1933 was 8441, as compared to 15,897 in 1929.[53]

The key provision of the tool and die code, which was approved on November 17, 1933, was its hours clause. The basic work week was fixed at forty hours, but in peak demand periods, if "no unemployed workers possessing the necessary skill to perform said production work" were available, the employees might average not more than forty-eight hours per week for not more than eight weeks in any six-month period. These limitations did not apply to employees on emergency, repair, or maintenance work, "or to very special cases where restriction of hours of highly skilled workers would unavoidably reduce or delay production, or to employees engaged in try-out, and/or installation work where products of the industry must be tried out and/or installed or demonstrated in the user's plant." When non-salaried employees worked more than eight hours per day or forty-eight hours per week, their overtime was to be compensated at not less than time-and-a-half.[54]

What these provisions seemed to mean was that job-shop employees, assuming that the peak period clause could be invoked for the full sixteen weeks, which was questionable considering the prevailing amount of unemployment, could work a greater number of hours *per year* than their counterparts in the forty-two hour group in the main plants (2208 hours as compared to 2184 hours); but the latter could work unlimited hours during any particular week, as long as they averaged out at forty-two hours per week for the year, whereas most of the job-shop employees could work unlimited hours for only sixteen weeks and for only eight weeks during the tooling-up period. Also, the job-shop workers, including even the minority who were exempted from all limitations on their hours of employment, had to be paid time-and-a-half whenever they exceeded forty-eight hours per week, whereas this was not true of the forty-two hour group in the automobile industry until after January 31, 1935. All this, however, is, to a degree, hypothetical. The language of the job-shop code regarding hours was ambiguous and confusing, and the employers hesitated to invoke the various tolerances permitting work beyond forty hours per week lest they be charged with noncompliance.[55]

The difference in the hours provisions of the two codes did not become a major issue until the fall of 1934,[56] when the automobile manufacturers were preparing for the introduction of their new models. Convinced that they would have to work their employees long hours in order to meet the demands placed upon their shops by the automobile manufacturers, uncertain whether they could invoke the peak period provisions in their code, and fearful that their tool and die makers, unless permitted to work additional hours, would be drained off to the automobile plants, where they could work unlimited hours during the peak period, the Institute members in the Detroit area sought to have the hours provisions of their code brought into line with those of the automobile code. On September 29, 1934, the fifty-nine Detroit members of the Institute, who were organized into the Automotive Tool and Die Manufacturers Association, were granted an exemption from the hours provision of the tool and die code until October 31, 1934, provided that the overtime provisions of the code remained in effect. Prior to the expiration date of the exemption the N.R.A. was to decide whether the job-shop industry should be given hours parity with the automobile industry or, failing this, whether the exemption should be renewed. The exemption permitted the Detroit job-shop employers to work their skilled employees forty-eight hours per week and to exceed these limits provided an overtime rate was paid.[57]

The Institute contended that there were simply not enough skilled tool and die makers in the Detroit area to perform the necessary work in the hours permitted by the job-shop code. This view was sharply challenged by officials of the M.E.S.A., who claimed that there were at least twelve hundred unemployed tool and die makers in the area —tool and die makers, Matthew Smith of the M.E.S.A. declared, were "cluttering up the sidewalks" of Detroit—and that the alleged shortage existed only because the job-shop employers refused to hire union labor. The M.E.S.A. consequently saw no need for increasing the permitted hours of labor in the industry and was angered that it had not been consulted before the exemption had been granted.

Whether there was a shortage or a surplus of tool and die makers in the Detroit area was a difficult question for N.R.A. officials to decide. There were perhaps fifteen to twenty thousand tool and die makers and workers in related job classifications in the Detroit area (of whom 35–40 per cent worked in the job shops during the peak season), and it is obvious that there was some unemployment among them even during the peak production months of 1934; but how many of the unemployed were sufficiently skilled to do the work that had to be performed was another matter. The best evidence seemed to indicate that there was a shortage of highly skilled workers in at least a few job classifications although by no means in most job categories.[58]

N.R.A. officials who looked into the matter did not find much evidence for the Institute allegation that the hours provisions of its code were causing member firms to lose skilled employees to the competing tool and die rooms of the main plants. Few workers seemed to be transferring from the job shops to the automobile plants; and where transfers did occur, it was not because of the hours question—the hours actually worked in the tool rooms of the main plants during the peak season were not too different from the hours of labor in the job shops—but because of superior working conditions in the automobile plants and the possibility of steadier, year-round employment.[59]

Failing during the period the Detroit exemption was in effect to secure a change in the job-shop code that would give the special tool, die, and machine shop industry hours parity with the automobile manufacturers, the Institute sought to have its exemption continued for an additional month. This request was considered at an informal N.R.A. hearing on October 31, but the data submitted by the Institute did not seem adequate to N.R.A. officials to justify granting the request. Following the hearing, A. H. Caesar, the deputy administrator in charge of the job-shop code, sought the aid of the N.R.A.'s Research and Planning Division, the N.R.A. advisory boards, compliance officials in Detroit, and labor representatives in an effort to gather further information on which a decision to resolve the problem could be made. Various alternatives were considered to meet the situation: an interpretation to clarify the hours provisions of the code, the amendment of the code to permit unlimited weekly hours of labor provided an overtime rate was paid for hours of labor in excess of forty-eight per week, and the amendment of the auto code to bring it into line with the job-shop code. A procedure was worked out by Caesar in December 1934, permitting job-shop employers in emergency situations to secure temporary ten-day exemptions from the hours provisions of their code provided time-and-one-half was paid for overtime. Also, late in January 1935, N.R.A. officials agreed to grant an exemption to job-shop employers adversely affected by the hours differential in the two codes if the auto code, whose renewal was then pending, was extended without change.[60]

The amendment of the auto code on January 31, 1935, to provide for the payment of time-and-a-half for work beyond forty-eight hours per week removed a cost advantage that the automobile manufacturers had heretofore enjoyed as compared to the job-shop employers, and this coupled with the passing of the peak season for the industry diminished chances for any change in the job-shop code or for the granting of any long-term exemption. The procedure that Caesar had devised in December to deal with emergency situations remained in effect, however. Although this arrangement worked out "fairly successfully," the job-shop employers were far from satisfied, and they continued to complain that they were losing "considerable business" to the automobile and parts plants because of the insufficiency of the job-shop code hours.[61] The statistics of the industry for the N.R.A. period are too inadequate, however, to permit one to determine the validity of this allegation.

In a report to the President on January 28, 1935, the National Industrial Recovery Board (N.I.R.B.), which had replaced Johnson on

September 27, 1934, at the head of the N.R.A., advised that steps should be taken to bring the provisions of the automobile code and of related codes into "coherent relationship." As the result of this suggestion, Donald Nelson, director of code administration, appointed a committee consisting of Kilbourne Johnston [*sic*], the general's son, Barton W. Murray, administrator of the N.R.A. division to which the automobile code was assigned, and Karl J. Ammerman to study the harmonization of codes "reasonably" related to the automobile code. The working member of the committee was Ammerman, who was unquestionably the best informed of the three on the subject.

After studying the provisions of forty-four separate codes, Ammerman concluded that the only important point of conflict between the automobile code and the codes of industries related to the automobile industry was the insufficient flexibility of the maximum hour provisions in the latter. This had made it difficult for the related industries to meet the demands of the automobile manufacturers during the period of peak automobile production and had led them on forty-four occasions to request exemptions from the hours provisions of their codes. To meet this situation, Ammerman recommended that a common hours clause be incorporated in the automobile code and the codes related to it. By the time Ammerman made his final report, however, the Supreme Court had struck down the N.I.R.A., and his recommendations were left to gather dust in the N.R.A. archives.[62]

One of the major objectives of the N.I.R.A. was to stimulate the re-employment of workers by a general reduction of the hours of labor. In the automobile industry, a substantial amount of re-employment took place during the period the N.I.R.A. was in effect. Total factory employment in plants covered by the code, which had risen from 162,200 in March 1933 to 223,094 in September 1933, the month the code went into effect, fell off during the remainder of the year as production declined but rose sharply with increasing output after December 1933, to reach a peak of 368,565 in April 1934. Employment then declined, but at the low point of the year, the month of October, total employment was still approximately 22,000 above what it had been in October 1933. The rising curve of production following the October trough led to increased employment, which reached a peak of 379,714 in April 1935, the last full month the code was in effect. Average factory employment for the year 1934 in automobile and body plants exceeded that for 1933 by 45 per cent, and average employment for the first five months of 1935 was 3.3 per cent greater than for the same months in 1934.[63]

The re-employment record of the automobile industry during the

N.R.A. period compared very favorably with that of other manufacturing industries. Whereas the number of wage earners in all manufacturing industries, according to B.L.S. figures, increased 29.7 per cent between May 1933 and May 1935, employment in automobile and body plants increased 93.7 per cent during the same period. An A.F. of L. study of the employment record of twenty major industries between July 1933 and July 1934 placed the automobile industry at the top of the list.[64]

The gains in employment in the automobile manufacturing industry between 1933 and 1935 reflect something more than the volatile reaction to depression and recovery of a consumer durable goods industry as compared to manufacturing as a whole. Whereas, according to B.L.S. and census figures, the average number of wage earners in manufacturing as a whole in 1934 was 75.1 per cent of the comparable 1929 total, average automobile employment in 1934 was 87.7 per cent of the estimated 1929 average. The employment of wage earners in the automobile manufacturing industry in May 1935 was at least 89.7 per cent of the estimated number of automobile wage earners in May 1929, but the employment of wage earners in manufacturing as a whole in May 1935 was only 77.5 per cent of the 1929 average.[65]

The mere recital of employment figures, however, leaves unanswered the basic question of whether shorter hours, as distinct from the upturn of the economy, were responsible for the increased employment in the industry. With production on the increase during the code period, the weekly hours of labor in the industry rose above the very low level of 1932, but they remained well below the prevailing standards of the 1920's. Whereas the average work week of N.A.C.C. factory employees had been 45.6 hours in 1929, automobile factory employees worked an average of 33.8 hours per week from November 1933 to August 1934, and 36.9 hours per week from October 1934 to July 1935.[66]

It would appear that fewer employees would have been engaged by the industry at longer hours of labor, particularly during the months of peak production, had not the code stood in the way. Thus, in a study for the Automobile Manufacturers Association of the effect of the limitation of hours on automobile employment during the year 1934, the economist Dr. David Friday found that member companies had worked their employees 40 per cent fewer total hours in 1934 than in 1929 and had produced 43 per cent fewer cars but that the maximum number of employees engaged during the peak month of 1934 had been only 5 per cent below the comparable figure for 1929. Had member firms worked their employees the same average weekly hours in 1934 as in 1929, they would have employed an average of 118,000 persons for the year rather than the 166,140 persons actually employed because of the shorter hours in effect.[67]   This, of course, assumes that employers would have followed their 1929 hours policy had they been free to do so, which cannot be demonstrated, but it does seem evident that without the code, and with production on the increase, longer hours would have been worked and fewer employees would have been taken on than was actually the case.

Throughout the Blue Eagle era, the automobile manufacturers resisted efforts to tighten the hours provisions of their code and argued that the relevant code terms should, if anything, be made more elastic. The industry contended that it could not even reach the permitted level of hours because of unavoidable interruptions in production schedules and because it was impossible to co-ordinate perfectly the flow of materials from outside parts suppliers with work in all departments of a plant.   It complained that the shorter work week limited the annual earnings of automobile workers and contributed materially to the unusual instability of automobile employment during the year 1934.   The increase in the number of short-term employees, it was argued, added to hiring, training, and supervision costs and led to increased spoilage of material.

If a still shorter work week were imposed on the industry and were not compensated for by a higher wage, the automobile workers, the A.M.A. contended, would be reduced to a subsistence level.   If, on the other hand, shorter hours were offset by higher wages, costs and prices would rise, demand would fall, and unemployment would result.   The automobile manufacturers similarly insisted that an overtime rate for work beyond forty hours per week was not a solution for the hours problem since the automobile companies could not afford to pay the higher rate.   "The automobile industry's life," the A.M.A. declared on April 17, 1935, "depends upon flexibility in working hours without penalties." [68]   That this was an altogether too pessimistic prognosis of the effect on the longevity of the patient of the forty-hour week with an overtime rate was to be demonstrated in later years when union contracts and then the Fair Labor Standards Act compelled the automobile manufacturers to work under the precise conditions which they had been predicting would have such baleful effects upon the industry.

IV

Less complex problems were raised by the implementation of the wage provisions of the auto code than by the implementation of its hours clauses, and the terms of the code with respect to wages did not in themselves compel any significant change in the policies of the automobile companies. In the final analysis, however, the N.I.R.A. left its mark on the wage policy of the automobile companies just as it did on other aspects of the relationship of employer and employee in the industry.

In establishing a minimum wage of forty-three cents per hour in cities of over 500,000 population, the automobile code placed itself among the less than 10 per cent of the codes that provided for minimum wages of more than forty cents per hour.[69] As noted, however, the minima set by the auto code were below prevailing wage rates in the industry. The wages of only 10,762 factory employees (4.8 per cent of the total) had to be raised as the result of the code minima, and a substantial proportion of this number, relatively speaking, were women. Thus G.M. as the result of the code had to raise the wages of only 3.3 per cent (1638) of its male employees but of 18.5 per cent (599) of its female workers; and Chrysler, in its Detroit plants, had to increase the pay of only 0.825 per cent (324) of its male employees but of 7.37 per cent (216) of its female workers. The independent body plants were most affected by the minimum wages stipulated by the code. Briggs, for example, had to increase the wages of all of its 1788 female workers and of 22.5 per cent (2005) of its male employees.[70]

The differentials in the minimum wage rates sanctioned by the auto code for smaller communities and for apprentices and learners do not appear to have affected the geographical structure or the employment practices of the industry to any significant degree. There is no evidence that production was shifted from the larger cities to the smaller towns to take advantage of the lower minimum wages permitted in the latter and not the slightest indication that apprentices and learners, a very negligible factor in the industry in any event, displaced other workers. The Women's Bureau of the Department of Labor complained in the fall of 1933 that employers in some plants had substituted women for men on a variety of job assignments, but, on the other hand, the necessity of paying women the same minimum rate as men for the same work and the limitation imposed by the code on the number of women who could be paid a below-minimum rate probably resulted in the upgrading of some female laborers, particularly in the body plants, where women workers constituted perhaps 10 per cent of the labor force.[71]

Despite the fact that the levels it established were not very realistic, the minimum-wage section of the automobile code remained intact during the life of the N.I.R.A. The code authority opposed the raising of the minimum wage, much desired by organized labor, and it similarly objected to the lowering of the minimum wage in the South, the goal of the Corbitt Motor Company. The industry was able to point to a record of virtually perfect compliance with the minimum-wage provisions of its code, including the 5 per cent limitation, but in view of the nature of this section of the document, any other result would have been cause for great surprise.[72]

Since most automobile workers at the time the code was adopted were receiving more than the stipulated wage minima, the code provisions regarding workers in the above-minimum category were potentially of great significance for the industry. Like forty other codes, the automobile code simply stated that there should be an "equitable adjustment in all pay schedules of factory employees above the minimum." Neither the code nor the N.R.A., however, provided any guidance as to what constituted an "equitable adjustment," with the result that the automobile manufacturers were free to interpret the phrase as they pleased. They contended that it was unnecessary for the N.R.A. to establish a particular formula for their instruction since varying job requirements and the differences in skill of employees would automatically serve to maintain wage differentials above the minimum. The record of the industry during the N.R.A. period supports the employers' position on this matter, for despite the vagueness of the equitable adjustment formula, the differentials in hourly rates between skilled and unskilled automobile workers were actually slightly greater in 1934 than they had been in 1929 and were substantially larger than the differentials for the years 1930–32.[73]

One of the principal objectives of the N.I.R.A. was the increase in consumer purchasing power, a goal toward whose attainment the automobile manufacturing industry contributed in a very substantial manner. Whereas weekly payrolls in all manufacturing industries increased approximately 60.4 per cent between May 1933 and May 1935, the factory payrolls of automobile and body plants increased approximately 133 per cent during the same period. Weekly payrolls in all manufacturing industries in 1934, according to B.L.S. figures, were 56.7 per cent of the weekly payrolls in the same industries in 1929, but weekly factory payrolls in automobile and body plants in 1934 were 67.3 per cent of the corresponding 1929 figure. The industry's total payroll for factory employees, which was just under $20 million during the first month the code was in effect, rose to over $42 million in April 1934, fell to about $22.5 million in September 1934, and then increased again to over $48 million in April 1935. The total automobile factory payroll for the months October 1934 to July 1935 exceeded the total payroll for the period November 1933 to August 1934 by 26.7 per cent.[74]

The increase in factory payrolls in the automobile industry during the N.R.A. era was more a reflection of re-employment in the industry than of higher hourly rates, but the latter were also a factor. Improving economic conditions would in themselves undoubtedly have persuaded the automobile manufacturers to increase the wages of their factory employees, but the pressure in this direction resulting from the N.I.R.A. should not be underestimated. N.A.C.C. members substantially boosted the wages of their employees while their code was being drafted partly to improve their bargaining power in code negotiations. They decided to raise wages by an additional 10 per cent in March 1934, again with a view to strengthening their position with the administration, their workers, and the public at a time when the A.F. of L. federal labor unions in their plants, for whose existence the N.I.R.A. was largely responsible, were threatening an industry-wide strike.

In September 1933 the average hourly wage of automobile factory employees was 65.6 cents per hour as compared to 57.2 cents for N.A.C.C. employees during the first six months of 1933. This figure rose to 72.4 cents in April 1934, which slightly exceeded the average hourly rate in the industry during the prosperity year 1929. The average hourly rate during the remainder of the code period remained near the April 1934 figure. Average weekly earnings of automobile factory employees were $20.72 in September 1933, about $23.50 for the period November 1933–August 1934, and about $27.20 for the period October 1934–July 1935, well below the average weekly wage of $32.74 for N.A.C.C. employees in 1929. Similarly, the average annual wage of all hourly rated employees in plants of N.A.C.C. members, although it rose from $744 during the model year 1933–34 to $1003 during the model year 1934–35, fell considerably short of the estimated 1929 average of $1688.[75] The failure of weekly and annual wages during the code period to keep pace with hourly rates in so far as comparisons with 1929 are concerned is explained by the shorter hours and the more irregular employment of the N.R.A. years. The instability of employment was one of the most serious problems of the automobile industry, but, as we shall see, the N.R.A. and the Roosevelt administration were at least partly responsible for the steps taken by the automobile manufacturers between 1933 and 1935 to regularize the work of their factory employees.

Average hourly and weekly wages in the automobile industry during the entire N.R.A. period increased more than the cost of living did, and weekly wages increased more than weekly wages in manufacturing as a whole. Between June 1933 and May 1935 the cost of living according to the National Industrial Conference Board increased by 13.8 per cent, but average hourly wages in automobile and body plants increased by 29 per cent during this period, and average weekly wages by 22 per cent. In manufacturing as a whole during these months, average hourly wages rose by 36 per cent and average weekly wages by 18.5 per cent.[76]

It was during the period that the Recovery Act was in effect that the automobile manufacturers began to abandon the complicated methods of wage payment that had come into vogue in the 1920's in most automobile plants other than those of the Ford Motor Company. The shift to a straight hourly rate began in the spring of 1934, and within a year the older systems of pay had been jettisoned in most of the main plants, although piece rates continued to be common in the parts plants. The employers made the change largely because of the opposition of organized labor to existing methods of pay. The purpose of the action, as one observer noted, was to keep labor "quiet" "in the undercover struggle going on in defense of the open shop." Many workers had long objected to the group and piece methods of pay utilized in the industry, but it was not until the automobile employers were confronted by the A.F. of L. federal labor unions spawned by the N.I.R.A. that they decided to remove a grievance of the workers that might otherwise have caused them to gravitate in a union direction.

In making the change, employers undoubtedly assumed that time and motion studies and a closer supervision of workers by foremen would make it possible to maintain desired production levels without the use of incentive pay systems. The plants that shifted to hourly rates are reported to have experienced a drop in output soon thereafter, but for the year 1934 as a whole production per man hour in the combined motor vehicle industries (there are no comparable figures for the automobile manufacturing industry alone) increased slightly, and a still further gain was registered in 1935. It is, of course, almost impossible to relate either increases or decreases in output to any single factor, but at all events the change in the method of wage payment does not appear to have brought any significant reduction in the efficiency of the automobile worker.[77]

V

As already noted, the automobile manufacturers refused from the start to deal with the subject of trade practices in their code. When asked by the N.I.R.B. for its views on the subject of price fixing, the code authority declared categorically on January 8, 1935, that it was opposed to any trade practices whose object was "price fixing, price maintenance or production control." Trade practices of this sort, it was declared, led to the "regimentation of business and to the sacrifice of efficiency." "We favor free and open competition under regulations laid down by Congress to prevent anti-social practices," the A.M.A. stated.[78]

Although the industry boasted of its lack of interest in the codification of trade practices and of its aversion to price fixing and price maintenance, its statements on these subjects cannot be taken entirely at their face value. It is true that the N.A.C.C. made no effort whatsoever to incorporate any trade practices in its code, but this was, as already indicated, because of the nature of the industry and of the relationship among the automobile manufacturers and because the disturbing trade practices in the automobile field were at the retail level, and these, for code purposes, became the problem of the motor vehicle dealers rather than of the motor vehicle manufacturers. It might also be noted that a supplement to the auto code applying to the funeral vehicle and ambulance manufacturing industry, which included such firms as Cadillac and Studebaker, provided for the control of prices at which funeral vehicles and ambulances were sold to jobbers, distributors, and dealers and contained a list of unfair trade practices.[79]

When the automobile manufacturers referred to their opposition to price fixing and price maintenance, they were referring only to *agreements among themselves* regarding the prices for their products. As we have seen, Association members exchanged price information, and, of greater importance, they all set the prices at which their vehicles and accessories were to be sold by their dealers. It was the latter fact that led F. W. A. Vesper, the president of the National Automobile Dealers' Association (N.A.D.A.), to inquire whether the code authority's statement of January 8, 1935, was to be construed as an attack on the dealers' code, which contained a resale price maintenance clause. Vesper noted that the dealers under their code simply maintained the prices "arbitrarily set by manufacturers." "Manufacturers," he remonstrated, "have always exercised absolute control of the prices of finished automobiles to consumers" and had even on occasion cancelled the franchises of dealers who did not observe list prices. Reeves assured Vesper that the January 8 communication was not intended to apply to the dealers' code,[80] which was tantamount to an admission that the automobile manufacturers, despite their statement to the N.I.R.B., did not object to price maintenance as long as they determined the prices.

As was previously indicated, one of the reasons the automobile manufacturers did not wish to include trade practices in the auto code was their unwillingness to have their relations with their suppliers or their dealers subjected to federal regulation. The industry clearly demonstrated its determination to preserve its freedom of action in these areas of its affairs in its reaction to the codes of the wholesale automotive trade and of the motor vehicle retail trade.

The wholesale automotive trade supplied a variety of retail outlets with replacement parts, accessories, and service tools and equipment for the maintenance, repair, and servicing of motor vehicles. The automobile manufacturers were themselves in direct competition with the independent automotive wholesalers since they supplied their dealers with parts and accessories for resale that they themselves had fabricated or that they had purchased from the parts manufacturers. The parts manufacturers sold products for the automotive after-market to parts jobbers, mail order houses, and chain stores, but the automobile manufacturers, who fabricated only about 30 per cent of their own parts, were the best customers of the parts makers.

The automobile companies normally accounted for at least 30–40 per cent of the wholesale automotive trade in terms of value, and in 1929, at least, the dollar value of their sales of replacement parts exceeded the value of the replacement parts the parts manufacturers supplied to other outlets for distribution. This portion of their business was of considerable value to the automobile manufacturers since they realized a larger profit per dollar of sales on parts and accessories than they did on motor vehicles. As a matter of fact, the Ford Motor Company between 1933 and 1935 netted a larger absolute profit on domestic parts sales than on domestic motor vehicle sales.[81]

Despite the important position that they occupied in the structure of the wholesale automotive trade, the automobile manufacturers did not participate in the drafting of the wholesalers' code, a task which was undertaken by representatives of more than five hundred independent wholesalers. Shortly before the hearing on the proposed code, which was held on October 21, 1933, the N.A.C.C. indicated to the National Administrative Committee of the Wholesale Automotive Trade that it wished to have the automobile manufacturing industry excepted from the code. At the public hearing, this request was supported in a brief filed for the Sales Managers Committee of the N.A.C.C. by Grant B. Sturgis of G.M. The N.A.C.C. objected particularly to sections in the proposed code dealing with resale price maintenance and with "coercion" in wholesale distribution. As drafted, the code provided that, subject to conditions prescribed by the Administrator, wholesalers should have the right to contract with manufacturers and retailers to observe the manufacturers' resale prices on branded or trademarked merchandise. Quoting, billing, or selling an article of automotive merchandise at less than the manufacturer's suggested resale price was to be deemed an unfair method of competition. Also specified as an unfair method of competition was "the practice of coercion in the wholesale distribution of automotive products in any form whatsoever or through the instrumentality of any devices whatsoever." [82]

These provisions of the proposed code were, in part at least, designed by the wholesalers to protect themselves against the competition of the automobile manufacturers. The jobbers were interested in the maintenance of price schedules fixed by the suppliers because they contended that the auto manufacturer, since he purchased a large volume of both original equipment and replacement parts, was able to use his superior buying power as compared to the independent wholesaler as "a whip lash" to secure parts at prices considerably below what the independent jobber had to pay for the same products. This enabled the auto manufacturers to provide their dealers with higher discounts on these parts than the jobbers (to the extent to which they were not excluded from this market altogether) could afford to offer them and also to set resale prices which permitted the dealers to undersell the retail outlets serviced by the wholesale automotive trade. As the result of this "unfair and destructive competition in price," the automobile manufacturers, it was charged, were creating a monopoly in the distribution of automobile parts.[83]

The coercion language of the proposed code was directed at the clauses in the contracts of automobile dealers which restricted the parts that they handled pretty largely to those supplied or authorized by the automobile manufacturers and thus confined the wholesalers' share of the dealer market to the sale of obsolete parts and of accessories the automobile manufacturers did not themselves handle. To the jobbers, the privileged relationship between the manufacturer and the dealer was "one of the most insidious means of breaking down the fundamentals of fair trade practice" and competition. The independent wholesalers further complained that the manufacturers were not content simply to supply their dealers with replacement parts but that they were entering the general wholesale trade through their wholesale departments and subsidiary or controlled wholesale outlets, like the Chrysler Parts Corporation, and were supplying their dealers and independent garages with shop equipment, accessories, and service materials in direct competition with the jobbers.[84]

The automobile manufacturers sought to be excepted from the wholesale automotive code partly on the grounds that although they were responsible for "a very substantial part" of the wholesale automotive business, they had not participated in the formulation of the code. This was a specious argument, since the N.A.C.C. had shown no inclination to take part in the drafting of the code when this had been suggested by the wholesalers.[85] On the specific subject of resale price maintenance, the N.A.C.C. pointed out that if the proposed clause were put into effect, the automobile manufacturer who purchased parts for resale from independent parts manufacturers would have to accept the prices that they set but would be able to set his own prices on the identical parts if he fabricated them himself. As a result, the N.A.C.C. warned, the auto manufacturer might decide to produce a larger share of the parts that he used to the detriment of the independent parts manufacturer.[86]

The N.A.C.C. also contended that the auto manufacturer was not really a wholesaler when he sold a product that he had ordered produced for resale purposes. The merchandise in question, the manufacturers inaccurately claimed, was "a small and incidental part" of factory sales to retail outlets, and the harm that would result from the disruption of the existing relationship between the manufacturer and his dealer was greater than any benefit that would accrue to the fabricators of the merchandise or to the independent wholesalers. The whole intent of the proposal, the N.A.C.C. insisted, was the transfer of business from those who had it to those who wished to take it away from them.

The N.A.C.C., furthermore, wanted the wholesale code to state specifically that the coercion language did not apply to the contractual relationship of the automobile manufacturers and their dealers. The exclusive-dealer type contract was required, the Chamber contended, as an assurance to the car owner that he could always obtain genuine replacement parts and proper service for his vehicle. Following the code hearing, a vain effort was made by the parties concerned and the N.R.A. to devise code language that would protect the vehicle manufacturers' interest in the automobile owner but which would not exclude the independent wholesalers from the dealer market. When Ammerman at one of the post-hearing sessions contended that exclusive-dealer contracts were monopolistic, Nicholas Kelley retorted that the automobile manufacturers were not asking for anything that they did not already have and that the legality of these contracts had not been questioned before. If this were true, Ammerman observed, the clause could be left in the code without qualification, and the N.A.C.C. now decided to pursue the matter no further.[87]

When approved on December 18, 1933, the code thus contained the original language regarding coercion. A compromise was reached, however, on the resale price maintenance provision. The code stated that it had been alleged that unfair and discriminatory practices existed in the trade which tended to eliminate or oppress small business and to promote monopoly. The code authority of the wholesale automotive trade was therefore to designate representatives to co-operate with representatives of the N.A.C.C., the A.P.E.M., and the Emergency National Committee of the Motor Vehicle Retailing Trade in a study of these alleged practices. The fact-finding committee was to report to the Administrator within ninety days, and if he concluded that the practices complained of existed, the resale price provisions were to be put into effect. These provisions made it an unfair method of competition for any member of the trade to sell a branded or trade-marked item at a lower price or on more favorable terms than in the currently published resale schedule of the manufacturer of the item. Since the code applied to the sale to retailers of automotive merchandise by any person, whether he purchased or manufactured the merchandise, the wholesale activities of the automobile manufacturers were obviously covered.[88]

A chairman of the fact-finding committee was not selected until February 16, 1934, when Ammerman appointed H. Bertram Lewis, then the head of his own advertising agency and a former vice-president of the Packard Motor Car Company of New York and of the Commercial Credit Corporation. The most important meeting of the committee was held on March 6. In an elaborate brief presented at the meeting by Harry W. Anderson of G.M., the N.A.C.C. argued that the resale price maintenance provisions of the code would unduly complicate the operating practices of the automobile manufacturers. As written, the Chamber explained, they would require the car maker to observe the resale schedules of different parts manufacturers who had been engaged to fabricate the same part and would compel him to conform to list prices that might not be competitive with prices being observed by a motor car manufacturer in the same price class or with the prices set by a vehicle maker who produced the same part himself. To complicate matters further, the N.A.C.C. pointed out, the resale price provisions did not apply to non-trademarked parts nor even to trademarked parts for which no resale schedules had been set by their producer.

The N.A.C.C. denied in its brief that the vehicle manufacturers had engaged in price cutting and pointed out that the list prices set by the automobile manufacturers on their parts were sometimes above the list prices for duplicated parts that the jobbers suggested for their outlets.   The N.A.C.C. was most effective in refuting charges that unfair trade practices were being employed that tended to oppress or eliminate the independents and to promote monopoly.   It presented figures which showed that between 1929 and 1933 the dollar value of parts sales by thirteen automobile manufacturers (all the important ones but Ford) had decreased by 55.8 per cent and their parts sales per vehicle in operation by 53.7 per cent whereas during the same period the dollar value of jobber sales had increased 9.2 per cent and jobber sales per vehicle in operation had increased 32.5 per cent.   It was true that the dollar value of the sales of individual wholesalers had decreased by 54.3 per cent, but this was because the number of wholesalers had doubled during these depression years.   The wholesalers, for their part, did not present the kind of data necessary to support their contention of oppression and the development of monopoly in the wholesale trade.

Although the N.A.C.C. wished to be entirely exempted from the operation of the resale price maintenance section of the wholesalers' code, it indicated its willingness to agree to resale price maintenance provided that the prices were set by the owner of the brand or the trademark—the vehicle manufacturer was frequently the owner of trademarks on parts that he did not himself manufacture but which had been made to his specifications—and provided a new section were added making it an unfair method of competition for any member of the trade to sell at a price lower than was suggested in the resale schedule of the owner of the trademarked or branded item an article without a trademark or brand but which was made in imitation of the distinctive design and characteristic appearance of branded or trademarked merchandise.   This latter provision was designed to deal with the problem of the manufacture and distribution of "gyp" or substandard parts.   This compromise was acceptable to the various groups represented on the fact-finding committee but not to the N.R.A.   It appears that N.R.A. officials concluded that insufficient data had been presented to justify invoking the resale price maintenance section of the code even in the modified form recommended by the auto group.[89]

The result was that the fact-finding committee was reconvened, and the wholesalers tried once again to prove their charges.   The N.R.A., which was at the time looking askance at schemes of price fixing,[90] remained unconvinced, however, and on the advice of the Research and Planning Division, which had examined the data submitted, Assistant Deputy Administrator Everitt informed the code authority of the wholesale automotive trade on July 7 that the evidence did not justify putting the resale price maintenance provisions of the code into effect. This brought an angry retort from E. T. Satchel, president of the Motor and Equipment Wholesalers Association. "Frankly," Satchell declared, "I have never read a weaker, or more transparent effort on the part of a man in a responsible position to perform an unpleasant duty." [91]

Although the resale price maintenance article of the wholesale automotive code was thus never put into effect, which meant that the automobile manufacturers were free, as before, to suggest list prices on parts to their dealers whether or not they had manufactured the parts themselves, the language of the code would seem to indicate that the wholesale operations of the vehicle manufacturers were subject to the remaining terms of the code.[92] This point, however, was never really pressed by the N.R.A., undoubtedly because both the jobbers and the automobile manufacturers concluded that the matter was no longer of sufficient importance to warrant giving it any further attention.

Not only were the automobile manufacturers thus able to resist efforts of the wholesalers to use their code as a means of limiting the freedom of action of the vehicle makers in dealing with their parts suppliers, but they also succeeded in preventing the N.R.A. from injecting itself into the even more sensitive area of factory-dealer relations. N.R.A. officials had assumed that following the approval of the automobile manufacturing code the N.A.C.C. would soon submit a supplementary code of trade practices and that it would touch on at least some aspects of the relationship of factory and dealer. When the automobile dealers prepared their code, some of them would have liked to include provisions defining this relationship, but the dealers' code committee was assured by N.R.A. officials that the manufacturers were likely to deal with this problem in a supplement to their own code.[93]

The result was that the motor vehicle retailing code, which was approved on October 3, 1933, left the status quo with regard to factory-dealer relationships undisturbed. The key provisions of the code concerned the pricing of automobiles and automobile parts and accessories and the valuation of used cars. New cars were to be sold to consumers for not less than the factory list price plus certain specified additional charges, and, similarly, the retail price for parts, ac-

cessories, and supplies was to be the published list price of the manufacturer, except for sales to duly authorized dealers, associate or
subdealers, or established service dealers. The value of a used car
was to be the average price the public in any market area was paying for the vehicle as ascertained by the N.A.D.A. from sworn statements regarding retail sales. In an effort to get at the problem of
the so-called "junk cars," the 20 per cent of sales at the lowest prices
during the previous period were to be excluded in the determination
of used-car values. The dealer was not to allow more for a used car
than the price computed as above, less a minimum selling, handling,
and reconditioning charge determined according to a fixed schedule.[94]

In dealing with the automobile manufacturers and the N.R.A.
following the adoption of the retail code, the leadership of the N.A.D.A.
was most concerned about manufacturer support for the used-car provision of the dealers' code and the problem of fleet sales, and relatively little effort was made to involve the N.R.A. in other aspects of
the factory-dealer relationship about which dealers had been complaining for some time.[95] Unlike the N.A.D.A., however, individual
dealers did not hesitate to bring their grievances to the attention of
the N.R.A., the most aggressive in this regard being S. M. Heimlich
of Long Branch, New Jersey, the spokesman for the Monmouth County
Auto Dealers Association and the Automotive Dealers Association of
New Jersey. Only Heimlich of all the dealers appeared at the N.R.A.
"squawkers convention" of late February and early March 1934 to
complain about the status of the dealer vis-à-vis the factory and to
charge that the "very existence" of the dealers was at stake because
factory-dealer relations were not regulated by the automobile code.[96]

Many dealers, in a sense, would have liked to see the N.R.A. use
its power and influence to strengthen their collective-bargaining power
as compared to the power of the manufacturers just as organized
labor looked to Washington to equalize the bargaining power of employer and employee. "No labor that I ever knew of in this country,"
one dealer wrote to General Johnson, "has been so much under the
thumb of ruthless big business as the poor auto dealer." Heimlich
complained that the dealers were not afforded any "group recognition" by the manufacturers and had no voice in their decisions and
urged the establishment of a board of arbitration for the industry,
composed of manufacturer, dealer, and government representatives,
to resolve factory-dealer disputes.[97] N.R.A. officials who were responsible for automotive codes did not, however, see it as their responsibility to strengthen dealer bargaining power or to improve dealer
contracts, however much some of them would have liked to see as-

pects of this subject governed by a fair-trade supplement to the automobile code.[98]

The dealers were particularly interested in securing the support of the manufacturers for the used-car provision of their code. They viewed this provision as the heart of their code and as the means of cutting the losses they had been suffering on trade-ins during the period of low demand since 1929. Truly effective enforcement of this clause, they believed, required the aid of the factories; the N.A.D.A. wanted the manufacturers to advise their dealers that those who did not comply with the code, and particularly with its used-car section, would be put out of business. The failure of manufacturers to cooperate in the enforcement of the code, declared a petition circulated in the summer of 1934 by the Michigan Automotive Trade Association, would be viewed as "a yardstick of the merchandising principles and attitude of said manufacturers toward legitimate business and their dealers." President Vesper of the N.A.D.A. informed the presidents of the automobile companies and their sales managers that the "smart manufacturer" would build up good will among his dealers by eliminating the "chiseler." [99]

The N.A.D.A., however, failed at any time during the code period to gain the unanimous and unqualified support of the factories for the used-car provision of the dealer code. The manufacturers had previously shown some interest in the reconditioning and junking of used cars, but they feared that any substantial reduction in trade-in allowances, which for most car buyers was tantamount to an increase in the price of new cars, would discourage the sale and production of passenger vehicles. It was for this reason that the N.A.C.C. had informed the N.A.D.A. before the public hearing on the dealer code that although it would be willing to support a 10 per cent deduction for junk cars in determining trade-in allowances, it could not support the proposed 20 per cent deduction.[100]

Of the various automobile manufacturers, the Ford Motor Company co-operated most closely with its dealers in the enforcement of their code. Ford branch managers were instructed to cancel the contracts of dealers who continued to violate the code after fair warning had been given. Alfred P. Sloan, Jr., similarly, would have liked the N.A.C.C. to devise a plan to aid compliance with the dealer code. He informed Macauley on July 30, 1934, that the used-car article had eliminated "the 'horse-trading' feature" from automobile purchasing and had made it "a standard merchandising proposition" and that it had resulted in "a very important reduction in used car losses" of G.M. dealers. The question, Sloan thought, was whether the manufacturers wished "to go the standardized route or the route of chaos." In throwing their influence against the code, which Sloan regarded as the policy of the automobile companies in so far as they had any policy on the matter, the automobile manufacturers had apparently voted for "chaos," and Sloan would have liked to see something done about this.[101]

Nothing was done by the N.A.C.C., however, undoubtedly because there was, as Sloan informed the N.R.A. at a later time, "more or less of a difference of opinion" among the manufacturers regarding the desirability of the dealers' code altogether. G.M., Chrysler, and other manufacturers advised their field staffs to support compliance, but since the dealers continued to complain to the end of the N.I.R.A. about the lack of "active factory support" for the used-car clause, this advice may not have been taken too seriously. At all events, the manufacturers, with the possible exception of Ford, were disinclined to go beyond exhortation to punitive action.[102]

Officially, the automobile companies took the position that whatever their personal views of the code might be, there were legal obstacles in the way of any effective action on their part to secure code compliance. Thus Reeves informed the Pennsylvania Automotive Association on September 17, 1934, that an individual manufacturer would be inviting a law suit if he canceled a dealer's franchise for noncompliance with the code and that the manufacturers as a group might be prosecuted under the antitrust laws if they agreed among themselves not to award a franchise to a dealer who had lost his franchise because of a code violation.[103] The manufacturers protested too much, however; the problem could have been easily solved by the incorporation of a provision in the automobile manufacturing code making it an unfair trade practice for a company to continue contractual relationships with a dealer who had violated the used-car provision of the retail code.[104] Had the N.R.A. approved such a clause, and it is a reasonable guess that it would have, the manufacturers could have ceased worrying about the likelihood of law suits.

Although individual dealers ignored the used-car provision of the motor vehicle retailing code when they found it necessary or convenient to do so, the dealers as a whole reduced their used-car losses substantially while their code was in effect.[105] They complained, however, that the savings on this phase of their business were offset by reduced discounts on equipment and smaller markups for freight and handling (the so-called "pack"). This charge was substantiated in so far as 255 Pennsylvania dealers and distributors were concerned in a study conducted for the Pennsylvania Automotive Association by

Edward Payton. Payton's figures indicated that the dealers whose records he had examined had sustained a gross loss of $758,256 (before selling expenses) on used-car sales of $11,494,236 in 1933 as compared to a gross loss of $18,130 on sales of $13,543,794 in 1934, a reduction of 98 per cent on a volume that had increased by 18 per cent. At the same time, however, Payton found that the gross profit on new-car sales of these dealers in 1934 was $804,587 less than it would have been had 1933 discounts and markups remained in effect. The dealers, if 1933 and 1934 sales are compared, thus lost $64,461 more in new-car gross profits than they saved on used-car transactions.[106]

Like the used-car provision of the dealer code, the code requirement that new cars be sold at list prices led to discord between automobile manufacturers and automobile dealers. As written, this section of the code prevented the dealers from selling cars at a discount to government agencies or to private fleet buyers. At the time the code was drafted, the dealers were apparently unconcerned about the limitation on fleet sales, partly because they had been led to believe that the subject would be covered in a fair-trade supplement to the auto code and partly because they did not want to include in their own code any reference to the granting of quantity discounts lest this provide an opening for the evasion of the list-price requirement. Also, fleet sales before 1933 had generally been arranged by the manufacturer rather than by the dealer, and the latter had become involved in the transaction only when used cars were traded in by the fleet purchaser and in the physical delivery of the new vehicles.[107]

Following the approval of the dealer code, the automobile manufacturers remained free to offer quantity discounts whereas the dealers were in effect debarred from selling to fleet accounts. Yet fleet buyers appeared at dealer showrooms and after agreeing to purchase a car presented a fleet order from the manufacturer entitling the purchaser to a discount. The dealer felt obligated by his contract to honor such orders, which meant that he not only had to accept a lower profit on the transaction than was permitted him on vehicles sold to nonfleet buyers but that he also violated his code. The anomalous position in which the dealer was thus placed persuaded President Vesper of the N.A.D.A. at the end of October 1933 to call for the entire elimination of fleet discounts. After conferring with the manufacturers in Detroit late in November, Vesper reported that all the companies but G.M. were "keen to cut ... out" fleet sales. G.M., it turned out, was seeking to expand sales of this type by increasing the discounts for quantity purchasers and was informing prospective buyers that discounts were now available only from the factory. Vesper protested in vain to G.M. that fleet sales placed the company in competition with its dealers and impaired their morale. He urged G.M. to show greater concern for its dealers, who sold 95 per cent of its cars, than for fleet purchasers, who bought only 5 per cent of its output.[108]

Failing to secure an agreement from the manufacturers to discontinue fleet sales, Vesper sought an arrangement that would permit the dealer to sell to fleet accounts without violating his code. Negotiations between the dealer code authority and the Sales Managers Committee of the N.A.C.C. led to an agreement early in January 1934 that seemed to solve the problem. A fleet purchaser was defined as one who spent at least $15,000 (exclusive of transportation charges, taxes, extra equipment, and so forth) on new cars in a twelve-month period. All sales to fleet purchasers were to be made by the dealers at list prices, but the dealer discount on cars sold to fleet accounts was to be 3 per cent less than the normal dealer discount. The fleet buyer was to receive a refund of 3 per cent from the manufacturer, who was free to refund an even greater percentage of the list price depending on the total amount paid for new vehicles by the fleet purchaser.[109]

Despite this arrangement, which the N.R.A. accepted as in conformity with the dealers' code, the factories continued to engage in direct sales to fleet accounts. This persuaded Vesper on April 21, 1934, to take the extreme position that whenever the manufacturer sold a vehicle directly to a consumer, he became a retailer and was subject to the motor vehicle retailing code. The manufacturers, he asserted, could resolve the problem either by providing for fleet sales in their code or by adhering strictly to the January agreement.[110]

Although the N.R.A. had previously assumed that the automobile manufacturers were not subject to the retail code when they made fleet sales, Vesper's interpretation of April 21, 1934, came to be accepted as valid. Since this meant that quantity purchasers could receive discounts from neither the dealers nor the manufacturers and that there could be no competitive bidding for government business, Ammerman concluded that it would be necessary to stay the provisions of the dealers' code at least in so far as factory sales to fleet buyers were concerned. He suggested the adoption of this procedure on June 20 and also recommended that all government agencies and, in addition, private purchasers who operated ten or more vehicles, or bought at least five vehicles in a twelve-month period, or whose net purchases exceeded $15,000 in a twelve-month period should be classified as fleet buyers.[111]

Vesper objected both to the proposed definition of a fleet purchaser and to the idea of limiting fleet sales to the factories. He did not protest the classification of government agencies as fleet buyers, but he was opposed to the use of ownership of a particular number of vehicles as a criterion for the determination of fleet status. This principle had been included by Ammerman at the behest of the N.A.C.C.'s Motor Truck Manufacturers' Committee on Trade Practices, but, as Vesper pointed out, the owner of the minimum number of vehicles specified would, by this standard, be entitled to a discount no matter how few cars or trucks he added to his fleet in any particular year. Vesper would have liked quantity sales to be restricted to the dealers, but if no agreement could be reached on this point, he thought that any stay of the retail code with regard to fleet sales should apply to dealers as well as manufacturers so that the two would at least be placed on an equal footing.[112]

Following hearings and conferences on the subject which failed to result in an agreement between the manufacturers and the dealers, the N.R.A. decided on July 31, 1934, to stay the list-price provision of the motor vehicle retailing code for both dealers and manufacturers in so far as sales to government agencies were concerned. The question of fleet sales to nongovernment purchasers was referred to a committee of dealer and factory representatives, which was to make appropriate recommendations to the N.R.A. No recommendations emerged from the committee, however, and thus to the day the N.I.R.A. lapsed, the issue of fleet sales remained a sore point between dealers and manufacturers.[113]

Although the N.I.R.A. failed to produce any significant change in the relationship of dealer and manufacturer,[114] the reduction in used-car losses resulting from the code caused the dealers to view their experience under the Blue Eagle as "brief but happy." When their code lapsed, they continued to look to the federal government for assistance, and although they failed to persuade Congress or the Federal Trade Commission to agree to some new plan governing used-car allowances, they were responsible for the Withrow Resolution, which led to a significant Federal Trade Commission study of the motor vehicle industry.[115]

VI

The extent to which the N.I.R.A. in and of itself contributed to the improved economic condition of the automobile industry after 1933 is almost impossible to calculate since it is exceedingly difficult to isolate for analysis from among the totality of factors affecting the industry the impact of this one statute alone. It does appear though that the increase in purchasing power for which the N.I.R.A. was in part responsible and the more hopeful attitude initially engendered by the New Deal recovery program as a whole stimulated the purchase of consumer durable goods like automobiles.

The automobile manufacturers themselves thought that "the change in the general sentiment of the country" produced by the advent of Roosevelt and the New Deal was to a considerable degree responsible for the spurt in the industry that began in the spring of 1933 even before the N.I.R.A. was enacted and that continued during the next few months. As the year drew to a close and the New Year began, President Macauley conceded that the N.R.A. had been "of much benefit to the fundamental industries of the country," and Edsel Ford and others commented favorably on the effect of the statute on purchasing power. Joseph B. Graham, president of Graham-Paige, looked forward to increased auto sales for 1934 as "the natural result of the success evidenced in President Roosevelt's Recovery program." When the leaders of the industry gathered in New York in January 1934 for their annual show dinner, the President congratulated them by letter for their contribution to recovery. "I realize," he wrote, "that this contribution was made in spite of handicaps which might have proved literally crushing to men of less dauntless spirit...." The automobile manufacturers responded to these remarks with a "great ovation." [116]

The continued improvement in the industry in 1934 persuaded the major producers to expend funds for the enlargement of capacity and the modernization of plant facilities. Donald Richberg, a partisan witness on the subject, to be sure, reported to the President on August 25, 1934, that the "phenomenal advance" in the production and sale of automobiles could be attributed to the increase in purchasing power and to the increased security of employment resulting from the N.I.R.A. Seven months later Richberg informed Congress that not one automobile manufacturer in conversations with him during the preceding two months had disputed the fact that the improvement in the industry was due to the increased purchasing power resulting from the N.I.R.A. and the A.A.A. The automobile industry, he contended, had benefited more from these two programs than any other industry in the nation. [117]

The recovery of the automobile manufacturing industry during the years 1933 to 1935 was a recovery, however, only of the strong. The Big Three's share of new passenger-car registrations rose from 82.45 per cent in 1932 to 90.07 per cent in 1933, 91.92 per cent in 1934, and 92.20 per cent during the first six months of 1935. [118]   The major independents, Hudson, Nash, Packard, and Studebaker, after seeing their share of the new-car market drop from 10 per cent in 1932 to 6.39 per cent in 1933, pretty much held their own for the remainder of the N.I.R.A. period, but the minor independents all but disappeared from the industry, their share of new passenger-car registrations dropping from 7.55 per cent in 1932 to 1.7 per cent in 1935. Such names as Franklin, Continental, and American Austin were added to the long list of names of passenger cars that had been unable to survive in the industry.[119]

In serious trouble as the result of falling demand after 1929, the smaller companies continued to find it difficult to compete even after the general automobile outlook began to improve in 1933, and for this state of affairs the N.I.R.A. and the automobile code were at least in part responsible. G.M. estimated at the end of October 1933 that higher wages and shorter hours had added $21 per car to the cost of building new cars, but the company noted that car prices had not been raised as a result. Price increases on their new models of 10–15 per cent were announced by most of the automobile companies in December 1933 and January 1934; and in April, after they had raised the wages of their employees 10 per cent, all of the important producers but Ford raised prices an additional $20 to $300. These price increases were largely rescinded in June, however, because the sale of cars whose prices had gone up declined contra-seasonally in May whereas Ford sales increased.[120] Thus, although unit labor costs rose considerably during 1934,[121] the price of automobiles remained virtually the same. The stronger companies, their volume expanding, sought to maintain their profit margins by increasing their investment in labor-saving machinery and by having a larger proportion of their parts fabricated by the lower-cost outside parts suppliers,[122] but the weaker concerns, their working capital depleted, in too shaky a position to raise new funds, and unable to increase their volume were driven to the wall.[123]

Although their economic position improved considerably between 1933 and 1935, the major automobile manufacturers were far from pleased with the effects of the N.I.R.A. What troubled them the most was the ferment among their workers for which Section 7(a) seemed responsible. The possibility that strong unions would be established in the industry which would challenge their heretofore uncontested authority to determine the conditions of labor in their plants was something the automobile manufacturers found it difficult to contemplate with any degree of equanimity.

V

THE A.F. OF L. AND ITS RIVALS

I

"The need of the moment," William Green advised William Collins after the auto code had been approved, "is organization, complete organization if possible, so that the chosen representatives of [the] organized automobile workers may speak with authority" for them.[1] Because the A.F. of L., however, failed to organize a substantial proportion of the men and women who toiled in the automobile plants, it was unable to "speak with authority" for them during the N.R.A. years.

For the failure of the Federation to achieve greater organizational success in the automobile industry, there were many reasons. Some of the problems the A.F. of L. faced were the result of its use of the federal labor union as the means by which to enroll auto workers in the Federation. In contrast to the trade autonomy that normally prevailed in the A.F. of L., federal labor unions were regarded as "wards" of the Federation, and although they could elect their own officers, the A.F. of L., in theory at least and sometimes in practice,[2] exercised direct control over most of their other activities. This naturally raised the question of the rights of the rank and file, which plagued the A.F. of L. throughout the period.

Also, although federal labor union members paid dues of only $1 per month, thirty-five cents of this sum was sent to the A. F. of L., whereas the international and national unions paid a per capita tax of only one cent per member per month. Moreover, when a federal labor union went on strike, it learned that the A.F. of L. was ready to offer its "moral support" and the aid of a local representative but that the local was not entitled to benefits from the defense fund, despite its per capita tax, unless it had been in continuous good standing for one year. President Green might argue that the A.F. of L. performed "tremendous services" for its federal labor unions by seeking favorable code terms and beneficial legislation and in other ways, but some auto workers felt that they had received much too little from the

Federation in return for their per capita tax. "We have fought our fight alone," Carl Shipley, the president of the strong Bendix local, complained to Green with some justice on April 29, 1934.[3] From the start, the auto unionists, particularly outside of Michigan, were largely thrown on their own resources, and perhaps this accounts for the fierce independence they were later to display.

The use of the federal labor union also created a problem of co-ordination of effort among the automobile locals. The 183 federal labor unions ultimately chartered in the automobile and parts industries had a direct relationship to the A.F. of L. but, at the outset at least, no relationship at all to one another. The national representative of the A.F. of L. for the industry, who had his office in Detroit, was able to exercise a degree of control over federal labor unions in the Detroit area, but he had almost no contact with the locals outside of Michigan. Collins tried to establish some sense of unity in Detroit by establishing a Detroit district council [4] to represent the city's automobile federal labor unions, and he also periodically called together the officers of the various Michigan auto locals to discuss problems of mutual concern; but not until June 1934 was a National Council set up for the organized auto workers, and not until August 1935 was an international union of automobile workers created.

Since the United Automobile Workers (U.A.W.) Federal Labor Unions, as they were referred to from the start, were free to accept any plant worker not already in an A.F. of L. union, they were temporarily at least of an industrial character. However, inasmuch as the federal labor unions were regarded as a recruiting device for the trade unions, the likelihood was that the skilled workers in these locals would at some future date be parceled out among the craft unions.[5] Although the relentless technological progress in the manufacturing of automobiles had reduced the percentage of highly skilled workers in the industry and, as Green observed, had "practically wiped out" craft lines, organizations such as the International Association of Machinists (I.A.M.) and the Metal Polishers International Union were jealous of their jurisdictional rights, and the I.A.M. in particular persistently and vehemently opposed the inclusion of all workers in an auto plant in a single union. The craft unions had no intention of admitting the bulk of the automobile workers into their own ranks—the Metal Polishers, one of their members later recalled, "wanted to build a fence around themselves even in the big plants" [6] —but they insisted that their jurisdictional rights be respected.

The I.A.M. claimed jurisdiction over machinists on machinery and equipment maintenance work and those building and repairing tools and dies and working on experimental work in plants where autos were fabricated and assembled. It also maintained that parts plants operated independently of an auto plant and separately owned were "entirely" under its jurisdiction. Although the I.A.M. had failed almost completely to organize workers in these categories, President A. O. Wharton and General Vice-President H. W. Brown insisted that the federal labor unions must not "serve as a recruiting station for those who should have properly been directed to our Association" and demanded that U.A.W. members who fell within the I.A.M.'s jurisdiction should be transferred immediately. They contended that machinists and tool and die makers had been attracted to the federal labor unions because their initiation fees and dues were lower than those charged by the I.A.M. and that this had placed the I.A.M. in an unfavorable light. Brown dismissed as "silly" Collins' claim that I.A.M. interference with the federal labor unions would "seriously" damage the campaign of organization in the automobile industry.[7]

As president of the A.F. of L., William Green had no choice but to advise Collins and other organizers that the jurisdictional rights of the I.A.M. and other national and international unions would have to be respected. Green was aware, however, that this was easier said than done. He counseled Collins during the early months of the auto campaign that if auto workers could not be persuaded to join the union within whose jurisdiction they fell, they should be taken into the federal labor unions, and he flatly informed Wharton at the Executive Council meeting of May 1934 that he was "thoroughly convinced that it [was] impossible to organize mass production workers in the automobile industry unless we organize them in Federal Labor Unions." Annoyed by Wharton's constant complaints of his failure to co-operate with the I.A.M. in the organization of the mass-production industries, Green retorted that it was not the A.F. of L.'s fault if the workers in these industries had become "mass minded" and suggested that "we ought to be broad minded enough to understand the situation."[8] But Green's views were not the views of the majority of the Executive Council, and the A.F. of L. president, in the end, had neither the strength nor the influence to make his ideas prevail over those of his craft-minded colleagues.

To the members of the federal labor unions, there was always the possibility that the craftsmen in their midst would be transferred to one of the national or international unions. Collins feared that his work with the Hudson local, virtually the only strong auto local in Detroit, would be "frustrated" by the I.A.M. "We face our work here with more temerity so far as the Machinists are concerned," he advised

Green, "than we do in facing the united hostility of the Employers' Association." Shipley, who thought that the craft unions simply wanted "to absorb the results of our efforts," protested to the A.F. of L. president that craft-union jurisdictional claims constituted "one of the greatest hindrances of organization" and warned that if the attempt were made to place auto workers in the craft unions, it would "kill" auto unionism.[9] The attempt was made, and although it did not "kill" auto unionism, it certainly reduced substantially the A.F. of L.'s chances of keeping the auto workers within its ranks.

Another difficulty the Federation faced in its efforts to organize the automobile workers resulted from the A.F. of L. rule that a local could not remain in good standing if it were in arrears for three months in the payment of its per capita tax. Individual members of federal labor unions were also suspended if they did not pay dues for three months, and they could gain reinstatement only by paying in the fourth month the arrearage in the monthly per capita tax that a federal labor union paid on its members, plus dues for the current month. Since many workers in the depressed and highly seasonal automobile industry were often unemployed for more than three successive months, the dues problem was a serious one for the struggling U.A.W. locals.

Again and again Collins and others pointed out to Green that some special provision would have to be made to permit the unemployed automobile worker to remain in good standing. The A.F. of L. president, who appreciated the seriousness of the problem, agreed in a conference with union leaders late in August 1934 that no union member should be suspended if unemployment prevented him from paying his dues for more than three months, but he did not commit himself to the support of a U.A.W. proposal that unemployed workers who were delinquent in their dues should not be required to pay their dues arrearage when they resumed work.

At the A.F. of L. convention of October 1934, the representative of one of the U.A.W. locals proposed that there be a moratorium on the payment of back dues for a period of one year beginning October 1, 1934, so that the U.A.W. could bring delinquent members back into the union fold. The resolutions committee recommended against this proposal, however, and it was unanimously rejected. Another of the U.A.W. representatives at the convention warned that if the dues problem were not dealt with realistically, the automobile workers would join organizations that had lower dues than the A.F. of L. or would throw in their lot with the company unions, which charged no dues at all. The problem of dues arrearage was not, however, satisfactorily resolved while the N.I.R.A. remained in effect.[10]

The failure of the A.F. of L. to make an all-out effort in its campaign to organize the auto workers also helps to explain its relative lack of success during the years 1933–35. The Federation, a member of the National Council of United Automobile Workers later declared, "could have organized all the automobile workers by the middle of 1935 if they had sent the right number of people in to do it. And the people with the right kind of orders to do it." "It was not easy, believe me," to secure A.F. of L. help in those days, a former president of the Cleveland Fisher Body local recalled many years later. "They did very little...." "They seemed to be satisfied to have us organized," another auto unionist declared, "but they did not give us the leadership to make our organization effective.... It appeared to me as if they were afraid to make an effective move. We were being retarded."

During the entire period from July 1, 1933, to February 15, 1934, the Detroit headquarters of the A.F. of L. spent only $5692 on organization work, exclusive of the salaries of regular organizers. Funds were never plentiful enough for the task at hand, and in October 1933 Collins had to eliminate some of the special organizers he was using and to reduce his distribution of literature. More funds were eventually made available, but even the $36,049 spent on the Detroit office between October 14, 1934, and June 29, 1935, was a small sum considering the magnitude of the job confronting the A.F. of L. and the opportunity the N.I.R.A. presented. The latter sum, incidentally, was less than the A.F. of L.'s income from the per capita tax for auto unionists during the same period.[11]

Not only was an insufficient number of organizers engaged for the task at hand, particularly during the critical early months of the campaign, but the A.F. of L. was also often disappointed in its expectation that the central labor unions would be of assistance. Collins found that the C.L.U. in Pontiac had to be aroused "from its dead ashes," that the C.L.U. in Muskegon was defunct, and that the Flint C.L.U. was of little assistance. He complained that even "with all this so-called Labor Movement in Detroit," it was difficult to find anyone in that key city who could carry the A.F. of L. message to the auto workers. The situation was little better outside of Michigan. The Cleveland Metal Trades Council "made a joke of our desire to organize" the White Motor plant, Wyndham Mortimer recalled. "You can't organize the hunkies out there," the secretary of the Council declared in response to a request for assistance from some of the workers at the White plant. When employees of the Ford plant in Richmond, California, approached the local A.F. of L. for aid, they were "flatly turned down" because Federation officials in the area feared that the organization of these workers would lead to jurisdictional disputes and because they did not believe that auto workers were "intelligent enough to be organized at that time." [12]

The A.F. of L. was particularly defective in the leadership that it supplied to the auto industry. Although the handful of organizers the Detroit office engaged were drawn from the automobile plants, the organizers the A.F. of L. assigned to the industry knew precious little about automobile shop conditions even though they were familiar with the "technique of joint relations." "We had Organizers that came into our plant," the president of one of the U.A.W. locals declared, "who did not know what the hell the automobile industry was, they didn't know one thing about it." Collins' principal trade-union experience had been in the field of street railways, and Francis Dillon, who replaced Collins on October 15, 1934, as the A.F. of L.'s national representative in the auto industry, had gained his experience with the Pattern Makers' League. On the other hand, the men from the ranks who became officers of the new locals were usually without trade-union experience, were unskilled in collective bargaining, and tended to be overly anxious for quick results.

Neither Collins nor Dillon had the force or the imagination necessary to lead a campaign so fraught with difficulties as the A.F. of L.'s organizing drive in the automobile industry. Collins, his correspondence indicates, was a chronic pessimist who saw only the difficulties that faced him rather than the opportunity that was before him. He seems to have believed that if success were to attend his efforts, it would be the result of government support or "good luck" rather than because of the exertions of the A.F. of L. or of the workers themselves. Dillon, a conservative and colorless unionist, specialized in a rather turgid sort of oratory rather than in aggressive, dynamic action to promote organization. As the auto workers gained in experience, he declared on March 2, 1935, they would learn that the labor movement, "above all else, must move cautiously." [13]

What Dillon said was not altogether untrue, but the A.F. of L.'s lack of militancy, its excess of caution, limited its effectiveness and its appeal to the auto workers. From the very beginning of the auto campaign, the Federation made it clear that it was simply trying to aid the workers to realize the goals of the N.I.R.A. and that it had no intention of fomenting strife. It attempted to convince the employers at the same time that it was a "good" union and that both labor and management would benefit if recognition were extended to the workers. When the automobile manufacturers were not swayed by this appeal, the A.F. of L. did not seek to win the argument by resort to the strike weapon but rather looked to government agencies for assistance. Again and again as Collins lamented the slow progress of the organizing drive, he expressed the opinion that improvement would come if only the National Labor Board, the N.R.A., or the President himself intervened or if Congress investigated the administration of the auto code.

Both Collins, who told the auto manufacturers that "I never voted for a strike in my life. I have always opposed them," and Dillon, who was afraid of "making a mistake which would bring to our people disaster," backed away from the use of the strike weapon. Edward McGrady bluntly told Collins that he was a "Softie" and that "he had not been hard-boiled enough in his handling of the labor situation in Detroit." [14] There were, to be sure, some strikes in the auto industry during the N.R.A. era, but they were called by the federal labor unions themselves, often without the knowledge and generally without the advance approval of the A.F. of L.

Conscious of its limited membership in the auto industry and of the generally depressed state of the economy, the A.F. of L. hesitated to risk a showdown with the automobile manufacturers in the economic field and was reluctant to support or to expand strikes initiated by its federal labor unions. One can well understand the caution of the A.F. of L., even though the demand for automobiles was on the upswing, but the Federation was too timid for its own good. Neither Collins nor Dillon seemed to realize that the auto workers, like workers in general, were more likely to join a union under strike conditions than otherwise, that "Once they were released from the plant," to quote a U.A.W. member with regard to one of the auto strikes of the period, "they felt their own freedom." [15] It was, after all, a strike at the Bower Roller Bearing Company in September 1933 that helped, momentarily, to put the auto locals on the map in Detroit. It was strikes in the Toledo parts plants, at the Seaman Body plant in Milwaukee, at the Nash plants in Racine and Kenosha, and at the Hupp plant in Detroit that helped to entrench unionism in the affected companies. And it was an unauthorized strike at the Toledo Chevrolet plant that gave the A.F. of L. its greatest victory in the auto field during the N.R.A. years. The A.F. of L. was unquestionably wise to recognize, at long last, the crucial role that government could play in the organization of the unorganized, but as the auto workers were themselves to demonstrate after they broke away from the Federation, bold action in the economic field was a necessary supplement to government assistance in winning the day for unionism against the giants of the automobile industry.

The marked seasonality of automobile employment coupled with the heavy unemployment resulting from the depression further complicated the A.F. of L.'s task in the automobile industry. With seasonal layoffs and outright discharge staring them in the face, automobile workers were reluctant to risk the displeasure of their employers by aligning themselves with a trade union. Fear, as Collins recognized, was one of the A.F. of L.'s greatest problems in the automobile industry.[16]

The nature of the labor force in the automobile industry was a further deterrent to unionization. The overwhelming majority of the automobile workers were not only without the personal experience or the family background in trade unionism that might have made them susceptible to the appeal of union organizers, but most of them were easily replaceable because of their lack of any significant degree of skill. The presence of a considerable number of Negroes and foreign-born in the automobile plants, particularly in the Detroit area, also posed a problem for the A.F. of L. The opposition of the Negro to the Federation because of the racial discrimination practiced by some of its affiliates, the racial antagonism between Negro and white workers in the automobile plants, the Negro support for the antiunion Ford Motor Company, which employed more Negroes than any other automobile firm and discriminated against them less in the assignment of jobs, and the higher rate of unemployment among Negro than among white automobile workers all deterred the Negroes from responding to union entreaties. As for the foreign-born, except for Hamtramck, where Polish-speaking Alexander Marks functioned for a while, the A.F. of L. was reluctant to use special organizers who could appeal to the immigrant-nationality groups in the industry. This was partly because of a lack of finances and partly because of fear that it would have a divisive effect. Whatever the causes, Collins found that the Negroes and the foreign-born were not coming to his meetings and that it was a "tremendous problem" to persuade them to join the federal labor unions.[17]

Another handicap that the A.F. of L. faced in Detroit was the poor reputation that organized labor enjoyed in that long-time stronghold of the open shop. Its public image already tarnished as the result of the incessant criticism of unfriendly employers and their allies, the labor movement in Detroit suffered a further loss in prestige in the depression when the city's notorious Purple Gang successfully invaded the trade-union field. The labor movement in Detroit, Collins informed Green, is "regarded as just a racket with no ideals and principles." There was a "distinct underground feeling" against the Detroit Federation of Labor even among the few auto workers the A.F. of L. was able to enroll in Detroit, and the city's federal labor unions were reluctant to join the D.F. of L., as they were expected to do. There was, moreover, bad blood between Collins and Frank Martel. Collins, who had tangled with the D.F. of L. president when he (Collins) had served as an organizer in Michigan in the 1920's, had been reluctant to accept his Detroit assignment because he did not relish the idea of having to work with Martel. Martel was equally displeased by Collins' presence in the motor city, possibly because the D.F. of L. president wished the auto organizing work in Detroit to be directed by the Detroit Federation, which, it will be recalled, had launched its own campaign in the industry before Collins had arrived on the scene.[18]

The communists, whether enrolled in the A.W.U. or in the federal labor unions in the auto plants, were a constant source of annoyance to the A.F. of L. They were forever sniping at the leadership of the Federation, at its lack of militancy, and its alleged collaboration with the employers. Much to the annoyance of the A.F. of L., the communists played a key role in some of the strongest U.A.W. locals, such as the Seaman Body local in Milwaukee and the White Motor local in Cleveland. Collins, who in his first speech after arriving in Detroit to take charge of the A.F. of L. campaign had stated that there was "no place" for the communists in the A.F. of L., advised the federal labor unions to oust any communists who were disrupting their work. Dillon complained to Green that the communists within the federal labor unions made more difficult the task of organizing the inexperienced automobile workers, to which the A.F. of L. president replied that the Federation classified the communists with the company unions and G.M. as constituting "an opposition to the bona fide trade union movement which we must meet and overcome." When Green was told that the Seaman Body local was "infested" with communists and that they were engaging in "nefarious schemes" to gain control of the organization, he advised A.F. of L. organizer Paul Smith to "Deal with the situation vigorously." Either the local must be an A.F. of L. local, he declared, or its charter revoked.[19]

Finally, and of crucial importance, the A.F. of L. had to contend with the aggressive and implacable opposition of the automobile manufacturers to independent unionism in their plants. Whereas Section 7(a) to the A.F. of L. meant an opportunity to organize the automobile workers, to the employers in the industry it represented a dangerous threat to existing employer-employee relations. No one had previously challenged the authority of the automobile manufacturers to manage their own labor affairs, and the automobile companies had not found it necessary to pay very much attention to the subject of industrial relations. The federal labor unions that developed in the industry after June 1933 were unquestionably viewed with alarm by the employers less because they were thought likely to raise the cost of automobile production than because they threatened to circumscribe the customary prerogatives of management. What Robert E. Lane has said of the reaction of businessmen in general to the labor legislation of the New Deal era applies to the automobile manufacturers in their response to Section 7(a): the danger posed was not one of economics but of "cost in status, in conceptions of the self, in freedom to make certain traditional decisions, in the [possible] disruption of once familiar and stable areas of managerial discretion." [20]

Under the circumstances, it is not at all surprising that the automobile employers, almost without exception, were prepared to do whatever was necessary to preserve as much of the pre-1933 pattern of industrial relations as was possible. In practice, this meant discrimination against union workers, the use of espionage, the establishment of company unions, and a narrow construction of the representation and bargaining rights of trade-union officials. William M. Leiserson, the first executive secretary of the N.L.B., reported to Frances Perkins that when he was in Detroit in December 1933 "automobile manufacturers told me frankly that section 7a was a mistake and they did not intend to live up to it." [21]

Given the high rate of discharge, layoff, and rehiring in the automobile industry, it is not surprising that the U.A.W. suspected that employers took advantage of the situation to discriminate against union officers and union members. Collins complained again and again of wholesale discrimination by Chrysler and G.M., and he attributed his difficulties in organizing the industry, in part, to the fear that this tactic inspired in the workers. Discrimination, he told Morrison on July 28, 1933, was his "biggest problem." David Lano, the financial secretary of the Flint Chevrolet local, protested to the N.L.B. on December 27, 1933, that the company had instituted a campaign of "complete extermination" against the union. He wildly charged at a later time that twelve hundred union members in Flint had lost their jobs "through intimidation, coercion and threats." [22]

Discrimination was more easily charged than proved, however, and it is almost impossible to determine the extent to which the automobile companies actually employed this antiunion weapon. There is some evidence, though, that discrimination was practiced by the employers. The Detroit Regional Labor Board thus found in a few instances prior to March 25, 1934, that particular automobile workers had been treated unfairly because of their union affiliation. While the Automobile Labor Board (A.L.B.) functioned (March 29, 1934–June 16, 1935), employers voluntarily reinstated 1129 workers who had brought charges of unfair treatment to the board—one may assume that the automobile companies in most instances preferred not to see these complaints carried to a decision—and, in addition, the board in a few cases decided, in effect, that discrimination had been practiced. In its final report, however, the A.L.B., which was generally inclined to give the employers the benefit of the doubt, stated that discrimination because of union membership was not by June 1935 "a problem of any magnitude in the automobile manufacturing industry, and had not been for some months previously." [23] Certainly, the A.F. of L. exaggerated the extent to which discrimination was practiced in the industry, and there was a tendency on the part of union leaders to assume that when unionists were laid off or discharged the cause for this action was their union affiliation. As Collins was aware, however, the fear of discrimination on the part of the insecure auto worker was as important a deterrent to organization as discrimination itself.

Most of the facts concerning espionage in the auto industry were not publicly aired until the La Follette Committee hearings of 1936 and following. It is not surprising that the enactment of Section 7(a) spurred private detective agencies engaged in espionage activities to offer their services to industrial clients. The superintendent of Pinkerton's National Detective Agency thus wrote to one automobile manufacturer in August 1933 that Section 7(a) had "placed in the hands of Labor . . . the greatest weapon ever known in the history of modern industry." "You should be interested in knowing," he counseled, "what your employees are planning and thinking, and particularly what outside influences are being brought to bear." The Ford Motor Company, which hardly needed the advice, was urged by a Corporations Auxiliary Company district manager "to keep fully informed on what is going on in your organization. Avoid the inconvenience and expense of being taken unawares. Take advantage of the constructive leadership our service establishes." [24]

The automobile companies were not at all reluctant to "take advantage of the constructive leadership" that the detective agencies offered. The La Follette Committee concluded that "perhaps no-where" was the correlation between labor organizing activities and ex-penditures for spy services "more marked than in the automobile in-dustry." Espionage, the committee concluded, was the industry's "first line of defense against labor organizations." [25]

G.M., in particular, resorted to labor espionage on an extensive scale. Espionage services were contracted for by the labor-relations division of the corporation, by the personnel directors of Chevrolet and Fisher Body, and by individual plant managers. G.M. was Pinkerton's largest industrial client; the corporation, according to in-complete figures, was billed for over $100,000 by Pinkerton in 1934 and for over $200,000 in 1935. But G.M. did not rely on Pinkerton alone; it used at least fourteen other detective agencies and even ar-ranged for some of its spies to check on others of its spies. The company spent approximately $1 million on labor espionage between January 1, 1934, and July 31, 1936.[26]

The services rendered to G.M. by the detective agencies it utilized were various. In an effort to keep track of U.A.W. activities, the Pinkerton agency on several occasions maintained an office next door, or at least as close as possible, to the Detroit headquarters of the automobile workers in the Hoffman Building. When the company's Toledo Chevrolet plant was struck in April 1935, G.M. "flooded" Toledo with spies. These spies served their turn on the picket line and not only shadowed union officials but also Assistant Secretary of Labor McGrady, who had come to the city to mediate the dispute.

Some of G.M.'s labor spies performed their duties while simul-taneously serving as union officials. Thus Lyle Letteer, a Pinker-ton operative but also a Chevrolet employee and an elected official of the Atlanta Chevrolet and Fisher Body local, was able to take union records to the local Pinkerton office to be copied and was reporting on union activities to his Pinkerton superiors at the same time that the union was pressing charges against Chevrolet because it had laid him off from his job. Three of the thirteen members of the Flint Fed-erated Executive Council, which represented the U.A.W. locals in Flint, were Corporations Auxiliary Company labor spies, and the La Follette Committee attributed to labor espionage the decline of the Flint automobile union membership from 26,000 in February 1934 to 120 in 1936.[27]

Chrysler relied for its labor espionage on the Corporations Auxil-iary Company; thirty-eight of the latter's operatives served in Chrysler plants in 1933, forty-five in 1934, and thirty-eight in 1935. Herman L. Weckler, a Chrysler official with responsibilities in the area of labor relations, observed with unsuspecting candor that the company spied in order to maintain "proper employee relations." Chrysler, Weckler noted, used espionage agents as "the background on which we built our whole structure." [28]

The Ford Motor Company did not employ any outside detective agency for espionage purposes but only because the task was handled with frightening thoroughness by its own Service Department. Commanded by Harry Bennett, former choir boy, sailor, and pugilist and a man who maintained "open relations with the Detroit underworld," the Ford Service Department kept Ford employees under close surveillance and, as one Ford employee of the time later recalled, "did a terrorizing job psychologically." Ford workers knew, as Keith Sward put it, that "only a fraction of the activity of Ford Service was visible and above-board. The rest was underground. The feeling spread, therefore, that no one at Ford's could afford to trust his neighbor." [29]

The smaller automobile manufacturing companies and the automobile parts concerns followed the lead of the Big Three in seeking to thwart union activity in their plants by resorting to labor espionage. Corporations Auxiliary, for example, had among its clients such firms as Hupp Motor Car Corporation, Graham-Paige Motors Corporation, Packard Motor Car Company, Briggs Manufacturing Company, E. G. Budd Manufacturing Company, Kelsey Hayes Wheel Company, and also the Automotive Tool and Die Manufacturers Association. The National Metal Trades Association supplied espionage and strike services as of August 30, 1934, to Hudson, Briggs, Nash, and Electric Auto-Lite, and, incidentally, to the N.A.C.C. itself.[30]

The labor espionage engaged in by the motor vehicle companies unquestionably added to the auto worker's sense of insecurity and limited the effectiveness of the federal labor unions that were established in the industry. Collins complained that the workers on occasion had to meet in basements in order to avoid detection, and R. J. Thomas, when president of the U.A.W., recalled for a Congressional committee "how we American auto workers in those years had to meet in secret, as though we were in some Fascist or other dictatorial countries [*sic*], in order to exercise without fear of reprisal our right to form a labor union." [31]

Although discrimination and espionage were tactics that could be utilized to weaken independent unionism and to limit its appeal to the worker, the employers in the industry did not regard these means as sufficient in themselves to remove the threat to the traditional relationship of employer and employee posed by Section 7(a). The A.F.

of L. and other labor organizations were telling automobile workers that their right to organize and bargain collectively could be realized only if they joined an independent union; but, the automobile manufacturers reasoned, could not the possible desire of their employees for some sort of collective relationship with their employers be satisfied, and the outside union rendered "superfluous," if employee representation were provided for through some company-union plan?[32] Although the automobile manufacturers had not previously made use of the company-union device, the enactment of the N.I.R.A. persuaded the overwhelming majority of them,[33] as it did so many other employers, that the company union was the most effective means of coping with the frightening implications of Section 7(a). The company unions in the automobile industry were thus the product of management's fears rather than of the workers' hopes, and this made them suspect from the start from the employees' point of view.

Taking the position that the employees were unlikely to form a shop union "until they are shown how," management assumed the initiative in drawing up the various plans of employee representation. The basic plan for G.M. plants was drafted under the direction of Merle C. Hale, slated to become the corporation's director of industrial relations, following a meeting of divisional managers in July 1933 at which it was decided to establish employee associations on a company-wide basis. "We have made this plan your plan," declared E. F. Fisher in submitting the plan to Fisher Body employees. Walter Chrysler similarly informed Chrysler employees in presenting the Chrysler plan to them, "I am proposing for your consideration a plan of Employees' Representation in our plants."[34]

Only the Chrysler Corporation and the few concerns that copied its plan permitted their employees to vote on whether or not they wished to accept the employee-representation scheme presented to them. In all the other automobile plants, the employees were simply invited to nominate and elect employee representatives in accordance with the procedure outlined in the particular plan; but they were not asked to ballot on the adoption of the plan itself. The elections that put the new plans into effect were generally staged by temporary employee election committees appointed by the management. In some instances, the members of the committee and perhaps a few other employees had been given an opportunity prior to the election to criticize the proposed scheme.[35]

The employers pointed with pride to the high percentage of eligible employees who participated in the elections that put the company-union plans into effect. Approximately 78 per cent of

G.M.'s employees in twenty Michigan plants voted in the elections of September 1933 that launched the G.M. plans. Chrysler Corporation reported that 86 per cent of its employees had accepted its plan, Dodge that almost 90 per cent had expressed approval, and Hudson that 91.9 per cent of its employees had voted in its first election. It would be a mistake, however, to interpret the large vote in company-union elections as an indication of worker support for the plans. Since, with the exception of the Chrysler type, the plans went into effect regardless of the number of workers who voted, employees must have concluded that they might as well cast their ballots for the candidates they favored. Many workers, undoubtedly, were afraid to abstain. The voting, after all, was done in the plant under the eyes of company officials, and the foremen generally let it be known that they expected a large turnout. In the Fisher Body plant in Cleveland, according to the affidavit of twenty employees, the machines were stopped to permit the employees to vote, the foremen led their men to the polling places, and supervisory personnel looked on as the workers cast their ballots.

The fear that workers who did not vote would be discriminated against was so pervasive that Collins found it necessary to advise union members to participate in the elections. The fact that one was a member of another labor organization did not, of course, prevent him from voting in a company-union election; and in some instances officers or members of the U.A.W. locals were elected to employee-association posts. Finally, some of the early plans, such as those of G.M. and Hudson, tied membership in the company union to insurance benefits and savings plans and thus gave workers an additional incentive to participate. It is not difficult in view of all of these considerations to understand why the N.L.B. specifically ruled that the election of employee representatives could not in itself be interpreted as constituting employee approval of a company-union plan.[36]

It may be argued that a large majority of Chrysler Corporation employees specifically endorsed the Chrysler plan, but it is doubtful that their vote indicated enthusiastic approval of the scheme. Fear was unquestionably a factor in the Chrysler plants as it was elsewhere. Also, since the workers were not asked to choose among alternative organizations but simply to express their opinion of the company's plan, they may very well have decided to try out a scheme that obviously had management support, that cost them nothing, and that might even be of some help. Significantly, when the Chrysler employees some months later cast their ballots in the A.L.B. elections and were permitted to designate the affiliation of the candidates they favored, only 96 of the 41,029 voters (approximately 0.2 of 1 per cent) expressed a preference for the company-union plans in their plants.[37]

The various employee-association plans [38] put into effect in the automobile industry provided for the division of the plants into voting districts and for primary and final elections leading to the designation of one employee representative for approximately every two hundred or three hundred workers to serve on the employee or works council. In a few plants all payroll employees were permitted to vote in the elections, but in most plants the suffrage was confined to those who met certain minimum qualifications or who were members of the association. Typically, to qualify for voting privileges or for membership in the association, one had to be twenty-one years of age, a citizen, and an employee of at least ninety days' service. Eligibility for election to the employee or works council was usually limited to nonsupervisory employees who had been with the company for one year, were at least twenty-one years of age, and were citizens. Employee representatives had to be employed in the district which they represented and generally had to vacate their position if they left the company, were transferred to another district, were promoted to a supervisory job, or, under the Chrysler plan, if they missed two consecutive meetings without being excused. Most plans set forth a procedure by which employee representatives could be recalled.

Management was present in greater or lesser degree in all the plans. The constitutions generally provided that management was to bear the cost of the plan, was to provide the meeting place for the employee representatives, and was to pay them for time spent on employee-association business. The Chrysler plan provided for the appointment by the company of management representatives equal in number to the employee representatives who were to sit with the employee representatives in a joint council, and also a "management's special representative" who was to be the nonvoting chairman of the joint council and who was to be the official representative of management in negotiation with the employee representatives. Decisions by the joint council could be taken only by a two-thirds vote, with management and employee representatives having an equal vote. The Hudson plan also provided for management representatives who served in alternate months on joint committees with the employee representatives and who met with all the employee representatives in an annual conference, but unlike the Chrysler plan, the decisions in joint meetings apparently did not require a two-thirds majority.

The plans of the G.M. divisions did not call for management representatives or for formal joint meetings. The Chevrolet model, for example, specified that the plant manager or his representative was to attend the meetings of the employee representatives only at their request; and the Fisher Body plan stipulated that the plant manager or someone designated by him was to attend council meeting solely in an advisory and consultative capacity.

All the plans established a grievance procedure permitting individual employees to carry their complaints by stages, either directly or through the works council, to the top management and possibly to arbitration. The Chevrolet constitution called for the general management of the division to discuss with a committee consisting of the chairmen of all the Chevrolet works councils those grievances which affected all the plants of the division, but this procedure was never invoked.

The Chrysler plan made no provision for its amendment, but this was exceptional. The Buick constitution could be amended by a two-thirds vote of the employee committee, the Packard plan by a two-thirds vote of the membership, the Hupp plan by a two-thirds vote of the employees' committee or a majority vote of the membership, and the Fisher Body plan by the unanimous agreement of the works council *and the plant manager.* The Hudson plan provided for amendment by a two-thirds vote of the joint committee on rules or a concurrent majority of the employee representatives and the management representatives at their annual conference. Even these limitations on the amendment process, however, did not satisfy Roy Chapin, the president of the company. "I don't think that we ought to permit any changes in the bylaws of the Hudson Industrial Association without the approval of Mr. Wollering [director of manufacturing] and myself," he wrote to a subordinate on January 19, 1934.[39]

All in all, it is difficult to reconcile the company-union plans of the automobile manufacturing industry with the rights supposedly guaranteed to employees by Section 7(a). The section, to be sure, did not rule out company unions per se, but it did assert the right of employees to organize and to bargain collectively through representatives of their own choosing and did say that they were to be free from employer interference or coercion in designating their representatives and in self-organization. The company-union plans, drafted and financed by the employers and generally not submitted to the workers for approval, were hardly examples of self-organization, and many workers felt themselves "coerced" into voting. Not all employees were permitted to vote under most of the plans, and none of the plans permitted the employees to select such representatives as they pleased. They could not, for example, choose someone who did not work in the plant or even someone who was not employed in their district, and management could easily dispose of troublesome representatives by simply transferring them to another district or by discharging them on one pretext or another. Under the Chrysler plan, employee representatives could not take action unless at least one-third of the management representatives agreed with them. The Hudson and the Fisher Body plans could not be amended without the consent of management, and the Chrysler plan could not be amended at all.[40]

All of these questions that suggest themselves concerning the consonance of the automobile company-union plans with the requirements of Section 7(a) are quite apart from the more fundamental question as to whether a company-sponsored and company-dominated employee association of the type established in the automobile industry in 1933, which does not have the ability to strike—and thus has no choice but to accept the employer's decision on issues in contention—can ever engage in really meaningful collective bargaining with management. In contrast to the local independent union of today, not a single automobile company union in the N.R.A. era negotiated a contract with its employer, and there were no company union strikes in the industry.

The company was so conspicuous a factor in the operation of most of the employee-association plans that it was difficult for the workers to view the company unions as their own organizations. Once a plan was put into effect, the company paid all the expenses of the works council, gave it the use of company bulletin boards, and permitted it to solicit membership on company property and often on company time. As a source friendly to G.M. conceded, the employee associations were "difficult to maintain as going organizations without constant stimulation on the part of management even to the point of actual domination in managing and keeping them alive." [41]

It would be a mistake, however, to assume that the company union was entirely a negative factor in the evolution of labor-management relations in the automobile industry. If nothing else, the company union provided a mechanism by which management could be made aware of employee complaints about working conditions. "We have been ashamed of conditions brought to our attention by men in the plants," one automobile employer admitted. C. C. Carlton, secretary of the Motor Wheel Corporation, which had not had a meeting with its employees for thirty years prior to the establishment of its company union, conceded to Robert Lea that "We have not been close enough to our own employees. They have labored for us under conditions which were not ideal, but, as no one called it to our attention, we either did not know about it or overlooked it." [42]

The grievance procedure set forth in the company-union plans provided a means of adjusting the complaints of individual workers and enabled automobile employees, for the first time really, to appeal the decisions of their foremen to a higher authority. Management, indeed, tended to see the plans primarily as a means of dealing with the concerns of the individual worker rather than with the collective problems of the employees as a whole. Thus at a meeting of the joint works council of the Chrysler Highland Park plant, the management special representative stated with regard to the Chrysler company-union plan, "While Mr. W. P. Chrysler's message [submitting the plan] was addressed to the employees . . . *it referred to individual employees.* Under this 'Plan' *the employee* who feels he has not been given a square deal may take up his grievance with his representative and through the regular procedure to the Joint Council and the management." [43]

The individual grievances that management most readily adjusted were those dealing with housekeeping questions such as sanitation and ventilation and with alleged favoritism in the plant rather than with the bread-and-butter issues of wages and hours. "The Works Council," declared a union official who had once been an employee at the Chevrolet Gear and Axle plant, "never got around to discuss anything but broken windows and safety hazards. When some unruly committeeman had the temerity to mention wages or seniority, the company representatives promptly sidetracked the discussions into less dangerous channels." In rejecting a works council request for the adjustment of some wage inequities, the management of the Chrysler Highland Park plant stated that the decision in this matter was "a question of management" that could not be "assigned to any group who do not have the experience and training for this kind of work." [44]

In some plants the company unions did have a fairly successful record in securing the adjustment of individual complaints concerning such matters as wage inequities, but management was normally reluctant to "bargain" with employee-association representatives about the wages and hours of plant workers as a whole. The works council of the Chrysler Highland Park plant was categorically informed that management did not wish it to "undertake the responsibility of controlling the application of increases or decreases [of pay] in general for the organization." [45]

Just as the company union provided the individual worker who was not afraid to avail himself of its procedures with a means for seeking the adjustment of his grievances, so it provided experience in the bargaining process for both employer and employee. This was of some importance in an industry where no negotiation of any sort between labor and management had previously taken place. At least a few workers were now given some idea of managerial problems, and management, for the first time in the history of the industry, was forced to pay some attention to the subject of labor relations and to develop a technique of dealing with employee representatives.[46] Also, the company-union device, although it was not appreciated at the time by labor or management, may very well have contributed, at least in a minor way, to the development of employee sentiment in favor of industrial rather than craft unionism. By including all the workers in a plant in a single organization, the company union like the plant federal labor union served to remind the workers of their common interests rather than of their differences.

If the testimony of company-union representatives before the A.L.B. can be trusted, the employee-association plans worked better in the G.M. plants than in the Chrysler plants. Several G.M. company-union representatives expressed satisfaction with the operation of their plans and pointed to various improvements in working conditions since the company unions had been established, whereas the Chrysler representatives had little good to say of their employee associations. The difference in the reaction of the employee representatives in the two corporations probably stemmed from a dissatisfaction with the joint-council type of plan used by Chrysler and from the less intransigent attitude in dealing with their workers of at least some of the G.M. plant managers. Among the plans of the independent automobile companies, the Hudson Industrial Association appears to have enjoyed the greatest success.[47]

In order to demonstrate to their employees that there was no reason for them to form an outside union, management in the automobile industry was prone to attribute improvements in wages, hours, and working conditions to the efforts of the company unions. Whether this tactic, coupled with the obvious fact that management favored the company unions, won friends for the employee associations among the automobile workers and deterred a substantial number of them from joining the U.A.W. is hard to say. In the A.L.B.

balloting of 1934–35, 13.3 per cent (21,744) of the 163,150 employees who voted in the nominating elections appeared to express a preference for the employee associations, which was a slightly larger figure than the 12.9 per cent (21,128) of the employees who appeared to favor one of the outside unions. It is possible that this vote indicates that the company unions enjoyed about as much support among the automobile workers as the outside unions did, but, on the other hand, it must be noted that the A.L.B. elections were not designed to yield a result indicative of the comparative strength of the competing employee organizations in the industry and the A.F. of L. was boycotting the elections whereas the company unions were not.[48]

The A.F. of L. came to regard the company union as its "greatest menace" in the automobile industry, and it protested again and again that the automobile companies were using the employee associations as a means of avoiding genuine collective bargaining. At the N.R.A. conference of late February 1934, Collins charged that every company union in the industry had been "initiated, paid for, and put in operation by company executives" and that management dominated the employee associations once they had been established.[49]

The views expressed by Collins won support within the N.R.A. William H. Davis, the N.R.A. Compliance Director, declared on March 6, 1934, that the company-union plans in the automobile and steel industries in particular were in violation of Section 7(a) and that the N.R.A. would seek to outlaw these plans through "mass action." The next day General Johnson told code-authority representatives that although there was "no law prohibiting a company union as such if there is no interposition by employers, and if the men freely choose it, . . . 99 times out of 100 you and I know that this is not the case." [50]

In so far as the automobile industry was concerned, the "mass action" against company unions of which Davis had spoken consisted of an authorization by the National Compliance Director to the state of Michigan N.R.A. Compliance Director to engage a special investigator, Henry A. Campeau, to look into Collins' charges and any other allegations of the violation of Section 7(a). Campeau submitted reports to his superiors on a number of company-union plans, and his efforts were supplemented by the Compliance Division in Washington, which also examined some of the employee-association constitutions. The information gathered tended to substantiate Collins' charges, but before any action could be taken, the A.L.B. had been established to preside over labor-management relations in the automobile industry, and the Compliance Division, consequently, referred the entire matter to the new agency.[51] From that point forward, the issue of company unionism in the industry became intertwined with the efforts of the A.L.B. to establish a new pattern of employee representation in the automobile plants.

II

Like the U.A.W. locals, the union rivals of the A.F. of L. were also seeking in the face of determined employer opposition to win a place for themselves in the automobile industry. Among the Federation's competitors, the most impressive gains were made by the fledgling Mechanics Educational Society of America, which took the strike route in a bold effort to gain the support of the tool and die makers.[52]

Since the M.E.S.A. had enjoyed a measure of success in organizing Flint tool and die makers, the executive committee of the union's Flint unit requested the managements of Buick, Chevrolet, and AC Spark Plug early in September 1933 to boost the average hourly wages of tool and die makers from eighty-five cents to $1.50, to agree to a work week of thirty-seven-and-a-half hours,[53] and to recognize the union. Only the Chevrolet management seemed amenable to these demands, and agreement between the two sides seemed close at a September 19 conference, by which time the union had reduced its wage request to $1.00 per hour. Two days later, however, William S. Knudsen, president of the Chevrolet division, acting on the advice of Chester M. Culver, the general manager of the Employers' Association of Detroit, took the position that if Chevrolet granted the M.E.S.A. request for a wage increase, this would have repercussions on wage rates for tool and die makers throughout the trade area and he would therefore have to consult with other signers of the auto code.[54]

Without awaiting the result of any talks that Knudsen might have with fellow automobile manufacturers, the M.E.S.A. committee quickly secured the approval of the Flint membership for a strike, which was ordered on September 21. The M.E.S.A. estimated that 1850 workers, allegedly 90 per cent of the tool and die makers in the companies affected, responded to the strike call. This claim was undoubtedly exaggerated and was sharply challenged by the employers, but the A.F. of L. organizer for the automobile industry in Flint, hardly a friend of the M.E.S.A., conceded that "they cleaned the shops out pretty well." [55]

The M.E.S.A. leaders in Flint felt certain that the strike in Flint had little chance of success if the work of the struck plants were simply transferred to Detroit and Pontiac. It was thus logical for them to argue that tool and die departments in other G.M. plants in the Detroit area and the various job shops making tools and dies for G.M. should also be struck. The Flint committee therefore visited Detroit and requested support for its strike. Responding to this appeal, the Detroit leadership of the organization decided to take a strike vote of the entire Detroit membership. At the time this vote was taken, no formal demands had been presented by the M.E.S.A. to any of the Detroit employers affected, although there had been some negotiation with the management of Fisher Body.[56]

Many of the M.E.S.A. Detroit members were less than enthusiastic about going on strike. Not only were they aware that no demands had been submitted to their employers, but they were also annoyed that the Flint M.E.S.A. had struck without securing the consent of the parent organization in Detroit, an action made possible by the lack of centralized control in the M.E.S.A. structure. Although the M.E.S.A. claimed a membership of more than nine thousand in Detroit, only four thousand workers, according to its own count, participated in the strike vote, which was held from September 23 to 25. Jay J. Griffen, who was to become chairman of the M.E.S.A. joint strike committee, announced at the time that the vote in favor of the strike was between twenty and twenty-five to one, but the M.E.S.A. conceded at a later date that the strike vote was actually carried by only "a small majority." [57]

The strike in Detroit was ordered on September 26. According to the employers, thirty-five hundred workers responded to the strike call immediately, and the maximum number of strikers during the course of the walkout was sixty-three hundred. Of this total, three thousand strikers, the employers indicated, were drawn from the job shops, and thirty-three hundred from the main plants. This represented, if the M.E.S.A. figures as to the distribution of tool and die makers in Detroit are accurate, 75 per cent of the tool and die makers working in the job shops and about 34 per cent of those working in the main plants. The M.E.S.A. contended that the strikers ultimately numbered fourteen thousand, an obvious exaggeration since this would have meant 100 per cent support of the strike among the tool and die makers, which even the M.E.S.A. did not claim. At all events, the strike affected most of the main plants in Detroit—the Ford Motor Company was a conspicuous exception—fifty-seven job shops associated with the Automotive Tool and Die Manufacturers Association (A.T. and D.M.A.), and sixty independent job shops. The strike also spread to Pontiac, where six hundred employees of the Pontiac Motor Company quit their jobs on September 26.[58]

The strikers did not officially agree to a set of joint strike demands until September 28, two days after the strike had begun. They called for a 25 per cent wage increase and a minimum rate of $1 an hour for bench men and ninety cents for affiliated machine men, a work week of forty hours and an understanding that any change from this standard would be negotiated with a view to enabling the greatest possible number of tool and die makers to be retained in employment, and a policy of no discrimination against strikers. The strikers also agreed that there should be no return to work without a settlement. The M.E.S.A. mailed these demands to the employers, but the inexperienced strike leaders failed to accompany their proposals with a request for a conference.[59]

The walkout was perfectly timed from the point of view of the strikers since it came during the period of model changeover when tool and die makers were in particular demand. The auto manufacturers tried to meet this problem by dispatching some of their work to cities not affected by the strike. The M.E.S.A., in turn, sought to counter this action by threatening to spread the walkout to plants to which the struck work was transferred, but it did not have the power to carry out this threat, and the strike remained confined to Flint, Detroit, and Pontiac. The M.E.S.A. did, however, learn from this experience that it would have to organize tool and die makers in outlying areas, and it did, as a matter of fact, spread its organization to Cleveland during the course of the dispute.

It is difficult to estimate the dollar volume of the tool and die work that left the Detroit area as the result of the strike. Toward the end of the walkout, the employers placed the total at somewhere between $10 and $20 million, but they undoubtedly exaggerated the figures in an effort to persuade the strikers to return to work while jobs remained for at least some of them. Some work was transferred from the struck plants, but at the same time that the jobbers were insisting that they had "in very large part" lost the business on which employment in their shops depended, they were sending letters to some of the strikers inviting them to return to work and were also advertising, without apparent success, for labor in the East. The fact remains that large contracts for tools and dies were available to many Detroit job shops when the strike ended and that most of the strikers were reengaged. As Knudsen conceded, the Detroit automobile manufacturers were "set . . . back quite a bit" by the strike, which, along with the lack of any significant alteration in its 1933 model, helps to explain why the Ford Motor Company, the only major Detroit automobile manufacturer unaffected by the walkout, was the first large producer to introduce its 1934 models and to be ready for prompt delivery.[60]

In addition to efforts to weaken striker morale by pointing to the work that was allegedly leaving the area, the employers also resorted to the familiar strike tactic of proclaiming that the strikers were rapidly returning to their jobs.   To the extent that strikers remained away from work, the employers contended that this was the result of the "terroristic" methods employed by the M.E.S.A.   Where the truth lies regarding these claims by the employers and the counterclaims of the union is not easily determined.   The strike, apparently, was "immediately effective" in the large job shops in Detroit, where the bulk of the M.E.S.A. membership in the city was concentrated, and at Fisher Body and Ternstedt, but it was less successful elsewhere.   In some plants, wage rates were already above the minimum demanded by the M.E.S.A., and so the workers concerned saw little reason for the strike.   Similarly, there was no great enthusiasm for the walkout among many of the tool and die makers of the main plants, where working conditions were generally better than they were in the job shops and where the M.E.S.A. had fewer members.   Unquestionably, some of the strikers drifted back to work before the strike was officially terminated, although the return to work was not as great as the employers indicated.[61]   In order to dissuade strikers from returning to their jobs and to persuade nonstrikers to join the ranks of those on the outside, the M.E.S.A. resorted to intensive picketing and undoubtedly employed strong-arm methods as well.[62]   Just how many strikers would have returned to work had such tactics not been employed it is impossible, however, to say.

The imminent spread of the strike to the Detroit area caused the M.E.S.A. on September 25 to wire Senator Wagner that the situation was "out of control."   Already displeased by the precipitate calling of the Flint strike, Wagner immediately informed the M.E.S.A. that he would send John Carmody, an industrial engineer working for the N.L.B. and later to become a member of the National Labor Relations Board and then the head of the Rural Electrification Administration, to conciliate the dispute; but the receipt of this information did not prevent the walkout.

The strike committee let it be known at once that it wished to treat the strikes in Flint, Detroit, and Pontiac as a single dispute and to negotiate a single settlement covering all the struck plants.   The managements of the affected Flint and Pontiac plants, all of them parts of the G.M. empire, were, however, opposed to joint negotiations; and, to make the situation even more difficult, the Detroit auto manufacturers contended that because of dissimilar conditions, the strikes in the main plants in Detroit and the job shops would also have to be treated separately. The insistence of the employers on separate negotiations, which complicated the strike problem for the M.E.S.A., was inconsistent with Knudsen's previous contention that a wage increase in one major plant in the area affected wage rates throughout the district, and is also difficult to reconcile with the request of the Detroit automobile manufacturers to Chester Culver to act as advisor to the job-shop owners even though they were not members of the Employers' Association. Culver's service to the job shops, he later recalled, was strictly "in the interest of the auto makers." [63]

Carmody, who arrived on the scene on September 28, quickly determined that the key to a settlement lay in the hands of the automobile manufacturers. The jobbers and the M.E.S.A., it appeared, were not too far apart on the issues in dispute, and particularly on the wage question, but the M.E.S.A. was unwilling to make a separate settlement with the jobbers lest this enable the automobile manufacturers to transfer the work of their tool and die departments to the job shops and thus to withstand the strikers' pressure on the main plants. Although Knudsen's committee of Detroit auto manufacturers had resolved not to meet with strikers and took the position that since the M.E.S.A. had walked out without presenting demands, there was nothing about which to negotiate, Carmody was able to arrange a conference on September 30 between a M.E.S.A. committee and Knudsen and two of his associates. This conference, however, and subsequent efforts by Carmody failed to break the deadlock.

The N.L.B. mediator placed the blame for his inability to resolve the dispute squarely on the Detroit auto manufacturers. He was convinced that he could have worked out a settlement had the conflict been confined to the Detroit job shops or even to Flint and the job shops, but he believed that the spread of the strike to the main plants in Detroit had thwarted his peace efforts. "The Detroit automobile manufacturers," he stated publicly, "are slow in recognizing that under the industrial set-up by the NRA they are face-to-face with a wholly new relationship between them and their employees." In Carmody's view, the automobile manufacturers were simply not complying with the requirements of Section 7(a). "The essence of the matter," he later reported to Wagner, "is the question of whether these men are required to deal with representatives duly elected with a view not merely to discussing their working conditions but to arrive at some definite agreement that will be workable." Carmody concluded that the wise course under the circumstances was to refer the dispute to Washington.[64]

By the time Carmody reached this conclusion the M.E.S.A. leadership had come to doubt very seriously the organization's ability to win the strike by its own efforts. It was because of this pessimistic estimate of the situation that the strike leaders permitted the "progressives" and communists in the union's ranks to take the lead in urging production workers to join the walkout and also, for the first time, indicated their willingness to have the dispute referred to Washington.

Its membership limited to skilled craftsmen, the M.E.S.A. prior to the strike had shown no interest in the production workers in the automobile plants. As a matter of fact, just before the Detroit strike began, Griffen had informed a labor reporter that if a strike developed, it would be unnecessary for the M.E.S.A. to persuade production workers to join the walkout because a strike of tool and die makers would in itself tie up production sufficiently to force the auto plants to cease operations.[65] Despite this remark, the M.E.S.A. would no doubt have welcomed the support of the A.F. of L. and the automobile production workers that the Federation had been able to organize, but from the A.F. of L. point of view the M.E.S.A. was a dual organization that was trespassing on the domain of the I.A.M. Collins consequently let it be known that the U.A.W. would pursue a policy of strict neutrality with regard to the strike.[66]

Even before the strike the left-wingers in the M.E.S.A. had been attacking the union leadership for its failure to organize production workers and to become an industrial union. After the strike began, the communists became increasingly critical of the M.E.S.A. leadership. Matthew Smith and Griffen in particular were assailed for opposing the formation of a rank-and-file strike committee, for refusing to permit members of the communist organization of the unemployed to reinforce M.E.S.A. picket lines, for failing to tie up Ford, and, above all, for not calling out the production workers. The strike leaders, at the outset, largely ignored the communist criticism of their policies, but when the walkout failed to bring the halt to automobile production that Griffen had predicted and striker morale began to sag, the left-wingers were given their chance. John Anderson, who the next year was to become a candidate for governor of Michigan on the Communist party ticket, presided at M.E.S.A. mass meetings of October 12 and 13 at which communists were much in evidence and at which there was talk of another "march on Dearborn" and of calling out the production workers and thus bringing about a general automobile strike. "Russia drove out the capitalists and is getting along very nicely. We can do the same," declared Phil Raymond of the Auto Workers Union at the October 13 meeting.

Communist rhetoric did not, however, persuade the unskilled and semiskilled automobile workers to join the strike. The largely unorganized production workers, who had previously been altogether ignored by the M.E.S.A. and had played absolutely no part in the formulation of strike decisions, saw little reason to quit their jobs at the behest of the M.E.S.A., much less of the communists. Also, although it was a favorable time for a strike of tool and die makers, it was, because of the heavy seasonal layoffs, an inauspicious period of the year for a walkout of production workers.[67]

A second indication that the M.E.S.A. had concluded that it could no longer win the strike by the exercise of its economic power alone was the increasing desire of its leadership, in contrast to the views expressed at the beginning of the strike, "to take the matter to the more liberal atmosphere of Washington, away from the reactionary atmosphere of Detroit." The M.E.S.A. was consequently elated when Senator Wagner on October 13, after being apprised of Carmody's views on the subject, invited representatives of the auto manufacturers, the job-shop owners, and the M.E.S.A. to come to Washington on October 18 to confer with the N.L.B. The M.E.S.A.'s enthusiasm was not, however, shared by the auto manufacturers, who decided not to accept the N.L.B.'s invitation.[68]

At the October 18 hearing, N.L.B. members criticized the M.E.S.A. for staging a walkout before submitting demands and for not specifically requesting a conference with the employers when strike demands finally were submitted. As for the M.E.S.A. desire for joint negotiations with the various companies involved in the strike, Gerard Swope, president of General Electric and an industry member of the board, declared that the N.L.B. could direct individual employers to negotiate in accordance with the law but it could not insist on joint negotiations or joint settlements. The N.L.B., consequently, instructed the M.E.S.A. to return to Detroit and to request a conference of each of the affected employers to discuss strike demands. Annoyed by this ruling and by N.L.B. criticism of its tactics and realizing that the M.E.S.A. would now have to return from Washington with empty hands, Smith protested that "the Labor Board is trying to get rid of a shabby problem, so they are throwing us back to Detroit." [69]

Anxious to bring the strike to a conclusion, the M.E.S.A. felt that it had no alternative but to accept the N.L.B.'s advice and to resubmit its terms to the employers but this time with a request for a con-

ference.   In addition to the three original proposals, the M.E.S.A. now
added a demand for union recognition, without however indicating
what it meant by the term.   At a mass meeting of October 22 the
strikers agreed that although the negotiations would have to be separate, the settlements with the various employers should be identical,
and there should be no return to work until agreements had been
reached with all the struck plants.   Subcommittees of the strike committee were set up to negotiate settlements with the individual job
shops and the automobile companies, but they were unable during
the next few days to come to terms with the employers.[70]

The frustration of the strikers as the result of the failure of the
M.E.S.A. to gain support for its position from the N.L.B. and its inability to negotiate strike settlements manifested itself late in October
in aggressive action directed against the property of the employers.
The most serious trouble occurred on October 30,[71] when a motorized
crowd of twenty-five hundred to three thousand rioters attacked eight
job shops, smashed one thousand windows, and burned a considerable
number of blueprints and tool diagrams.   The rioting began at about
ten in the morning and continued until late in the afternoon, when the
police, who had been one step behind the mob throughout the day,
finally caught up with a group of the vandals and arrested eight of
them.   Temporarily subdued, the rioters visited one more plant before the day was out.   The M.E.S.A. promptly disclaimed responsibility for the violence, and Griffen repudiated the acts of vandalism,
but Matthew Smith admitted at a later time that although the M.E.S.A.
had not advised the action, it was not opposed to what had taken place,
and its repudiation was only for the record.[72]

The violence of October 30 was the storm before the calm, and
the strikers within the next ten days reached settlements with most of
the companies involved.   Pay increases of at least five cents per hour
were secured from some of the smaller shops, but the terms of settlement with the main plants and with the companies affiliated with the
A.T. and D.M.A. provided for no change in the existing wage scales,
which ranged from sixty to seventy-five cents per hour for the semiskilled and superannuated to ninety-five cents to $1.05 per hour for
die leaders.   The hours question had already been disposed of for
the main plants by the provisions of the auto code, and it was in the
process of being worked out for the job shops in the code of the special tool, die, and machine shop industry.   The disputants also agreed
that there was to be no discrimination by either party as the result
of strike activities, and preference in re-employment was to be given
the strikers.   Although not specifically mentioned in any of the agree-

ments, the contract method of wage payment does not appear to have survived the strike.

The employers refused to sign a contract with the M.E.S.A., and since the union did not wish to leave the agreements a matter of verbal understanding only, the N.L.B.'s Detroit Regional Labor Board, for the settlements which it had helped to arrange, used the device of submitting letters to the disputants containing the terms agreed upon, which brought the board in as a witness. The M.E.S.A. proclaimed that it had secured "satisfactory recognition" at least in the job shops, by which it no doubt meant that it had been recognized as the spokesman for its members in these plants, but its status in the main plants does not appear to have been one whit altered.[73]

Although the M.E.S.A. registered some gains as the result of the strike, it had fallen considerably short of a complete victory in so far as the attainment of its principal strike demands was concerned. This failure was partly the result of the tactics pursued by the organization's inexperienced leadership, which had called the strike in Flint without having exhausted the process of negotiation and had then brought out the Detroit and Pontiac tool and die makers without presenting any demands to their employers and when these workers were less than enthusiastic about striking. The strikers' cause was weakened also by the inability of the M.E.S.A. to enlist the all-out support of tool and die makers in the main plants and to gain the adherence of the production workers. The chance of victory was further diminished to the extent that the main plants were able to farm out their tool and die work to shops outside the Detroit area that were not affected by the strike.[74]

Despite its limited success in attaining its strike demands, the M.E.S.A. achieved what may very well have been the major objective of the strike: it had proved itself as a union. The strike, as Matthew Smith later declared, "placed the MESA once and for all on the map as a force to be reckoned with in trade unionism." If nothing else, the M.E.S.A. had demonstrated to the skilled workers in whom it was primarily interested that it was unafraid to challenge even the giants in the automobile industry. Membership in the organization doubled during the strike, reaching 21,375 by the time the dispute was over; and Elizabeth McCracken later recalled that although she had been the only employee in the M.E.S.A. Detroit office when the strike began, eight girls were soon working there and were doing nothing but accepting membership applications.[75] By its strike, the M.E.S.A. had won for itself a position in the trade-union structure that it has not since relinquished.

The strike seems to have convinced the leaders of the M.E.S.A. that it was necessary to give their organization a more definite structure and also to make some provision for the enrollment of production workers. In January 1934 the membership elected the union's first national officers, with the key position in the organization, that of general secretary, going to the fiery Matthew Smith. Smith, who had migrated to the United States from England, where he had been active in the shop steward movement, was to retain this post until his death in 1958.

The admission of production workers into the M.E.S.A. was provided for at the organization's first convention in February 1934. The constitution and bylaws, which were tentatively adopted at this convention, established two classes of membership in the organization: membership in Section 1 of a M.E.S.A. local was open to workers who manufactured or repaired tools, dies, jigs, fixtures, and machinery; production workers could henceforth be enrolled in a separate but parallel Section 2. The provision for the entry of production workers seemed to M.E.S.A. leaders, in the abstract, to make their organization less vulnerable to the seasonality of automobile production. It was assumed that during the period of model changeover, Section 1 members would remain employed and that when their employment was curtailed, Section 2 members would be returned to work.[76]

By deciding to enroll production workers, the M.E.S.A. became a competitor of the U.A.W. locals just as it already was a competitor of the I.A.M. It created a special corps of organizers to seek members among the production workers, but the efforts of these organizers were not attended by any conspicuous success. As the decision to segregate the production workers indicates, the skilled workers in the M.E.S.A. continued to see themselves and their problems as quite distinct from the unskilled and their problems. Under the circumstances, it is not surprising that the production workers, who hesitated to join any union, were not especially enthusiastic about the prospects of membership in the M.E.S.A.[77]

The reluctance of the production workers to accept the offer of second-class citizenship in the M.E.S.A. persuaded the delegates to the M.E.S.A. convention of January 1935 to abolish the section plan and to provide for the integration in the same locals of the skilled and the unskilled in the automobile industry and the allied metal trades, a practice that was already being followed by the M.E.S.A. locals in Cleveland. This action made the M.E.S.A., in theory, a full-blown industrial union, but in practice, the appeal of the organization continued to be to the tool and die makers, and the production workers in the M.E.S.A.'s ranks remained a distinct and an unimportant minority.[78]

Ideologically, or at least rhetorically, the M.E.S.A. was to the left of the A.F. of L. The M.E.S.A., Smith declared, did not accept the idea that the employer was entitled to a profit. "Its immediate task," he proclaimed, "is to temper wage slavery; its ultimate goal is to function in a planned society as a national instrument of production, cooperating with a recast distributive system to make a Brave New World." At the 1935 convention Smith announced that the M.E.S.A. "must take its place as a revolutionary, industrial organization." The union's goal, he later declared in the M.E.S.A.'s official organ, was "the communal ownership of the means of life."[79] However radical these remarks may appear and however faithfully they reflected the personal views of socialistically inclined M.E.S.A. leaders like Smith, they did not, in practice, cause the M.E.S.A. during the N.I.R.A. years to follow a pattern of economic behavior that differed very greatly from that of unions that phrased their objectives in the more conventional language of Samuel Gompers and William Green.

The M.E.S.A. liked to point out that in contrast to the A.F. of L. it did not depend on the N.I.R.A. to advance its objectives. "We don't meander with the NRA . . . ," Smith boasted, "but fight any encroachments of the bosses by direct action in the plants concerned." Similarly, Smith declared that he did not believe that "any code means anything as far as giving the workers any rights are concerned. . . . We feel that labor can obtain its needs only by the power of organization." The M.E.S.A. was also critical of the government labor boards that developed while the N.I.R.A. was in effect and attacked them, in the words of President Jesse Chapman, as "sops to labor which actually work in the interests of the employers."[80] Despite these remarks, however, the M.E.S.A. could not afford to ignore government agencies like the N.R.A. and the N.L.B. that played such a large role in the area of labor relations. It was very much concerned with the provisions of the special tool, die, and machine shop code; it urged that public hearings be held on the automobile code and was prepared to submit its own code proposals should the occasion permit;[81] it turned to the N.L.B. for help during its great strike in the fall of 1933; and it did not hesitate to resort to labor-board machinery when it believed that employers were discriminating against M.E.S.A. members.

It remained true, nevertheless, that the M.E.S.A. placed somewhat more faith in the strike and somewhat less faith in government aid than the U.A.W. did. Smith in particular saw the strike or the threat of a strike as labor's chief weapon. "No strike," he once observed, "is a lost strike. You weed out the chaff and find out who are your 'real' unionists." It may very well have been because of such views and because Smith, as one M.E.S.A. member recalled, "still was mad at the world, particularly employers," that the M.E.S.A. leadership secured the reluctant consent of the membership for an ill-advised and poorly timed strike against the job shops in April 1934.[82]

As already noted, the N.A.C.C. on March 13, 1934, at a time when the U.A.W. was threatening a large-scale strike, recommended to its members that they grant their employees a 10 per cent wage increase and that they also reduce the hours of employment by an equivalent amount. The membership complied with the wage recommendation and extended the increase not only to production workers but also to tool and die makers. A similar increase was not, however, granted to their employees by the job-shop owners, who were not members of the N.A.C.C. This brought the job shops, both the independents and those affiliated with the A.T. and D.M.A., into conflict with the M.E.S.A., which demanded that they increase wages 20 per cent and reduce working hours to thirty-six per week or face a strike. When its demands were rejected, the M.E.S.A. on April 12 struck eighty-three of the more than 160 job shops in the Detroit area, forty-seven of the struck plants being affiliated with the A.T. and D.M.A. A few of the independents had met the M.E.S.A. terms prior to April 12 and were therefore spared a strike.[83]

Since the spring months were a period of slack production and reduced employment in the tool and die industry, the M.E.S.A. could not have picked a worse time to apply its economic pressure. Recognizing that the idea of a walkout was not particularly popular with employed tool and die makers, the organization requested that each striker remove his tools from his place of employment and turn them over to M.E.S.A. headquarters for storage in a bonded warehouse for the duration of the strike. This tactic would presumably prevent the premature return to work of disgruntled strikers. Smith claimed that fifteen hundred strikers complied with this request, which, if true, would still have been less than half of the tool and die makers the M.E.S.A. alleged were on strike. Nonstriking M.E.S.A. members were expected to assume part of the cost of strike, which could hardly have made the walkout very popular with them.

Within a relatively short time after the strike was initiated, strikers began drifting back to work, and on May 2, with the strike obviously lost, the M.E.S.A., in a face-saving gesture, authorized strikers to return to job shops that were observing the minimum M.E.S.A. wage scale for the Detroit area even though no wage increase had been conceded. This, despite M.E.S.A. denials, was the effective end of the strike, and although a few of the job shops had granted wage increases, the majority of the strikers returned to work without having won any of their demands.[84]

The communists and the self-styled "progressives" in the M.E.S.A.'s ranks, in what must have sounded like a familiar refrain to Smith and Griffen, criticized the M.E.S.A. strike leadership for not having spread the strike to the main plants and to the production workers, for not having engaged in mass picketing, and for having failed to form a united front with the A.W.U. and the U.A.W. Nettled by this criticism and believing, quite correctly, that its only purpose was to create dissension within the organization, the Detroit district committee of the M.E.S.A. expelled John Anderson and John Mack, the two leading "progressives" in the organization, and declared that it would purge all known communists in the M.E.S.A. ranks. Anderson's local reinstated him to membership by a narrow vote, and Anderson charged that Smith was using the issue of a red scare to conceal his deficiencies as a leader. Anderson was decisively defeated, however, when he contested the position of general secretary with Smith in the M.E.S.A. elections of December 1934, and communist efforts to unseat Smith at the January 1935 convention also came to naught. The communists remained in control of three of M.E.S.A.'s Detroit locals—Elizabeth McCracken later supposed that the M.E.S.A. "had most of the Communists in Detroit as members"—but they were unable to seize control of the national organization.[85]

The defeat the M.E.S.A. suffered in the strike of April 1934 did not, in the long run, seriously impair its appeal to the tool and die makers in the auto industry. By December 1934 it had established thirty-one locals across the country, and the next month it claimed a membership of about 38,000. As Collins had conceded some months earlier, it had practically driven the I.A.M. "out of the picture" in the automobile industry. Also, whereas the U.A.W. had been able to make very little headway among the automobile workers in Detroit, about two-thirds of the M.E.S.A. membership was concentrated in the motor city, and the M.E.S.A., for a time, was even able to penetrate the antiunion barricades of the Ford Motor Company. When the N.I.R.A. was declared unconstitutional in May 1935, the Detroit membership of the M.E.S.A. in the automobile industry was greater than the Detroit membership of the U.A.W. and the I.A.M. combined.[86]

III

The I.W.W. made its major effort to win adherents among the automobile workers in the summer and early fall of 1933. In an effort to draw a contrast between itself and the A.F. of L., it directed its appeal to the automobile workers as a militant, rank-and-file controlled industrial union with low dues and initiation fees and open to all workers regardless of their skill, sex, color, or nationality. It distributed more than two million pieces of literature during these months, held numerous meetings at plant gates, and even initiated six-day-a-week broadcasts over a Dearborn radio station. In September, Metal and Machinery Workers Industrial Union No. 440 moved its Detroit headquarters into larger quarters, "One Big Union Hall," which, the editor of the *Industrial Worker* later described as "a lavish front for the growing union; in the kitchen back of it, the organizers survived on bread and beans and slept on benches." [87]

The I.W.W. organizing drive in Detroit centered on the Murray Body plant, where working conditions were notoriously poor, but members were also enlisted in a few other plants, and brief on-the-job strikes were staged by Wobblies in August at the Briggs Highland Park plant and in one of the Chrysler plants. The Murray Body campaign, which was spearheaded by veterans of the Briggs strike of early 1933, met with considerable success. By the end of August 1933 the I.W.W. had enrolled about one thousand members in the plant—it had only two members there when the membership drive began in the previous month—and had achieved a position of real strength in the metal finishing department in particular. [88]

When the Murray Body management in September 1933, as production tapered off, began laying off a substantial proportion of its work force, some of the I.W.W. members in the plant quite incorrectly assumed that discrimination was being practiced against unionists, and they became impatient for action. Although the time was hardly propitious for a strike and the national leadership was opposed to a walkout, the union negotiating committee was instructed by the membership on September 26 to call a strike unless the company agreed to recognize the union shop committee and to spread the work among the available employees by shortening the hours of labor. When the Murray Body management the next morning, the same morning that the M.E.S.A. began its strike in Detroit, promised not to discriminate against unionists but otherwise gave a noncommittal reply to the I.W.W. demands, the negotiating committee decided on an immediate strike, and at least one half of the approximately three thousand employees in the plant quit their jobs.[89]

The I.W.W. failed to win support for its strike from the few A.F. of L. members in the plant, and it was unable to achieve "negotiational unity" with the M.E.S.A., which was also striking the plant. In a vain effort to discourage nonstrikers from remaining at work and to force the management to close down the plant, the I.W.W. engaged in aggressive picketing at the plant and arranged for "visitations" at the homes of those who remained at their jobs. A relief kitchen was opened in the strike area, and efforts were made to raise funds by the use of strike-relief coin cans and a "Strikers' Hard Time Dance." Money, however, was always in short supply, and the hard-pressed union was forced during the course of the strike to cancel its radio program and to vacate its new hall.[90]

Although the official I.W.W. position was that strikes were to be won on the picket line rather than with the aid of government, the strike leadership seems to have appreciated from the start that the I.W.W. was unlikely in a period of declining production to bring the Murray Body management to terms by its own efforts. At the outset it was the management rather than the I.W.W. that opposed the efforts of the Detroit Compliance Board to arrange a settlement, and as the strike dragged on without any real prospect of union success, it was the I.W.W. on October 28 that appealed to the newly established Detroit Regional Labor Board to arrange a conference with the management. The board transmitted this request to Murray Body, but C. W. Avery, the corporation's president, replied on November 6 that the company had a full complement of workers in the plant and that there was therefore no issue before the board. When the board, apparently on the assumption that no violation of Section 7(a) was involved in the dispute, ruled that this reply closed the case, the secretary of Metal and Machinery Workers Industrial Union No. 440, as directed by the strikers, angrily replied that this decision demonstrated the complete subservience of the board to Murray Body and that both the Compliance Board and the Regional Labor Board were "wholly incompetent to handle labor disputes and quite untrustworthy." At a meeting on the same day that this letter was written, November 9, the strikers, without having won a single concession from the management, voted to call off the strike.[91]

"The loss of the Murray strike," F. W. Thompson, the chairman of the strike committee and of the I.W.W.'s General Executive Board, later observed, "was the loss of the campaign in Detroit," but this was not so evident to the I.W.W. leadership at the time as it was later to become. The *Industrial Worker* conceded with masterly under-statement that the Wobblies had suffered "a slight setback," but in accordance with standard I.W.W. doctrine that a strike was never really lost, it hopefully contended that the dispute had resulted in the development of "a corps of first-rate industrial unionists" and that the strikers had "learned what the class struggle really means in the auto industry." The General Executive Board at its session of late November and early December 1933 referred to the "excellent prog-ress made in the auto industry," and there continued to be talk dur-ing the remainder of the N.R.A. period of a "big organizing drive" and the ultimate general strike that would bring victory in the in-dustry. Only the most optimistic Wobblies, however, could have interpreted the few on-the-job strikes of 1934, staged mainly by I.W.W. metal finishers, as a prelude to the realization of the organi-zation's objectives in the industry. The members recruited by the union before the Murray Body strike dwindled away after the strike, and all that remained of the I.W.W. in Detroit was a small number of "the unswerving Finns and Hungarians." [92] The workers in the auto industry were eventually to join "one big union," but whatever consolation the handful of Wobblies might have derived from this fact must have been tempered by the realization that the I.W.W. it-self by that time had, for all practical purposes, disappeared from the industry.

IV

In the sphere of automobile unionism the N.I.R.A. period for the communists was a time of transition from the dual unionism of the T.U.U.L. and the A.W.U. to the policy of the united front. [93] Com-munist activity among the workers in the automobile industry was carried on at two levels: the A.W.U. was offered to the workers as the union that they should join, but at the same time every effort was made to build up a communist-controlled and influenced rank-and-file op-position within the U.A.W. locals and the M.E.S.A. In the end, the A.W.U. was dissolved, and its members were instructed to join either the U.A.W. or the M.E.S.A.

The failure of the A.W.U. to attract more than a handful of auto workers—the membership reached an estimated peak of fifteen hun-dred in September 1933—was a cause for constant complaint by com-munist functionaries. John Schmies, a Communist party district or-ganizer and a member of the A.W.U.'s National Executive Board, lamented in October 1933 that the A.W.U. had "declined all the way down the line," whereas the A.F. of L. and even the I.W.W. were making "deep inroads among sections of automobile workers." The A.W.U. was exhorted to win over the unorganized and the rank and file in the competing unions. Ways had to be found "to electrify the rising spirit for organization among the auto masses."

The communist leadership was not only dissatisfied with the progress of the A.W.U., but it also found little reason for self-congratulation in the results of communist efforts to penetrate the U.A.W. The Political Bureau of the Central Committee of the Communist party complained in January 1934 that the work of the party within the A.F. of L. was "very weak." Without neglecting the A.W.U., the party was instructed to pay "the most serious attention" to the organization of "opposition work" in the A.F. of L. The objective of communist activity was to "isolate the A.F. of L. leaders within their unions and win over the local A.F. of L. organizations." [94]

In pursuit of their twin objectives of strengthening the A.W.U. and boring from within the A.F. of L. and the M.E.S.A., the communists resorted to the tactic of constant criticism of the leadership and policies of their rivals while at the same time urging a united-front approach as the best means of furthering labor objectives in the industry. The A.W.U. and the communists harped particularly on the lack of militancy of the A.F. of L. leadership, on "their pussy-footing policy of delay-delay-delay." When strikes did occur, the communists invariably and monotonously criticized the A.F. of L. for failure to establish rank-and-file strike committees representing all departments of the plant involved and for refusing to engage in mass picketing and to permit the communist Unemployed Councils to augment the picket line. The strikers were cautioned to insist that strike negotiations with the management should include the rank and file and not just the union leadership and that any settlement of the strike should be submitted to the vote of the strikers. All strike settlements were ritualistically reviled by the communists as sell-outs, the inevitable result of the failure of the social-fascist leadership to conduct the strike in the manner prescribed by the communists.[95]

The criticism of the A.F. of L. and the M.E.S.A. leadership went hand in hand with efforts of the A.W.U. and the communists to promote a united front of automobile workers at the plant level and in the industry as a whole. As a first step in the united-front drive the communists urged the union of the rank and file within each plant so that a common front of workers could be presented to the employers. This type of co-operation at the plant level, the communists contended, would expose the "misleaders" of labor, who feared mass action, and would lay the basis for the ultimate goal, the establishment of a single industrial union for the industry as a whole.[96]

As part of a two-month organizing drive launched on November 13, 1933, and in order to promote the idea of a united front, the A.W.U. invited the A.F. of L., the M.E.S.A., the I.W.W., the Unemployed Councils, shop organizations, fraternal organizations, and even the unorganized to a united-front conference in Detroit on December 17, 1933. The leadership of the A.W.U.'s rivals ignored the conference call, but the A.W.U., whose reputation for reportorial accuracy leaves something to be desired, insisted that among the 224 delegates who attended were representatives of all the principal organizations in the automobile-union field. To the surprise of no one, the conference adopted the usual A.W.U. grab bag of proposals for inclusion in the automobile code and for enactment by Congress.[97]

In the latter part of March 1934, while the A.F. of L. was negotiating in Washington for the settlement of a threatened major automobile strike, the A.W.U., in order to capitalize on what appeared to be a rank-and-file desire to challenge the giants of the industry in the economic field, scheduled another united-front conference, this time for the purpose of planning strike action. The A.W.U. claimed an attendance at the conference of 146 persons representing thirty thousand workers, but by the time the delegates assembled on March 25, the strike threat had evaporated, and a settlement had been arranged. The conference then dutifully and predictably decided on a "united" mass effort to "fight the sellout," but the rhetoric expended in pursuance of this objective resulted in no immediate gain for the A.W.U. nor in any united-front action of any consequence either.[98]

Although the communists following the March conference continued to call for the strengthening of the A.W.U., the union remained the "weakest link" of the party in the Detroit district. The auto workers almost completely ignored the A.W.U., notwithstanding its appeal that it was the only "militant union" in the industry and that in contrast to the A.F. of L., it was committed to industrial unionism and to control by the rank and file. Increasingly, therefore, the communists directed their main attention in the industry away from the A.W.U. and toward an effort to build up opposition sentiment within the U.A.W. and the M.E.S.A. In December 1934 the A.W.U. was officially dissolved, and its members were instructed to join the U.A.W. locals if they were production workers and the M.E.S.A. if they were tool and die makers. The former A.W.U. members were told to build these two unions into "powerful mass organizations controlled by the rank and file and through united struggle to lay the basis for one union in the industry." [99]

At the time this decision was made there were only 450 members in the twenty-one locals of the A.W.U., and only a handful of even this pitifully small number were actually employed in the automobile factories.[100] The former A.W.U. members were, however, unionists of some experience, and their addition to the communists and fellow travelers who had previously enrolled in the U.A.W. gave to the communists a nucleus of adherents within the organization, whose ranks were so largely made up of persons without previous union experience, that was out of all proportion to the small numbers involved.

Striking a pose of self-sacrifice, the communists explained their decision to disband their almost nonexistent automobile union as the result of their "burning desire for unity" and as consistent with long-standing A.W.U. efforts to promote a united front among the automobile workers. For the remaining months that the N.I.R.A. was in effect, the communists adhered rigidly to the line that the principal objective of unionists in the automobile industry should be the establishment forthwith of "one powerful International union within the A.F. of L., controlled by the auto workers themselves and basing itself on a policy of struggle against the employers for better conditions." [101] Displeased with the slow progress in this direction being made by the A.F. of L. leadership, the communists and their friends in the U.A.W. locals, among other unionists to be sure, sought to stimulate action leading toward the establishment of an international union. Although unable to form an automobile workers' union of their own, the communists were by no means willing to surrender the important field of automobile unionism to their erstwhile rivals. They were determined that when an international union of automobile workers was finally created, the communists, who had been noisily striving for this goal for some time, would not be without influence in its ranks.

VI

REPRESENTATIVES OF THEIR OWN CHOOSING

I

THE CLASH BETWEEN automobile labor and automobile management in the Detroit area fell within the purview first of the N.R.A. Compliance Board in Detroit and then of the Detroit Regional Labor Board. The Compliance Board was formally organized on September 18, 1933. It consisted of two representatives of labor, two representatives of the employers, a consumer representative, a lawyer, and a chairman, Abner E. Larned, elected by the other six members. A retired manufacturer of men's clothing, Larned had previously served as chairman of the Detroit Recovery Committee.

Organized labor in Detroit was far from satisfied with either the composition or the behavior of the Compliance Board. Frank Martel complained to Senator Wagner early in October 1933 that the board was made up of four representatives of the commercial class and only two representatives of labor; and William Collins, speaking for twenty U.A.W. locals, urged Wagner on October 18 to establish a regional labor board in Detroit because the Compliance Board had failed to secure the reinstatement of workers whom the A.F. of L. believed had been the victims of discrimination. The Compliance Board, on the other hand, was favorably viewed by Detroit businessmen. Harvey Campbell, vice-president and secretary of the Detroit Board of Commerce, protested to Wagner that the establishment in Detroit of a regional labor board would be a "direct slap" at the Compliance Board, which enjoyed the confidence of the community, and would lead only to confusion.[1]

The National Labor Board, which by the end of September had emerged the victor in a jurisdictional conflict with the N.R.A. as to whether it or the N.R.A. Compliance Boards should deal with labor disputes, pushed ahead with its plan of establishing regional labor boards across the country, including a board in Detroit, despite the complaints of some employers. The Detroit board, which held its first session on October 30, consisted of five employer and five employee representatives, with Larned serving as the impartial chairman. None of the union representatives spoke directly for the U.A.W. locals, whereas four of the five employer representatives were related in one way or another to the automobile industry.[2]

Although he had urged the establishment of a regional labor board, Collins was soon complaining about the "lumbering processes" of the tribunal and about its handling of discrimination and representation cases. As might perhaps have been expected from a board of the bipartisan type, the employer and employee members tended to interpret the evidence differently, and organized labor thought that Larned, himself a businessman, was too inclined to side with the employer representatives. Collins protested within a few weeks after the Detroit board had been established that it was a "6-5" board; and the board's labor members went so far as to request Senator Wagner on January 6, 1934, to replace the employer members because a majority of them were using their position on the board to deny the workers their rights, and to dismiss Larned because he was "a very staunch partisan on behalf of the employers."[3] In February 1934 the board was reorganized. The Rev. Frederick Siedenburg, formerly a dean at the University of Detroit, became vice-chairman, and a labor representative and an employer representative were added to the panel. Larned resigned his position on May 1, and Siedenburg then became the board's chairman.[4]

The A.F. of L. preferred Siedenburg to Larned, but it now had new cause for complaint because the labor representative added to the board was none other than Matthew Smith, the general secretary of the M.E.S.A., which from the A.F. of L.'s point of view was a dual union. Apparently Frank Martel had indicated to the N.L.B. that he had no objection to Smith's serving on the board since he represented a substantial group of workers in the Detroit area, which was true; but other A.F. of L. officials made it clear to the N.L.B. that they did not welcome the appointment since it permitted the representative of a dual union to pass on issues affecting "bona fide" labor organizations. Senator Wagner was soon being advised that Smith was not a citizen and also that the M.E.S.A. might be controlled by communists. Siedenburg was accordingly asked by the N.L.B. to look into these charges and to ascertain whether Smith or his wife was a communist. Siedenburg, who quite properly did not question Smith about his wife, reported back that Smith had informed him that he was not a communist and that he had not become a citizen because he was a pacifist. Some of the Detroit board members

were convinced, however, that Smith had "strong communistic lean-
ings," but this was undoubtedly because they confused socialism
with communism and because Smith, who enjoyed turning a radical
phrase, had probably shocked his more conservative listeners with
strong talk.

Siedenburg did not express his own views on the issue of Smith's
radicalism, but he did not regard the M.E.S.A. general secretary as
well qualified for service on the board. The N.L.B. made no effort
to supplant Smith, but the fiery M.E.S.A. leader resigned of his own
volition on May 21, 1934. In a caustic letter to Wagner, he explained
that the board had been of some value during the first few months
of his service because at least the small and medium-sized concerns
had paid it some heed, even though the larger corporations had ignored it. "Now," however, he remarked, "even one-horse employers
treat Board recommendations with derision." [5]

Whereas the A.F. of L., initially at least, looked on the regional
board as an ally in its efforts to establish itself in the automobile industry, management in the industry viewed the tribunal with some
suspicion. The N.A.C.C. from the start had believed that any labor
board established with jurisdiction over the automobile industry
should be attached to the code authority and should be of a nonpartisan rather than a bipartisan character, but the Detroit board failed to
meet both of these conditions. The automobile companies replied
politely to the board's requests for information, but they refused to
appear at its hearings or to comply with its decisions. In declining
to obey a board decision in a discrimination case, Chrysler Corporation
thus advised the tribunal that it wished to co-operate with it but that
it did not "admit" the jurisdiction of the board and had not "consented
. . . to your Board's making findings in regard to this Corporation, and
does not consent." With tongue in cheek—or so it must have seemed
to the board—the corporation declared that it desired "to express its
great respect for the Board." Similarly, in submitting requested data
to the board, Max F. Wollering wrote for Hudson that "We are not
aware, nor do we recognize any right of the Labor Board to say, who
shall or who shall not be employed by this Company, nor shall there
be anything binding on us in any finding or recommendation made by
this Board. . . ." [6]

The automobile manufacturers were undoubtedly fortified in their
recalcitrance by the knowledge that the legal status of the N.L.B. was
by no means unassailable. The board had been established without
specific legislative authorization, and it was not until December 16,
1933, that it was accorded recognition and its functions defined even

in an executive order. The board, moreover, was without enforcement powers of its own. An executive order of February 1, 1934, provided that the N.L.B. was to report cases of noncompliance to the Administrator for Industrial Recovery "for appropriate action." This was altered by a new executive order of February 23, which authorized the board when faced with defiance of its orders to report its findings and to make appropriate recommendations to the Attorney General or to the Compliance Division of the N.R.A. The Compliance Division was specifically ordered not to review the findings of the N.L.B.[7]

II

During the autumn months of declining automobile production following the adoption of the automobile code the organization work of the A.F. of L. in Flint and Pontiac met with some success, but in Detroit, union membership, as Collins ruefully reported to Green, increased at a snail's pace. Even when production began its upward climb in December and January, Collins continued to report "a letdown" in interest.[8] In March 1934 Collins was able to involve both the N.L.B. and the President in the automobile labor question, but up to that time the U.A.W. locals had failed to attain their two major objectives: the improvement of the automobile code and the establishment of a satisfactory relationship with the automobile manufacturers.

The necessity of amending the auto code before it expired on December 31, 1933, was expressed by the officers of twenty-two Michigan federal labor unions who were meeting in Detroit on November 5. Green promised the U.A.W. locals that he would deal with the situation "as forcefully as circumstances will permit." The chief changes required, according to the A.F. of L. president, were the representation of labor on the automobile code authority, the establishment of a joint industrial-relations board for the industry, and the removal of the merit clause. The Labor Advisory Board echoed Green's opinions, and it too requested that the code be amended.[9]

The N.A.C.C. in the meantime was also giving some thought to the scheduled expiration of its code. It was particularly concerned about the relationship of the automobile manufacturing code to other automotive codes and the status of the merit clause in view of President Roosevelt's aforementioned letter of October 19 forbidding the further use in codes of language interpreting Section 7(a). The majority of the Chamber membership apparently favored the renewal of the code without change, but there was reported to be a "strong group" within the industry that was prepared to let the code expire altogether, even if this meant the imposition of a code by the President. *Automotive Industries* quoted one automobile executive as saying, "It's just a question as to whether manufacturers want to be seduced or raped."

The decision taken by the N.A.C.C. was to request an extension of the auto code without change on the grounds that it had not been in effect for a sufficiently long time to determine its value. Only the merit clause seemed to be a stumbling block to renewal, but Johnson allayed management's apprehension on this score by declaring on December 15 that this was "a matter of complete indifference" to him in view of the President's statement of October 19. Johnson was undoubtedly willing to let the industry have its way because of the impressive contribution it was making to the recovery program. On December 18, 1933, the code was consequently renewed without change until September 4, 1934. In his letter of transmittal to the President, Johnson pointed out that between July and September N.A.C.C. payrolls had increased 16 per cent and N.A.C.C. employment 20 per cent but that total man hours of Chamber employees had decreased 8 per cent, which meant that the code was accomplishing the purposes of Title I of the N.I.R.A.[10]

To Green's protests, Johnson, echoing the manufacturers, replied that the code had not been in effect long enough "to constitute a real test," that the existence of the N.L.B. made unwise the establishment of a separate industrial-relations board for the automobile industry, and that the merit clause was a "purely academic issue." The moral to be drawn from the A.F. of L. defeat on the issue of the code's extension, Green correctly informed the auto workers, was that "it is not alone the law which is going to help us. We must depend very largely upon our own efforts." Collins complained that the renewal of the code without a public hearing had contributed to a decline of interest in unionism among the auto workers. When a few weeks later the N.R.A. further disappointed the U.A.W. by permitting the industry to raise the average weekly hours of most of its factory employees from thirty-five to forty, Collins and two hundred officers of the U.A.W. locals protested to President Roosevelt that "Unless we can depend on you to right these wrongs ... we have no hope for the success of the NRA." Collins carried his complaints about the industry and its code to an N.R.A. conference on February 27, 1934, but although he won the praise of Johnson for being "reasonable and intelligent," he won little else.[11]

Unsuccessful in securing any change in the automobile code during the first months of its operation, the U.A.W. locals were also largely frustrated in their efforts to secure the kind of recognition they sought from their employers. In most automobile plants, to be sure, the U.A.W. simply did not have a sufficiently large membership to pose as the representative of the workers for collective-bargaining purposes, a fact which Green was willing enough to admit in private. "We are in no position yet," he stated to the auto locals in January 1934, "to demand collective bargaining." Green's advice was to "prepare the way by frequent conferences with the employers, by strengthening our position in every possible way, by keeping the union as much before the employer as possible." [12]

In only one instance in the Detroit area during 1933 did Collins, and "somewhat reluctantly" at that, permit a federal labor union to seek by strike action to redress its grievances against management. The concern involved was the Bower Roller Bearing Company, a small parts maker which had laid off 143 of its 688 employees on September 1 because of a reduction in its business volume. The federal labor union in the plant, which had succeeded in organizing perhaps 50 per cent of the employees, charged that the company had discriminated against union members in the layoff and also contended that the company had obstructed genuine collective bargaining by refusing to recognize the local and by converting an employee welfare organization into a company union (the Bower NIRA Association).

The strike began on September 18, and according to a Department of Labor conciliator was "approximately ninety percent effective." The president of the company, Silas A. Strickland, quickly brought the dispute to the attention of the newly organized N.R.A. Compliance Board in Detroit and stated, in rebuttal of the U.A.W. charges, that he had not discriminated against union members, had not, indeed, even known at the time of the layoff that there was an A.F. of L. organization in the plant, and that the Bower NIRA Association had been organized by the employees themselves and they had joined it voluntarily. Whether or not Strickland was correct in denying discrimination, it is impossible to say, but it is evident that the company itself, not its employees, had established the inside union and was contributing to its support.[13]

A settlement of the strike was quickly arranged by the Compliance Board on September 19. The agreement provided that the rights of employees as set forth in Section 7(a) were to be recognized by both labor and management in the plant. All those employed just prior to the strike were to be returned to their jobs, and the workers who had been previously laid off were to be given preference in rehiring, if qualified, before new employees were engaged. Finally, all grievances that could not be adjusted by negotiation between management and a committee representing the union employees were to be referred to the Compliance Board for "arbitration and adjustment." [14]

The Bower local had not been successful in securing the immediate return to work of all those who it claimed had been improperly laid off, but it had nevertheless made an important stride forward. "This first victory in the enforcement of the extremely difficult problem of discrimination," an observer friendly to labor advised the N.L.B., "and this first step in the recognition of the union will mean a great deal toward the establishment of a real union in the city." [15] The benefits that accrued to the Bower local as the result of the strike were, in the final analysis, to be dissipated, and a second strike called on March 19, 1934, after continual differences between the union and the management, ended disastrously for the local; but there is, nevertheless, some truth in the observation of the *Detroit Labor News* that the A.F. of L. had "won its spurs" in the automobile industry in this one-day strike.[16] If nothing else, the newly organized auto workers had demonstrated that, however few their numbers, they were a factor to be reckoned with in the automobile plants.

Following the Bower strike and prior to March 25, 1934, the A.F. of L. in its efforts to organize the auto workers in Detroit and Michigan eschewed the strike weapon and relied primarily on the machinery of the N.L.B. and its Detroit Regional Labor Board to redress union grievances against the automobile employers. To the regional board organized labor brought its complaints of discrimination and of the alleged failure of management to recognize the unions and their representatives and to bargain with them in good faith.

Cases of alleged discrimination involving more than one hundred automobile unionists were submitted to the regional labor board before March 25, 1934, by the U.A.W., the M.E.S.A., the S.D.E., and the Metal Polishers Union. G.M. was the defendant in almost two-thirds of these cases, and the Chrysler Corporation in about one-quarter of them. The procedure of the board was to forward the complaints of discrimination to the companies concerned for their comments and then to pass on the replies to the complainants. Generally, what the union interpreted as discrimination, the management defended as the result of some infraction of company rules, unsatisfactory job performance, or simply a required reduction of force. Rarely were the facts in a case sufficiently clear to resolve all doubts as to whether labor or management's version of what had occurred was nearer the truth. If the company's reply did not satisfy the complainant and thus cause a withdrawal of the case or if some settlement had not in the meantime been reached, the board might delegate one or two of its members to speak with the management in an effort to compose the issue. In one instance, the board enlisted the aid of a Flint rabbi and a priest in investigating several complaints of discrimination directed against the management of the Flint Chevrolet plant.[17]

When efforts to settle discrimination cases by informal means failed, the board scheduled a formal hearing and then rendered a decision. In three cases—one involving an employee of the Chrysler Kercheval plant, another involving Al Cook, the president of the U.A.W. local in the Fisher No. 1 plant in Flint, and the third dealing with an employee of the Marvel Carburetor Company—the regional board found that the employees concerned had been the victims of discrimination,[18] but their employers refused to comply with rulings that they be rehired. In a case involving a metal polisher at the Plymouth plant, the board without specifically ruling that discrimination had occurred nevertheless found that the company had dealt unfairly with the complainant and advised the management to make a thorough investigation with a view to re-employing him.[19] In one unusual case, the Ford Motor Company, in responding to a M.E.S.A. allegation of discrimination in the discharge of one of its members, offered to prove that union affiliation was not the cause by agreeing to hire any union member suggested by the M.E.S.A. to replace the discharged worker. The case was settled on this basis.[20]

When management refused to comply with a regional board decision, the N.L.B. itself assumed jurisdiction of the case, but before it could hand down a decision on any of the automobile discrimination cases that were before it, the Automobile Labor Board, which was attached to the N.R.A. and was entirely independent of the N.L.B., had been established, and cases involving the automobile manufacturing industry, including those pending before the regional board, were transferred to the new agency. The N.L.B. and its regional boards continued to deal with discrimination cases in the automobile parts industry that the disputants could not agree to submit to the A.L.B.

On only two occasions prior to the establishment of the A.L.B. did the Detroit regional board have before it the question of the legality of the company unions established in the automobile industry. The S.D.E. charged in December 1933 that the Hudson management had used coercive tactics in establishing the Hudson Industrial Association, but the regional board rejected this accusation. Collins complained to the board about the legality of the company unions in the Chrysler Jefferson and Kercheval plants, but his allegation lacked specificity and was not made the subject of a board decision.[21]   As shall be noted, the U.A.W. carried its complaints about the automobile company unions to the N.L.B. in hearings of March 14 and 15, 1934, designed to avert a threatened strike in the industry.

The most significant issue which the U.A.W. locals in Michigan brought before the Detroit regional board was the charge that the employers refused to confer and to bargain with them and were thus violating the terms of Section 7(a).   When the federal labor unions first approached the automobile companies to confer regarding working conditions, they were generally advised that a substantial majority of the employees of the plant had already decided to establish some sort of employee-representation plan and that any grievances of the workers should therefore be referred to the works council.   In taking this position, management was in effect endorsing the idea that the representatives selected by the majority of the workers should have the exclusive right to bargain for all the workers in the plant.[22]

In December 1933 and January 1934 the automobile manufacturers, guided by the advice of William J. Cronin, began to insist when approached by union representatives for bargaining purposes that they would have to know precisely which of their employees had authorized the union committee to bargain on their behalf.   The argument advanced was the logical one that since Section 7(a) authorized employees to bargain through representatives of their own choosing, the employers would violate the statute if they bargained with union representatives on behalf of employees who had not specifically authorized these representatives to speak for them.   The union representatives were therefore asked to furnish a list of the persons for whom they had been authorized to speak and "satisfactory evidence" that these workers wished the union committee to bargain for them.[23]

In accepting this new interpretation of Section 7(a), the automobile manufacturers were abandoning their earlier support of majority rule in the choice of representatives for collective-bargaining purposes. Undoubtedly this decision reflected a growing fear on the part of the employers that a majority of their employees might prefer a trade union to a company union if they were given the opportunity to express themselves freely on this point.   The Cronin interpretation of Section 7(a), in contrast, left the door open for each group in a plant to select its own representatives and for individuals who wished to do so to bargain for themselves.   This made it unlikely that the employees in the foreseeable future would be able to present a united trade-union front to their employers for collective-bargaining purposes.

The A.F. of L., unwittingly, had played a part in the shaping of management's new interpretation of Section 7(a). Cronin had obtained a copy of a William Green letter of January 8, 1934, in which the A.F. of L. president had informed the U.A.W. locals that the time had come for them "to make effective use" of Section 7(a). "That no question may arise as to the right of the union to represent the members in all dealings with the employers," Green wrote, "it would be well to have each member execute an individual authorization of such representation.... If question arises later—as it almost certainly will—of the union's position, you will have these authorizations to submit to the company."[24]

Despite Green's letter, however, when employers began to request the submission of membership lists as a prelude to collective bargaining, union officials stated that they could not comply because to do so would be to invite discrimination against union members. In January and February 1934 several of the stronger U.A.W. locals in Michigan insisted that the proper way to determine representation rights was through elections conducted by the N.L.B. This position was in accord with the existing practice of the N.L.B. and with an executive order of February 1, 1934, that authorized the board to hold elections whenever "a substantial number" of the employees in a particular unit requested the use of this procedure for choosing representatives to engage in collective bargaining with their employer. The executive order, moreover, endorsed the principle of majority rule to which the A.F. of L. had become committed. The representatives selected by a majority of those voting, the order stated, were "to represent all the employees eligible to participate in such an election."[25]

Although the language of the executive order appeared to reject the concept of collective-bargaining pluralism that the automobile employers had espoused, the latter were able to take refuge in an interpretation of the President's order, issued on February 3, by the two most powerful officials in the N.R.A., General Johnson and Donald Richberg. The executive order of February 1, they bewilderingly stated, did not restrict the right of minorities or of individuals in a bargaining unit to deal with the employers. It simply provided a method by which a majority might select representatives who would serve as the "representatives of the will of the majority of the employees eligible to join in that selection." For good measure, Johnson and Richberg added that it was false to assume that employees might not freely choose a company union as their representative. At odds with the N.R.A. regarding the interpretation of Section 7(a), the

N.L.B. ignored the Johnson-Richberg statement and in its decision of March 1 in the Denver Tramway case specifically endorsed the principle of majority rule.[26]

Precedent in the conflict between the advocates of majority rule and exclusive representation and the defenders of some form of collective-bargaining pluralism was on the side of majority rule, although the issue had not previously been formulated in precisely the same fashion. Prior to World War I the vast majority of employers engaged only in individual bargaining with their employees, but where unions were sufficiently strong to negotiate agreements with management, the terms of the contract normally applied to all the workers of the particular craft or plant. Similarly, when employers during and after World War I established employee-representation plans in their plants, they did not normally look upon the company union as one of several organizations with which they would have collective dealings but rather as the sole spokesman for their employees.

As late as November 1933, some four months after the N.I.R.A. had become law, the vast majority of American employers in manufacturing and mining still resorted to only one type of bargaining with their employees. Either they engaged exclusively in individual bargaining, exclusively in collective bargaining with a trade union, or exclusively in collective bargaining with a company union. A study by the National Industrial Conference Board revealed that as of November 1933 only 7.4 per cent of 3314 manufacturing and mining concerns on which data had been obtained resorted to a combination of individual and collective bargaining or to bargaining with both a trade union and a company union.[27]

In so far as the federal government had previously expressed itself on the subject of collective bargaining, it too had espoused the principle of majority rule. Although the National War Labor Board, in three of its representation elections, instructed its examiner to provide for minority representation "wherever practicable," it specifically endorsed the concept of majority rule in formulating its general plan for the election of shop committees; and, similarly, the Railroad Labor Board created by the Transportation Act of 1920 had ruled that the majority of any craft or class of employees "shall have the right to determine what organization shall represent members of such craft or class. Such organization," it stated, "shall have the right to make an agreement which shall apply to all employees in such craft or class." [28]

Election requests were submitted to the N.L.B. and the Detroit regional board by the Fisher Body No. 1 local in Flint on January 19; the five principal U.A.W. locals in Flint on February 13, and then, after this request had been denied, by the Buick local alone; and by the local in the Pontiac Fisher Body plant on March 1. The regional board rejected the request of the five Flint locals because the evidence, in its opinion, did not indicate a refusal on the part of management to meet with the union representatives. The board decided in favor of an election at the Pontiac Fisher Body plant since it found that this accorded with the wishes of the required "substantial number" of plant employees, and it asked its committee of Flint clergymen, which was already looking into complaints of discrimination by Chevrolet workers, to investigate the election request of the Buick local.[29] Before any further action resulted, however, the threatened automobile dispute of March 1934, which will be examined below, transferred the conflict between automobile labor and automobile management to the nation's capital, and the resulting settlement took away from the N.L.B. its power to hold elections in the automobile manufacturing plants.

III

The struggle between employer and employee in the automobile industry was not confined to the great auto centers of Michigan. Outside of the state, as in Michigan itself, the conflicting interests of labor and management led to occasional strikes and to N.L.B. efforts to compose these disputes and to settle, in accordance with its interpretation of Section 7(a), other automobile labor matters brought to its attention.

As in Michigan, the U.A.W. locals outside of the motor state that enjoyed the greatest success were those in the plants of the independent auto producers and in the parts plants. Independents like Nash, Studebaker, and White were in a far more precarious financial and market position than the Big Three and hence less able to resist union pressure. The parts companies were also vulnerable since many of them felt that they could not afford prolonged labor strife lest their inability to deliver their product on schedule would cause them to lose business to their numerous competitors or to the main plants themselves. Because of inferior working conditions, employee dissatisfaction was also greater in the parts plants than in the main plants—the workers looked upon the parts plants as the "sweat shops" of the industry.

The gains of the U.A.W. locals outside Michigan cannot, however, be attributed entirely to the character of the opposition or to the fact that the power of the Big Three was concentrated in Michigan. Removed from the restraining influence of the A.F. of L.'s national representative in the auto industry, several of the non-Michigan locals were considerably more militant than their Michigan counterparts. This greater daring brought them occasional success in their struggles with management and also won them adherents among the automobile workers in the plants that they were seeking to organize. Throughout the period of the N.R.A., the membership of the U.A.W. locals outside of Michigan was substantially greater than the membership inside the Wolverine state.

Of the employer-employee conflicts in the automobile industry outside of Michigan, few received greater attention during the N.I.R.A. years than the dispute between the union and the management of the Edward G. Budd Manufacturing Company of Philadelphia, maker of bodies and other steel products for several of the automobile concerns. The Budd federal labor union was chartered on September 19, 1933, following a mass meeting of Budd employees on August 30 at which the decision had been made to affiliate with the A.F. of L. Edward G. Budd looked with disfavor on this effort to organize his workers and was particularly disturbed by A.F. of L. exhortations to his employees that they must join the union to receive the benefits of the N.I.R.A. He would have preferred "to have gone on in the old way," but in an effort to counter the threat to his managerial prerogatives posed by an outside union and because he believed it would make his men "easier in their minds," Budd, like so many of his fellow automobile manufacturers, decided to take the initiative in establishing a company union in his plant. The workers were informed of this decision by notices posted on the company time clocks on September 1, two days after the A.F. of L. mass meeting for Budd employees.

On September 5 the company distributed a brief preliminary announcement among its employees concerning the establishment of a Budd Employee Representative Association and requesting the workers to elect employee representatives to conduct the business of the proposed organization. Seventy-nine per cent of the employees voted in the nominating election of September 5, and 92 per cent (3263 of the 3519 eligible), in the final election of September 7. Union officials later informed the N.L.B. that the foremen in the plant insisted that the men cast a ballot and "We were all scared to not vote for fear of our jobs." Following the election, the company submitted a proposed constitution for the employee association to the nineteen elected representatives, and they accepted the plan, which was of the usual company-union type, without modification. The management made it known that it expected the employee representatives to prevent "outside interference" in company affairs and "to correct the false impression" allegedly being created among their constituents by the A.F. of L.[30]

Membership in the Budd U.A.W. local was limited to the workers, largely semiskilled and unskilled, in the production and shipping departments of the plant. The union claimed that twelve hundred Budd employees as of November 13, 1933, had paid their full initiation fees and that another twenty-three hundred had applied for membership. This was undoubtedly an exaggeration since only about twenty-five hundred workers were identified with the production and shipping departments and, at most, twenty-three hundred of these were actually at work on November 13, along with about nineteen hundred additional employees in other departments of the plant. The union had paid a per capita tax to the A.F. of L. in October on only 157 members, but this figure almost certainly understated union strength and support.[31]

A three-man union committee met with Delmer S. Harder, the Budd works manager, on November 13, expressed to him the union's desire for recognition as a basis for collective bargaining, and was informed that the company had already established an employee association for this purpose. When this conversation was reported to the union membership, the decision was taken to strike the company. The strike was initiated on November 14, when, according to the local, two thousand workers from the production and shipping departments quit their jobs, to be joined by other union members and sympathizers who had been laid off prior to the strike because of the slackening of production. The company claimed that only five hundred to six hundred employees had quit work, and in characteristic employer fashion insisted that most of these were out "either through intimidation or coercion." The company continued to operate the plant and on November 20 began hiring new employees, including some persons who had previously worked for the company but had not been employed on the day of the strike. According to figures compiled for Budd by the accounting firm of Price, Waterhouse and Company, the plant work force averaged 4352 a day for the week ending November 11; 3993 for the week ending November 18; 4592 for the week ending November 25; and 4678 for the week ending December 2. These figures do not indicate the precise number who struck on November 14 although they make it clear that Budd was able to replenish his labor force within a few days after the strike. Budd later conceded that the number of strikers exceeded one thousand, but this figure probably included employees laid off prior to the walkout who joined the original Budd strikers.[32]

The Philadelphia Regional Labor Board assumed jurisdiction of the Budd dispute on November 15 and after failing to effect a settlement rendered its decision on November 23. In an opinion which had for all practical purposes been written by Milton S. Handler, the N.L.B.'s General Counsel, the tribunal criticized the local for having failed to avail itself of the N.L.B. machinery before going on strike and for not giving the company a reasonable amount of time to consider the merit of its proposals. At the same time, the board raised the question as to whether company sponsorship and drafting of the employee-representation plan, the limitations that the plan placed on the choice of representatives and the right to vote, and the failure of the company to permit the employees to indicate their approval or disapproval of the plan were consistent with the self-organization of workers for which Section 7(a) provided. The board ruled that the strike should be called off at once, that the strikers should be reinstated without discrimination as rapidly as work became available, that an election should be held under regional board auspices within ninety days so that employees could indicate whom they wished to represent them, and that any misunderstandings concerning the decision should be reported to the board.[33]

When Budd refused to comply with the regional board decision, partly on the grounds that the holding of a new election would reflect on the authority of the employee representatives to speak for the company's workers, the N.L.B. assumed jurisdiction of the case. A hearing was held in Washington on December 7 and 8, but only union representatives attended. Budd, who had appeared before the regional board, did, however, submit a lengthy memorandum to the N.L.B. defending the company's position. As far as Budd was concerned, the dispute had come to an end, and the only task remaining for the N.L.B. was to advise the strikers to apply for work.[34]

In its decision in the case, which was issued on December 14, 1933, the N.L.B., like the regional board, criticized the union for its precipitate calling of the strike and verbally chastised the management for interfering with the self-organization of its employees, for its summary rejection of the union's demands on November 13, and for its defiance of the regional board. The N.L.B. noted that the question as to whether the union was entitled to recognition depended on how representative an organization it was, and that this could have been ascertained by "patient discussion" or, failing this, by a regional board election. If the committee represented a majority of the employees, the management had erred in refusing to bargain with it unless other representatives had previously been chosen in a bona fide election, which the Budd company-union election was not. The N.L.B. ruled that the strike should be called off at once, that the strikers should be promptly reinstated without discrimination and with priority over workers who had been newly engaged after the regional board had assumed jurisdiction of the case, and that an election should be held in thirty days under the direction of the N.L.B.[35] Although the decision did not specifically place the N.L.B.'s stamp of approval on the doctrine of majority rule, it did indicate that when there was any doubt as to the right of a particular organization to represent a substantial number of employees, the proper way to resolve the doubt was by an election. Unlike the regional board decision, the N.L.B. ruling made it clear that not only did strikers remain employees but in a dispute involving a violation of Section 7(a), they were to be returned to their jobs in preference to newly engaged workers. This view of the status of strikers was one which neither Budd nor his fellow automobile manufacturers were disposed to accept.

The union at a mass meeting of December 16 accepted the N.L.B. decision and ordered its men to return to work on December 18. Budd, however, remained defiant. He informed Senator Wagner by letter that nothing in the N.I.R.A. or the automobile code required the company to hold an election and that for it to do so would be tantamount to repudiating the loyal employees who had stood by it during the preceding five weeks. Nor would he consent to replace persons on the payroll by those who had quit his employ on November 14. He did, however, hope to re-employ many of the strikers as business improved. Actually, Budd was satisfied that the new workers he had taken on were of a "better grade" than those who had quit his employ, and, as he privately informed a Ford executive, he was disinclined "to take these strikers back excepting a few at a time as we are convinced of their loyalty." The leaders of the strike and those who had engaged in violence would "never be permitted in our shop." [36]

On December 18 at 5:00 A.M. more than two thousand persons, not all of them strikers or even Budd workers who had been laid off before the strike, gathered at the gates of the Budd plant in search of employment. The company interviewed 1368 of the job applicants that day, but it hired only twenty-nine of them. Budd, who obviously viewed strikers as evil persons and "conspirators," was of the opinion that the bulk of the men seeking work did not really want jobs but were rather "playing a part in the game that was meant to disorganize our shop." Interviewers of the job applicants had been instructed to refer applicants about whom they were "suspicious" to personnel manager Edwin H. McIlwain. When asked at a later date how he determined whom to re-employ, Budd stated that "personal character" was the sole consideration, but he conceded that when an organization had acted as the U.A.W. had in his plant, that is, had committed the sin of striking, "we have to be careful about how we take those men in." The company was indeed "careful" about the re-employment of strikers, and by early January 1934 it had returned only fifty-nine of them to their jobs.[37]

Despairing that the company would comply with its decision, the N.L.B. on January 11, 1934, in its first resort to the N.R.A.'s compliance machinery, referred the Budd case to Compliance Director William H. Davis with the recommendation that "immediate action be taken to compel compliance." Refusing to accept the N.L.B.'s finding on the facts, the Compliance Division scheduled a hearing on the case before the National Compliance Board.[38] The board's decision, which was submitted to General Johnson on February 17, was based squarely on the issue of self-organization rather than on whether there had been any violation of the right of Budd employees to bargain collectively with their employer.

Davis and his advisors found that the requirements of Section 7(a) regarding self-organization had been observed neither in the establishment of the company union nor in its subsequent operation. The decision noted that the employee representatives in their meetings with company representatives had discussed questions that were not properly the concern of management, such as the qualification of employee representatives, and that changes in the plan were improperly subject to the veto of the company. It was pointed out, however, that the employee representatives had redrafted the plan and now wished to submit it to the employees as a basis for self-organization. It was therefore recommended that there should be an election among the employees, supervised by the National Compliance Director, to ascertain whether they desired any form of self-organization and, if so, whether they preferred an inside, an outside, or some other form of organization. The ballot was to include the new plan drafted by the employee-association representatives, and full opportunity was to be given to the employees to indicate their views regarding the salient features of the plan and also regarding a tentative agreement with the company prepared by the nineteen employee representatives. The submission of the revised employee-association plan was to be accompanied by a statement prepared by the National Compliance Director outlining the basic questions involved in the plan. Finally, as business permitted, Budd was to re-employ all the strikers still out of work and available for re-employment. If the company did not accept these recommendations, it was proposed that its Blue Eagle should be removed, its government contracts canceled, and the case referred to the Attorney General.[39]

The Compliance Board's recommendations, as Budd pointed out, were "in line with the Company's wishes throughout" [40] and hardly seem consistent with Davis' justly earned reputation for fair dealing. Not only did the decision give a privileged position on the ballot to the company-union plan, but also it did not require the company to give the strikers priority in re-employment over "loyal" employees, nor did it appear to grant the suffrage in the proposed election to those still on strike despite the fact that the N.L.B. had indicated that strikers were to be considered employees and had advised Davis not to hold the election until those who walked out on November 14 had been reinstated. The Compliance Board also ignored the N.L.B.'s advice that the production and shipping departments should be allowed to decide for themselves whether they wished these two departments alone, rather than the plant as a whole, to serve as the appropriate bargaining unit for representation purposes.

The union indicated that it did not object to the election provided that it were held off company property, that the strikers who had not been re-employed were permitted to vote, and that the outside union, like the inside union, were given an opportunity to explain its purposes. It protested the recommendation concerning the rehiring of strikers as meaning that some of those who had quit work would never be re-employed, which was a fair inference considering Budd's interpretation of the phrase "available for re-employment" to exclude not only those who had taken jobs elsewhere but also those guilty of violence or of "fomenting" the strike.[41]

In substantial accordance with Davis' recommendations, the N.R.A. announced on March 5 that an election would be held four days later, under the National Compliance Director's control, to permit the employees in the plant to determine whether they wished self-organization through the employee-representation plan, the A.F. of L. federal labor union, or some other agency, or whether they were opposed to self-organization. Since this order ignored the conditions for an election stipulated by the Budd local, the union immediately protested to General Johnson. Davis defended the Compliance Board's decision, but on March 8 the National Compliance Director, acting for the

N.R.A., ordered the election postponed for ten days to give the N.R.A. Administrator an opportunity to consider the union's protest.[42]

The employee representatives of the Budd company union decided to go ahead with the scheduled election despite the announced postponement, and Budd stated that "It is not within my province to stand in the way of this election, nor to influence the result." Of the 5762 employees who voted, 3152 expressed a preference for the employee-association plan; 1995 for the U.A.W. local; 261 for other organizations; 229 were opposed to self-organization; and 125 ballots were void. Budd pointed out that even if all the strikers who had not been re-employed, then estimated by the union as eight hundred, had been permitted to vote and had expressed a preference for the U.A.W., the company union would still have won the election. If Budd was shocked that almost two thousand of his "loyal" employees had voted for the U.A.W. despite their employer's well-known views on the virtues of outside unions, he gave no indication of that fact. In rebuttal to Budd, the local contended that if eight hundred newly engaged employees had been replaced before the election by eight hundred strikers, as it thought should have been done, the union would have won the election even though it had been wrongly held on company property.[43]

The union view of the election was seconded by N.R.A. Assistant Administrator Edward McGrady, who denounced the election as "illegal" and as "in defiance" of Johnson. "Just what do these people think General Johnson's orders are for?" McGrady indignantly asked. Johnson himself stated that he would disregard the poll, and he sent his friend Robert Lea to Philadelphia to "see Budd and try to get him to let us hold an election *off* company property and *including* strikers still unemployed." Following conferences between the N.R.A. and Budd, Johnson on March 17, in a statement that was designed to placate Budd but which the general must have surmised would antagonize the union, ordered a new election for March 20. The N.R.A. Administrator declared that he regarded the Budd matter as "most unfortunate," but he indicated, with questionable accuracy, that Budd had acted "in complete good faith," had supported the N.R.A., and had complied with the law. He noted that the indications were that the scheme of employee representation was "desired by the majority of the men" but that there was some doubt as to whether in arriving at this "state of the law," all employees had been accorded their full rights. In order "to purge the situation of this condition" and to permit production and employment to continue, he was proposing an election to be held outside the plant by his representative. Employees on the payroll as of March 15, 1934, and also employees on the payroll on the date of the strike but not currently employed were to be permitted to vote. The company-union plan was to continue in effect unless *a majority of those eligible* voted in the affirmative on the question, "Do you favor the United Automobile Workers Federal Labor Union 18763 to represent you in Collective Bargaining?" [44]

The U.A.W. local, obviously doubtful that it could secure a majority unless the strikers replaced those who had taken their jobs and the latter were denied the vote, decided to ignore the election. An A.F. of L. representative in Philadelphia stated that Johnson had not been "an impartial referee." The general, he declared, "has been liberal in his praise and consideration for Budd, but no General can stuff this 'Nicaraguan election' down our throats." The company union, the burden of proof now placed squarely on its opponents, also advised Budd employees to boycott the election. The advice of both the strikers and the company union was heeded, and to Johnson's chagrin, only about fifty persons participated in the election.[45]

Although the N.R.A. considered the poll "a closed incident," it continued to negotiate with Budd for a settlement of the dispute. Budd indicated that he was willing, as business permitted, to re-employ "a substantial proportion" of the strikers who were good workers, but the events of the preceding several months, as he interpreted them, simply confirmed his unfavorable opinion of unions and strikers. In an unmistakable revelation of Budd's views on the subject, his attorney expressed concern to the N.R.A. about the tendency of "the striking kind" to soldier on the job, the probability that the strikers if re-employed would "stir up further trouble," and the likelihood that some of them would be "sent in coached to frame a complaint for discharge in violation of the NRA." [46]

The general settlement in Washington late in March 1934 of a contemplated widespread automobile strike had as one of its by-products the arrangement on March 29 of peace terms that brought the Budd strike, at long last, to a close. The company agreed to re-employ one striker for every two men hired in the production and the shipping departments during the ensuing ninety days and to observe the terms of the general automobile settlement with regard to layoffs. Finally, Budd, "on his own initiative," offered to undertake a clean-up operation at the plant to relieve the distress of the strikers.[47]

The strike had ended in an utter rout for the local, and within a short time the federal labor union in the plant had vanished from the automobile scene. The strike was indicative in some ways of the shortcomings of the A.F. of L.'s organization campaign in the automobile industry. Not until a month after the walkout had begun did President Green become aware, at least in an official way, of the existence of the dispute. He thereupon advised an A.F. of L. representative in Philadelphia, who had already done so on his own, to assist the strikers but at the same time to explain to them that they were not entitled to receive financial aid from the Federation because they had not been affiliated for a full year. The strikers also discovered that their affiliation with the A.F. of L. did not necessarily mean that their strike would be supported by Federation members in the Budd plant who were outside the jurisdiction of the federal labor union. The pattern makers in the plant, who apparently were strongly organized, gave the strikers no support whatsoever, nor did Budd's A.F. of L. machinists in any appreciable number heed the plea of the U.A.W. to join the striking production and shipping-department employees.[48] The conclusion undoubtedly drawn by some of the strikers was that all the workers in an automobile plant should be included in a single industrial union rather than fragmented in several unions.

Just as the Budd strike was indicative of the weakness of the A.F. of L. in the automoile industry so it was revelatory of the inability of the N.L.B. to compel a recalcitrant employer to comply with its interpretation of Section 7(a). President Roosevelt, partly because of the Budd case, sought to strengthen the N.L.B. by his executive order of December 16, 1933, but Budd remained defiant. When the case passed into its hands, the N.R.A., as was sometimes its habit, took a more tolerant view of the employer's behavior than the N.L.B. had done, but it too proved unable to resolve the dispute until the union had become so enfeebled that it was no longer in a position to resist.

The differences between employer and employee in the automobile industry regarding the interpretation of Section 7(a) were nowhere more conspicuously in evidence than in the dispute involving Federal Labor Union No. 18839 and the Houde Engineering Corporation of Buffalo, New York, manufacturer of shock absorbers and other automobile parts and also of refrigerator parts. Following the organization of the U.A.W. local late in the summer of 1933, a "loose-knit" athletic association that had been functioning in the plant for several years was suddenly transformed, with the company's "moral blessing," into a full-fledged company union, the Houde Welfare and Athletic Association of Employees.[49]

On November 4, 1933, at a time when employment in the plant had been reduced from a level of about fifteen hundred to about 750, of whom the union claimed 481 members or applicants for membership, a committee of union officials presented a set of demands to Ralph Peo, vice-president and general manager of the firm, who had successfully "dodged" the local's representatives for more than two weeks. Peo, completely unaccustomed to dealing with union representatives and unwilling to concede that Section 7(a) had changed the law of labor relations in the United States, informed the committee that he would not negotiate with the union officials as the representatives of any of Houde's employees until he was supplied with the names of the workers who had specifically authorized these officials to be their spokesmen in dealing with the management. The union refused to comply with this request because it feared that the company would use such a list to discriminate against union members. That the local had reason to be concerned about this matter was indicated by the fact that four union officials, including the president of the local, had been laid off between September 28 and October 19 and although they were good workers were not rehired when the company substantially increased its labor force beginning in December.[50]

When the intercession of a federal conciliator failed to bring a change in Peo's position—the company had the conciliator "investigated" and was "insistent" in seeking to ascertain how he had become involved in the case—the local turned to the Buffalo Regional Labor Board for assistance. The regional board heard the case on December 28, and following the advice of Benedict Wolf, the executive secretary of the N.L.B., ruled on January 2, 1934, that the executive secretary of the Buffalo board, Daniel B. Shortal, should compare a list of the company's employees with a list of union members and should then certify his findings to the complainant and the respondent. Peo transmitted the list to Shortal on the condition, among others, that the latter's certification of the results must include the number of union members and the names of all Houde employees who had authorized the union committee to represent them.

The regional board refused to accept the list under the conditions stipulated by Peo, and board efforts to get the Houde general manager to reconsider his position were unavailing. Under the circumstances, the board apparently thought it unnecessary to ascertain the exact size of the union membership, and it simply informed Peo on January 16 that it had been demonstrated to its "entire satisfaction" that the union officials in question were "the duly accredited representatives of a certain group" of Houde employees and that the company should therefore negotiate with them "at once." Asserting that the controversy was not even within its jurisdiction, Peo advised the board that he would not comply with its decision. Not only had the board failed to supply him with any evidence for its conclusions, but nothing in Section 7(a) nor in the parts code, he stated, required him to bargain with a union as such or with union representatives as distinguished from employee representatives.[51]

Following the regional board decision, the Houde local sought once again to negotiate with Peo, but the Houde general manager adamantly insisted on the submission of a membership list as a precondition for any discussion with union officials. The local thereupon scheduled a strike for January 30, 1934, but the N.L.B., to avoid this, stepped into the dispute on January 29 and scheduled a hearing for February 6. Peo, however, was no more impressed with the N.L.B. than with its regional agencies. He advised the board that it was without jurisdiction in the case since there was no dispute and that even if there were a dispute, the board was powerless to intervene without the consent of both parties. The issue of whether agents should be required to submit evidence of their authority to act for their principals was, he argued, purely a question of law, and if an arbitration tribunal were invited to pass on such a matter, it should be a body that was "judicially impartial and free from bias." With all due respect for the board, Peo added, "we are not satisfied that all the members thereof satisfy that arbitral test."[52]

No management representative was thus present when the N.L.B. hearing on the Houde case took place on February 6. The board decision, announced on March 8, met squarely the central question posed by the dispute: was an employer obligated to bargain with union officials purporting to speak for some of his employees if these officials refused to divulge the names of those they represented? When an employer challenged employee representatives as the Houde management had, the resolution of the issue, the board declared, was through the election process, with the company then being obligated, in accordance with the Denver Tramway decision, to bargain with the representatives selected by the majority of its employees. Under these circumstances it would be unnecessary for the union to divulge the names of its members to the management. The Buffalo Regional Labor Board was therefore instructed to hold an election among the Houde employees if it were asked to do so by a "substantial number" of workers.[53]

On the same day that it rendered the Houde decision, the N.L.B., in the Hall Baking case, unequivocally proclaimed for the first time that a labor organization *as such* and not just individual union members or a union committee in its collective capacity could claim recognition as a "representative" within the meaning of the term as used in

Section 7(a).[54] The touchy and symbolically important question of recognition had thus been resolved by the board in a manner entirely satisfactory from the union point of view but hardly pleasing to Peo or most other employers.

Having satisfied itself that a substantial number of Houde employees desired an election, the Buffalo board arranged for a poll to be held on March 21, 1934. All nonsupervisory personnel were permitted to participate, and they were asked to choose between Federal Labor Union No. 18839 and the Houde Welfare and Athletic Association, which had requested, "nay, almost demanded," a position on the ballot. The victory went to the U.A.W. by a vote of 1105 to 674, with four hundred not voting. Peo, as could have been expected, raised some questions about the payroll list he had been asked to submit and about the election rules and the nature of the ballot, but Shortal was in no mood to listen to any more of the Houde official's complaints. "It appears somewhat evident to the Board," he wrote to Peo, "that your Company has created obstacles and has developed technicalities before and since the perfectly legal election...." [55]

If Shortal or the N.L.B. thought that the results of an election conducted under the auspices of an agency of the United States government would cause Peo to retreat, they seriously underestimated their adversary. In meetings with union officials following the election, Peo informed them that he would accept the union committee as representing "a certain group" of the company's employees who had selected them, but not as the exclusive bargaining agency for the plant's workers, that he would continue to bargain with minority groups, that he would not recognize the federal labor union as such nor would he negotiate with it, and that he would not sign an agreement with any employee representatives regarding wages, hours, and working conditions or the question of recognition.[56] The federal government had begun a battle with the Houde management that was still to be unresolved when the N.I.R.A. was declared unconstitutional.

As in the Houde plant so in the Bendix plant in South Bend, Indiana, and in some of the parts plants in Toledo, U.A.W. locals were able to establish themselves in some strength, but like automobile locals elsewhere they had to contend with the implacable opposition of the employers. The Bendix Products Corporation, manufacturer of a variety of automobile parts and accessories, was, like the Houde Company, subject to the automobile parts code. Its employees had not previously been unionized, but the enactment of the N.I.R.A. led late in July 1933 to the chartering of Federal Labor Union No. 18347 for the Bendix plant workers. Like so many other concerns, the company sought to counter this threat to its customary prerogatives by launching a company union. It informed its workers on September 12 that in compliance with the request of "a large number of employees," it was recommending a plan designed to provide "a more effective contact" between employer and employee regarding conditions of work. Carl Shipley, who became president of the U.A.W. local in October, complained that in the election of company-union representatives, the workers were "coerced and intimidated against to the extreme." From the U.A.W.'s point of view, the company union acquired a reputation for "no dues, no benefits; just a lot of bull!" [57]

In the months following the employee-association election, the U.A.W. local charged that the management was discriminating against union members, including the local's "executive backbone," and that it was continuing to promote the company union. Dissatisfied with the company's behavior, the union early in January 1934 petitioned the N.L.B. for an election, and in the succeeding weeks it threatened to strike if the company did not mend its ways. Undoubtedly aware that perhaps one-half of its employees were union members or had applied for union membership and that a strike might cause it to lose business at a time when production was rising, the Bendix management in the middle of February agreed to a pay increase of 5 per cent as of March 1 and an additional 5 per cent increase on June 1. The plant federal labor union had failed to secure a signed agreement, but it had nevertheless established itself in strength, and it was destined to play an important part in the movement to form an international union of automobile workers.[58]

Whereas the U.A.W. locals in the Houde and Bendix plants only threatened to strike, Federal Labor Union No. 18384 actually brought out the workers in several of Toledo's parts plants in a brief strike in February 1934. Local 18384 was unique among the U.A.W. locals in that it served not one but rather all of Toledo's numerous automobile parts and main plants. Working conditions in these plants were, on the whole, inferior to conditions in the Detroit auto plants, and wages in particular were "strikingly lower." [59]

At the beginning of February 1934, the inexperienced and somewhat confused business agent of the Toledo local, Thomas J. Ramsey, failed in an effort to secure a contract and recognition from the Spicer Manufacturing Company, the principal producer outside of the main plants themselves of the universal joints used in automobiles. Charles A. Dana, the president of the company and a second cousin of the famous newspaperman of the same name, informed Philip C. Nash, the president of Toledo University and the chairman of the Toledo Sub-Regional Labor Board, that the company had five different associations of workers in its plant and had always tried "to satisfy their ideas of how we should best conduct this Industry," but apparently he had no intention of negotiating with "outsiders" like Ramsey. As a matter of fact, Dana decided sometime after Ramsey approached him to set up an inside union in his plant, and he arranged to have representatives for this organization selected on February 22.[60]

Dana's action triggered a strike by the U.A.W. local the next day not only at the Spicer plant, where about two thousand workers walked out, but also at the Logan Gear Company, the Bingham Stamping and Tool Company, and the Electric Auto-Lite Company, where an additional fifteen hundred to sixteen hundred workers quit their jobs. The principal demands of the union were recognition and a wage increase to sixty-five cents per hour—the local alleged that the companies were paying but forty cents per hour to common labor, the normal parts code minimum for male labor, and forty to fifty cents per hour to skilled workers.[61] The strike was generally effective at the Spicer plant and only somewhat less so at Bingham and Logan Gear, but Electric Auto-Lite was hardly affected by the walkout, and Ramsey himself on February 24, although he changed his mind later, urged the few striking Auto-Lite workers to return to their jobs. The strike was supported by the I.A.M., the International Brotherhood of Blacksmiths, Drop Forgers, and Helpers, and, despite the "frosty reception" accorded it by the A.F. of L. craft unions, the M.E.S.A.[62]

Although all four employers declared themselves unable to meet the union's wage demands,[63] Logan Gear and Bingham began hiring new workers at a 5 per cent increase on February 27, and Auto-Lite put a similar increase into effect the next day. The Spicer Company, which alone of the four firms had been completely shut down, announced on February 27 that it would reopen the next day and that it too would increase wage rates by 5 per cent and would also make adjustments in base rates and group prices which would further augment the take-home pay of its employees.

The granting of a 5 per cent wage increase which would be effective until April 1 and which would permit a careful consideration of the wage problem in the meantime had first been suggested to the disputants by Nash but had been rejected by the union. Ramsey, who had called the proffered pay boost "a lousy, measly" increase and had said that he would "hope to be stricken dead" before presenting such "a contemptible offer" to the strikers, had second thoughts on the question, however. With the aid of Department of Labor Conciliator

Hugh D. Friel, who had played an important part in arranging the settlement, and with the possible knowledge that the employers were prepared to break the strike if it continued any longer, he persuaded the workers at a mass meeting of February 28 to accept peace terms calling for the 5 per cent increase and for certain additional adjustments at the Spicer plant, which raised the total wage increase at that plant, according to Dana, to 12 per cent. All those who had been working on February 23 were to be considered employees and were to be returned to their old jobs not later than March 5 unless the shop committee of the particular plant agreed that this could not be done because of a loss of orders, a change of work, or the like. Negotiations were to take place between the companies and the federal labor union in an effort to work out improved standards that would become effective on April 1. Any increase in wages beyond the 5 per cent that might be agreed upon by that date was to be applied retroactively to March 1 for the machinists and the blacksmiths. There was to be no strike or lockout at any of the plants "so long as peaceful methods for adjusting differences have not been exhausted." [64]

The agreement fell short of meeting the demands originally advanced by the U.A.W., but it left the local in a strong position in the Spicer, Logan Gear, and Bingham plants. The union had failed to make an impression on the Electric Auto-Lite plant, but within a few months it would be ready once again to test its strength, in dramatic fashion, against this most important of the Toledo automobile parts companies.

As in Toledo, resort to the strike weapon was instrumental in firmly establishing unionism at the Nash Motors Company plants in Kenosha and Racine, Wisconsin, and the Seaman Body plant in Milwaukee, which made bodies for Nash cars. The labor difficulties in the Nash-Seaman Body complex came to the fore initially at the Kenosha Nash plant, where members of Federal Labor Union No. 19008 were disturbed because of the company's decision late in October 1933 to introduce a company union of the Chrysler type but more importantly because of the new piece-work schedules applied to the final assembly line. The Nash management in establishing the production line for the new 1934 models had set an hourly rate for the workers on the line, but as the line began to operate more smoothly, the company introduced a new piece rate. Although Charles W. Nash, the chairman of the board of Nash Motors, alleged that the workers on the final assembly line on the afternoon shift earned 17½ per cent more the first day the piece rate was in effect than they had earned on the previous hourly rate and pleaded with the men to give the new rate a fair trial, about two hundred men on the final assembly line, complaining that the piece rates had substantially cut their earnings, went on strike on November 9. Nash thereupon shut down the entire plant, which idled about three thousand workers.[65]

The dispute was mediated by John A. Lapp, the secretary of the Chicago Regional Labor Board, who succeeded in effecting a settlement on November 21. Nash agreed to recognize any committee chosen by the company's employees to work out arrangements for the resumption of work or to deal with future difficulties, to bargain with a committee of three selected to represent the final assembly line and with similar committees in other departments of the plant, to refer to an arbitrator acceptable to both sides any point on which management and a workers' committee were unable to agree, and to restore each of the strikers to the job that he had held before the walkout. It was also agreed that the piece-rate schedule should be given a ten-day trial.[66]

Following the return of the Kenosha strikers to their jobs, the hourly earnings of the assembly-line workers increased substantially,[67] but the dispute between Nash and the final assembly line remained unresolved. The company and the local decided late in December to arbitrate their differences, but they could not agree among themselves on the arbitrator, and the Chicago Regional Labor Board was unable to break the deadlock. The union president, Eugene Stauder, complained to the board that the company was simply "dodging" and, ominously, that it "might as well be taught a lesson." The executive secretary of the board later agreed with the local that the Nash management had "not been sincere" in the implementation of the November agreement.[68]

While the Kenosha local remained at loggerheads with the Nash management, the Racine and Seaman Body locals, which had been ready to support the Kenosha workers during the November strike,[69] also attempted to secure an increase in wages. Submitting identical demands to their employers, both locals at the end of January requested a 20 per cent wage increase, a sixty cent per hour minimum, certain changes in the group pay system, and employer adherence to the principle of seniority. It might have been anticipated that both Nash and Seaman Body would find it difficult to meet these demands since both companies had lost money in 1932 and 1933, and the sale of Nash cars had fallen from over fifty thousand in 1930 to a mere 11,353 in 1933. The Seaman Body management explained to the union representatives that the 57½ cent average hourly rate of its employees was above the rate paid for similar work in Milwaukee and that it simply could not afford to pay any more until increased volume cut unit costs.[70]

Rebuffed in its demands, the Seaman local voted on February 16 to strike, a decision that brought Carl Steffensen of the Chicago board hurrying to Milwaukee in an effort to mediate the dispute at both the Seaman Body and the Racine Nash plants. Steffensen helped to arrange an agreement calling for a 10 per cent increase [71] at Seaman Body and for the recognition of seniority in so far as this was consistent with the merit clause of the automobile code. Since Nash was its sole customer, Seaman Body made its acceptance of these terms contingent on the Racine employees remaining at their jobs.

The Nash management, reluctant to undergo a strike at a time when it was bringing out its new 1934 models and was hoping to increase its meager share of the automobile market, indicated its willingness to grant its Racine and Kenosha employees the same terms as Seaman Body offered its employees, but the Racine local was dissatisfied with this partial victory and called its members out on strike on February 21. The Seaman Body local followed suit five days later, and the Kenosha local on March 1. Within a short time, twelve hundred employees were on strike at the Racine plant, sixteen hundred at the Kenosha plant, and eighteen hundred at Seaman Body. The Nash management made no real effort to operate its plants, with the result that the strike was pursued in orderly fashion in both Racine and Kenosha. Seaman Body, on the other hand, tried to keep its plant open with a much reduced force of workers. This caused the union to engage in mass picketing of the plant, which led to frequent clashes between the police and the pickets and between strikers and nonstrikers.[72]

The three locals, which had agreed to remain on strike until an agreement acceptable to all of them had been effected, now confronted the management with a common set of demands. In addition to the wage and seniority proposals they had previously advanced, they now requested the two companies to recognize a general union committee in each plant for collective-bargaining purposes [73] and to promise not to discriminate against union workers and to give them preference in rehiring. To these demands were added a separate set of proposals submitted by the I.A.M. local in the Kenosha plant on behalf of its members.[74]

Demonstrating the potency of the strike weapon as a means of organizing the unorganized, the Nash and Seaman locals increased their membership during the early days of March. At a conference on March 9 at Kenosha, P. A. Donoghue, who had been dispatched to the scene of the trouble by the N.L.B., informed Seaman Body and Nash management representatives that a check of union membership lists indicated that the union committees represented a majority of the workers in the three plants and that in accordance with the principles set forth by the N.L.B., the companies would have to negotiate with the union representatives for all the employees in their plants. This advice was no more acceptable to Nash and Seaman Body officials than it was to other automobile manufacturers.[75]

The official reply of the Nash and Seaman Body managements to the union proposals was submitted to the employees of the three plants on March 16. Both companies, following the lead of automobile employers elsewhere, stated that they would bargain with the union committees in their plants as representing only those workers who had authorized these officials to speak for them. The companies indicated once again their willingness to increase wages 10 per cent. They promised not to discriminate against employees because of their participation in the strike or their union membership but rejected as illegal the proposal that union men be given preference in rehiring. The three locals rejected the reply to their demands as ignoring the "collectivity of the workers," [76] and here the matter rested while the attention of labor and management in the three plants turned to Washington, where the N.L.B., General Johnson, and the President himself were taking turns at trying to stave off a threatened large-scale strike in the automobile industry involving some of the major producers. Efforts to settle the Nash and Seaman Body strikes would be resumed only after the greater threat to peace in the automobile industry had been dispelled.

As at Nash Motors and Seaman Body so at the White Motor Company plant in Cleveland an aggressive A.F. of L. federal labor union was able to take advantage of the precarious economic position of an independent motor vehicle producer and, by militant action, establish itself as one of the strongest locals in the automobile industry. White Motor, a truck manufacturer, had been losing money steadily since 1930, and during the first six months of 1933 had sustained a loss of $2 million. Despite this fact, the company, in August 1933, in conformity with N.A.C.C. policy, had boosted wage rates 10 per cent. Early in December 1933, at a time when the company was employing approximately twenty-five hundred workers, Federal Labor Union No. 18463, which seems to have been infiltrated by communists or at least by communist sympathizers, voted to strike unless the company raised wages, improved working conditions, and recognized the union. The management succeeded in convincing the local that it could not afford a general wage increase at that time; but it committed itself in an agreement reached with the union on December 18 to readjust wage rates on classified jobs with a view to removing any wage inequities, and to pay the day rate for all hours worked, including hours in which piece-work earnings fell below the minimum hourly rate. Most important of all, the company agreed to deal with all duly appointed or elected representatives of the employees, including the shop committee of the U.A.W. local.[77]

The cautious strike policy of the A.F. of L. did not sit well with at least some members of the White Motor local, and President George Lehman informed Green on February 27, 1934, that it had been necessary for A.F. of L. organizer George A. McKinnon "to go to bat" for the A.F. of L. president in order to counter criticism of the Federation. Green had advised caution when the local, on its own initiative, scheduled a strike for February 28, 1934, should the company not grant a 20 per cent wage increase. The strike was averted when White agreed to raise the minimum rate of common labor from forty-three to fifty-one cents, the rate of the semiskilled from sixty to sixty-seven cents, and the rates of workers in the top brackets by five cents. When asked whether the threatened strike had been authorized by Green, the chairman of the strike committee, Wyndham Mortimer, later to become a U.A.W. vice-president and described by Benjamin Stolberg as "a Stalinist from the very beginning," allegedly replied, "Hell no! We did not expect him to. We took the right in our own hands. We had enough of his telegrams telling us to do nothing." [78] Mortimer's local, as it turned out, was to play a key role in the dramatic events that culminated in the decision of the U.A.W. to leave the A.F. of L. and to throw in its lot with the fledging Committee for Industrial Organization.

The efforts of the A.F. of L. to organize the automobile workers outside of Michigan were by no means confined to the plants of the independents and the automobile parts companies. The Ford Motor Company, as we have seen, had to contend with strikes at its Chester and Edgewater plants, and G.M. similarly had to deal with the grievances of newly formed federal labor unions in the non-Michigan sector of its far-flung empire, particularly, in the months before April 1934, in St. Louis and Atlanta.

The Chevrolet and Fisher Body workers in St. Louis and Atlanta were each served by a single federal labor union. The St. Louis U.A.W. local appears to have been the stronger of the two, with a membership as of August 30, 1933, consisting of a majority of the twenty-five hundred to three thousand employees then at work and probably a majority of the thirty-five hundred to forty-five hundred workers engaged during the period of peak production. Like the U.A.W. locals in so many other plants, both of the federal labor unions began complaining soon after their formation that management was discriminating against union members in layoffs and rehiring, was coercing employees to join the plant company unions, and was refusing to bargain with union officers. Both locals took their complaints to the regional labor board in their area, but management refused to attend the board hearings.

The St. Louis Regional Labor Board handed down a decision on February 13, 1934, that supported the St. Louis local's charges, but the union was soon protesting that neither company was complying with the ruling. It requested the N.L.B. to compel the two companies to observe the decision, and it also petitioned for an N.L.B. representation election. The Atlanta Regional Labor Board drafted but did not make public a decision that accepted the Atlanta union's complaints against Fisher Body; and, in response to the local's petition, it ordered an election for the Chevrolet plant. Before anything further could be done to implement the St. Louis and Atlanta decisions, however, jurisdiction over labor matters in the automobile manufacturing industry had been taken out of the hands of the N.L.B. and its regional boards and vested in the A.L.B.[79]

IV

Early in February 1934, as dissatisfaction mounted among the U.A.W. locals because of alleged employer discrimination against union members and the failure of the unionists to secure the kind of recognition from management that they sought, William Collins decided that some "aggressive action" by the A.F. of L. in the industry was necessary both to strengthen union morale and to demonstrate the superiority of the independent union over the company union. On February 6, consequently, he advised the U.A.W. locals to seek a 20 per cent wage increase from their employers and also to urge Congress to provide for labor representation on the automobile code authority and for the enforcement of the decisions of the N.L.B. and the provisions of the automobile code. When the automobile companies failed to meet the union demands—"they might as well reach for the moon," Knudsen later said of the wage request—or to redress union grievances, strike sentiment began to gather strength among the organized automobile workers, who were anxious, as new unionists are apt to be, to test their strength against their employers. Conciliator Robert H. Pilkington informed the N.L.B. at the end of February that labor leaders in the Michigan auto centers were having difficulty restraining union members from going on strike. Pilkington feared that "a strike among any great number of persons in any shop would precipitate a strike in all of them." [80]

When the fourth conference of officers of the Michigan U.A.W. locals gathered in Lansing on March 4, 1934, strike talk was in the air, and it was decided that four of the locals that were in "fairly good shape," namely the Buick, Flint Fisher Body No. 1 and No. 2, and Hudson locals, should immediately present wage and hour demands to their employers and should call for a reply within forty-eight hours. [81] The officers and the rank and file were deadly serious about striking if these demands were not met, and there was a strong desire to spread the strike to all the plants where the U.A.W. had been unable to gain recognition, but William Collins had no intention of permitting a strike to be called. A chronic pessimist about union prospects in the industry and about the potentiality of the strike weapon and convinced that the automobile workers lacked the necessary funds and leadership to stage a successful walkout against the giants of the industry, Collins was actually using the threat of a work stoppage in this key industry to bring about federal intervention and a government-sponsored settlement that would give the automobile workers courage. [82]

Collins, who had already asked the N.L.B. on March 1 to send in an investigator lest it prove impossible to avoid a strike, therefore quickly called the threatening situation to the attention of the President and warned him that if strikes were called against the four plants, there was a "serious possibility" that other automobile plants would also become involved. Making no reference to the specific demands of the four locals, Collins charged the employers with the violation of Section 7(a) and the automobile code and appealed to the President for whatever assistance he could give the automobile workers in their effort to secure the objectives of the N.I.R.A. and particularly the right to organize and to bargain collectively. Collins' warning to the President had the desired effect. The N.L.B., at the President's behest and on the advice of Conciliator James F. Dewey, who in response to Collins' request of March 1 had been sent to Detroit by the board to investigate the situation, assumed jurisdiction of the case on March 5 and by promising that hearings on the dispute would be held in Washington on March 14, and because "the President had asked it," was able to get the impending strikes postponed. [83]

On the eve of the hearings the board of directors of the N.A.C.C., in a move calculated to win favor with the administration, the public, and the automobile workers, announced that in response to the recent request of the President and General Johnson to the codified industries, they had recommended to Chamber members that they reduce average weekly hours from forty to thirty-six, effective March 31, and that they increase wages by an equivalent 10 per cent.[84] This decision helped to remove the wage-and-hour question from the automobile labor dispute, but as Collins' telegram of March 7 to the President indicated, Section 7(a) rather than specific bread-and-butter demands had become the crucial issue in contention in so far as the U.A.W. was concerned.

At the automobile hearings of March 14 and 15, described by the *New York Times* as "the most important conference held under the auspices of the Labor Board," Collins and the representatives of ten U.A.W. locals testified that the automobile manufacturers had discriminated against union workers, had imposed company unions on their employees, and had refused to confer with union representatives. Collins called for the holding of N.L.B. elections in the automobile plants and the application of the principle of majority rule to the selection of employee representatives for collective-bargaining purposes. Representatives of the company unions in the Buick and Flint Chevrolet plants, who had been sent to Washington at company expense, sought to refute the arguments of union representatives regarding the ineffectiveness of the employee associations in the industry.

Management's part in the hearing was limited to the reading of statements by William S. Knudsen, by then executive vice-president of G.M., and A. E. Barit, vice-president and treasurer of Hudson, both of whom appeared "informally" only, out of "respect" for the N.L.B Knudsen stated that G.M. was prepared to deal with all cases of alleged discrimination or code violation on their merits, but "so far as we know, there are none such." G.M., he declared, would bargain with union representatives for the employees they could prove they represented, but despite the N.L.B. decision in the Hall Baking case, it would not recognize the union as such, nor would it enter into a contract with it on behalf of its employees. Challenging the authority of the N.L.B., Knudsen flatly asserted that G.M. must "decline to make any commitment or accept any obligation with respect to any election that may be resorted to." Barit indicated that his company viewed the issues before the N.L.B. in much the same way that G.M. did.[85]

The recalcitrant attitude of management placed the N.L.B. in a difficult position. "You are sitting right on top of a volcano right now, aren't you?" R. C. Jacobson of the Chicago regional board wrote to Benedict Wolf of the N.L.B. The board could not mediate the dispute because management refused to co-operate with it. Had the board decided to hold an election in any of the main plants, its decision almost certainly would have been appealed by the employers to the courts, and the representation issue in the industry would have remained unresolved pending judicial determination of the case. Perplexed as to the course it should follow, the N.L.B. met the challenge to its authority and prestige by doing nothing, which led General Johnson to intervene and to take the dispute out of its hands altogether. Johnson explained that although only two companies had appeared before the N.L.B., the strike threatened the entire industry, and he had therefore decided to submit the matter to the industry's code authority so that the difficulty might be composed "not only as to the two companies and not only as to this occasion but as to all companies and other occasions that might arise." [86]

The automobile companies were concerned at this time not only about the threat of a strike in the industry but also with the possibility that the issue as between them and their employees regarding the nature of labor relations in the industry would be resolved in favor of the A.F. of L. by the enactment of Senator Wagner's Labor Disputes Bill, which had been introduced in the Senate on March 1, 1934, and which answered in a manner satisfactory to organized labor most of the questions raised by the vague language of Section 7(a). The measure asserted the right of employees to organize and to join labor organizations and specified and made illegal certain unfair labor practices on the part of employers that might circumscribe this right. Employers could not impair the rights of employees by "interference, influence, restraint, favor, coercion, or lockout, or by any other means." They could not refuse to recognize or to deal with employee representatives or "to fail to exert every reasonable effort to make and maintain agreements with such representatives." The employer-dominated company union was in effect declared illegal, and the practice of discrimination to encourage membership or nonmembership in any organization was prohibited. Closed-shop agreements with a union representing the majority of the employees in a given unit were specifically sanctioned. An independent tripartite National Labor Board was provided for in the bill, and its orders were made enforceable in the district courts. The board was authorized to settle representation disputes by holding elections or by "any other appropriate method," but the measure did not specify whether majority rule was to apply in the choice of representatives.[87]

In an effort "to throw the full weight of the Chamber" against a measure regarded as "destructive of the best interests of the industry and the public," the N.A.C.C. on March 12 established an operations committee of ten members to head up an extensive public-relations campaign. The committee utilized the services of the advertising firm, Campbell-Ewald Company, and at one time a staff of twenty-two persons was engaged in executing the committee's plans. "Every conceivable avenue of approach to the problem," the committee accurately reported, "was explored and every available media pressed into service." During the next three weeks the committee, in combating the Wagner Bill and in defending the position of the automobile industry in the pending automobile labor dispute, was responsible for the mounting of three newspaper advertisement campaigns and four radio activities; the issuance of nine press releases; the distribution of more than 1,250,000 handbills and pieces of mail; the printing of two extra editions of the *Automotive Daily News,* which were distributed to thirty thousand automobile dealers, seven thousand newspaper editors, six hundred thousand automobile stockholders, and other "influential and interested people"; and the preparation of a six-page analysis of the bill as it affected small printshops, which was distributed to thirteen thousand newspaper publishers over the signature of the Newspaper Editorial Association. By April 10 the committee had spent almost $185,000 in its effort to gain acceptance for the N.A.C.C.'s views of what was proper and improper in the sphere of labor-management relations.[88]

The N.A.C.C. contended in its attack on the Wagner Bill that the A.F. of L., having failed to persuade employees to join the Federation and to compel industry to recognize it as the spokesman for the nation's workers, was seeking now to force unionization by law. If it succeeded, the union card rather than merit would become the basis for employment, and every person in the United States would be placed "virtually at the mercy" of the A.F. of L. The Wagner Bill, which imposed penalties on employers but ignored the coercive tactics of unions, was an open invitation to the closed shop and "labor dictatorship."

The N.A.C.C. coupled its criticism of the Wagner Bill with a sharp attack on the position of the A.F. of L. in the pending automobile labor dispute. The Federation was seeking by the strike route to accomplish the same results in the automobile industry as the Wagner Bill was likely to produce in the country as a whole. The automobile manufacturers were neither coercing their employees nor discriminating against them and, as the law required, were willing to meet the duly accredited representatives of any group on behalf of the members of that group. The A.F. of L., by contrast, was seeking to impose itself on all the automobile workers and was trying to make it appear that the N.I.R.A. intended it to be the spokesman for labor as a whole. It was not really interested in the success of the automobile industry and wished to represent the workers only to extract dues from them and to dictate their working conditions. "The issue," the N.A.C.C. stated, "is union domination." [89]

The A.F. of L., although unable to match the expenditure of the N.A.C.C., replied in kind to the verbal barrage of the employers. The real issue, said William Green in rebuttal to the N.A.C.C.'s definition as to what was at stake, was not union domination but whether automobile workers were free to organize and to bargain collectively through representatives of their own choosing without coercion by employers. The A.F. of L. repeated the charges put forward at the N.L.B. automobile hearings that the employers in the industry were violating Section 7(a) with impunity, and contended that the Wagner Bill was therefore necessary to secure for the workers the rights guaranteed to them by the N.I.R.A. and the automobile code.[90]

The exchange of propaganda blows between the A.F. of L. and the N.A.C.C. was but the public expression of the differences between the two antagonists which General Johnson was seeking privately to compose. In order to permit Johnson to arrange a settlement, the union representatives who had testified before the N.L.B. recommended to their locals on March 16 that strike action be deferred until March 21. When Johnson, however, failed to find a solution to the dispute that was satisfactory to both sides and as additional U.A.W. locals voted to strike, Collins on March 19 let it be known that the only way the scheduled walkout could now be avoided was through "the direct intervention of the President." The next day President Roosevelt stepped into the dispute. He told Johnson to invite a committee of automobile manufacturers to Washington, and he himself wired Collins to defer action until the President could confer with both sides.[91]

Collins carried Roosevelt's message to a conference of U.A.W. leaders meeting in Pontiac on March 20 and gained their assent to place the union case before the President. He and his aides, however, still had to contact the automobile centers where walkouts were scheduled to convince the U.A.W. locals to defer strike action. The workers, who were gathered in mass meetings, were told that a request from President Roosevelt simply could not be refused. "You have a wonderful man down there in the White House," Collins told the Hudson meeting, "and he is trying hard to raise wages and working conditions." The unionists heeded the appeal of their leaders because, as one U.A.W. official declared, "The President has given labor its first chance in many years, and we are endeavoring to show our gratitude to him by agreeing to his request." Although the A.F. of L. leaders did not really want a strike and were not prepared to conduct one, it is doubtful if they could have stayed the scheduled work stoppage had not President Roosevelt personally intervened.[92]

By the time the President acted, the automobile labor dispute had come to center on two issues: the form that employee representation should assume and the question of discrimination. The A.F. of L., as we have seen, contended that the representatives of a majority of the workers in a given plant, as determined by an N.L.B. election, should bargain for all the workers. The N.A.C.C., however, insisted that Section 7(a), properly interpreted, required the employers to deal with the accredited representatives of all groups in a plant, regardless of their size, and that individuals who desired to bargain for themselves also had a perfect right to do so. If an organization wished to establish its right to bargain for its members, it must submit a membership list to the employer. Although the question of lists had seemingly been disposed of by the N.L.B.'s decision of March 8 in the Houde case and the issue of majority rule by the President's executive order of February 1, 1934, and the N.L.B. decision of March 1 in the Denver Tramway case, the automobile manufacturers made it perfectly clear that they simply would not accept the principle of majority rule for which the A.F. of L. was contending. "We cannot yield on this issue," Macauley informed the President on March 21, "and if that means a strike, a strike will have to come." [93]

With regard to the issue of discrimination, the N.A.C.C. proposed that charges of discrimination should be brought before a three-man industrial-relations committee appointed by the code authority, with its findings subject to appeal to a board of review composed of three men, not identified with the industry, appointed by the N.R.A. The proposal was a modification of the N.A.C.C. plan for a labor complaints agency advanced in January 1934. The A.F. of L., for its part, wanted the adjudication of discrimination cases entirely divorced from the code authority, on which it had no representation, and vested in a government-appointed joint industrial-relations board whose decisions would be final.[94]

As a mediator in the automobile dispute, the President could not help but be concerned with the potential danger to the recovery program posed by the threatened automobile strike. As *Iron Age* declared, the automobile industry was "the spearhead in the Roosevelt administration's drive toward recovery." One-quarter of the national increase in payrolls between January and February 1934 was accounted for by the automobile industry alone. Since the President at that time, as Francis Biddle has suggested, placed the short-term need of spurring recovery ahead of the long-term desirability of establishing a more satisfactory relationship between employer and employee in American society, it was likely that he would do whatever he could to stave off a strike in the vital automobile industry.[95]

The President had also to weigh the relative strength of the two antagonists. Although March was a month of heavy production in the industry, the manufacturers seemed determined not to recognize the A.F. of L. "as such" nor to contract with it on behalf of their employees, even if this meant a strike. Against this determination of the manufacturers the President had few weapons to employ other than to threaten to support the Wagner Bill, then before the Senate and likely to pass if made an administration measure. It is possible, although he denied it, that the President hinted to the automobile manufacturers that their failure to accept a settlement would make the passage of the bill more likely.[96]

It must have been obvious to Roosevelt, who, as Francis Biddle has observed, had "a strong sense of the incidence of power," that the bargaining strength of the A.F. of L. in the industry was considerably less than that of management and that the A.F. of L. leadership was less determined to stand by its position regardless of the consequences. Although the Federation had developed fairly strong locals in the G.M. plants in Flint, it had, with the exception of the Hudson Motor Car Company, made very little progress in the main plants in Detroit. The A.F. of L. claimed sixty thousand federal labor union members among the 470,000 hourly workers in the combined motor vehicle industries as of March 1934, but the paid-up membership of the U.A.W. at the time was actually just a little over thirty-two thousand, and this total, it must be remembered, included membership in the various parts plants and in main plants not directly involved in the dispute.[97] On the other hand, the dues-paying membership figure unquestionably understated the number of workers who were in some way attached to the U.A.W. and the number who would have supported it had a strike actually come. Thus James Dewey, after sizing up the strike prospects in Detroit and Flint, advised the Conciliation Service that "If this situation breaks it will involve a tremendous number of people." [98]

Although the outlook for the A.F. of L. was thus not quite as bleak as the paid-up membership figures for the U.A.W. locals indicated, the cautious President Green, unable to determine the number of workers who would actually walk out if a strike were called and how these untested unionists and their friends would conduct themselves under pressure, was in agreement with Collins in preferring a settlement that would yield the U.A.W. some gain to a work stoppage that might cause it to lose everything. President Roosevelt must have been aware that the A.F. of L. leadership, fearful of the consequences of an unsuccessful strike, was prepared to accept half a loaf, or even less. Richard Byrd, one of the key figures in the union delegation that negotiated with the President, later stated with some truth that the union leaders accepted the settlement "because we knew we would be licked if we didn't take it." [99]

The auto manufacturers were represented in Washington by Alvan Macauley, Alfred P. Sloan, Jr., Walter Chrysler, Roy Chapin, Charles Nash, Donaldson Brown, John T. Smith, a G.M. attorney, and Nicholas Kelley, counsel for Chrysler. The union delegation of twenty-eight, headed by Green and Collins, included representatives from fifteen different U.A.W. locals. The negotiations continued from March 21 to March 25, but the manufacturers, who did not share Johnson's willingness to "sit down with the Devil himself, if . . . it would make hell any cooler," refused throughout to meet union representatives face to face. Both sides met frequently with Johnson, and in addition President Roosevelt, who devoted a great deal of his time to the matter, saw the manufacturers twice and some or all of the union men on three occasions. [100]

On the issue of discrimination, the employers, faced with A.F. of L. opposition, receded from their original position with regard to an adjudicating agency linked to the code authority; and the final settlement that was agreed upon, in addition to barring discrimination against employees "because of their labor affiliations or for any other unfair or unjust reason," provided that questions of discrimination would be passed on by a board—subsequently established as the Automobile Labor Board—composed of a labor representative, an industry representative, and a neutral arbiter. [101] The board was to be set up by the N.R.A. and was to be responsible to the President. The N.A.C.C. was insistent that the labor representative must not be a member of the A.F. of L., allegedly because of the minority status of the Federation in the industry. The union delegation naturally objected to this condition, and the issue was ultimately compromised. Although no mention was made of the point in the settlement, it was understood by both sides that the union group would nominate the labor representative but that he would not be an "outside" organizer like Collins. This arrangement was probably quite satisfactory to the officials of the federal labor unions who were associated with Green and Collins in the negotiations. Some of them not only thought that Collins was more a handicap than an aid to them in securing their objectives, but they also resented his efforts to exclude from the union delegation the representatives from the locals at the Seaman Body, Nash, St. Louis Fisher Body and Chevrolet, and Cleveland Fisher Body plants who were present in Washington but who had not been invited there by Collins as part of the official union delegation.[102]

Closely related to the issue of discrimination was that of seniority or, more accurately, job tenure, for if the manner by which an automobile worker acquired tenure could be defined, it would be possible to determine with greater objectivity than previously had been true whether discrimination had been practiced by management in the layoff and rehiring of individual employees. The A.F. of L. delegation would have liked length of service to be the sole determinant in the calculation of job-tenure rights, whereas the automobile manufacturers, who had fought so hard to include a merit clause in their code, regarded the efficiency of the worker, as determined by his employer, as the most important consideration in establishing the order of layoff and rehiring. The President, for his part, thought that marital and family status should be a major factor in job-tenure calculations. The terms agreed upon represented a synthesis of these three positions. The settlement provided that in reductions and increases of force, "such human relationships as married men with families shall come first and then seniority, individual skill and efficient service." After these factors had been taken into account, "no greater proportion of outside union employees similarly situated" were to be laid off than of "other employees." In his amplifying remarks accompanying the settlement, the President declared that "we have for the first time written into an industrial settlement a definite rule for the equitable handling of reductions and increases of forces."[103] He might also have noted that by placing dependency and length of service ahead of efficiency, the order of layoff and rehiring specified in the settlement seemingly contravened, or at least modified, the merit clause of the automobile code.

The thorniest problem in the negotiations, as could have been anticipated, was the definition of the phrase "representatives of their own choosing" as it was used in Section 7(a). Despite the protection against discrimination afforded union members by the settlement, the union group remained reluctant to submit membership lists to management in order to establish representation rights. Since the union representatives did, however, indicate a willingness to turn over such lists to the President, it was finally agreed that the new Automobile Labor Board, which would be responsible to the President, should have access to both membership lists and payrolls. The board was to pass on all questions of representation as well as of discharge and discrimination, and its decisions were to be final and binding on both sides. The settlement did not specifically state that the board would determine representation by comparing lists and payrolls, but it would seem that this procedure rather than the holding of elections was contemplated. This was definitely to the disadvantage of the union since many employees who might have voted for the U.A.W. in an election could not be counted as union members [104] on the basis of a membership list.

The settlement also stated that there would be no basis for a claim of discrimination unless membership lists had been disclosed to an employer but that no such disclosure should be made "without specific direction of the President." This provision was puzzling to say the least. Although discrimination against union members was seemingly illegal under Section 7(a) and was specifically forbidden by the settlement, an automobile worker, apparently, could not validly claim that he had been the victim of discrimination unless a membership list had been presented to his employer and the President had ordered its disclosure.[105]

On the crucial question of the form that representation was to take, management, with the aid of the President, won a major victory. The concept of majority rule, about which Roosevelt, according to Francis Biddle, was never "enthusiastic," was rejected in favor of a system of proportional representation. The employers agreed to bargain with the "freely chosen representatives of groups," and if there was more than one group in a plant, each bargaining committee was to have "total membership pro rata to the number of men each member represents." Although this formula ran counter to his own executive order of February 1 and to the policy of the N.L.B., the President accepted the idea with apparent delight. In his amplifying remarks, he asserted that the settlement "charted a new course in social engineering in the United States." For the first time in a large industry, he declared, a basis had been provided on which "a more comprehensive, a more adequate and a more equitable system of industrial relations may be built than ever before. It is my hope that this system may develop into a kind of works council in industry in which all groups of employees, whatever may be their choice of organization or form of representation, may participate in joint conferences with their employers." The settlement itself did not specifically state whether there was to be a single bargaining committee in each plant with membership allocated to the various groups in proportion to their strength or whether each group was to meet separately with the employer. The President's amplifying remarks quoted above indicate that there was to be a single works council in each plant, but the union representatives, who claimed that they had not seen this statement prior to its publication, insisted that the President had assured them that each employee group would meet separately with management.[106]

The President's amplifying remarks suggest that he thought proportional representation a proper mode for collective bargaining in all industries, but he informed his press conference on June 15, 1934, that the question of minority representation was one that had "to be worked out in each individual case." [107]   The President was thus not really establishing general principles to govern the choice of representatives for collective bargaining but was simply attempting to find a solution for the particular problem that confronted him. As it worked out, the formula of proportional representation, despite the wishes of many employers, was applied to no other industry.

The President made the victory of the employers complete on the issue of representation and collective bargaining by complying with the N.A.C.C.'s request that he make it clear that the A.F. of L. was in error in implying to automobile workers that the federal government favored the Federation and that employees had to join a trade union to secure their rights under the N.I.R.A. "The government," the settlement stated, "favors no particular union or particular form of employee organization or representation. The government's only duty is to secure absolute and uninfluenced freedom of choice without coercion, restraint or intimidation from any source." Thus, the company union was, in effect, sanctioned as long as employees had not been coerced into joining it, and union coercion was put on a par with employer coercion. The President, moreover, indicated in his amplifying remarks that the N.I.R.A. was not a one-sided statute and that employee organizations had to recognize their responsibilities as well as to assert their rights. Industry's obligations were set forth in the law, and it was therefore not improper to expect employee organizations "to observe the same ethical and moral responsibilities." [108]

These remarks of the President and the settlement's reference to the protection of workers from coercion from any source might seem to support the view that the N.I.R.A. conferred obligations on management without commensurate benefits, but this was hardly in accord with the facts. Section 7(a) was, after all, placed in the act to balance the obvious privileges the statute accorded employers and was not designed to impose any obligations, moral or otherwise, on employee organizations.[109] The language of the settlement on this point and the President's amplifying statement appear to be more consonant with the thinking behind the Taft-Hartley Act of a later era, when unions had become powerful, than with the philosophy of the early New Deal years that led to the passage in 1935 of the National Labor Relations Act.

On March 25, with the dispute still unresolved, the manufacturers presented their final terms to Johnson in the form of a virtual ultimatum. The union delegation, for its part, wired the President that their constituents were pressing for "immediate and decisive action" and that a statement from the White House was "imperative to control the situation." The deadlock was broken by the President on that day, and he was able to announce the terms of the agreement. The President diplomatically praised both sides for their co-operation and declared the result to be "one of the most encouraging incidents of the Recovery Program." [110]

The employers, by their own admission, were "tremendously happy over the outcome in Washington." They had, of course, made concessions with regard to discrimination and job tenure, in agreeing to abide by the decisions of a labor board that was entirely divorced from the code authority and that would include an A.F. of L. member, and in assenting to the establishment of union representation rights on the basis of membership lists submitted to a government tribunal rather than to themselves; but they had gained far more than they had lost. Not only had a strike been averted in the midst of the production season, but the application of the majority-rule principle to the automobile industry had been staved off, and there apparently were to be no N.L.B.-type elections among the automobile workers. Moreover, the automobile manufacturers were now able to tell their employees that they did not have to join a union to secure the benefits of the N.I.R.A., that the President and the N.R.A. did not favor the outside union over the company union, and that employee-representation schemes were perfectly legal as long as they were freely adopted. The contrary claims of "unscrupulous" labor organizers, the automobile companies informed their employees, were "definitely, positively and unquestionably refuted and denied by the President himself. . . ." [111]

The A.F. of L. had less reason than the employers to be satisfied with the results of the settlement. It had, to be sure, made some gains,[112] but it had capitulated on the crucial questions of majority rule and elections and had, in effect, accepted the idea that self-organization did not necessarily mean an outside union.[113] William Green, for a time, although recognizing that it was not an "ideal agreement," defended the settlement in public and in private, and some members of the union delegation claimed "a tremendous victory"; but Arthur Law, the president of the Pontiac Fisher Body local, came closer to the truth when he stated that "The settlement is not what the boys wanted originally." Perhaps the President's most important contribution to the settlement was in persuading the union representatives to accept peace terms that were not in accord with their basic demands when the negotiations began. Arthur Greer, president of the Hudson local, Richard Byrd, secretary of the Pontiac local, John Bailey, president of the Buick local, and Al Cook, president of the Flint Fisher Body No. 1 local, who along with Green and Collins did most of the negotiating with the President for the union group, were flattered at being admitted into the Presidential presence and were impressed with Roosevelt's knowledge of labor affairs, his sympathy for their problems, and his assurances that the law would be enforced. From the union point of view, the "outstanding point of the settlement was that President Roosevelt would protect the workers." "He asked us to trust him," Byrd declared, "and we will." [114]

The resolution of the automobile labor dispute without a strike brought praise of the President in many circles. The *New York Times* thought that Roosevelt had given evidence of "diplomatic skill of the highest order." *Iron Age* commented on the President's "masterly handling of the situation" and his qualities of "leadership," and the *Nation,* which was critical of the terms of the agreement, called the President "the most skilful political prestidigitator the country has ever known." [115] Businessmen and sources friendly to the business point of view generally praised the terms of the settlement and expressed the hope that its principles would "control not only in this dispute but in future industrial disagreements" as well.[116]

Labor sources to the left of the A.F. of L. and left-wing opinion in general were critical of the settlement and viewed it as a defeat for the A.F. of L. Matthew Smith of the M.E.S.A. quite understandably complained that minorities of the highly skilled would "lose their identity" in any scheme of proportional representation, a fact which the craft-minded A.F. of L. seems to have overlooked. Smith described the settlement as "a Versailles Treaty of industry," which possessed "more germs for future industrial strife than [the] pre-dispute set-up." No one, however, quite matched the stream of abuse that poured forth from the A.W.U. and the communists, much discomfited that the threat of a large-scale automobile strike had been averted by the settlement. The settlement, the communists charged, was the result of "gigantic treachery" and was "a blow against the whole American working class." The A.F. of L. and the President, who were really "two sets of spokesmen" for the N.A.C.C., had co-operated to secure a victory for the auto manufacturers, and Roosevelt had revealed himself as "the company union strikebreaking president." The most accurate analysis of the settlement from a source friendly to organized labor came from the *New Republic,* which editorialized that the settlement had "saved" the automobile workers "from the consequences of possible defeat without giving them the fruits of possible victory." [117]

The settlement was particularly damaging to the prestige and influence of the N.L.B. Not only had a key dispute been taken out of its hands and the automobile manufacturing industry removed from its jurisdiction, but its precedents with regard to such vital matters as majority rule, the disclosure of membership lists, and election procedures had been completely ignored. Following the settlement, as Lorwin and Wubnig have pointed out, "the NLB lapsed into a lethargy and torpor from which it never emerged." [118]

The principles of the settlement were naturally seized on by the automobile manufacturers and industrial spokesmen in general to combat the pending Wagner Labor Disputes Bill. Attorney Hal H. Smith, representing the N.A.C.C., told the Senate Committee on Education and Labor, which was holding hearings on the measure, that the theory of the settlement was "radically" different from that of the Wagner Bill. He complained that the proposed new labor measure was one-sided in that it specified unfair labor practices by employers but not by employees, that it substituted a tribunal for the "free agreement" between parties that had produced the automobile settlement, and that the procedures to be followed by the tribunal were inequitable. Alfred P. Sloan, Jr., protested that the Wagner Bill, unlike the automobile settlement, failed to proscribe coercive methods by organized labor and failed to protect minorities, and he contended that separate labor boards for particular industries were preferable to a single national board that could not possibly be familiar with the specific problems of the nation's various businesses.

The attack on the pending bill by automobile spokesmen was seconded by James A. Emery for the N.A.M. and Henry I. Harriman for the United States Chamber of Commerce. Harriman told the Senate Committee on Education and Labor that the settlement made "entirely unnecessary" most of the provisions of the Wagner Bill, that all that was required now was an amendment to Section 7(a) protecting employees from coercion from any source, and that the principle of proportional representation should be applied generally.[119]

Realizing, as the President informed his press conference, that the automobile agreement had "changed the character" of things, Senator Wagner altered his measure to bring it more in line with the principles of the settlement. He revised the definition of unfair labor practices to permit an employer to introduce a company union, afforded permission to the states to prohibit union security arrangements regardless of the terms of the national statute, and added language asserting the right of individuals or minorities to present grievances to their employers. As finally reported out by Senator Walsh's Committee on Education and Labor on May 26, the bill, which was now entitled the National Industrial Adjustment Bill, permitted employers to initiate company unions and to pay company-union representatives subject to regulations drawn up by the Department of Labor. The obligation to bargain, included in Wagner's original bill, was now omitted. A five-man National Industrial Adjustment Board, to be set up within the Department of Labor, was authorized to use either majority rule or proportional representation as the basis for the selection of employee representatives. The measure specified that although the representatives of the majority might negotiate an agreement for a particular unit, the minority was to retain the right to present grievances to the employer.[120]

The N.A.C.C. was as little pleased with Walsh's National Industrial Adjustment Bill as it had been with Wagner's original measure. A five-man committee of automobile manufacturers visited President Roosevelt on June 5 and advised against new labor legislation which would depart from the principles of the automobile settlement and "which might confuse the existing labor situation." The President, who obviously believed that the support of the automobile and other major industries was essential to the success of his recovery program, assured the automobile manufacturers, as one of them put it, that "it was not his expectation to change our labor settlement."[121]

A mounting labor crisis in the steel industry convinced the President, however, that some new labor legislation was required, but he desired a noncontroversial measure that could be quickly enacted and would not antagonize business supporters of the N.I.R.A. The proper formula, as the President saw it, was embodied in Public Resolution

44, which was submitted to the Congress by the White House on June 13, quickly passed both houses, and was signed by the President on June 19, 1934. The new measure authorized the President to establish a board or boards to investigate the activities of employers or employees in any controversy arising under Section 7(a) or which obstructed or threatened to obstruct interstate commerce. The boards which the President might establish were authorized to conduct representation elections, the first time this procedure had been sanctioned by statute, but whether majority rule or proportional representation was to apply to the choice of representatives was not specified.

As authorized by Public Resolution 44, President Roosevelt on June 29, 1934, by executive order, created the National Labor Relations Board (N.L.R.B.). The board was empowered to investigate employer and employee activities as specified in the resolution, to hold elections, to make findings regarding complaints of the violation of Section 7(a), and, on the request of labor and management, to serve as "a board of voluntary arbitration." It was furthermore authorized to study the activities of other government labor boards to determine whether they should be designated as special boards as provided by P.R. 44, to receive reports from such boards, and to hear appeals from them if this was recommended by one of the boards, if there was a division of opinion on a board, or if the N.L.R.B. believed that a review would serve the public interest. The new board began to function on July 9, and the N.L.B. thereupon passed from the scene.[122] The exact relationship of the N.L.R.B. to the A.L.B. was not spelled out in the President's executive order of June 29, and it was to be some months before this problem was fully resolved.

The settlement, understandably enough, was viewed by General Johnson as a victory for the N.R.A. in its long-standing battle with the N.L.B. for jurisdiction over collective-bargaining issues and labor disputes arising under the N.I.R.A. and the codes. Late in March, therefore, the general issued an administrative order calling for the establishment in every codified industry of both labor complaints and labor disputes committees or, if the industry's code made no provision for either type of committee, a single industrial-relations committee to deal with both complaints and disputes. The order, however, as Lorwin and Wubnig have pointed out, "proved to be little more than a scrap of paper," partly because of the opposition of the L.A.B. to the establishment of such committees in nonunionized industries where, presumably, they would be dominated by the employers. With the enactment of P.R. 44 and the establishment of the

N.L.R.B., the N.R.A. once again was "relegated to a secondary place in the field of labor relations and in the settlement of labor disputes." [123]

As Collins had anticipated, the publicity resulting from the display of interest in the problems of the automobile industry by the N.L.B. and the President had proved a decided boon to the U.A.W. The "faith in Washington during the early months of the NRA," Edward A. Wieck has written, "was almost of a religious intensity, strongly tinged with patriotic fervor." The executive secretary of the Detroit Regional Labor Board reported to the N.L.B. on March 9 that as a result of the N.L.B.'s scheduled hearings on the industry, organization work was proceeding "at a very rapid rate" and that even the Detroit locals were being "greatly strengthened." In Flint, according to the *Flint Weekly Review* of March 16, union offices were "crowded day and night with applicants," and one local had gained three thousand new members in only four days. [124] Should the implementation of the settlement demonstrate that the A.F. of L. had erred in not permitting a strike to be called and that it had placed altogether too much faith in Washington, the results were likely to be damaging to the prospects of the Federation in the automobile industry.

In the final analysis, the full significance of the automobile labor settlement of March 25, 1934, would depend on the manner in which its provisions were interpreted and implemented by the new Automobile Labor Board. The membership of that board and its conception of its role were thus likely to be of crucial importance to the subsequent course of labor relations in the automobile manufacturing industry.

VII

THE AUTOMOBILE LABOR BOARD

ON MARCH 27, two days after he had arranged the terms of the automobile labor settlement, the President announced the membership of the new Automobile Labor Board. The neutral chairman selected was Leo Wolman, the employer representative was Nicholas Kelley, and the labor representative was Richard Byrd.

Wolman, a short, plump man with thinning hair, was forty-four years old at the time of his appointment and had had experience in academic life, the labor movement, and government. He had served as an investigator for the Commission on Industrial Relations, as chief of the section of production statistics of the War Industries Board, and as an economist at the Versailles Conference. A member of the research staff of the National Bureau of Economic Research, he had joined the Columbia economics department in 1931 after having taught at Johns Hopkins, Hobart, the University of Michigan, and the New School for Social Research. Wolman was a specialist in the area of industrial relations and had served between 1920 and 1931 as the director of research for the Amalgamated Clothing Workers.

When Franklin D. Roosevelt was governor of New York, Frances Perkins brought Wolman to the governor's attention, and Roosevelt in 1931 selected him as the state's technical expert on the Interstate Commission on Unemployment Insurance. After the enactment of the N.I.R.A., Perkins was probably responsible for Wolman's appointment as chairman of the Labor Advisory Board and as a member of the N.L.B. By the time of the March 25 settlement, a "marked coolness" had developed between Wolman and the A.F. of L., and Wolman, who in late February had wanted to resign from the N.L.B., had virtually decided to quit the N.R.A. altogether. General Johnson apparently wanted his son Kilbourne to receive the post of A.L.B. chairman, and the names of several other possibilities for the job were brought forward; but Perkins preferred Wolman, and the President persuaded him to accept the appointment. Both organized labor and management acquiesced in the President's choice "with some hesitation." [1]

Wolman came to the chairmanship of the A.L.B. firm in the conviction that the established pattern of industrial relations in the automobile industry could not be changed overnight regardless of the language of federal statutes or Presidential labor settlements. Progress in this area could be achieved only slowly, and given the superior power of the employers as compared to organized labor in the industry, no step forward could be taken without the manufacturers' support. The employers, Wolman candidly told the representatives of one of the A.L.B.'s bargaining agencies, could not "stomach" unionism, and it was wrong to think that they would alter their ways simply because of board orders. "I don't give a damn what the law is," the A.L.B. chairman bluntly stated, "even the courts cannot order them to do it and get away with it." The development of true collective bargaining in the industry required patience and time. "You have to edge it in. They [the employers] have to get accustomed to it." [2]

Pleased with Wolman's conduct of the A.L.B.'s business and his obvious deference to them, the automobile manufacturers co-operated with and praised the board and generally, although not quite to the extent that the A.L.B. indicated, complied with its decisions. [3] The automobile unionists, by contrast, came increasingly to view the board with suspicion, and as their attack on the A.L.B. and its chairman mounted, Wolman found it easier and easier to see the management point of view and to find fault with the official union position and with the union leadership.

Nicholas Kelley, the Chrysler Corporation counsel whom the employers had nominated as their representative on the board, was the son of the prominent social worker Florence Kelley and had served as Assistant Secretary of the Treasury under Wilson. The ruddy-complexioned and gray-haired Kelley was noted for the incisiveness of his mind and the breadth of his understanding of the industry's labor problems. He enjoyed the respect of the manufacturers and was viewed as fair-minded by the workers who came in contact with the A.L.B. [4] Wolman and Kelley were in basic agreement regarding the policies and role of the A.L.B., and there is no indication that they differed on any matters, major or minor, the board was called upon to decide.

Richard Byrd, nominated as the labor representative on the board by the officers of the U.A.W. federal labor unions who were present in Washington when the March 25 settlement was negotiated, had been born in Shiloh, Indiana, forty-two years before the President appointed him to the A.L.B. He moved to Detroit shortly before World War I, after having won a second place in the discus at the 1912 Olympic games. He worked for a time as a clerk at the Ford Motor Company, but following the entry of the United States into World War I, he joined the Marine Corps and rose from the rank of private to that of first lieutenant. After the war he worked in the copper mines in Nevada and then, beginning in 1925, for Fisher Body. Like millions of other Americans, he lost his job during the depression, but in August 1933 was hired by G.M. Truck in Pontiac. He was laid off shortly thereafter and became quite active in the plant's federal labor union.

At a time when nearly all of the automobile unionists were inexperienced and had difficulty articulating their views, the talent of oratory could carry one far in the union hierarchy. Thus Byrd, who knew relatively little about the labor movement but who was viewed by his associates as "a pleasing and forceful speaker," rose to a position of local leadership in the U.A.W. ranks. We can only guess why his fellow U.A.W. officers selected him from their midst as the labor representative on the board, but perhaps it was because they were impressed with his oratory and thought he knew "just a little bit more" than they did and because he, unlike the other candidates for the position, had come in their eyes to stand for the autonomy of the U.A.W. locals as opposed to the concept of centralized control by the Federation, which the local officials associated with Collins and Green.[5]

Collins looked upon Byrd as the representative of the A.F. of L. on the new labor board and expected him not only to adhere to the Federation's interpretation of the settlement but also to work with the A.F. of L.'s Detroit staff in the preparation of cases to submit to the A.L.B. If Byrd ever viewed his role on the board precisely as Collins did, which is doubtful, he did not do so for long. He liked to think of himself as the representative of all of the workers in the automobile industry rather than of just the small minority of A.F. of L. members, and he did not believe that what was good for the U.A.W. locals was necessarily good for the automobile workers as a whole. Within a few months after taking office he broke with the Federation and although publicly claiming to favor no particular labor organization, became the unofficial spokesman on the A.L.B. for a new labor association composed of a few of the U.A.W. locals that had severed their tie with the A.F. of L.[6]

Although he occasionally appraised the issues before the A.L.B. in much the same manner as the labor leadership in the industry did, Byrd was a totally ineffective defender of the trade-union point of view on the board. His lack of knowledge of the subject was matched, despite his reputation to the contrary, by a lamentable inability to phrase his thoughts in lucid and coherent language. He seems genuinely to have believed in "industrial democracy" and rank-and-file control as desirable elements in the sphere of industrial relations and trade unionism, but he was distressingly vague when it came to describing the institutional arrangements necessary to give substance to these concepts.[7]

Although "big, strong hands, a sharp nose and a belligerent chin" may have created an impression of strength, Byrd was a weak person who allowed himself to be dominated by his fellow board members. The secretary of the St. Louis U.A.W. local reported that when some of the union's members appeared before the A.L.B. in September 1934, "Wolman spoke and snapped his fingers to Byrd, much the same as you would to a pet poodle, or some other animal. We were so surprised that we could hardly speak." When Byrd objected to a mode of procedure or a decision favored by the board's chairman or its industry member, Wolman and Kelley were nearly always able to convince him to accept their judgment or at least not to protest publicly. Not until March 21, 1935, did Byrd officially dissent from one of the board's decisions, although the A.L.B. records make it clear that he had privately disapproved of the board's rulings in some earlier cases.[8] The A.F. of L. insisted that Byrd had been persuaded to agree that decisions of the A.L.B. should be unanimous, a charge that the board officially denied. Byrd's own rather curious explanation of his behavior was that during the first year of the A.L.B.'s existence he believed that the filing of dissenting opinions "would hamper the board's work without accomplishing any good end." [9]

In carrying out its assignment, the A.L.B., unlike the N.L.B. and the N.L.R.B., made no use of regional subagencies to hear cases in the first instance. All of the board's hearings were conducted by the board members themselves or by Professor Alfred H. Williams, chairman of the department of industry at the Wharton School of Commerce and Finance and a former member of the N.R.A.'s Consumers' Advisory Board, who was appointed executive secretary of the A.L.B. on June 20, 1934; Professor Francis E. Ross of the School of Business Administration of the University of Michigan, the board's chief accountant and later Williams' unofficial successor; or Professor Z. Clark Dickinson, a University of Michigan economist who served as an A.L.B. hearings officer.[10]

The failure of the A.L.B. to decentralize its operations and the fact that Wolman and Kelley devoted only part of their time to A.L.B.

business necessarily led to delays in the holding of hearings and the rendering of decisions. It was not at all unusual for three months or more to elapse between the time a case was filed and the final decision was rendered. This delay worked to the disadvantage of the workers who alleged discrimination or the misapplication of the board's seniority rules since the complainants were without "waiting power" and since the A.L.B., as we shall see, never ordered employers to give back pay to workers who had been improperly treated. As Byrd conceded, delay was not only hard on the individual but damaging to union morale.[11] Some workers, at least, must have concluded that their jobs were more secure if they remained outside the union and thus presumably in the good graces of their employers than if they relied on the A.L.B. for their protection.

From the start the A.L.B., like the N.L.B. and the N.L.R.B., decided that in so far as it was possible to do so, it would seek to dispose of the matters brought to its attention by negotiation with the parties concerned. Since the legal sanctions supporting the settlement were regarded as "slight and unimportant," the board believed that its success depended on securing the voluntary agreement of employer and employee rather than on issuing orders. As Wolman indicated on one occasion, the A.L.B. was not interested in rendering decisions just "for the purpose of showing anybody up." Only when it could not dispose of complaints by voluntary procedures did the board order a hearing. Hearings were held in the A.L.B.'s Detroit office or in or near the plant involved and were highly informal in character. In an effort to get at the "guts" of the case, the board allowed the parties to the dispute and the witnesses they brought with them to ask questions freely in examination and cross-examination. The board did not normally ask for affidavits, and it had no authority to subpoena documents or witnesses or to swear witnesses, but it did not regard these limitations on its powers as of any significance, despite the complaints of the A.F. of L.[12]

The decisions issued by the A.L.B., which Wolman hyperbolically regarded as "more valuable than any labor contract," were, unlike at least some of the decisions of the N.L.B. and the N.L.R.B., extremely brief in character and did not adequately state the pertinent facts upon which the rulings were based.[13] In all, the board issued 244 decisions, the first on May 23, 1934, the last on May 21, 1935. Only three of the decisions—one relating to wages and two concerning the A.L.B. elections—dealt with subjects other than discrimination and seniority. Virtually all of the cases which led to A.L.B. decisions were brought to the board by the U.A.W.; a mere handful of cases were initiated by individuals without a union connection, by independent labor organizations, or by company unions. G.M. divisions were involved in 171 decisions, units of the Chrysler Corporation in nineteen decisions, the independent auto manufacturers in twenty-six decisions, and automobile parts manufacturers in twenty-eight decisions. The management position was supported by the A.L.B. in its decisions about three times as frequently as the labor position, although this fact in itself does not indicate any prejudice on the board's part.[14] In several of its decisions the A.L.B. praised the behavior of management, but it never had kind words for the unions, and in some instances it specifically criticized the manner in which labor had presented its case.[15]

From the outset, Wolman, who was ever the pragmatist, let it be known that the A.L.B. would decide matters on a case-by-case basis rather than by seeking to formulate principles which would be of general application. Ignoring the work of the N.L.B. and the principles regarding labor relations that could have been derived from its decisions, Wolman announced on March 29, 1934, that since there were no precedents for the board to follow, it "would have to build its own road which it expects to travel." The board was normally reluctant to answer questions raised by labor or management concerning its position on the subjects within its jurisdiction unless these questions were posed in an A.L.B. hearing or were related to a specific case under consideration or on which a decision had been announced. Thus, even after the board had devised a set of rules to govern the order of layoff and rehiring, it refused to interpret the meaning of these rules apart from its decisions in particular cases.[16]

The jurisdiction of the A.L.B. extended originally only to the automobile manufacturing industry. Johnson, however, issued an administrative order on April 27, 1934, authorizing the board to deal with questions of representation, discharge, and discrimination arising within the automobile parts industry provided that the parties involved subscribed "in full" to the principles of the President's settlement. The general may have been prompted to take this step by the knowledge that the A.P.E.M. believed that "it would be a fine thing" if the A.L.B. were allowed to handle parts cases until the industry, in accordance with the recent N.R.A. recommendation, established its own industrial-relations committee. After Johnson issued the order, the A.P.E.M. code authority advised industry members that the principles of the settlement were "absolutely fair and we can not see how either Labor or ourselves can refuse to have our problems settled on this basis." [17]

Because it was necessary to secure the approval of both parties to a dispute, relatively few parts cases actually came before the A.L.B. for decision. Management, faced with the choice of having a case go to the N.L.R.B. or the A.L.B., generally preferred the A.L.B., but the U.A.W., as its antagonism toward the A.L.B. mounted, became increasingly reluctant to permit complaints in which it was concerned to be brought before the Wolman board. During the summer months of 1934 the A.F. of L. and its U.A.W. locals began pressing for the establishment of a separate board for the parts industry. Wolman seemed to have no objection to this idea, and the A.P.E.M. was not unwilling provided the new board functioned "in the same manner" as the A.L.B. Although the A.F. of L. initially contended that it favored a separate board simply because this was preferable to having some parts cases decided by the N.L.R.B. and some by the A.L.B., it became evident by the late summer that the A.F. of L. would have acquiesced only in a parts board that did not function "in the same manner" as the A.L.B., which forestalled any possible agreement on the subject with the parts manufacturers.[18]

Since the Ford Motor Company had not been a party to the settlement and the settlement had not been incorporated in the automobile code, the A.L.B. was undecided as to whether its jurisdiction encompassed the Ford plants. The subject could not be ignored because the M.E.S.A. was protesting that Ford was discriminating against its members. Reluctant to let these complaints go to the N.L.R.B., Wolman began to refer them to the Ford Motor Company, but when a company official in reply indicated what action, if any, the company had taken in the case, the A.L.B. generally pursued the matter no further.[19] Ford was never asked to attend an A.L.B. hearing and was not the subject of a single board decision. When the board eventually put an election plan into effect in the industry, no effort was made to poll employees of the Ford Motor Company.

The most troublesome of the Ford labor cases in which the A.L.B. had a hand and one which revealed the tender manner in which the board approached problems involving the company concerned M.E.S.A. member Ellef S. Clark. Clark complained to the N.R.A. late in April 1934 that "several hundred" M.E.S.A. members working in the rolling mill tool room at the Rouge plant had been indefinitely laid off. The N.R.A. referred the matter to Wolman, who expressed doubt as to the board's jurisdiction in the case but nevertheless forwarded the complaint to Ford. Most of the men involved had been re-employed by this time, but Clark was not among them, and Wolman suggested that Clark be asked for additional information with

regard to his original complaint.   Clark supplied the requested data
to the N.R.A. Compliance Division early in June, and the information
was passed on to Wolman.   Franklin S. Pollak, the counsel of the
Compliance Division, who thought that Clark had "a pretty strong
prima facie case," tried in vain during the next two months to secure
an opinion from the A.L.B. on how to proceed in the matter.   Finally
on August 2, Wolman, following Kelley's advice, wrote Pollak that if
he had sufficient evidence he should arrange for the Attorney General
to prosecute.

Reluctant to take this step and despairing of solving the problem
through the A.L.B., Pollak turned the case over to the N.L.R.B.; but
now Wolman decided that the matter was indeed within the A.L.B.'s
jurisdiction, and so the N.L.R.B. on September 14 sent the A.L.B. the
Clark file.   Not until October 29, however, did Wolman get in touch
with the Ford Motor Company to ascertain why Clark had not been
re-employed.   The A.L.B. chairman was informed on November 8
that Clark would be rehired when work was available for him, but
the year ended with Clark still unemployed.

On January 8, 1935, Francis Biddle, the N.L.R.B. chairman, tried
his hand at spurring the A.L.B. into action.   "The case is so stale,"
he wrote Wolman, "that I should appreciate your handling it as
promptly as possible. . . ."   Ten days later, Wolman wrote to William
J. Cameron to inquire about Clark, but the unfortunate Clark still
remained without work.   "I seem to be the victim of circumstances
over which I have no control," he understandably enough wrote to
Wolman, "my employer being unwilling to give me a square deal, and
the government being unable to enforce its laws."   Finally, at the
end of January and more than nine months after he had been laid off,
Clark was able to advise the A.L.B. that he had been re-employed.
He attributed this happy ending to his dolorous story not to the A.L.B.
nor to any other agency of the United States government but to the
intervention on his behalf of Ford's Sociological Department.   Clark
might also have noted that if Ford's objective in laying off the M.E.S.A.
members had been the destruction of the union in the Rouge, the
company had attained its goal: although the employees concerned
had been returned to work, they seem to have decided that their jobs
would be more secure if they gave up their union membership.[20]

The subjects over which the A.L.B. had jurisdiction were limited
by the settlement to representation, discharge, and discrimination,
but there was nothing to prevent the board from dealing with other
matters of concern to employer and employee provided that the
parties involved were agreeable to its intercession.   Although the

A.L.B., initially, would have liked to broaden the scope of its authority, in only one instance during its entire history was it invited by employer and employee to arbitrate a question falling outside its defined jurisdiction. The disputants were the Plymouth Motor Corporation and the employees of one plant department, and the issue was the wages paid the workers.[21] That the A.L.B. was not asked on subsequent occasions to render judgments in other wage disputes was undoubtedly due to management's conviction that the determination of wages was a managerial prerogative that should not be surrendered even to a friendly government agency [22] and to the A.F. of L.'s adherence to its traditional view that wages above the minimum should, under normal circumstances, be fixed by collective bargaining and, also, after August 1934, to its distrust of the A.L.B.

For a brief period after it was established, it appeared that the A.L.B. would concern itself with the crucial question of the stabilization of automobile employment. Wolman, in April 1934, suggested various means by which this goal might be realized and declared that "The whole situation indicates the necessity for action from outside the industry, by some such board or government agency as the present board or by a voluntary grouping together of the manufacturers to effect such a programme, probably under the direction of a personal representative of the President...." Although the press reported the A.L.B. to be devoting an increasing proportion of its time to this subject [23] and although Wolman, who had gained experience in dealing with the problem of irregular employment as the research director for the Amalgamated Clothing Workers, may have fancied himself as the President's "personal representative" in this field, the A.L.B. chairman many years later could not remember that the board had ever really concerned itself with the stabilization of automobile employment.[24]

Since the A.L.B. had been established by the President primarily to maintain peace in the automobile industry, it is not surprising that the first major task to which the board devoted its attention after it set up shop in Detroit on March 29 was the settlement of the Nash-Seaman Body dispute, the one strike then taking place in the industry. After conferring in Detroit with management representatives, the A.L.B. members traveled to Racine for further discussion with the disputants and to aid in arranging a settlement. On April 5 the board announced peace terms that were acceptable to the management but that remained subject to the ratification of the strikers. The two companies agreed to return the strikers to work without discrimination as rapidly as production warranted and in not more than two weeks.

The companies were "to bargain collectively with representatives freely chosen by those employees for whom they are to act," which accorded with the position of management on this point from the beginning of the dispute. In layoffs and rehiring, Nash and Seaman agreed to follow the procedure outlined in the President's settlement. Matching the pay increase already put into effect at Seaman Body, Nash agreed to raise the wages of factory workers in the Racine plant 10 per cent above the levels prevailing when the strike began, and the wages of Kenosha workers were to be brought up to the new Racine levels. Both companies agreed to adjust base rates that were "clearly inequitable." Finally, it was stipulated that minimum earnings in the three plants would be not less than fifty cents per hour (as compared to forty-four cents before the strike) for male piece-work or group-work operators and for sweepers, chiphaulers, and stock chasers, and not less than forty-four cents per hour (as compared to forty cents before the walkout) for female piece workers or group-work operators.[25]

The Racine strikers accepted the settlement by an overwhelming vote, but neither the Kenosha nor the Seaman Body strikers were satisfied with the A.L.B. proposals. At Kenosha, the principal concern was the wage clause of the settlement. Since the base rates at Kenosha at the time the strike began were higher than those at Racine, the settlement would have yielded Kenosha workers at most a 5 per cent increase as compared to the 10 per cent increase for the strikers at the other two plants. For this reason, the Kenosha local on April 6, after "two hours of bedlam," rejected the A.L.B. terms by a nineteen hundred to one hundred vote.[26]

The situation at Seaman Body was complicated by the fact that the company had engaged a considerable number of new workers in an effort to continue its operations during the strike, and the union, despite management assurances that there was ample work for strikers and nonstrikers alike, insisted that all the strikebreakers must be discharged forthwith. After first accepting the strike terms, the Seaman strikers reconsidered, and on April 7 decisively rejected the A.L.B. proposals. Since the strikers at the three plants had agreed that they would not return to work until terms acceptable to all three locals had been devised, the decision of the Kenosha and Seaman Body workers meant that the strike continued at all three plants. With no place to send its bodies and running out of storage space, Seaman Body finally decided to close down its plant beginning April 9.[27]

When the A.L.B. proved itself unable to break the deadlock at the Kenosha Nash plant and at Seaman Body, the unions and the management attempted to resolve their differences by direct negotiation. Both sides were anxious for a settlement, the unions because the strikers had been without work for more than a month, the companies, already hard-pressed financially, because they wished to be able to stock Nash dealers with cars to take advantage of the heavy spring demand and to repair the financial losses they had already sustained in 1934.[28]

The wage issue at the Kenosha plant was quickly settled when Nash promised that each Kenosha worker would receive at least a 5 per cent increase and that wage boosts would range up to 17.2 per cent for some employees. It proved more difficult to resolve the strikebreaker question at the Seaman Body plant, but on April 15, 1934, after the local had rejected a compromise proposed by the management, terms satisfactory to the strikers were arranged, and the walkout at all three plants was brought to a close. Seaman Body now agreed to re-employ all strikers forthwith, including strikers hired before November who had been laid off in January 1934 and about one hundred strikers who had been engaged after November. Management was to employ such additional men as it required only after the strikers had been returned to their jobs, which meant that workers newly engaged during the strike were not to receive jobs until all the strikers had been re-employed. The original A.L.B. terms were otherwise left intact, except that preference in subsequent layoffs and rehirings was to be given to Seaman Body workers who had been on the company payroll before the strike. This clause was designed to reassure the strikers that the company in the future would not take advantage of the order of layoff and rehiring provided by the March 25 settlement to return strikebreakers and new workers with large numbers of dependents in preference to unmarried strikers with records of long service.[29] Short of barring strikebreakers from further employment at the Seaman Body plant, the strikers thus succeeded in winning their point that, in principle at least, the advantage in terms of employment after a strike should be with the strikers rather than with the workers who had taken their jobs. Like the Kenosha local, the Seaman Body local had gained additional concessions from management by refusing to accept the original A.L.B. terms.

Following the strike settlement of April 18 the U.A.W. locals in the Nash and Seaman Body plants continued to gain in strength. Just as the company union at the Kenosha plant had failed to survive the strike of November 1933, so the inside unions at both the Racine Nash plant and at Seaman Body ceased to exist after the 1934 strike. The Nash and Seaman Body managements henceforth negotiated with union committees without questioning their authority to speak for the factory employees, and the three locals came to be among the most powerful of the federal labor unions in the entire automobile industry. They had clearly demonstrated that in certain circumstances at least militancy was not without its rewards in the campaign to organize the automobile workers.[30]

No sooner had it returned to Michigan following its not altogether successful attempt to compose the Nash-Seaman Body strike than the A.L.B. was confronted by a strike in Detroit at the Motor Products plant, fabricator of an extensive line of automobile parts. The immediate cause of the strike was a reduction in the piece rates of electric platers (from 87.9 cents to 83.4 cents per hour) resulting from the hurried setting of new rates by the company at the start of the 1934 production season. The employees in other departments of the plant were also dissatisfied with their wages, which ranged from forty cents to $1.00 per hour, and, in addition, there was some complaint that the company was replacing male workers with female workers in order to shave its costs. William Collins counseled the Motor Products unionists not to strike, but the local, which contained a communist-organized rank-and-file opposition group that had been severely critical of the A.F. of L. leadership, ignored the advice. Approximately fifteen hundred workers walked out on April 5, and this resulted in the shutting down of the entire plant and the consequent idling of a total of 5600 employees. Within a few days, eighteen thousand more workers were thrown out of work when Hudson was forced to shut down because of the interruption in the flow of parts from Motor Products.[31]

Although the A.L.B. had not yet received any authorization to deal with labor problems in the parts industry, apparently neither the union nor the management objected to the board's attempt to mediate the dispute. Following a conference with the disputants, which was also attended by Assistant Secretary of Labor McGrady, the A.L.B. on April 7 worked out a settlement which was acceptable to the employers and which the union leadership agreed to submit to the strikers. The agreement provided for consultation between the union shop steward and the company's time-study man whenever there was a dispute concerning the piece-work rate that had been established for a particular job. Certain changes desired by the workers were to be made in the method of computing the group bonus. The company was to pay its platers 87.9 cents per hour, which was the old rate, and also the difference between what they would have earned at this rate and the 83.4 cents per hour that they had been receiving during the previous two weeks. No woman was to be hired to replace a male employee unless the displaced male received a job that was satisfactory to him in terms of pay and the amount of work available. The order of lay-off and rehiring and the minimum earnings for men and women were to be the same as provided in the A.L.B.'s proposed settlement for the Nash-Seaman Body dispute. The company was to pay the employees at the rate of fifty cents per hour for waiting time in excess of one hour a day for which the employees were not themselves responsible, and, finally, the employees were to agree that in the event of a dispute with the management, they would remain at work until one of the parties had presented the case to the A.L.B. and reported back to the workers.[32]

Although the A.L.B. terms represented a considerable gain for the union, including a substantial pay boost for its unskilled members, many of the strikers were dissatisfied because no provision had been made for a wage increase for the semiskilled and skilled workers. The result was that the strikers at a meeting of April 8 overwhelmingly rejected the A.L.B. terms, a decision which the board received "with something like consternation." John H. French, the acting manager of the plant, thereupon informed the A.L.B. that he intended to put the new rates into effect regardless of the union's action and that he would hire new workers after giving the strikers twenty-four hours to return to their jobs. French's plan, which if implemented could only have exacerbated an already tense situation, prompted Edward McGrady to inject himself more prominently into the dispute. He persuaded French to agree to a 10 per cent wage increase for the skilled and the semiskilled provided the strikers returned to work on April 10. The new wage concessions broke the strike deadlock, and at a meeting of April 9 the local, responding to the urgings of McGrady, Byrd, and Collins, accepted the terms of settlement and called off the walkout.[33]

Just as it had been unable on its own to bring the Nash and Seaman Body strikes to a close so the A.L.B. had required aid in the settlement of the Motor Products strike. Its assistance was not even called for when the M.E.S.A. in April staged its ill-advised strike against the Detroit job shops, nor, as we shall see, when the U.A.W.'s Toledo local during the same month struck the Electric Auto-Lite Company in one of the most bitter labor conflicts of the entire N.R.A. period. The A.L.B. was, however, to re-enter the strike picture late in April when several Fisher Body locals either went on strike or threatened to do so unless the board intervened. But this story, related as it is to the more general subject of the evolution of collective-bargaining procedures in the industry after the President's settlement, will be recounted at a later time.

Apart from the obvious necessity of attempting to bring to a conclusion any strikes that were plaguing the industry when it assumed office, Wolman concluded as the result of the N.L.B. auto hearings and his talks with N.A.C.C. and A.F. of L. representatives before he left for Detroit that the most urgent task for the board was to deal with the problem of alleged discrimination by the automobile companies against union members. The elimination of discrimination, real or fancied, the A.L.B. chairman believed, would help to "eradicate such fear as may have existed in the minds" of the automobile workers and would lead to more amicable relations between labor and management.[34]

Kelley agreed with Wolman on the order of A.L.B. priorities, but Byrd dissented. He urged his fellow board members to concentrate first on the question of representation, for once this problem was settled, organized labor could itself deal with cases of discrimination through direct negotiation with management. Delay in resolving the representation issue, however, meant that the spring production peak would come to an end before the board could provide for a more effective collective-bargaining relationship in the industry, and the workers would then remain at a bargaining disadvantage until production once again resumed its upward climb. Byrd's views on this subject were understandably shared by Collins and most of the U.A.W. officials, but as was usual in the operation of the A.L.B., the wishes of Wolman and Kelley prevailed.[35]

The very first day that it convened in Detroit the A.L.B. invited Collins to submit to the board discrimination cases on which the A.F. of L. wished action. Collins very shortly presented a list of forty-one Flint cases and informed the press that "many, many more [cases] will come later." Like the N.L.B. and the N.L.R.B., the A.L.B. tried to settle the discrimination complaints brought to its attention by voluntary procedures, and only when the employer was unwilling to reinstate the complainant voluntarily or was unable to convince him that his charges were groundless did the board schedule a hearing and then render a decision on the case. Using this approach, the A.L.B. was able to secure the reinstatement without a hearing or decision of 1129 of the 2348 workers involved in complaints of discrimination, and an additional 742 workers dropped their cases or allowed them to lapse.[36]

Although the reinstatement by the employers of so many workers seemed like a victory for the individuals who alleged discrimination and for the union representatives who had pressed their claims, the A.F. of L. was far from satisfied with the results. Having, in effect, "underwritten" the settlement, the Federation was anxious to have the board demonstrate to the more timid auto workers that it had the power and the will to deal decisively with employer tactics such as discrimination that violated Section 7(a) and the code and that limited the appeal of outside unionism, and the A.F. of L. did not believe that the A.L.B.'s approach to the problem served this purpose. The A.L.B.'s procedures, union representatives charged, simply permitted employers to re-engage workers against whom they had discriminated without any admission of guilt and, indeed, as an act of seeming generosity. There was, moreover, no guarantee that these workers would be returned to their old or similar jobs or that they would be paid at the same rate as before their discharge or layoff. Thus, some of the Flint workers whom G.M. had agreed to take back were soon complaining about the terms of their re-employment, and, in the end, the A.L.B. had to hear their cases and decide the merit of their claims.[37]

Wolman's response to union criticism of the A.L.B.'s procedure in handling discrimination cases was that the board could not possibly hear all the complaints that were submitted to it, that its interest was in the re-employment of the workers who alleged foul play rather than in proving discrimination, and that its methods were designed to secure the return to work of a maximum number of workers in a minimum amount of time. The employers, if anything, were to be praised for their evident "desire to cooperate with the Board" and for not insisting upon compliance with the terms of the settlement regarding the submission of union membership lists in discrimination cases. It was "an interesting commentary on the good faith of all concerned," the A.L.B. declared in its final report, that no employer ever questioned the claim of a union or its officers to represent an individual alleging discrimination.[38]

When voluntary procedures failed, the board had to decide on the basis of the testimony presented at its hearings whether discrimination had been practiced by the employer as alleged. This was ordinarily an extremely difficult matter to determine since the testimony presented tended to be contradictory, and the motivation of the defendant, which was at the heart of every case, was not necessarily self-evident. The decisions, generally, went against the workers, but this was to have been expected. The employers, after all, given the nature of the A.L.B.'s procedures, allowed only those cases to come to a decision that they believed they were likely to win, and these cases were argued before the board by able counsel.

The A.F. of L. would also have preferred to submit only those claims that were backed by solid evidence, but this was easier said than done. To retain the loyalty of its members and to show its aggressiveness, it felt itself under obligation to push the claims of unionists who alleged discrimination even though the evidence on which they based their charges was of the most tenuous sort. It was natural, given the high rate of labor turnover in the automobile industry and the known attitude of the employers regarding unionism, for some unionists to assume that separation from their job was solely the result of their labor affiliation, and the A.F. of L. representatives in the industry, who undoubtedly shared these assumptions to some degree, believed that they had little choice but to support U.A.W. members in their allegations of foul play. In arguing union cases before the A.L.B., moreover, the Detroit office of the A.F. of L. could not command legal talent comparable to that available to the employers, and this plus the fact that the insecure automobile workers were reluctant to serve as witnesses in hearings at which employer representatives were also present further handicapped the Federation in its efforts to prove discrimination to the satisfaction of the A.L.B.[39]

In decisions in discrimination cases that were favorable to the employer, the A.L.B. would simply indicate its agreement with the defendant that the complainant had been dismissed or laid off because of "insubordination," "violation of shop rules," "lack of interest in his work," "interfering with work," "inefficiency," "unsatisfactory work," and so forth.[40] The A.L.B. was inclined to accept reasons of this sort as the sole cause for the discharge of an aggrieved employee although one suspects that in some cases at least other considerations were also involved. Union representatives became increasingly suspicious about the objectivity of the board in reaching these decisions. After all, had not Wolman told them on May 2, 1934, before a single decision had been rendered by the A.L.B. and while numerous claims of discrimination were under adjudication, that G.M., the chief target of the discrimination claims, was unconcerned as to whether or not its employees were active unionists?[41]

The A.L.B. stated explicitly in several cases in which the employer defense was upheld that discrimination had not been practiced or that unionism had not been an issue in the case. On occasion, the A.L.B. in its opinions made it a point to praise the fairness of a particular company in treating its employees. In its very first decision, for example, the A.L.B. categorically stated that it was the general policy of Hudson not to discriminate against its employees for union activities. In a key decision involving Al Cook, the president of the Fisher Body No. 1 local of Flint, the A.L.B., in reversing a Detroit Regional Labor Board decision that Cook had been the victim of discrimination, declared that the company, far from discriminating against the complainant, had "gone out of its way to show him consideration" and that Cook had been "officious and troublesome over a period of several years." Since the Cook case had become something of a *cause célèbre* as far as the U.A.W. locals were concerned, this decision in particular antagonized automobile unionists.[42]

In some cases, not only was the company upheld but the union presentation of its claim was attacked. The union attorney in one case was charged with "pettifogging" and the union complainant with a lack of frankness, whereas the company's treatment of the complainant was lauded. Wolman, in an obvious attack on the union's presentation in another case, appended a note to one of the board's earliest decisions stating that it was "undesirable for those representing parties to take up long hours with irrelevancies in simple cases. It will facilitate the work of the Board if those who assist in presenting cases do so with good temper and politeness."[43] Remarks of this sort did not win friends for the board among the U.A.W. leadership.

The A.L.B. found for the complainant in some discrimination cases, but not once did it state in so many words that the defendant had actually discriminated against the protesting worker. The A.F. of L. complained about this and also charged that the A.L.B. never really ordered that an individual be returned to employment. The latter allegation, however, is not supported by the facts. In several of its cases, the board ruled that the complainant should be returned to work by a certain date, that he be returned promptly and without prejudice, or that he be returned "forthwith," on the basis of his seniority, to work that he could do.[44]

In contrast to the N.L.B. and the N.L.R.B., even in cases in which the A.L.B. decided in favor of the complainant, it rarely specified that he be re-employed at the same rate of pay that he had been earning at the time of his discharge or layoff, and it never required the employer to return a worker to his old or a similar job or to pay him back wages for working time that he had lost as the result of discrimination.[45] Employers sometimes took advantage of the A.L.B.'s leniency to return workers to jobs that they found less satisfactory than their former work and which carried lower rates of pay, although this happened primarily to employees who were returned without an A.L.B.

hearing or following strike settlements arranged by the board which called for the re-employment of strikers without discrimination.[46] Whatever reason the employer might give to explain the necessity for the changed conditions of employment when an employee who alleged discrimination was returned to work, it appeared to the workers that even when the A.L.B. was able to arrange for the re-employment of union members, their lot in the plant was not an easy one and they were being made to pay the price for their union membership and for complaining to the A.L.B.

Wolman contended in an early A.L.B. hearing involving discrimination cases at the Fisher Body No. 1 plant in Flint that the board could not insist that a complainant be returned to his former job because of the conditions that might obtain in a particular plant at a particular time, but he reported that he had nevertheless advised the company that a man returned to employment should not be penalized in any way and that every effort should be made to give him the same work. He conceded that he was dissatisfied with the way the problem had been handled at the plant—Byrd stated flatly that the men had not "been given a square deal"—and he indicated that he failed to understand why a small number of men could not be returned to their previous jobs in a factory of such large size. The A.L.B.'s advice to employees who were returned to work as the result of its intercession was to take whatever jobs were offered them and then to complain to the board if the work was beyond their skill or their pay was less than it had formerly been. A reinstated worker who quit the new job that had been offered him, regardless of its nature, could not appeal to the board since it took the position that a quit closed the case.[47]

There is no evidence that Wolman or the A.L.B. ever put any real pressure on the employers to play fair with the workers the board ordered reinstated. Responding to union complaints on this score, the A.L.B. chairman asserted, "You cannot do this thing perfectly. This is a big revolution." A year earlier, he insisted, the employers would not have returned the complainants altogether or would have returned them when it pleased the company to do so, and, consequently, a certain amount of imperfection had to be tolerated.[48] It is difficult, however, to accept the reasoning of Wolman on this point. If the board could tell the employer to reinstate a worker, it could tell him to re-employ the complainant at his former job and his former rate of pay. If altered conditions in the plant made this impossible, it should have been the responsibility of the employer to prove the point to the A.L.B. and not the responsibility of the employee to initiate a new complaint while he worked at an inferior job. As was so often the case, Wolman was simply reluctant to take a step that might antagonize the employers in the automobile industry.

Wolman conceded that the A.L.B. had the power to order back pay and that the decision to do so might speed up employer action in discrimination cases, but he was unwilling to put any such policy into effect. In a conference with the members of the works councils of several Chrysler plants, he pointed out that many of the complaints of discrimination with which the A.L.B. had to deal had originated before the board was created, when there was "a great deal of monkey business" in the industry, and that it was therefore sufficient under the circumstances to secure the reinstatement of aggrieved workers rather than to "try to remedy everything that was wrong in the industry." [49] This, certainly, was a specious argument. Discrimination, the N.L.B. had ruled, had been made illegal by Section 7(a), which was a part of the automobile code, and the settlement had simply confirmed this point. The employer was no less guilty of violating the code if the discriminatory act had taken place in the six-month period before the A.L.B. was established than if it had occurred in the ensuing six months. It is a sufficient commentary on Wolman's argument to note that the board treated complaints that originated entirely after March 25, 1934, no differently from cases that originated before that date. No employer was penalized in the slightest for discriminating against a union worker, the automobile code and the N.I.R.A. to the contrary notwithstanding.

In some discrimination cases, the A.L.B., apparently believing that the employer had dealt too harshly with a worker in discharging him for a particular offense, ruled that the discharge should be interpreted as a "disciplinary lay-off" and that the complainant should be re-employed. The concept of the disciplinary layoff seems to have been a novel one in the automobile industry, and the employers, as Kelley remembered it, reacted to the idea with some surprise but without challenge.[50] The A.L.B. also advised the G.M. management at least that it might be wise to reinstate certain employees who had become "centers of attraction" even though the A.L.B. had upheld their discharge. In a meeting with G.M. executives on November 15, 1934, the board specifically advised the return of Al Cook to some kind of work and counseled a lenient attitude in borderline cases that had been decided in the employers' favor.[51] The A.L.B. was obviously aware that the circumstances in particular cases were far more complex than the brief statement of the facts in its decisions might indicate.

Whatever the weaknesses of its procedures, it seems evident that the presence of the A.L.B. served to deter the employers from resort to discrimination as a weapon to combat unionism and probably lessened the fear of some workers that membership in a union might cost them their jobs.   Wolman observed in September 1935 that there had been some instances of discrimination in the industry during the latter half of 1933 and the early months of 1934, but he thought that the number of cases had been greatly reduced following the establishment of the A.L.B.   Less than half of the board's 244 decisions dealt with discrimination as such, and Wolman regarded this number as surprisingly small considering the size of the industry, the extent of its labor turnover, and the previous attitude of the automobile companies toward unionism.   In its report of February 1935 the A.L.B. concluded that discrimination due to unionism "is not a problem of any magnitude at the present time and has not been for some time in the past." [52]

Although the A.L.B. judgment on this matter was concurred in, to a degree, by W. Ellison Chalmers, who aided the Detroit office of the U.A.W. in preparing cases for submission to the A.L.B., it would appear to err somewhat on the optimistic side.   Complaints of discrimination, as Lorwin and Wubnig have pointed out, were a more prominent factor in the work of the A.L.B. than of any other labor board in the N.R.A. period, and the number of these complaints that came to a decision grossly understates the extent to which discrimination was probably practiced in the industry.   One has to assume, for example, that a substantial number of the employees the automobile companies voluntarily returned to their jobs after they had filed complaints of discrimination with the A.L.B. were out of work for reasons other than the seasonality of the industry and the depressed state of the economy.   The workers, moreover, were not unmindful of the risks they might run if they carried their complaints to the board.   The employee who alleged discrimination, Byrd noted, "incurs, unquestionably in most cases, the displeasure of his supervisory force, and suffers thereby in future employment regardless of the decision of the Board...." [53]

Although discrimination cases continued to be brought to the board as long as it remained in existence, within a few months after the March 25 settlement the number of seniority cases began to exceed the number of discrimination cases.   It is not, however, always possible to distinguish between the two types of cases since the question posed in a seniority case might very well be whether discrimination had been practiced in the application of the board's seniority rules.

The automobile employers in the years before the March 25 settlement did not necessarily lay off and rehire employees in an entirely haphazard manner, but they were under no obligation to observe any particular order of layoff and rehiring, and they had not worked out any rules regarding the relative weight to be assigned to such factors as efficiency, number of dependents, and length of service. The settlement dealt with this subject in very general terms, and then on May 18, 1934, after having consulted with both labor and management on the matter,[54] the A.L.B. issued a set of rules which defined in a more precise manner the order which employers were to follow in reductions and increases of force. Employees hired after September 1, 1933 (Class A), were the first to be laid off, regardless of their marital status and the number of their dependents, unless they could be placed in Class D. Next to be laid off (Class B) were those hired before September 1, 1933, who were unmarried and without dependents, unless they had a long record of service or were in Class D. Next in the order of layoff (Class C) were employees hired before September 1, 1933, who were married and those who had dependents. Employees of less service in Classes B and C were to be laid off before employees of longer service, service being determined on a yearly basis. Finally, employees (Class D) whose work in the judgment of management was essential to the operation of the plant and to production or who had received special training or who had exceptional ability might be hired, retained, and re-employed in preference to employees in Classes A, B, and C. When the work force was increased, the order of layoff was simply to be reversed, but no provision was made for the return to work of Class A employees.

The A.L.B. rules further specified that length of service was to be determined from the date of employment in the plant or similar plants of the same employer rather than by the length of employment in the particular group or department or on a particular job. Other things being equal, the skill and efficiency of the employees, as judged by the management, was to determine preference in both layoff and rehiring. Cases of discharge or quitting, as distinguished from layoffs, were to be indicated clearly, and the reasons for same given. Finally, the A.L.B. specified the kinds of records employers were to keep to permit the board to ascertain without difficulty whether its rules were being observed.[55]

In issuing its rules, the A.L.B. stated that it was merely implementing the principles of the President's settlement, but, actually, by giving Class D employees preference over men with dependents and long service, it was altering the order of layoff and rehiring specified in the March 25 agreement. The A.L.B. rules also ignored the requirement of the settlement that after the various factors determining the order of layoff and rehiring had been considered, "no greater proportion of outside union employees similarly situated shall be laid off than of other employees," but this omission never became an issue in the implementation of the rules.

The A.L.B. rules of May 18, 1934, remained unmodified until January 18, 1935, when the board simply substituted a one-year criterion for its original September 1, 1933, standard. Thus, Class A employees were henceforth those hired less than one year prior to the decrease in force, and Class B and C workers had to have been hired one year or more before the decrease in force.[56]

More than half of the A.L.B.'s decisions involved questions of seniority, and, for the most part, employee complaints were found by the board to be unjustified. This was a not unexpected result since what was involved in the observance of the board's rules was simply the keeping of accurate records by the employer and their honest use in the determination of the order of layoff and rehiring. The complainants, who were not given access to employer records, frequently did not have their facts straight or simply did not understand the A.L.B. rules.[57]

Class A employees, as the A.L.B. saw it, were, in effect, on probation and had no claim whatsoever on their job. New employees could be rehired in preference to them, and they could be recalled in any order the management saw fit regardless of the number of their dependents and the length of their service. In defending the establishment of this category, Wolman argued that since the automobile industry was the first nonunionized industry to agree to follow definite layoff and rehiring procedures, the employers had to be given some freedom in the recruitment of their labor force. "You have got to give them some leeway in repayment for getting general seniority,"[58] the A.L.B. chairman declared. It was, of course, perfectly reasonable to require an employee to serve a probationary period before he acquired some right to his job, and the automobile unionists raised no objection to this principle.

Length of service as compared to number of dependents was the basic issue presented by the B and C categories established by the A.L.B. rules. It was obvious from the rules that if two employees had the same terms of service, the employee in Class B who was unmarried and had no dependents was to be laid off before the employee in Class C. What was not clear was how much longer service a Class B employee needed to warrant preference in employment over a Class C worker. Byrd suggested that this problem be solved in a precise manner by assigning to each worker a number derived by multiplying the number of months he had served by the number of his dependents and then laying off the workers with the lowest numbers first. Thus a man with five dependents who had worked twenty months would be assigned the number one hundred and would have seniority over unmarried employees with fewer than one hundred months of service unless the latter could be placed in Class D. Seaman Body, at least, seems to have followed the Byrd formula in determining the order of layoff and rehiring of its employees.[59] Fisher Body treated marriage as the equivalent of two years of service, but Chevrolet, for a time, laid off all single men before laying off married men or men with dependents, a practice that violated A.L.B. rules. It proved impossible, actually, for the A.L.B. to lay down a precise rule regarding the relative weight to be assigned to dependency and length of service with the result that the employees became dissatisfied with dependency as a factor in determining the order of layoff and rehiring.[60]

The A.L.B. layoff and rehiring rules afforded no clues as to the status of married women employees, and the practice with regard to their employment seems to have varied from plant to plant. The Fisher Body plant in Janesville laid off married women before employees in Class A, to which the U.A.W. local in the plant objected. The Buick local, on the other hand, was dissatisfied because the company would not give job preference to single women over married women with employed husbands. The A.L.B. did not think that it was proper for G.M. to treat married women like single men in determining the layoff order but nevertheless said that it would not object to this procedure as long as it was applied uniformly.[61]

The A.L.B. rules specified that service was to be determined on a yearly basis, but no one was altogether certain what this meant. Thus, the automobile parts companies, many of which followed the A.L.B. rules, assumed that the number of months an employee worked in any particular year was of no importance in determining length of service. G.M. totaled the number of months its employees had worked and then classified them by years for tenure purposes. Thus, employees who had worked from twelve to twenty-three months were placed in a single group, and within the group employees of longer service enjoyed no advantage over employees of lesser service. Seaman Body on the other hand determined length of service in accordance with the total number of months each employee had worked, and the A.L.B. indicated its preference for this plan, despite the language of its May 18 rules. Layoff time was not included in the calculation of seniority, although some unionists believed that it should be, and, similarly, the time a worker was on strike was not added to his period of service, even though Byrd thought this a sensible idea. By the same token, a worker did not acquire extra seniority for having worked during a strike.[62]

It was agreed by all concerned that a quit or a valid discharge constituted a break in the worker's service in so far as seniority calculations were concerned, but there was a difference of opinion regarding the length of the layoff period that should constitute a break in service. The A.L.B. declared that it would accept any reasonable rule regarding this matter so long as it was fairly and uniformly applied. Some employers, like Chrysler, interpreted a layoff of six months as a break in service, and the criterion at Seaman Body was three years, but the more general practice was for the employers to follow a one-year rule. G.M. adhered to a one-year criterion, but only if employees who had already been laid off for six months specifically requested that their seniority be maintained for an additional six months. When a laid-off employee took a job with another employer, he did not, according to A.L.B. interpretation, break his service with his first employer in so far as the calculation of his seniority was concerned.[63]

The Class D category provided by the A.L.B. layoff and rehiring rules was interpreted by G.M. to embrace "those men who because of their versatility, experience and efficiency are used as a nucleus group around which the production force is built up." The U.A.W. recognized that some employees were entitled to the privileged status of Class D, but it believed that too many workers were being placed in this group and that this opened the way for "an almost unlimited amount of favoritism." It therefore urged, and in this it was supported by Byrd, that the determination of the employees to be placed in Class D should be jointly made by the union and the management rather than by the management alone.

On the whole, the employers do not appear to have abused the Class D privilege, but when A.L.B. official Z. Clark Dickinson learned that the Chrysler Jefferson plant had placed 20 per cent of its employees in three groups in the plant in Class D and by so doing had been able to justify its failure to re-employ a union official, he concluded that this action gave "some color to the charge that such classification is being used to evade the seniority scheme." [64] It might also be noted that employers did not hesitate to give preference in layoff and rehiring to more skilled employees in Classes B and C regardless of the length of their service or the number of their dependents as compared to other employees in these same categories. Although this seemed to violate the A.L.B.'s rule that skill and efficiency were to be taken into account outside of Class D only if other things were equal, the board upheld the management on this point in the cases that came to its attention.[65]

Quite apart from the Class D category, the A.L.B. agreed with the employers that there were certain jobs in the plant, such as those involved in the designing and engineering of the product, to which the seniority rules did not apply and in the disposition of which the management must be given a free hand. Similarly, the A.L.B. ruled that management must have "wide latitude" in the employment of its supervisory force and that the seniority rules, therefore, did not protect foremen.[66]

In decisions regarding its rule that seniority was to be determined by the length of an employee's service in the plant rather than in a group or in a department or on a particular job in the plant, the A.L.B. explained that an employee who would otherwise be laid off was to be transferred to the job of another employee in the plant who was junior to him in length of service but only if there was work in the plant for which the employee of longer service was qualified, that is, as the A.L.B. defined it, "work for which he is available immediately in the circumstances in which it has to be done." The A.L.B. also ruled that an employee could transfer his seniority to another plant of the same employer if the change in employment was made at the request of the employer. This was contrary to the wishes of the A.F. of L., which contended that an employee should be permitted to retain seniority as compared to other employees only in the plant in which he was originally employed.[67]

As for the rule that cases of discharge or quitting as distinguished from layoffs were to be clearly indicated on the employee's record, Wolman stipulated that this did not require a company to notify its laid-off employees that they would be rehired during the next production season, although the A.L.B. apparently regarded this as a desirable procedure. The board, at the same time, disapproved of the practice of using a layoff as the means of actually terminating an employee's service.[68]

In decisions in seniority cases in which it found for the employee, the A.L.B. would state that the complainant should be returned promptly to work that he could do, that he should be returned to work on the basis of his seniority, that he should be substituted for men working who had less seniority than he, that his seniority should be calculated as though he had not been laid off, or that he should be returned to work with the seniority that he would have had if he had not been discharged and with the period of the discharge to be included in his service. When the employer was upheld in seniority cases, the A.L.B. would generally state that the management had not erred in the action that it had taken.[69]

The A.L.B. decision in favor of the employer in a seniority case involving the layoff of Robert Giroux, a Pontiac Motor Company employee, was particularly galling to U.A.W. officials, and properly so. The A.L.B. stated that Giroux's representatives had not given the board the facts that would have permitted it to determine that his layoff had been unjustified. The board had not been told the day from which his seniority should rank, the department in which he should have a job, or the individuals in the plant whom he was eligible to "bump." Collins protested that the union, which had not been given access to company records, had presented whatever data it could, that the board should have secured from the company such additional information as it needed to render a decision, that the union should not be placed in the position of having to indicate who should be laid off to provide a place for an employee who had been the victim of discrimination, and that the A.L.B.'s remarks in the decision concerning the union's presentation of its case were "gratuitous, unfair and inaccurate."[70] The Giroux case involved only one worker, but the nature of the board's remarks was symptomatic of an attitude toward the U.A.W. that, to say the least, annoyed the union leadership.

The A.L.B. did not object to some deviation from its layoff and rehiring rules provided that this was mutually agreeable to the employer and employees concerned. As Alfred Williams informed one employer, "The Board does not feel itself necessarily bound to impose upon the Industry a uniform method of calculating seniority. Any reasonable system that is agreeable to both parties, the Board is not inclined to interfere with." As a consequence, some of the stronger U.A.W. locals were able to secure layoff and rehiring arrangements that were more to their liking than the procedures specified by the A.L.B. The Seaman Body local and the management agreed that layoff and rehiring should be on "a straight seniority basis by operation groups," except that when production began, Class D employees were to be the first recalled. Similarly, at the International

Harvester plant in Springfield, Ohio, marriage and dependency were not considered a factor in the calculation of seniority, and the order of layoff and rehiring was determined by service alone.[71]

On the whole, it would appear that the employers administered the A.L.B.'s seniority rules in a nondiscriminatory manner, and, as Chalmers pointed out, when one considers the number of employees in the industry, "surprisingly few" cases involving the violation of the seniority rules were brought to the board's attention. Concerns like G.M., as the firm's director of industrial relations declared, made an effort in implementing the May 18 rules "to avoid all possible cases of discrimination." [72]

Whatever their imperfections, the A.L.B. layoff and rehiring rules were a major step forward in the area of industrial relations in the automobile industry, an industry in which the sameness of the jobs and the high rate of labor turnover made the calculation of seniority peculiarly important from the point of view of the employees. The rules gave the automobile factory worker a measure of security on the job that he had never before enjoyed and "a substantial degree of protection from unfair foremen." With the application of the May 18 rules, the automobile industry became the first in the country to follow "uniform seniority rules on an industry-wide basis."

After the N.I.R.A. was declared unconstitutional, G.M. and other companies continued to apply the A.L.B. rules until the U.A.W. was able to win approval for layoff and rehiring procedures that were more acceptable to it than the original A.L.B. rules and which made length of service the principal factor in the determination of job tenure. The provision in the early U.A.W. contracts, however, for a six-month probationary period for employees before they acquired a seniority status and the preference in employment despite length of service given to employees whose skills were deemed vital by management to the operation of the plant suggest the continuing influence of the A.L.B. rules even after 1935.[73]

Finally, the A.L.B. layoff and rehiring rules were not without their effect on the internal administrative structure of the automobile companies. The implementation of the rules required the careful keeping of service records and the determination of the order of layoff and rehiring on the basis of these records. These were obviously tasks that could better be performed by staff officials than by individual foremen, with the result that central employment offices of the corporations, where they were not already doing so, began to assume functions with regard to firing, layoff, and rehiring that had formerly been the responsibility of the plant supervision. Similarly, the necessity of adjusting employee complaints of discrimination and of quickly disposing of cases that might otherwise have led to an adverse A.L.B. ruling and possible damage to the public image of the company were matters more safely entrusted to a central industrial-relations staff than to individual plant foremen.   Thus, the adjustment of the discrimination cases in Flint which Collins submitted to the A.L.B. soon after its formation was *"the first purely administrative duty* in collective bargaining assumed by the industrial relations staff" of G.M.[74]

VIII

THE A.L.B. AND COLLECTIVE BARGAINING

I

"THE MOST CONTENTIOUS of the issues confronting the Board," as the A.L.B. recognized in its report of February 1935, was that of "achieving and enforcing processes of genuine collective bargaining." Organized labor was, in the end, more critical of the A.L.B.'s performance in this area than in any other phase of its work, but Wolman and Kelley believed the union's complaints to be without substance. The A.L.B. thought that part of the difficulty, at least, stemmed from the obvious lack of experience and skill in collective bargaining of both labor and management and from the tendency of the unionists to confuse the process of bargaining with the results desired therefrom. It is easy to sympathize with the A.L.B. in this matter since, as a prominent union official of the time later recalled, "One would have to recognize the fact that practically everybody . . . that was functioning at that time, both on the part of management as well as labor, was in pretty much of a high state of confusion. Nobody knew where they were going, or why." [1]

The A.L.B. argued in its final report that little could have been accomplished by collective bargaining in the automobile industry during the period of the board's existence in view of the high hourly wage rates already being paid by the automobile manufacturers and the excess number of employees on company payrolls as the result of management efforts to spread the work. [2] This observation, however, accurate as it might be, ignored the fact that the automobile unions were interested not only in improved wages and hours but also in their status in the industry and in gaining recognition as the representative of the workers, and it was for this reason that they attached so much importance to the manner in which they were received by their employers.

Wolman's advice to the auto unionists when they complained of management's alleged refusal to bargain with them or to accord them the recognition they sought was to be patient and to appreciate how difficult it had been for the automobile employers to adjust to the requirements of Section 7(a) and how much improvement in labor-management relations there had been in the industry since 1933. "You have to go through a period of inequality of conditions in different plants," Wolman advised the officers of the U.A.W. Flint locals.[3] In view of the law on the subject, however, the automobile unions did not understand why "inequality of conditions" had to be tolerated.

When it assumed office, the A.L.B. did not believe, in view of what it regarded as "the state of excitement" in the industry, that the time was propitious for the introduction of a plan to implement the theory of collective bargaining expressed in the March 25 settlement. It did, however, advise the employers that they would have to meet with representatives of all labor groups in the industry in "bona fide collective bargaining" and without favoring one group over another. To "avoid friction," the board specifically requested that there be no solicitation of membership during working hours by either company or outside-union representatives.[4]

In order to provide evidence of its majority status in at least some of the automobile plants and to establish its right to bargain for the members that it claimed, the A.F. of L., as soon as the A.L.B. took office, began to submit to the board membership lists of some of the U.A.W. locals. Within a short time, the A.L.B. had in its hands the lists of fourteen automobile locals, all but two of them in G.M. plants, and only one of them, the Hudson local, in a Detroit automobile plant. To verify these lists, the A.L.B. engaged the services of Francis E. Ross, and Ross eventually hired a staff of ten persons to aid him in this task.[5]

The verification of the union lists proved to be no easy matter. The lists included the names of fully paid-up union members, employees who had paid only part of their union obligations, and workers who had simply signed union membership blanks but had paid neither the required initiation fee nor union dues. Under the circumstances, it was difficult to determine which of the names on the lists could be included within the settlement's definition of an outside-union member as one who was "a paid-up member in good standing" or who was "legally obligated to pay up." To complicate matters further, the employers requested the A.L.B. to establish the authenticity of the names appearing on the union membership blanks by comparing them with independently gathered signatures, a procedure the A.L.B. declined to follow because of the obvious difficulties involved. A final problem posed by the U.A.W. membership lists was that they included the names of workers who belonged to, or were at least claimed as members by, other labor organizations, and particularly by the company unions.[6]

Had the A.L.B. wished to use union membership lists as a basis for establishing a plan of representation in the automobile industry, it could have made an arbitrary definition of what constituted membership or could have discussed the matter with labor and management representatives in an attempt to arrive at some mutually agreeable solution of the problem. As it was, despite the difficulties presented by the lists, the board did have them all verified, and it did advise the Jackson Motor Shaft Company that a comparison of its payroll with the membership list of the plant's U.A.W. local revealed that over half of the firm's employees were members of the union. In the end, however, the A.L.B. decided that a plan of proportional representation could not be introduced in the automobile industry on the basis of lists of claimed union membership and that elections would have to be held for this purpose. This was unquestionably a sound conclusion considering the nature of the lists, but the failure of the board to explain to the A.F. of L. why it had found the lists inadequate served but to exacerbate the already strained relations between the union and the board.[7]

Unwilling to wait until the A.L.B. completed the verification of the union membership lists that had been submitted to it, several U.A.W. locals sought conferences with management early in April 1934 to discuss union grievances and to present demands. Following one of these conferences, at the Fisher Body plant in Cleveland on April 10, the local jubilantly announced that it had been "officially" recognized by the management for purposes of collective bargaining. If by this statement the union meant to create the impression that it had been recognized as the exclusive bargaining agency for the Cleveland Fisher Body employees, it certainly was overstating management's conception of what had taken place. The plant manager, L. R. Scafe, explained following the conference that the company had "recognized these men as representatives of a number of workers in the plant. I don't know how many they represent, nor whom they represent," Scafe declared, "but I do know they represent someone." The plant manager made it clear, however, that the company union would continue to be the agency through which the majority of the company's employees dealt with the management. The conference, as a matter of fact, had not changed the status of the U.A.W. in the plant in the slightest, and the local had claimed "recognition" because the term had a high prestige value at a time when the U.A.W.

was struggling to exist in the industry. "By meeting with us," declared Paul Miley, the local's president, a few days after the conference and after the union's assertion of recognition had been challenged, "we claim that they recognized the union. However," Miley lamely concluded, "anybody's guess is as good as mine." [8]

The top Fisher Body and G.M. management, which, like the other automobile manufacturers, attached as much symbolic importance to the concept of recognition as union officials did, was perturbed at the statement given out by the Cleveland Fisher Body local following the April 10 conference. E. F. Fisher insisted that the local had simply been granted an "informal conference" and that it would remain for the A.L.B. to determine the right of the U.A.W. to represent any employees in the Fisher Body plants. William Knudsen advised the A.L.B. that G.M. would not confer with the local in the Flint Fisher Body No. 1 plant unless it was clearly understood that such a conference was not to be construed as a recognition by G.M. of the U.A.W. as such or as a recognition that the persons granted the conference represented any employees other than those whom they could prove they represented on the basis of a union membership list.[9]

The A.L.B. tried to meet this problem on a general basis and to smooth ruffled feelings by issuing a statement on April 16 requesting that the employers grant conferences to union representatives without waiting for the A.L.B. to complete its verification of union membership lists. The board stated that the lists which it had already received indicated that in the plants concerned "organized groups of varying sizes, some of them large, now exist." When a union submitted a membership list, it was the opinion of the board that the employers should confer with union representatives while the list was being verified, but it was to be understood that such conferences were not to be interpreted as "recognition of the union as such" nor were employee spokesmen to be regarded as representing employees other than those whom it would ultimately be determined that they represented on the basis of verified membership lists.[10]

The A.L.B.'s April 16 statement provided a basis on which meetings between employers and employees could take place in at least those plants for which union membership lists had been submitted. Following the issuance of the statement, conferences were held at several of the automobile plants, but the results were uniformly disappointing to the union representatives. The Cleveland Fisher Body local conferred with the management on April 18 and submitted demands which, among other things, called for a 20 per cent wage increase, a minimum wage of seventy-five cents per hour, an overtime rate, and a signed contract. Perturbed because the company delayed a reply to its proposals and because of what it believed was the management's continued support of the company union, the Cleveland local, which claimed 4500 of the plant's 8500 employees, decided at a "turbulent" meeting of April 21 to strike the plant the next day. The strike came off as scheduled, and the management, allegedly to avoid violence against nonunion workers, closed down the plant. In a public statement, the company declared that it would not enter into an agreement with "so-called representatives" of the employees, who could not prove "conclusively" that they had been selected without coercion as the March 25 settlement required. The company pointed out that its average wage of eighty-three cents per hour for males and fifty-four cents per hour for females was the highest for comparable work in the automobile industry and in the city of Cleveland and that the union's wage demands were preposterous.[11]

The Cleveland Fisher Body plant was "perhaps the most important link in the chain of Fisher shops," and since it made body stampings for Chevrolet, Pontiac, and Buick cars, a prolonged strike there would have seriously affected G.M.'s auto production. Efforts by the A.L.B. to resolve the dispute were unavailing,[12] and in the meantime the strike spread to St. Louis, Kansas City, and North Tarrytown. In all three instances, the plant unions involved were, for the time being, outside the A.F. of L.

The St. Louis local, which had been seeking in vain prior to March 25 to secure a representation election and company compliance with a regional labor board decision in the union's favor, carried its complaints after March 25 to the new A.L.B. Disturbed both by the terms of the settlement and by Collins' treatment of the St. Louis representatives who were in Washington at the time of the settlement, the local seceded from the A.F. of L. and on April 2 established the Federated Automobile Workers of America.[13]

Nettled by the management's treatment of its discrimination claims, the local, on April 23, 1934, the same day that the Cleveland Fisher Body union began its walkout, struck both Chevrolet and Fisher Body. Although the local pulled out most of the forty-five hundred employees of the two companies, G.M. continued to operate the St. Louis plant during the first days of the strike. This led to the usual hostilities between strikers and nonstrikers—one striker was stabbed to death —and created a problem in employer-employee relations that was to remain unresolved during the life of the N.I.R.A.[14]

At North Tarrytown, New York, the Chevrolet and Fisher Body

employees, who had been completely ignored by the A.F. of L., had established their own organization, the Federated Automotive Association (F.A.A.). The union's difficulties with the local G.M. management went back to the end of March 1934, when, according to the union, one of the organization's members had been the victim of discrimination. The A.L.B. failed to compose the issue, with the result that the F.A.A. on April 24 declared a strike against both Fisher Body and Chevrolet. This, at least, was the F.A.A.'s version of what had happened. G.M. stubbornly insisted that there was no strike in North Tarrytown, that it had been forced to lay off some workers there because of a shortage of materials resulting from the Cleveland strike, and that these laid-off workers had then decided to regard themselves as strikers. Whatever the truth in the matter, the F.A.A. had the support of only a handful of Chevrolet workers and a somewhat larger number of Fisher Body workers among the more than five thousand employed in the two plants.[15]

In Kansas City (actually Leeds, Missouri) an A.F. of L. federal labor union had been formed for the workers in the Fisher Body-Chevrolet plant (the two companies, as in St. Louis, were housed under one roof), but following the lead of St. Louis, the Kansas City unionists, early in April, left the A.F. of L. and became Local No. 2 of the Federated Automobile Workers of America. The vice-president and later president of the local was Homer Martin, a thirty-one year old graduate of William Jewell College and a former pastor of the Leeds Baptist church who had been removed from his pulpit in 1932 because of his support of the workingman. He had then taken a job in the Kansas City Chevrolet plant, from which he had been either discharged or laid off in March 1934, allegedly because of his union activities.[16] The Kansas City unionists complained to the A.L.B. that Chevrolet and Fisher Body were discriminating against union members, were actively promoting the company unions in the plant, and had refused to bargain with and to recognize the outside union. The local plant managers, in the words of Edward G. Shaw, the Chevrolet plant manager, contended that they had not refused "to bargain with the employees as employees" but that they had refused "to bargain with a union."

Martin conferred with the A.L.B. in Detroit on April 27 and then issued a statement praising the board members as "men who are capable and desirous of developing a constructive policy which will result in tremendous social and industrial progress." Despite Martin's high opinion of the A.L.B., which was soon to be revised downward, his union did not have sufficient confidence in the board to permit it to mediate the dispute between employer and employee that had developed in Kansas City. On April 30 the Kansas City union, disregarding Martin's advice, joined the strike movement in the G.M. empire that had been triggered by the Cleveland Fisher Body strike.

Of the approximately 2300 persons employed by the two companies at that time, only fifty to sixty Chevrolet workers joined the walkout, but the Fisher Body employees apparently supported the strike in strength. As in St. Louis and North Tarrytown, G.M. kept its Kansas City plant open despite the walkout and with the usual consequences. Strikers tangled with the police and with nonstrikers, and according to Martin the strike was soon "developing into a civil war." One striker was hospitalized with meningitis, which the union attributed to a blow on the head that he had received at the scene of the dispute, and two other strikers were shot.[17]

Although the plea of the Cleveland Fisher Body local for support in its strike had, in effect, been answered by plant unions no longer affiliated with the A.F. of L., none of the U.A.W. locals in Fisher Body plants outside of Cleveland joined in the strike movement. Sentiment to challenge G.M. in the economic field did however develop in the Fisher Body No. 1 local in Flint and in the Fisher Body and Chevrolet locals in Janesville, Wisconsin, and Atlanta because of the unsatisfactory nature of the conferences between union representatives and local G.M. officials. Anxious as always to avoid a strike or at least to keep it localized, Collins informed the A.L.B. on April 27 of the difficulties Fisher Body locals were experiencing in their efforts to engage in collective bargaining with their employers and suggested that the way to cope with this problem and to avert a further spread of the strike was by a summit conference between the top Fisher management and representatives of the U.A.W. locals involved.[18]

Collins' suggestion met with the approval of the A.L.B. and was not opposed by G.M. executives, who were undoubtedly concerned lest the corporation's production of motor vehicles be seriously curtailed by the prolongation of the Cleveland strike at a time when the demand for automobiles was rising.[19] Insisting, however, that they would not confer with strikers, G.M. officials would not consent to the admission of Cleveland Fisher Body union representatives to the proposed meeting unless the Cleveland strike were first terminated. This condition, on which the success of any top-level conference seemed to hinge, was acceptable to the A.F. of L. leadership, which regarded a conference with the G.M. management and a demonstration of the Federation's conservatism as of greater long-range significance for the cause of automobile unionism than a continuation of the Cleveland strike.   Collins and Green, as a matter of fact, were not particularly optimistic that the Cleveland strike, which some automobile unionists thought would eventually tie up G.M. production, could successfully be maintained very much longer.   They feared that G.M. would within a few days reopen the plant with strikebreakers, and there was also the possibility that the plant company union would be successful in its suit for an injunction, initiated on April 28, to prevent the U.A.W. local from interfering with the entry of "loyal" workers into the plant.   The great majority of the employees, the president of the company union asserted, wished to work but they had been "beaten up, pushed around and threatened so that they are afraid to go to the plant, and when they go there they can't get in."

Under pressure from the A.F. of L., unwilling to go it alone, and promised by the A.L.B. that strikers would be permitted to return to their jobs without discrimination, the Cleveland local, whose membership had increased substantially during the walkout, voted on April 29 to call off its strike.[20]   The way was thus cleared for leading G.M. executives to meet for the first time with top A.F. of L. officials and with U.A.W. representatives from more than one plant.   The conference, which began on April 30 and continued until May 2, was held in the G.M. building in Detroit.   Knudsen and Charles T. Fisher represented G.M.; Collins and his staff and representatives of eight Fisher Body locals spoke for the U.A.W.; and the A.L.B. presided over the discussion.   Knudsen would not agree to the admission of union representatives from Kansas City and North Tarrytown because "we don't propose to deal with men on strike," but at the same time he inconsistently maintained that there was no strike in the G.M. plants in these two cities.

The principal subject of discussion at the conference was the manner in which bargaining between the U.A.W. locals and Fisher Body should take place.   Knudsen stoutly insisted that specific issues would have to be discussed at the plant level, but this raised the question as to whether company union, U.A.W., and other outside union representatives were to meet separately with local Fisher Body officials or in a single body.   The employers favored a joint meeting with the various employee groups, but the union officials claimed that meetings of this sort had not been intended by the settlement, that the employees were unlikely to be able to present a solid front to the employer in joint sessions, and that if company-union representatives were included in the employee group, the management would really be represented on both sides of the bargaining table.   Wolman and Kelley sided with the employers on this issue, as did Byrd to some extent, and Wolman argued that the issues would become "all muddled up" if separate employee groups went in to see the management. The union officials, therefore, reluctantly accepted Knudsen's suggestion that in Cleveland and Pontiac at least the representatives of the various organizations in the plant should meet jointly with the management, and it was further agreed that top G.M. and union officials should also attend these conferences. It was understood, but not specifically provided, that conferences would also be held at the other Fisher Body plants and that matters that could not be settled satisfactorily on a local basis would be taken up at a later time with the A.L.B.[21]

Union-management meetings of the type prescribed by the Fisher Body conference were held in Pontiac and Cleveland but nowhere else. At the Pontiac meeting on May 8, the company-union representatives, to the annoyance of the A.F. of L., indicated that they were not dissatisfied with plant conditions. The management promised to investigate the complaints of the U.A.W. local, most of which dealt with the general question of discrimination against union members. The Cleveland negotiations began on May 9, and once again the U.A.W. and the company-union representatives failed to present a common front. The U.A.W. repeated its demand for an overtime rate of time-and-one-half, but the company union indicated that it would be satisfied with time-and-one-third.[22]

"You can not blend these two groups," William Green had declared with regard to joint trade-union, company-union meetings with management, and nothing that happened in the collective-bargaining sessions in Pontiac and Cleveland caused the A.F. of L. to revise this judgment. Perhaps because of the U.A.W.'s determined opposition to the procedure, the A.L.B. did not require that the practice of joint meetings be continued in the other Fisher Body plants, or anywhere else for that matter, but simply stipulated, as it had from the beginning, that in accordance with the endorsement of collective-bargaining pluralism in the settlement, management must bargain with all bona fide labor organizations, a requirement that was not always observed by any means.[23] The board had nothing further to say regarding the composition of employee bargaining committees until December 7, 1934, nor did it until that date prescribe a plan of proportional representation for the industry.

Negotiations to bring an end to the strike at the St. Louis Fisher Body and Chevrolet plant were initiated by the A.L.B. on April 30, 1934, by which time all production at the plant had ceased, but the strike was not officially halted until May 7. Because of the inept-

ness of Richard Byrd or perhaps because Wolman and Kelley failed
to keep their colleague informed of what they were doing, the settlement terms to which the union ultimately agreed were not the same
as the terms that the management had offered and that the majority
of the board had accepted as the official strike agreement. Knudsen
had informed the board on May 2 that because of reduced production
schedules G.M. would be unable to re-employ all the strikers but that
the two companies would be able to use twenty-two hundred workers
immediately. The first to be taken back, the G.M. executive vice-
president declared, would be the employees required to re-establish
the production line, and they would be followed back to work by
men with dependents. In anticipation of the layoff and rehiring rules
soon to be announced by the A.L.B., Knudsen specified that service
with the company prior to September 1, 1933, was to be a condition of
re-employment. Wolman informed the union's president, John Bostwick, of the G.M. terms and advised him further that it was the
A.L.B.'s understanding that as production increased, former employees
would be taken back in the order Knudsen had indicated and without
discrimination against strikers and also that these employees would be
re-engaged after the next layoff before any new workers were hired.

Before the union responded one way or another to these proposals, Richard Byrd arrived in St. Louis on May 6 and secured the
local's agreement to end the strike but on terms different from those
set forth in Knudsen's letter to Wolman of May 2. The statement of
agreement, which Byrd signed for the A.L.B., provided that employees
who had worked for the company prior to September 1, 1933, would
be the first recalled to work or interviewed for re-employment and that
certain departments that required additional employees after the first
group had been recalled would also engage men whose service with
the companies began after September 1, 1933. Byrd's terms made no
reference to a priority group required to re-establish the production
line nor to men with dependents, and they certainly left the impression that the strikers whose employment antedated September 1, 1933,
would be quickly returned to work. Since most of the strikers fell
into this category, union officials assumed that the 118 persons against
whom they were still alleging discrimination would soon be back at
their jobs.[24]

The implementation of the St. Louis strike terms—the A.L.B. regarded Knudsen's May 2 proposals rather than Byrd's May 6 terms as
the official settlement—embittered the relations between the St. Louis
local and G.M. and between the local and the A.L.B. In resuming
production at the plant, G.M. gave first preference to those who had

worked during the strike regardless of their seniority as compared to strikers. Although Knudsen's terms did not specifically call for any such order of re-employment, the A.L.B. did not object to this procedure. As the board apparently interpreted the strike settlement, G.M. in resuming operations could favor nonstrikers over strikers, but once the next layoff occurred, the nonstrikers were to lose their preferred position and were to retain only the seniority to which they were entitled on the basis of the length of their service and the number of their dependents.[25]

The local complained bitterly and continuously to the A.L.B. not only about the preference initially given to nonstrikers but also that the two companies were hiring employees whose service had begun after September 1, 1933, and even new employees, in preference to some of the older workers, that among employees whose service had antedated September 1, 1933, the companies did not always give preference in re-employment to the more senior employees and those with the most dependents, that physical examinations were being used as an excuse to deny strikers their jobs, that great pressure was put on re-employed strikers to join the company unions in the two firms, and, finally, that strikers were often returned to far less desirable jobs than they had previously held.[26]

That neither Fisher Body nor Chevrolet was making any serious effort to comply with the St. Louis strike settlement became evident when Francis Ross in June 1934 checked the employment records of the two firms. Ross reported to the A.L.B. that these records seemed to indicate that 310 Chevrolet workers and at least 151 Fisher Body workers who were entitled to jobs had not been re-employed. It is also clear that Chevrolet in particular found exceedingly disagreeable assignments for some of the strikers whom it had called back to work. The job of installing wheels on trucks or of hanging wheels on the conveyor line was given to workers who had not previously performed this kind of demanding and disagreeable work. It was natural for the local to look upon these job assignments as a company tactic to "kill off" strikers and to disrupt the union. The A.L.B. later ordered the company to rehire some of the workers who had been discharged for inability to perform their new assignments, but, as was its practice, the board refused to do anything for workers who had quit their new jobs for one reason or another.[27]

Aware that Fisher Body and Chevrolet were not complying with the strike settlement terms, Wolman on June 21, after earlier letters had had very little effect, wrote sharply to Knudsen and Charles T. Fisher that large numbers of persons who should have been returned to their jobs had still not been re-employed and that unless the matter were cleared up within a week, the A.L.B. would "have to consider issuing an order returning the appropriate people to their jobs, and displacing those of lesser service." Fisher Body and Chevrolet responded to this warning with sufficient alacrity to satisfy the A.L.B., and the board did not find it necessary to issue an order of the kind that Wolman had threatened.[28]   The St. Louis unionists might have been comforted to know that the A.L.B. had put some pressure on G.M. to comply with the strike settlement, but Wolman, who did not hesitate to criticize the unions publicly, had used the channels of private communication to indicate the board's displeasure with management's behavior.   The whole episode also reveals that the record of employer compliance with A.L.B. policies and rulings was not quite as perfect as Wolman sometimes indicated.

The slowness of the A.L.B. in dealing with the post-strike situation in St. Louis and the ineffectiveness, as the union saw it, of the board's efforts led the St. Louis local, which soon after the strike had reaffiliated with the A.F. of L., to become increasingly discouraged with the A.L.B. as a labor-relations tribunal.   After the union's secretary had earlier complained that the "total efforts" of the board to settle St. Louis discrimination cases had amounted to "exactly nil," the executive board of the local advised the A.L.B. on November 23, 1934, that the union had voted to have no further dealings with the board.   The A.L.B. tried thereafter to contact individual St. Louis Fisher Body and Chevrolet workers to ascertain if they wished to have their cases heard, but apparently most St. Louis unionists after November refused to let the board handle their complaints.   "The labor board to my knowledge," one of the local's members wrote to the A.L.B., "is nothing but a double crossing outfit, that should be wiped out of the Automobile workers [sic] mind." [29]

The St. Louis local in its long and unhappy battle with Fisher Body and Chevrolet had become disillusioned not only with the A.L.B. but also with the A.F. of L.   The local officers, who became identified with the "progressive" opposition to the Federation's leadership in the automobile industry, were distressed at the lack of support the St. Louis unionists had received from the Federation and also at the "spirit of pacifism" that they believed "permeates the organization in the Detroit area."   At the end of May the local voted for the ouster of Francis Dillon as the chairman of the National Council that the A.F. of L. had set up for the automobile industry, and Dillon, in retaliation, removed the St. Louis officers from their posts.[30]

After having thoroughly confused the situation in St. Louis, Byrd moved on to Kansas City, where the strike was going badly for the workers and the union itself, which had rejoined the A.F. of L., seemed on the verge of collapse. With distressing consistency, Byrd muddied the waters once again by negotiating a strike settlement with the union and the local plant management that differed from the settlement which the majority of the board arranged with William Knudsen and which it treated as the official settlement. The accounts of the peace negotiations in Kansas City are not entirely clear, but it would seem that Byrd appeared at a union meeting on the evening of May 6 and secured the approval of the local for the end of the walkout on the basis of the return of the strikers to work without discrimination and with the A.L.B. to adjust all disputed cases. Later that evening Byrd met in a Kansas City hotel with Homer Martin and another union official and with the Chevrolet and Fisher Body plant managers to work out the precise details of the settlement. The terms agreed on, which were subject to the approval of the local management's supervisors in Detroit, were then telephoned to the A.L.B. by its labor member.

The Byrd strike agreement called for the re-employment without discrimination of the 53 or 54 Chevrolet strikers "subject to the best possible arrangement" the plant manager could make "to avoid possible trouble in the plant." Both companies were to re-engage injured men, whether or not they had gone on strike, as soon as production and the state of their health permitted, and they were to re-employ all strikers without discrimination before hiring any new employees for the same class of work.[31]

The agreement negotiated in Detroit on May 7 between Knudsen and the A.L.B. majority, possibly in ignorance of the terms Byrd had arranged, provided that the men on the Chevrolet payroll on April 27, that is, just prior to the strike, were to be rehired when needed but were to be given priority over entirely new employees. The Fisher Body strikers were also to be rehired before new employees were engaged, but no one was to be laid off to provide a place for strikers. Unlike the St. Louis strike settlement, the Kansas City agreement did not commit G.M. to rehire anyone at once and did not provide for the preferential treatment of employees with dependents and who had service records with the companies antedating September 1, 1933.[32] These terms, if union officials are to be believed, were not conveyed to the local until June 4, but the A.L.B. on May 12 did promise the union's president, as he put it, that the union would be given a "square deal" in the re-employment of "all strikers, 'lay offs' and 'discharges'" and that there would be a "complete settlement" of the Kansas City troubles within one week.[33]

As it turned out, there was not to be a "complete settlement" of the Kansas City case during the life of the A.L.B., much less within the week following May 12. Like the St. Louis local after the settlement of its strike, the Kansas City local bombarded the A.L.B. with complaints that Chevrolet and Fisher Body were not living up to the terms of the agreement. It was alleged that the two companies retained "scabs and rats" and refused to rehire strikers who should have been re-employed and that workers who had been returned to their jobs had then been laid off while nonstrikers with less seniority had been retained.[34]

The union complaints, although frequently exaggerated, were not altogether without substance. Ignoring the settlement, which required him to re-employ strikers before hiring new employees, the manager of the Fisher Body plant, on the day following the termination of the strike, had made up his work force from among persons who appeared at the factory in quest of jobs regardless of whether or not the settlement made them eligible for employment. When Wolman phoned him about this, the plant manager professed to be ignorant of any official agreement concluding the strike. The A.L.B. chairman, who was himself a bit confused regarding the terms of the strike settlement, protested to Knudsen on June 8 that the strikers were to be returned in the order of their seniority before new men were engaged. Knudsen reminded the A.L.B. chairman that the settlement had made no mention of seniority, but by this time the A.L.B.'s seniority rules were in effect, and presumably they superseded the Kansas City strike terms with regard to the re-employment of the strikers. At all events, it was decided that the A.L.B. would check the employment records of the two firms to ascertain if the settlement terms were being observed. The search of the records, conducted by Francis Ross, indicated that as of June 22 ninety-nine Chevrolet workers and seventy-six Fisher Body workers who had not been re-employed might have been "entitled to jobs."[35]   Once again, as in St. Louis, the record of employer compliance left something to be desired.

Like its counterpart in St. Louis, the Kansas City local was dissatisfied with the slowness with which the A.L.B. addressed itself to employee complaints and its failure to adjust these complaints to the satisfaction of the union. "Don't send any more promises," the president of the local wired Byrd on June 2. "We were in better shape before agreement." Homer Martin complained on August 2 that "the

Board is so darned slow that the people lose all hope," and later in the month he informed Collins, in disgust, that "No Board will ever get an opportunity to again put an end to a strike here." Forgetting that only a week previously he had advised Collins that the strike had already been lost when Byrd appeared on the Kansas City scene and that the wise course had been "to throw the thing into the lap of the Board and save as much as possible of our swiftly breaking union," Martin decided on August 15 that the unionists had been defeated because "we foolishly put our trust in the Board." Since the companies were "not doing any more than they had to in order to hold that damn Board," he began talking grandiloquently in January 1935 of a march on Washington or of securing an injunction to restrain Fisher Body and Chevrolet from violating the strike settlement, but Francis Dillon thought as little of these ideas as the local plant managers thought of Martin's proposal to have Kansas City cases transferred from the A.L.B. to the N.L.R.B.[36] With his union's membership dwindling to the vanishing point, Martin was hoping for some dramatic action that would impress the automobile workers and attract them once again to the union cause.

The "foolish strike" in North Tarrytown, to use Collins' phrase, was brought to an end by May 11 by direct negotiation between Knudsen and Wolman but apparently without official approval of the settlement terms by the union. The agreement provided that the strikers would be returned to work before new men were hired and in accordance with the March 25 settlement but that no one would be laid off to make a place for a striker. Otto Kleinert, the president of the Tarrytown local, which soon after the strike became a regular A.F. of L. federal labor union, declared himself to be "entirely dissatisfied" with these terms, but his union was in no position to resist their implementation.[37]

Although several of the Fisher Body federal labor unions complained that the summit conference of April 30–May 2, 1934, had failed to produce any change in the attitude of local Fisher Body officials regarding the status and grievances of the federal labor unions in their plants, only the Fisher Body No. 1 local in Flint resorted to a strike to gain its demands. The unionists in the plant were mainly concerned about production standards and the piece rates set by management for work on a new and smaller Buick body, but the tension between the local and the company was heightened by the insistence of the management that company-union representatives should sit in with outside union officials in discussions with the employer.

The strike began on May 10 and was terminated a week later on the basis of a settlement worked out by the A.L.B. in consultation with Knudsen, Charles T. Fisher, and Francis Dillon. The agreement simply provided that the management would discuss the various employee grievances with a committee of worker representatives, but since company-union officials were to be excluded from the conferences between the U.A.W. and the employer, the A.F. of L. leadership declared itself pleased with the outcome. There was little change, however, in working conditions in the plant or in the status of the union following the settlement.[38]

The termination of the Flint walkout brought to an end the strike movement of April and May 1934 in the plants of the Fisher Body Company. All of the U.A.W. federal labor unions concerned had sought by the strike route to establish a more satisfactory collective-bargaining relationship with the Fisher Body management, but the settlements arranged by the A.L.B. left employer-employee relations substantially as they had been before the walkouts. In the months that followed the strikes, the federal labor unions failed to secure the recognition that they sought, and they found it increasingly difficult to attract the automobile workers to the U.A.W. cause.

With the return of the Fisher Body workers to their jobs, the automobile manufacturing industry was entirely free of strikes, but the peace of the parts industry was marred by a strike in Toledo directed against the Electric Auto-Lite Company and two other parts manufacturers. The A.L.B. could have intervened in this strike only with the consent of both parties to the dispute, but initially the management and later the union refused to allow the issues in contention to be referred to the Wolman board. The Toledo local, in the end, won its strike on the picket line; and, unlike the Fisher Body locals, it secured signed contracts from its employer antagonists and established itself as one of the strongest of all the U.A.W. federal labor unions.

The strike of Toledo's Federal Labor Union No. 18384 was directed against the Electric Auto-Lite Company, the Bingham Stamping and Tool Company, and the Logan Gear Company. The three concerns were interlocked in ownership in that Bingham was completely owned by Logan Gear, and C. O. Miniger, the president of Auto-Lite, and Daniel Kelly, the vice-president and general manager of the firm, were Logan Gear stockholders. The Electric Auto-Lite management was not particularly popular in Toledo because of Miniger's prominent connection with the failure in 1932 of the Ohio Bank and the Security Bank.[39] This may account for the fact that public sentiment in Toledo during most of the dispute was on the side of the strikers.

It will be recalled that a brief strike against Auto-Lite and the other two companies had been terminated on February 28 on the understanding that the companies and the union would negotiate in an effort to agree upon improved standards that would become effective on April 1 and that there would be no strike or lockout "so long as peaceful methods of adjusting differences have not been exhausted." When the bargaining for new terms of employment was initiated, the union demanded, among other things, a 20 per cent wage increase and what the employers interpreted as a closed shop.[40] Electric Auto-Lite, the most important of the three concerns involved, granted a 5 per cent increase to its workers at the beginning of April, and it appears that the union would have settled for an additional 5 per cent from Auto-Lite and a matching 10 per cent increase from the other two companies. Bingham and Logan Gear, which were in serious financial difficulties, were unwilling, however, to increase the wages of their workers, and Electric Auto-Lite, although in a much stronger financial position than the other two, regarded its 5 per cent increase as sufficient. The differences between the local and the employers on the union-security question also could not be reconciled, with the result that the union struck the Bingham plant on April 11, Electric Auto-Lite on April 13, and Logan Gear on April 17.[41]

The union succeeded in pulling out at least 75 per cent of Bingham's 538 employees, about five hundred of the seventeen hundred Auto-Lite employees, and a minority of the eight hundred Logan Gear workers. All three concerns continued to operate despite the walkout and hired new workers to replace the strikers. Bingham stated that it would rehire strikers as long as there was a place for them, but Electric Auto-Lite announced that the strikers had lost their jobs and that it would rehire only those who were staying away from work because they had been intimidated. All three concerns indicated by the first of May that they had all the employees that they needed, and J. A. Minch, Auto-Lite's vice-president, asserted that as far as his company was concerned, the strike was over.[42]

On April 17, after there had been some scuffling between strikers and nonstrikers in front of the Auto-Lite plant, Common Pleas Judge Roy Stuart, on the application of Auto-Lite and Bingham, issued a restraining order limiting the number of pickets at the Auto-Lite plant to fifty (twenty-five at each of two gates to which the entry of workers was confined) and at the Bingham plant to twenty-five, and prohibiting all picketing by the Socialist party, the Lucas County (Toledo) Unemployed Council, the Lucas County Unemployed League, and all nonunion personnel.[43] The communist-controlled Unemployed Councils and the National Unemployed League, which had been formed by the Conference for Progressive Labor Action and was closely linked with A. J. Muste's American Workers party, itself an outgrowth of the C.P.L.A., not only sought to promote the interests of the jobless by agitating for adequate relief measures and against evictions and foreclosures but also, on occasion, supported the strikes of employed workers. During the February Toledo strike the A.W.U. and the Lucas County Unemployed Council had called for the mass picketing of the struck plants and had talked about closing the Auto-Lite factory as "tight as hell," but in the April strike it was the Musteites and the Lucas County Unemployed League that played the key role in support of the strikers. Since the strikers had received little assistance at the outset from the Toledo Central Labor Union, with which they were not affiliated, and none at all from the A.F. of L. itself, they were willing to accept the aid of the Musteites and may, indeed, have solicited it.[44]

After the restraining order was issued, Lucas County Sheriff David Krieger requested the county commissioners for funds to engage special deputies to help protect the property of the struck concerns. Krieger probably took this action because the Toledo municipal government, hard-pressed financially, had laid off a substantial proportion of the city's police force in the weeks before the strike and had reduced the wages of the remainder. The sheriff's application was denied, however, on the grounds that it had not been demonstrated that the city's police were incapable of dealing with the situation. Krieger thereupon, following the advice of Judge Stuart, appointed 150 deputies on his own responsibility, and Auto-Lite and Bingham—one is reminded of the Pullman strike of 1894—supplied the funds to compensate them.[45] The special deputies were a source of trouble throughout the remainder of the strike.

While hearings were underway to determine whether a temporary injunction should be issued, the union expressed its willingness to submit the dispute to the A.L.B. for arbitration, but the management of the three concerns, although agreeable to the board's participation in so far as questions of discrimination, discharge, and representation were concerned, refused to permit the key issues in contention to go before the tribunal. The three companies informed the A.L.B. that they would not dismiss any of their current employees to make room for strikers, would not allow the question of the closed shop to go before the A.L.B. since they were advised that the closed shop was illegal, and, most important of all, that they would not submit the matter of a wage increase to arbitration since this was basically a question as to whether "they shall be put out of business by being required to pay increased wages." [46]

During the first two weeks of May it became increasingly evident that the strike was going badly for the workers. The M.E.S.A., which controlled the tool and die room in the Auto-Lite plant and had refused to cross the U.A.W. picket lines, agreed on May 7 to let its sixty-two Auto-Lite members return to their jobs because, as M.E.S.A. President Chapman put it, "We feel now that the strike is lost." [47] The secretary of the Toledo C.L.U., Otto W. Brach, reported to Frank Morrison on May 4 that "We are in a desperate situation." As C.L.U. officials saw it, the real opponent of organized labor in the strike was Toledo's Merchants and Manufacturers' Association, which the union leaders believed was seeking not only to destroy the U.A.W. local but to extirpate the union forces in Toledo in general.

Believing that the future of unionism in Toledo was at stake in the Auto-Lite strike, the C.L.U. on May 3 adopted the recommendations of its committee of twenty-three, which represented all the affiliated crafts and trades in the city, instructing union members not to cross the strikers' picket lines, protesting the restraining order against mass picketing, and raising the possibility that the protection of the trade-union interests of the city against the "tyranny" of the employers might necessitate the calling of a general strike. William Green, who thought that the Auto-Lite strike should not even have been called, was dismayed at the prospect that the end result of the walkout might now be a general strike. He wrote Brach on May 17 that he had depended on persons like him "to prevent strike action at a time when conditions were unfavorable." Expressing fear that a situation might develop in Toledo that would cause "great injury" to the labor movement, he cautioned that a sympathetic strike was "a serious matter and should not be ordered except under the most grave circumstances and conditions." On the same day he instructed A.F. of L. organizer Coleman Claherty to proceed from Akron to Toledo and to "speak plainly to the organized workers and their friends there if in your judgment the situation requires you to do so." [48]

Judge Stuart on May 14 issued a temporary injunction against mass picketing and restraining eighty-five nonunion members who had been accused of violence and illegal picketing from appearing in the vicinity of the plant. Both the Unemployed League and the Unemployed Council ignored the order and, as they had been doing for some days, advised the strikers to do likewise. From this point forward, the strike, which had appeared to be lost, was aggressively pursued, and the violence that finally occurred became increasingly predictable. On the fifteenth of May, 107 persons were arrested in front of the Auto-Lite plant for violating the May 14 injunction, and the next day forty-six persons, of whom twenty-four were cited for contempt, were detained for the same reason. Most of those arrested were members of the Unemployed League and were neither strikers nor U.A.W. members. When three additional Auto-Lite pickets were arrested on May 17, a mob of over two hundred strike sympathizers stormed the jail and threatened to break down the doors and to "get" both Stuart and Krieger. Hearings on the contempt charge began in Judge Stuart's court the next day while mobs demonstrated and sang in the courthouse corridors.[49]

Judge Stuart on May 15 issued a permanent injunction against picketing by the twenty-four strike sympathizers and by the Unemployed Council and the Unemployed League, but Thomas J. Ramsey, the union's business agent, who officially at least had been critical of the role that outsiders had begun to play in the strike, announced that mass picketing would continue regardless of court orders. On the afternoon of May 22, as the pickets marched in a continuous circle before the main gate of the Auto-Lite plant and a large crowd of spectators, eventually numbering about two thousand, gathered to observe the proceedings, Minch ordered the day shift to remain in the plant beyond the scheduled time for its departure. When the nonstrikers began to leave the plant two hours after their usual quitting time, there were clashes between them and the pickets and between the pickets and the police, and quiet was not restored until 7:30 P.M. George D. Welles, attorney for Auto-Lite and for the Auto-Lite Council, an inside union that was seeking an injunction against all picketing, stated that "A situation of anarchy exists in this city" and that fifteen hundred "Russianized agitators" were trying to close the plant. The *Toledo News-Bee*, which was not unfriendly to the strikers and was highly critical of Krieger's "company-paid deputies," blamed the rioting, with some justification, on "lawless agitators who do not want a settlement, and who have no desire to work anywhere, but who are looking for trouble and trying to incite it."[50]

The events of May 22, as it turned out, were of a tepid character as compared to the dramatic happenings of the next day. The strikers and their sympathizers massed before the Auto-Lite plant and, despite the efforts of the city police, prevented the workers on the day shift from leaving the factory. Wild rioting followed when Krieger's deputies, operating from inside the plant, used gas guns and grenades to drive back the mob.[51] With a large crowd that eventually numbered an estimated eight thousand persons looking on, the rioters stormed the plant, breaking windows, tearing down fences, and even attempting to set the property on fire. The mob broke into the plant at three points at 1:00 A.M. on the twenty-fourth but was driven off by gas bombs. Hostilities continued throughout the early hours of the morning after a "nightlong reign of terror" that kept sixteen hundred to eighteen hundred workers imprisoned in the plant. Ralph Lind, the executive secretary of the Cleveland Regional Labor Board, advised the N.L.B. that not a window had been left in the plant—"The Auto-Lite is now in reality an Open Shop," the rioters grimly joked—and that a "whole hell of [a] lot" had been wounded.[52]

The violence of May 23 set in operation a series of actions that led ultimately to the settlement of the Toledo strike, although that hardly appeared to be the shape of things on the morning of the twenty-fourth. Governor George White of Ohio sent National Guardsmen into Toledo that morning "to save the lives of the beleaguered employees and restore law and order." White acted on the "urgent request" of Sheriff Krieger and the recommendation of Ansel R. Cleary, representing Ohio's State N.R.A. Compliance Director, and only after Auto-Lite officials had assured him that they would be willing to submit the dispute to arbitration. By May 25 there were 1350 Guardsmen in Toledo, which made this show of force "the largest military display in peace time in the history of Ohio" to that date. The Auto-Lite employees, who had spent the night in the plant, were now sent home, and the plant was closed down, but the siege of the factory continued.[53]

The Guardsmen on May 24 first tried to disperse the picketers with bayonets, but when this failed to achieve the desired result, vomiting and tear gas were used, which caused the strikers and their sympathizers to barricade themselves on the porches of private homes near the plant. Fighting between the mob and the troops raged throughout the day on the twenty-fourth and then broke out again on the afternoon of the twenty-fifth before an audience that, according to police estimates, reached twenty thousand in the early evening. A night of bitter fighting on the twenty-fifth was followed by still more violence the next day as the National Guardsmen laid down a heavy blanket of gas and used their bayonets against the rioters while the strikers and their friends hurled bricks, bottles, and assorted other objects at the militia. Two of the strike sympathizers were killed by Guardsmen bullets on May 24, dozens of persons were injured, scores were temporarily jailed, and a considerable amount of property in the vicinity of the plant was damaged.[54]

During the rioting of May 23 the police arrested five of the ringleaders for violation of the picketing injunction. Among them were one member of the Lucas County Unemployed Council and three Musteites, including Louis F. Budenz, the executive secretary of the American Workers party. Just prior to his arrest Budenz, who had apparently conceived the idea of the deliberate violation of the injunction, had publicly proclaimed that "We are here to smash the injunction once and for all." When he and his cohorts were put on trial, their defense was led by Arthur Garfield Hays, who had been sent into Toledo for the purpose by the American Civil Liberties Union. The Musteites, of course, made much of the use of National Guardsmen in the strike and the killing of two strike sympathizers; and not to be outdone by their rivals, who in the weird communist lexicon were labeled as "'left' social-fascists," the communists mobilized their entire apparatus of front organizations to protest the "murders" committed by the "troops of the capitalist government" and the "bloodthirsty . . . Roosevelt New Dealers." Unlike the Musteites, however, the communists, despite a great deal of violent rhetoric and efforts to promote the usual united front to support and extend the strike, played only a very limited part in the proceedings. John Williamson, state organizer of the Communist party in Ohio, conceded that the A.W.U. "played no role during the strike." The Communist party itself, he thought, was handicapped in the strike "by its prior isolation from the Auto-Lite workers and the trade union movement generally." [55]

The use of troops in the Auto-Lite strike antagonized the locals affiliated with the Toledo C.L.U. and increased the pressures building up for a general strike. An impending strike by the Toledo local of the International Brotherhood of Electrical Workers against Toledo Edison,[56] originally scheduled for May 28 but postponed until May 31 and once again until June 1, would in itself have paralyzed the industrial life of the city, and it began to appear that unless this strike could be averted, the dreaded general strike would surely be called. At a C.L.U. meeting on the night of May 31 it was announced that ninety-five of the 103 affiliated Toledo locals had pledged themselves to support a mass walkout should this become necessary. The decision to call the strike was entrusted to the committee of twenty-three, whose chairman announced that unless immediate action were taken by President Roosevelt to restore labor peace in Toledo, the date for the general strike would be set in forty-eight hours.[57]

Department of Labor Conciliator E. H. Dunnigan had been seeking since May 15 to head off the Toledo Edison strike. The violence of May 23 persuaded Secretary of Labor Perkins, however, that the explosive Toledo situation required an additional federal peacemaker, and she therefore appointed Charles P. Taft, the son of William Howard Taft, as a special mediator. Taft and Dunnigan were joined in the effort to bring industrial peace to Toledo by Ralph Lind, who was assigned to the city by Senator Wagner, the N.L.B. chairman.[58]

When Taft arrived in Toledo on May 24, he found company officials "very much wrought up" over the violence at the Auto-Lite plant and "quite unable to appreciate" his "suggestion that after all every kid likes to throw a rock once in a while and that while the violence was not to be condoned, it certainly was understandable." [59] Taft's initial efforts to break the strike deadlock proved to be unavailing. The union rejected his proposal that the closed Auto-Lite plant be allowed to operate while the points at issue were submitted to the A.L.B. for binding arbitration, and the Auto-Lite management and the Auto-Lite Council were equally unwilling to accept a suggestion that, pending arbitration, the plant remain closed or that the strikers, who numbered about five hundred, be permitted to replace the five hundred or so employees who had been hired since the strike began. The question of reopening the plant was, in the end, settled by Governor White, who announced that he would not permit Auto-Lite to resume production under military protection, which meant, for all practical purposes, that the plant would remain closed until strike terms could be arranged.[60]

Chances for a settlement improved at the end of May when both Miniger and Ramsey, the latter after thinking about the matter "out in the woods," receded from their earlier positions and submitted new proposals that were very similar in content. Ramsey, whom Taft regarded as "utterly inexperienced and temperamentally unqualified to handle the job," was by this time being aided by A.F. of L. organizer T. N. Taylor and also by W. Ellison Chalmers, a member of Collins' staff. Claherty had earlier advised Green that the Toledo strike required the presence of a trained union man, but the A.F. of L. president, in a pathetic reply on May 25, confessed that "I hardly know what to do in this situation at the present moment" since he did not have a single trained organizer to assign to the city. Taylor and Chalmers finally came to Ramsey's aid, however, and they played an important part in the negotiations that led to the settlement of the strike.[61]

A major obstacle to the ending of the strike was removed on June 1 when Dunnigan and Taft, after many days of patient effort, finally secured an agreement on the key wage issue in the Toledo Edison dispute, and the electrical workers called off their threatened strike. News of this decision ended talk of a general strike in Toledo, much to the discomfiture of the Musteites and the communists. The Ohio National Guard was withdrawn from the city on June 2, and three days later Lind was able to report to the N.L.B. that "The battle of Toledo is officially settled and the peace treaties in the form of working agreements for a six months period have been signed." [62]

The signed strike settlements provided that the three companies would negotiate with the company unions and the federal labor union in their plants and would not "discriminate against, intimidate or coerce" any employee because of his membership or nonmembership in any group. Layoff and rehiring procedures were to be governed by the A.L.B.'s seniority rules except that the workers were to share in the determination of who was to be placed in Class D and the September 1, 1933, date specified in the May 19 rules was altered to February 23, 1934, the date the previous parts strike began. All strikers were to be returned to their jobs as rapidly as possible and within one week from the date of the agreement, and employees on the payroll on June 1 were to be retained as the companies saw fit, which meant that strikers were given job preference over nonstrikers. If layoffs became necessary, employees not on the payroll on February 23 were to be the first to be let go. Auto-Lite agreed to put an additional 5 per cent wage increase into effect when the plant reopened and specified that the minimum hourly rates of its employees would be not less than 5 per cent above the code minima. Bingham and Logan Gear, which, unlike Auto-Lite, had not granted a 5 per cent wage increase on April 1, also promised a 5 per cent pay boost in all hourly and base rates.[63]

In a separate agreement of June 4 Bingham and Logan Gear gave the executive shop committee of the federal labor union the privilege of appointing a certified public accountant within ten days to check the books of the two companies to ascertain if their combined operations for the year up to that date had resulted in a profit or loss. If the union failed to appoint the accountant within the allotted time or if he reported that the companies were losing money, the wage rates provided in the agreement were to remain in effect for six months. If he reported a profit for the two companies, the question of a wage increase to be effective as of June 1 was to be determined for each company by a board of four members, two of whom would be appointed by the employer and two by the union. If these four-man boards could not come to a decision, a fifth member was to be appointed to each board by the other four members or, if they could not agree among themselves, by the A.L.B. When this agreement was invoked, it was discovered that the companies had suffered a combined net loss of $92,268.02 for the first five months of 1934 and were therefore not required to exceed the 5 per cent increase provided for in the strike agreement.[64]

Although Federal Labor Union No. 18384 had failed to gain all of its strike demands and although its treasury had been depleted, it emerged from the Auto-Lite strike as one of the strongest of the U.A.W. locals. It had been tested under fire, had proved its ability to hold its ranks together during a long and bitter strike, and had secured signed contracts which recognized its status in the companies concerned. The A.F. of L. eventually contributed $1000 to help the union defray the legal expenses that it had incurred during the strike, but the local quite rightly believed that what it had achieved, it had achieved without the tangible assistance of the Federation. The aid which it had received on the picket line and which had helped it to win a limited victory was provided by left-wing groups that were highly critical of the A.F. of L., and although these groups in no sense controlled the local, the Musteites in particular gave it a progressive, even radical, tone that caused it to be impatient with the cautious conservatism of the Federation.[65] This difference in outlook between the local and the A.F. of L. proved to be of considerable importance when the federal labor union in March 1935 extended its organizing efforts from the parts plants, where it had enjoyed so much success, to the Chevrolet plant, which it had previously been unable to unionize.

The A.L.B. had been given no opportunity to apply its policies with regard to collective bargaining to the settlement of the Auto-Lite strike. The Toledo local, like most of the other U.A.W. locals, viewed with alarm the later efforts of the Wolman board to implement a plan of proportional representation in the automobile manufacturing industry, and it was the likelihood that this scheme would be put into effect at the Toledo Chevrolet plant that caused Federal Labor Union No. 18384 once again to employ the strike weapon that it had successfully utilized against the Electric Auto-Lite Company.

II

As previously noted, the automobile manufacturers viewed the terms of the March 25 settlement as "fully in accord with the principles of dealing with employees which were adopted by the automobile industry when representation plans or so-called company unions first came into effect." Following the settlement, the employers and the company unions stressed in literature disseminated among the automobile workers that contrary to the allegations of "unscrupulous" labor organizers, the employee associations were regarded as "perfectly legal" by the President and the A.L.B. and it was consequently foolish for a worker to pay dues to an outside labor organization when he could be better represented and at no cost to himself by fellow employees who were thoroughly familiar with his problems.[66]

Wolman and Kelley appear to have regarded the automobile company union as just another labor organization, and they simply insisted that the employers must not discriminate in its favor. Thus, upon taking office, the A.L.B., it will be recalled, had stipulated that neither company unions nor outside unions were to be permitted to solicit membership during working hours, and, similarly, the board ruled following the Fisher Body conference that employers must not discriminate among the representatives of different labor groups in the use of bulletin boards. In a further effort to clarify the rights of individuals and groups under the law and the settlement, the A.L.B. in a statement of May 26 announced that membership in any organized group was "not . . . a necessary qualification for continued employment. The Board is desirous that further irritation should cease."[67]

Some of the employers, and particularly the divisions of G.M., concluded as the result of the N.L.B. automobile hearings of March 1934 and the settlement that followed that the time had come to revise the employee-association constitutions so as to make somewhat less obvious the connection between the management and the inside unions. At a meeting of G.M. divisional managers on March 27, 1934, it was agreed that it would be wise to remove from the constitutions and bylaws of the associations all references to the relationship of the company unions and the management, to eliminate all restrictions on employee membership, and even to remove all eligibility requirements for representatives provided that the status of the works council in the particular plant was "absolutely secure."[68]

Changes in the structure of the employee associations were soon forthcoming in the various G.M. divisions. In the Fisher Body plants in Cleveland, Kansas City, and St. Louis, at least, the revisions were prepared by a committee of the employee association with the aid of a company attorney. One of the major changes made in the Fisher Body plans, which brought them in line with other G.M. plans, was to limit participation in the company union to actual members of the association. In the Fisher Body No. 1 plant in Flint, membership was thus opened to all nonsupervisory employees who had been with the company for fifteen days. An employee had to file an application to become a member, and he remained a member for six months after he had been laid off. The insertion of the membership requirement in the plans was obviously intended to give the company unions a definite status as labor organizations in the eyes of the A.L.B. and also to enable them to provide the board with membership lists should it decide to set up some sort of pro rata representation scheme on the basis of such lists.[69]

The Fisher Body No. 1 revised plan limited the eligibility for service on the employees' council to association members who were over twenty-one, were employed in the particular voting division, and had been with the company for over a year, but the Cadillac plan—apparently the company union was regarded as "absolutely secure" there—did not impose the latter two restrictions. The new Fisher Body plans no longer provided for the automatic presence of the management at company-union meetings and also deprived the management of any role in the amendment process. Although there continued to be neither initiation fees nor membership dues, the plans no longer stated that the costs were to be assumed by the company, and at least in some G.M. divisions the employee associations tried to raise their own funds by dances, athletic events, raffles, and the like. In recognition of the presence of the A.L.B., grievances under the modified plans could be carried, as a final resort, to the "duly constituted Labor Board or tribunal now or hereafter in existence, having jurisdiction to determine such disputes." [70]

Despite the alterations in their structure in the plants of the G.M. divisions, in Hudson,[71] and in some other automobile concerns, and despite A.L.B. rulings, the employee associations continued to be favored by management. The employers thus continued to make bulletin-board space available to the company unions but not to their rivals; they sometimes permitted the company unions, but not the outside labor organizations, to solicit membership on company time and on company property; and some of them supplied the names and addresses of employees to the employee associations but not to the U.A.W. Hudson, until the A.L.B. intervened, mailed company-union membership application blanks to new employees along with the forms to obtain group insurance; and in the AC Spark Plug plant only company-union members, for a time, were permitted to participate in the G.M. Savings and Investment Fund plan, although the management alleged that this had been done in error. The A.F. of L. complained bitterly about employer discrimination in favor of the company unions and called for appropriate A.L.B. action, but the board was just as loath to act on the Federation's protests as it had been on the information previously supplied to it by the N.R.A.'s Compliance Division which pointed to the possible illegality of the company-union plans in the industry.[72]

The most troublesome of the questions pertaining to the company unions that required the attention of the A.L.B. was whether to permit the employee associations to hold their scheduled annual elections in the summer of 1934 and what stance the board should take with regard to the newly chosen representatives when elections were held in contravention of A.L.B. orders. The manner in which the A.L.B. reacted to this problem antagonized the outside unions in the industry and raised serious questions about the board's impartiality.

When Wolman learned on June 14 that the Cadillac company union had held a nominating election the previous day and was planning its final election for the next week, he immediately informed Knudsen in unambiguous language that it was the opinion of the A.L.B. that *all* elections within the industry should be postponed until such time as the A.L.B. was prepared to promulgate its own rules regarding the representation of the workers. The board followed up this action on July 17 by issuing a statement that it had suspended all elections under the plant representation plans until the board had itself laid down rules regarding employee representation.[73]

Despite the clear intent of this statement and despite the fact that the A.L.B. reiterated its ruling in response to petitions from company unions and in conferences with works-council representatives, company-union elections were held in the industry in the summer of 1934 with either the open or covert support of the management in the plants concerned. The elections were generally not held on company property, but the employers supplied the election machinery, paid the election expenses, supplied election officials with lists of eligible employees, permitted employees to vote on company time, and, in some cases, allowed their foremen to urge the employees to participate.

When the A.L.B. questioned works-council representatives about these elections, they generally responded that they had not been informed of the July 17 order, which employers were required to post, or that they believed that it was not improper to hold an election provided the voting did not take place on company property.[74]

The employers, who had conveniently ignored the July 17 ruling, also chose to argue that Kelley had given them to understand that the ban on elections applied only to elections held on company property. In further defense of management's negligence in applying the A.L.B.'s policy, G.M. officials like Alfred Marshall, Chevrolet's director of personnel relations, and Charles E. Wilson, later to become the corporation's president, lamely contended that once the employer had advised the workers of the July 17 order, which, to be sure, they sometimes failed to do, the issue was between the A.L.B. and the employee associations, not between the A.L.B. and the employers. Since G.M. officials had provided material assistance to the company unions in the conduct of their elections, this thesis, which Wolman, incredibly, accepted as reasonable, will not bear serious examination.[75]

Although the A.L.B. did not act as expeditiously as it might have to forestall company-union elections that it knew were to be held, it did at least take the position as late as September 5 that it would not recognize the representatives who had been victorious in these elections. The board was actually preparing to issue a statement to this effect, but it retreated in the face of employer opposition, and on September 18, 1934, announced that although the company-union elections, which had been held as the result of a "misunderstanding" in contravention of the July 17 ruling, were invalid, until the board issued its own regulations pertaining to representation and held its own elections the employers, as "a temporary expedient" and "to avoid confusion," might meet with the newly elected representatives as "unofficial interim representatives of such employees as wish to have these representatives act for them."[76] In this mystifying and tortuously reasoned statement, the A.L.B., which was so quick to criticize union behavior of which it did not approve, not only generously construed as a mere "misunderstanding" the refusal of some of the automobile manufacturers to comply with one of its rulings but failed also to adhere to its own oft-stated position regarding the status of the newly elected representatives.

It should hardly have been a matter for surprise that the A.L.B.'s reaction to the company-union elections intensified the doubts of the outside unions regarding the impartiality of the board. Even Arthur Greer, the president of the Hudson local of the Associated Automobile Workers of America, which, unlike the A.F. of L., had been friendly to the A.L.B., wrote to President Roosevelt that his organization could no longer be expected to deal with a tribunal that was so obviously biased in favor of the employers, and he urged the President to dismiss the A.L.B.'s chairman. Charles E. Wyzanski, Jr., the Solicitor of the Department of Labor, regarded Greer's letter, with its description of the A.L.B.'s policy reversal concerning the company-union elections, as "dynamite," but Wolman pragmatically defended the board's action to Frances Perkins as "the only practical way to deal with a somewhat troublesome and confused matter." It would not have been in accord with the settlement, he explained, to deprive the employees of all representation, and, anyhow, there had been little change in the personnel of the works councils as a result of the elections.[77]

A few weeks before the A.L.B. issued its September 18 statement, G.M., in an effort to provide uniform guidance for its various divisions with respect to employee representation and to inform its employees and the public of the policies which it intended to follow in the sphere of collective bargaining, adopted a corporation policy statement regarding labor-management relations. The statement was mailed to G.M. employees on October 12, with an accompanying letter from Alfred P. Sloan, Jr., in which the G.M. president declared that the corporation recognized collective bargaining as "a constructive step forward" and that it was its intention "not only to continue the idea, but to develop it."

In the statement itself, the G.M. management asserted its belief that there was "no real conflict of interests between employers and employees" and no reason why the problems as between them could not be settled *within the organization*. The company wished to make it clear, however, that its endorsement of collective bargaining did "not imply the assumption by the employee of a voice in those affairs of management which management, by its very nature, must ultimately decide upon its own responsibility." Similarly, although controversial questions of fact might be submitted to arbitration, there could be no referral to impartial agencies of issues which, if compromised, might adversely affect "the long-term interests of the business."

Division managers were advised that they did not satisfy the requirements of collective bargaining merely by listening to employee proposals and that they must make every effort to arrive at a satisfactory agreement. They were reminded, however, that mere membership in a labor or employee organization did not in itself establish the right of the organization to represent its members in collective bargaining; representatives for this purpose would have to be specifically chosen by the employees, and the fact of this choice would have to be established. Although employees were to be given "entire freedom with respect to the selection and form and rules of their organization and their selection of representatives," management remained free to aid or advise an employee organization in developing or implementing plans for the benefit of employees, provided that all employees could participate in the enjoyment of these benefits on a nondiscriminatory basis. If an outside union sought to coerce employees to become members, the divisional management was to investigate and to refer the matter to G.M.'s industrial-relations department. The possibility that coercion might be used to enroll members in an inside union was ignored, but the statement did make it explicit that the A.L.B. ban on the solicitation of membership on company time applied to the employee associations as well as to the outside unions.

Each division was instructed to establish a definite plan providing for a conference with an employee or group five days after the receipt of a written notice setting forth the purpose of the meeting. The division was to report to the G.M. executive vice-president the grievances that could not be satisfactorily adjusted. Employees or their representatives were also permitted to take their grievances to the corporation's department of industrial relations. If the latter found that company policies had been violated or that the matter in contention was beyond the scope of divisional authority, it was to refer the facts through the group executive to the executive vice-president, who was to report on the issue to the executive committee.[78]

Although the G.M. statement, which introduced no radical changes in existing company policy, can hardly be considered earthshaking in view of the requirements of Section 7(a) and the interpretation of the section by various labor boards, it was hyperbolically described by the *Michigan Manufacturer and Financial Record* as "the most striking labor document which has been issued in the history of American industry," and even the A.F. of L.'s Frank Morrison, despite the obvious preference for the inside union evidenced in the statement, declared that it was "a step forward beyond any position the motor companies have taken heretofore." Francis Dillon, however, was less impressed with the document. He denounced the statement as an "insult" to the intelligence of the automobile workers, and an A.F. of L. broadside put out by the Detroit office asked the automobile worker if he knew that "Mr. Alfred P. Sloan, Jr. proposes to make a union for you, compel you to belong, form its rules, select its officers and dominate its policy?" [79]

Trying a different approach, Dillon wrote to Sloan on November 6 requesting him, in view of the recently published G.M. statement, to meet with the accredited representatives of the organized automobile workers in order to work out a joint agreement. Sloan advised Dillon to take up his request through "established channels," but Dillon replied some days later that the G.M. divisional managers did not conform to the corporation's announced policies and that the G.M. plan of labor relations, which no one was legally obligated to follow, was "unfair" and "unworkable" and was designed to thwart the development of "free and independent" unionism.[80]

G.M. thought sufficiently well of its collective-bargaining statement to reissue it in July 1935 and March 1937, and to maintain it as the official view of the corporation until it was superseded by the G.M.-U.AW. contract of 1940.[81]   The A.L.B. had no comment to make on the G.M. statement, but it was soon to announce a plan of its own to implement the concept of proportional representation embodied in the President's settlement of March 25, 1934.

IX

THE A.F. OF L., THE U.A.W., AND THE A.L.B.

I

THE CHARACTER OF THE AUTOMOBILE SETTLEMENT of March 25, 1934, and its failure to bring any immediate improvement in the relations of employer and employee in the automobile industry were a source of profound discouragement to the workers who had rallied to the union cause when the likelihood of a strike and then of Presidential intervention promised some dramatic change in the status and the working conditions of the industry's employees. As Tracy Doll has observed, "A great many people at that time believed that a union was a slot machine that you threw a quarter in. If you did not hit the jackpot, you walked away." The result was that the executive secretary of the Detroit Regional Labor Board found, a few weeks after the settlement, that it had resulted in a "decided decrease in interest" in the A.F. of L. "Everybody said we got sold down the river," a member of the U.A.W.'s National Council later remembered. According to the recollection of another U.A.W. stalwart, the automobile workers "started dropping out [of the federal labor unions] as rapidly or more so than they joined up." [1] In the Michigan auto towns and especially in Detroit, the U.A.W. locals were never again during the N.R.A. period to have the degree of support among the automobile workers that they had enjoyed in the few weeks preceding the settlement.

As the membership of the U.A.W. locals continued to dwindle in the months following the settlement,[2] the automobile unionists increasingly came to believe that they had made an almost fatal mistake in failing to strike and in agreeing to the settlement and the establishment of the A.L.B. "That day," lamented Delmer Minzey, the president of the AC Spark Plug local, "was the turning point of our Unions. On that day when we answered the plea of the President as patriotic citizens and gave up the opportunity to force justice from a heartless and cold-blooded employer who knows not the meaning of honor, we wrote doom into the pages of our history for the only chance the Automobile workers have ever had to establish protection for their jobs and a living wage, and decent working conditions.... where last March we had a splendid union which was progressing rapidly toward the establishing of a voice for the workers in the industry today we have only a handful of the faithful.... The morale of our people is broken and where there was hope there is now only fear and despair." [3]

To the automobile unionists who viewed the situation as Minzey did, President Roosevelt had incurred obligations to the workers of the industry, and they clung to the hope that "our great President will somehow learn the truth in time and will keep his promise to those who toil in the Automobile Industry." "We stood by the President when he needed us," declared the A.F. of L.'s national representative in the industry in November 1934; "now we need him and he must not fail us...." [4] The organized automobile workers were to learn, however, that as long as the N.I.R.A. continued in effect the President would not be inclined to support their position too vigorously if this involved the risk of a break with the powerful automobile manufacturers.

Having endorsed the settlement and approved the establishment of the A.L.B., the A.F. of L. leadership in the automobile industry was puzzled as to the stance it should take with regard to the board once automobile unionists became dissatisfied with its procedures. When the officers of sixty U.A.W. locals gathered in Detroit on April 8, 1934, there was talk of a strike and of asking Byrd to resign from the board in protest against its behavior, but Collins checked any action along these lines in favor of a telegram to the President the next day criticizing the A.L.B.'s handling of discrimination cases and its reliance on the techniques of mediation and conciliation and calling for "positive decisions and pronouncements by the Board definitely defining the rights" of the auto workers. If the chairman of the board was unwilling to carry out the terms of the settlement, the officers advised the President, he should be removed from his job. In similar vein, if somewhat more crudely, David Lano of the Flint Chevrolet local wired Johnson that he should "either compell [sic] Wohlman [sic] to execute his duty according to your promise to us or throw him out of there and put some one in there that will or there will be hell to pay." [5]

The U.A.W. wire to the President did not mean that the A.F. of L. was thinking of severing relations with the A.L.B. The same conference of officers that was responsible for the message of criticism to the President drew up an analysis of the settlement that stressed what the automobile unionists would gain from its terms and from the establishment of the A.L.B. At a similar conference in Pontiac the next week Collins, whose position was reinforced by a message from Green, responded to U.A.W. criticism of the board with a plea for patience and stated that the A.L.B. was "setting up machinery which will work." Early in May he advised the U.A.W. locals that it was their "clear duty ... to go along with that Board in the attempt to work out a method of real collective bargaining in the industry." William Green protested in May that the board was not "functioning properly and constructively," but he nevertheless observed toward the end of the next month that the A.L.B. had "served to remedy a lot of wrongs, settle a lot of grievances and act as a stabilizing force." [6]

II

By the time Green made the remarks noted above, he was well aware that several of the U.A.W. federal labor unions were not only dissatisfied with the March 25 settlement and the A.F. of L.'s continued support of the A.L.B. but also with the failure of the Federation to create an international union of automobile workers. Two of the locals in particular, the St. Louis Chevrolet and Fisher Body local and the Bendix local, had from an early date been concerned about the lack of contact among the automobile unionists and, without any authorization from above, had sought to bring some kind of unity to the dispersed federal labor unions in the industry.

The St. Louis local was interested almost from the day it was chartered in establishing an international union of automobile workers and in some kind of co-ordinated effort among the automobile locals to secure improved code terms. At a meeting of the local on September 22, 1933, a motion was carried to give the union's representative to the forthcoming A.F. of L. convention "the right to contact the proper other representatives with the purpose of forming a National Organization with St. Louis as Headquarters." In November, in anticipation of expected hearings on the automobile code, the local drew up its own code terms and not only decided to send a representative to Green to discuss the matter but also dispatched a letter to all the U.A.W. locals suggesting that they notify the A.F. of L. of their agreement with the St. Louis proposals, if this were the fact, and also recommending that when the hearings on the code were held, each local should send a representative to Washington so that "joint conclusions" could be reached by the auto workers with regard to questions of mutual concern.[7]

At its November 15 meeting the St. Louis local decided to send a delegation to Detroit to contact the auto workers there and to gain their support both for the St. Louis code revisions and for the plans to "organize a National Committee." The result of this decision was a conference in Detroit on December 5 that was attended by representatives from U.A.W. locals in St. Louis, Atlanta, Cleveland, and Wisconsin and at which perhaps ten other locals were represented by proxies. George Darner, the chairman of the St. Louis "Committee to Form [a] National Committee to act for all Auto Workers," reported to the St. Louis members that the Chevrolet and Fisher Body locals represented at the conference were "sold on the idea" of a national organization but that other locals were "skeptical" since they believed that St. Louis was interested in the project "for personal gain." A. J. Pickett, who although chairman of the Employees Committee of the Brotherhood of Railway Clerks was a member of the St. Louis Committee to Form a National Committee, defiantly told the meeting that St. Louis would "continue to carry out its policies regardless of Detroit lagging behind and let Detroit fall in line when they [*sic*] are ready."

Following its meeting of December 22 the St. Louis local sent Pickett to Washington to suggest to Green that the A.F. of L. "form a National Committee for Auto Workers." It is doubtful that Green responded with any enthusiasm to this suggestion, but this did not discourage the St. Louis union. At a meeting of the local on January 17, 1934, a resolution was adopted urging the A.F. of L. Executive Council, in view of the fact that the individual U.A.W. locals were "without a common weapon to combat the policies of the organized industry" and were thus "impotent," to authorize the formation of a "National Committee to represent the Workers in the ENTIRE INDUSTRY." [8] The St. Louis local, however, had no more success in advancing this idea than attended its efforts to have the U.A.W. federal labor unions draw up common proposals for the revision of the auto code.

Like the St. Louis local, the Bendix federal labor union, as it informed William Green late in September 1933, was interested in uniting the U.A.W. locals so that they could "meet the problems of the automotive industry in a collective way." Carl Shipley, the president of the local, wrote the Federation's president on April 29, 1934, recommending the establishment of an executive committee selected from the officers of the U.A.W. federal labor unions that could be supplied with the data necessary to enable it to meet with the automobile employers to work out uniform wage scales and working conditions for the industry as a whole and in this way to cope with the problem of interfirm competition. Green, in reply, indicated that the A.F. of L. would be pleased to collect the necessary data and make it available to the locals—he was, indeed, willing to set up a research office in Detroit to aid the auto workers in gathering information for collective-bargaining purposes and to have the Detroit office put out a weekly news letter so that the scattered federal labor unions could be kept informed of one another's activities—[9] but he ignored Shipley's suggestion concerning the establishment of an executive committee. He undoubtedly regarded the formation of any such body as simply a first step leading to the establishment of an international union, and believed that the A.F. of L. "could not even consider" the creation of an international until it was assured that the "internal situation" among the auto locals was "favorable" to action of this kind and that the organization would be self-sustaining.[10]

That the Bendix federal labor union was indeed thinking in terms of an international became evident on May 24 when it decided to invite the U.A.W. locals interested in the establishment of an international to a conference in the expectation that "This action will save many Locals that are weakening through lack of closer contact . . . [with] other Locals." Representatives from eight U.A.W. federal labor unions, including the strong Bendix, Studebaker, Kenosha Nash, and Racine Nash locals, attended the conference, which was held in Chicago on June 3; and among the delegates were such A.F. of L. stalwarts as Al Cook, the president of the Flint Fisher Body No. 1 local, and Samuel R. Isard, the chairman of the Detroit District Council of the U.A.W. The key resolution approved by the conference —it was presented by the Bendix local—called on the A.F. of L. to convoke a convention of U.A.W. federal labor union delegates not later than July 1, 1934, "to Consider the adviseability [*sic*] of Forming a Control [Central?] Body for the Guidance and Conduct" of the federal labor unions in the automobile industry. Although the South Bend representatives at the convention believed that their locals "were not getting cooperation" from the Federation, Cook reported to Collins that "every man there refused to even consider withdrawing from the A.F. of L." [11]

The pressure from certain of the U.A.W. locals [12] for the better co-ordination of the work of the federal labor unions or for the establishment at an early date of an international union was vocally supported by the communists, who from the start had been calling for some sort of united front among the various labor organizations in the industry and who had stressed the ultimate need for a single industrial union of automobile workers. The communists, however, were initially a bit vague regarding the procedure to be followed in establishing the auto international and as to whether the proposed organization was to consist only of the independent unions outside the A.F. of L. or whether the U.A.W. locals, or at least the "militant" members thereof, were also to be included.[13]

Collins' reaction to the unauthorized activities initiated by the St. Louis and Bendix locals was to suggest the calling of a meeting of the U.A.W. federal labor unions to bring the "underground discussion" of an international into the open and to expose the persons involved and the methods being employed. The more experienced Green, however, counseled against this proposal. It would be wiser, he advised, to call a national conference of auto workers to discuss "a specific constructive program." The best way to convince the auto workers that they were not yet ready for an international was to make them aware of the size of the organizing task before them.[14]

Following a meeting with Green, Collins began to lay plans for a conference of auto locals to be held on June 23–24, 1934, for the purpose of setting up a national council to serve principally as an advisory agency to the national representative of the A.F. of L. in the automobile industry. The council, as Collins envisioned it, would include eleven members elected by the delegates and apportioned among the locals on a geographic basis, would meet only at the call of the A.F. of L. national representative, would aid him in his organizing work, and, to meet the criticism of the Bendix local, would help to gather information that would assist the auto workers in bargaining with their employers. In advance of the conference, Collins worked out the chief resolutions to be passed by the delegates and the bylaws of the proposed council.[15]

One hundred and twenty-seven delegates representing seventy-seven locals gathered in Detroit on June 23 for the two-day conference. The key question they considered was whether to accept Collins' plan for a weak national council or to resolve in favor of the establishment of an international. Those who were inclined in the latter direction—included among them were delegates from some of the strongest U.A.W. locals—were by no means agreed as to the method of reaching their goal. One group, which included the delegates from the powerful Hudson local, led by President Arthur Greer, accepted the idea of a "National Executive Council" as a temporary expedient but wanted it to have "full authority to guide the National Policies of our Organization," to appoint one of its own members "to conduct a central office under direction of the Council," and to develop "the procedure and program" for the establishment of an international union "at the earliest feasible time." The Hudson local was anti-Collins, was resentful of the tight control the A.F. of L. exercised over its federal labor unions in the Detroit area, and feared that it would ultimately be ordered to surrender the skilled workers among its members to the craft unions. It was prepared to secede from the A.F. of L. if it could not win approval from the conference for its proposals regarding a national council and an international union. At least one secret caucus was held by this group in Detroit prior to the opening of the conference, and according to Homer Martin, who was present at the meeting, the principal figure at the session was none other than Richard Byrd. As Martin recalled the discussion some weeks later, "it was plainly the attitude of Byrd and Greer... that the Federation was hindering [*sic*] and that it would be... best to withdraw from it." [16]

A second group, which included delegates from the strong Studebaker and Bendix locals and the Chrysler Jefferson and Kercheval plants local, wished the A.F. of L. executive council to provide for the prompt establishment of an auto workers' international. A third faction, led by Wyndham Mortimer, the president of the powerful White Motor local, and taking a position that paralleled the communist line, also called for the immediate establishment of an international, industrial union controlled by the rank and file and apparently including the M.E.S.A. and the A.W.U. Underlying the demand of many of the delegates for a course of action with regard to an international that was at variance with the wishes of the A.F. of L. leadership was a mounting antagonism toward the policies and practices of the Federation in the automobile industry. Michael Manning, who was one of the delegates to the June conference, was "astounded" at "the amount of hate, downright hate, these guys had for the AFL." [17]

William Green, who was present at the conference, told the delegates that the A.F. of L. sympathized with the desire for an international and wanted it "at the earliest possible moment" that the auto workers provided evidence that they had created "a permanent self-sustaining organization." Aware, however, that the U.A.W. locals had only about eighteen thousand paid-up members, Green thought that "a slower approach" was needed. If an international were launched prematurely, he told the delegates, a divisive campaign for office would "tear you asunder." With Green and Collins throwing their weight behind the idea of a national council, the resolutions committee, which, like the other committees, had been handpicked by Collins, recommended nonconcurrence with the various resolutions calling for an international, and this was accepted by the convention over the opposition of fifty delegates.   The committee then secured the conference's approval of Collins' project for a National Council of United Automobile Workers Federal Labor Unions.[18]

The delicate matter of jurisdiction was also raised at the conference, and some of the delegates pressed Green to promise that the U.A.W. locals would not be deterred from enrolling automobile workers because of their craft and would not be forced to surrender the skilled workers who were already federal labor union members. Green, of course, was in no position to make any such promises.   He indicated that there would be no change in the existing structure for the organization of the industry, but at the same time he noted that the rights of the craft unions had to be respected in so far as it was possible to do so, and he advised delegates to bear in mind that the craft unions were the bulwark of the Federation and supplied the money for the organization of the production workers.   It is doubtful that the delegates concerned about the jurisdictional problem and those who felt that the federal labor unions were already paying more in per capita taxes to the Federation than they received from it in services were altogether satisfied with Green's analysis of the importance of the craft unions.   On the other hand, the International Association of Machinists, the most aggressive of the A.F. of L. affiliates in combating the jurisdictional pretensions of the U.A.W., was discomfited because its Detroit business agent had been excluded from the conference; and Vice-President Brown complained that the composition of the automobile council "created more than ever the atmosphere for an Industrial Union for the entire automobile industry." [19]

In addition to the jurisdictional problem and the question of an international, the June conference also brought to the surface the discontent of some of the federal labor unions with the A.F. of L. organizers in the industry.   Not only was there opposition to Collins but also to the quantity and the quality of the organizers in the field.   The Bendix local thought that the organizers should be drawn from the ranks of the U.A.W. locals and proposed that each federal labor union should send one or more qualified members to a special meeting from which forty or more persons should be selected to organize new locals and to help those already in existence.   This resolution apparently never came to a vote, but the delegates indicated their displeasure with the organizers the Federation had assigned to the industry by voting them off the floor of the convention and onto the platform.[20]

When the conference supported its resolutions committee on the issue of an international union of automobile workers, twenty-five delegates, headed by Arthur Greer, bolted the meeting. This act of defiance took on added significance several weeks later when the Hudson local, the G.M. Truck local of Pontiac, and the Olds local of Lansing seceded from the A.F. of L. to form the Associated Automobile Workers of America (A.A.W.A.).

The A.A.W.A. pointed to the "dictatorial methods" of the A.F. of L. as one of the chief reasons for its defection from the Federation. Greer charged that his group had been "steam-rollered out of the picture" at the June conference and that the new council was just "a rubber stamp" of the Federation and was "controlled by a Federation clique that has grown more autocratic than democratic." The A.A.W.A. also complained about the high dues of the A.F. of L., its cautious strike policy, and its growing criticism of Richard Byrd, and it insisted that an organization led by workers in the plants was more likely to succeed in the automobile industry than one dominated by "outside" leaders.[21]

The A.F. of L. charged that management was behind the secession movement, and union men sometimes referred to the A.A.W.A. as an "outside company union." It is difficult, however, to make a definite judgment on this point on the basis of the available evidence. It is true that A.A.W.A. locals tended to deal with management on a more friendly basis than the U.A.W. did. Also, Arthur Greer, who was the key figure in the organization and who was eventually to become an international representative of the U.A.W., was some years later accused of being a Pinkerton agent and thereupon dropped out of the labor movement. On the other hand, the demands of the A.A.W.A. with regards to wages, hours, and working conditions did not differ materially from those of the U.A.W., and Merle C. Hale, G.M.'s director of industrial relations, privately viewed the organization as progressive, if not radical, whereas he thought the A.F. of L. to be conservative.[22]

The individual locals of the A.A.W.A. enjoyed virtually complete autonomy, although some effort was made to link them together in a national organization. A temporary executive council to plan a constitutional convention was named at a preliminary conference of A.A.W.A. locals early in September 1934, and somewhat later in the year a national council was established which included one representative from each of the locals and to which each local payed a per capita tax. The structure was loose enough to permit the A.A.W.A.

in June 1935 to grant a charter to the Automobile and Garage Workers of America, an organization of mechanics and service-station attendants.[23]

Although there was some sentiment for the A.A.W.A. in a few other U.A.W. locals, the A.F. of L. succeeded in confining the secession movement to the three federal labor unions indicated.[24] The Federation, however, was unable to dislodge the A.A.W.A. in the three plants where it had become established. The most serious loss from the U.A.W. point of view was the Hudson local, which was the only strong federal labor union the A.F. of L. had been able to establish in the main plants in Detroit. The A.A.W.A. in June 1935 claimed a membership of thirty-one thousand, but it is doubtful if its maximum strength in the automobile industry greatly exceeded ten thousand members.[25]

In the midst of the crisis stemming from the secession of some of the U.A.W. locals, Collins was dealt another heavy blow when the Detroit F. of L., on August 1, 1934, approved a resolution requesting Green to remove the A.F. of L.'s national representative from his post. The action of the Detroit F. of L. was not altogether unexpected considering the strained relations between Collins and Martel; but coming at a time when the outlook for the U.A.W. in the industry, by Collins' own admission, was "not bright" and when the A.F. of L. national representative was seeking to contain a secession movement, the resolution made Collins' position virtually untenable. Collins, who never seems to have enjoyed his work in Detroit—Michael Manning thought that Collins "didn't have any particular interest in organizing automobile workers"—had asked Green as early as June 25, 1934, to be transferred back to New York, and Green had promised to call him East when circumstances permitted. The death of Hugh Frayne, who headed the A.F. of L. office in New York, provided the Federation's president with the occasion to assign Collins to the post Frayne had held and to appoint Francis Dillon the A.F. of L. national representative in the automobile industry. Collins left proclaming that the "seed of Trade-Union organization has been sown" in the industry, and the Detroit District Council praised his "pioneering service" to the automobile workers.[26]

Dillon, described by Rose Pesotta as "the cartoon prototype of a union official, pot-bellied, always with a large cigar," had been serving as an organizer in the automobile industry since February 1934. He was of a more buoyant nature than Collins and was less inclined to see the dark side of things, but he lacked aggressiveness and was never able to win the confidence of the automobile workers. When he assumed his new post on October 15, 1934, he stated that the "foundation of a great and powerful organization" had already been laid in the automobile industry and that the task now was the "construction of the superstructure."[27] In the event, Dillon found that the "superstructure" that he hoped to rear rested on a dangerously shaky foundation.

In their efforts to organize the automobile industry following the conference of June 1934, Collins and Dillon could presumably have turned to the National Council for assistance. The elected members were Michael J. Manning of Kelsey-Hayes, Herbert W. Richardson of Flint Fisher Body No. 2, Clyde W. Cooke of Lansing Fisher Body, and John W. Pickering of Pontiac, who represented Michigan; Thomas J. Ramsey of Electric Auto-Lite and George J. Lehman of White Motor, who represented Ohio; Ed Hall of Seaman Body, who represented Wisconsin; Forrest G. Woods of Studebaker, who represented Indiana and Illinois; Fred C. Pieper of Atlanta Fisher Body, who represented Georgia, Tennessee, Louisiana, and West Virginia; Homer Martin, formerly of Kansas City Fisher Body, who represented Arkansas, Iowa, Missouri, and California; and Otto Kleinert of Tarrytown Fisher Body, who represented New York, Pennsylvania, New Jersey, and Connecticut.[28] The Council, from the A.F. of L. point of view, provided a convenient mechanism for co-ordinating the activities of the federal labor unions while at the same time permitting a deferral of a final decision on the difficult jurisdictional question. The A.F. of L. had used the same organizational device in the rubber industry, but unlike the auto council, the council for the rubber workers, which was established on June 4, 1934, included representatives of sixteen craft locals in the industry as well as representatives of the federal labor unions.[29]

As it turned out, the National Council met on only three occasions, and it did not play a particularly important role in the development of organization in the automobile industry. Dillon used some of the Council members for organizing work to a limited extent, but when Ed Hall suggested that Council members were the logical persons to be employed in an "intensive organizing campaign" since they were themselves auto workers and would therefore enjoy the confidence of the rank and file, Dillon did not take too kindly to the proposal. "We have many people in the Organization who regard themselves qualified to be great Labor leaders," he sarcastically wrote to Martin, "but unfortunately some of them will never be." He was trying, he patronizingly noted, to give assignments to Council members "gradually" so that he could ascertain their abilities and provide an opportunity for them to understand the labor movement and to develop their talents. Partly because of the rejection of his proposal, Hall rather bitterly and unjustly concluded that Dillon was "more interested in preventing organization than he was in establishing it." [30]

The Council members saw relatively little of one another, but Dillon did not seem particularly anxious to have the Council meet more frequently than it did. When Martin on December 8, 1934, at a moment of crisis for the organized automobile workers, suggested that the Council should meet in Detroit to consider the situation, Dillon replied that the idea of a Detroit meeting was "absolutely impossible of fulfillment." The time was inauspicious, he declared, because of the "uncertainty of things" and the "rapidity" with which events were shaping themselves. [31] Although his reply was in the negative, Dillon actually offered the best possible reason for the convening of the National Council.

Dillon not only seemed reluctant to call the National Council into session, but he was also very much opposed to having individual Council members assume any policy initiatives. He let the Council members know, as Hall accurately recalled, that "he was the boss," and "he made no bones about it." On one occasion, in April 1935, when he learned that Homer Martin and Fred Pieper were discussing the possibility of an automobile strike with several of the locals, Dillon, even though both men had apparently made it clear that any final decision would rest with the A.F. of L. national representative, told them "very plainly" that Council members were to submit their suggestions to his office. To act as Martin and Pieper had could lead only to "confusion, misunderstanding and ultimate disaster." He simply would not permit "irresponsible individuals" to direct the policies of the organization. "I want to tell you quite frankly," he wrote Martin, "I don't like this procedure and I don't want to see it continued and it is not going to continue." [32]

Council member Forrest Woods suggested in August 1934 that the Council was the logical agency to negotiate an industry-wide agreement with the automobile manufacturers to supersede the code and to do away with the "old competition plea." He thought that this was "the only course open too [sic] the Council if we are to properly interpret and carry out the wishes of the Auto Workers." Martin regarded this suggestion as "to the point," and Hall also thought it a fine idea. Dillon asked each of the Council members for his views on the proposal, but he noted that the Council would have to conform to the decisions reached at the forthcoming A.F. of L. convention. [33]   In the end, it was Green who approached the A.M.A. to discuss a possible automobile contract and not the National Council.

On the whole, the Council members were a cautious lot who followed Dillon's advice and who, as members of the great army of the unemployed—Manning later recalled that he was the only one of the group with a steady job—were beholden to the A.F. of L. national representative for the occasional assignments that brought them some income. There was, however, some dissent in the Council from A.F. of L. policies and particularly from its excessive caution regarding the use of the strike weapon. "Why waste any more time organizing," Hall asked Martin on November 14. "It is now time to act. I am doing everything in my power to bring this thing to a head. . . . We have everything to gain and nothing to lose. There is only one way to put presser [*sic*] on industrialist[s] [and that] is [to] use drastic action." With these militant sentiments Kleinert and Pieper, at least, agreed.[34]

Although the National Council proved to be of little value in the organization of the automobile workers, it did help to give a certain prominence to individuals who were eventually to play important roles in the U.A.W. Homer Martin was later to serve as the U.A.W.'s first elected president, Hall as a U.A.W. vice-president, and Pieper as a member of the union's executive board.

The decision of the June 1934 conference to form a National Council for the automobile industry did not satisfy the more militant, progressive members of the U.A.W. federal labor unions who favored more rapid progress in the direction of the establishment of an international union of automobile workers. The principal center of disaffection after the June conference was the nine U.A.W. locals in Cleveland, which some time after the conference and without any authorization from the A.F. of L. set up their own Auto Council for the city to promote the establishment within the Federation of an international, industrial union controlled by the rank and file. The president of the Cleveland Auto Council was Wyndham Mortimer of the White Motor local. Mortimer, who had grown up in the coal fields of Pennsylvania "in an atmosphere of unionization and strikes" and had joined the United Mine Workers when he was only sixteen, was one of the more experienced trade unionists in the U.A.W. ranks and although an undeviating follower of the communist line enjoyed the support of many auto unionists who did not share his social philosophy.[35]

At a conference on August 18, 1934, the Cleveland U.A.W. locals expressed dissatisfaction with the National Council and proposed that a preliminary national conference of all automobile federal labor unions be held in Cleveland on September 16 looking toward the ultimate establishment of an international, industrial union. After hearing a report on the Cleveland situation from George Lehman, the National Council, at its second meeting late in August 1934, announced that the Cleveland Auto Council had been established without the authorization of the A.F. of L. or the constituent locals, that it was being used for "Communistic propaganda," and that its call for the September 16 conference was designed to mislead the workers. Collins informed the U.A.W. federal labor unions that the proposed meeting was "simply a part of the destructive methods pursued by Communists in their efforts to disrupt and destroy trade unions." [36]

Despite the warnings of the A.F. of L., the conference was held in Cleveland on September 16, as scheduled. More than forty delegates were present, although it is uncertain how many of them were authorized by their locals to attend. The principal resolution, presented by Mortimer, attributed the decline of the U.A.W. locals to the leadership of the A.F. of L. and its failure to establish an auto international. The A.F. of L.'s "sabotaging efforts" to prevent strikes and its commitment to craft unionism were denounced, and it was decided to work for an international union on industrial lines and controlled by the rank and file.[37]

A second unauthorized rump conference was held in Flint on November 10, and the delegates once again approved a resolution calling for an international, industrial union under rank-and-file control. The A.F. of L. Executive Council was petitioned to convene a constitutional convention for this purpose about March 1, 1935, and also to call a conference of the U.A.W. locals to form an organizing committee.[38]

President Green of the A.F. of L. thought the demand for the prompt establishment of an international union premature. Such a step, he had indicated from the start, should not be taken until the auto workers had gained additional trade-union experience, had developed effective leadership, and had been able to assure the Federation that the organization would be "self-sustaining." He was particularly annoyed by the naïveté of those who thought that the mere establishment of an international would solve the organizational problems in the automobile industry. With considerable insight into the shape of things to come, he wrote to Carl Shipley on November 26, 1934:

You seem to think that the establishment of a national or international union among the automobile workers would solve all your difficulties and bring about a perfect, ideal state. Please accept this prediction from one who has had training in a wide field of organizing work. When a national or international union of automobile workers is formed, you will still find that the ideal state has not been reached; that condemnation will be indulged in by impetuous members, that serious internal problems will be presented, and fights of the most bitter kind take place between those who seek to secure and exercise control over the international union.[39]

The subject of an international union of auto workers received attention at the annual A.F. of L. convention of October 1934 in San Francisco. Resolutions were introduced by a delegate from the White Motor local, the key union in the rump movement for an international, importuning the convention to call a constitutional convention not later than December 1, 1934, for the purpose of forming an international; by a Buick delegate, requesting the A.F. of L. to ask the various international unions to relinquish their jurisdictional claims over the entire auto industry; and by a delegate from the Bendix local, empowering the Executive Council to establish an international with complete industrial jurisdiction, directed by men selected from the ranks, and advised by and receiving the support of the A.F. of L. These proposals were referred to the committee on resolutions, which in an ambivalent report to the convention left open the controversial question of occupational jurisdiction and directed the A.F. of L. Executive Council to issue charters for internationals in several mass-production industries, including the automotive, and with the A.F. of L. for a "provisional period" to direct their policies, administer their affairs, and designate their officers.

Following the presentation of the report of the committee on resolutions, President Wharton of the I.A.M., who, as Mark Perlman has said, "could feel nothing but mistrust for the enthusiasm of the industrial unionists," inquired as to the meaning of the phrase "automotive industry" and asked for assurances that "the rights of existing organizations within reason are recognized." The question of craft versus industrial unionism was then inconclusively debated, with the White Motor delegate charging that the craft unions were trying "to break us up" and with Matthew Woll, in a remark that illuminated the point of view of many of the craft unionists, stating that the report dealt more with the unorganized "and perhaps unorganizable" than it did with the subject of craft versus industrial unionism. In the end the report was unanimously adopted, "upon which," according to the official proceedings of the convention, "the delegates arose and applauded in an enthusiastic manner." The unanimous adoption of the report suggests that the delegates read into it whatever they pleased and that the foes of industrial unionism felt secure as long as the final decision regarding the jurisdiction of the new internationals rested with the craft-union-minded Executive Council.[40]

The Cleveland U.A.W. locals did not regard the decision of the San Francisco convention as sufficient reason for them to desist in their independent efforts to establish an international union. Officials of six of the locals therefore issued a call for another conference to be held in Detroit on January 26, 1935. The conference announcement attacked the decision of the San Francisco convention to place the proposed international under the provisional control of the A.F. of L. and charged that the craft unions, which dominated the Executive Council, would not bring the "proper sympathy and understanding" to the question of jurisdiction. The document referred to "the false policies pursued by the top officialdom of the A.F. of L." and criticized the Federation's alleged no-strike policy and its reliance on "strike-breaking arbitration boards." Dillon charged that the convention call was "written in the language of the Communists" and warned that any individual who attended the meeting would be violating his obligations as a member of the A.F. of L. The A.F. of L. did not err in its assumption that the rump movement for an international was in part at least the result of communist machinations, but it might well have paid heed to the fact that, whether communist-influenced or not, the demand for a complete industrial jurisdiction for the international union and for rank-and-file control struck a responsive chord among the auto workers, the vast majority of whom knew little about communism and were not then as concerned about the presence of communists in their midst as they were later to become.[41]

According to the *Daily Worker*, thirty-nine delegates from nineteen U.A.W. federal labor unions attended the Detroit conference of January 26, 1935. A letter and a delegation were dispatched to the National Council urging it to call a constitutional convention at once to establish an international, industrial union and also to convene a conference of auto workers to lay plans for "a united general strike" in the automobile and parts industries.[42] We must pause, however, before considering the response of the National Council to these requests.

III

Frustrated by the continued decline in the U.A.W.'s fortunes following the June conference, the A.F. of L. leadership began to lash out at the A.L.B. as the primary source of the Federation's difficulties in the automobile industry. In the first months after the March 25 settlement the A.F. of L., although reluctant to make an all-out attack on the board, had nevertheless complained about its preference for disposing of the problems before it by mediation and conciliation rather than by issuing orders, the slowness with which it acted, the inadequate protection that it provided for union members who were returned to work after they had complained of discrimination, the alleged unfairness of some of its decisions, its failure to make any use of the union membership lists submitted to it or to order elections to establish representation rights, its insufficient concern with management efforts to promote company unions, and its interpretation of the layoff and rehiring rules. These criticisms of the board continued to be voiced throughout the life of the agency, but of greater concern to the A.F. of L. during the summer months of 1934 was the behavior of the labor member of the board, Richard Byrd.

The A.F. of L.'s disenchantment with Byrd began to set in after it became apparent that he had bungled the job in his efforts in early May to settle the strikes in St. Louis and Kansas City. No comment was made by the A.F. of L. or the U.A.W. when Byrd in leaving Kansas City declared that although the A.L.B. did not object to dealing with the representatives of the auto locals in the various plants, it was "not negotiating with the American Federation of Labor," but this statement must certainly have aroused the suspicions of the Federation. Homer Martin soon concluded that Byrd's behavior in Kansas City had been disgraceful and that he was "a dangerous character" who should be exposed and removed.[43]

The A.F. of L. was also displeased that Byrd seemed to be going along with his colleagues on the board in actions and decisions of which the Federation disapproved. When the A.L.B. in handing down one of its rulings stated that Byrd had not participated in the rendering of the decision, Collins bitterly commented that this was a "gratuitous" remark since Byrd had not as yet rendered any decisions as far as organized labor was concerned.[44]

The breaking point in the relationship between the A.F. of L. and Richard Byrd was reached when the A.L.B.'s labor member participated in at least one of the secret caucuses in Detroit just preceding the opening of the June conference and allegedly supported the idea of an international auto workers union that would be outside the A.F. of L. During the course of the conference itself, Byrd, according to Homer Martin, opposed the official policy of the Federation and "cussed the whole A.F. of L. movement." Collins was not entirely in error when he complained that Byrd had become "the center of activity for all of those officers of Federal Labor Unions who have ambitions but nothing else, in their efforts to destroy or promote themselves into a job." [45]

There seems to be no doubt that Byrd played a part in the movement that led to the establishment of the A.A.W.A. "It would appear," G.M.'s Merle Hale observed, "that during this entire period the labor representative on the Board has acted as their [A.A.W.A.'s] counselor and advisor, if not indeed a stimulator of their plans." The locals that formed the A.A.W.A. were quick to defend Byrd against U.A.W. criticism, and Byrd was their defender before the board. When the Hudson local alleged that it had been discriminated against by the company during the course of the A.L.B. election in the plant, Byrd stated to his colleagues that "If this Board sits supinely by and permits continuation of this unfair treatment for the only free union which has given us its support and backing we are just no damned good and should get the hell out of this job." The A.A.W.A., he declared, had "made a showing [in the election] for which we are all glad." Byrd's own G.M. Truck local joined the A.A.W.A., and the A.L.B. labor member subsequently admitted that he was a member of the organization.[46]

William Green suggested as early as June 28, 1934, that Byrd should be dropped from the Board because of his alleged lack of understanding of his duties as a labor member, but the A.F. of L. opposition to Byrd did not really come to a head until the National Council met in Detroit from July 9 to 14, 1934, in its first session. According to the official proceedings of the meeting, Collins during the course of the session asked Byrd to refute the charges against him, and Byrd "admitted his activities among several of the Unions" and conceded that he had agreed that the decisions of the A.L.B. should be unanimous. He did not reply when Collins asked him if he regarded himself as competent to represent the interests of labor on the board. The National Council thereupon agreed unanimously that Byrd should resign from the board, and Collins so advised Green.[47]

Acting on this advice, Green instructed A.F. of L. attorney Charlton Ogburn on July 23 to inform Wolman that "under no circumstances can we cooperate with the Automobile Labor Board if Mr. Byrd is to remain a member," and the A.F. of L. president discussed with Secretary of Labor Perkins the possibility of removing Byrd from the tribunal. Perkins thought that this would be difficult to accomplish since the labor member had been appointed to his position by the President, and thus, presumably, only the President could remove him. In a letter of July 26 to Wolman, in which it detailed its complaints against Byrd, the National Council alleged that Byrd had advised the Detroit office of the A.F. of L. of his intention to resign, and the Council indicated its desire that he be replaced with a competent labor representative. Wolman stated in reply, however, that he did not regard some of the statements in the letter as "accurate" and that he was therefore returning it without transmitting it to the President.[48] Despite the opposition of the A.F. of L., Byrd remained on the A.L.B. as long as it continued in existence. This was to be one cause but, in the final analysis, not the most important one, for the decision of the Federation to attempt to sever its connection with the Wolman board.

X

PROPORTIONAL REPRESENTATION AND
MAJORITY RULE

I

THE A.F. OF L. DID NOT CEASE to complain about the continued presence of Richard Byrd on the A.L.B., but by the end of August 1934 its criticism of the settlement and the board had come to focus on a far more important issue: proportional representation. The A.F. of L. simply could not reconcile itself to the fact that representation for collective bargaining in the automobile manufacturing industry was to be determined on the basis of proportional representation whereas majority rule prevailed, at least in theory, everywhere else. Why, asked the A.F. of L., should not the President on the basis of Public Resolution 44 establish a board for the automobile industry similar to the one that he had appointed for the steel industry and order it, as he had ordered the Steel Labor Relations Board on June 28, 1934, to conduct elections on the principle of majority rule? [1] Pointing up the issue even more sharply for the A.F. of L. was the N.L.R.B. decision of August 30, 1934, in the Houde case, in favor of majority rule. Since the decision involved a U.A.W. federal labor union in an automobile parts plant, the A.F. of L. could not help but wonder why the same principle should not be applied to workers in the main plants.

In the Houde case, it will be recalled that although Federal Labor Union No. 18839 had secured a majority of the votes cast in the election of March 21, 1934, Ralph Peo, the Houde general manager, had informed union officials that he would not recognize the union nor would he accept the union committee as the sole bargaining agency for the company's employees. A subcommittee of the Buffalo Regional Labor Board held a hearing on the case on April 12, which Peo did not attend, and ruled the same day that the Houde company and the federal labor union should "proceed at once" to negotiate an agreement, which should be reduced to writing, and that the federal labor union should be recognized by the company as "the exclusive bargaining agency" for Houde employees. When Houde indicated that it would not abide by this decision, Daniel Shortal, the executive secretary of the Buffalo board, advised the N.L.B. that "it was apparent that the Company has been from the very out-set determined to use all obstructionistic tactics and forms of procrastination for the purpose of defeating the purposes of Section 7 (a)." [2]

The N.L.B. thereupon stepped into the picture and held still another hearing on the case on May 3, but Peo, denying that the board had jurisdiction, refused to attend. Following the hearing, the N.L.B. tried to settle the affair by negotiation, but its efforts proved unavailing. Before the board could issue a decision, however, it had been replaced by the N.L.R.B., which decided to hear the case *de novo* on July 24. As Paul M. Herzog of the N.L.R.B. staff stated, "The case squarely presents the issue decided by the old Board [N.L.B.] in the Denver Railway case." This time Peo appeared at the hearing, accompanied by M. C. Mason, the secretary and counsel of the company. Mason attacked the principle of exclusive representation and contended that Section 7(a) gave employees the "right to organize into as many groups as they please." He pointed out that in accordance with this interpretation of the law, the company had been negotiating separately with representatives of the federal labor union and of the Houde Welfare and Athletic Association and indicated that it was also willing to negotiate with a composite committee of the sort envisioned by the President's settlement. He thought the company would benefit if the "conflicting views" of the minority were available to it. Peo, who proudly informed the board that his plant was "operated entirely with American born white help," receded from his former position and now declared that he would be willing to sign an agreement with the union but only if it represented 100 per cent of his employees. [3]

The N.L.R.B. issued its long-awaited and crucially important decision in the Houde case on August 30. The board stated that the right of employees to bargain as set forth in Section 7(a) implied the correlative duty of the employers to bargain with them, that the purpose of bargaining was to reach an agreement, and that the employers had to negotiate in good faith with this objective in view. It found that the Houde practice of dealing with one group and then with the other defeated the purposes of Section 7(a), enabled the company to favor one employee group over another, and "was calculated to confuse the employees, to make them uncertain which organization they should from time to time adhere to, and to maintain a permanent and artificial division in the ranks." Even if this tactic did not impair the effectiveness of collective bargaining, it forestalled the working out of collective labor agreements and thus served "to nullify the purposes of the statute."

The company conceded, the decision noted, that a collective agreement covering the terms of employment would have to apply to all the workers in the plant. The practical way to achieve this purpose, the N.L.R.B. asserted, was by the negotiation of an agreement with the representatives of the majority of the employees. The alternative method suggested by the company, namely, negotiation with a composite committee, would "on its face be just and democratic." If labor and management, as in the automobile industry, agreed to bargain in this manner, there would be no conflict with the statute since it permitted the majority to devise "any fair plan of representation" that they desired. But in the absence of such an agreement, the suggested procedure "would have hindered true collective bargaining even more effectively than the policies heretofore pursued by the company.... This vision of an employer dealing with a divided committee and calling in individual employees to assist the company in arriving at a decision is certainly far from what Section 7(a) must have contemplated in guaranteeing the right of collective bargaining." The board therefore concluded that "the only interpretation of Section 7(a) which can give effect to its purposes is that the representatives of the majority should constitute the exclusive bargaining agency for collective bargaining with the employer." Congress, it argued, in providing for elections, "necessarily rejected plural bargaining, and almost as certainly endorsed majority rule." The N.L.R.B. cautioned that its majority-rule decision did not mean that employees were obligated to join the organization that represented the majority, did not establish the closed shop, and did not prevent individual employees or groups of employees from presenting grievances to and conferring with their employers and from associating together for their mutual benefit.

The N.L.R.B. found that the Houde company had interfered with the self-organization of its employees and had, in effect, refused to bargain; and the board ruled that unless the company within ten days notified the N.L.R.B. in writing that it had recognized Federal Labor Union No. 18839 as the exclusive bargaining agency for its employees and that when requested it would negotiate with it and seek in good faith to arrive at a collective agreement covering the terms of employment of all employees who had been permitted to vote in the March election, the case would be referred to the N.R.A. and the enforcement agencies of the federal government for "appropriate action." [4] Thus the N.L.R.B., like the N.L.B. in the Denver Tramway case, rejected a pluralistic approach to the choice of employee representatives for collective bargaining and found in favor of majority rule. It reserved to the majority of employees the right to adopt a plan of proportional representation if they so desired, but it was in error in citing the automobile settlement as an example of an agreement of this type since the A.F. of L. at the time of the settlement represented considerably less than a majority of the automobile workers.

Newspapers that approved the Houde decision thought that it made the collective-bargaining clause of the N.I.R.A. "a reality," whereas the opposition saw it as a "gratuitous over-ruling" of the President's settlement of March 25 and the concept of proportional representation. The Houde Corporation quite naturally found the decision "erroneous, contrary to the law, unjust and totally unenforceable" and declared that it would not comply with it. Its position on the majority-rule question, the company noted, was in accord with the Johnson-Richberg interpretation of Section 7(a) and the President's settlement.[5]

Houde was supported by the N.A.M. in its refusal to comply with the N.L.R.B. decision. The directors of the N.A.M. advised employers, "until competent judicial authority has declared otherwise," to ignore the ruling and to abide by interpretations upholding the right of the minority to bargain. William Green attacked the N.A.M. position as "a challenge to the government" and as being virtually "a conspiracy to violate the law." [6]

Houde's defiance of the N.L.R.B. decision led General Johnson on September 14 to inform the company that it could no longer display the Blue Eagle, which meant that it would not be eligible to receive government contracts. In referring the case to the Justice Department, the N.L.R.B. stated that its chief concern was to have the concept of majority rule "judicially affirmed." The Justice Department preferred a "stronger case" on the facts, but it agreed to take Houde to court. A bill of complaint in equity was accordingly filed on November 30 in the United States district court in Buffalo. This initiated an involved legal battle between Houde and the federal government that remained unresolved when the Schechter decision caused the N.L.R.B. to inform the union and the company that the board was "closing its file" on the case.[7] The principle of majority rule that the N.L.R.B. had announced in the case was to become the law of the land, however, when the National Labor Relations Act went into effect a short time thereafter.

The day following the N.L.R.B. decision in the Houde case, the National Council of the U.A.W., fearful that the A.L.B. would soon introduce a representation plan of its own, announced its intention of withdrawing the federal labor unions from the President's settlement of March 25, 1934. Green conveyed this decision to President Roosevelt in a letter of September 11, 1934, in which he informed the Chief Executive that attorney Charlton Ogburn had advised him that since the settlement was simply an agreement between two parties and was of "no fixed duration of time," the A.F. of L. could withdraw from it by giving notice to the President and the automobile manufacturers. Green noted that since the date of the settlement the concept of majority rule had been endorsed in the President's executive order establishing the Steel Labor Relations Board, in the amendments of June 1934 to the Railway Labor Act, and in the Houde decision, and that the automobile workers should not be denied the opportunity of availing themselves of this principle "merely because of the unfortunate situation in which these automobile workers find themselves with the present Automobile Labor Board." As requested by the National Council, Green asked the President to establish a statutory board for the automobile and parts industries like the Steel Labor Relations Board or the N.L.R.B., and, pending such action, to permit the automobile workers to bring to the N.L.R.B. their petitions for elections and their complaints involving Section 7(a).[8]

The A.M.A., to which Green sent a copy of his letter, was not at all pleased with the A.F. of L.'s attempt to terminate the March 25 settlement. Walter Chrysler on September 13 called the President's secretary, Marvin McIntyre, and expressed the hope that the President would "try to talk him [Green] out of it." Through Frances Perkins, Roosevelt requested Green to withhold the September 11 letter from publication until he (Green) could discuss the matter with the Secretary of Labor. Perkins, in turn, later asked the A.F. of L. president not to release the letter until he had talked with the President, but a subsequent conference with the Chief Executive did not cause Green to change his mind. For the moment, however, he took no public action to sever the connection between the A.F. of L. and the A.L.B.[9]

Any hope that the A.F. of L and the U.A.W. would reconsider their position with regard to the A.L.B. was dashed on December 7 when the board made public an election plan designed to provide each of the plants under its jurisdiction with a bargaining agency whose membership would be determined on the basis of proportional representation. As already noted, the March 25 settlement did not mention the

word "election," and there is reason to believe that the expectation
at the time was that the A.L.B. would determine employee representation by comparing union membership lists and company payrolls. As we have seen, however, the board found the lists defective,
and it came to believe that some kind of formal machinery was necessary to remove any suspicion that employers were not bargaining in
good faith. It delayed the formulation of an election plan because
it had assigned a higher priority initially to the settlement of strikes
in the industry and the attack on the problem of discrimination and
job tenure; and by the time these matters had been resolved to the
A.L.B.'s satisfaction, the seasonal layoffs had begun, and it was therefore believed necessary to wait until production resumed its upward
curve and employment increased.[10]

Although the A.L.B. was criticized for devising an election plan
based on the concept of proportional representation, it should be noted
that the settlement under which the board was operating called for
the establishment of bargaining committees on a pro rata basis and
that, at all events, there was no organized majority group in the automobile industry. There was thus justice in Wolman's remark at the
time that "The real issue in the automobile industry has not been
and is not whether there shall be majority rule but by what means
the several minorities should have representation in bargaining with
the managements." [11]

The A.L.B. plan called for the division of each plant into voting
districts. All nonsupervisory employees working at the time of the
election and workers who had been temporarily laid off, except those
in Class A, were eligible to vote. In the nominating election, each
voter was to nominate one person, who did not have to be an employee, to represent his district, and he could, if he desired, "indicate the group, if any, with which his nominee is identified." The
names of the two persons receiving the highest number of votes in a
district in the primary were to appear on the ballot for the final election according to their affiliation, if any had been indicated. The
tabulation of the primary votes would determine the relative proportion of representatives on the bargaining agency to which each group
containing "a substantial number" [12] of voters was entitled. Voters
who expressed no group affiliation for their nominee were placed in
a single unaffiliated group. If the representatives victorious in the
final election did not provide the proportional representation to which
a group was entitled on the basis of its primary vote, the A.L.B. was
to add to the bargaining agency a sufficient number of additional representatives from among the defeated candidates of that group re-

ceiving the highest number of votes. Thus, for example, in the Buick nominating election, the unaffiliated group received 5611 votes, the A.F. of L. 1116 votes, and the Buick Employees Association 545 votes. In the final election, candidates designated as unaffiliated were victorious in twenty-three of the districts, and a candidate designated as A.F. of L. in the remaining district. To provide proportional representation, the A.L.B. had to add to the bargaining agency four representatives from among the defeated candidates who had been designated by the voters as A.F. of L. candidates and two representatives designated as affiliated with the Buick Employees Association.[13]

The A.L.B. elections were supervised by Francis E. Ross, who was aided by a staff of election officials that numbered 166 at its peak in April 1935. Prior to the holding of an election, the A.L.B. or one of its agents met with employee representatives in the plant in order to explain the board's complicated plan. Since only the A.A.W.A. of the outside labor organizations in the industry co-operated with the A.L.B. in the holding of its elections, these conferences were normally attended only by representatives of the company unions and, in the few plants where it had any strength, the A.A.W.A. Representatives of the various organizations in the plant were also invited to observe the counting of the ballots, and the A.L.B. took pride in the fact that in none of its elections was a recount demanded.[14]

In delimiting the election districts, the A.L.B. generally followed the pattern of districting already employed in the company-union elections unless the employees in the pre-election conferences convinced election officials of the wisdom of some other plan. Normally, the election districts were established on a geographical basis, but in the Hudson plant, at least, the criterion for districting was the type of work performed. The number of persons in an election district ranged from eight to eight hundred, but the population of the typical district was three hundred.[15]

The A.L.B. plan was applied only at the plant level, and the plant as a whole was accepted as the appropriate bargaining unit. In thus establishing its bargaining agencies on an industrial rather than a craft basis, the A.L.B. was following the practice not only of the company unions and, to a degree, of the U.A.W. federal labor unions but also of the National War Labor Board: in plants where there was no established machinery for collective bargaining, the National War Labor Board had tended to favor the creation of shop committees which represented the workers as a whole regardless of craft.[16]

Quite apart from its attempt to carry out a scheme of proportional representation, the A.L.B. plan differed markedly from the election procedures then being employed by other government labor boards. Whereas nearly all other representation elections originated in a complaint of a trade union that it was being denied recognition, the A.L.B. plan was applied to most of the plants subject to the automobile manufacturing code whether an organized group desired an election or not. This caused critics of the plan to charge that the plan violated the principle of self-organization set forth in Section 7(a). Elections among employees, the opponents of the A.L.B. scheme charged, were solely their own affair, and the government was to intervene only when asked to do so by a substantial number of the workers involved. If the majority of workers in a bargaining unit did not wish to engage in collective bargaining or to choose representatives for this purpose, they should not be forced to do so by a government labor board.[17]

Normally, also, the elections held by other government labor boards involved a straight choice between a company union and a trade union,[18] whereas in the A.L.B. elections an individual could not vote for an organization at all. Moreover, he was not, strictly speaking, to indicate his own affiliation, if he had any, but only the affiliation of his candidate, assuming he knew what that affiliation was and was inclined to write it on the ballot.[19] If the voter was uninformed, careless, confused, or for any reason afraid, the easiest way of voting was to omit any mention of his candidate's affiliation.

Wolman defended the A.L.B. plan's emphasis on voting for individuals rather than for organizations on the grounds that this enabled the worker to pick his own representatives whereas when he selected an organization, it was the organization that then determined the person or persons who were to speak for him. If the purpose of the elections, however, was to indicate the relative strength of the various groups in a plant, the voters should have had a greater opportunity to register their support for the organization, if any, that they favored. As the plan operated, the most popular or best-known individual in the district was apt to emerge the victor. And whether the victorious candidate was a former company-union official or a trade-union member, at least a plurality of those who voted for him were as likely as not to fail to specify any affiliation for him. Thus, in the Cadillac plant, where the first A.L.B. election was held, although ten of the sixteen elected members of the bargaining agency were former company-union representatives and six were A.F. of L. members, fourteen were elected as unaffiliated persons. It was similarly possible for a voter to designate a candidate as affiliated with an organized group to which he did not belong, and this too sometimes occurred. A candidate victorious in the primary had to accept the affiliation attributed to him by a plurality of those voting for him whether the designation was accurate or not.[20]

The necessity of adding representatives to the bargaining agency to achieve proportional representation gave rise to certain oddities. Thus, a candidate who did not secure enough votes to win in his district might, in the end, be added to the bargaining agency to represent the plant as a whole. Also, the total vote a defeated candidate received in the primary was less important in determining whether he should be added to the bargaining agency to achieve proportional representation than was the vote he received under a particular affiliation. Thus, for purposes of selection as an A.F. of L. representative to complete the make-up of a bargaining agency, a candidate who was designated as A.F. of L. by twenty-four voters and as unaffiliated by twenty-three voters ranked ahead of a candidate designated as A.F. of L. by 150 voters but as unaffiliated by 151 voters.[21]

Since the voters in the A.L.B. elections did not specifically choose between organizations but selected only individuals to represent them, it was unnecessary for the board to make explicit provision for a "no union" vote. Of course, it was possible, although not entirely accurate, to interpret the failure of a voter to designate an affiliation for his candidate as a "no union" vote, and the A.L.B. did, in effect, follow this practice.[22] The A.L.B. election plan was, as a matter of fact, biased in favor of the unaffiliated "group," since voters were placed in this category without having to designate that their candidates were "unaffiliated" whereas the proportionate strength of organized groups was determined by the number of voters who went to the trouble of writing in a specific affiliation for their candidate.

In its use of nominating and final elections, in its choice of election districts, and in holding its elections on company property, the A.L.B. tended to follow the pattern of the company-union elections. But under the A.L.B. plan, in contrast to the company-union plans, an individual could vote for whomever he pleased, and not just for an employee of the same district, and the election machinery was entirely in the hands of a government agency. To some, indeed, the A.L.B. plan appeared to be an "experiment in labor democracy," and certainly it did give every worker full opportunity to vote for the *person* he wished to represent his district.

In establishing a single bargaining agency for most of the plants under its jurisdiction, the A.L.B. was fulfilling the hope the President had expressed in his amplifying remarks accompanying the settlement. It must be noted, however, that the settlement specifically stated that the government favored "no particular form of employee organization or representation." It would seem that the A.L.B. plan, which did provide for a particular form of employee representation, was not entirely consistent with this proclamation of neutrality.

Although heralded as such, the A.L.B. election plan was not a plan of proportional representation in the sense in which the political scientist uses the term. "It is not even a species of the same genus," declared Emmett L. Bennett, director of the Municipal Reference Bureau. The use of primaries, single-member districts, and plurality counting disqualified the plan as one of proportional representation in the eyes of the political scientist.[23]

There is no question that many voters found the A.L.B.'s rather intricate election plan difficult to understand. "The greatest confusion exists in what is the purpose of the vote," Harry W. Anderson, executive in charge of G.M.'s labor staff, reported to the A.L.B. The A.L.B. official conducting the election in Atlanta found that "a great many of these 'Hill Billies' just don't know what it is all about." The conferences which the Board held with the newly elected bargaining agencies also indicated that the understanding of the A.L.B. plan was less than perfect. "In my opinion," a representative of the Chevrolet Gear and Axle plant declared, "the election was the worst set up I ever heard of, and the guy that made that plan . . . should make one more plan like that and then go and jump in the river." [24]

Although Wolman regarded the A.L.B. elections as "the most fundamental thing which is being done in American industrial relations," the A.F. of L., the M.E.S.A., and the S.D.E. all decided to boycott the elections. The M.E.S.A. and the S.D.E. objected to the election plan because they realized that there were simply not enough tool and die makers or designing engineers in any one auto plant to enable them to gain any significant representation on the bargaining agencies.[25] The A.F. of L. leadership complained that Dillon had not received the full details of the scheme until it had been announced to the press, despite promises by Wolman on several occasions that he would consult with the A.F. of L. before issuing a plan of representation. The Federation opposed the holding of the elections in the automobile plants, where foremen could observe who voted and where every vote was allegedly "a vote of fear and coercion." It charged that the A.L.B. had decided to hold its first elections in Detroit rather than in the plants for which the A.F. of L. had previously submitted membership lists because it knew that the U.A.W. was unusually weak in the motor city. Ross explained, however, that although other regions would be covered in due course, Detroit was the logical starting place for the elections since the A.L.B. headquarters were in the city and it was also more convenient and economical to have the entire election staff working in one area at a particular time.

The A.F. of L. did not object to the idea of elections per se, but it thought that they should be held only at the request of the employees, that the choice should be between a company union and a trade union, and that majority rule should prevail in the selection of representatives.[26]   Although the A.F. of L. had agreed to the President's settlement in March 1934, it had come to believe that proportional representation would "nullify and ultimately destroy" independent unionism. It must also have been apparent to the A.F. of L. leadership that if the A.L.B. bargaining agencies became the medium through which bargaining took place in the auto plants, the auto workers would see little point in paying dues to a labor union.   Undoubtedly, this was in Dillon's mind when he charged that the A.L.B. was sponsoring "a National company dominated, controlled and financed union, designed to destroy American Federation of Labor independent organizations." [27]

In an effort to head off the A.L.B. elections, the A.F. of L. turned to the N.L.R.B. and by so doing brought to the surface a smoldering jurisdictional conflict between it and the Wolman board.   Individual U.A.W. locals like those in St. Louis and Atlanta, dissatisfied with the manner in which the A.L.B. had acted on their grievances, had for some time been seeking to interest the N.L.R.B. in their problems, much to Wolman's annoyance.   On one occasion, when the N.L.R.B., prodded by the Atlanta local, had requested the A.L.B. chairman for information concerning the Atlanta situation, Wolman had tartly replied that it was sufficient to inform the Atlanta union that the N.L.R.B. did not have jurisdiction over its affairs.   An N.L.R.B. staff member sent Wolman's reply on to the Atlanta board with the comment: "Winter is coming—b-r-r-r!"   The N.L.R.B. some weeks later advised Wolman that it had "paramount authority" over issues arising under Section 7(a), but in the end it had to advise the Atlanta regional board that jurisdiction lay with the A.L.B.[28]

As its reports to the President make clear, the N.L.R.B. was quite critical of bipartisan-type labor boards like the A.L.B.   Such boards, it contended, lacked the "dispassionate approach" required for the interpretation of Section 7(a), and their neutral chairman was inevitably placed in a difficult position.   The N.L.R.B., which already enjoyed some appellate jurisdiction, was of the opinion that it should be "ultimately responsible" for the interpretation of Section 7(a), that the decisions of all labor boards should be subject to its review. "The inadequacies of a particular board," it informed the President, "should not be allowed to interfere with the extension of the principle of collective bargaining to the workers coming under the protection of the statute." That the A.L.B. was one of the boards about whose "inadequacies" the N.L.R.B. was concerned is evident from a report on the various industrial-relations boards which was prepared early in 1935 at the behest of the N.L.R.B. but which the administration did not permit to be made public.[29]

With the first A.L.B. election at the Cadillac plant impending, Ogburn wired the N.L.R.B. to intervene and to halt the poll. Although N.L.R.B. chairman Francis Biddle had "grave doubts" about his board's jurisdiction in the matter, when asked by newsmen on December 13 if the N.L.R.B. could deal with the situation created by the refusal of the A.F. of L. to participate in the A.L.B. elections, he stated that "we'll let no technicalities stand in the way of settling any difficulty in a manner fair to both sides." In response to another query as to whether the board would intervene if the A.L.B. had "broken down," Biddle replied, "We would certainly give it most serious consideration and if the board has not produced results we would intervene." The N.L.R.B. discussed the question of its jurisdiction at some length the next day, and the other members of the board, as Biddle later recollected, thought that he had been "a bit too expansive" at his press conference. At all events, after the meeting the board issued a statement that it did not propose to intervene in the A.L.B. election and that it had "very grave doubts as to its jurisdiction to hear any automobile cases."[30]

Already miffed at the N.L.R.B.'s assumption of jurisdiction in a case arising under the newspaper code that in his opinion should have gone to the Newspaper Industrial Board, Donald Richberg, then the executive director of the National Emergency Council, thought that the controversy over jurisdiction in the automobile labor field further pointed up the need for giving the N.L.R.B. "a correct understanding of its functions" lest "it serve as the agency for upsetting every effort to adjust labor relations under the NRA codes." The issue was resolved on January 22, 1935, when Roosevelt informed Biddle, in a statement prepared by Richberg and Louis Howe and which Biddle has criticized as "clumsy" and lacking in "frankness," that the N.L.R.B. was without authority to intervene when a code provided for the adjudication of complaints of violation of the code's labor provisions and some agency had been established to which appeals could be taken and which was empowered to make final and enforceable decisions.[31] The A.L.B. was an agency of the type described by the President except that its authority was in no sense derived from the automobile code. This deficiency was to be quickly remedied, however, with the result that the N.L.R.B. was stripped of jurisdiction over all cases arising within the automobile manufacturing industry. Just as the N.L.B. had come off second best when it sought to apply its principles to the automobile labor field so the N.L.R.B. was also rebuffed when it seemed that it might seek to exercise review power over the actions of the A.L.B. and the code boards. Biddle complained to the President that "We believe that this limitation of our functions will impair our usefulness and authority," and Biddle's two associates on the board had to be dissuaded from resigning, but the order stood.[32] Once again the President had, in effect, sided with the automobile manufacturers and against the U.A.W.

The character of the A.L.B. elections and the failure of the A.F. of L. to halt them, combined with the apparent desire of many of the U.A.W. locals to sever their relationship with the A.L.B., persuaded Green to take the action that he had originally proposed in his letter to the President of September 11, 1934. On January 8, 1935, the A.F. of L. president wrote to the A.M.A. to announce the Federation's withdrawal from "participation in the work and decisions" of the A.L.B. Acting on the advice of Frances Perkins, he stated that the A.F. of L. wished to meet with A.M.A. representatives to agree on a new tribunal to replace the A.L.B. When the A.M.A. refused to confer with him on the subject, Green on January 24 publicly announced that the A.F. of L. would have "nothing more to do" with the A.L.B.[33]

Green naively assumed that the announced withdrawal of the A.F. of L. from the settlement deprived the A.L.B. of legal standing and that it would therefore "pass out of the picture," [34] but nothing of this sort occurred. The A.L.B. continued to hold its elections, and it invited individual workers to submit their complaints to the board. Since a new board was not created to replace the Wolman board, the U.A.W. locals in the main plants thus found themselves after January 1935 without a government tribunal to which they could take their complaints against their employers. This was a turn of events that the auto unionists had not anticipated, and some of them were more than a little displeased as a result. The Janesville Fisher Body and Chevrolet locals, for example, advised Green and Dillon on April 6 that unless the A.F. of L. was able to make some arrangement by April 10 for the adjudication of Janesville cases, they would submit their complaints to the A.L.B. Not knowing where to turn, Dillon sought the aid of Frances Perkins in the disposition of a long list of cases, all of them involving G.M., but the issue was still unresolved when the N.I.R.A. was declared unconstitutional.[35]

Undeterred by the opposition of the A.F. of L. and other labor organizations, the A.L.B. between December 19, 1934, and April 23, 1935, held sixty-three nominating elections and sixty-two final elections.[36] A total of 163,150 persons voted in the nominating elections and 161,907 in the final elections. The total for the nominating elections represented 85 per cent of those eligible to vote and 89 per cent of those working on the day of the elections.[37] Of those voting in the primaries, 68.6 per cent did not indicate any affiliation for their candidate, 13.3 per cent indicated that their candidate belonged to one or another of the employee associations, 8.6 per cent that their candidate was affiliated with the A.F. of L., and 3.7 per cent that their candidate was identified with the A.A.W.A. In all, 784 representatives were elected, and the A.L.B. added 126 representatives to the bargaining agencies to achieve proportional representation. The largest bargaining agency, at the Hudson plant, had seventy-two members; several bargaining agencies consisted of only five members.[38]

The A.L.B. elections, of course, were held only in plants subject to the code of the automobile manufacturing industry. Since the A.L.B., however, was uncertain of its jurisdiction over Ford, which had not been a party to the March 25 settlement, no elections were held among workers of the Ford Motor Company. Nor were any elections scheduled for the plants of Nash, Seaman Body, Studebaker, White Motor, and a few other companies where the U.A.W. was strong, apparently because neither the management nor the employees desired an election, and the A.L.B. did not wish to disturb the reasonably harmonious relations that prevailed. The A.F. of L., by a strike threat, blocked an election at the Detroit plant of the Hupp Motor Car Corporation, and a strike prevented the A.L.B. from holding the final election at the Toledo Chevrolet plant.[39]

The A.F. of L. fared very poorly in the first eleven elections held in Detroit as only 4 per cent of the voters indicated that their candidate was affiliated with the Federation. The A.F. of L. picked up strength outside Detroit, but only in the Toledo Chevrolet plant and the Los Angeles Chrysler plant did a majority of the voters express a preference for candidates that they identified with the Federation. The A.F. of L. did, however, win at least 30 per cent of the vote in the International Harvester plant in Fort Wayne, the International Motor Company plant in Plainfield, New Jersey, the Willys-Overland plant in Los Angeles, the Chevrolet plants in Oakland, California, and Indianapolis, and in the Fisher Body Fleetwood plant in Detroit, where a belated election was held.

In the Toledo Chevrolet primary, the business agent of the Toledo U.A.W. local emerged victorious in all eight of the plant's districts, securing 1327 of the 2140 votes cast. Had the U.A.W. local permitted a final election to be held in the plant and had the union's business agent again been the victor in all or some of the districts, the A.L.B. would have had to assign him more than one vote on the bargaining agency so as to give the A.F. of L. the proportional representation to which its primary vote entitled it. A similar situation was created in the Oakland Chevrolet plant, where Sidney Jacobs of the I.A.M. was victorious in seven of the eight districts in the primary election. In the final election, however, Jacobs, who in the meantime had accused the management of using "the rottenest [methods] any human brain could conceive" to defeat him, won in only two districts. As a result, he was presumably entitled to two votes on the plant bargaining agency.[40]

The A.F. of L. boycott of the elections was particularly effective in the Fisher Body plants in Norwood, Atlanta, Kansas City, and Cleveland, in the Chevrolet plant in Atlanta, and in the Willys-Overland plant in Toledo. In the elections in these plants, the percentage of the voters was considerably below the average for the elections as a whole. In the Atlanta primaries, at least, the A.F. of L. seems to have used "intimidation and coercion" in an effort to discourage voting, and some of the unionists were "so aroused," according to the A.L.B. official in charge of the election, "that they threatened to stab the men of the Works Council who were doing some campaigning in the shop." The A.F. of L. decision to boycott the elections not only reduced the total vote in several plant elections but also caused higher officials of the organization to refuse to serve on the bargaining agencies on the occasions when the votes they received entitled them to do so. In some instances, the bargaining agencies did not have their full complement of A.F. of L. members because of the refusal of unionists to serve.[41]

In defiance of the official A.F. of L. position, the U.A.W. federal labor unions in the International Harvester plant in Fort Wayne and the Fisher Body Fleetwood plant in Detroit urged the voters to elect candidates affiliated with the A.F. of L., and the locals emerged with 33.6 per cent of the primary vote in the former plant and 31.9 per cent in the latter.[42] It is perfectly apparent that had the Federation decided to participate in the elections rather than to boycott them, it would have won a substantially larger percentage of the total vote than it actually did. Given the nature of the A.L.B. elections, campaigning was necessary if an organization expected any large number of voters not only to select candidates who were members of the organization but to go to the trouble of writing in the affiliation of these candidates.

The A.A.W.A. made a respectable showing in the three plants in which its strength in the automobile industry was concentrated, winning 37.8 per cent of the primary vote in the Hudson plant, 34.5 per cent in the G.M. Truck plant, and 42.2 per cent in the Olds plant. Candidates whom the voters identified with an employee association won a majority of the votes in the International Harvester plants in Springfield and Fort Wayne and the Fisher Body and Chevrolet plant in Kansas City, and in addition company unions won at least 30 per cent of the vote in primary elections at Hudson, Packard, Reo, AC Spark Plug, Atlanta Fisher Body, St. Louis Chevrolet and Fisher Body, and the Chevrolet plants in Bloomfield and Indianapolis. In none of the plants of the Chrysler Corporation did candidates affiliated with the employee associations win as much as 1.5 per cent of the primary vote.[43]

Unlike the federal labor unions in the main plants, U.A.W. and other A.F. of L. locals in the parts plants could turn to the N.L.R.B. in an effort to have the principle of majority rule applied to the choice of representatives for collective-bargaining purposes. In addition to the Houde local, A.F. of L. unions in the Guide Lamp, Bendix, and Kelsey-Hayes plants all became involved in N.L.R.B. representation cases in which the principle of majority rule was at stake.

The controversy between the Guide Lamp Corporation, a G.M. subsidiary that manufactured head and tail lamps for G.M. and Chrysler cars, and Local 52 of the A.F. of L.'s Metal Polishers International Union originated in the fall of 1933 when the local, which claimed it represented 90 per cent of the employees in the polishing, buffing, and plating departments of the plant, sought a conference with the management. Taking a position the automobile and parts manufacturers were soon to abandon and the automobile unionists were to adopt, F. L. Burke, the plant manager, replied to this request on October 27 by standing on the doctrine of majority rule. He pointed out that Guide Lamp had already recognized the Guide Employees' Association, a company union the management had helped to establish, and stated, "We feel that we should deal with the representatives of all Guide employees, and not with individual groups, even though that group might represent a majority of men in a single department. If we begin the practice of negotiation with each group which presents itself, we will not be complying with the provisions of the N.R.A., and a great deal of confusion would result." The management was glad to consider the grievances of any employee or group, "but any negotiations or collective bargaining must be with the committee representing the great majority of our employees." [44]

On February 28, 1934, after having failed to secure the recognition it sought from the management, the local turned to the Indianapolis Regional Labor Board for assistance. The board on March 19, 1934, conducted an election among the employees of ten departments of the plant in which Local 52 defeated the Guide Employees' Association by a vote of 329 to 286. When the union, however, attempted early in April to secure an agreement covering the ten departments, the local plant management, reinforced by the presence of G.M.'s Harry Anderson, abandoned its earlier support of majority rule and expediently sought refuge in the principles embodied in the March 25 settlement. To forestall a regional labor board hearing scheduled for June 28, Anderson sought to have the case transferred to the A.L.B., but since the local would not agree to this, jurisdiction remained with the N.L.B., then in the final days of its existence. On July 2, following a hearing that the management did not attend, the Indianapolis board ordered G.M. to meet with the representatives of Local 52 as the spokesmen for all the employees in the ten departments eligible for membership in the Metal Polishers Union.[45]

The failure of Guide Lamp to comply with the regional board's ruling led the N.L.R.B. to step into the case. At an N.L.R.B. hearing of August 13 the company attorney, Henry M. Hogan, proposed proportional representation as the solution for the problem at issue and argued that the minority in the plant had "a greater interest at stake than people subject to outside domination." The N.L.R.B., in its decision of September 4, however, followed the Houde precedent and concluded that the company's insistence on bargaining with the minority was "essentially a reluctance to bargain collectively at all." The company was instructed to "make every reasonable effort" to enter into an agreement with Local 52 as the exclusive bargaining agency for all the employees eligible to participate in the March 19 election. When Guide Lamp indicated that it would not comply with the N.L.R.B. decision, the National Industrial Recovery Board took away its right to display the Blue Eagle, but the enforcement of the N.L.R.B. decision was delayed while the company sought to test its validity in the courts. The case had not yet come to a judicial decision when the N.I.R.A. was declared unconstitutional.[46]

The strong Bendix local, which had been thwarted in its efforts to secure a representation election in the months before the March 25 settlement, made another attempt on September 14, 1934, when it submitted an election petition bearing 848 names to the Chicago Regional Labor Board. Following a hearing on the case, the regional board ruled on November 7 that a poll of the employees was in the public interest and recommended to the N.L.R.B. that an election be held "as soon as it is practicable to do so." The N.L.R.B. scheduled a hearing on the Bendix case for November 30, but the company asked for a postponement on the grounds that it might otherwise lose a substantial portion of its Ford business and since Vincent Bendix, who was in charge of the firm's labor relations, was out of the country. In return for a postponement, the company agreed to make certain concessions to the union. This promised reward took the form of a "memorandum of company policy" that included layoff and rehiring provisions that came closer to satisfying the union's desire for straight seniority than the A.L.B.'s rules did. The company also agreed to pursue a policy of strict neutrality with regard to the employee association, which it maintained was consistent with existing company practice. Shipley optimistically assumed that the employee association was now "all but buried officially." [47]

The assumption of the regional director of the Chicago board that Vincent Bendix's presence would in itself solve the representation problem at the Bendix plant was given a rude jolt when the Bendix official refused to grant the union the exclusive bargaining rights that it was seeking. The many-times postponed N.L.R.B. hearing was finally held on January 14, 1935; and, as might have been expected, the board in its decision of January 25 ordered a representation election among the firm's hourly rated employees as of that date. Vincent Bendix, who was no more inclined than other automotive employers to accept the principle of exclusive representation, forestalled the implementation of the decision by seeking a court review, and once again the demise of the N.R.A. occurred before the case could be judicially resolved. [48]

The union did not emerge from its contest with the Bendix Corporation without some further gain for itself, however. A few days after the N.L.R.B. decision, the company, following negotiations between Vincent Bendix and the U.A.W. local, granted its employees a 5 per cent wage increase and adjustments in individual base rates and made a verbal promise to reimburse employees who had been unjustly dismissed. Carl Shipley informed Green that the company had "done all [that was] possible under [the] circumstances," and Green replied that "You have demonstrated what can be accomplished through organization and through collective bargaining." [49]   The Bendix local had indeed demonstrated the importance of organization, and when the N.I.R.A. came to a close, it was in a position to play a large part in the affairs of the organized automobile workers.

One week before the N.L.R.B. handed down its decision in the Bendix case, Charlton Ogburn submitted a petition to the board calling for an election among the factory employees of Kelsey-Hayes, manufacturer of wheels and other automobile parts and one of the few U.A.W. strongholds in the Detroit area.   The election was necessary, the A.F. of L. attorney argued, because the presence of a company union in the plant created "a spirit of rivalry" and denied the union majority the "full right" of collective bargaining.   The N.L.R.B. stepped into the case after the company indicated that it would not accept the principle of majority rule—the law firm representing Kelsey-Hayes later referred to this as an "un-American doctrine"— and would continue to bargain with all organized groups in the plant and also with individuals who wished to do so.   Following hearings in Detroit and Washington, the N.L.R.B. on April 10, 1935, found that the company's practice of meeting with both the company union and the federal labor union made for ineffective bargaining and ordered that a representation election be held in two weeks; but the Kelsey-Hayes management prevented the decree from going into immediate effect by seeking a court review.[50]

Judging by the action of Kelsey-Hayes and the similar behavior of Guide Lamp, Bendix, and Houde, it seems perfectly clear that had the President or the A.L.B. sought to apply the principle of majority rule to the choice of employee representatives in the main plants, the automobile manufacturers would have fought the decision in the courts.   They were willing to co-operate with the A.L.B. in the implementation of a scheme of proportional representation, but it would be a long time before they would be ready to concede that the majority-rule principle was here to stay.

II

As the new bargaining agencies were elected in the various plants, the A.L.B. or its agents held conferences with the representatives to discuss the scope of their duties and the procedures to be followed. The A.L.B. thought that it could not formulate rules for the operation of the agencies until it had had a chance to talk with a good many of them.   At the same time, it was aware that most of the representatives knew very little about the nature of collective bargaining, and that it might therefore be well to discuss the subject with them. Wolman, in particular, tried to persuade the representatives to take a pragmatic view of the bargaining process and not to expect too much from it. "There are no miracles in collective bargaining," he cautioned the representatives. Byrd realistically remarked that the only "miracle" would be if the A.L.B. plan proved successful.[51]

The conferences of the A.L.B. with the new bargaining agencies revealed rather clearly the difficulties the agencies were likely to encounter and the problems presented by the board's plan of proportional representation. There was, for example, the question of the relationship of the bargaining agency to other organizations of employees. Wolman stated that the bargaining agency was the only "official body for all the employees," but at the same time he indicated that the companies, if requested to do so, would also have to meet with outside groups on behalf of the persons they represented and with individuals who wished to bargain for themselves.[52]

The representatives, for the most part, found it difficult to distinguish between the new bargaining agencies and the old company unions. "You are no company Union," Wolman told one group of representatives, and he was at pains to point out that the employee associations no longer enjoyed a privileged position in the plants and that they could not serve as the medium through which bargaining took place. However, as Robert Briggs, one of the A.L.B.'s agents, conceded, it was difficult to convince the men that the companies were not responsible for the new scheme. The fact that so many former company-union officials were elected to positions on the bargaining agencies only added to the confusion.[53]

The A.L.B. did not help to relieve the representatives' concern about this matter by the position it took with regard to the pay of representatives for time spent on official business and the place where the bargaining agency should meet. From the start, Wolman expressed the view that the companies, rather than the A.L.B., should pay the representatives, but he thought, at the outset, that some arrangement should be devised that would remove any resulting suspicion that management was influencing the representatives. It was necessary, he said, to find "a method of payment whereby the men are free." No such method was worked out, however, and this may have lessened the appeal of the bargaining agencies to at least some of the automobile workers. To be sure, the automobile unionists were later to insist that the automobile companies pay union stewards their regular wage rate for the time that they spent in dealing with employee grievances, but during this earlier period, when the struggling outside unions were anxious to contrast their independence of the employer with the dependence of the company unions, the pay of employee representatives assumed a symbolic importance which it was not later to have.

Wolman also preferred that the men meet in the plant, and he did not understand why some representatives were opposed to this. He made it clear that the A.L.B. would not pay the expenses of meetings held off the premises. He did not even see why the representatives should object to having the company supply a secretary to record the minutes of the meetings of the bargaining agency. After all, he declared, the secretary could always be told what should not be included in the minutes.[54]

The bargaining agencies in their conferences with the A.L.B. raised some troublesome questions concerning the role of the representative who was not an employee and the functions of the designated as distinguished from the elected representative. Was the representative who was not an employee to be paid for his services, and did he have a right to enter the plant when he saw fit? Could the designated representative handle complaints arising in any district in the plant? Was he subject to recall, and in what manner could he be replaced if his position became vacant?[55] The A.L.B. had to take these questions under advisement, and actually it found no answers for some of them.

The size of the bargaining agency was a matter of some concern to the members of the larger bargaining agencies, and they wondered if the task of bargaining could be assigned to a small committee of the agency. The A.L.B. was opposed to this idea and thought it important that the entire bargaining agency should bargain for the men. Wolman did concede, however, that a bargaining agency of fifty-nine members was a cumbersome group and that it would have to work through committees on many issues.[56]

The main concern of the representatives was how the bargaining agency could be used to gain higher wages and improved working conditions for the men. It was in the raising of this question that the representatives became aware of the essential weakness of the new plan. The representatives were more or less familiar with the fact that the company unions had successfully disposed of many housekeeping problems in the plants and had been able to secure individual rate adjustments, but they expected something more from a plan that was under government auspices. The representatives were, consequently, generally disturbed to learn that although the A.L.B., as the settlement provided, retained jurisdiction over questions of discrimination, discharge, and representation, it had no jurisdiction with regard to wages and working conditions unless both sides agreed to permit it to mediate or arbitrate. Since the representatives correctly assumed that the bargaining agencies did not have the ability to strike, they thought that the A.L.B. should come to their assistance when they were deadlocked with their employer over some fundamental issue. The problem, as the men saw it, was well illustrated in the following conversation that took place between Wolman and Elmer Ratzloff of the Dodge bargaining agency:

Dr. Wolman: What you are asking me is if you make a request for a wage increase, will you get it?

Ratzloff: Yes.

Wolman: How should I know?

Ratzloff: The fact that I made the request, will that have any bearing? In other words, will that help get it?

Wolman: It might. . . . It may be a sound one which they can grant, and it may not.

Ratzloff: Suppose I know it is sound and it is refused, we have no recourse to the Board?

Wolman: You have no recourse to the Board.

Ratzloff: That is all there is. It drops right there?

Wolman: Yes.

Ratzloff: So our power is very limited.

Wolman: What kind of power do you think you should have?

Ratzloff: What we ought to have is if we make a request for higher wages—

Wolman: You should get it?

Ratzloff: No. Should we get it? I think we should.

Wolman: You think you should have power, if you make a demand for higher wages it must be granted?

Ratzloff: Just as much power as they have to say no.

Wolman: Nobody ever has that power.

Ratzloff: We will take [make] a request for higher wages and . . . naturally the company will say anything that will appear reasonable to us will be unreasonable to them. . . .

Wolman: Oh, no, that is not the way it works. After all negotiation takes skill. . . . You have to work out these things where you can listen to their arguments and they listen to your arguments and if they say no, they finally convince you and if you say yes, you finally convince them. . . .

Ratzloff: I fail to agree with you, for the reason that we will take these plants that have outside unions, when they have a certain power behind them, they have the force.[57]

In similar vein, an unaffiliated representative told Edward Wieck: "In the vital matter of wages and working conditions we can do nothing. We can only ask the employer about them, and if refused that ends it. We have no right to force them, no one to appeal to if the employer stands pat. As a representative I have no power. The company only has to refuse." [58]

Wolman's assurances that reason would prevail hardly convinced the representatives. He told the bargaining agencies, also, that the A.L.B. would try to help them if they were in a jam, and in response to a question, he assured the men that they could strike if they so desired. The representatives knew, however, that this was an empty right as long as they had no organization at their back. "If we don't build ourselves up to have power why it will be just merely no to everything we want," declared one of the representatives. [59]

Representatives who thought that the bargaining agencies should have information on conditions in other auto plants as well as their own and who saw advantages to be derived from multiplant bargaining were also troubled that no arrangements were being made by the A.L.B. to co-ordinate the activities of the various bargaining agencies. Thus Patrick V. McNamara of the Chrysler Kercheval bargaining agency, later to become a United States senator from Michigan, asked Byrd if the A.L.B. had any plans for "a central committee of men from the different plants." When Byrd replied that it was not the A.L.B.'s responsibility to deal with this problem, McNamara retorted, "What the hell good are you going to do then?" [60]

While the A.L.B. delayed the issuance of any rules applying to the operation of the bargaining agencies, G.M. and Chrysler, possibly at Wolman's suggestion, stepped into the void and issued instructions of their own. These instructions reveal rather clearly that from the management point of view the new bargaining agency was simply the company union in a somewhat different guise. Both companies drew up their rules without consulting with the bargaining agencies in their plants, and neither gave any indication that the rules were in any way subject to negotiation. The A.L.B., to be sure, informed the bargaining agencies that the instructions were only suggestions, [61] but the documents themselves provide no evidence that the companies viewed them in this light.

The G.M. instructions, while conceding that collective negotiation of the terms of employment was one of the purposes of the new plan, categorically stated that the determination of wages and hours was exclusively the prerogative of management. The bargaining agencies, the G.M. rules provided, were to meet on company premises twice a month, once without management representatives present and once in a joint meeting with the management. The procedure for handling grievances was spelled out, with provision made for referring matters within its jurisdiction to the A.L.B.

Representatives not employed in the plant were denied access to it but were given access to the conference room for bargaining-agency meetings. Individual employees who so desired could bargain separately with the management. No dues or assessments were to be levied or collected by the bargaining agency, nor was any representative to solicit membership for an organization on the premises. The company would compensate employed representatives at their usual rate for time spent during regular shift hours on bargaining-agency business.[62]

The Chrysler policy statement followed the company's employee-representation plan formula in providing for the separate meetings of the bargaining agency and the management representatives, who equaled the employee representatives in number, and for their common meetings as a works council. The statement indicated the conduct the company expected of the employees and their representatives in their relationship with one another and imposed the same restrictions on the nonemployed representatives as the G.M. instructions did.[63]

Finally, on April 12, by which time forty-eight bargaining agencies were already functioning, the A.L.B. issued its own "Rules and Instructions on Bargaining Agencies." The rules provided that representatives were to serve for one year and were to be subject to recall by a majority of the eligible voters of the district they represented. The representatives added to the bargaining agency for purposes of proportional representation were not to represent the members of any district but were to serve on the bargaining agency itself on equal terms with other members. It was proper for employers to pay representatives for time spent during their regular shift hours on bargaining-agency business and, by mutual agreement, for time spent outside shift hours as well. It was not to be considered a breach of the A.L.B.'s rules regarding layoff and rehiring if a representative was continued in his employment as long as a substantial number of his constituents were at work.

Aware that neither the representatives nor management had had much experience in collective bargaining, the A.L.B. included in its instructions advice concerning the collective-bargaining process. The employers and the bargaining agencies were counseled "to deal sincerely and fairly with one another" and to seek by negotiation "the best balance between the economic requirements of the business and the just aspirations of the employees." Employers ware asked to accompany their decisions regarding issues in contention with explanations and, where possible, evidence, and to make available to the bargaining agencies and the representatives the facilities necessary for studying the facts relating to disputed matters. Employee representatives were advised to keep their constituents informed of the status of questions being negotiated and were charged with the responsibility of aiding in maintaining discipline in the plants. The A.L.B. thought that efforts should be made to adjust issues between the representatives and lower management before these issues were taken up by the bargaining agency with the employer. It advised also that the arrangements for collective bargaining would be facilitated if matters within the A.L.B.'s jurisdiction were brought to its attention by the bargaining agencies only after the procedure of negotiation in the plants had been utilized.[64]

Richard Byrd thought that the A.L.B.'s instructions would contribute to "the arrival of industrial democracy," but the A.F. of L. charged that there could be no "freedom of action" by the representatives as long as they were paid by the company. It attacked the attempt by a government agency to guide the bargaining agencies and declared that the A.L.B. could not foist "this un-American Fascist philosophy" on the workers. Not all the bargaining agencies were pleased with the A.L.B.'s rules either. The Packard unit rejected the instructions as "discriminatory," and the association of officers of the agencies, about which more will be said later, found the rules "lacking of everything that would be of any value to us, the elected representatives, in dealing collectively with the manufacturers in this industry." [65]

One of the chief weaknesses of the A.L.B.'s rules was that they failed to distinguish the bargaining agencies from the company unions sufficiently to give the workers a sense that the new organizations were independent of company control. The A.L.B. rules also make it appear that the board thought that sweet reasonableness would prevail in the realm of collective bargaining if only the facts were made available, and that the question of power was not really vital to the process. Furthermore, the board's rules raised the question as to whether the attempt of a government body to guide the bargaining agencies by rules and instructions was any more consistent with the concept of self-organization than were the efforts at company guidance embodied in the Chrysler and G.M. instructions. As a report prepared for the first N.L.R.B. indicated, even before the A.L.B. rules were announced: "If proportional representation is proving to be in practice the sort of device which requires a governmental agency to lay down rules and regulations as to how the workers shall go about the process of bargaining, the whole procedure becomes far removed from that ideal of self-organization of the workers for collective bargaining which is the corner stone of Section 7(a)." [66]

Some of the bargaining agencies began to function as early as January 1935, but most of them did not take up their duties until March or April. On the advice of the A.L.B. the new agencies drew up rules of procedure to govern their relations with management. These rules, generally adopted with the consent of the employers, were on the whole quite similar to the instructions already promulgated by G.M. and Chrysler and the regulations that had governed the company unions. In some plants, indeed, the new bargaining agency simply adopted the existing company-union constitution with a minimum of changes. The Chevrolet Commercial Body unit went so far as to include in its "Articles of Association" the same membership rules as applied to the plant employee-representation plan, and Byrd, consequently, had to remind the group of the necessity of recognizing the difference between a bargaining agency and a "private organization." [67]

The plans adopted by the bargaining agencies usually called for two meetings a month, one of them a joint meeting with the management. Despite the advice of the A.L.B., some of the bargaining agencies assigned the task of bargaining with the management to a select committee. The Hudson body, interestingly enough, allocated the membership of its Negotiations Committee and its Rules Committee in proportion to the strength of the three groups represented on the agency, the A.A.W.A., the Hudson Industrial Association, and the unaffiliated group. The same bargaining agency later agreed that its three officers should also represent these three affiliations.[68] Decisions within the bargaining agencies, insofar as can be determined, were reached by majority rule.

The bargaining agencies adopted a variety of procedures for the handling of grievances. In some plants, the individual employee was to take his grievance to his foreman, to begin with, but in other plants grievances were to be brought initially to the district representative. Matters within the jurisdiction of the A.L.B. could, of course, be carried to the board whether or not the rules made provision for this. The Cadillac plan permitted subjects outside the A.L.B.'s jurisdiction to be carried by stages to G.M.'s Department of Industrial Relations. The Olds rules provided for carrying grievances to the president of G.M. and, failing a settlement at this level, to the A.L.B. Some of the agencies arranged with their employers to permit the ultimate referral of all disputes to the A.L.B.[69]

The role of the representative, whether elected or designated and whether an employee or not, was largely defined by the company rules and the A.L.B. instructions previously noted. The representative added to the bargaining agency for purposes of proportional representation played a less important role in the plant than did the elected representative since he had no constituency of his own and was not permitted to deal with the grievances arising in any particular district unless and until they came before the bargaining agency as a whole. No provision was made for the recall of the designated representative nor for filling his post should it become vacant for one reason or another.

The lot of the representative who was not an employee was a difficult one since he did not enjoy the same access to his constituents as the employed representative did. One of the best known of the outside representatives, Arthur Greer, the president of the Hudson local of the A.A.W.A. and the chairman of the Hudson bargaining agency's Negotiations Committee, was recalled by his constituents allegedly because he was not an employee of the district he represented and was thus presumably unfamiliar with its problems.[70]

As the A.L.B. had advised, the bargaining-agency regulations provided for the company to pay employee representatives for time spent on bargaining-agency business and, generally, to meet the expenses of the agency as well. Some of the groups did raise their own funds to meet the expenses of running the agency, and those units which held all or some of their meetings outside the plant did so at their own expense. The A.A.W.A. and the Hudson Industrial Association, for example, shared the expenses incurred by the Hudson bargaining agency and paid the cost of its meetings, all of which were held outside the plant.[71]

One of the fundamental questions raised by the bargaining agencies was whether the representatives should have access to the wage and service records of all their constituents so that they could more intelligently deal with wage, seniority, and discrimination problems. The position of the employers was that individual records would be provided in specific cases but that records would not be made available generally. Wolman supported management in this stand. He distinguished between dealing with trouble and looking for trouble and cautioned that the general availability of the data in question would only increase the grievances of the men.[72]

Traditionally, the chief criticism of proportional representation in collective bargaining has been that it tends to pit a divided labor group against a single employer; and it was principally for this reason that the A.F. of L. and such advocates of majority rule as the members of the first N.L.R.B. viewed with disfavor the concept the A.L.B. was trying to implement.[73] Although this is a legitimate criticism of proportional representation, it presupposes the existence on the bargaining committee of organized groups with probably conflicting goals. Actually, however, because of the nature of the A.L.B. plan and the weakness of organized groups in the auto industry, the A.L.B. bargaining agencies were principally composed of unaffiliated representatives rather than the representatives of strongly organized groups. There was not a single agency whose membership was dominated by rival trade unions, and the Hudson bargaining agency was the only one in a major plant in which a well-organized and successful company union and a potent outside union were represented in strength.[74]

The antagonism between the two Hudson groups was reflected in the functioning of the bargaining agency. As John Kehrig, the temporary chairman of the bargaining agency, informed the A.L.B. with regard to these two rivals, "affiliations will not be forgotten." The two groups did not wish to sit with one another, and the A.A.W.A. asked if it might bargain separately with the management for the districts it represented. Although Wolman saw no reason why different groups on a bargaining agency should not be able to reach unanimous agreement, the minutes of the meetings of the Hudson bargaining agency indicate that "affiliations will not be forgotten." [75]

As previously noted, one of the great weaknesses of the bargaining agencies established under the A.L.B. plan was their lack of power. Byrd recognized this fact and actually advised the secretary of the Cadillac bargaining agency to use "every quiet and peaceful persuasion to get the men to organize behind the representatives." He thought the workers should join some union and that the unions should "cooperate through the official machinery." [76]

No bargaining agency was more concerned with the question of organization than was the Dodge main plant body. Conscious of its lack of bargaining power, the Dodge agency eventually formed an important new independent auto union, one which was later to merge with the U.A.W. This fact gives the Dodge group a distinction enjoyed by no other A.L.B. bargaining agency.

The Dodge bargaining agency consisted of fifty-three members, all of whom were designated as unaffiliated; and following its practice under the Chrysler works-council plan, the company appointed an equal number of management representatives to sit with the employee representatives in the monthly joint meetings and designated one of its officials as special management representative and chairman of the joint meetings. The employee representatives, who had expected the new bargaining agency to be a stronger and more independent body than the old company union, were disturbed by this management action.[77]

From the start, the Dodge bargaining agency displayed an independent spirit, and its members "vaguely" saw "the organizational opportunity that was provided by the get-together." At a meeting of February 19, 1935, the employee representatives agreed to meet on company property, as the company wished, but only if they could invite to their meetings any outside person whom they pleased. Also, the men agreed to accept pay from the company only for meetings held inside the plant. James Reid, one of the representatives, pointed out to the men that if they intended to secure their rights, they would have to organize. "Individually," he noted, "we don't amount to a row of pins."[78]

When the company soon after this meeting distributed its aforementioned "Policy for Works Council and Employees Representatives Meetings," J. M. Campbell, then the temporary chairman of the bargaining agency, protested this action to the A.L.B. as "dictatorial." "We maintain," Campbell informed the Board, "that we as duly elected Employee Representatives alone have the authority to say how, when and where we may best use our office for betterment of our constituents...."[79]

At its February 26 meeting, after Secretary Richard Frankensteen, who as a college graduate with a winning personality and a certain amount of oratorical talent was emerging as the key figure in the organization, had reported that the operating manager of the plant had refused to comply with several demands presented to him by the agency's executive committee, the bargaining agency went a bit further on the road to independence. It voted not to permit the company clerk to take the minutes of its meetings any longer, collected a small sum to defray the expenses of the secretary's office, and appointed a committee to find a meeting place for the group outside the plant.[80]

The first regular joint meeting of the bargaining agency and the management representatives under the new plan took place on March 5. Believing that it was impossible for a group of 106 persons to engage in real bargaining on issues of importance, the employee representatives decided in advance not to bring up any matters pertaining to wages and hours. The discussion was consequently confined to such subjects as sanitation in the plant, ventilation, and the quality of food and the size of the milk bottle sold by the lunch wagon. At subsequent meetings of the bargaining agency that month, meetings held outside the plant, a majority of the representatives decided that henceforth the task of bargaining for the men should be entrusted to the executive committee of the bargaining agency rather than to the bargaining agency as a whole. It was further decided to initiate the organization of the Dodge workers and to sell tickets for a mass meeting on March 31 designed to spur the organization of Dodge employees and to acquaint them with their rights under the N.I.R.A.[81]

When the Dodge management refused to bargain with the executive committee and insisted that the committee's requests would be answered only at the joint meetings, President Campbell and Secretary Frankensteen informed Walter Chrysler by letter on March 23 that the representatives would not meet with the management until the company had appointed a committee composed of persons with authority to bind the company and small enough to reach decisions. Campbell, the same day, also complained about the company's behavior to the A.L.B. and insisted that unless the board came to the aid of the bargaining agency, all the efforts of the federal government to provide for collective bargaining in the Dodge plant "will have done no good whatever." [82]

The letters of March 23 led to a meeting on March 27 between a committee of the bargaining agency and six high Chrysler officials and to a conference of the executive officers of the various Chrysler bargaining agencies with the A.L.B. on March 28. At the March 27 meeting the company officials discussed with the bargaining-agency committee the principal issues that were troubling the representatives but rejected their request that bargaining be conducted by small groups from both sides rather than by the works council as a whole.[83]

The next day the Dodge bargaining-agency officers complained to the A.L.B. about the character of collective bargaining under the A.L.B. plan. Frankensteen remarked that the men had expected that the new plan would have "a few teeth" in it but that actually it was not an improvement over the company union. When Nicholas Kelley argued that it was better for all fifty-three members of the bargaining agency, rather than just a small group, to gain experience in collective bargaining, Frankensteen retorted, "We are not after experience. We are after results."

With regard to the efforts of the bargaining agency "to put across organization," Wolman pointed out that it was not the business of a representative to organize anyone and that no individual could use his position on a bargaining agency for this purpose.   Frankensteen, however, replied that his constituents had elected him to secure better working conditions, and if he could bargain more effectively for them as the result of having an organization at his back, he was within his rights in seeking to accomplish that objective.   Reid declared that a majority of the men favored organization and only if an organization were formed would it be possible for a representative to take time off from his job in the plant to make a study of the questions the men wished discussed with the company.[84]

During April the new organization of the Dodge employees began to take shape.   Since the men did not wish to join the A.F. of L., because of its allegedly dictatorial control over its federal labor unions and its craft-union bias, the officers decided to establish a new independent organization, to which they gave the name "Automotive Industrial Workers' Association."   When cards were distributed among the workers asking whether they would support an independent organization of employees, more than fourteen thousand of them replied in the affirmative.[85]

The Chrysler management indicated its displeasure with the organizational developments in the Dodge plant at a special meeting of the bargaining agency on April 19.   "This thing here isn't working out the way it was supposed to work at all," declared W. J. O'Neill, Chrysler vice-president in charge of manufacturing.   As management saw it, it was not necessary for the employees to have an independent organization in order for them to bargain collectively.   "Organization," declared Chrysler's Herman L. Weckler, "is not a part of collective bargaining."   It was the job of the representative simply to find out what his constituents desired and then to report this to the management.   L. L. Colbert, then a Chrysler attorney, agreed with Weckler.   It was the duty of the bargaining-agency members, he declared, to represent the men, not to organize them.   O'Neill's advice to the representatives was to go "a little easy here.   You will get just as far.   You don't need any union around here.   We will deal with you just the same."

The representatives took a different view of collective bargaining and insisted that the only way the bargaining agency could gain the power to bargain effectively was through organization.   The representatives were undoubtedly correct in so arguing, but whether they were exceeding their authority by using their position to promote an independent organization and to solicit support for it on company property was another matter, and it was agreed that this issue should be taken to the A.L.B.[86]

Before the A.L.B. on April 23 the Chrysler management, which was soon to yield on the issue of the size of the bargaining group, stated its view that meetings of the bargaining agency on company property should be for collective-bargaining purposes only and that if representatives wished to address meetings off the premises called for organizing purposes, they should do so in their capacity as individuals and not as members of the bargaining agency. The A.L.B. also took the position that the bargaining agency, as such, must not be used to promote organization, and the representatives agreed to abide by this ruling.[87] The distinction the A.L.B. and the company tried to draw, however, was a meaningless one in practice. The representatives were, after all, the elected leaders of the workers, and it made little difference to their constituents whether they were addressed by their leaders as individuals or as members of the bargaining agency.

In the months following the April 23 conference, the A.I.W.A. grew in strength and spread its organization to several other automobile plants in the Detroit area. Richard Frankensteen was eventually to be elected president of the group, and R. J. Thomas, the president of the Chrysler Kercheval plant local of the A.I.W.A., was to be elected first vice-president. Since some of the organization's leaders regarded Father Charles E. Coughlin as the person who had "done more toward educating the working class than any other living man," the Royal Oak priest was looked to as the A.I.W.A.'s "advisor and supporter." By the fall of 1935 the A.I.W.A. was claiming twenty-four thousand members. Significantly, the strength of the organization was entirely in the Detroit area, where the A.F. of L. had failed altogether to organize the auto workers.[88]

As previously noted, not only were some members of the bargaining agencies concerned about the problem of organization but also about the lack of co-ordination among the units in the various plants. Thus, at its first regular meeting, the Cadillac bargaining agency decided to suggest to the other bargaining agencies that they unite to form a national automobile employees' association for collective-bargaining purposes. Byrd also made clear on several occasions his desire "to hook the bargaining agencies up together," and he told the Dodge agency on February 14 that he looked forward to the "eventual development of a bigger organization than just your plant." No concrete action was taken, however, to co-ordinate the activities of the bargaining agencies until March 23, when the officers of sixteen of the bargaining agencies in the Detroit area banded together to form the Officers Association of Automobile Industrial Employees. The chairman of the group was Patrick V. McNamara of the Chrysler Kercheval plant bargaining agency.

The announced purpose of the new organization was to forge the bargaining agencies into "one solid unit" so that they might "coordinate constructive ideas to bargain collectively for a mutual benefit." Significantly, at their first meeting, the officers announced their support of the pending National Labor Relations Bill, which endorsed the idea of majority rule rather than proportional representation as the basis for establishing bargaining rights.

The Officers Association was out of sympathy with the A.L.B. and charged it with being "always cautious to rule in such a manner that is entirely in favor of the employer and seemingly never able to grasp even for a moment the point of view of the employee." At a meeting late in April, the officers petitioned President Roosevelt to remove Wolman and Byrd from the A.L.B., the former for his alleged "lack of cooperation," the latter for his alleged incompetence. At the same meeting the officers adopted a resolution advising the representatives of the various bargaining agencies to join a union of their choice.[89]

Initiated with the intention of co-ordinating the endeavors of the bargaining agencies, the Officers Association decided in August 1935, after the N.I.R.A. had lapsed, to take on the task of co-ordinating the activities of the various organized groups in the automobile industry—the A.F. of L., the A.A.W.A., the A.I.W.A., the M.E.S.A., and such bargaining agencies as continued to function. Its efforts led to the establishment of the Brotherhood of Allied Automobile Workers, but the A.F. of L. and the M.E.S.A. refused to participate in the new organization, and such strength as it had derived principally from the A.A.W.A. With the establishment of the Brotherhood, the Officers Association ceased to function. During its brief existence, it did not engage in any multiplant bargaining, and it is doubtful that the exchange of information that it promoted strengthened the bargaining agencies in any material sense. The Association was, at best, a symbol of unity rather than a real unifying force.[90]

The product of the A.L.B.'s interpretation of the President's settlement of March 25, 1934, and, in the last analysis, of Section 7(a) of the N.I.R.A., the bargaining agencies ceased to be of any real significance in the automobile industry after the N.I.R.A. was declared unconstitutional on May 27, 1935. Most of the agencies soon became inactive, although some of them were kept alive until 1937, when the validation of the Wagner Act convinced most employers that the bargaining agencies could not be used as a substitute for independent unionism. Those agencies that did survive the end of the N.I.R.A. do not appear to have played a particularly important role in the collective-bargaining process in the automobile industry.[91]

Because of the short period of time during which most of the bargaining agencies functioned, it is difficult to evaluate their work and the effectiveness of proportional representation as a method of determining representation rights.   Naturally, the members of the A.L.B. viewed the agencies in a favorable light.   In their final report, they stated their belief that "in the majority of instances the agencies acted as effective representatives of the interests of their constituents, that the issues they discussed with representatives of employers were no different and no fewer in number than under any system of collective bargaining, that the percentage of successful outcome [*sic*] to negotiations was no less here than elsewhere, and that, except in one bargaining agency [Hudson?], representatives of different labor groups serving on the same bargaining agency had little difficulty in getting along with one another."

This estimate by the A.L.B. errs on the optimistic side.   The bargaining agencies certainly had the right to discuss any subject they pleased with management, but, as Anthony Lucheck has pointed out, "The extent of their bargaining power was limited to reasoning with employers."   Even in this latter respect, it must be noted, the representatives of the bargaining agencies were under a handicap.   Although they generally knew more about shop conditions in the industry than the professional A.F. of L. organizers did, they lacked experience and skill in bargaining and adequate time to prepare their arguments.

In many respects the bargaining agencies were simply "a continuation of the company union," and it would appear that the workers increasingly viewed them in this light.   Like the company unions, they functioned successfully in dealing with the housekeeping problems in the auto plants, but they were far less successful in tackling the bread-and-butter issues in which the workers were more interested. "The other part [housekeeping matters] don't mean a damn," Frankensteen told a group of Chrysler officials.   "They [the men] want more money." [92]

The experiment in proportional representation in the automobile industry was not, however, without significance for the future.   Like the company unions, the A.L.B. bargaining agencies provided some experience in collective bargaining for both employer and employee in an industry where such experience was badly needed.[93]   It brought to the fore a future U.A.W. vice-president in Richard Frankensteen and a future U.A.W. president in R. J. Thomas.   It led to the organization of the A.I.W.A.—Frankensteen said that A.I.W.A. members were referred to as "the illegitimate sons of the Wolman board" [94]—which was later to add its strength to the U.A.W., and it convinced many automobile workers that there was no organizational alternative to outside unionism as an agency for promoting their interests. It demonstrated that the selection of representatives on the basis of proportional representation but without the support of organizations was unlikely to produce realistic collective bargaining. At the same time, it did not shed too much light on the effectiveness of proportional representation as a method for determining the composition of employee bargaining agencies when strongly organized competing groups are present in the bargaining unit, although the experience of the Hudson bargaining agency casts doubt on the workability of proportional representation under these circumstances also. At all events, Congress in passing the Wagner Act and the President in signing it decided that majority rule was to prevail in the realm of collective bargaining, and within a relatively short time an interesting, if brief, experiment in labor relations in the nation's premier industry was all but forgotten.

XI

THE A.F. OF L. AND THE CODE

THWARTED IN ITS EFFORTS to bargain to a successful conclusion with the automobile manufacturers, convinced that the A.L.B. was a hindrance rather than an aid to unionism in the automobile industry, the A.F. of L. looked to the amendment of the automobile code as the means of improving the lot of the automobile workers. Just prior to its first expiration date, the code, it will be recalled, had been extended without change until September 4, 1934. The A.F. of L. and the U.A.W. were determined that before the code was once again renewed, there should be a public hearing at which the organized automobile workers would be given an opportunity to express their views about working conditions in the industry and about needed changes in the code. As early as July 10, 1934, William Green had advised Johnson that the Labor Advisory Board, of which the A.F. of L. president was then the acting chairman, believed it essential that hearings be held on the code before its scheduled expiration date because it was the only code containing a merit clause, its wage provisions were not consistent with the current practices of the industry, its hours provisions were unenforceable, its labor provisions in general departed from N.R.A. standards, and related and subsidiary industries were constantly seeking exemptions from the labor clauses of their codes so as to make them conform to the loosely drawn provisions of the automobile code.[1]

In anticipation of hearings on the code, the L.A.B. and the A.F. of L. drafted a set of proposals—they appear to have been largely the work of W. Ellison Chalmers—which called for the radical alteration of the salient provisions of the automobile code. The two organizations proposed that the hours of labor in the industry be reduced to thirty per week and no more than eight per day, except for employees engaged in emergency repair work on the employers' equipment and provided they were paid time-and-a-half for hours above the daily and weekly maxima for other workers. To provide for the peak period of automobile production, the normal hourly limits were not to apply for ten weeks during the year, but time-and-a-half was to be paid during this period for working hours above eight per day and forty per week, and the overtime hours were to be limited to eight per week. The A.F. of L. and the L.A.B. were prepared to charge that such re-employment as had occurred in the industry since the code had gone into effect was attributable to the increased demand for automobiles rather than the hours provisions of the code, that too many workers were exempted from the weekly hours limitations set forth in the code, that the suggested thirty-hour week was only slightly below the average weekly hours of employment of factory workers in the industry during the preceding year, and that the recommended provision for the peak period was consistent with current N.R.A. practice whereas the averaging clause of the automobile code was not. No effort was made to estimate the extent of re-employment that would occur if the proposed hours provisions were implemented or what effect they would have on the cost of producing automobiles.

The L.A.B. and the A.F. of L. recommended the simplification of the methods of wage payment used in the industry, a minimum wage of seventy cents per hour, and the adjustment of rates above the minimum so as to preserve the differentials prevailing before the effective date of the code. The labor groups conceded that hourly rates in the industry had reached 1929 levels, but they insisted that low annual earnings and the relatively strong financial position of the industry justified both higher minimum and above-minimum rates.

To deal with the troublesome problem of the irregularity of automobile employment, the L.A.B. and the A.F. of L., which at the time of the original code hearings had advanced the concept of dismissal pay, now recommended that when an employee was laid off, he should receive one-half of his average weekly earnings for the preceding six months or less of his last continuous employment for each week that he remained unemployed until the total period of his unemployment and his last continuous employment reached thirty-nine weeks. No employee, however, was to be eligible to receive unemployment compensation during the first two weeks of his unemployment. When an employee worked less than fifteen hours in any particular week, he was to be paid an employment benefit to bring his total earnings for the week up to the equivalent of fifteen hours of pay. Workers who were dismissed after having been employed for at least two weeks were to receive an additional week's compensation. The proponents of the unemployment compensation plan looked upon it as a means of en-

couraging the stabilization of automobile employment without, however, having examined its full implications and without indicating
how it was to be financed and how expensive it was apt to be. They
undoubtedly advanced their scheme for bargaining purposes only since
they could hardly have expected much support for the idea either
from the employers or the N.R.A. Finally, the L.A.B. and the
A.F. of L. proposed the elimination of the merit clause from the code
and the inclusion of certain provisions relating to child labor, safety
and health, the contracting out of work, and so forth, that had become
standard for N.R.A. codes.[2]

Undoubtedly appreciating that there was some justification for
the L.A.B. and A.F. of L. demand that the automobile code be reopened, General Johnson announced on August 17, 1934, that a public
hearing would be held on the document ten days later, but the scheduled hearing was abruptly canceled the next day, ostensibly because
the employers had not yet submitted their proposals for the extension
of the code. The Automobile Manufacturers Association was, as
a matter of fact, prepared to accept a continuation of the code only if
it could be assured that the status quo, particularly as defined by the
March 25 settlement, would not be disturbed. Acting for the A.M.A.,
which was determined "to budge not an inch" from its position, Walter
Chrysler informed Johnson on August 31 that unless assurances could
be given that the code would remain unaltered, the industry, in his
"private opinion," would not apply for an extension. The A.M.A. was
aware that its failure to agree to a renewal of the code "would probably result in little short of a brawl and would undoubtedly involve
litigation with the Government," but it assumed, correctly as it turned
out, that the administration and the N.R.A. desired "to get by September 4th with the least possible trouble."[3]

The U.A.W. National Council, which held its second session in
Washington from August 28 to August 31, met on August 31 with
George A. Lynch, acting N.R.A. Administrator, to present the A.F. of L.
code proposals and to complain about "the many ways" in which the
document was "totally inadequate to accomplish the purposes of the
President and the Recovery Act." On the very same day, however,
Johnson, acceding to the wishes of the automobile manufacturers,
secured Green's reluctant consent to the extension of the code for sixty
days (until November 3, 1934) and with the understanding—so Johnson informed the President—that the March 25 settlement would "continue in effect."[4] If the information the general supplied the President was accurate—and it must be said that Johnson was not in the

best physical condition at the time [5]—Green was going back on his word when on September 11, as noted above, he wrote to Roosevelt in an effort to withdraw the A.F. of L. from the settlement.

In securing Green's consent for a sixty-day extension of the code, Johnson had apparently promised the A.F. of L. president that there would be a public hearing on the document before it was once again extended.[6] In preparation for this event, W. Ellison Chalmers, acting once again for both the A.F. of L. and the L.A.B., prepared a set of amendments to the code and buttressed his proposals with an analysis of the document that was based on a "useful but highly inadequate" investigation conducted by the Bureau of Labor Statistics and on information supplied by the Research and Planning Division from the altogether inadequate monthly reports submitted to the N.R.A. by the automobile companies. Chalmers concluded that the automobile industry had profited "enormously" from the N.R.A. but had done very little to spread or to stabilize employment or to increase purchasing power.

The changes in the labor provisions of the code that Chalmers recommended were virtually identical to the proposals that the A.F. of L. and the L.A.B. had advanced in August,[7] but they appear to have been modified within the L.A.B. prior to their transmission to the N.I.R.B. In their final form, the L.A.B. recommendations, which enjoyed the support of the A.F. of L., called for a thirty-hour week, except for a peak period of ten weeks when thirty-six hours would be permitted; an overtime rate of time-and-one-half; a weekly wage that was to be not less for thirty hours than it had been for forty hours in June 1933, and not less for thirty-six hours than for forty-eight hours as of the same date; an annnual minimum wage of $1000; and limitation of the employees excepted from the hourly limitations to executives and managerial personnel receiving more than $35 per week, outside salesmen, and workers engaged in emergency maintenance and repair tasks.

In defense of its proposals the L.A.B. noted that the thirty-hour week would work no real hardship on the industry during the nonpeak period; that the hours specified for the period of maximum production would have increased employment by 8 per cent during the peak production months of March and April 1934; that the weekly wages it was proposing would require an increase of only three cents per hour over the June 1934 figures for the industry; that 70 per cent of the eighty-nine codes in the equipment section of the N.R.A., which included the automobile industry, required an overtime rate; that the

limitation of the excepted occupations was consistent with current
N.R.A. practice; that 55 per cent of the automobile manufacturing employees received less than $1000 in 1933 and that the average annual
wage for the industry in 1933 was only about $850 as compared to
$1475 in 1929 (the 1929 figure was estimated by the A.M.A. as
$1688); and that the implementation of the minimum annual-wage
provision, which would have amounted to a guarantee of about forty-
five weeks of employment per year, assuming a thirty-hour week and
an average hourly wage of 74.4 cents, the industry average for October 1934, would be an important spur to the stabilization of automobile employment.[8] From its original support of a dismissal wage, the
A.F. of L., which had previously shown very little interest in the subject, had now advanced to an espousal of the concept of an annual
minimum wage as the best means of dealing with the unsolved problem of the irregularity of automobile employment. The A.F. of L.
was to adhere to this position, about which so much was to be heard
in the industry at a later time, as long as the automobile code remained in effect.[9]

Both the A.F. of L. and the L.A.B. formally requested that a hearing on the code be held prior to its November 3 expiration date, but
the National Industrial Recovery Board, aware that the A.M.A. was
not prepared to accept any amendments to the code, failed to act
on this request. The result was that the question of the code's renewal passed from the board's hands into those of the President.
Roosevelt was willing to go along with the industry's desire for the
extension of the code without change, but he did think that the question of the stabilization of automobile employment required further
attention. As the result of his conversations with the automobile
workers at the time of the March settlement, he had become impressed
with the fact that because of irregularity of employment, the relatively
high hourly wages paid by the industry did not necessarily become
translated into adequate annual earnings. Richard Byrd had told
him that "the homes of my neighborhood are hovels, rooms without
carpets, walls without paper, no modern conveniences and children
undernourished." The President, therefore, probably at the suggestion of Sidney Hillman, president of the Amalgamated Clothing Workers of America and the labor member of the N.I.R.B., proposed to
the manufacturers' committee of Sloan, Donaldson Brown, and Walter
Chrysler an administration study of the problem of the regularization
of automobile employment. The A.M.A. representatives responded
that the industry had already made "substantial progress" in its efforts

to stabilize employment, that they had neither "the right nor the power" to agree to the proposed inquiry, and that they did not "in any sense" consent to its being made.[10]

Undoubtedly anxious, particularly with Congressional elections in the offing, to assuage the pain of the A.F. of L. at having to accept an unamended code for a third time, Roosevelt decided to push ahead with the inquiry despite the opposition of the A.M.A. On November 2, consequently, the President, in an unusual move, personally announced the extension of the code until February 1, 1935, but at the same time declared his intent to institute a study which, he hoped, would "contribute toward improvements in stabilizing employment in the industry and reducing further the effects of the seasonal factors." Stating publicly that he had "not asked the manufacturers to agree that such an inquiry should be made"—he would have been more accurate had he declared that they had not agreed that it should be made—he indicated that the study would be initiated under his executive powers. In a letter to Green and A.M.A. President Macauley, Roosevelt, without being specific, wrote that he had "no hesitation" in telling them "that there are a number of matters connected with this code with which I have never been fully satisfied." He expressed his desire to confer with the two men before initiating the contemplated inquiry and declared that he would decide whether a public hearing on the code was required after the government study had been completed.[11]

As the President had anticipated, the A.F. of L. high command's disappointment at the failure of the N.R.A. to hold a public hearing on the automobile code was "very greatly counteracted"—to use Green's phrase—by the decision to have a study made of the problem of irregular automobile employment. Some automobile union leaders were also pleased that a showdown with the automobile employers had been avoided at a time that would not have been "good for us" and that the code had been extended not for the life of the N.I.R.A., as the A.M.A. had originally requested, but only until February 1, 1935, which was in the midst of the automobile production season and was thus "the most advantageous time" from the workers' point of view.[12]

In his November 2 letter to Green and Macauley the President made reference to a study of the problem of the regularization of automobile employment that the auto manufacturers had pledged themselves to make in their code and on which they were obligated to report by December 1, 1933. The task of drafting the required report had been assigned by Macauley in October to a "Continuous

Employment Committee" consisting of M. A. Cudlip of Packard as chairman, N. C. Dezendorf of G.M., and I. T. O'Brien of Chrysler.[13]

Although the Cudlip committee was the first of its kind in the industry, the automobile manufacturers had not previously been unconcerned with the problem of irregular production and employment; and even during the halcyon and prosperous 1920's, individual manufacturers had attempted by one means or another to level their production curve. Some producers during the mid-1920's had sought to stabilize production by introducing their new models during the summer months, but the industry as a whole viewed the staggered introduction of new models as disruptive even though the results were not entirely unsatisfactory from the point of view of individual companies. The increase of exports during the winter months was another means utilized by some manufacturers to cope with the problem of irregular output, but this had little effect on the industry in the aggregate. There was also some interest in winter production for storage by dealers, but only the dealers who sold the most popular makes were willing to co-operate with the manufacturers to any extent in this effort. The most notable attempt to regularize automobile production before 1929 was the Packard "Level Production Plan," which was introduced in 1927 and continued until the depression, when falling sales forced its abandonment. In so far as automobile employers considered the problem of regularization in the 1920's, it was in the interests of sound business policy rather than to provide their employees with steadier jobs and higher annual wages.[14] Annual wages in the industry tended to be relatively high, and it was thought that the automobile workers could find other jobs during the period of their layoff to supplement the wages they received from their primary employers.

The depression, as previously noted, aggravated the problem of irregular production and employment in the automobile industry. The manufacturers proved to be too optimistic in their sales forecasts for 1930, 1931, and 1932, with the result that a greater percentage of the total annual production was concentrated in the early months of the year than had been true in 1929 and earlier years. Irregularity of employment was also enhanced to the extent that the industry co-operated in the national program to spread the available work among as many employees as possible.[15]

Although the automobile code was probably responsible for "the first concerted attempt to regularize output in the automobile industry," the declining fortunes of the industry during the depression years and the concomitant increase in the seasonality of production and employment were stimulants that might in themselves have produced a similar response. It was obvious that the existing degree of irregularity was disadvantageous both to the automobile producers and to their workers. For the employer, it meant increased overhead costs since he had to maintain surplus production facilities which were utilized only during the months of peak production. The high rate of labor turnover required him to maintain a larger employment department than might otherwise have been necessary and added to the expense that he incurred in training his employees. The workers added to his labor force during the months of peak production tended to be less efficient than his regular employees, and this resulted in the excessive waste and spoilage of materials. To the automobile worker, the seasonal pattern of automobile production meant irregular employment, low annual wages, and the lack of any sense of job security.[16]

In preparing its report, the Cudlip committee attempted "to minimize the possibility of further reports to the Administrator and at the same time to avoid committing the Industry." The report was completed on November 14, 1933, and was then approved by the N.A.C.C. with only "minor changes." It was transmitted to the N.R.A. on December 1, 1933.[17]

The N.A.C.C., in its report, attributed the irregularity of employment in the industry to the seasonal variation in consumer demand, the difficulty of forecasting sales with a high degree of accuracy, and the practice of introducing new annual models. It pointed out that continuous production could be achieved only if some way were found to influence the seasonal trend of automobile purchases or if cars and parts could be stored in advance of sales. The report declared that the experiments already undertaken by various manufacturers indicated that there was no panacea for the problem but that there were at least four measures that might be employed to good effect.

More stable employment could be obtained, it was argued, if new models were introduced in the late summer or early fall, rather than in January, and the N.A.C.C. stated that it would attempt to persuade its members to follow this practice. This recommendation was based on the fact that the introduction of a new model tended to stimulate demand regardless of the time of the year when the event took place. The existing practice of introducing new models shortly after the first of the year simply accentuated the already heavy spring demand for new cars, thereby "superimposing a new model urge on top of a normal seasonal urge." If new models were introduced in the late summer or the fall, however, this would raise demand in the sluggish final quarter of the year and would lower the spring peak, thus producing a more level production curve for the year as a whole. It would mean that the summer months just before the new models were introduced would be the period of lowest production, which was the least objectionable time of the year from the workers' point of view. It would provide the manufacturers with ample time to liquidate the previous year's models and would permit them to stock their dealers with new models during the quiet months preceding the spring peak. It would facilitate the training of men to work on the new models at a time when the industry was not being pressed to supply the dealers with vehicles to meet the spring demand, thus resulting in more efficient and continuous production. It would also, as was later pointed out, reduce the fixed capital requirements for the production of a given annual volume since a lessening of demand during the spring peak would decrease the amount of equipment needed to turn out vehicles during the busiest months of the year.[18]

No specific date on which new models should be introduced was suggested in the December 1933 report, but Stephen DuBrul of G.M. later prepared a supplementary report that pointed to November 1 as the "theoretical ideal date" for the introduction of new passenger-car models. DuBrul arrived at this conclusion after determining the "normal or average" seasonal trend of new passenger-car sales, the degree to which a new model stimulated purchases in the month of its introduction and in succeeding months, the rate at which production could be built up most efficiently after the new model was introduced, the maximum inventory of cars the dealers could carry, the probable carry-over of the old model when the new-model announcement was made, and the employment limitations imposed by the code.[19] The automobile manufacturers were later to decide, however, that it was impractical to fix a specific date on which all the new passenger-car models should appear.

The introduction of new models in the summer or fall, according to the N.A.C.C. report, would make it easier for the automobile manufacturers to produce cars and parts for storage in advance of sales and thus to provide employment when the demand for vehicles was low. The Chamber agreed to recommend to those of its members who had not already done so that they seek to determine the extent to which the advance production of cars and parts would be feasible for them. The building of car and parts inventories on any large scale had previously been rendered difficult by the fact that new models were announced in January, which meant that a high rate of production was required for the succeeding months simply to meet the peak spring demand. A uniform fall or summer announcement date, however, would provide additional months of production both to accommodate spring purchasers and to build up inventories of cars and parts.

Actually, the storage of finished vehicles on any large scale would have been an enormously difficult and costly operation. The automobile is an item of considerable size, with a low value in proportion to its bulk, and is thus expensive to store. It would have been extremely difficult to anticipate the demand for each model type and color of a particular make even if it had been possible—and the automobile manufacturers insisted that it was not—to forecast accurately the total demand for the make as a whole. Stored vehicles, moreover, required special care if they were not to deteriorate, and this added to their cost. Only the automobile dealers, as a matter of fact, had economical facilities available for storage, and Stephen DuBrul estimated that the peak inventory that they could handle, including cars in transit, was about 16 per cent of the annual demand for a particular vehicle.[20]

The objections to the storage of finished vehicles did not, however, apply to the storage of parts. With a uniform fall announcement date, it would be possible for the automobile manufacturers, if they so desired, to produce such units as motors, front and rear axles, transmissions, and steering gears during the late fall and winter months of otherwise low production and to bank these parts for use in April, May, and June. Employees who worked on parts and unit assemblies in the winter could then be shifted to the assembling of finished vehicles in the spring.[21]

In addition to its endorsement of a new model announcement date and of advance storage, the N.A.C.C. in its report agreed to recommend a more careful classification of employees by the individual manufacturers so that workers could be transferred from one department to another rather than being laid off, and also to pool its members' estimates of the probable volume of industry sales so as to arrive at a more reliable total on the basis of which the individual manufacturer could forecast his own sales. The N.A.C.C. concluded that the circumstances affecting each manufacturer were so varied that reliance in achieving greater stabilization of employment would have to be placed primarily on the individual employer, with the Chamber providing supplementary guidance.[22]

Of the various other methods that had been suggested at one time or another as likely to produce greater stabilization of employment, the N.A.C.C. report took particular notice only of the possible use of seasonal price adjustments to influence consumer demand. This approach, however, was rejected by the Chamber as likely to have an unsettling effect on the retail market since, it was alleged, it would intensify price competition among the manufacturers, would cause the consumer to have less regard for the industry's price structure and to desire the lowest price for the year no matter when he made his purchase, and would penalize the volume lines since their field stocks, which would be affected by any price adjustments, were greater than those of other automobile manufacturers. It might also have been noted that it would have been difficult for the manufacturers to determine the precise degree of price adjustment required at any particular time of the year to achieve the desired results.[23]

The suggestion that less frequent model changes might lead to greater regularity of employment, an idea that was soon to be endorsed by Frances Perkins, was rejected in the N.A.C.C. report on the grounds that the practice of introducing new models annually served to increase demand and employment and had promoted the growth of the industry.[24] No attention was given in the report to the proposal that the introduction of the various new models be staggered during the year so as to even out consumer purchases, and there was little support for this idea in the industry, as statements of a later date indicate. The automobile manufacturers thought that it would be difficult to determine the different dates that new models should be introduced without discriminating among the various manufacturers; and it was believed that the public, at all events, would delay its purchase of new cars until all the models were available. Also, it appeared that although the staggered introduction of new models might regularize employment for the industry as a whole, it was less likely to have the same result for the individual worker, who would still be subject to the production vicissitudes of the plant in which he was employed. The dealers, in particular, were opposed to the plan since it would make the liquidation of obsolete models a year-round affair and thus, in the words of the president of the National Automobile Dealers' Association, would "throw the trade into a continuous state of turmoil." [25]

The N.A.C.C. commented critically on William Green's plea at the code hearings for shorter hours of labor as a means of spreading the work, but the report ignored devices such as dismissal pay,[26] unemployment compensation, and the guaranteed annual wage that organized labor was later to advance to achieve more regular employment. At no time during the N.I.R.A. period did these A.F. of L. proposals receive the industry's endorsement, but in October 1934, in a report which attacked the concept of nationwide, compulsory unemployment insurance, the A.M.A. did not rule out the possibility that individual industries might wish to develop programs to cope with unemployment that would include an unemployment-reserve plan.[27]

The N.A.C.C.'s December 1 report was hailed by Lawrence Seltzer as a "sincere attempt to deal constructively" with the problem of the regularization of automobile employment. The Detroit economist thought that the particular measures proposed in the report were "immediately practicable" and that the N.A.C.C. should be encouraged to implement them.[28]   Curiously, however, although N.R.A. officials as early as September 1933 had consulted with the N.A.C.C. about the possibility of having the manufacturers introduce their new car models in November of that year,[29] there was no follow-up on the N.A.C.C. report prior to the November 1934 renewal of the code. Apparently the N.R.A. officials within whose jurisdiction the automobile code fell, and their superiors in the organization, were simply too busy to concern themselves with problems that were not constantly being thrust before them.

As it turned out, the year 1934 was one of the worst in the industry's history in so far as the regularity of employment was concerned. The annual layoff rate rose to an astronomical 90.41 as compared to 77.65 in 1933 and 49.73 in 1930, the annual total separation rate to 117.3 as compared to 96.96 in 1933 and 70.15 in 1930, and the annual accession rate to 144.23 as compared to 116.59 in 1933 and 56.98 in 1930.[30]   What this high degree of irregularity meant for the automobile worker can be gleaned from the employment record of one of the nation's largest automobile firms.   During the first year the automobile code was in effect (September 4, 1933–September 4, 1934), almost 20 per cent of the net number of hourly rated male employees (total number minus those who quit, were discharged, or died) of this concern worked less than twenty weeks, and 56.2 per cent of them worked less than forty weeks.   Of the net number of males employed, 27.6 per cent earned less than $500 for the year, and an additional 34.1 per cent earned between $500 and $999.   On the other hand, 60.5 per cent of the net payroll was disbursed to male employees who earned in excess of $1000 for the year, and 66.8 per cent of the net payroll went to male employees who worked an average of forty-six weeks or more.[31]

The substantial amount of labor turnover in the automobile industry in 1934 was explained in part by work spreading resulting from the limitation on the hours of labor imposed by the code, but it also reflected the altered nature of employer-employee relations for which Section 7(a) was primarily responsible. Thus, the tool and die strike of the fall of 1933 delayed work on the 1934 models and led to the employment during the early months of 1934 of a larger number of temporary employees than was usual at this time of the year. The threat of a large-scale strike in the industry in March caused the automobile manufacturers to build up a larger inventory of finished cars than they would otherwise have done, and this meant a greater relative decline in production and employment during the second half of the year. The automobile producers also complained that the shifting policies of the New Deal increased the uncertainty regarding production requirements from month to month and led to "unusually large adjustments in employment." [32]

Despite the high degree of labor turnover in the automobile industry in 1934, the automobile manufacturers took no definite action to implement the recommendations contained in the December 1933 report to the N.R.A. until the evidence of Presidential concern expressed at the time the code was renewed in November 1934 "provided the last necessary impulse to achievement." Employment policies in the industry that had always been questionable from a cost point of view "now," to cite one automobile company observer, "became dangerous from a political point of view"; and for an industry that was so conscious of the public-relations impact of its policies, the wisdom of early action became evident. On December 5, 1934, an A.M.A. committee that had been studying the problem submitted a report which recommended that the various passenger-car producers agree to introduce their new car models between August 1 and October 1 or, at the latest, November 1. If the date of introduction were delayed much beyond October 1, it was argued, the possible stimulation of sales during the remainder of the year would be too limited to produce very much additional employment.[33]

The arguments presented in the committee's report were convincing to the A.M.A. membership, and on December 11 they adopted a resolution announcing their intention, beginning in 1935, to confine the annual announcement of new passenger-car models as nearly as possible to the month of October. Since it was thought that the practical operating difficulties in scheduling the production of new models, the limitations of physical equipment, and the consideration that had to be shown employees in the tool manufacturing plants producing machinery for the new models made it undesirable and impracticable for all manufacturers to announce their new models at the same time, it was further decided that members who introduced their models within a sixty-day period before or after October 1 would not be violating the agreement. The resolution authorized the A.M.A. board of directors to take the action necessary to secure the greatest degree of co-operation from the membership in the implementation of the decision, and with that purpose in mind it was decided that the first automobile show at which the new models would be exhibited was to be held not later than November 5.[34]

The text of the A.M.A.'s December 11 resolution was not officially filed with the N.R.A. until January 31, 1935, and was not made public until the next day, allegedly because of fears on the part of the manufacturers that an immediate announcement would disrupt plans for the introduction of the 1935 models at the January 1935 show. When the public announcement of the decision was finally made, the A.M.A. bravely stated that the automobile industry compared favorably with many other industries in so far as the stabilization of employment was concerned but that "its position in the forefront of American industry" required it to take the lead in this field. There was no suggestion in the A.M.A. statement that the N.R.A. or the President had played a part in making the industry somewhat more mindful of its responsibilities to its employees and the public at large than it might otherwise have been.[35]

By the time the A.M.A. officially resolved to experiment with the fall introduction of new passenger-car models the federal government's inquiry into the stabilization of automobile employment was already under way. The A.F. of L. had proposed that the study be conducted by a bipartisan commission made up of representatives of management and labor and chaired by an official of the federal government, but the President accepted the advice of Frances Perkins, Donald Richberg, and S. Clay Williams and assigned the task to the Research and Planning Division of the N.R.A., with the Bureau of Labor Statistics and other agencies of the federal government to render it assistance. The letter of instruction that the President on November 21 dispatched to Williams as chairman of the N.I.R.B. stipulated that the study was to deal with the "possibilities of regularizing employment and *otherwise improving the conditions of labor*" in the automobile industry. This represented a significant broadening of the scope of the inquiry, although it was incorrectly stated in the letter that the President had indicated at the time the code had been extended that the study was to be of this nature. The N.I.R.B. was instructed to review the report resulting from the inquiry and to transmit it to the President with a statement of the board's views regarding the feasibility and the methods of carrying out the recommendations contained in the document. The N.I.R.B. was to take no further action on the subject until the interested parties had been given "ample opportunity" to review the results of the study and to present their views on the issues that had been raised.[36]

The over-all responsibility for the inquiry fell to Leon Henderson, the stocky, energetic, and outspoken chairman of the Research and Planning Division. Henderson, who had served on the War Industries Board as an army captain and had taught economics at Carnegie Tech, came to the N.R.A. after having been deputy secretary of Pennsylvania under Governor Gifford Pinchot and having gained a reputation as a foe of the loan sharks while working for the Russell Sage Foundation. He became a "conspicuous figure" in Washington because of his unusual habits of dress—he wore old khaki pants and sneakers to work—and he won his job, according to his own account, "by hollering." The actual task of planning and organizing the study and of preparing the preliminary report was delegated by Henderson to Richard Lansburgh, the associate director of the Research and Planning Division and the acting chief of its statistical section. Lansburgh had previously taught business administration at the University of Pennsylvania and had worked in Detroit as a business consultant.[37]

The Research and Planning Division was assisted in compiling the data for the study by the Bureau of Labor Statistics, the Women's Bureau, the Department of Public Welfare of Detroit, and the Federal Emergency Relief Administration. Several attempts were made by Research and Planning Division officials to arrange a meeting with Wolman to gain his views on the subject of the inquiry, but all to no avail. The complaints of some workers about the A.L.B.'s seniority rules, which occasioned the only reference to the board in the division's report, were, however, discussed with Francis Ross before the report was completed.[38]

Organized labor in the automobile industry looked upon the Henderson inquiry as a grand opportunity to air its grievances concerning working conditions in the automobile plants. Dillon brought to the attention of the President and the interested government agencies the subjects the A.F. of L. thought should be investigated, and he instructed the members of the National Council and the officers and members of the various U.A.W. locals to see to it that the "proper evidence" was presented at the hearings in their area. William Green assigned James Wilson, a former president of the Pattern Makers' League and a former member of the Executive Council, to aid Dillon in presenting the A.F. of L. point of view in the Detroit hearings, and he advised A.F. of L. officials in the industry to "do everything possible to see that we are well represented." The M.E.S.A. and the S.D.E. aided the Research and Planning Division in the gathering of some of its data, and representatives of the two organizations, as well as of the A.A.W.A. and the A.W.U., testified at the Detroit hearings.[39]

The A.M.A., which seems to have lacked confidence in Henderson and Lansburgh, was far more reluctant than organized labor to cooperate with the N.R.A. inquiry, although the manufacturers do appear to have supplied the Bureau of Labor Statistics and Henderson's staff with most of the statistical data that they requested, including DuBrul's analysis of the theoretical ideal date for the introduction of new passenger-car models. Henderson went over the outline of the inquiry with Reeves and Pyke Johnson, and he and members of his staff discussed the subjects under investigation with A.M.A. representatives and with officials of the various automobile companies. The Research and Planning Division chief was far from satisfied, however, with the reaction of the automobile manufacturers to the inquiry. He complained that pertinent data that he had requested had not been supplied to him, and he was probably also annoyed by the decision of the A.M.A. not to testify at the hearings held in Detroit and elsewhere. There appears to have been a division of opinion among A.M.A. members regarding the wisdom of this decision, but those who favored abstention, largely because they feared that the inquiry would be hostile to the management point of view, prevailed.[40]

The A.M.A. preferred that there be no public hearings in Detroit, a view that Donald Richberg shared since he believed that such an inquiry might stir up labor trouble in the motor city. After receiving complaints about the scheduled Detroit hearings "from two or three of 'our friends'" in the automobile industry, Marvin McIntyre discussed the subject with Roosevelt, who suggested the possibility of a hearing in Washington over which the President himself would preside. McIntyre, who admitted that he was "a babe in the woods" about such matters, told the President that this was impractical, although, as he informed Henderson, he could not understand why the N.R.A. had "walked right out into the center of things where it [a hearing] would provoke ten times as much notice." Henderson, however, advised McIntyre that if the hearing were removed from Detroit, "it would destroy the possibility of getting an accurate picture because the labor group would feel that they were badly treated." After further discussion within the administration, it was decided to go ahead with the Detroit hearings.[41]

Henderson, Lansburgh, and Isadore Lubin, the director of the

Bureau of Labor Statistics, were present in Detroit on December 15, 1934, to initiate the testimony-taking phase of the inquiry before an overflow audience in the Masonic Temple. Those who testified were advised in this as in all subsequent hearings that no presentations were to be made concerning Section 7(a) and similar issues within the jurisdiction of special labor boards, but this restriction was more honored in the breach than in the observance. The Detroit hearings lasted for two days, with Henderson presiding over the public phase of the proceedings while two of his assistants, Harry Weiss and Thomas Kelly, heard some of the witnesses in private. Virtually every organized labor group in the automobile industry was represented among the sixty-three witnesses at the Detroit hearings, whereas not a single management representative asked to be heard.

The Detroit hearings were followed by additional hearings during the next ten days in many of the cities where automobiles were manufactured and assembled and where automobile parts were fabricated—in the Michigan automobile towns of Flint, Lansing, Muskegon, and Jackson, and in Indianapolis, St. Louis, Milwaukee, South Bend, Cleveland, Buffalo, Philadelphia, Toledo, and Dayton. The hearings in all of these cities were confidential in nature, and the testimony was taken by either Weiss or Kelly. In all, 389 witnesses testified in the hearings outside Detroit, the vast majority of whom were trade-union officials or employed or unemployed automobile workers who had joined the U.A.W. locals. Even more workers would have testified, Weiss was convinced, had not fear of their employers kept them away. Some of the witnesses worked in the automobile parts plants rather than in the main plants, but it had previously been decided that the parts industry would have to be brought within the scope of the inquiry. A few management people testified at the hearings outside Detroit—a representative of the Wisconsin Automotive Trades Association, who complained about factory-dealer relationships; the manager of the production division of the bankrupt Pierce Arrow Motor Company, who suggested the introduction of new models every two or three years rather than annually as a means of stabilizing employment; and some members of the special tool, die, and machine shop industry in Dayton, who expressed concern about the pressures placed upon the tool and die shops by the automobile manufacturers and about the competition of the "captive" tool rooms —but the A.M.A., as in Detroit, boycotted the hearings.[42]

As might have been expected, workers who had grievances against their employers were very much in evidence at the hearings. Kelly, however, was confident that the employees who testified represented an adequate cross section of the labor force in the industry, and Weiss thought that the conditions about which they complained were typical of the industry as a whole.   The witnesses were not under oath and were not subject to cross examination, and many of them had great difficulty expressing themselves, but the two investigators, whose sympathies were obviously with the workers, were certain that their accounts were substantially true.[43]   On the whole, the witnesses devoted most of their testimony to a criticism of working conditions in the industry rather than to a presentation of the means by which greater regularization of employment conditions could be attained or the hazards of seasonal employment could be counteracted.   Among the remedies suggested for the problem of irregular employment were the guaranteed annual wage (ranging from $1500 to $3000), unemployment insurance, some form of supplementary compensation during short work weeks, the thirty-hour week, and an overtime rate.

Weiss concluded that the most frequently mentioned grievance was the speed-up and the stretch out ("They are getting more production with less men"; "The speed is unbearable"; the work makes you "a physical . . . and nervous wreck"), and he believed that this was the cause for "the conflagration that appears . . . imminent in the automobile industry."   The "most important grievance" of the workers, Weiss thought, was their low annual income, but generally, as he noted, those who testified did not blame this condition on their employers.   Kelly, on the basis of the testimony he had heard, concluded that the inadequacy of annual earnings was the most commonly mentioned subject but that the alleged speed-up was the grievance "most vehemently recorded."   Kelly himself was convinced by the testimony that "only those of great physical capacity survive as wage earners in the automobile industry."   "Thus," he declared, "is human misery embraced as an opportunity to reduce the cost of building an automobile."

The workers also complained about unfair and complicated methods of compensation in the industry—it "takes a certified public accountant to figure the wages"; uncompensated work; the failure of employers to share the work; allegedly unfair deductions from their wages for group insurance and welfare plans; the A.L.B. seniority rules, which many workers simply did not understand; the displacement of older workers—"The most tragic situation in the industry," according to Weiss; technological unemployment; the substitution of female for male labor; the use of the parts plants as "the sweat shops of the automotive industry"; inadequate safety and health standards; employer espionage (the auto plants are "riddled with spies and stool pigeons"; there is an "atmosphere of fear" in the plants); the provisions of the code, about which there seemed to be utter confusion; and alleged violations and evasions of code provisions. The A.F. of L., at least, was convinced that many of these grievances could be readily disposed of if only the employers would recognize the U.A.W. locals in their plants and bargain with them in good faith.[44]

Weiss, on the basis of what he had heard, thought that the least the N.R.A. could do for the automobile workers was to permit them to present their grievances to an administrative agency that would have the power to alter the code. He contended that the faith of the workers in the N.R.A. had been "badly shattered" and that prompt action was necessary to restore it. Kelly also concluded, somewhat melodramatically, that "to stay the spread of hot discontent and abandon," it was necessary "to offer to the rational worker some tangible evidence of the sincere desire to lift him from his present pit of despair and lost hope." Neither of the men had a good word to say about the automobile manufacturers.[45]

In addition to the testimony taken at the hearings, Henderson invited interested parties to submit their views in writing. Labor organizations, automobile dealers, and a few other businessmen both inside and outside the industry availed themselves of this opportunity, but the A.M.A. passed up this means of making its position known, just as it had foregone the chance to testify at the hearings.[46]

The Henderson Report—its official title was Preliminary Report on Study of Regularization of Employment and Improvement of Labor Conditions in the Automobile Industry—was transmitted to the President and the N.I.R.B. on January 23, 1935. It had been hastily prepared and, as Henderson informed the N.I.R.B., was only preliminary in nature. Not all the relevant information had been collected by the investigators, and even some of the data that had been gathered had not been completely tabulated at the time the report was submitted. It was conceded in the summary of the document that the report painted "a rather dark picture" of the industry, but this was attributed to the fact that the subject of the inquiry made unnecessary an "inclusive review" of the industry's accomplishments and that the purpose of the report was to improve conditions to which "insufficient attention" had been devoted in the past.[47] It might also have been noted that much of the information on which the report was based had been supplied by critics of the industry, but for this state of affairs the automobile manufacturers themselves were at least partly to blame.

The industry had changed to such a degree, the report observed, that its structure was "socially inadequate to meet its responsibilities accruing out of the changes" and to achieve the lower costs, the better labor relations, and the general progress expected of "our leading industry." The report found fault with the methods employed by the automobile manufacturers in purchasing parts from their suppliers and blamed the automobile companies for the poor working conditions, the irregular employment, and the abnormal production costs of the parts makers. It charged that the manufacturers were insufficiently concerned with the welfare of their dealers and had given "very little active support" to the crucial trade-in provision of the dealers' code. The report was especially critical of working conditions in the automobile plants, basing its conclusions in this regard pretty much on the testimony taken at the hearings and the summary of this testimony provided by Weiss and Kelly. It asserted that the speed-up and the uncertainty of employment—the "spectre" haunting the auto worker—were making the industry a difficult one in which to work. Although admitting that the records were inadequate, the report nevertheless declared that it was the opinion of those who conducted the survey that the man hours of labor per automobile produced had decreased "tremendously" since 1929. It conceded that technological advances in the industry gave the automobile consumer a value that was "unexcelled by any other industry" and that some concerns had been able to operate at a profit only because of the economies resulting from laborsaving devices, but, at the same time, it contended that time-study men were setting jobs on "a speed-up basis that puts production demands beyond human capability to produce day after day."

The report complained that the industry's procedures for the layoff and rehiring of workers were "inequitable" and that the A.L.B. rules were not the solution for the problem and were being used by the employers to discriminate against the workers. Men over forty years of age, it declared, found it difficult to secure a job in the industry or to be rehired after they had been laid off, and it observed that it was "socially and economically indefensible" for the industry to regard its employees as superannuated ten to twenty years before this was true of similar employees in other industries. It took notice of the special problems of the tool and die makers, the decline in the annual earnings of tool and die engineers, and the low annual income of auto workers in general. Although the subject of collective bargaining was outside the scope of the inquiry, the report nevertheless offered the opinion that many of the complaints of the auto workers would disappear if facilities for collective bargaining were "fully extended." This, of course, accorded exactly with the views of the A.F. of L.

The report considered the various proposals that had been made to bring about more stable employment in the industry, something that it conceded was "actively desired" by the automobile manufacturers, and concluded that the fall introduction of new models was "the present key to any major regularization of employment." Without specifically indicating that its own analysis of this problem rested heavily on data supplied by the A.M.A., the report noted that this subject had been "explored exhaustively" by the industry, and it specifically recommended that the administration should assist the automobile manufacturers in putting the idea into effect. If the proposal were implemented, it was argued, the hours of labor of all automobile factory employees could be limited to forty per week except for an eight-week period during which forty-eight hours per week would be permitted, with time-and-a-half being paid for all hours above forty.[48]

The Henderson Report was not publicly released until February 7, 1935, after the automobile code had once again been renewed. Although it had appeared from the President's letter to Williams of November 21 that the report would not be issued until the interested parties had been given an opportunity to review and comment on its findings, neither management nor labor had even been sent a copy of the study prior to its release. Organized labor was, of course, delighted with the document. The report, Green noted enthusiastically, bore out "every contention" the A.F. of L. had been making during the previous year-and-a-half about labor conditions in the industry. Although the report had been hurriedly put together and although it was not free from error, it required no great imagination to see that the prestige of what was supposed to be an "impartial government study" could henceforth be used by labor leaders in the industry to document their charges against the automobile companies. The automobile manufacturers had for some time been pointing to themselves as model employers, but now, in what was reputed to be "the first comprehensive investigation of the automobile industry made by a neutral agency," the automobile companies were pictured as woefully deficient in the sphere of human relations however progressive they might be in the area of production technique. In this, it would seem, lay the chief significance of the Henderson Report in the long run.

Organized labor's pleasure with the character of the Henderson Report was more than matched by the pain of the automobile manufacturers, for the report, as the *New York Times* remarked in a disapproving editorial, painted "an almost nightmarish picture" of labor conditions in the industry.   Following a meeting on February 14 of the A.M.A.'s "Special Committee on the President's Survey," it was decided to address a letter of protest to the administration and in the meantime to assign the various sections of the report to members of the industry for a "close and critical analysis." [49]

In its letter of complaint, which was addressed to S. Clay Williams on February 19, the A.M.A. stated that it had expected that the report would contain "a disinterested and sober appraisal of the facts," but that even as a preliminary effort it could not withstand the criticism of anyone familiar with the true state of affairs in the industry.   The report would have been of a different sort, the A.M.A. observed, had it been submitted to the industry prior to its publication, as had been promised.   The authors of the report were chided for having relied so largely on the "recklessly false" statements of the A.F. of L. on the one hand and, on the other hand, for having plagiarized the "one correct conclusion" in the document—the endorsement of the fall introduction of models—from an industry report that had been given to the investigators.   Specifically, the letter charged that the report presented no evidence to support its allegations concerning the displacement of older workers in the industry; that despite its complaints about layoff and rehiring procedures, the automobile industry, unlike other industries, was following a set of job-tenure rules prescribed by a government labor board; that the impression created by the report that a substantial number of automobile workers were being replaced by machines was belied by the fact that more man hours of labor were expended per car produced by A.M.A. members in 1934 than in 1929, despite the trend toward the purchase and production of lower-priced cars; and that the document's animadversions concerning the low annual income of automobile workers failed to take notice of the N.I.R.A.'s effect on the hours of employment and were inconsistent with the recommendation for still further reductions in the hours of work.   A more elaborate analysis of the report, the letter concluded, "would merely cumulate the evidence of its inaccuracies, faulty data, distortions of information, and careless interpretation of facts." [50]

The Ford Motor Company was also publicly critical of the character of the Henderson Report.   Ford's spokesman, William J. Cameron, pointed out that about 41 per cent of Ford's employees in and around Detroit were over forty years of age and that the company imposed no arbitrary age limit on employment, that 198.5 hours of labor, on the average, went into every Ford car produced in 1934 as compared to 191.8 hours per Ford car in 1929, and that irregularity of employment in the Ford plants could be attributed to the annual introduction of new models, a practice that Ford had long opposed. "There are indications, however," Cameron could not resist saying, "that those who disrupted the continuity of work in the motor industry are growing tired of their new system." [51]

The A.M.A. had apparently hoped that the section-by-section analysis of the Henderson Report that it had ordered would enable it to refute the document in detail and to discredit it in the eyes of the public. The analysis was completed by February 23, but although it pointed out many shortcomings and errors in the report and contained a defense of industry practices that had been criticized, it was insufficiently factual in character to serve as a complete answer to the government study. Early in March the A.M.A. sent out a questionnaire to the automobile companies subject to the code in an effort to elicit information to counteract the "unfortunate public impressions gained from the report, and to put the industry in a position to meet governmental and other agencies on the basis of fact as to the issues involved." The following month the A.M.A. hired the economist Dr. David Friday to compile data on wages, hours, and working conditions in the industry that could be used to answer the recent criticism of the automobile manufacturers and to provide the public and the government with fuller information about industry practices.[52] The Henderson Report had made the industry even more public-relations conscious and even more wary of the federal government than it had previously been.

All in all the Henderson Report was neither the "sound, accurate," and "scientific" document that Charlton Ogburn found it to be nor a "hodge-podge of bald allegations and vitriolic indictments of The Industry's policies," to cite the opinion of an automobile company staff member. As the automobile manufacturers charged, it was prepared hurriedly and under pressure and by men who had very little previous knowledge of the automobile industry. It tended to view the industry through the eyes of the A.F. of L., the parts makers, and the dealers and only rarely through the eyes of the automobile manufacturers themselves, and it was consequently "restricted . . . too much to the darker phases of the industry's record." [53] Its conclusions were not always supported by evidence and in some instances were simply contrary to fact—the assertions of the report concerning the displacement of workers by labor-saving machines and the premature superannuation of the industry's employees are cases in point.[54] The allegations of the report regarding a speed-up were also very much exaggerated although not without some basis in fact. Output per man hour in the combined motor vehicle industries, according to the Bureau of Labor Statistics, rose from a depression low of 69.4 in 1932 (1939 = 100) to 83.8 in 1933 and 85.2 in 1934, but the 1934 figure was only slightly above that of 1929 (84.2). The spread of employment and the high degree of labor turnover probably militated against any really spectacular gains in productivity during the first year the code was in effect.[55]

The report, however, had more to commend it than its opponents were willing to admit. Stephen DuBrul of G.M. grudgingly conceded that its analysis of the possibilities of regularizing employment was "fairly satisfactory," and the section of the report dealing with working conditions was not entirely inaccurate even if it was overdrawn. Working conditions in the industry were far from ideal, and the report was correct in its assertions that the automobile workers were insecure, that their employment was much too irregular, that their annual incomes were too low, and that the industry's methods of compensation were too complicated. Time was to reveal, moreover, that the report was, to a degree at least, correct in its judgment that many of the complaints of the workers would disappear once facilities for collective bargaining were "fully extended." The report was a reminder to the automobile manufacturers that the United States had changed since 1929 and that in the era of the N.I.R.A. and the New Deal employers could no longer emphasize production alone; they would henceforth have to pay greater attention to the conditions under which their employees worked.[56]

At the time the Henderson Report was submitted to the President and the N.I.R.B., the renewal of the automobile code had once again become a subject of concern within both the administration and the A.F. of L., and the manner in which the President disposed of this matter served to make the automobile-labor question "the primary labor-Administration issue." William Green on January 17, 1935, called the expiration date of the code to the President's attention and informed him that in accordance with the November 21 letter to Williams, the A.F. of L. was assuming that it would be given an opportunity to review the findings of the Henderson Report and the recommendations of the N.I.R.B. based thereon and that it was preparing to present proposals for the amendment of the code either in a public hearing or in conferences with the President and his representatives and the employers. "Speaking for the workers in this industry," Green wrote the President, "I cannot urge too strongly that the code be not again renewed in its present form." [57]

Both the A.F. of L. and the L.A.B. subsequently let it be known that they preferred no code at all to the extension of the existing code without change. The A.F. of L. sought to clarify its position further by publicly announcing on January 24, as we have seen, that it would have nothing more to do with the A.L.B.; and Charlton Ogburn, in a letter to the President a few days later, reminded the Chief Executive of the A.F. of L. view that its withdrawal from the settlement terminated the agreement and thus deprived the A.L.B. of its "legal status." "The automobile labor problem," Ogburn stated to the President without too much exaggeration, "is today by far the most serious labor problem in America."

The proposed A.F. of L.-L.A.B. amendments to the automobile code, which were ready for submission on January 21, differed somewhat from the demands the two groups had been prepared to submit prior to the previous two extensions of the code, although the arguments to support the proposals had changed not at all. The hours of labor, designed to achieve greater re-employment in the industry than had occurred in 1934, were now set at seven (rather than eight) per day and thirty per week during all but the ten weeks of peak production, when an eight-hour day and a thirty-six hour week were permitted. Tool and die makers, however, were to be allowed to work an eight-hour day and a forty-hour week during the peak period provided that each member of the industry contracted for his tools and dies only from employers who conformed to wage and hour standards at least as stringent as those proposed for the auto code. Hours in excess of those stipulated were to be compensated at a rate of time-and-one-half and were not to exceed two hours per day and eight hours per week. Also, no employee whose period of employment with his employer exceeded the production period on the current model was to be laid off until the working schedule of his department or of the plant as a whole had been reduced to at least twenty-four hours per week.

The A.F. of L. and the L.A.B. recommended the same wage rates that they had proposed prior to the November extension of the code except that the figure for the guaranteed annual wage was increased from $1000 to $1500, a sum that the labor groups argued was still less than the level set by the Michigan Department of Labor and Industry for a minimum health and decency standard of living. The A.F. of L. and the L.A.B. brief conceded that "a number of practical problems" were involved in the implementation of this proposal, but the two organizations thought that the details could "safely be left" to the collective-bargaining process. "Only a penalty as stringent as this,"

Green was prepared to contend, "can be expected to secure a translation of the pious wishes about stabilization into actuality."

Frustrated in previous efforts to have the auto code altered, the L.A.B. and the A.F. of L. intended to state at the hoped-for public hearing that if the code were extended without the amendments the two groups favored, it would be tantamount to a confession by the N.R.A. that it was "powerless to compel or induce this great Industry to bear its share of the costs of recovery, even in the face of large and increasing profits." [58]   In the event, the A.F. of L. not only failed to secure a revision of the code along the lines of its January proposals, but it was not even given the opportunity to air its demands in public or to discuss them with the President.

Three days after the A.F. of L. and the L.A.B. had completed the formulation of their code proposals, the N.I.R.B. transmitted to the President its own more modest recommendations for changes in the code.   The board endorsed the idea of introducing new car models in the fall and recommended that the forty-hour week be applied to all workers in the industry, with forty-eight hours permitted provided time-and-a-half were paid for hours in excess of forty.   It suggested that the controversial merit clause "be handled in such way as the President finds feasible in the light of the negotiations with the interested parties," but it indicated to the Chief Executive that a majority of the board thought that the clause should be "deleted." [59]

The N.I.R.B. met with the President on January 28 and transmitted to him at that time its comments on the Henderson Report. The board reminded the President of the exploratory character of the study, but it nevertheless endorsed once again the document's recommendation concerning the fall introduction of new models and, without supporting the relevant recommendations of the report or reaffirming its own previously expressed views on the subject, also advised that the hours provisions of the code should be revised in co-operation with the industry.   Most important of all, the N.I.R.B. used the occasion to declare that "There is no blinking the fact that industrial relations in this industry call for constructive treatment" and to recommend that consideration be given to the advisability of establishing "a comprehensive Automotive Industry Labor Relations Board" under the authority of the N.I.R.A. and Public Resolution 44.   This recommendation, of course, constituted an admission that in the view of the N.I.R.B. the March 25 settlement and the A.L.B. had proved less than satisfactory. [60]

Although the Henderson Report and the N.I.R.B. leaned in the direction of the A.F. of L. in their view of the automobile code and of industrial relations in the automobile industry, the President in the few days before the code was renewed received information from other sources that were less friendly to the A.F. of L. He was also undoubtedly apprised of the fact that, statistically at least, the Federation could not properly claim to be the spokesman for the automobile workers. The President's chief advisor in the code negotiations was Donald Richberg, whom the President as early as January 15 had advised, along with S. Clay Williams, to "get active in the Automobile Code matter." Once the friend of many labor leaders, Richberg had become increasingly suspicious of the A.F. of L. He had become impressed with the independence of the auto workers and their reluctance to affiliate with the Federation and had concluded that the A.F. of L. was seeking "the forceful, involuntary organization of workers," which he considered a "crazy idea." He complained that "there is a habit among many of the [labor] organizations of insisting that a public official must be thoroughly partisan, merely an advocate of whatever position regular labor organizations take, or else he is an enemy." [61]

From George L. Berry, a vice-president of the A.F. of L. and the president of the International Printing Pressmen and Assistants' Union, and from Leo Wolman, the President in the last few days of January received reports on the automobile labor situation that were not particularly favorable to the A.F. of L. Berry, who was an advocate of industrial unionism, believed that organized labor had "failed to take advantage of the splendid opportunities for constructive industrial statesmanship" created by the N.I.R.A. because of "the antiquated policy that has become rather an obsession with the American Federation of Labor." After an investigation of the labor situation in Detroit that he had been requested to make by the President, Berry on January 29, in a none too lucid report, remarked on "the absolute absence of discipline" among the automobile workers and mistakenly warned that "a very sizable percentage" of them were "obviously tending toward communistic points of view." He advised the President that the federal government was justified in saying to the automobile workers that it was not disposed to come to their assistance until they had achieved "adequate representation in order to give practical consideration to their demands for collective bargaining." [62]

Wolman saw Roosevelt on January 30 and later recalled having told him that the A.F. of L. was being fairly treated in the automobile industry. He undoubtedly advised the President that the A.F. of L. spoke for only a small minority of automobile workers since less than

5 per cent of the 46,211 voters in the A.L.B. elections to that date had identified their candidates as affiliated with the Federation. The A.L.B. election rules, to be sure, did not make it easy for an organization to register its true strength, and the A.F. of L. was boycotting the poll, but the fact remains that in the plants in Detroit where the first elections were held, the A.F. of L. had practically no membership at all. Its total paid-up membership in January 1935 was just under twenty-six thousand, and the bulk of this number were in parts plants not covered by the automobile manufacturing code and in main plants outside of Detroit.[63] The paid-up membership figures certainly understated the A.F. of L.'s effective strength in the automobile industry, but it must nonetheless have been evident to the President that there was little muscle behind the Federation code proposals and scant likelihood that the automobile workers would strike if the A.F. of L.'s demands were not met.

In the negotiations in Washington immediately preceding the extension of the code, the administration consulted with management representatives but ignored the A.F. of L. As the final terms were being hammered out, the N.I.R.B., through Richberg, transmitted a verbal report to the White House apparently to the effect that a majority of the board were opposed to the extension of the code in the form contemplated by Roosevelt and the A.M.A. It was perhaps for this reason that when the President on January 31, 1935, announced the extension of the code until June 16, 1935, the date the N.I.R.A. itself was scheduled to lapse, his executive order did not carry the usual indication that the action had been recommended by the N.I.R.B. This time the responsibility was the President's alone.[64]

Declaring that "No backward steps are taken," the President approved three amendments to the code. "As a means of facilitating regularization of employment in the industry," the manufacturers were authorized and requested to enter into agreements with one another respecting the fall announcement of new models. The A.M.A. had already agreed to implement this policy, but the inclusion of the provision in the code protected the Association from the possibility of antitrust prosecution and made more likely the co-operation of "reluctant competitors" such as Ford in carrying out the program. Richberg observed that the provision meant that "those who are supported by the automobile industry will be fully supported by it," although he conceded that fewer employees would now be engaged by the industry during the period of peak production.[65]

A second amendment to the code stipulated that employees were to be paid time-and-a-half for work in excess of forty-eight hours per week, not, as the N.I.R.B. had recommended, for hours over forty, nor, as the A.F. of L. had proposed, for hours above thirty or above thirty-six during the peak period. This provision, which Richberg described as "an automatic leveler of employment," was in part at least designed to bring the automobile code more in line with the hours provision of the special tool, die, and machine shop code. Although only about 17 per cent of the automobile manufacturing industry's 344,128 employees as of January 1935 were permitted to work over forty-eight hours per week and thus to take advantage of this provision, its inclusion in the code was resisted by the manufacturers to the last minute.[66]

Finally, the code now stipulated that the industry was to comply with the March 25 settlement, which was confirmed and continued. This provision, which removed all doubts concerning the N.L.R.B.'s lack of jurisdiction over the A.L.B., was unquestionably included in the code as a rejoinder to the A.F. of L.'s interpretation of the nature of the settlement and in the face of the Federation's decision to have nothing more to do with the Wolman board. A few days later, in a letter to Charlton Ogburn that Richberg had drafted, the President returned to this point and specifically rejected the A.F. of L.'s analysis of the March 25 agreement. The President asserted that the A.L.B. had been established under the authority of the N.I.R.A., that it was responsible to the President, and that it was for him to determine whether it was fulfilling its duties and for how long it should be permitted to continue. The A.L.B. elections, he stated, in words that must have stung the A.F. of L., would "provide for the first time conclusive evidence of how and by whom the employees desire to be represented," and it was therefore assumed that any organization of automobile employees, or one "claiming to represent such employees, would avail itself fully of the opportunity to establish the authentic character of its representation." [67]

The President's announcement of the extension of the code threw the A.F. of L. into an uproar. Not only had the administration failed once again to hold hearings on the code, but, the A.F. of L. charged, it had not even consulted with the workers' representatives despite alleged promises of the President to do so.[68] The code had been "imposed" on labor "in paternal fashion." "I want to say to you," Green told a Senate subcommittee, "that we protest against that automobile code. We will not accept it. We will not recognize it. We will not yield to it."

Reluctant to direct its attack at a very popular President, the A.F. of L. charged, in Dillon's words, that "somebody or a group of individuals deliberately prevented the President from having placed before him the situation as it really exists." The A.F. of L. included Leo Wolman in this "deliberate and malicious conspiracy," but its sharpest thrusts were reserved for Donald Richberg, whom John L. Lewis characterized as "a traitor to organized labor" and "recreant in his obligations as a public servant." "Mr. Richberg," Lewis declared in the florid language for which he was becoming famous, "secretly conspired with the leaders of the automobile industry to deceive the President and bludgeon labor. Like medieval ruffians they lay in secret during the day and emerged after nightfall to perpetrate their deeds and announce the consummation of their plot." "For Mr. Richberg . . . ," the United Mine Workers' president grandiloquently stated, "springing from the loins of labor as he did . . . and at whose breast he suckled . . . I express my personal contempt." [69]

At his press conference of February 1, in response to the criticism by the Federation, the President insisted that Green was in error when he stated that the A.F. of L. had not been consulted prior to the extension of the code. The A.F. of L. had made its position clear by correspondence, Roosevelt declared, and the administration had known its views for over a month. The President, however, was speaking only a half truth. The A.F. of L. had indeed made its views known concerning the A.L.B., and it had expressed its opinion concerning the code in the Henderson hearings, but it had not been given an opportunity to present the detailed recommendations for changes in the code that it had drafted in January, and it had not been asked to comment on the specific amendments incorporated in the January 31 extension. At the same press conference the President referred to the A.L.B. as his "baby," but he denied, despite this admission of paternity, that the board had been written into the code and insisted that "it was merely a continuation of the board." The President, however, was splitting hairs. The A.L.B., it is true, was not mentioned in the code, but the confirmation of the settlement in the code was also a confirmation of the A.L.B., which was an integral part of the settlement.[70]

If the A.F. of L. was reluctant to attack the President, the communists and the so-called "progressives" within the U.A.W. seized on the renewal of the code as an opportunity to belabor the President, the N.R.A., the New Deal, and the leadership of the A.F. of L. itself. The *Daily Worker* referred to the code renewal as "a part of the whole anti-labor policy of the New Deal" and declared that it was not Richberg who had deceived the President but the President who had deceived the workers. The time had arrived, declared the Central Committee of the Communist party, in a familiar refrain, for a "united front" effort to unionize the auto workers and to prepare for a strike. Wyndham Mortimer proclaimed that the auto workers would henceforth have to "ignore" the N.R.A. and the codes, which "have run us into a blind alley," and John Soltis, the president of the Cleveland Hupp local, observed that the leadership for a united-front movement would have to come from the rank and file rather than from William Green. The M.E.S.A. also viewed the renewal of the code as "another effort to dupe the auto workers," and concluded that "The Administration is still batting 1000 for the automobile manufacturers." [71]

Even some of the more cautious members of the U.A.W. thought that the A.F. of L. had come to the end of the road in its policy of co-operation with the President and the N.R.A. Thus, the normally conservative National Council member John W. Pickering, who viewed the January 31 extension of the code as "about as raw a deal as Labor has ever had put over [on] them," wrote his fellow Council members, "Well Brothers, it looks like we will have to take things into our own hands, if the automobile worker is to have anything to say regarding his own welfare. It appears that the President has stepped over onto the other side of the fence, the same as all good Presidents have done in the past, when the Big Shots of Industry and Finance cracked the whip.... As I see it we will either sink or swim on our own initiative. We have sat around long enough waiting for the Government to help us out." [72]

So serious did the rift between the administration and the A.F. of L. appear that the *New York Times* thought that organized labor and the New Deal had come to a parting of the ways, and the *Nation* wondered if the New Deal itself had come to an end. Louis Stark, the labor reporter of the *New York Times*, believed that the negotiations for the extension of the code had "brought the administration definitely out into the open as anti A.F. of L." The administration, he declared, had concluded that the Federation would be unable to organize the mass-production industries other than coal and was hoping, it was being whispered, that proportional representation would "supplant the present form of trade-union organization." [73]

The newspaper speculation that the A.F. of L. would break or had broken with the administration and that it would call a strike in the automobile industry to show its displeasure with the treatment that it had received in Washington was rather wide of the mark. The A.F. of L. leadership at that time did not have the kind of confidence in the strength of its organization, particularly in the automobile industry, to give it the courage to challenge Roosevelt and the New Deal and to seek in the economic field what it was unable to gain through the process of negotiation. On February 6 Green sought a conference with the President in order that the newly enlarged A.F. of L. Executive Council might "talk to him about our common problems." George Berry, himself a member of the Executive Council, correctly informed Marvin McIntyre that "the situation is largely one of pride," and Berry prepared some remarks for the President which, he thought, would "completely remove the tension." [74]

The conference took place on February 11. Green read a seven-page statement in which, among other things, he defined the A.F. of L.'s position with regard to the automobile code, the settlement, and the A.L.B. In response, the President declared that "No one can disregard the importance of the American Federation of Labor as one of the great and outstanding institutions of the country. It has been my purpose to recognize this in every practical and logical way, and I have no intention of changing my point of view." He reiterated his belief in the "necessity" and "soundness" of the principle of collective bargaining and in the value of the "highly developed organization of both employees and employers." Organization, however, the President significantly remarked, had to be voluntary; it could not be compelled by the federal government. The A.F. of L. let it be known that the meeting was "very satisfactory"—John Frey later complained that Green became "quite soft" when Roosevelt "turned his blandishments" on him—but, as the *New York Times* observed editorially, the President had yielded nothing in re-establishing good relations with the A.F. of L. [75]

At his press conference of February 8, 1935, the President replied in the negative when asked whether in view of the Henderson Report, which had just been made public, the question of the automobile code would receive any consideration prior to its next expiration date. [76] As it turned out, the code that the A.F. of L. had declared it would not "recognize" and to which it would not "yield" remained without further alteration as long as the N.I.R.A. continued in effect.

XII

TOWARD AN INTERNATIONAL UNION

I

TEN DAYS AFTER the A.F. of L. Executive Council met with the President in an effort to reconcile the differences between them that had been brought to a head by the recent extension of the automobile code, Senator Robert Wagner, who had failed during the previous year to secure the enactment of his Labor Disputes Bill, introduced a new National Labor Relations Bill designed to make effective the terms of Section 7(a) and to embody in legislative form some of the basic principles regarding labor relations that had been proclaimed by the N.L.B. and the N.L.R.B. The A.F. of L., which had been frustrated in its efforts to scuttle the March 25 settlement and the A.L.B., saw in the new measure the opportunity of achieving by the legislative route what it had been unable to win from the N.R.A. and the President. The A.M.A., in contrast, which had helped to defeat Wagner's 1934 bill, correctly interpreted the New York senator's new measure as a repudiation of the principles that governed labor relations in the automobile industry, and it therefore joined in the campaign to secure the bill's defeat.

The National Labor Relations Bill reasserted the right of employees to self-organization and to bargain collectively through representatives of their own choosing. It declared that it would be an "unfair labor practice" for an employer (1) to "interfere with, restrain, or coerce" employees in the exercise of this right; (2) to dominate or to interfere with a labor organization or to contribute to its support; (3) to discriminate against employees for the purpose of encouraging or discouraging membership in a labor organization; (4) to discriminate against an employee for filing charges or giving testimony under the measure; and (5)—this provision was added by the Senate Committee on Education and Labor—to refuse to bargain with employee representatives. The bill established a three-man nonpartisan National Labor Relations Board to carry out its terms and authorized the board to issue orders requiring the cessation by employers of unfair labor practices and to appeal to the federal circuit courts for the enforcement of these orders.

"Convinced" by the experience of the A.L.B. that "pluralism provoked confusion and strife, defeating collective bargaining," the draftsmen of Wagner's 1935 bill included a provision in the measure that specifically endorsed the principle of majority rule in the designation of employee representatives. The bill authorized the N.L.R.B. to hold elections when necessary to determine whom the employees wished to represent them and lodged in the board the power to determine the appropriate unit for collective-bargaining purposes. It declared that nothing in the measure was designed to prevent an employer from concluding an agreement with a labor organization requiring union membership as a condition of employment as long as the union represented a majority of the employees and was not maintained as the result of an unfair labor practice.[1]

In so far as labor relations in the automobile industry were concerned, the most significant feature of Wagner's National Labor Relations Bill was its endorsement of the concept of majority rule. The A.F. of L. had long since concluded that the application of the majority-rule principle to the choice of employee representatives was the indispensable prerequisite for effective collective bargaining. "The errors made in the President's settlement," Charlton Ogburn argued, "should not be perpetuated, but should be removed from the area of industrial relations as speedily as possible." Proportional representation, in the A.F. of L.'s view, destroyed the "united front" the employees must of necessity oppose to the power of management and enabled the employer to play off one group against the other and thus to frustrate the bargaining process. Real collective bargaining required that the employees' bargaining committee have back of it "an organization united and capable of being militant, if necessary" —a condition that the A.L.B.'s representation plan made impossible of fulfillment.[2]

The A.F. of L. pushed its attack on proportional representation and the A.L.B. in the Senate hearings on the Wagner bill, which opened on March 11, 1935, and in the House hearings, which began two days later. Ranging themselves alongside the Federation and the U.A.W. on this issue were some of the federal government's leading authorities in the sphere of labor relations, including the chairman of the N.L.R.B., Francis Biddle, and the former board chairman and the principal architect of the Houde decision, Lloyd K. Garrison. Both men contended, to use Biddle's words, that "an employer who refuses to recognize the majority rule right does not intend to bargain collectively in any realistic sense." This was perhaps an overly harsh judgment of employer defenders of proportional representation, but it is difficult to escape the conclusion that in the American context, at least, proportional representation is unlikely to result in very meaningful bargaining. Although it can be defended on grounds of equity and as militating against the premature freezing of the organizational status quo in favor of one labor group or another, it invites factionalism among the workers and seems likely to reduce the strength and cohesiveness of the employee bargaining agency.[3] The experience of the automobile industry with the device was admittedly brief and, as we have seen, not completely relevant, but at the same time it did nothing to weaken the arguments of the proponents of majority rule.

The A.M.A. launched its assault on the National Labor Relations Bill on March 29, 1935, when Robert Graham argued the Association's case before the Senate Committee on Education and Labor. The automobile manufacturers charged that the measure was "wholly one-sided" since it condemned unfair labor practices by employers but, unlike the March 25 settlement, ignored the tactics of intimidation and coercion resorted to by labor unions. The balance between labor and management, the A.M.A. argued, must be held even, and the employee's "inalienable right to work" must be protected against "coercion from any source whatsoever." Supporters of the bill met this argument by insisting that union behavior was already policed by the courts and by state and local laws and that the measure, as drafted, was required if equalization of bargaining power, which was one of its major objectives, was to be attained.

The A.M.A., as might have been expected, attacked the majority-rule principle and insisted that where the A.F. of L. was in the majority, it would coerce the minority and management by seeking the closed shop, and where it was in the minority, it would seek to disrupt the status quo. Graham wondered if the Federation, in view of its showing in the A.L.B. elections, really favored majority rule, but he assumed that the organization expected the N.L.R.B. to carve out bargaining units in which the A.F. of L. would be able to win a majority position even though it was in the minority in the plant as a whole.

The A.M.A. also objected to the Wagner bill on procedural grounds. The measure, it charged, gave the N.L.R.B. "inquisitorial powers" and made it complainant, prosecutor, and judge. This criticism, of course, was a criticism of the administrative process itself and overlooked the fact that N.L.R.B. decisions were to be subject to judicial review.

If the bill were enacted, the A.M.A. complained, the company union would be outlawed, the closed shop would be imposed on American business, and the A.F. of L. would be aided in its efforts to make itself the "undisputed czar" of the workers and to force them to "pay tribute" to it in order to hold their jobs. The measure would make membership in a union rather than merit the basis of employment and "would stifle the initiative that has made the automobile industry great." The A.M.A., finally, urged Congress not to approve legislation which was so contrary to the principles of the President's March 25 settlement and that was likely to disturb "the peaceful relations" that prevailed in the industry.[4]

After the Senate Committee on Education and Labor completed its hearings on the Wagner Bill on April 2, the A.M.A. summarized its position on the proposed legislation for the President, and its executive committee asked Association members to enlist the co-operation of their dealers and suppliers in the fight against the measure. When the committee reported the bill out on May 2, the A.M.A. intensified its campaign of opposition. Members were urged to contact their senators and congressmen and the chairman of the Senate Committee on Education and Labor, to get in touch with their dealers and suppliers once again, and to send them an A.M.A. pamphlet that recapitulated the manufacturers' arguments against the bill.

On May 16, the day the Senate defeated an amendment to the bill barring coercion from any source and then passed the measure by a lopsided 63-12 vote, the automobile manufacturers, "in case publicity were necessary," prepared a statement in which they promised to live up to the principles of the automobile settlement but not to submit "to the deadening hand of irresponsible labor organizations." They stated categorically that they would refuse to sign an agreement with a trade union and would not recognize the principle of exclusive representation. This time, however, the A.M.A. was fighting a losing battle. The President, who had so often sided with the automobile manufacturers in the past and who had contributed so importantly to the sidetracking of Wagner's 1934 bill, now went over to the opposition. With the N.R.A. coming apart at the seams and with tension mounting between the White House and the business community, Roosevelt on May 24, three days before the Supreme Court declared the N.I.R.A. unconstitutional, finally agreed to support the National Labor Relations Bill, subject to the adjustment of some differences concerning the measure between some of the President's advisors and Senator Wagner. On June 27 the measure was approved by both houses of Congress, and on July 5 it became law.[5]

The enactment of the National Labor Relations Act constituted an official repudiation by Congress and the President of the principles of the automobile settlement and particularly of the concept of proportional representation. The Senate Committee on Education and Labor declared in its report on the bill that employees were unable to approach employers "in a friendly spirit" if they were "divided among themselves," that "long experience" had demonstrated that majority rule was best for both labor and management, and that the making of agreements was "impracticable" in its absence. The House Labor Committee, in its report on the bill, referred to the N.L.R.B.'s criticism of proportional representation in the Houde case and cited the Guide Lamp case as evidence that the employers themselves invoked the majority-rule principle as "the excuse" for refusing to deal with trade unions. "It is apparent," the House committee declared, "that those who oppose majority rule in effect oppose collective bargaining and the making of collection [collective] agreements as the end thereof, by seeking to create conditions making such accomplishment impossible." Secretary of Commerce Daniel Roper advised the President not to sign the measure since it conflicted with the principles of employer-employee relations that he had enunciated in the automobile settlement of 1934, but the President apparently no longer wished to follow the "new course in social engineering" that he had once said was charted by the terms of the settlement.[6]

II

Its support of the National Labor Relations Bill indicates that the A.F. of L. leadership in the automobile industry was still counting heavily on government assistance to supplement its organizational efforts. The failure of the Federation to secure the amendments to the automobile code that it had sought and its disillusionment with the A.L.B. and the President's settlement had, for some time, however, caused the A.F. of L. leadership to talk as though the Federation was more likely to prosper in the industry if it depended less on government and more on the strike weapon and its own organizational efforts.

The A.F. of L. had recognized as early as September 1, 1934, that there was "no hope" of getting G.M. to bargain "honestly" with the auto workers without "a show of force" and that it would take "swarms of men" or a strike to bring Ford to terms. When the code was renewed early in November 1934, without the public hearing the A.F. of L. had requested, Dillon wrote to the members of the National Council and to the various U.A.W. locals urging them to advise William Green that it was important to launch an "intensive organizing campaign" among the automobile workers so that they would be able to exercise their economic power to secure a consideration of their grievances. Green replied that he hoped a campaign could "soon" be launched and that he wanted to devote as much time as possible to the effort, but he had little more in mind than the delivery of a few speeches to labor mass meetings. The year ended without the organizing drive having proceeded beyond the talk stage.[7]

After having discussed some of the problems of the U.A.W. federal labor unions with Green in the middle of January 1935, Dillon at the end of the month announced that the A.F. of L. president would address mass meetings in the various automobile centers between February 17 and February 24 and that the automobile workers were preparing to submit demands to their employers for recognition and improved working conditions. Testifying in Washington on January 30 on the employment provisions of the codes, Dillon menacingly stated that if the automobile manufacturers did not mend their ways, he would no longer counsel their employees to refrain from the use of their economic power. Belligerent talk of this sort was also heard in U.A.W. circles following the renewal of the automobile code on January 31, 1935, and there was some speculation, as has been noted, that the A.F. of L. would resort to the strike weapon to indicate its displeasure with the administration and to wrest from the automobile manufacturers the improvements in the terms of employment that it had failed to incorporate in the code.[8]

As he set out on his tour of the auto centers, Green hailed his journey as part of "a grand drive for [the] complete organization" of the auto workers, and he did not rule out the possibility of a strike should that become necessary. He spoke to six thousand persons in Cleveland on his first stop, and Dillon, who was with him, boldly stated that "we are here to see if you are prepared to move out and stay out when the order comes." From Cleveland, Green journeyed to Toledo, St. Louis, and South Bend, before appearing in Detroit on February 23 for a nationwide broadcast. Prior to his Detroit address Green stated to newsmen that "We are not talking of pulling a strike. We haven't made any such plans," but during the course of his speech, which he delivered before a live audience of about fifteen hundred persons, he was enthusiastically applauded when he intimated that the A.F. of L. would do nothing to prevent the automobile workers from striking if that was their desire and results could not be achieved in any other way.[9]

Green met with the members of the National Council while in Detroit and assured them of A.F. of L. support, but, at the same time, he cautioned against hasty action. The Council, two days later, approved a formal letter to Green designating the A.F. of L. as its bargaining agency in the automobile industry and naming Green as its representative to negotiate a contract with the automobile manufacturers. "We express to you candidly," the letter stated, "that under no consideration will the automobile worker continue to work under conditions as they prevail in this industry today." A few days later the National Council instructed the U.A.W. locals to designate Green as their representative in bargaining with the auto companies and to take strike votes authorizing the A.F. of L. president to call a strike through the National Council if the automobile manufacturers refused to accede to demands to bargain collectively. "Never before," the letter to the federal labor unions declared, "have so large a group of workers within our country been compelled to toil under such intolerable conditions and at excessive speeds for so long a period of time as have the men and women employed in the automobile industry." Since the pleas of the workers had gone unheeded by both the employers and the federal government, the time had come for the U.A.W. locals to mobilize their strength so that their representatives "may have in their hands the power necessary to enforce your demands." The locals were instructed, however, that there was to be no strike unless it had been authorized by Green through the National Council.[10] The decision to order a work stoppage rested therefore in the hands of the cautious president of the A.F. of L.

As authorized by the National Council, and later by the U.A.W. locals, Green wrote to Alfred Reeves on February 27, 1935, requesting a conference with the automobile manufacturers affiliated with the A.M.A. to negotiate an agreement respecting wages, hours, and working conditions. Reeves replied on March 7 that the A.M.A. was not itself an employer and therefore had no occasion to bargain with workers or to arrange such conferences as Green had suggested. The individual A.M.A. members, Reeves noted, negotiated regularly with the A.L.B. bargaining agencies in their plants and were also willing to meet with other duly accredited representatives of their employees. He branded the A.F. of L. attempt to withdraw from the President's settlement and the strike votes then being taken as "acts of unprovoked aggression against the welfare of the employees in the industry and against the progress of recovery" and insisted, quite correctly, that since it represented only "a small minority" of the automobile workers, the Federation had "no just claim to be spokesman for the automobile workers generally." [11]

Both Green and Dillon criticized Reeves' reply to Green's letter, and Dillon stated that the strike vote then being taken was "the only avenue left by which these workers may adjust or correct their grievances." Green, however, if only for the record, followed the course of action that seemed to be suggested by Reeves' letter and wrote directly to the automobile companies requesting conferences with them on behalf of their employees. The A.F. of L. president could hardly have been surprised when he was informed in a typical reply that in so far as representatives of "special groups" were "duly accredited," they could take up "suitable questions" with the management "in the regular way." [12]

The stage thus seemed to be set for the long-talked-about automobile strike, and Dillon let it be known on April 9 that all but a few of the 176 U.A.W. locals had authorized Green to order a work stoppage when he thought the time proper. Whatever the meaning of the strike vote, it is perfectly apparent that there was strong sentiment for a strike within the ranks of the organized automobile workers. The strong Cleveland locals, in particular, had been urging such action for some time. The rump convention that they had convoked in Detroit on January 26, 1935, had called on the National Council to convene a national auto workers' conference to decide on a "united general strike" in the automobile and parts industries, and had urged the establishment of departmental and plant committees and city-wide organizational and negotiating committees to prepare for strike action.

The Cleveland Fisher Body local submitted demands to the management in February, and when they were rejected, Louis Spisak, the president of the local, wired Green, "We are depending on you for immediate action with General Motors. We are ready." All the Cleveland automobile locals voted in favor of a strike when the question was put to them in response to the request of Dillon and the National Council, and the Cleveland Auto Council on March 10 recommended the calling of a conference of the U.A.W. federal labor unions to plan a walkout. The Fisher Body local not only urged the National Council to set a strike date but sent delegates to the G.M. locals in Flint to seek joint action for a work stoppage. The latter step was in line with the promptings of the communists and the Musteites, who were urging the locals to by-pass Green and the A.F. of L. leadership and to take strike preparations into their own hands. [13]

Despite their public statements, it is doubtful that Dillon and Green ever really contemplated a major strike in the automobile industry in the spring of 1935. On March 25, while the various locals were taking their strike votes, Dillon wired Roosevelt that "ruthless discharges" of unionists by the automobile manufacturers had precipitated a crisis in employer-employee relations in the industry that could be resolved only by Presidential intervention. Apparently Dillon, who was later to observe that "It's almost got to the point where a worker who has a stomach ache or gets fired, wants the President of the United States to do something about it" and to state that the auto workers would have to learn to rely on themselves, did not think that the situation about which he complained could be dealt with by the U.A.W. without White House support.[14]

Dillon did permit the Detroit Hupp local to go out on strike on April 5, but this was a strike against a weak independent which was then involved in a damaging factional fight for the control of the company. Dillon called the walkout "undoubtedly the most effective and enthusiastically supported demonstration of automobile workers ever to be conducted in the City of Detroit," and the *Detroit Labor News* described the strike settlement as "The first full and complete victory in the automobile industry." [15] The Hupp success, however, did not cause Dillon to abandon his customary caution and to favor strike action against the more powerful automobile concerns. When, during the course of the strike, Joseph Wood of the St. Louis local complained that St. Louis U.A.W. members thought that "a spirit of pacifism permeates the organization in the Detroit area," Dillon replied that he was dealing with "a tremendously difficult problem," that the "odds against us are terrific," and that therefore it was "unavoidable that we should proceed with some caution...." [16]

The final decision for a work stoppage rested with Green, but he had advised Carl Shipley as early as February 7, 1935, that a strike simply did not fit in with the A.F. of L.'s plans. Green later informed the Executive Council that the auto workers "wanted to engage in a general strike but I stopped that. I said, you are in no position to engage in a general strike." Like Dillon, Green probably thought of the strike drive and strike vote as simply a means of strengthening the A.F. of L. in its efforts to bargain with the automobile manufacturers and to gain support for the passage of the National Labor Relations Bill. The automobile executive who referred to the strike drive as simply an "A.F. of L. sales promotion campaign" was certainly not far from the mark.[17]

It must be said in explanation of Green and Dillon's caution that the two men were painfully aware of the limited membership of the U.A.W. and of the weakened condition of many of the federal labor unions. The U.A.W., at this time, had strong locals in the Studebaker, White Motor, Seaman Body, and Nash plants and in several of the

automobile parts plants, but some of these locals enjoyed amicable relations with their employers, and Green and Dillon were understandably loathe to ask them to strike.[18] In most of the other automobile
plants, in contrast, the problem for the A.F. of L. was not one of
strength but of weakness. Charles O. Madden, the president of the
Pontiac local, reported to Green on March 2, 1935, at a time when the
three G.M. plants in the city employed about twelve thousand persons, that the Pontiac federal labor union had not more than twenty
active members, the Fisher Body local had even fewer members, and
the G.M. Truck local had none. After surveying the situation in Flint,
where union membership had plummeted following the March 25
settlement, Homer Martin wrote Dillon on March 28, 1935, that "It is
going to take a while to build the Locals back...." The St. Louis
local had not paid a per capita tax since June 1934, and Martin had
told Dillon in explanation of the small per capita tax paid by the Kansas City local that it was "more or less of a miracle that we have saved
the unions at all." In the Detroit main plants, as James Dewey and
P. W. Chappell had reported to the Department of Labor on January
19 in an analysis of the degree of organization in the automobile industry, the U.A.W. had "practically no membership at all." Although
Dewey and Chappell unquestionably overestimated the strength of the
U.A.W. in such G.M. strongholds as Flint and Pontiac, they had nevertheless concluded that "an effective strike cannot be staged at the
present time." [19]

Under the circumstances, it is not surprising that Green and Dillon
thought that a major strike in the automobile industry would be a
disaster for the U.A.W. Both men, however, underestimated the potentiality of the strike as an organizational device. It was, indeed,
precisely for this reason that some of the members of the National
Council thought a strike should be called. Thus, Otto Kleinert wrote
Martin in December 1934 that his local was "shot completely" but that
he was unworried. "The first constructive militant step the A.F.L.
takes," he explained, "will be the spark that is now so badly needed."
Similarly, Fred Pieper, who wrote Martin in March 1935 that it
seemed to him that "we are moving rather slow" and that "The boys
are getting a little uneasy," thought that his local could double its
membership if a strike were called.

Pieper was convinced that a strike against G.M. was absolutely
essential to the well-being and future of the U.A.W. If the A.F. of L.
could not strike G.M. in the Detroit area, he wrote Dillon on April
11, it should "bend every effort" to close as many G.M. assembly plants
outside Detroit as possible. Every person he had contacted, Pieper

asserted, believed that the A.F. of L. had gone as far as it could in peaceful efforts to secure recognition and collective bargaining, and that "the only means we have now is to strike.... One thing is certain and that is, we must prove to the Automobile workers that we can help them...." Pieper thought that the U.A.W. locals had more support among the automobile workers and would prove stronger in a strike than Dillon was inclined to believe. At all events, as he wrote Martin the next day, he had concluded that "We must do something; that is for sure. Unless we can prove to these men that we are willing to give them a chance to help themselves, I am afraid our membership will decrease a good deal within the next thirty days.... To be very frank," Pieper concluded, "I don't know of any thing else to do except strike." [20]

When Pieper in his letter to Dillon of April 11 listed the G.M. plants outside Detroit where he thought a strike would be effective,[21] he did not include the Toledo Chrevolet plant. It was here, however, that a strike began on April 23 that brought Chevrolet production all over the United States to a standstill, caused G.M. to retreat from its announced policy of refusing to negotiate with strikers, and resulted in an agreement that a future U.A.W. president hailed at the time as "our greatest single step forward." [22] The Toledo Chevrolet strike was the most important staged in the automobile manufacturing industry during the period the N.I.R.A. was in effect.

Just what part, if any, the A.F. of L. leadership played in the calling of the Toledo strike is a matter for conjecture. The Toledo local did not request permission to strike, and, officially, the strike was unauthorized. However, W. Ellison Chalmers has maintained that Dillon, whom he was assisting at the time, actually welcomed the strike —an opinion shared by Department of Labor Conciliator Thomas J. Williams—since he feared that the A.L.B. bargaining agencies were about "to eliminate the Federation as an independent bargaining agency." According to Chalmers, Dillon was unwilling to authorize the strike officially because he did not wish to accept responsibility for its possible failure, but he did suggest to T. N. Taylor, an A.F. of L. organizer in Ohio, that he hint to the leaders of the Toledo local that it might be a good idea to force the issue with the company. It is possible that this is an accurate account of what actually took place, but it is hard to reconcile this interpretation with the obvious reluctance of Green and Dillon to challenge G.M. in the economic field and with Dillon's unqualified statement to Green when the strike was concluded that the union had not consulted with him prior to the walkout and that the strike had not received the approval of his office.

At all events, once the strike developed, Green promptly announced that the facilities of the A.F. of L. would be extended to the strikers, and he told Dillon, "We should support these people in Toledo."[23]

The U.A.W. local involved in the strike was the same Federal Labor Union No. 18384 that had conducted the great Auto-Lite strike in the spring of 1934. It had successfully organized Toledo's parts plants, and it held signed contracts with many of them, but until the end of March 1935 it had failed to organize the Chevrolet plant. The latter was an exceedingly important link in the G.M. chain of plants since it was the only one then making Chevrolet and Pontiac transmissions. A successful strike at the Toledo Chevrolet plant was bound to have repercussions for G.M. as a whole.

When the A.L.B. announced late in March 1935 that it would hold a nominating election in the Chevrolet plant on April 9, the leadership of the Toledo local, several of whom were Musteites,[24] realized that the time had come to make a determined effort to organize the plant. There were only a handful of Chevrolet workers in the local when the campaign began, but the employees, who were dissatisfied with the level of their wages and with wage differentials in the plant, were evidently ripe for organization since they flocked to the U.A.W.'s banners. The paid-up membership of the local increased from two thousand in March to four thousand in April, and at least half of this increase was accounted for by the Chevrolet plant.[25]

The A.F. of L. leadership, consistent with the organization's policy, advised the Chevrolet workers to boycott the A.L.B. election, but this counsel was ignored. In the April 9 primary, 1327 of the 2140 employees who voted designated Fred Schwake, the local's business agent, as their candidate, and he emerged victorious in all of the plant's eight districts. According to the A.L.B.'s election rules, Schwake, in the final election scheduled for April 24, was to face the candidate with the next highest number of votes in each of the eight districts. Had Schwake won in each of the districts in the final election, as seemed likely, the A.L.B. would have added to the plant bargaining agency from among the defeated candidates a sufficient number of representatives to afford the voters who had indicated no affiliation for their candidate representation in proportion to their total strength as evidenced in the nominating election.[26] The union, however, did not wait for this contingency to develop. It quickly drafted a tentative agreement, modeled on the contracts it already had signed with the Toledo parts plants, mailed it to the company on April 16, and its executive shop committee discussed the document with the management on April 18. When the committee reported to a union meeting of April 20 that it had failed to reach an understanding with the company on fundamental issues, it was given the authority to call a strike if this seemed necessary.[27]

Negotiations between the union and the company were resumed on April 22. The union was represented by Schwake and its executive shop committee, and the company negotiators included not only the local management but also William S. Knudsen, executive vice-president of G.M., Marvin E. Coyle, the president of Chevrolet, C. E. Wetherald, the vice-president of Chevrolet, and Hugh Dean, the manufacturing manager of the Chevrolet division. The presence of these men indicates the importance that G.M. attached to the threatening Toledo situation. Although the company in the counterproposals that it presented to the union on April 22 met several of the union's terms, the differences between the two groups were substantial. The issues in contention involved hours, wages, seniority, the timing of jobs, and so forth, but what particularly disturbed the union was the company's refusal to grant exclusive bargaining rights, which would have involved a departure from the principles of the settlement, and a signed contract.[28]

The union was also antagonized by other factors that were not directly related to the contract negotiations. It thought that the conferences which the company was holding with small groups of employees were designed to discourage support for the union in the forthcoming final election, although the company insisted that it was simply trying to explain A.L.B. election procedures, a task normally assumed by the board itself. The union found additional reason for concern in the fact that although the primary elections at the Toledo Chevrolet plant and the Toledo Willys-Overland plant had been held on the same date, the final election at Chevrolet was scheduled for a week later than the final election at Willys. Was not the purpose of this delay to give the Chevrolet management more time to defeat the union? The union also thought that the company was itself preparing for a "showdown strike" since it was hiring extra guards and having wire netting placed over the windows of the plant.[29]

The management presumed at the close of the conference on April 22, which had continued throughout the day, that negotiations were to be resumed at a later time, but the union's executive shop committee decided that night to strike the plant the next morning. Union committeemen appeared in the plant at 6:00 A.M., when the morning shift began, and went from department to department announcing the strike. Approximately six hundred employees promptly walked out, and a few minutes later the management sent out the remaining five hundred workers. The second shift, of approximately twelve hundred employees, did not report for work, and the plant was thus completely shut down.[30]

From the beginning of the strike to its end the union maintained a completely effective, round-the-clock picket line at the Chevrolet plant. "The workers," Conciliator Thomas J. Williams found, "are in absolute control, as it pertains to the plant. I have never seen anything like it...." In contrast to the situation that prevailed during the Electric Auto-Lite strike, the union, despite the presence of some "radicals" on the strike committee, excluded from its picket line communists and Musteites and members of their satellite organizations of the unemployed. "This strike," Schwake declared, "is our own affair, and we'll keep it clean or know the reason why." Not only was discipline maintained on the picket line, but, in marked contrast to the Auto-Lite strike, the Chevrolet strike was free of violence. The company deserves a great deal of credit for this happy occurrence since, remembering the trouble that had developed at the Auto-Lite plant, it decided not to operate the Chevrolet plant for the duration of the strike.[31]

The company, to be sure, did not rely entirely on its economic power in this contest with the union. It is possible that two of the union officials were employees of Pinkerton's National Detective Agency, which was performing labor espionage services for G.M., and some of the strikers manning the picket line were actually Pinkerton agents. The La Follette Committee, as has been indicated, later found that G.M. had "flooded" Toledo with labor spies as a result of the strike, and Merle C. Hale, who had been G.M.'s director of industrial relations, admitted to the committee, "I tried to keep track of the union activities very definitely." Both Dillon and Taylor were put under surveillance, and Pinkerton agents also had instructions to shadow the chairman of the strike committee. When Edward F. McGrady, Assistant Secretary of Labor, was sent in to mediate the strike, Pinkerton men took a hotel room next to his in a vain attempt to listen in on his conversations. Preparing for the worst, the Chevrolet division bought $6874.80 worth of gas equipment during the strike, including 288 long-range projectiles and 288 grenades.[32]

Although management presented a united front to the employees, there was division in the camp of the strikers between the A.F. of L. leadership and the nine-man strike committee.[33] The committee was headed by the twenty-three year old James Roland, who had played a key role in the fight against the injunction in the Auto-Lite strike and had later become chairman of the local's executive shop committee in the Chevrolet plant. Dillon, who gave the strike his personal attention, pursued a cautious policy and was prepared to settle for less than a complete victory. Dubious about the objectives of at least some members of the strike committee, he was determined to keep control of the strike in his own hands and was, on the whole, successful in doing so. The strike committee, as Dillon knew, was tinged with radicalism. Roland, who had joined the Unemployed League after losing his Chevrolet job,[34] and at least one or two others were under the influence of A. J. Muste and his Workers party; and the committee also included Robert C. Travis, later prominent in the U.A.W. and described by Max M. Kampelman as "a man with a long pedigree of Communist activity." Both the Musteites and the communists attacked the A.F. of L.'s conduct of the strike and urged the strike committee to run the strike itself without regard to the wishes of Dillon and the Federation.[35]

Occupying a middle ground between Dillon and the strike committee was the executive committee of the union, and particularly the union's president, Ellsworth Kramer, and its financial secretary, George Addes. Fred Schwake was also a member of this middle group. The executive committee and Schwake, like the strike committee, had their differences with the A.F. of L.—Williams thought the Toledo local was an A.F. of L. local "in name only"—and were equally committed to local control of the strike,[36] but, at the same time, they were not under the influence of Muste or the communists, and they supported Dillon, as we shall see, on several crucial occasions.

One of the fundamental issues raised between Dillon and the strike committee was the question of spreading the strike to other G.M. locals and thus presumably putting additional pressure on the company. The strike committee pictured the walkout as not simply "a fight against the local management . . . but against the entire anti-labor policy of General Motors." Consistent with the advice of the Musteites and the communists, but not necessarily for this reason, the strike committee, and the executive committee to some degree as well, were anxious to have other G.M. locals join Toledo on strike and to have them all pursue a common strike policy, regardless of the wishes of the A.F. of L. In support of this position, a union mass meeting of April 29 resolved that all G.M. locals should go out on strike and should remain out until all of them had won signed contracts. Roland stated bluntly that the locals should not wait for the permission of the A.F. of L. to strike because such permission would not be forthcoming.[37]

In conformity with its desire to "expand" the strike, the strike committee on April 18 dispatched six carloads of workers to Detroit to picket the G.M. building and thus to point the finger at what it regarded as the real source of the workers' troubles. The strike committee and the union executive committee also sent emissaries to Flint, Norwood, Ohio, Cleveland, and elsewhere to contact G.M. locals, and delegations from various G.M. federal labor unions were received in Toledo. *"It has all the appearance of developing into a general strike,"* Conciliator Thomas J. Williams concluded on April 30.

The policy of spreading the strike met with only limited success, however. The Norwood Chevrolet and Fisher Body leadership, after conferring with the Toledo group, drew up strike demands that were almost identical with Toledo's, and the local then staged a walkout on April 30. Following a conference in Toledo on April 28, officers of the Cleveland Fisher Body local decided on a strike and gained the membership's consent for this action the next day; but before the walkout occurred, the company on April 30 closed the plant, allegedly because of a lack of transmissions. The union, whose representatives had told the Toledo strikers that they would "close the whole city of Cleveland if necessary," then converted the shutdown into a strike. A similar situation occurred in Atlanta, where the local was contemplating joint action with other U.A.W. federal labor unions in G.M. plants and where, Fred Pieper wrote Martin, "the men are anxious to take their place in the present skirmish." Before the local arrived at a firm decision to strike, however, G.M. shut down the plant, again because of a lack of transmissions; and following the Cleveland pattern, the local on May 3 voted in favor of a strike.[38]

The Toledo local failed to persuade G.M. workers other than those in Norwood, Cleveland, and Atlanta to join the walkout, largely, it would seem, because the local organizations did not wish to strike without Dillon's consent.[39] Other Chevrolet plants and Fisher Body plants making Chevrolet bodies—in Janesville, Kansas City, St. Louis, Baltimore, Tarrytown, and Buffalo—were forced to shut down, however, simply because of a lack of transmissions. Altogether some thirty-two thousand workers were idled as the result of the Toledo strike.[40]

Dillon had little sympathy for the strike committee's policy of spreading the strike: Roland was not incorrect in his later recollection that A.F. of L. officials "felt they could not handle it [the strike] if it went national." To be sure, in order to increase the A.F. of L.'s bargaining power, Dillon hinted on occasion that all the G.M. locals might be called out on strike if G.M. proved adamant; but, privately, he did not believe that most of the G.M. federal labor unions had the strength to challenge the company, and so he sought to localize the strike. Similarly, Dillon opposed the establishment of a general strike committee, embracing the various G.M. plants, to conduct strike negotiations. Thus, when the Toledo strike committee on May 10 issued invitations for a conference of G.M. locals to be held in Toledo on May 12 ostensibly to co-ordinate strike demands but perhaps also to set up a joint strike committee which would settle the strike as it saw fit, Dillon persuaded the executive committee of the union to repudiate the call and influenced most of the locals concerned not to send delegates, with the result that the conference was not held.[41]

The crucial test of strength between Dillon and the strike committee with regard to the spread of the strike, a test that Dillon won, involved the great Buick plant in Flint. If this plant, which made parts not only for the Buick but also for the Oldsmobile and the Cadillac, could have been shut down successfully, G.M.'s position would have been considerably weakened. Dillon, however, did not think the Buick local was strong enough to win a strike and so was determined to prevent the walkout the strike committee desired. The Buick local had voted to strike on May 6 if the Toledo strike was not settled by then, but it gave its executive board discretion to defer the strike "if it seemed advisable." A union trustee many years later thought that the local had not been strong enough to "carry on an intensive strike" but that it could have closed down the plant for a brief period.

Fearing that a Buick strike would be called, Dillon, whom the union trustee quoted above described as one of those " 'wait and see and let's drag it out' guys," rushed to Flint on May 5 to plead at a union meeting that the strike be delayed pending the outcome of negotiations in Toledo. Although there was some heckling from the audience, the union's executive board agreed to support Dillon, and a strike was averted. When the Toledo strike did not quickly yield to settlement, however, the executive board decided on May 11 to strike on May 14 regardless of developments in Toledo. "It is a question of survival of the union here," declared the president of the local in expressing the opinion of the executive board, "and further delay would be fatal." But there was to be no strike at the Buick plant. On May 11 and 12 an agreement to end the Toledo strike was negotiated, and Dillon informed Louis Hart, the A.F. of L. organizer in Flint, that he would recommend its acceptance to a meeting of the strikers on May 13 and that he did not favor a walkout at Buick. Bowing to Dillon's wishes, the Buick executive board agreed to defer a Buick strike at a wild meeting of the local on the night of May 13. About thirty to thirty-five Toledo strikers were present, and when it was announced that there would be no strike the next day, they demanded the floor. The president of the local thereupon adjourned the meeting. Before order could be restored, it proved necessary to turn out the lights and to hustle the Toledo strikers from the room.[42]

Dillon also differed with the strike committee on the question of complying with the company's demand, made on the first day of the strike, that the terms it had offered the union on April 22 be submitted to a vote of Chevrolet employees. The strike committee stated that it would ignore the company's request for a referendum, but Dillon, fearing that the strike leaders had antagonized public opinion by their stand, announced from Washington on April 24 that the strikers would vote on the company proposals at a meeting on April 26. He also conferred with Perkins and McGrady on the twenty-fourth and warned them of the possible spread of the strike. The Department of Labor responded by assigning veteran conciliator Thomas J. Williams to the dispute. Realizing that this decision effectively by-passed the A.L.B., Dillon triumphantly proclaimed with regard to the board, "it's all washed up. We will have nothing more to do with it." The A.L.B., for its part, canceled on April 24 the final election scheduled for the Chevrolet plant on that day.[43]

Dillon was the chief speaker at the union meeting of April 26, which was attended by approximately sixteen hundred persons. The company proposals were unanimously rejected by the assembled throng, and then a resolution to resume negotiations was unanimously adopted. Although this reasonable behavior by the union placed the company on the spot, G.M. made it clear on the twenty-seventh that it would not "resume negotiations with the strikers while they remain on strike" and that it would not under any circumstances grant the union exclusive bargaining rights since this was contrary to the terms of the President's settlement. The strike committee, in rebuttal, insisted that the walkout of all the employees proved its right to negotiate for the workers as a whole and declared that it would not agree to Knudsen's condition of a return to work prior to the resumption of negotiations because this meant the acceptance, in effect, of the company's terms.[44]

Efforts during the next few days to break the deadlock between the company and the union proved unavailing,[45] and in the meantime a back-to-work movement threatened to undermine the union's position. The movement was initiated on April 29 when ten Toledo employees conferred in Detroit with Richard Byrd, informed him that 75 per cent of the employees were opposed to the strike, and requested the A.L.B. to poll the workers by mail ballot to ascertain whether they were willing to return to work. Four days later an Independent Workers Association (I.W.A.) was formed and began circulating petitions calling for a return to work on the company's terms or, failing that, for a vote of the employees by secret ballot on the company's proposals. The next night, May 4, the organization held a meeting which was attended by sixteen hundred persons, all alleged to be Chevrolet employees. At least fourteen hundred of those present endorsed by a rising vote the twin proposals supported by the petitions. The next day the I.W.A. presented its petitions, allegedly bearing fourteen hundred signatures, to Chevrolet's president, Marvin Coyle, and to the A.L.B.[46]

It is difficult to ascertain how bona fide this back-to-work movement was. The strike committee charged that the new organization was "company owned, controlled and managed" and that it was a "strikebreaking agency" designed to destroy the power of organized labor in Toledo and in the automobile industry in general. It claimed that the company had itself recruited the members, that it had signed up persons who had not worked for the company for years, and that it had threatened to blacklist union members who refused to approve the company's proposals. The committee insisted that the May 4 meeting was a farce, contending that the officers of the union and the members of the strike committee had not been permitted to enter the hall and that the signing of the petition was a condition of admission.[47] Whatever the merit of the union charges, one thing was made clear by later developments: the back-to-work petitions grossly exaggerated the number of Chevrolet employees who were willing to return to their jobs at that time on the basis of the company's proposals.

Whether the back-to-work movement was genuine or not, Dillon realized that the action taken by an apparent majority of the Chevrolet employees placed the union very much on the defensive and that it would have to take some affirmative action if it were to enjoy any public support for its position. He therefore proposed to the strike committee on May 5 that it agree to permit the Department of Labor, rather than the hated A.L.B., to conduct a poll among the employees to ascertain whether they favored the company's proposals. The strike committee was far from enthusiastic about this suggestion, but Dillon finally won the committee's consent. McGrady, who had stepped into the dispute on April 30, and Williams then carried the idea to Detroit and secured G.M.'s approval, "after some hesitation" on the company's part.[48]   As it turned out, Dillon's proposal proved to be the key factor in the settlement of the strike.

Opposition to Dillon's plan was immediately and strongly expressed by Charlton Ogburn, whom Dillon had brought into the strike negotiations.   It was up to the union itself, with the aid of the A.F. of L., Ogburn advised Dillon, to determine if it wished to continue the strike.   It would be an "extremely bad precedent" to permit a strike called by a union to be settled by all the employees whether they were union members or not.   With seventeen G.M. plants already closed, the Toledo local was in a position "to force important concessions," but the poll Dillon was proposing would "end the strike and the union will be humiliated with nothing but defeat to point to."   If the attendance at the I.W.A. meeting of May 4 had been accurately reported, Dillon would be leading the Toledo officers "to the slaughter," and the A.F. of L. "might as well fold up in the automobile industry."   Dillon, however, thought the poll "indispensable to a proper solution" of the Toledo question and stated that he would go ahead with the idea unless Green directed him otherwise.   Ogburn then carried his objections to the A.F. of L. president, and Green did express to Dillon his "apprehension" concerning the poll, but no change in plans was made.[49]

The balloting, which was confined to the production workers in the Chevrolet plant, was held on May 8.   The voters were asked simply to indicate on their ballots whether they approved or disapproved of the company's proposals as listed in the Toledo newspapers on April 23.   Williams, who along with McGrady was in charge of the poll, later complained privately that "Much pressure, most of it unfair, was brought to bear on me to phrase the terms in the ballot favorable to the Company."   In a joint statement, McGrady and Williams announced that it was their understanding that if a majority of the voters favored the company's proposals, there would be an immediate return to work.   If the proposals were rejected, the two men would seek to have negotiations resumed at once.[50]

The result of the voting was a clear victory for the union.   Despite the fact that the company's proposals promised some improvement of existing working conditions, 1251 employees rejected the company's offer, whereas only 605 indicated their approval.   Even if all the 369 eligible employees who did not vote were I.W.A. adherents, there was nothing in the balloting to indicate that the I.W.A. had the degree of support among the workers that it had claimed.   Dillon, his judgment vindicated, immediately announced that the poll proved that

G.M.'s labor policy was "unsatisfactory to the great majority" of its employees and that the company would now have to negotiate directly with the accredited representatives of the A.F. of L. "We today occupy an enviable position," Dillon, with some reason, informed Green. Not only had the union proved its right to speak for the majority of the strikers, but it was easy to interpret the poll as a repudiation of the A.L.B. and a victory, at least in an oblique sense, for the concept of majority rule. Knudsen, who had refused to negotiate with strikers at the time of the Cleveland Fisher Body strike in April 1934, realized that the poll made it difficult for G.M. to continue to insist that it would not negotiate with the Toledo strikers; and so after conferring with Williams and McGrady in Detroit on May 9, he stated that "We will negotiate directly with the committee." A conference was accordingly scheduled for May 11 in Toledo.[51]

Representing the company at the May 11 conference were Knudsen, Coyle, Wetherald, Alfred G. Gulliver, the Toledo plant general manager, and J. T. Smith, a G.M. attorney. The union was represented by the strike committee,[52] Schwake, Dillon, and James A. Wilson, whom Green had sent to Toledo as his personal representative. McGrady and Williams were also present. The conference began at 9:00 A.M. and did not break up until 3:00 A.M. the next morning, by which time the weary negotiators had finally arrived at an agreement. The terms agreed on did not, on paper, differ greatly from the company's proposals of April 22, but the union did register some additional gains. As before, the company refused to sign a contract and agreed simply to post the settlement on its bulletin boards and to file a copy with the Department of Labor. But now the settlement was entitled "Memorandum of negotiations between Chevrolet . . . and Employees represented by a Committee in behalf of . . . Federal Labor Union No. 18384," which indicated that the union had had something to do with working out the terms, a point that Knudsen had previously refused to concede.[53] The company did not grant the union exclusive bargaining rights and simply agreed, as before, to meet with duly accredited employee representatives upon all questions at issue. There seems, however, to have been an "informal understanding" that no final A.L.B. election was to be held at the plant and that the company would not seek to convert the I.W.A. into a company union. This left the union, *de facto,* as Knudsen privately conceded, the sole bargaining agent in the plant.[54] Knudsen also promised to confer with Dillon and the local shop committees at other G.M. plants. This was of some importance to Dillon since to counter the strike committee's plea for a common strike policy, he had assured the G.M. locals that he would insist on the application of the Toledo terms to G.M. employees generally.[55]

With regard to seniority, the May 12 agreement stated that the company was operating under seniority rules established by authority of the President but that the executive shop committee and the company would try to reconcile their viewpoints concerning the application of these rules. This at least presented the possibility that the union could alter the application of the rules in its favor. The company also improved its wage offer. Whereas it had previously proposed a 5 per cent increase, it now promised an increase of not less than four cents per hour to all employees, which represented an 8 per cent increase for those receiving the minimum fifty cents per hour. Finally, the company now agreed that the executive shop committee would have the right to confer with the company on the timing of any jobs the committee believed incorrectly timed, whereas previously the company had agreed only to furnish information on times, on request, to the proper department.[56]

Although Dillon realized that the union had failed to gain many of its principal demands, he decided to recommend the acceptance of the agreement to the strikers. Dillon reached this decision partly because Knudsen had made it clear to him that this was the company's final offer and that the Toledo plant would be dismantled if the terms were rejected. More could have been gained only if additional G.M. locals, such as the Buick federal labor union, had been called out and G.M. was, as a consequence, forced into submission, but this also involved the risk of losing everything, and the cautious Dillon did not believe that other G.M. locals were strong enough for such a contest. Dillon also felt that for the union to settle on the basis of the May 12 agreement would have a good effect on public opinion and would help to convince G.M. that the A.F. of L. was a reasonable and responsible organization.

Wilson also took the position, as he reported to Green, that "This was the best that could be done at this time." It was not what the men wanted, and the failure to secure a signed agreement gave persons like Muste an opportunity to do "their dirty work," but "still it is progress and lays the ground work for a future relation that would be good." The members of the strike committee did not, however, share this view and were particularly angered that the settlement did not include a signed contract. After all, the local had not called off the Auto-Lite strike without winning a signed agreement, and G.M. too could be brought to terms if only the Buick workers were called out. The strike leaders refused consequently to give the agreement their blessing.[57]

The settlement still required the approval of the strikers, who met on the evening of May 13 in Toledo's Civic Auditorium to render their verdict. The meeting, as the *Toledo News-Bee* reported, was "marked by dramatic highlights such as seldom have been equalled in all the colorful history of the labor movement in Toledo." [58] Approximately fifteen hundred workers, some of whom had been rehearsed for the occasion by the strike leaders who opposed the settlement, were gathered inside the auditorium, while outside the inner doors Communist and Workers party literature was being passed out attacking Dillon and advising the strikers to hold out for all their demands. When Dillon arrived, he was warned by a guard posted at the entrance, "I'm afraid you won't get a very good reception," and when he entered the auditorium itself, he was greeted with boos and jeers. A resolution was offered from the floor and carried which permitted only members of the strike committee to address the crowd and which, contrary to A.F. of L. regulations, specifically excluded Dillon. Dillon angrily countered this move by declaring that the union was no longer part of the A.F. of L. "They're out, they're out," he told reporters as he stalked from the auditorium and returned to his hotel.

Dillon's action caught the strike leaders by surprise, and the executive committee, which had no desire to see the union expelled from the A.F. of L., assumed the initiative in securing the withdrawal of the resolution that had barred Dillon from speaking. Addes thereupon phoned Dillon and asked him to return. While Dillon was absent, all of the strike committee members but Roland had spoken, and only one of them had specifically urged acceptance of the agreement.[59] Dillon, on his return, spoke for thirty minutes and pleaded for a favorable vote on the settlement. Some gains had been registered, he said, and it was simply impossible at the moment to win anything further. G.M. would not, unhappily, sign a contract. Yes, he had advised the Buick local not to strike, but this was because he did not wish to see the "slaughter of innocent people." Dillon even had to deny that he owned G.M. stock. When Dillon finished speaking, Roland took the floor and urged that the agreement be rejected. Dillon thereupon told Roland that he was "out" if the settlement was turned down, but he did not, as was later charged, threaten to expel the union as a whole if the terms were rejected.

While the ballots were being distributed, Schwake went over the agreement point by point and indicated the gains that had been made, although he did not specifically urge acceptance. This action may have turned the tide in favor of the agreement because of the confidence reposed in the local's business agent by the rank and file. When the vote was announced—732 to 385 in favor of acceptance— Roland exploded. "Are you a lot of yellow mice, or are you men?" he asked of the strikers. Roland demanded another vote, but the audience was beginning to thin by that time. The bitter-end foes of the agreement thereupon gathered on the stage and decided to continue the strike. The next morning a small handful of strikers set up picket lines about the plant, but Dillon ordered them to disperse "forthwith" on pain of losing their membership in the A.F. of L. At the same time he lifted the suspension of the union that he had proclaimed the previous night.[60]

On the morning of May 15 the Toledo Chevrolet workers returned to their jobs without incident, and with their return the strike movement in the G.M. plants came to an end. The strikes in Norwood and Atlanta were called off, with Dillon giving assurances that the "basic principles" of the Toledo settlement would be applied to the affected plants. Cleveland's Fisher Body workers voted on May 14 to return to work, and the Buick local also voted to accept the Toledo terms in so far as they were applicable.[61]

The view of the A.F. of L. and its friends was that the best terms possible had been gained and that a foundation had been laid on which a solid future could be built. The *American Federationist* proudly stated that "For the first time in history one of the major automobile manufacturing concerns ... has agreed to recognize and meet with a spokesman for its employees." [62] There was some exaggeration in this statement, but when one considers how little the A.F. of L. had accomplished in the auto industry up to that time, it is easy to understand its jubilation.

In contrast to the official A.F. of L. view, the "progressives" in the Toledo local and the more aggressive-minded federal labor unions in the industry thought that the Federation, because of its opposition to militant action, had capitulated when it would have been possible to tie up G.M. as a whole and to win the original union demands. It was not G.M. that had blocked the workers from gaining their objectives but the "perfidious treachery" of Dillon, whose only interest, in the view of members of the strike committee, was "to settle the strike and under any kind of conditions and get us back to work." George Darner, of the St. Louis local, who was in Toledo during part of the strike, wired his local that Dillon had "sold out" the automobile workers, and he refused even to discuss the issue with the A.F. of L. national representative. Darner's colleague Joseph Wood also thought that "a wonderful opportunity was muffed at Toledo." [63]

The auto manufacturers, for their part, pointed to the fact that the union had failed to win its principal demands—a signed contract and exclusive bargaining rights—that management had successfully resisted inroads on its prerogatives originally sought by the union, and that the A.L.B.'s seniority rules had not been altered. However management explained it, though, the union had won a status in the plant and a position of power that it had not previously enjoyed. The business press recognized that the A.F. of L. had staged a comeback in the auto industry when it seemed to be on the ropes and had demonstrated that it was a "power to be reckoned with." [64] More importantly, the strike had demonstrated that the Big Three in the automobile industry were not invulnerable to union pressure and that "even a small group of workers, willing to fight," could "successfully cripple a giant organization like the Chevrolet Corp." [65] It is more than a coincidence that Robert Travis, a member of the Toledo Chevrolet strike committee, was later to play a key role in the great Flint sit-down strike that caused G.M. to sign a contract with the U.A.W. and to grant it exclusive bargaining rights, in effect, for a six-month period.

The Toledo strike dealt a smashing blow to the prestige of the A.L.B. Not only were the board and its policies partly responsible for the strike, but the A.L.B. had been excluded from the strike picture from the beginning to the end, and it had been forced to cancel the final election scheduled for the Chevrolet plant. It is doubtful whether the A.L.B. could have long survived the Toledo strike even if the N.I.R.A. had not soon been declared unconstitutional, since even the employers now had some doubts as to its effectiveness. [66]

The Toledo settlement was followed by further negotiations in May and June between Dillon and G.M. executives in Cleveland, Norwood, [67] Atlanta, Janesville, and Kansas City. As the result of these meetings agreements were concluded which were roughly similar to the Toledo settlement and in which the company recognized the A.F. of L. shop committees as the spokesmen for the union's members. Dillon, who wrote to Green that he had "never . . . before been treated with greater courtesy nor observed a more favorable reaction upon the part of employers to the adopted policies and principles of the American Federation of Labor than I have observed upon the high executives of this great corporation," was exceedingly optimistic about the results of these conferences. After he had conferred with Knudsen, Coyle, and E. Fisher at Norwood and Atlanta, he informed Green that these G.M. officials had "acknowledged the fundamental fallacy of the company union" and, as he later reported, had recognized the A.F. of L. shop committees as "the duly constituted Bargaining Agency of our Organization within plants of the corporation where our Unions existed." He had been assured that the future policy of G.M. with regard to the A.F. of L. would be determined by "the ability and competency of these committees to function" and to see that negotiated agreements were carried out. "I am confident," Dillon declared, "that the United Automobile Workers are upon the way to the achievement of great things." [68]

Dillon, as later events were to show, was too optimistic about G.M.'s good will with regard to automobile unionism. His words were to turn particularly sour in Toledo, for the company in the fall of 1935 removed about 50 per cent of the machinery from the Toledo plant to Saginaw and Muncie, thus displacing anywhere from nine hundred to twelve hundred workers. From the union point of view, this appeared to be entirely an act of revenge, but the company was also made aware by the Toledo strike that it was unwise for it to concentrate the production of a key part in a single plant, particularly if there was a strong union in that plant. The strike had caught G.M. "napping," but as Knudsen had informed Conciliator Williams, the company was determined "never to be in such a position again." [69]

The Toledo strike had important consequences for the future of the A.F. of L. in the automobile industry. It helped, as we shall see, to persuade Green that the time had come to call a constitutional convention to establish an international union, but, at the same time, it served to weaken the A.F. of L.'s control over the organized auto workers. The A.F. of L. had triumphed over the local strike committee in the running of the strike, but in so doing it widened the cleavage that had been developing between the Federation's leadership in the industry and the more militant elements of the rank and file. This was apparent in Toledo in particular, but it also had implications for the U.A.W. as a whole. Less than two weeks after the Toledo settlement had been approved, the Toledo local adopted a resolution introduced by Roland attacking Dillon's conduct of the strike and petitioning the A.F. of L. to deprive him of his credentials as an organizer and to repudiate his conduct. Green rejected the charges against Dillon as "false and without foundation," and declared that they were inspired by "real enemies" of the A.F. of L., which was in a sense true; but be that as it may, Roland was not incorrect in his later judgment that the Toledo Chevrolet strike was "the beginning of Dillon's downfall." When delegates of the U.A.W. federal labor unions gathered in Detroit on August 26, 1935, in constitutional convention, the pronounced opposition to Dillon centered largely on his handling of the Toledo strike.[70]

But we must retreat for a moment to trace the steps that led finally to the establishment of the new international union of automobile workers. It will be recalled that the San Francisco convention of the A.F. of L. had directed the Executive Council to issue a charter for such a union and to direct its affairs for a "provisional period." When the Executive Council met in Washington beginning on January 29, 1935, to discuss the San Francisco decision, Michael Manning, Forrest Woods, and Otto Kleinert were present as representatives of the National Council, along with Francis Dillon, to request that the Detroit office of the A.F. of L. be strengthened by the assignment to it of additional organizers, preferably automobile workers, and by the establishment of a periodical, and that the A.F. of L. commit itself to the chartering of an international union for the industry and to the calling of a constitutional convention to meet in Detroit during the slack season on a date to be determined by President Green. Manning later remembered that the reception accorded the National Council representatives was "cool but civil" and that only John L. Lewis showed them any "consideration." [71]

The principal issue in contention in the Executive Council debate on the establishment of an automobile international was the jurisdiction to be accorded the new union. The point of view of the craft unionists on the Council was summed up by William Hutcheson of the Carpenters when he declared, "I do not believe we should give them [the automobile workers] a charter so broad that they could go out and claim any employee that might be employed by these automobile manufacturers." Wharton of the Machinists asserted that there were twenty-five thousand tool and die makers in the industry over whom the I.A.M. claimed jurisdiction, and representatives of the electricians, the plumbers, and the bricklayers insisted that the maintenance men in the automobile plants fell within their jurisdiction. William Green, who understood the feelings of the automobile workers on the jurisdictional issue far better than most of his colleagues on the Executive Council did, tried to persuade Council members to deal with the situation as it was and not as they wished it to be. "It is impossible for us," he told them, "to attempt to organize along our old lines in the automobile industry.... I must confess to you that I am come, you will come, and all of us will always come face to face with the fact, not a theory but a situation actually existing, that if organization is to be established in the automobile industry it will be upon a basis that the workers employed in this mass production industry must join an organization en masse. We cannot separate them." Whatever the Executive Council instructed him to do, he would "try to carry out but I will be the target of criticism," Green accurately predicted, "and I know we will fail."

John L. Lewis urged the Executive Council to postpone a decision on the jurisdictional issue until organization had been achieved. "Contention over the fruits of victory," he sensibly advised, should "be deferred until we have some of the fruits in our possession." With this thought in mind, Lewis on February 12 presented a motion calling for the issuance of a charter "at once"; the designation of the officers of the new union by the president of the A.F. of L. for a temporary period to be determined by the Executive Council; the inauguration of an active organizing campaign to achieve "complete organization" as soon as possible; the provision to the new union of funds "within the proper limitations" of the A.F. of L., organizing assistance, and facilities for publicity, including a newspaper; and the referral to the Executive Council of "questions of overlapping jurisdiction."

The craft unionists on the Council were, however, unwilling to leave the question of jurisdiction for future determination. George Harrison of the Railway Clerks proposed that Lewis' motion be amended to include a definition of the charter as embracing "all employees directly engaged in the manufacture of parts (not including tools, dies and machinery) and assembling of those parts into completed automobiles but not including job or contract shops manufacturing parts or any other employee engaged in said automobile production plants." Only Lewis, Dubinsky, and one other member of the Executive Council opposed Harrison's motion, and it was with the charter amendment included that Lewis' original motion was passed.[72] This left the projected union with only a semi-industrial jurisdiction and made a reality of the fear of many auto unionists that, in the end, they would not be permitted to include in their organization all the workers in and around the automobile plants regardless of their craft. Although the motion carried the instruction to issue a charter "at once," the Executive Council either then or subsequently authorized the Federation's officers to form the international when in their judgment it was "appropriate and convenient" to do so.[73]

At the third session of the National Council of the U.A.W., which was held in Detroit from February 23 to March 2, 1935, Ed Hall moved that the Council go on record as recommending to the president of the A.F. of L. that a constitutional convention to establish an international, industrial union be held in July or August, or even sooner if in Green's opinion this was desirable; but the motion was tabled, and the Council then simply accepted and endorsed Green's statement regarding the action recently taken on the subject by the Executive Council. The militant Cleveland unionists had sent a delegation to the Council, headed by Mortimer, to press for a constitutional convention, but Mortimer was later advised by mail that in view of the "tense situation" in the industry, the National Council realized the need for A.F. of L. support and had therefore asked that the charter which the Executive Council had authorized Green to issue be held in abeyance for the time being. Mortimer agreed that the calling of a constitutional convention would have to wait until the strike issue then pending was resolved, but he wanted assurances that the new union would operate "on an uncompromising industrial and rank and file basis." [74]

Long annoyed by the unwillingness of the Cleveland U.A.W. locals, particularly those in the Fisher Body and White Motor plants, to conform to the policies of the A.F. of L. with regard to an international and a general strike in the automobile industry, Dillon decided soon after the close of the National Council meeting that the time had come for vigorous counteraction. He flew to Cleveland early in April and warned the Fisher Body officers that their charter would be revoked if they continued to support individuals and groups not in sympathy with the A.F. of L. He told them that T. N. Taylor would be placed in charge of the federal labor union and that he expected them to co-operate with the A.F. of L. organizer in educating the local's members to their responsibilities. Dillon informed Green that he intended to return to Cleveland to pursue the same course with the White Motor local "for there are certain individuals in Cleveland that must get out of those Local Unions and they are going to be put out." Green, who had previously advised that Mortimer should be ejected from office if he were a communist, complimented Dillon for talking "direct and plain" to the federal labor union officers in Cleveland. [75]

Disaffection with the policies of the A.F. of L. regarding the proposed international was not, however, confined to the Cleveland locals. When the terms of the charter first became known some weeks after the February–March session of the National Council, several members of the Council were somewhat less than pleased at the jurisdictional limitations that were to be imposed on the auto international. Ed Hall complained to Homer Martin that "According to the set-up, as I see it, the Auto workers International wont [*sic*] amount to a *darn*." Hall thought that the automobile unions should prepare to make "a big fight" at the constitutional convention, and he did not believe that the charter as worded should be accepted. For-rest Woods, on the other hand, thought that the convention should accept the charter but should protest its jurisdictional limitations and should instruct the officers of the new international to carry the pro-test to the A.F. of L. Executive Council and, if necessary, the A.F. of L. convention. If this procedure did not bring relief, another consti-tutional convention should be called "to consider and formulate further plans." [76]

What was likely to happen if the automobile unionists failed to secure an out-and-out industrial jurisdiction was indicated by Carl Shipley in a letter of May 27, 1935, to John L. Lewis. Dillon, Shipley reported, had told him that the craft unions would claim the skilled workers in the federal labor unions. "We say like h— they will and if it is ever ordered and enforced there will be one more independent union. . . . If you have to follow through to a split which we don't want only as a last resort, I believe," Shipley predicted with unerring accuracy, "It will be an easy matter to get the Automobile Industry, because now they are discontented. . . . Are they [A.F. of L. Execu-tive Council] going to loose [*sic*] this chance to organize America be-cause of Craft Jealousies?" [77]

At the Executive Council meeting of April 30–May 7, 1935, Green reported that the U.A.W. federal labor unions were paying per capita tax on twenty thousand members but that this was probably only half of the actual membership. He thought that an organization of thirty thousand paid-up members would be self-sustaining and ex-pressed the hope that the situation would "clarify" in the near future so that he could issue the call for a constitutional convention to estab-lish an international union. The Toledo strike and the subsequent conferences between G.M. and the U.A.W. federal labor unions in various G.M. plants apparently helped to "clarify" matters and to persuade Green and Dillon that it was now "appropriate and con-venient" to convene the constitutional convention. The two men met on the subject on June 17, about three weeks after the N.I.R.A. had been declared unconstitutional, following which Dillon an-nounced that preparations would be made for a convention beginning on August 26 to launch the international. The replies to a question-naire sent out by the A.F. of L. president to the various auto locals on June 19 indicated overwhelming support for the idea.[78]

When the Schechter decision ended the N.I.R.A. experiment and as the A.F. of L. prepared for the auto workers' constitutional convention, the total paid-up membership of the U.A.W. federal labor unions was 22,687, which was approximately 5.4 per cent of the 421,000 wage earners employed in the automobile manufacturing and automobile parts industries as of June 1935. The paid-up membership figure, although a rock-bottom indication of U.A.W. strength, nevertheless reveals how inadequate were the results of the A.F. of L.'s organizing efforts in the automobile industry. The Federation had experienced its greatest organizational failure in the Detroit citadel of the automobile manufacturing industry and in the other automobile cities of Michigan. Here, where the power of the Big Three was massed, where the reputation of the A.F. of L. was at low ebb, and where Collins and then Dillon had kept a tight rein on the federal labor unions, the Federation had simply been unable to win the favor of the auto workers. There were only 2197 paid-up members in the various Detroit locals, and a mere 1413 additional members in the Michigan locals outside Detroit. The U.A.W. had only nineteen paid-up members in Ford's giant Rouge plant, 178 in the Chrysler Corporation plants in Detroit, 423 in the G.M. Detroit plants, and 707 in the five G.M. plants in Flint. The U.A.W. federal labor union in the Detroit Gear plant was the largest auto local in the motor city, and it had only 432 paid-up members.[79]

In so far as automobile workers were organized in Detroit, they belonged in the main to unions that were not affiliated with the A.F. of L. Thus, the Associated Automobile Workers of America had achieved a position of power in the Hudson plant, the Automotive Industrial Workers' Association was building its strength in the Chrysler plants and in a few other Detroit factories, and the core of the M.E.S.A. membership was in Detroit. The total membership of these three independents was almost certainly greater than the total membership of the U.A.W. federal labor unions. This would suggest that perhaps 10 to 15 per cent of the factory workers in the automobile and automobile parts industries belonged to some outside union organization as of June 1935.

The strength of the U.A.W. when the N.I.R.A. came to an end was concentrated outside of Michigan—in the Studebaker and Bendix locals in South Bend, the White Motor local in Cleveland, the hybrid Toledo local, the Nash locals in Racine and Kenosha, the Seaman Body local in Milwaukee, the Norwood Chevrolet and Fisher Body local, and the Janesville Fisher Body local. Over fifteen thousand of the paid-up members of the organization belonged to these nine federal labor unions.[80] They were, in the main, locals that had had their differences with the A.F. of L. leadership. They were committed to a more militant policy than that pursued by the Federation and were determined to resist any raids on their membership by the craft unions. Also, communists, Musteites, Socialists, and other left-wing groups had played an important part in the establishment of some of these locals—the Toledo and White Motor locals are conspicuous examples—and it would not have been too difficult to predict on the eve of the U.A.W. constitutional convention that the clash of ideologies in the new international would be something to behold.

As of August 26, 1935, when the U.A.W. constitutional convention opened, the auto workers, according to Francis Dillon, had been able to secure signed contracts from only sixteen companies in the automobile manufacturing and automobile parts industries. Fourteen of these contracts had been negotiated by federal labor unions in the parts plants, eight of them by the Toledo local alone. Only the factory employees of White Motor and Pierce Arrow among the automobile manufacturers were covered by signed contracts.[81]

Although they did not hold signed contracts, the federal labor unions in the Studebaker, Nash, Seaman Body, and Hupp plants enjoyed a satisfactory collective relationship with their employers. Speaking for the Wisconsin U.A.W. locals, Ed Hall thus told Harry Weiss during the course of the Henderson inquiry that until the other automobile manufacturers improved the terms under which their employees labored, Nash had gone as far as it safely could in meeting union demands regarding wages, seniority, and other working conditions. Studebaker bargained with its workers on the basis of a "company statement of policy" and oral agreements rather than a signed contract, but employer-employee relations in the plant appear to have been excellent. Undoubtedly, the precarious position of Studebaker and the other independent automobile manufacturers, as compared to the Big Three, caused them to seek the goodwill of their workers and to co-operate with rather than oppose the federal labor unions in their plants.[82]

Where U.A.W. locals had been able to secure signed contracts or had played a part in the formulation of company statements of policy or memoranda of agreement, they had generally been able to make provisions for such matters as an overtime rate for hours in excess of eight per day and for work on Sundays and holidays, call-in pay, payment for dead time, reinstatement with back pay of employees against whom discrimination had been proved, seniority by service alone or joint union-management determination of efficiency if seniority was modified by a merit clause, the retiming of jobs when this was requested by an employee, and arbitration of disputes. The U.A.W. local in the Young Radiator Company plant in Racine had been recognized in a contract of March 13, 1935, as the exclusive representative of the company's factory employees, and the Toledo local had been able to secure a contract from the Bingham Stamping Company in October 1934 which called for the management to teach time-study methods to the union's executive shop committee and "to arbitrate wages in regard to the rise in the cost of living." The kinds of provisions that the future international union of automobile workers would seek to have incorporated in contracts with the automobile companies were thus forecast to a degree in these first U.A.W. agreements.[83]

Although the number of union members constituted but a small percentage of the factory employees in the main and parts plants and although signed union contracts were a rarity in the industry, unionism by the end of the N.R.A. era had gained a foothold in the automobile industry from which it was not to be dislodged. It had, moreover, become apparent to the organized automobile workers that if their union were to prosper in the industry, it would have to acquire jurisdiction over all the automobile workers and would have to have "the will and courage to fight when necessary."[84] The dramatic events in the automobile union field during the next two years were to demonstrate graphically how much the automobile workers had learned from their experiences during the Blue Eagle era.

XIII

AFTER THE BLUE EAGLE

I

WITHIN A FEW HOURS after the United States Supreme Court had declared the N.I.R.A. unconstitutional, Alvan Macauley, the president of the A.M.A., announced publicly that he did not believe the Court's decision would lead to any significant change in the labor policies of the automobile manufacturers. In similar vein, Alfred P. Sloan, Jr., although hailing the passing of the N.I.R.A. as "a vital step forward in promoting a sane industrial recovery," nevertheless assured G.M. employees, as other automobile and automobile parts manufacturers were assuring their employees, that the death of the Blue Eagle did not mean that wages would be cut.

In a fuller statement of the policies that it would pursue now that the code had lapsed, G.M. informed its divisions on June 6, 1935, that there would be no shift in the corporation's policy of dealing with groups of employees or with their representatives, that labor complaints would continue to be handled in accordance with the company's statement of August 15, 1934, on employer-employee relations, that there would be no blanket changes in wages and hours, and that the seniority rules then being followed would remain in force. A few days later the Packard Motor Company, in a statement to its employees, also announced that it did not intend to change its policies regarding wages, hours, collective bargaining, and employee grievances. Alvan Macauley, Packard's president, informed Roy Chapin that a pronouncement of this sort was necessary because "agitators of all kinds" were misrepresenting the company's attitude. He thought that the statement would "largely satisfy the men" without tying the company's hands.[1]

Despite these assurances that the status quo would be observed, there was considerable speculation that the industry would no longer heed the code-imposed limitations on the hours of labor about which it had so persistently and vehemently complained. Macauley remarked late in July 1935 that since the forty-hour week limited both the earnings of the automobile worker and the flexibility in the use of his labor force required of the employer, the hours of labor in the industry would, in the future, sometimes exceed the limits that had been set by the code. The automobile manufacturers had, however, become accustomed to a shorter work week than had been common in the 1920's, and they did not return to their earlier hours policy even though now free to do so. The average weekly hours of labor of wage earners in the motor vehicle industries were 37.1 in 1935, 38.5 in 1936, and 35.9 in 1937. When the U.A.W. gained recognition in 1937, it remembered the unhappy experience of the automobile workers with the averaging of hours under the code and insisted that union contracts stipulate a forty-hour week, with time-and-a-half for overtime and without deviation from this norm during the period of peak production. By the time the Fair Labor Standards Act went into effect, the forty-hour week had become the standard in the automobile industry, and, in part at least, this was a heritage of the Blue Eagle era.[2]

The demise of the N.I.R.A. did not cause the automobile industry to abandon either its plan to introduce new passenger-car models in the fall rather than in January or the remainder of its program to stabilize automobile employment. The A.M.A. announced on October 14, 1935, that the advance manufacture of subassemblies, interdepartmental transfers of employees, and better planning in individual plants had already resulted in three additional weeks of employment for the average automobile worker.[3] It was the fall introduction of models, however, that was viewed as the principal measure likely to lead to more regular employment, and the expectations in this regard were not to be disappointed. Domestic factory sales of automobiles during the period November 1935–January 1936 exceeded by approximately 500,000 units the total that might have been expected for these months on the basis of total factory sales for the model year 1935–36 as compared to the preceding two model years. The fifty million additional manhours of direct labor resulting from this increase, plus an estimated thirty million additional manhours during the last four months of 1935 resulting from the advance banking of subassemblies, were estimated to have provided full-time employment during the September–January period for ninety thousand persons in the automobile, bodies, and parts industries; to have narrowed the percentage change in the factory employment index in the combined industries from the lowest month to the highest month in the model year (September–August) from 103 in 1933–34 to 41 in

1935–36; and to have increased the number of male employees in auto and body plants enjoying steady jobs of forty-six or more weeks to 79 per cent of the average number employed during the model year 1935–36 as compared to 51 per cent of the average number employed in 1933–34 and 56 per cent in 1934–35.

The average annual earnings of the steadily employed male factory workers in A.M.A. plants were $1618 in 1935–36 as compared to $1454 in 1934–35 and $1317 in 1933–34, and the average individual annual earnings of all hourly rated automobile factory employees advanced to $1270 in the model year 1935–36 as compared to $1003 in 1934–35 and $744 in 1933–34. The annual layoff rate in the automobile and body industry was 51.46 in 1935 and 58.92 in 1936 as compared to 90.41 in 1934; the total annual separation rate declined from 117.30 in 1934 to 70.23 in 1935 and 77.86 in 1936; and the annual accession rate stood at 84.90 in 1935 and 88.92 in 1936 as compared to 144.23 in 1934. There was less labor turnover in the automobile and body industry in 1935 and in 1936 than in any year since 1930.[4]

The introduction of models in the fall, a legacy of the N.R.A. years, gave the automobile industry a production curve with two peaks, one in the fall and one in the spring, but both of these high points were below the spring production peak that had characterized the industry when models had been introduced in January. When C. Parker Anderson interviewed various automobile executives in 1946, he found universal agreement among them that the introduction of new models in the autumn had been "an important factor" in the regularization of both automobile sales and automobile employment.[5] At least partly as the result of prodding by the N.R.A., the industry had committed itself to a production schedule that proved to be of benefit both to the automobile workers and to the employers themselves.

The automobile industry's implementation of the fall new model program, authorized in the January 31, 1935, extension of the automobile code, and the continued observation by the automobile companies of most of the wage and hour standards of the N.R.A. code structure did not mean that the automobile manufacturers had in any way changed their views about the N.I.R.A. experiment. That this was so was clearly indicated in their reaction to a projected study of the industry by the N.R.A.'s Division of Review and to the efforts directed by George L. Berry, as the Coordinator for Industrial Cooperation, to attain some of the goals of the defunct N.I.R.A. by the voluntary action of business and labor in co-operation with the federal government.

An executive order of June 15, 1935, authorized a newly established N.R.A. Division of Review to prepare economic studies of the various trades and industries formerly subject to codes and to emphasize in these studies the code experience and the success or failure of the N.R.A. in dealing with the recognized problems of the industry. Various members of the new agency met with representatives of the A.M.A. in order to secure its co-operation in the projected study of the automobile industry; but no formal request for assistance was made until September 25, 1935, when L. C. Marshall, the director of the Division of Review, wrote to Alfred Reeves to assure the A.M.A. that a policy of co-operation would not involve the submission of an unlimited amount of data, that the approach of the division was "wholly objective and factual," and that it was "not investigating the Automobile Industry in order to uncover any alleged misdeeds or moral shortcomings."

Finding these assurances inadequate, Reeves replied for the A.M.A. that since the study was designed to determine the value of the automobile code and whether the problems of the industry should be treated by the "legislative or other governmental methods," it would be well for the division to know that the industry did not "believe that the problems before it were such as the Code could help to solve," that it had agreed to a code only because of its desire to co-operate with the President, and that "neither the industry nor its employees benefitted from the Code while it existed and neither have [*sic*] suffered any loss from its termination." The A.M.A. did, however, authorize David Friday to work with the automobile study unit in an advisory capacity and to determine in consultation with it the extent to which the industry could "usefully" assist the study group. Dr. Friday conferred with Division of Review personnel about the study and did comment on at least some portions of the final document during the course of its preparation, but apparently the degree of co-operation between the A.M.A. and the division was rather limited.[6]

The industry's wariness about submitting data to the Division of Review is explained not only by its retrospective and not altogether accurate opinion of the merits of the auto code but also in part by its belief that it had been unfairly dealt with in the Henderson Report. Thus, the first draft of Reeves' letter of reply to Marshall had stated that the Henderson Report, in the industry's opinion, was "so irresponsible in its statements and so unfair in its conclusions as to lead the industry to doubt the wisdom of a further attempt in the same direction." The statistical advisor for the automobile study informed his superior that the automobile industry had "a vast suspicion of the

NRA" because of the Henderson Report and that it wished to exercise "maximum supervision" over the material published in government reports because of the prominence attached to such documents and the faith that was placed in them.[7]

George L. Berry was appointed Coordinator for Industrial Co-operation by the President on September 26, 1935, and was instructed, among other things, to supervise conferences of industry, labor, and consumer representatives to consider "the best means of accelerating industrial recovery, eliminating unemployment, and maintaining business and labor standards." The A.M.A. was suspicious, to use the words of a report later submitted by Pyke Johnson, that the projected Berry conferences were "the first major move by the administration to sound out business sentiment on future industry-cooperation plans," and it assumed that since the administration was "skeptical about 'industry's ability to go it alone' . . . some type of government 'supervision' would be necessary." Consequently, when Berry wrote to the A.M.A. to enlist its co-operation, Reeves replied that the industry was "strongly opposed" to what Berry was proposing. "The variations in industry requirements," the A.M.A. general manager wrote, "do not permit of solution in mass meetings but rather require long and exhaustive study." The process of recovery was under way, and "to inject controversial and unsettling discussions into the picture would surely do more harm than good."

Berry replied that "further N.R.A. legislation" was not contemplated and that the conferences might even lead the participants to conclude that no action by Congress was required. He asked the industry to reconsider its position, but the A.M.A. once again responded in the negative. Although Berry informed the A.M.A. that the industry's refusal to participate was "to say the least inconceivable," the automobile manufacturers did not budge from their position: they refused, like so many other industrialists, to send representatives to the group conferences, and they had nothing to do with the ill-fated Council for Industrial Progress that grew out of the conferences.[8]

Although the automobile manufacturers claimed to be delighted that the N.I.R.A. was no longer the law of the land, it must have grieved them that the Schechter case also meant the demise of the President's settlement and of the A.L.B. At noon on June 15, 1935, the A.L.B. closed its Detroit office, and within a few weeks the National Labor Relations Act proclaimed majority rule rather than proportional representation to be the basis on which representatives were to be chosen for collective-bargaining purposes, and the N.L.R.B. replaced the A.L.B. as the government labor board with jurisdiction over the automobile manufacturing industry. Most of the automobile manufacturers decided that they simply would not comply with the new statute unless and until the Supreme Court upheld its constitutionality. "Majority rule," one of the automobile executives stated, "will not be recognized. Management will continue to bargain with individuals or representatives of all groups pending ultimate court determination." [9]

The drift of legislative policy in the area of labor relations was also disturbing to the erstwhile A.L.B. chairman, Leo Wolman. "If there was ever a law that was unenforceable," he declared in July, "it is the majority rule law. . . ." The purpose of the measure was to strengthen unionism, but the only kind of unionism that would survive was that which "grows on its own merit. This kind won't last." Wolman was also dubious about the wisdom of establishing a single labor-relations board for all of American industry. Its "brief experience," the A.L.B. declared in its final report, "offers clear evidence of the opportunity for usefulness of a government agency limited in its jurisdiction to a single industry and, therefore, close enough to the details of the problem under which it is empowered to deal." [10]

This was a judgment from which the U.A.W. violently dissented. The unionists felt that the A.L.B. had "materially weakened the union position" and that "The history of the board," to use the words of labor reporter Joe Brown, was "an almost unbroken record of defeats for the auto workers and the various auto unions and of cringing subservience to the auto manufacturers." As Ed Hall later observed, however, the A.F. of L. charges against the board "were made out of frustration, were made out of confusion and misunderstandings." [11] The A.L.B., to be sure, did not make the organizing task of the Federation in the automobile industry any easier, and there was substance to some of its criticisms of the board, but it was in error in assigning its lack of success in the industry to the A.L.B. The A.F. of L.'s difficulties were of a more fundamental nature, and it would have been in trouble even if a board more to its liking had been established. It was simply less painful for the Federation to attribute its failure to organize the automobile workers to the machinations of the A.L.B. than to wonder whether it was the policies of the A.F. of L. that were really to blame.

If the A.L.B. did not produce the "hell of a big change" in employer-employee relations that Wolman thought it had,[12] it did nevertheless leave its mark on the automobile industry. It secured the return to employment of several hundred workers who but for its intervention might have remained without work. It introduced the concept of job tenure by rule in the automobile industry and in so doing largely determined the order of layoff and rehiring in the industry until union contracts modified but, as we have seen, did not completely scrap the procedures that the board had established. Byrd was exaggerating when he said of the A.L.B. that "we got the foundation laid for real collective bargaining in the automotive industry," [13] but it is nevertheless true that the discussion of the terms of employment in the meetings of the A.L.B. bargaining agencies with the management represented a change from pre-N.I.R.A. days, although it did not differ essentially from the sort of negotiations that had previously taken place between the company unions and the automobile employers. It might also be recalled that the A.I.W.A. developed out of one of the A.L.B.'s bargaining agencies and that its membership at the time the N.I.R.A was declared unconstitutional greatly exceeded the combined membership of all of the U.A.W. federal labor unions in Michigan.

One of the President's chief purposes in establishing the A.L.B. was to avoid labor strife in the automobile industry, and some observers have given it the major credit for keeping the industry "relatively peaceful" from the time of the settlement to the end of the N.I.R.A.[14] This, however, is a conclusion that is difficult to support. The A.L.B. proposals in April 1934 for the settlement of the Nash and Seaman Body strikes and the Motor Products strike were rejected by the strikers; the board failed to avert strikes in various Fisher Body plants in April and May 1934 and in the Hupp and White Motor plants in April and May 1935; and, in a sense, it was the cause of the great Toledo Chevrolet strike. If there were not more strikes in the automobile manufacturing industry during the period that the A.L.B. presided over its industrial relations, it was because of policies pursued by the A.F. of L. rather than because of the restraining influence exerted by the board.

II

Three weeks after the A.L.B. submitted its final report, delegates from sixty-five U.A.W. federal labor unions gathered in Detroit for the constitutional convention of the International Union, United Automobile Workers of America, the first international to be launched by the A.F. of L. in one of the mass-production industries.[15] Francis Dillon informed the delegates that the credentials sent out from his office revealed that the dues-paying membership of the 148 U.A.W. locals was thirty-five thousand, but the A.F. of L.'s own figures indicate that the paid-up membership at the time was slightly less than twenty-six thousand.[16]

The two principal issues debated on the convention floor were the jurisdiction of the new union and the right of the delegates to choose their own officers. President Green stated in his opening address to the convention that the charter for the new union provided for "a broad advanced policy of organization of the production workers" but that the jurisdictional authority of other organizations, particularly over skilled mechanics in tool and die shops, would have to be respected.[17] The committee on constitution and laws, chaired by George Lehman, an A.F. of L. regular, called for acceptance of the charter, and Dillon informed the delegates that the decision of the Executive Council on this matter was binding on the convention; but several of the delegates expressed their belief that the authorized jurisdiction was altogether inadequate and that the new international should be permitted to organize all workers "in or around automobile or parts plants." Mortimer alleged that "the craft form of organization fits into the automobile industry like a square peg in a round hole," and Ed Hall warned, "I don't care what policy is laid down by the AFL executive council. Our members are going to remain in our local, so we favor drawing the jurisdiction clause very loosely."

The incomplete official convention proceedings state that the report of the committee on constitution and laws was approved "with but few dissenting votes," but the true feeling of the delegates on the jurisdictional issue was revealed in the unanimous vote then accorded a resolution previously introduced by Forrest Woods, the chairman of the resolutions committee, but which had been tabled pending the report of the Lehman committee. The Woods resolution stated that if the jurisdictional limitations imposed by the charter were allowed to stand, it would mean the "gradual disintegration" of the auto locals. It complained that the internationals awarded jurisdiction over some of the auto workers "have in the past made no considerable effort to organize these workers, but have instead, waited until . . . [they] were organized into Federal Labor Unions before manifesting any interest in . . . [them]." In accordance with the procedure that Woods had recommended before the convention, the resolution called for the acceptance of the charter but instructed the officers of the new international to protest the jurisdictional award to the president of the A.F. of L. and, if necessary, to the next A.F. of L. convention, and if satisfaction were not obtained "to formulate such plans and take such action as in their opinion may seem advisable."

The issue of the choice of officers for the new union appears to have produced even more discord in the convention than the jurisdictional limitations imposed by the charter. It will be recalled that the A.F. of L. Executive Council, in accordance with the decision of the San Francisco convention, had stipulated that for a temporary period to be determined by the Executive Council, the officers of the new international were to be designated by the president of the A.F. of L. In the weeks preceding the convention, some of the more conservative National Council members, dubious about the ability of the projected international to proceed "without further guidance and financial aid" from the A.F. of L. and ignoring the strong opposition to Dillon among the "progressives" in the U.A.W., indicated their belief that Green should appoint the A.F. of L.'s national representative in the automobile industry as the international's first president. Homer Martin, who generally told Dillon what he liked to hear, had written him on July 9 that this was the "attitude of most of the locals which I have contacted or know anything about, and it seems to me to be the sensible solution of the situation." The call to the August 26 convention had, however, stated that a constitution would be adopted and that "officers will be *elected* and installed." [18]

The issue came to a head on the first day of the convention when the resolutions committee moved that Green appoint Dillon as president and that the A.F. of L. pay his salary and expenses but that the remaining officers be elected by the delegates and their salaries paid by the international. Carl Shipley rose immediately to move that all the officers be nominated and elected from the floor and that they all be members of the U.A.W., which would have removed Dillon from consideration. Dillon thereupon turned the gavel over to Green, who ruled Shipley's motion out of order and stated that he could not alter the procedure laid down by the Executive Council, that Dillon would be at the head of the new organization, but that the delegates would be given the widest authority to elect the other officers and the members of the union's executive board. The motion of the resolutions committee was then put to a vote, but despite the remarks by Green it was defeated by a margin of 164.2 to 112.8. Included in the majority were the delegates from the Studebaker and Bendix locals of South Bend, the White Motor local of Cleveland, the Kenosha Nash local, the Toledo local, and the Norwood local, six of the seven largest U.A.W. locals. Only the Seaman Body local, the Janesville Fisher Body local, and the Racine Nash local, among the stronger federal labor unions, gave their support to Dillon.

During the next day of the convention Green met with some of the delegates in an effort to break the impasse. Some of the unionists present later reported the A.F. of L. president as having said that he would allow the delegates to nominate and elect all of the organization's officers and that Dillon would remain on the Federation's payroll only as an advisor to the international.[19] If this is an accurate account of what Green had said, he soon changed his mind, possibly because the opponents of Dillon had no agreed-upon candidate of their own to support, or possibly because of Dillon's hostility to the idea. Green reported to the convention on the twenty-ninth that he had hoped to find some way for the delegates to select the union's officers and then for him to designate them to serve for the required probationary period; but, he declared, he had concluded after discussing the matter with delegates whose judgment he respected that there was too much division of opinion in the convention to proceed along these lines and that only after the probationary period was ended would the union "be able to stand the shock" of division in its ranks. He had therefore decided to follow the instructions of the Executive Council literally and to appoint all the officers. He selected Dillon to serve as temporary president, Martin as vice-president, Hall as secretary-treasurer, and the remaining members of the National Council as members, along with the other three, of the union's General Executive Board.[20] There was no need for the convention to approve or disapprove his choices, Green declared, since he was simply carrying out the decision of the Executive Council.

Green's selection of all of the union's officers seems to have stunned the convention. Delegate Tom Johnson of the small Ford local called the action an "outrage," and Ellsworth Kramer, the president of the Toledo local, seconded by Robert Travis of the same union, moved that the convention rescind its earlier decision to accept the charter. Dillon, however, ruled this motion out of order, stating that the action taken was binding on the convention and that "if there be those here who cannot conform to the terms and provisions of this document, then they must leave." The indignant delegates then resolved "by what sounded like virtually a unanimous vote" to select a committee of seven to protest to the A.F. of L. Executive Council and, if necessary, to the next A.F. of L. convention Green's designation of all the officers of the new union and also, as it turned out, the jurisdictional limitations imposed by the charter. The seven delegates selected by the convention for this task included such prominent critics of the A.F. of L.'s policies in the industry as Wyndham Mortimer, Carl Shipley, George Addes, and Tom Johnson.[21]

The committee of seven, after being rebuffed by the A.F. of L. Executive Council—Mortimer later claimed that David Dubinsky and William Hutcheson wanted to know how many communists there were in the group [22]—carried its protest to the A.F. of L. convention in Atlantic City. The committee submitted a resolution requesting the convention to grant the U.A.W. exclusive jurisdiction over all workers in the automobile industry. The resolution made note of the failure of the craft unionists to organize the industry and contrasted with this failure the alleged success of many of the federal labor unions in organizing the automobile workers into "one mass Union." Now, however, the resolution complained, the U.A.W. federal labor unions were "being confounded, confused and all but torn apart because some old line Union would like to kill the fatted calf, made possible through the mass or industrial form of organization."

When the convention's committee on resolutions recommended nonconcurrence with this resolution, Carl Shipley offered a substitute but similar resolution requesting that the U.A.W. be granted "complete jurisdiction . . . over all employes in or around plants engaged in the manufacture of automobile parts and the assembling of such parts into completed automobiles." This motion was defended by Shipley, Mortimer, and Frank Martel, but it was sharply attacked by craft-union leaders. William Britton, the president and secretary-treasurer of the Metal Polishers International Union, who claimed that his union had organized 2462 of the thirty-one hundred to thirty-two hundred metal polishers, buffers, and platers in Detroit, protested that the approval of the resolution would "wipe us out of existence." Wharton of the I.A.M. noted with alarm that the passage of the resolution would lead to "practically one big union in the metal industry." His organization wished to aid the automobile workers, but it should not be asked "to eliminate" itself from the industry to the extent demanded by the resolution. Sidney Hillman, however, wondered what harm would befall the craft unions were they to relinquish jurisdiction over workers whom they would not organize anyhow and suggested that the matter be disposed of by the declaration of a three-year moratorium on jurisdictional conflicts in the industry. The craft unionists, who had already voted down a minority report emanating from the committee on resolutions that sought "to provide for the organization of workers in mass production and other industries upon industrial and plant lines, regardless of claims based upon the question of jurisdiction," were in no mood for compromise, however, and they defeated Shipley's substitute resolution by a vote of 104 to 125.

The committee of seven also asked the convention to approve a resolution that endorsed the calling of a special convention of the U.A.W. at "the earliest possible moment" and no later than March 1,

1936, so that the auto workers could elect their own officers. The resolution charged that Green's appointment of the officers of the new international "threatens the very life of our union" and alleged that U.A.W. members lacked confidence in the members of General Executive Board, which was simply the old National Council, because of their "inefficiency" and their "sorry record." The U.A.W. delegation was no more successful in gaining the support of the A.F. of L. convention on this issue, however, than on the jurisdictional question. Its resolution was referred to the Executive Council, which decided that no further action was necessary since both the Executive Council and the convention had "acted upon this matter." [23] Decisions taken at the Atlantic City convention of the A.F. of L. thus not only led to the formal establishment soon thereafter of the Committee for Industrial Organization but also made it virtually certain that the U.A.W. would eventually cast its lot with this new rival of the A.F. of L.

Although the appointment by Green of the U.A.W. officers seems to have antagonized a preponderant number of the delegates at the U.A.W. constitutional convention, Homer Martin informed the A.F. of L. president on September 4 that what he had done would "work out much better than any of us dreamed" and that he (Martin) would "work with Brother Dillon in every way possible." A month later the St. Louis local was similarly assured by Martin that Dillon was "the man for the job." [24] This was an opinion that does not seem to have been shared by very many automobile unionists, and it was one which Martin, who was inclined to bend with the wind, was soon to abandon himself.

Obviously disgruntled by the reluctance of the majority of the delegates at the Detroit convention to accept him as their leader, Dillon pursued a course of action during the months after the convention that lost him whatever support he might still have enjoyed among the automobile workers. After meeting briefly with the General Executive Board members immediately after the close of the Detroit convention, he did not call the group together again until just before the South Bend meeting in April 1936. Ostensibly because he had been instructed by Green "to economize in every possible way" in the establishment of the headquarters of the international, he temporarily discontinued the employment of Board members in organizing work and held up the reimbursement of the members of the committee of seven for the expenses that they had incurred in carrying the protests of the constitutional-convention delegates to the Executive Council and the A.F. of L. convention. To members of the Board and to "progressives" in the international, these actions of

Dillon undoubtedly appeared to have been motivated by considerations other than the need for economy.[25]

Of even greater importance in serving to widen the breach between the U.A.W.'s first president and an increasing number of its members were the tactics pursued by Dillon with regard to the granting of a charter to Toledo's Federal Labor Union No. 18384 and the participation of the U.A.W. in a strike at the Motor Products plant in Detroit that began on November 15, 1935. When the Toledo local applied for its charter from the new international, Dillon informed George Addes that it was the policy of the international to charter unions for individual plants but that he would seek authority from the General Executive Board to provide a single charter for Toledo for a probationary period, with the understanding that the officers of the local during the interim would educate the membership as to the advisability of accepting separate charters for each of the city's auto plants. Pointing to its past successes as a composite union, the Toledo local rejected this proposal as "very dangerous to our local," but Dillon, in what looked like an effort to gain revenge on an old enemy, adamantly refused to grant the Toledo auto workers a single charter.[26]

The strike against the Motor Products plant was called by Richard Frankensteen's A.I.W.A. following a wage dispute with the management. When the six hundred or so A.I.W.A. members in the plant walked out on November 15, the M.E.S.A., which had organized the firm's 153 tool and die makers and had participated in the prestrike negotiations, pulled its members from the plant in sympathy. A sizable number of the Motor Products workers belonged to the U.A.W. and the Metal Polishers International Union, and they too were forced from the plant the next day when the management decided to cease production.

A few days after the work stoppage began Matthew Smith of the M.E.S.A. invited the U.A.W. to join in the conduct of the strike, but Dillon replied that the A.F. of L. could not assume responsibility for a strike about which it had not previously been consulted. He attributed the lack of unity about which Smith complained to dual unions that had always been critical of the A.F. of L. and described the walkout as "the most ill-advised and unpopular strike ever called in Detroit." He insisted that the Motor Products management was willing to negotiate with its workers but did not know which of the several unions in the plant should be treated as their spokesman, and he therefore proposed a return to work pending an N.L.R.B. election. He summoned the strikers to vote on this issue, but the balloting was confined to U.A.W. members, who agreed to return to work on the terms Dillon had suggested. They were escorted into the plant on November 25 by the local union's shop committee and by the police, and within a few days the company claimed that thirty-one hundred men were at work in the plant as compared to an employment total of thirty-five hundred before the strike began.

When it became apparent after the U.A.W. returned to work that the Motor Products management, despite Dillon's previous assurances to the contrary, was anxious to "avoid" all unions rather than to recognize and deal with one, the U.A.W. local on December 8 voted to strike but left the timing of the walkout to the president of the local. A brief sitdown appears to have been staged in the plant on December 18, but Dillon, after conferring with the management, announced the U.A.W. withdrawal from the strike because it had "no possible chance of success." The M.E.S.A. and the A.I.W.A., however, continued the strike—the M.E.S.A. did not admit defeat until May 27, 1936—and denounced Dillon as a "Judas" and a strikebreaker.[27]

Opponents of Dillon within the U.A.W. were fearful that his tactics in the Motor Products strike would further weaken the U.A.W. position in Detroit and would make it impossible for the so-called independent unions, the A.I.W.A., the M.E.S.A., and the A.A.W.A., to merge with the U.A.W. once its probationary period came to an end. The independents, as a matter of fact, were already planning a merger of their own and were appealing to the U.A.W. rank and file to choose "between a delapidated [sic], reactionary group asking you to scab on your co-workers and ... a new mobile industrial organization, democratically controlled."[28] To many in the U.A.W., therefore, support of the Motor Products strike appeared to be of crucial importance to the future success of the international and to its very existence in the Detroit area.[29]

In the meantime President Dillon and Vice-President Martin were coming to a parting of the ways. Martin wrote Green on November 18 that Dillon had called him in the previous week and told him "in very strong language" that he was going to resign his position and quit the international. If Dillon really meant this, Martin observed, he should resign before the production season was "too far gone." Martin assured Green that he did not covet Dillon's position. A few days later Martin wrote to one of the A.F. of L. organizers that he had never been able to speak to Dillon "confidentially" and that Dillon had been "very cool" toward him since the convention. The feeling against Dillon was "very strong" among the great majority of the auto workers, Martin now discovered, and this antagonism had become "even more marked" since the convention.

In the latter part of November Martin journeyed to Cleveland and there met with local union leaders such as Mortimer who headed up the opposition to Dillon. He became increasingly aware of the desire of the auto workers for a full-fledged industrial union and of their interest in the C.I.O. "I find," he wrote, "that every where the Auto Workers are of the same opinion, they all want Lewis and will come out to hear him." While in Cleveland, Martin participated in the planning of a "giant" mass meeting at which John L. Lewis was to be the chief speaker. The meeting, which took place on January 19, 1936, "marked the formal entry of the CIO into the auto field." [30]

Secretary-Treasurer Ed Hall, like Martin, had also become disenchanted with Dillon. He appeared in South Bend in January 1936 and told the Studebaker workers, according to one account, what "a dirty rat" Dillon was. The Wisconsin delegates, he declared, were conscious of the mistake they had made in supporting Dillon at the constitutional convention and would "go down the line with the progressive groups 100%." Forrest Woods wrote Martin that all the members of the General Executive Board now realized that they had erred in opposing the majority at the constitutional convention on the issue of the union's presidency. [31]

When the A.F. of L. Executive Council met in its January 1936 session, Dillon advised that the election of new U.A.W. officers should be deferred at least until August, but the Executive Council, urged on by Martin, Hall, and Mortimer, who were also present, decided that the U.A.W.'s probationary period should come to an end no later than April 30. The craft-controlled Executive Council, however, did not alter its stand on the jurisdictional issue; on the contrary, it ordered the U.A.W. to withdraw the charters it had issued to forty-three different parts locals, and the members of these locals were instructed to join the craft unions that had jurisdiction over them. [32]

Seemingly emboldened by the decision of the Executive Council to bring the probationary period to an end in the near future and by the opposition to Dillon of several members of the General Executive Board, Vice-President Martin and Secretary-Treasurer Hall sought to oust Dillon from office even before the convention, scheduled to meet in South Bend on April 27, had an opportunity to elect a new slate of officers. They "assumed complete charge of the [Detroit] office" on February 9, and three days later Martin dramatically informed Delmond Garst of the St. Louis local that "Dillon is out! . . . We are in charge and propose to stay in complete charge until the convention." [33]

Proceeding as though the executive authority of the union were now vested in them, Martin and Hall quickly dispatched a charter to the Toledo local (Dillon, by the time they acted, had already granted a charter to the Toledo Chevrolet workers as Local 12, and so the charter presented by Martin and Hall applied only to the remainder of the old Federal Labor Union No. 18384, now reconstituted as Local 14); asked Hillman and Dubinsky for aid in organizing the Detroit auto workers; and decided to put "everything we have got" into the continuing Motor Products strike. Martin regarded the strike as "by far the most important issue in this territory" and thought that the U.A.W. could "make a lasting impression" on Detroit if it came to the aid of the strikers. He charged Dillon with having "completely bungled the job" and described the "situation" in Detroit as "the most pitiful I have ever seen." [34]

Despite Martin's statement that he was "out," Dillon refused to surrender his presidency. He denounced Hall and Martin as "low and infamous men," defended his action in the Motor Products strike, and announced that the charter issued to the Toledo local "isn't worth the paper it is written on so far as its legal status is concerned." Dillon was able to keep his office until the South Bend convention, but Martin, who was increasingly gaining the support of the auto workers "because he was what you might call an orator and he could hold the attention of any crowd that he talked to and he had a good education," had succeeded in establishing his independence of the unfortunate Dillon and had become the most popular figure in the U.A.W.[35] The "Caucus of Progressive auto unionists," as Dillon's organized opposition had come to identify itself, had been backing Wyndham Mortimer for the U.A.W. presidency, but Mortimer withdrew from the race shortly before the convention, and the progressives threw their support to Martin.[36]

In the eyes of the delegates who gathered in South Bend on April 27 for the opening of the second U.A.W. convention, "the prime purpose" of the meeting, to quote the managing editor of the Federated Press, "was to run Frank Dillon out of the convention and keep him out, and all others like him—and this was done with great relish." The left-wing group, in which Mortimer and Addes were the chief figures and which could count on the support of three of the four largest locals represented in the convention (Toledo Local 12, White Motor, Seaman Body), was firmly in control of the meeting. Indicative of the character of things to come was the obvious sympathy of the delegates for the C.I.O. and for industrial unionism and the presence in the convention of a large variety of ideological groups (Adolph Germer, who was there, thought at one point that the Socialists and communists had "taken over the convention"). Also present at the meeting were Richard Frankensteen of the A.I.W.A., Arthur Greer of the A.A.W.A., and John Anderson, the Detroit district representative of the M.E.S.A., and the remarks that they addressed to the delegates made it appear likely that the independents would soon cast their lot with the U.A.W.

After William Green informed the convention that the U.A.W.'s probationary period had terminated as of that moment, the delegates proceeded to elect their officers. Homer Martin was selected president; Wyndham Mortimer, first vice-president; Ed Hall, second vice-president; Walter N. Wells, third vice-president; George Addes, secretary-treasurer; and Delmond Garst, F. J. Michel, Lloyd T. Jones, Fred Pieper, Jack Kennedy, John Soltis, Lester Washburn, Walter Reuther, Willis Marrer, Frank Tucci, and Russell Merrill, members of the executive board.[37]   Most of the officers and board members were under thirty-five—Pieper and Reuther were under thirty—and every one of them had worked in an automobile plant, which reflected the long-standing antagonism of the auto workers to organizers and union officials without experience in the industry.

Virtually all of the international's officers had originally attracted the attention of the organized auto workers because of the role they had played in one of the U.A.W. federal labor unions during the N.R.A. period. Martin had been the president of the Kansas City local; Ed Hall, a welder by trade, had helped form the Seaman Body local; Mortimer was the president of the White Motor local and also of the Cleveland Auto Council; Wells had helped to organize the Detroit Gear local, which had the largest paid-up membership of any of the Detroit U.A.W. locals; Addes, who had worked as a metal finisher in the Willys-Overland plant, was the financial secretary of Local 12 of Toledo; Garst was the general executive secretary of the St. Louis local and had participated in the strike of April 1934; Michel had been recording secretary of the Racine Nash local and had been a leader in its 1934 strike; Jones had been active in the Briggs and Murray Body strikes of 1933 and the Motor Products strike of 1935; Pieper had been the leading figure in the Atlanta Chevrolet and Fisher Body local; Kennedy, a former member of the United Brotherhood of Carpenters and Joiners, had been active from the start in the Chrysler local and had become its president; Soltis, a one-time U.M.W. member, had been president of the Cleveland Hupp local and was the first vice-president of the Cleveland Auto Council; Lester Washburn had been a member of the Reo local since September 1933 and was serving as its recording secretary; Merrill, who contested the vice-presidency with Mortimer, had been active in the strong Studebaker local and had become its president; Tucci was the president of the North Tarrytown Chevrolet and Fisher Body local; and Willis Marrer had been recording secretary and then had been elected president of the militant Norwood local. The member of the board who was destined to play the leading role in the later history of the U.A.W., the twenty-eight year old Walter Reuther, had been absent from the United States during most of the time the N.I.R.A. had been in effect and had only recently begun to attract the attention of the auto workers.[38]

In May 1936, shortly after the close of the South Bend convention, both the A.I.W.A. and the A.A.W.A. joined the auto international. The M.E.S.A. National Administrative Committee declined an invitation to unite with the U.A.W. on the grounds that the latter's charter did not give it jurisdiction over skilled workers, but three Detroit locals of the M.E.S.A., which contained the bulk of the organization's communists, ignored the M.E.S.A. leadership and sought U.A.W. charters.[39] On July 2, 1936, the U.A.W. affiliated with the C.I.O., and it was soon to undertake the militant strike action that was to make it a far more important force in the automobile industry than it had ever been during the N.I.R.A. years.

The establishment of the U.A.W. as a full-fledged international union officered entirely by elected officials brought to a close a chapter in the labor history of the automobile industry that had begun with the enactment of the N.I.R.A. and the drafting of the automobile code. The experience of the industry under the Blue Eagle was a relatively brief one, but it is of significance not only for what it reveals of the nature of the N.I.R.A. and of the so-called first New Deal but also for its long-range consequences for the industry itself.

Some months after the Schechter decision, John Frey, the president of the A.F. of L.'s Metal Trades Department, commented that "Labor did have a voice in the NRA, but business had a greater voice and much more control of the situation." [40] What was true of the N.I.R.A. experience in general was true of the automobile code in particular, for the history of this code disclosed in exaggerated fashion that despite the talk of the partnership of government, industry, and labor in the implementation of the N.I.R.A., organized labor, where it did not have the power to challenge organized industry, was at best a limited partner. In their contests with the automobile manufacturers, the weakly organized auto workers almost always came out second best. Of all the codes, only the automobile code contained a merit clause, and only in the automobile industry was the formula of proportional representation applied to the choice of employee representatives for collective-bargaining purposes. The A.F. of L. failed to secure a public hearing on the auto code on any of the four occasions on which its life was extended, and such changes as were made in the code after its adoption were either opposed by the U.A.W. or did not go far enough to satisfy it. A provision for the averaging of hours was permitted to remain in the auto code even after the practice became contrary to N.R.A. policy; and in contrast to many other codes, an overtime provision was not added to the automobile code until January 31, 1935, and, even then, it applied to less than 20 per cent of the industry's employees. It is little wonder that a contemporary observer described the automobile code as "as rotten an egg as was ever hatched by the Blue Eagle" and that a U.A.W. president at a later time referred to it as "the No. 1 scandal . . . of the N.R.A." from the point of view of organized labor.[41]

Because the automobile manufacturing industry was regarded as the pacesetter of the economy, the automobile code "claimed the special solicitude of the N.R.A. and the President." [42]   The result was that the crucial decisions regarding the character of the code were made at the highest levels of the N.R.A. or by the President himself. As George Myrick, Jr., noted in October 1934, after having discussed a proposed change in the code with Barton W. Murray, the administrator of the N.R.A. division to which the code was assigned, "I gather that in the past as well as the present the fighting has been carried on at higher altitudes and he has only caught the echo of the guns." [43] No code was the object of so much Presidential attention as the automobile code, and it is an interesting commentary on the character not only of the N.R.A. but of the first New Deal itself that from the drafting of the automobile code until its expiration date, the President, at the moments of greatest crisis in the relations between automobile management and automobile labor, had leaned in the direction of management.

Although organized labor was inclined to dismiss the provisions of the automobile code as meaningless and to minimize the impact of the N.I.R.A. on the behavior of the automobile manufacturers, the N.I.R.A. and the automobile code had important long-range consequences for the automobile manufacturing industry. As we have seen, the N.I.R.A. was at least in part responsible for substantial increases in the hourly wages of automobile workers and the substitution in many automobile plants of a straight hourly rate for the complicated methods of wage payment then commonly employed in the industry. Because of the code the industry was unable to work the bulk of its employees as many hours per week during periods of peak production as it had in the years before 1933, and the industry did not return to its previous hours policy even after the code lapsed. The code also led to greater concern in the industry with the problem of irregular employment and speeded up the industry's decision to introduce new car models in the fall rather than shortly after the first of the year.

In the long run, the N.I.R.A. had its most important impact on the automobile industry in the area of labor organization. "I do not think there was any real urge for unionism," a former president of the Cleveland Fisher Body local later noted, "until the law [N.I.R.A.] made it possible or made it look like it was going to be possible to have a union without a lot of discharges and so forth." Green also conceded that the U.A.W. federal labor unions were established "under the inspiration of the National Recovery Act and as a result of it," [44] and the same might be said of the M.E.S.A., the A.A.W.A., and the A.I.W.A. Management in the industry, which had previously paid little attention to the subject of labor relations and had tended to be unaware of employee grievances, now had to develop a labor-relations policy, to designate particular officials or to establish industrial-relations departments to implement that policy, and to provide special training for foremen to acquaint them with their responsibilities in this area.[45]

The A.F. of L. and the independent unions, as it turned out, failed to organize a significant proportion of the automobile workers, and to many of the industry's employees Section 7(a) and the automobile code had fallen "far short of what they promised"; but to the employee who saw them "not in the light of what might have been, but against the darker background of what was," the changes they produced in employer-employee relations and the opportunity for the airing of employee grievances that they provided were, to quote one union official, "almost more than I ever expected to see happen in my lifetime." [46] The N.I.R.A. was declared unconstitutional on May 27, 1935, but industrial relations in the automobile manufacturing industry were never again to return to the conditions that had prevailed before June 16, 1933.

As Arthur Schlesinger, Jr., has pointed out, the "dismissal of the NRA has become an historian's and economist's cliché." [47] Relatively little scholarly attention has been devoted to the subject since the Schechter case, and the bulging archives of the agency have been largely neglected. It is not easy to generalize about the N.I.R.A. since its history is so much a history of individual codes rather than of policy formulated at the top and then uniformly applied, but if the experience of the automobile manufacturing industry is typical, the statute had a more enduring impact on the nation's industries and particularly on employer-employee relations than has generally been recognized. The records for a study of other codes are available in embarrassing abundance, and only when the full ramifications of the major codes have been explored will it be possible to render a more definitive judgment regarding the real significance of the National Industrial Recovery Act.

NOTES

NOTES TO CHAPTER I

¹ Ralph C. Epstein, *The Automobile Industry. Its Economic and Commercial Development* (Chicago, 1928), p. 3; Bureau of the Census, *Fifteenth Census of the United States, Manufactures: 1929*, II (Washington, 1933), 1220–21, 1224, 1228; Automobile Manufacturers Association (A.M.A.), *Automobile Facts and Figures, 1959–60*, pp. 3, 18. The automobile manufacturing industry as codified under the National Industrial Recovery Act is not synonymous with either branch of the motor vehicle industry as defined through 1937 by the Bureau of the Census and the Bureau of Labor Statistics since it included not only the manufacturers and assemblers of motor vehicles but also body manufacturers like Seaman and Fisher and such parts manufacturers as AC Spark Plug.

² Rae, *American Automobile Manufacturers: The First Forty Years* (Philadelphia, 1959), pp. 45–47; Epstein, *Automobile Industry*, pp. 39–40; Donald A. Moore, "The Automobile Industry," in Walter Adams, ed., *The Structure of American Industry* (Revised ed.; New York, 1954), pp. 278–80; C. O. Skinner to W. W. Rose, Oct. 31, 1934, Box 688, Records of the National Recovery Administration, National Archives, Washington, D.C. (henceforth, records in this group will be cited as N.R.A.).

³ Henry Ford, in his famous advertisement announcing the Model T, had declared, "I will build a motor car for the great multitude." Roger Burlingame, *Henry Ford* (Signet Key Book; New York, 1956), p. 48.

⁴ Epstein, *Automobile Industry*, pp. 102–17; Rae, *Automobile Manufacturers*, pp. 115, 153. The ratio of used cars sold to new cars sold increased from 58.7 per cent in 1919 to 128.6 per cent in 1929. The ratio of estimated annual sales of vehicles (new and old) to total registrations was 43.37 in 1919 and 38.36 in 1929. Theodore H. Smith, *The Marketing of Used Automobiles* (Columbus, Ohio, 1941), pp. 16–18.

⁵ Allan Nevins and Frank Ernest Hill, *Ford. The Times, the Man, the Company* (New York, 1954), pp. 237–38 (henceforth cited as *Ford*, Vol. I); Federal Trade Commission (F.T.C.), *Report on Motor Vehicle Industry*, 76 Cong., 1 Sess., *House Document No. 468* (Washington, 1939), p. 657. Although the company was originally capitalized at $150,000, only $100,000 in stock was actually issued. Nevins and Hill, *Ford*, I, 237n.

⁶ The cheapest Model T sold for $850 in 1908. In 1926 the price reached the all-time low figure of $290 for a stripped model which did not include a self-starter or demountable rims. Nevins and Hill, *Ford*, I, 646; Burlingame, *Ford*, p. 86.

⁷ Burlingame, *Ford*, pp. 43–52, 81–88; Nevins and Hill, *Ford*, I, 352–53,

387–414, 447–80; Nevins and Hill, *Ford. Expansion and Challenge, 1915–1933* (New York, 1957), pp. 379–478 (henceforth cited as *Ford,* Vol. II); Mark Adams, "The Automobile—A Luxury Becomes a Necessity," in Walton Hamilton *et al., Price and Price Policies* (New York, 1938), p. 42; Clair Wilcox, *Competition and Monopoly in American Industry,* Temporary National Economic Committee, *Monograph No. 21* (Washington, 1940), p. 195. The Ford Motor Co. was responsible for 56.2 per cent of the new car output or registrations in 1914; 35.2 per cent in 1926; 15.2 per cent in 1927; and 33.9 per cent in 1929. Simon N. Whitney, *Antitrust Policies: American Experience in Twenty Industries* (New York, 1958), I, 468.

⁸ Rae, *Automobile Manufacturers,* pp. 86–89, 110–12, 137–39; Whitney, *Antitrust Policies,* I, 470; E. D. Kennedy, *The Automobile Industry* (New York, 1941), pp. 48–58, 97–101, 108–10.

⁹ G.M. was responsible for 25 per cent of the new car output or registrations in 1909; 21.7 per cent in 1910; 42.5 per cent in 1927; 41.3 per cent in 1928; and 43.3 per cent in 1931. Whitney, *Antitrust Policies,* I, 468.

¹⁰ Rae, *Automobile Manufacturers,* pp. 143–45, 162–65; Whitney, *Antitrust Policies,* I, 470; National Recovery Administration, Research and Planning Division, Preliminary Report on Study of Regularization of Employment and Improvement of Labor Conditions in the Automobile Industry, Jan. 23, 1935, Appendix A, Exhibit 1 (henceforth cited as Henderson Report).

¹¹ Although it has been argued that there is a greater opportunity for smaller concerns in the manufacture of trucks than in the manufacture of passenger cars because the variety of demand for heavy trucks limits the degree to which mass production methods can be applied to their fabrication, the Big Three in 1929 accounted for a larger share of new truck registrations (81 per cent) than of new car registrations (75.8). Rae, *Automobile Manufacturers,* p. 99; Whitney, *Antitrust Policies,* I, 471; Henderson Report, Appendix A, Exhibits 2 and 3. Cf. Chapter IV, n. 118.

¹² Harold G. Vatter, "The Closure of Entry in the American Automobile Industry," *Oxford Economic Papers,* N.S., IV (Oct., 1952), 213–34; Epstein, *Automobile Industry,* pp. 39–40, 164; Lawrence H. Seltzer, *A Financial History of the Automobile Industry* (Boston, 1928), pp. 10–11, 19; Moore, "Automobile Industry," pp. 278–80, 294–99; Whitney, *Antitrust Policies,* I, 468, 472; Henderson Report, Appendix A, Exhibit 2.

¹³ Bureau of the Census, *Fifteenth Census, Manufactures: 1929,* II, 1220, 1223–24, 1228–29; *ibid.,* III (Washington, 1933), 258; Rae, *Automobile Manufacturers,* pp. 58–60; Moore, "Automobile Industry," p. 293.

¹⁴ Edward J. Stevens, "A Quarter of a Century of Progress in Employment Stabilization in the Automobile Industry" (1947), pp. 3–6, 17, Bureau of Industrial Relations Library, University of Michigan; Whitney, *Antitrust Policies,* I, 431–32.

¹⁵ A.M.A., *Stabilization of Employment in the Automobile Industry* (Feb. 25, 1936), pp. 8–10; National Automobile Chamber of Commerce (N.A.C.C.), *Facts and Figures, 1933,* p. 6; "Instability of Employment in the Automobile Industry," *Monthly Labor Review,* XXVIII (Feb., 1929), 20, 23.

¹⁶ Henderson Report, p. 23.

¹⁷ Skinner to Rose, Oct. 31, 1934, N.R.A. Box 688; W. Ellison Chalmers, "Collective Bargaining in the Automobile Industry" (Incomplete MS, 1935), VIII, 2–5; W. H. McPherson and Anthony Lucheck, "Automobiles," Twentieth

Century Fund, *How Collective Bargaining Works* (New York, 1942), pp. 573–75; Moore, "Automobile Industry," pp. 279–80, 318–19; Epstein, *Automobile Industry*, pp. 40–41; Whitney, *Antitrust Policies*, I, 431, 496–98; Adams, "Automobile," pp. 53–55; Henderson Report, pp. 25–30; Bureau of the Census, *Biennial Census of Manufactures, 1935* (Washington, 1938), p. 604. The average hourly wage of factory employees in the principal parts plants in 1929 was 58.61 cents as compared to 71.8 cents for factory employees in the plants of N.A.C.C. members. Hearing on Code of Fair Practices and Competition Presented by Automotive Parts and Equipment Manufacturing Industry, Oct. 3, 1933, p. 45, N.R.A. Box 7268. For labor turnover rates in the automobile manufacturing and automobile parts industries between 1931 and 1935, see "Labor Turn-over in the Automobile and Automobile Parts Industries, 1931 to 1935," *Monthly Labor Review*, XLII (May, 1936), 1320.

[18] Thirty-three per cent of motor vehicle sales by value were still handled by wholesale distributors in 1929. The wholesale distributor had largely been eliminated from the low-price field, but he continued to handle other price lines until World War II. His functions were eventually taken over by the factory sales organization of the various companies. The terms of the franchises held by the wholesale distributor and the retail dealer were prescribed by the manufacturer and were identical in nature. Paul H. Banner, "Competition in the Automobile Industry" (Ph.D. thesis, Harvard University, 1953), pp. 171–73, 178, 181; Charles M. Hewitt, *The Development of Automobile Franchises, Indiana Business Information Bulletin No. 37* (n.p., 1960), pp. 10, 12, 17; George F. Chambers, "Manufacturer-Dealer Relationships in the Automobile Industry" (Ph.D. thesis, University of Buffalo, 1958), pp. 40–41, 47–50.

[19] Rae, *Automobile Manufacturers*, pp. 46–47, 52; Hewitt, *Development of Automobile Franchises*, pp. 11, 13–21; Hewitt, *Automobile Franchise Agreements* (Homewood, Ill., 1956), pp. 85–88; Chambers, "Manufacturer-Dealer Relationships," pp. 50–51, 67–72, 143; The Reminiscences of W. C. Cowling, May, 1954, p. 25, Ford Archives, Dearborn, Michigan; Banner, "Competition in the Automobile Industry," pp. 224, 227; F.T.C., *Report on Motor Vehicle Industry*, pp. 95, 130–34, 181; George B. Myrick, Jr., *et al.*, "An Economic Survey of the Automobile Industry" (1936), Section Four, pp. 69–115, N.R.A. Box 8309; Epstein, *Automobile Industry*, pp. 136–37, 147–51; "Automobiles II.—The Dealer," *Fortune*, IV (Dec., 1931), 38–43+. See Myrick, Jr., *et al.*, "Economic Survey," Appendix B, N.R.A. Box 8310, for copies of several dealer franchises.

[20] Nevins and Hill, *Ford*, II, 535; interview with Pyke Johnson, Sept. 6, 1957.

[21] Nevins and Hill, *Ford*, I, 525, 533–35; Kennedy, *Automobile Industry*, p. 75.

[22] William H. McPherson, *Labor Relations in the Automobile Industry* (Washington, 1940), pp. 76–77; Bureau of Labor Statistics (B.L.S.), *Handbook of Labor Statistics, Bulletin No. 616* (Washington, 1936), p. 982; Bureau of the Census, *Historical Statistics of the United States Colonial Times to 1957* (Washington, 1960), p. 92. The hourly wages of male employees in the combined motor vehicle industries in 1922 ranged from 38.5 cents for apprentices to 93.1 cents for letterers, stripers, and varnishers. The hourly wages of female employees in the same year ranged from 35.2 cents for inspectors to 68 cents for "other skilled occupations." In 1928 male wages per hour ranged from 57.2 cents for apprentices to \$1.128 for dingmen, and female wages per hour from 39 cents for inspectors to 63.6 cents for lacquer rubbers. B.L.S., *Wages and Hours*

in the Motor Vehicle Industry: 1928, Bulletin No. 502 (Washington, 1930), pp. 1–2.

23 Nevins and Hill, *Ford*, I, 541, 551–67; II, 332–49, 353–54, 514–15, 518–20, 524–27.

24 B.L.S., *Health and Recreation Activities in Industrial Establishments, 1926, Bulletin No. 458* (Washington, 1928), pp. 4, 32, 39, 45, 60, 66; *Automotive Industries*, LIX (Aug. 4, 1928), 163; Robert W. Dunn, *Labor and Automobiles* (New York, 1929), pp. 148–56.

25 Nevins and Hill, *Ford*, I, 375–80, 513–15; II, 353, 493–94, 535–39; McPherson, *Labor Relations in the Automobile Industry*, pp. 13–14.

26 Nevins and Hill, *Ford*, I, 284–322, 415–43.

27 N.A.C.C., *Facts and Figures, 1933*, pp. 89–90, 93; McPherson, *Labor Relations in the Automobile Industry*, p. 11.

28 Rae, *Automobile Manufacturers*, pp. 80–81; Epstein, *Automobile Industry*, pp. 273–79; Whitney, *Antitrust Policies*, I, 485–86.

29 Pyke Johnson to Executive Committee, Nov. 29, 1935, enclosing Jo G. Roberts, "Automobile Industry Study Codes and Effect," Roy Chapin Papers, Michigan Historical Collections, Ann Arbor, Michigan; N.A.C.C., *Facts and Figures, 1933*, p. 93; *Automotive Industries*, LXIV (Jan. 10, 1931), 69; P. M. Heldt, "The Story of the National Automobile Show," *ibid.*, LXX (May 26, 1934), 643; Epstein, *Automobile Industry*, p. 236; W. Ellison Chalmers, "The Automobile Industry," in George Galloway *et al.*, *Industrial Planning under Codes* (New York, 1935), pp. 314–15, 317, 319.

30 F.T.C., *Report on Motor Vehicle Industry*, pp. 34, 48–58, 1065; Moore, "Automobile Industry," p. 301; Whitney, *Antitrust Policies*, I, 441; Reports of Meetings of Automotive Sales Research Conference, 1934, Chapin Papers.

31 F.T.C., *Report on Motor Vehicle Industry*, pp. 33, 49–50, 55, 1065–66; N.A.C.C. Bulletin, July 31, 1933, Volume A, N.R.A. Box 112; Homer B. Vanderblue, "Pricing Policies in the Automobile Industry," *Harvard Business Review*, XVII (Summer, 1939), 385–401; *ibid.*, XVIII (Autumn, 1939), 64–81; Wilcox, *Competition and Monopoly*, pp. 195–97; Banner, "Competition in the Automobile Industry," pp. 90, 104–06, 110, 121; Moore, "Automobile Industry," pp. 301, 304; Whitney, *Antitrust Policies*, I, 491. Prices were announced by the individual manufacturers on an f.o.b. basis at the beginning of the model year and were normally maintained throughout the model year despite the nature of the demand for the particular vehicle. In the 39 months from Jan. 1926 to Apr. 1929 there were only 5 month-to-month price changes. Wilcox, *Competition and Monopoly*, p. 196.

32 Whitney, *Antitrust Policies*, I, 490–91; *Motor*, XLIX (June 19, 1933), 44; Myrick, Jr., *et al.*, "Economic Survey," Section Five, p. 358, N.R.A. Box 8310.

33 Moore, "Automobile Industry," p. 280; Whitney, *Antitrust Policies*, I, 489; Banner, "Competition in the Automobile Industry," pp. 107–8; F.T.C., *Report on Motor Vehicle Industry*, p. 1074.

34 Stevens, "Quarter Century of Progress," pp. 5–12; N.A.C.C. Bulletin, July 31, 1933, Volume A, N.R.A. Box 112.

35 Arthur Pound, *Detroit Dynamic City* (New York, 1940), pp. 279–81; Philip Taft, *The Structure and Government of Labor Unions* (Cambridge, Mass., 1954), p. 215; Dunn, *Labor and Automobiles*, pp. 62–66; Writers' Program of the W.P.A., *Michigan: A Guide to the Wolverine State* (New York, 1941), pp. 107–8; Bureau of the Census, *Fifteenth Census of the United States: 1930, Popula-*

tion, IV (Washington, 1933), 803; *ibid.,* V (Washington, 1933), 468–70. Of the women employees, 19,032 were classified as operatives, 3567 as laborers, 5748 as clerks, 9527 as stenographers and typists, and 3373 as bookkeepers and cashiers. About 27 per cent of the employees in the industry as a whole were foreign-born, and only about 4 per cent were Negroes.

36 Taft, *Structure and Government of Labor Unions,* pp. 215–16; Pound, *Detroit,* p. 281. A few of the automobile workers had been members of the United Mine Workers of America or of the International Association of Machinists.

37 Eli Chinoy, *Automobile Workers and the American Dream* (Garden City, New York, 1955), p. 19; McPherson, *Labor Relations in the Automobile Industry,* pp. 7–8.

38 McPherson and Lucheck, "Automobiles," p. 576. Charles Reitell in 1924 classified 10–15 per cent of the workers in automobile machine shops and assembly plants as assemblers, 25–40 per cent as machine tenders, 5–10 per cent as skilled workers, 5 per cent as inspectors and testers, 15 per cent as helpers, and 10–15 per cent as laborers. "Machinery and Its Effect upon the Workers in the Automotive Industry," *Annals of the American Academy of Political and Social Science,* CXVI (Nov., 1924), 39.

39 Chinoy, *Automobile Workers,* pp. 70–72; Charles R. Walker and Robert H. Guest, *The Man on the Assembly Line* (Cambridge, Mass., 1952), pp. 10–11, 34–37; Anonymous to Roosevelt, Mar. 5, 1934, Thomas P. Jespersen to Hugh Johnson, Mar. 8, 1934, Edward Moore to Roosevelt, Jan. 16, 1933 [1934], N.R.A. Box 660; Oral History Interview of Nick Digaetano, Apr. 29, May 7, 1959, Michigan Historical Collections; Oral History Interview of Lew Michener, June 21, 1960, pp. 2–3, *ibid.* Chinoy's study was based on interviews in 1946, 1947, 1948, and 1951 with a small sample of automobile workers in a small plant located in Lansing. The Walker and Guest book is based on interviews, begun in the summer of 1949, with 180 automobile assembly-line workers employed at a new plant not in the Detroit area. The findings of the two studies regarding the attitude of automobile workers with respect to the content of their jobs seem applicable to an earlier period and to the Detroit area.

40 Bureau of the Census, *Historical Statistics,* p. 601; Nevins and Hill, *Ford,* II, 520–21.

41 "Success Story," *Fortune,* XII (Dec., 1935), 119; Mrs. J. W. Wallace to Mrs. Roosevelt, Oct. 11, 1933, N.R.A. Box 660; Reitell, "Machinery and Its Effect," p. 43; Walker and Guest, *Man on the Assembly Line,* pp. 52–54, 62.

42 Decisions #176 and #146. There is a complete file of the A.L.B. decisions in Automobile Labor Board (A.L.B.) Drawers 4084–4100, National Archives (the A.L.B. records are part of the N.R.A. Records), and a virtually complete file in the Bureau of Industrial Relations Library, University of Michigan. Unless otherwise indicated, A.L.B. decisions hereafter cited may be found in the Bureau of Industrial Relations Library.

43 A 1932 B.L.S. study of 11 unidentified auto and parts plants, with 49,955 employees, revealed that retention of employees at layoff time was based on efficiency in 2 plants, seniority in 4 plants, and family responsibility in 2 plants. "Hiring and Separation Methods in American Factories," *Monthly Labor Review,* XXXV (Nov., 1932), 1013. The Ford Motor Co. ignored seniority after 1921 and preferred younger workers for assembly-line jobs. Nevins and Hill, *Ford,* II, 534.

44 Fountain, *Union Guy* (New York, 1949), pp. 41–42. "The foreman in those days," another auto worker recalled, "held you right in the palm of his hand." Oral History Interview of Jack Palmer, July 23, 1960, p. 3, Michigan Historical Collections. See also Oral History Interview of Walter Schilling, Apr. 26, 1961, pp. 3–4, *ibid.;* Oral History Interview of Norman Bully, Oct. 12, 1961, p. 2, *ibid.;* and Oral History Interview of Charles K. Beckman, July 25, 1961, p. 5, *ibid.*

45 Harry Bennett, as told to Paul Marcus, *We Never Called Him Henry* (Gold Medal Books; New York, 1951), p. 109; Carl Raushenbush, *Fordism* (New York, 1937), p. 13.

46 B.L.S., *Bulletin No. 502*, pp. 1, 24. The average yearly wage of wage earners in the motor vehicle industry rose from $1431 in 1919 to $1675 in 1925. *Ibid.*, p. 24.

47 B.L.S., *Wages and Hours of Labor in the Motor Vehicle Industry: 1925, Bulletin No. 438* (Washington, 1927), p. 21; Fountain, *Union Guy*, p. 28; McPherson, *Labor Relations in the Automobile Industry*, p. 94; Oral History Interview of Joseph Ferriss, May 12, 1961, p. 4, Michigan Historical Collections; Oral History Interview of Joe Hattley, Aug. 4, 8, 1961, p. 6, *ibid.* The Briggs Manufacturing Co. stated early in 1933 that piece-work rates throughout the industry were scaled down as piece workers attained a degree of proficiency on a particular operation that permitted quantity production. Report of the Mayor's Non-Partisan Committee on Industrial Relations (the Fact-Finding Committee) in the Matter of the Strike at the Briggs Manufacturing Co., Feb. 21, 1933, p. 47, Michigan Historical Collections (hereafter cited as Briggs Fact-Finding Report). Four of the 99 plants studied by the B.L.S. for 1925 used a group piece system of wage payment. Three plants utilized a contract system. Where the latter plan was in effect, the labor cost of a particular order would be estimated, and the employees who worked on the order would be paid a straight time rate until the order was completed. If the estimate proved greater than the time rate cost, the difference between the estimated and the actual cost would be divided among those who had worked on the order according to their individual basic wage rates and the number of hours they had worked. B.L.S., *Bulletin No. 438*, p. 22.

48 B.L.S., *Bulletin No. 502*, pp. 16–21; N.R.A. Release No. 366, Aug. 18, 1933, pp. 59–61 (there is a complete file of N.R.A. releases in the N.R.A. Archives); Worden L. Barron to Roosevelt, Jan. 1, 1934, Moore to Roosevelt, Jan. 16, 1933 [1934], Albert A. Taylor to Frances Perkins, July 24, 1933, N.R.A. Box 660; Oral History Interview of Adam Poplawski, May 2, 1960, p. 2, Michigan Historical Collections; Digaetano interview, p. 49, *ibid.*

49 Samuel Romer, "That Detroit Strike," *Nation*, CXXXVI (Feb. 15, 1933), 167; Briggs Fact-Finding Report, p. 8; N.R.A. Release No. 366, Aug. 18, 1933, p. 53; Harry Weiss to Leon Henderson, Jan. 7, 1935, N.R.A. Box 8281; Oral History Interview of R. C. Ingram, Apr. 28, 1961, pp. 3–4, Michigan Historical Collections; Ferris interview, p. 3, *ibid.;* Oral History Interview of Patrick J. O'Malley, July 25, 1961, p. 4, *ibid.*

50 See Kennedy, *Automobile Industry*, pp. 115–37.

51 A.M.A., *Automobile Facts and Figures, 1959–60*, p. 3; *ibid., 1937*, p. 44; Bureau of the Census, *Biennial Census of Manufactures, 1935* (Washington, 1938), pp. 1148, 1150, 1156; Spurgeon Bell, *Productivity, Wages, and National*

Income (Washington, 1940), p. 286; John W. Scoville, *Behavior of the Automobile Industry in Depression* (n.p., 1936), p. 16.

52 Nevins and Hill, *Ford*, II, 572, 585–86; Bureau of the Census, *Biennial Census of Manufactures, 1935,* pp. 1150, 1156; Henderson Report, pp. 2–3, Appendix A, Exhibit 1; Rae, *Automobile Manufacturers,* pp. 191–92, 198.

53 Henderson Report, p. 4, Appendix A, Exhibits 1 and 2; F.T.C., *Report on Motor Vehicle Industry,* pp. 431, 491, 493, 597, 651; Rae, *Automobile Manufacturers,* p. 200; A.M.A., *Automobile Facts and Figures, 1937,* p. 10. On its parts and accessories group, G.M., before income taxes, earned $34,491,361 in 1930; $30,625,247 in 1931; and $10,398,858 in 1932. Chrysler enjoyed a net profit on its sales of parts and accessories of $2,570,397 in 1930; $1,418,719 in 1931; and $813,445 in 1932. Ford made a net profit of $18,343,320 on domestic sales of parts and accessories in 1930 but lost a total of about $13 million on this portion of its business in 1931 and 1932. See F.T.C. citation, above.

54 N.A.C.C., *Facts and Figures, 1929,* p. 34; *ibid., 1933,* p. 68; Chambers, "Manufacturer-Dealer Relationships," pp. 72–73; *Motor,* LXI (May, 1934), 74; *Automobile Trade Journal,* L (June, 1935), 18–19; N.A.C.C. Bulletin, Feb. 27, 1934, Acc. 203, Box 3, Ford Archives; *Automotive Daily News,* Jan. 14, 1935; Hearing on Code of Fair Practices and Competition Presented by the Motor Vehicle Retailing Trade, Sept. 18, 1933, pp. 98–100, N.R.A. Box 7267.

55 Weiss to Henderson, Jan. 7, 1935, N.R.A. Box 8281; Thomas H. Earl to Roosevelt, Jan. 7, 1934, N.R.A. Box 660; Irving Bernstein, *The Lean Years: A History of the American Worker, 1920–1933* (Boston, 1960), pp. 300–301; Helen Hall, "When Detroit's Out of Gear," *Survey,* LXIV (April 1, 1930), 9; Department of Public Welfare, *The Department of Public Welfare 1930 to 1940* (Detroit, n.d.), p. 84.

56 B.L.S., *Bulletin No. 616,* p. 982; N.R.A. Release No. 366, Aug. 18, 1933, p. 40; *Automotive Industries,* LXIX (Aug. 19, 1933), 201. Of 84,000 employees at Ford's Rouge and Highland Park plants in Apr. 1931, 50 per cent were working only 3 days a week. Samuel M. Levin, "The Ford Unemployment Policy," *American Labor Legislation Review,* XXII (June, 1932), 101–2.

57 Herman B. Byer and John Anker, "A Review of Factory Labor Turn-Over, 1930 to 1936," *Monthly Labor Review,* XLV (July, 1937), 157–58. The annual layoff rate in the automobile parts industry only rose from 86.87 in 1930 to 87.02 in 1932, and the total annual separation rate dropped from 116.90 in 1930 to 97.93 in 1932. *Ibid.*

58 Nevins and Hill, *Ford,* II, 529–31, 575, 588. The average hourly wage of N.A.C.C. employees dropped from 71.8 cents in 1929 to 60.3 cents in 1932, and the average hourly wage of Ford's Rouge employees from 92.245 cents to 78.825 cents during the same period. Statistics folders, N.R.A. Box 676; F.T.C., *Report on Motor Vehicle Industry,* p. 668.

59 B.L.S., *Bulletin No. 616,* p. 982; Bureau of the Census, *Historical Statistics,* pp. 92, 125–26; J. M. Hunter, *Wage Trends in Prosperity and Depression Prior to NRA,* N.R.A. Division of Review, *Work Materials No. 45* (Washington, 1936), p. 41; Leo Wolman, *Wages during the Depression,* National Bureau of Economic Research, *Bulletin No. 46* (May 1, 1933), p. 2; F.T.C., *Report on Motor Vehicle Industry,* p. 8.

60 Weiss to Henderson, Jan. 7, 1935, N.R.A. Box 8281; N.R.A. Release No. 366, Aug. 18, 1933, pp. 43, 61; Nevins and Hill, *Ford,* II, 587; John Palm to

Hugh S. Johnson, July 28, 1933, N.R.A. Box 661; Research Section, Research and Planning Division, Preliminary Report on Labor Productivity in the Automobile Manufacturing Industry, Sept. 20, 1934, pp. 6–7, N.R.A. Box 8281; Bureau of the Census, *Historical Statistics*, pp. 600–601. Cf. B.L.S., *Productivity and Unit Labor Cost in Selected Manufacturing Industries, 1919–1940* (Washington, 1942), pp. 1, 66; and Bell, *Productivity, Wages, and National Income*, p. 289.

⁶¹ A.F. of L., *Report of Proceedings of the Fifty-Fifth Annual Convention, 1935* (Washington, n.d.), pp. 739–40 (hereafter, A.F. of L. convention proceedings will be cited as *Proceedings*). The International Association of Machinists, which claimed jurisdiction over more automobile workers than any other craft union, had fewer than 1000 members in Detroit in 1929. Ten years previously it had claimed a Detroit membership of between 7000 and 10,000. Dunn, *Labor and Automobiles*, pp. 183–84.

⁶² A.F. of L., *Proceedings, 1910* (Washington, 1910), p. 279; *ibid., 1911* (Washington, 1911), pp. 126–27; *ibid., 1912* (Washington, 1912), pp. 320–21; *ibid., 1913* (Washington, 1913), pp. 240, 341; *ibid., 1914* (Washington, 1914), pp. 410–11; *ibid., 1917* (Washington, 1917), pp. 130, 369–70; *ibid., 1918* (Washington, 1918), p. 129; James O. Morris, *Conflict within the AFL: A Study of Craft versus Industrial Unionism, 1901–1938* (Ithaca, 1958), pp. 22–24; John A. Fitch, "The Clash over Industrial Unionism. Exhibit A—The Automobile Industry," *Survey Graphic*, XXV (Jan., 1936), 41–42; Dunn, *Labor and Automobiles*, pp. 186–91; U.A.A.V.W. Membership Book [1923], Collective Bargaining Agreements, B.L.S. Records, National Archives; Oral History Interview of Lester Johnson, June 3, 1959, pp. 7, 13, 17–19, 21–27, Michigan Historical Collections; Oral History Interview of the Rev. I. Paul Taylor, Nov. 2, 1960, p. 4, *ibid.*; Oral History Interview of Arthur Rohan, Aug. 14, 1961, pp. 10 ff., *ibid.*; Oral History Interview of Phil Raymond, Jan. 14, 1960, p. 2, *ibid.*

⁶³ Philip Taft, *The A.F. of L. in the Time of Gompers* (New York, 1957), p. 460.

⁶⁴ Taft, *The A.F. of L. from the Death of Gompers to the Merger* (New York, 1959), pp. 95–98; Morris, *Conflict within the AFL*, pp. 57–61; Lewis L. Lorwin, *The American Federation of Labor* (Washington, 1933), pp. 244–48; Dunn, *Labor and Automobiles*, pp. 178–79.

⁶⁵ Morris, *Conflict within the AFL*, p. 61. Smith resumed organizing efforts in Kenosha and Milwaukee in 1929 but without conspicuous success. *Ibid.*

⁶⁶ Fred Thompson, *The I.W.W. Its First Fifty Years (1905–1955)* (Chicago, 1955), pp. 74–75; Nevins and Hill, *Ford*, I, 379, 522; Organization Program for General Recruiting Union, Detroit Branch, I.W.W., Apr. 21, 1932, Joe Brown Collection, Wayne State University Archives, Detroit, Michigan.

⁶⁷ "The Structure and Membership of the Communist Party in the Detroit Area" (1936), Homer Martin Papers, Wayne State University Archives; Dunn, *Labor and Automobiles*, pp. 193–95; Johnson interview, p. 13, Michigan Historical Collections; Raymond interview, pp. 2–3, 5, *ibid.*; Oral History Interview of John Panzner, Apr. 20, 1959, p. 25, *ibid.*; Philip Bonosky, *Brother Bill McKie: Building the Union at Ford* (New York, 1953), pp. 39, 53; William Z. Foster, *From Bryan to Stalin* (London, [1937]), pp. 216–18, 239. The Detroit local was composed of all of the U.A.A.V.W. shop units in the city. The A.W.U. membership is given as 100 in 1930 in Leo Wolman, *Ebb and Flow in Trade Unionism* (New York, 1936), p. 144.

⁶⁸ Auto Workers Union Membership Book, Brown Collection.

[69] Employment at the Rouge fell from an average number of 101,069 in 1929 to 56,277 in 1932. F.T.C., *Report on Motor Vehicle Industry*, p. 668.

[70] Keith Sward, *The Legend of Henry Ford* (New York, 1948), pp. 231–42; Bernstein, *Lean Years*, pp. 432–34; Oral History Interview of Josephine Gomon, Dec. 22, 1959, p. 7, Michigan Historical Collections; Benjamin Gitlow, *The Whole of Their Lives* (New York, 1948), pp. 223–25. The most carefully researched account of the 1932 hunger march is Helen V. Barnes, "Frank Murphy and the Ford Hunger March of 1932" (MS, 1962, in possession of author).

[71] Ford hunger march handbills, Joseph A. Labadie Collection, University of Michigan General Library, Ann Arbor, Michigan; *Detroit News*, June 6, 1933.

[72] Edward A. Wieck, "The Automobile Workers under the NRA" (MS in possession of Mrs. E. A. Wieck, Aug., 1935), pp. 40–41; S.D.E., Bulletin No. 3, Nov. 19, 1933, N.R.A. Box 5371; *Designing Engineer*, I (Sept., 1934), 2; *The Society of Designing Engineers* . . . (pamphlet, Aug., 1936), Brown Collection. According to the business agent of the S.D.E., the average yearly wage of members who designed tools, dies, and special machines declined from $3218 in 1929 to $837 in 1933, and the average yearly wage of the designers of auto bodies, chassis, and motors from $4600 in 1928 to $1752 in 1933. House Committee on Labor, *Labor Disputes Act, Hearings on H.R. 6288*, 74 Cong., 1 Sess. (Washington, 1935), pp. 71–72. Not all of the members of the S.D.E. were in the automobile industry, but the greater portion of them were.

[73] Wieck, "Automobile Workers," p. 41; *Designing Engineer*, I (Sept., 1934), 2; *Detroit News*, May 22, 1935; William Foster to Roy Chapin, Sept. 11, 1933, Chapin Papers; stenographic reports of meetings of tool designers and Mr. Zwolinski, Sept. 13, 15, 1933, *ibid.*; *Hearings on H.R. 6288*, 74 Cong., 1 Sess., p. 68; Hearing on Regularizing Employment and Otherwise Improving the Conditions of Labor in the Automobile Industry, Detroit, Dec. 15, 1934, pp. 322–44, N.R.A. Box 7265.

[74] Anthony Lucheck, "Labor Organizations in the Automobile Industry" (MS in possession of Mr. Lucheck, [1936]), pp. 61–62; *Detroit News*, May 15, 1935; "Short-Lived Unions of Local Importance," typewritten draft in Brown Collection; Larry S. Davidow to Hugh L. Kerwin, May 31, 1935, Robert H. Pilkington to Kerwin, June 21, 1935, Conciliation Service File 182–462, National Archives (henceforth, Conciliation Service files will be cited as C.S.). The dingmen organized as a "welfare club" because they were afraid to identify themselves as union members. Oral History Interview of Larry S. Davidow, July 14, 1960, p. 7, Michigan Historical Collections.

[75] Gomon interview, pp. 12–13, 15, Michigan Historical Collections; Oral History Interview of Leon Pody, Nov. 28, 1959, Jan. 11, 1960, p. 11, *ibid.*; Briggs Fact-Finding Report, p. 21; Wieck, "Automobile Workers," p. 21; *Industrial Worker*, Jan. 9, 1934.

[76] Romer, "That Detroit Strike," pp. 167–68; Briggs Fact-Finding Report, p. 20; Summary of Final Report of Commissioner of Conciliation, Apr. 10, 1933, C.S. 170-7752. Briggs and Murray held "interlocking contracts" for Ford bodies, and the strike at one company forced a shutdown at the other. Murray Body workers were apparently planning a strike before the company closed down the plant. *Detroit News*, Jan. 26, 1933; Romer, "That Detroit Strike," p. 168. Ford circles suspiciously viewed the strike as "a part of sabotage by rivals to prevent them from bringing out a new model." Pilkington to Kerwin, Jan. 28, 1933, C.S. 170-7752.

[77] Briggs Fact-Finding Report, pp. 8–20, 51–52, 55; Romer, "That Detroit Strike," p. 167; Sward, *Legend of Henry Ford*, pp. 221–22; Pilkington to Kerwin, Feb. 2, 7, 1933, C.S. 170-7752.

[78] Briggs Fact-Finding Report, pp. 21, 30–35, 52–53; Gomon interview, p. 15, Michigan Historical Collections; Pody interview, pp. 2, 7–8, *ibid.;* Oral History Interview of John W. Anderson, Feb. 17–May 21, 1960, pp. 6, 7, 10–12, *ibid.* The role of the communists in the Briggs strike is emphasized in the material on the dispute in the Brown Collection.

[79] Cf. Briggs Fact-Finding Report, p. 40.

[80] *Ibid.,* pp. 23–30, 37–51, 57–58; Romer, "That Detroit Strike," p. 168; Pilkington to Kerwin, Feb. 7, 1933, C.S. 170-7752. When Walter Briggs saw the Fact-Finding Committee, he reportedly "banged the desk with his fists and called attention to the fact that he had reduced his own pay to a mere eighteen hundred dollars per month," that he had had to leave Florida because of the strike, and that butlers in fashionable Grosse Pointe who formerly had received $150 per month were now being paid only $75. *Ibid.*

[81] Wieck, "Automobile Workers," pp. 20–21; Pody interview, pp. 8–9, Michigan Historical Collections; Anderson interview, pp. 9, 16, *ibid.;* The Reminiscences of John P. Frey, 1957, p. 552, Oral History Research Office, Columbia University; American Industrial Association folder, Brown Collection; *Detroit News,* Aug. 16, 1933; *Labor Action,* Aug. 23, 1933; Lorwin, *A.F. of L.,* p. 265; N.R.A. Release, No. 366, Aug. 18, 1933, p. 99. The C.P.L.A. favored industrial unionism, organization of the unorganized in the basic industries, worker education to further the "class struggle," and independent political action. *Labor Action,* Dec. 1, 1934.

[82] Samuel I. Rosenman, compiler, *The Public Papers and Addresses of Franklin D. Roosevelt,* II: *The Year of Crisis, 1933* (New York, 1938), 246.

[83] Allen, *Since Yesterday* (Bantam Books; New York, 1961), p. 98; Raymond Moley, *After Seven Years* (New York, 1939), pp. 184–85; Charles Frederick Roos, *NRA Economic Planning* (Bloomington, Ind., 1937), pp. 17–20, 29–30, 32–34; Leverett S. Lyon *et al., The National Recovery Administration* (Washington, 1935), p. 26; Lyon *et al., Government and Economic Life,* II (Washington, 1940), 1036; Irving Bernstein, *The New Deal Collective Bargaining Policy* (Berkeley, 1950), pp. 26–27, 29, 37; Taft, *A.F. of L. from Death of Gompers,* pp. 41–42; Murray Edelman, "New Deal Sensitivity to Labor Interests," in Milton Derber and Edwin Young, eds., *Labor and the New Deal* (Madison, 1957), pp. 163–64, 176–77, 179–80; Arthur M. Schlesinger, Jr., *The Age of Roosevelt: The Coming of the New Deal* (Boston, 1959), pp. 87–94.

[84] Bernstein, *New Deal Collective Bargaining Policy,* pp. 29–31; Roos, *NRA Economic Planning,* pp. 30–32; *House Report No. 124, 73* Cong., 1 Sess., May 10, 1933, pp. 1–3.

[85] Bernstein, *New Deal Collective Bargaining Policy,* pp. 31–32; Schlesinger, Jr., *Coming of the New Deal,* pp. 96–97.

[86] The Reminiscences of Rexford G. Tugwell, 1950, pp. 47–48, Oral History Research Office, Columbia University; Bernstein, *New Deal Collective Bargaining Policy,* p. 32; [John Franklin Carter], *The New Dealers* (New York, 1934), pp. 31–32, 36; Schlesinger, Jr., *The Age of Roosevelt: The Crisis of the Old Order* (Boston, 1957), pp. 413–15; Schlesinger, Jr., *Coming of the New Deal,* p. 97; Matthew Josephson, "Profiles: The General," *New Yorker Magazine,* Aug. 18, 25, 1934; Josephson, *Sidney Hillman* (Garden City, New York, 1952), p. 366.

87 Bernstein, *New Deal Collective Bargaining Policy,* p. 32; Schlesinger, Jr., *Coming of the New Deal,* pp. 87–88, 97, 136; [Carter], *New Dealers,* pp. 38–40; Jonathan Mitchell, "Grand Vizier: Donald R. Richberg," *New Republic,* LXXXII (Apr. 24, 1935), 301–4; Bernstein, *Lean Years,* pp. 216, 397, 408; Donald Richberg, *The Rainbow* (Garden City, New York, 1936), pp. 50–52, 106–8.

88 Bernstein, *New Deal Collective Bargaining Policy,* pp. 32–33.

89 Title II of the statute authorized the expenditure of $3.3 billion for public works.

90 Lyon *et al., N.R.A.,* p. 12. The text of Title I is given in *ibid.,* pp. 889–902.

91 Section 2 of the Railway Labor Act made it "the duty" of the railroads and their employees "to exert every reasonable effort to make and maintain agreements" and to settle disputes. If possible, disputes were to be settled by representatives of labor and management who were to be chosen "without interference, influence, or coercion exercised by either party over the self-organization, or designation of representatives, by the other." The Supreme Court, in Texas and New Orleans Railroad Co. *v.* Brotherhood of Railway and Steamship Clerks (1930), ruled that the establishment and financial support by management of a company union and discrimination against union members and officers violated Section 2. Bernstein, *Lean Years,* pp. 217–18, 405–6. Employer interference with the right of their employees to organize and to bargain collectively had been proscribed by the principles that governed the conduct of the National War Labor Board in World War I. National War Labor Board, *Principles and Rules of Procedure* (Washington, 1919).

92 Bernstein, *New Deal Collective Bargaining Policy,* pp. 33–37; Lewis L. Lorwin and Arthur Wubnig, *Labor Relations Boards: The Regulation of Collective Bargaining under the National Industrial Recovery Act* (Washington, 1935), pp. 100–105; Grant N. Farr, *The Origins of Recent Labor Policy* (Boulder, Colorado, 1959), pp. 100–101.

93 Lyon *et al., N.R.A.,* pp. 41, 83–84, 123–24; N.R.A. *Bulletin No. 1,* June 16, 1933; Roos, *NRA Economic Planning,* pp. 45–47; Lyon *et al., Government and Economic Life,* II, 1049, 1051; Schlesinger, Jr., *Coming of the New Deal,* pp. 108–10.

94 *Public Papers and Addresses of F.D.R.,* II, 254–56; N.R.A., *Bulletin No. 1;* N.R.A., *Bulletin No. 2,* June 19, 1933; N.R.A. Release No. 30, July 6, 1933.

95 N.R.A. Release No. 30, July 6, 1933; Lyon *et al., N.R.A.,* pp. 39–40, 52; N.R.A., *Bulletin No. 3,* July 20, 1933. The terms of the P.R.A. are discussed in Chapter III.

96 N.R.A., *Bulletin No. 3.*

97 Josephson, "Profiles: The General," *New Yorker Magazine,* Aug. 25, 1934, p. 27; Schlesinger, Jr., *Coming of the New Deal,* pp. 112–16; Lyon *et al., N.R.A.,* pp. 52–53.

98 Lorwin and Wubnig, *Labor Relations Boards,* pp. 50–51, 61–62; N.A.M. to Members, July 26, 1933, Chapin Papers.

99 The S.I.R.B., created on June 16, 1933, consisted of the Secretary of Commerce as chairman, the Attorney General, the Secretary of the Interior, the Secretary of Agriculture, the Secretary of Labor, the Director of the Budget, the Administrator for Industrial Recovery, and the chairman of the F.T.C. It was intended to exercise "general supervisory control" over the N.R.A. Lyon *et al., N.R.A.,* pp. 41n, 43, 61.

100 Lorwin and Wubnig, *Labor Relations Boards,* pp. 59–60, 76; Proceedings

... of the S.I.R.B., Aug. 14, 1933, N.R.A. Box 8462; N.R.A. Releases Nos. 34, July 7, 1933, 136, July 29, 1933, 463, undated, 536, Aug. 29, 1933, 602, Sept. 1, 1933, 625, Sept 4, 1933.

101 Lorwin and Wubnig, *Labor Relations Boards,* pp. 87–95; *Decisions of the National Labor Board, August 1933—March 1934* (Washington, 1934), p. v.

102 Taft, *A.F. of L. from Death of Gompers,* p. 45; George Blackwood, "The United Automobile Workers of America, 1935–51" (Ph.D. thesis, University of Chicago, 1951), p. 36; Green to Collins, Apr. 10, May 31, Nov. 16, 29, 1926, June 30, 1933, Green to Executive Council, June 21, 1933, Green Letterbooks, A.F. of L.-C.I.O. Archives, Washington, D.C.; interview with Collins, Feb. 4, 1957.

103 *Detroit Labor News,* June 16, 23, 30, July 7, 1933; "Automobile Workers! Here Is Your Chance," circular in Brown Collection.

104 Collins to Green, July 15, 22, 1933, Collins to Frank Morrison, July 28, 1933, Collins File, A.F. of L.-C.I.O. Archives; Green to T. J. Conboy, June 16, 19, 1933, Green to Coleman Claherty, July 14, 1933, Green to Collins, July 24, 27, 1933, Paul J. Smith to Green, Aug. 1, 1933, Green Letterbooks; Chalmers, "Collective Bargaining," V, 23–24.

105 Collins to Green, July 15, 28, Aug. 12, 1933, Collins File; "Cooperative Plan of the American Federation of Labor to Provide Collective Bargaining for the United Automobile Workers of America," handbill in Case 209, Drawer 35, Records of the National Labor Board and the National Labor Relations Board, National Archives (henceforth, records in this group will be cited as N.L.B. or N.L.R.B.); Chalmers, "Collective Bargaining," V, 27–28, 32–33; Lucheck, "Labor Organizations," p. 46. A single federal labor union served both the Chevrolet and Fisher Body workers in such places as St. Louis, Kansas City, and Atlanta.

106 Collins to Green, June 23, July 15, 28, Aug. 5, 1933, Collins File; Green to Collins, June 30, 1933, Green Letterbooks; *Detroit Labor News,* July 21, 28, 1933. The initiation fee for a federal labor union member was $2, but Collins did not insist that the full amount be paid at once.

107 Harry Gannes, "The National Industrial Recovery Act...," *Communist,* XII (Aug., 1933), 770–83; *Michigan Worker,* July 1, Aug. 5, 1933; *Auto Workers News,* Aug., 1933; N.R.A. Release No. 366, Aug. 18, 1933, pp. 103–8.

108 A.W.U. pamphlet attached to Alexander Marks to Morrison, July 29, 1933, Marks File, A.F. of L.-C.I.O. Archives.

109 *Industrial Worker,* Sept. 5, 12, 1933.

110 Lucheck, "Labor Organizations," pp. 63–65; Collins to Green, Aug. 12, 1933, May 31, 1934, Collins File; *Detroit News,* Sept. 2, 1933; N.R.A. Release No. 366, Aug. 18, 1933, p. 94; *Labor Action,* Dec. 20, 1933; Chamber of Labor of North America folder, Brown Collection.

111 Where the contract system was in effect, tool and die makers bid on jobs, and the worker who offered to do the job in the fewest number of hours received the contract. He was paid only for the hours he had estimated it would take him to do the job regardless of the number of hours he actually worked.

112 Harry Dahlheimer, *A History of the Mechanics Educational Society of America in Detroit from Its Inception in 1933 through 1937* (Detroit, 1941), pp. 1–4, 5n; Joe Brown, "The MESA: Tool and Die Makers Organize and Strike," pp. 3–5, undated MS, Brown Collection; M.E.S.A. circular [Aug., 1933], *ibid.;* Matthew Smith, "Militant Labor in Detroit," *Nation,* CXXXVIII (May 16, 1934), 561; *The MESA. Why? When? Whither?* [1939]; Chalmers, "Collec-

tive Bargaining," IV, 1–2; interview with Matthew Smith, Apr. 10, 1957; Oral History Interview of Elizabeth McCracken, Dec. 23, 1959, pp. 2–3, Michigan Historical Collections; Oral History Interview of William Stevenson, July 6, 1961, pp. 7–9, *ibid*. The various accounts of the origins of the M.E.S.A. differ as to the exact month of its founding.

113 Wieck, "Automobile Workers," p. 38; Smith interview; Collins to Morrison, Sept. 23, 1933, Collins File; M.E.S.A. circular [Sept., 1933], Labadie Collection; A. O. Wharton to Green, Aug. 8, 1933, International Association of Machinists File, A.F. of L.-C.I.O. Archives; Morris, *Conflict within the AFL*, p. 154.

114 Hearing on Code of Fair Practices and Competition Presented by the Automobile Industry, Aug. 18, 1933, pp. 239–41, N.R.A. Box 7264.

NOTES TO CHAPTER II

1 Vandenberg to Roy Chapin, Apr. 1, 1933, Chapin to Vandenberg, Apr. 3, 1933, Chapin to Vandenberg and James Couzens, Apr. 6, 1933, copy of wire by Hutchinson, Apr. 5, 1933, Chapin Papers.

2 House Committee on Labor, *Thirty-Hour Week Bill, Hearings on S.158 . . . ,* 73 Cong., 1 Sess. (Washington, 1933), pp. 770–74, 778–80, 784, 787–94.

3 Total new passenger car and truck registrations in May 1933 were 181,167 as compared to 149,978 for May 1932, which was the first time since October 1929 that new registrations for any month were higher than registrations for the same month in the previous year. The industry continued to improve over its 1932 performance during the remainder of the year 1933. A.M.A., *Facts and Figures, 1937*, p. 7.

4 N.A.C.C. to Roosevelt, May 15, 1933, Oscar P. Pearson Papers, in possession of Mr. Pearson; P. Johnson to Chapin, May 22, 23, 26, 1933, Chapin to Couzens, May 25, 1933, Chapin Papers; N.A.C.C. General Bulletins No. G-1604, May 31, 1933, No. G-1609, June 6, 1933, *ibid.;* House Committee on Ways and Means, *National Industrial Recovery, Hearings on H.R. 5664*, 73 Cong., 1 Sess. (Washington, 1933), p. 188. As finally approved, the N.I.R.A. added a $\frac{1}{2}$ cent per gallon tax to the existing 1-cent tax.

5 P. Johnson to Chapin, May 22, 1933, P. Johnson, "An Analysis of the Position of the National Automobile Chamber of Commerce under the National Recovery Act," May 23, 1933, Chapin to P. Johnson, May 25, 1933, Chapin Papers; N.A.C.C. General Bulletin No. G-1603, May 27, 1933, Pearson Papers.

6 Senate Committee on Finance, *National Industrial Recovery, Hearings on S.1712 . . . ,* 73 Cong., 1 Sess. (Washington, 1933), pp. 371–72.

7 Chapin to P. Johnson, June 1, 1933, P. Johnson to Chapin, June 6, 1933, Chapin Papers; P. Johnson to Reeves (citing letter from Sloan), June 3, 1933, Pearson Papers.

8 P. Johnson to Chapin, June 2, 1933, Chapin Papers; N.A.C.C. General Bulletin No. G-1607, June 3, 1933, *ibid.*

9 P. Johnson to Chapin, June 3, 1933, *ibid.;* P. Johnson to A. C. Brown, June 3, 1933, P. Johnson to Sloan, June 3, 1933, Pearson Papers.

10 N.A.C.C. General Bulletins No. G-1603, May 27, 1933, No. G-1610, June 8, 1933, No. G-1612, June 16, 1933, Pearson Papers; Reeves to Sloan *et al.*, June 8, 1933, Chapin Papers; Reeves to H. Ford, June 15, 1933, E. Ford to Reeves, June 21, 1933, Accession 203, Box 3, Ford Archives.

11 *Iron Age*, CXXXI (June 22, 1933), 997; interview with William Cronin,

Apr. 9, 1957; interview with Nicholas Kelley, Feb. 5, 1957; *Detroit News,* June 18, 1933; pencil draft of report by Consumers' Advisory Board, N.R.A. Box 660.

12 *Detroit News,* July 22, 1933; Chapin to P. Johnson, June 1, 1933, Chapin Papers. N.A.C.C. members in May and June raised the wages of 36.8 per cent of their employees by less than 10 per cent and the wages of 37.7 per cent of their workers by more than 10 per cent. Forty-seven per cent of the N.A.C.C. employees received pay boosts of 10–14 per cent after July 1, and 51.2 per cent received increases of more than 15 per cent. "Wage Increases by Members of N.A.C.C.," N.R.A. Box 655.

13 Chapin to Herbert Hoover, Aug. 5, 1933, Chapin Papers.

14 P. Johnson to Chapin, May 17, 1933, Macauley to Chapin, June 26, 1933, P. Johnson to Macauley, June 29, 1933, Chapin Papers; P. Johnson, "An Analysis," May 23, 1933, *ibid.; Business Week,* July 29, 1933, p. 9.

15 Minutes of Meeting of June 22, 1933, of Committee on N.I.R.A., Acc. 203, Box 6, Ford Archives; Moekle memorandum for B. J. Craig, June 23, 1933, Acc. 203, Box 3, *ibid.*

16 Reeves to Brown *et al.,* June 27, 1933, Brown to Graham *et al.,* June 27, 1933, Acc. 203, Box 13, *ibid.; New York Times,* Feb. 6, 1961. I have been able to locate seven code drafts, dated June 14, July 6, 14, 18, 21, 26, and 28. The June 14 draft appears to have been one of two drafts prepared by Montague and submitted to the code committee on June 29. I have not been able to locate the second Montague draft. Copies of the code drafts may be found in the Chapin Papers and in Acc. 203, Box 3, Ford Archives.

17 Minutes of meeting of Committee on the N.I.R.A., July 11, 1933, Pearson Papers; Reeves to Brown, July 19, 1933, *ibid.;* code draft, July 21, 1933, Chapin Papers; Chapin to Macauley, June 22, 1933, *ibid.;* N.A.C.C. Bulletin, July 14, 1933, Acc. 203, Box 13, Ford Archives; *New York Times,* July 15, 1933.

18 Cronin interview; Hearing on Automotive Parts and Equipment Manufacturing Industry Proposed Amendments to the Code of Fair Competition, Feb. 27, 1935, N.R.A. Box 7268.

19 The issue was resolved by July 21.

20 "Passenger Car Trade Practices—Possible Codes," included with Reeves to E. Ford, June 19, 1933, Pearson Papers. Included in the Reeves list were such matters as the advertising of delivered prices for automobiles, control of used-car trade-in allowances, establishment of uniform discounts for fleet purchasers, advertising of price reductions on old models when new models were being brought out, limitation of production when field stocks were excessive, and the reduction of the number of models and options.

21 Minutes of June 29, Acc. 203, Box 13, Ford Archives; Moekle to N.A.C.C., July 14, 1933, Acc. 203, Box 3, *ibid.* Montague's June 14 draft, prepared independently of the committee, provided that no unit of the industry was to sell below cost as determined by a uniform method of accounting.

22 Minutes of June 29, 1933, Acc. 203, Box 13, Ford Archives; code draft of July 14, 1933, *ibid.;* Minutes of July 11, 1933, Pearson Papers; code drafts of July 6, 18, 21, 26, 28, Chapin Papers; *Detroit News,* July 12, 1933; *Iron Age,* CXXXII (July 27, 1933), 35. The quotation is taken from the code as finally adopted.

23 N.R.A., *Bulletin No. 3,* July 20, 1933.

24 McPherson, *Labor Relations in the Automobile Industry,* p. 69; statistics in N.R.A. Boxes 655 and 676.

25 Minutes of June 29, 1933, Acc. 203, Box 13, Ford Archives; Reeves to Brown *et al.*, July 10, 1933, *ibid.;* N.A.C.C. Bulletin, July 6, 1933, *ibid.;* code draft of July 14, 1933, Acc. 203, Box 3, *ibid.;* Reeves to Montague, July 24, 1933, *ibid.;* code drafts of July 21, 28, Chapin Papers.

26 N.R.A., *Bulletin No. 3,* July 20, 1933; statistics in N.R.A. Box 655. The N.R.A. subsequently explained that it did not necessarily mean that the total compensation of hourly rated employees whose wages were above the minimum were to be the same regardless of the extent to which their hours were reduced. It did not, however, intend "to turn this Reemployment Agreement into a mere share-the-work movement without a resulting increase of total purchasing power," and therefore it did insist upon some "equitable" adjustment upward for employees receiving above-minimum rates. The N.R.A. stated that employees paid by the day, week, or month were, however, to receive the same pay for a shorter day, week, or month. Interpretations of President's Reemployment Agreement, July 28, Aug. 3, 1933, Chapin Papers.

27 Reeves to Brown, July 19, 1933, Pearson Papers; interview with Pyke Johnson, Sept. 6, 1957; *Detroit News,* July 12, 1933; Chalmers, "Collective Bargaining," Preface, p. 1; G.M., Labor Relations Diary, Section 1 (1946), p. 1.

28 *Iron Age,* CXXXI (June 29, 1933), 1038-D; Minutes of June 29, 1933, Acc. 203, Box 13, Ford Archives; code draft of July 14, 1933, Acc. 203, Box 3, *ibid.;* code drafts of July 6, 21, 28, Chapin Papers.

29 Compare code drafts of July 6 and 28, 1933, Chapin Papers.

30 N.A.C.C. General Bulletin No. G-1623, July 27, 1933, Acc. 203, Box 5, Ford Archives.

31 *Automotive Industries,* LXIX (July 1, 1933), 1; Reeves to Brown, July 19, 1933, Pearson Papers; *Detroit News,* July 12, 1933; *Iron Age,* CXXXII (Aug. 3, 1933), 38-D.

32 *Detroit Free Press,* July 28, 1933.

33 Special Meeting of N.A.C.C. with General Johnson Held in General Motors Building, Detroit, July 28, 1933, Chapin Papers.

34 The source listed in the previous footnote is a transcript of the July 28 meeting.

35 During Sept. 1933, the first month the code was in effect, the average hourly earned rate for Ford's factory employees was 57.9 cents as compared to an industry average of 65.6 cents. Statistics folders, N.R.A. Box 676; George Myrick, Jr., *et al.*, "An Economic Survey of the Automobile Industry," Section Three, p. 52, N.R.A. Box 8309.

36 Johnson, *The Blue Eagle from Egg to Earth* (Garden City, N.Y., 1935), p. 238.

37 Proceedings of Meeting No. 9 of the S.I.R.B., Aug. 14, 1933, N.R.A. Box 8462.

38 *New York Times,* July 29, 30, 1933; *Detroit Free Press,* July 29, 1933.

39 *New York Times,* Aug. 2, 1933; *Detroit News,* Aug. 2, 1933; *Automotive Industries,* LXIX (Aug. 5, 1933), 143; *ibid.* (Aug. 12, 1933), 183; [Carter], *New Dealers,* pp. 42–53; Lawrence Seltzer to Leo Wolman, [Aug., 1933], N.R.A. Box 8174.

40 P. Johnson to Industrial Recovery Committee . . . , Aug. 3, 1933, Acc. 203, Box 13, Ford Archives; *Detroit News,* Aug. 10, 11, 1933; Edward R. Stettinius, Jr., to Lea, Aug. 10, 1933, Nash to H. Johnson, Aug. 11, 1933, Stettinius, Jr., to Lea, Aug. 16, 1933, N.R.A. Box 658.

41 Lyon *et al., N.R.A.,* pp. 428–29; J. R. Lane to Lea, Aug. 14, 1933, Milton Katz and C. M. Dinkins to Lea, Aug. 14, 1933, L.A.B. to Lea, Aug. 15, 1933, N.R.A. Box 662; notes on conference of Aug. 15, 1933, N.R.A. Box 656; Lorwin and Wubnig, *Labor Relations Boards,* pp. 60–66; *Detroit Free Press,* Aug. 13, 1933. As the result of the prehearing discussions, the N.A.C.C. agreed to indicate in the code that the minimum wage rates of factory employees were to apply regardless of whether a worker was compensated by the hour or the piece.   N.R.A. Release No. 345, Aug. 17, 1933.

42 Stenographic transcripts of the hearings are given in N.R.A. Release No. 366, Aug. 18, 1933, and in Hearing on Code of Fair Practices and Competition Presented by the Automobile Industry, Aug. 18, 1933, N.R.A. Box 7264.

43 Notes on conference of Aug. 15, 1933, N.R.A. Box 656.

44 N.R.A. Release No. 34, July 7, 1933.

45 Green pointed out that the annual net labor turnover rates for the combined motor vehicle industries exceeded the average rates for manufacturing as a whole by 68.6 per cent in 1930 and 51.8 per cent in 1932.

46 Seltzer to Wolman, undated, N.R.A. Box 8174; Joseph Geschelin, "What Has Been Done and May Be Done with the Dismissal Wage Idea," *Automotive Industries,* LXIX (Dec. 16, 1933), 734–36+; Everitt D. Hawkins to John Hamm, Dec. 13, 1934, and attached statement, "Dismissal Compensation in the Automobile Industry," N.R.A. Box 661.

47 The figures cited by Green indicated that total payrolls in the combined motor vehicle industries in June 1933 were only 35 per cent of the monthly average for 1929 whereas the volume of motor vehicle output in June 1933 was 55.5 per cent of the monthly average for 1929.   As noted above, however, manhour productivity in the industry declined during the depression.

48 Green gave no indication of what the character of such a fund should be.

49 Other persons who appeared at the public hearing were William Corbitt, the only manufacturer of automotive vehicles in the South, who called for a lower minimum wage for the South; Marion Wade Doyle, who appeared for the National League of Women Voters and opposed the differential for female laborers; William Collins; Peter and Sarah Fagan; A. J. Muste; and a representative of the Metal Polishers International Union.   Written briefs were filed by William J. Lavery, an industrial consultant, who advocated a definition in the code of manufacturer-dealer relationships; James E. Sidel, of the National Child Labor Committee, who protested the wage differential for employees under 21; the M.E.S.A.; and several of the A.F. of L. craft unions, which sought for the workers within their jurisdiction higher wages and shorter hours than the code provided.   Hearing on Code Presented by Automobile Industry, Aug. 18, 1933, *passim,* N.R.A. Box 7264; Sidel to Lea, Aug. 21, 1933, N.R.A. Box 112; D. W. Tracy to Lea, Aug. 17, 1933, W. W. Britton to Johnson, Aug. 15, 1933, N.R.A. Box 658; M. F. Garrett to Johnson, Aug. 18, 1933, N.R.A. Box 660.

50 The only territorial differential the L.A.B. was willing to accept was a North-South differential of two cents.   Seltzer to Lea, Aug. 24, 1933, N.R.A. Box 662.

51 There were only 2440 apprentices in the combined motor vehicle industries in 1930.   Bureau of the Census, *Fifteenth Census of the United States, 1930: Population,* V (Washington, 1933), 470.   The limitation of the differential for females to those not doing the same work as males was inserted in the code between the time of its submission and the public hearing.

52 "Supplemental Statement Submitted by the Code Committee of the Na-

tional Automobile Chamber of Commerce," N.R.A. Box 658; code drafts of Aug. 23 and 25, 1933, N.R.A. Box 655; *Detroit Free Press*, Aug. 20, 21, 22, 1933.

53 Seltzer to Lea, Aug. 24, 1933, N.R.A. Box 662. Seltzer had previously submitted a detailed criticism of Brown's presentation at the Aug. 18 hearing. Seltzer to Lea, Aug. 19, 1933, *ibid.*

54 As noted above, the provisions for equitable adjustment of pay schedules above the minimum and the requirement regarding the pay of females and apprentices were added after the submission of the N.A.C.C. supplementary brief of Aug. 23. Also, whereas previous versions of the code had made no mention of N.R.A. participation in code authority deliberations, the code now stated that the President or the Administrator might designate a representative to participate in conferences with the Chamber regarding the code and that he was to have access to the statistics whose collection by the N.A.C.C. the code required. The Chamber agreed to "hold itself in readiness to assist and keep the Administrator fully advised" and to meet with the Administrator's representative, as requested, to consider suggestions of the Administrator or of any member of the industry regarding the code. Cf. the code drafts of Aug. 23 and 25, 1933, N.R.A. Box 655.

55 *New York Times*, Aug. 24, 1933; *Detroit News*, Aug. 24, 1933.

56 N.R.A. Release No. 463, [Aug. 24, 1933]; *Detroit News*, Aug. 24, 1933.

57 *Detroit News*, Aug. 25, 1933; N.R.A., *Codes of Fair Competition*, I (Washington, 1933), 256.

58 *Detroit Free Press*, Aug. 26, 1933.

59 William N. Loucks to Lea, Aug. 21, 1933, N.R.A. Box 662; Loucks to Lea, Aug. 25, 1933, N.R.A. Box 655.

60 Code for the Automobile Manufacturing Industry, Report and Recommendations of A. E. McKinstry, Aug. 23, 1933, N.R.A. Box 662; Stettinius, Jr., to Lea, Aug. 25, 1933, N.R.A. Box 655.

61 Wolman to Johnson, Aug. 25, 1933; letter of Margaret S. Stabler (an L.A.B. secretary) to Frank Martel, in *Detroit Labor News*, Feb. 14, 1936. Wolman many years later had no recollection of a controversy within the L.A.B. over the merit clause. Interview with Wolman, Feb. 4. 1957.

62 Division of Economic Research and Planning, Report on the Automobile Manufacturing Code, Aug. 26, 1933, N.R.A. Box 662.

63 Report of the Deputy Administrator, Aug. 25, 1933, N.R.A. Box 655.

64 *New York Times*, Aug. 27, 1933; N.R.A. Release No. 523, Aug. 27, 1933; Green to Collins, Aug. 28, 1933, Green Letterbooks.

65 N.R.A. Release No. 366, Aug. 18, 1933, p. 34; *Michigan Manufacturer and Financial Record*, LII (Sept. 2, 1933), 14.

66 *Business Week*, Sept. 2, 1933, p. 3.

67 *Michigan Manufacturer and Financial Record*, LII (Sept. 2, 1933), 14; *Automotive Industries*, LXIX (Sept. 2, 1933), 267; *New York Times*, Aug. 29, 1933; Richard S. Childs, "How the Automobile Code Works," in Alfred M. Bingham and Selden Rodman, eds., *Challenge to the New Deal* (New York, 1934), pp. 113, 115; undated A.W.U. handbill, Chapin Papers; *Industrial Worker*, Sept. 5, 12, 1933.

68 Green to Collins, Aug. 28, 1933, Green Letterbooks; *New York Times*, Aug. 29, 1933; *American Federationist*, XL (Dec., 1933), 1332.

69 Green to Collins, Sept. 18, 1933, Green Letterbooks; Formal Conference, A.P.E.M., Sept. 20, 1933, N.R.A. Box 687.

70 *Detroit News*, Aug. 28, 1933; Chalmers, "Collective Bargaining," III, 10;

"Representatives of Their Own Choosing," *Conference Board Service Letter,* VI (Sept. 30, 1933), 67–68; memo from Richberg to Legal Division, Aug. 30, 1933, N.R.A. Box 654; *New York Times,* Aug. 23, 1933; L. N. Martin to Johnson, Oct. 20, 1933, N.R.A. Box 660.

71 *New York Times,* Sept. 1, 1933; *Detroit News,* Sept. 1, 1933; Lorwin and Wubnig, *Labor Relations Boards,* p. 76.

72 *New York Times,* Sept. 1, 7, 1933; transcript of Johnson press conference, Sept. 6, 1933, N.R.A. Box 8163. Johnson explained at his press conference that he had promised the automobile manufacturers "in an unguarded moment" that they could have such a clause in their code and so "there was nothing to do but let them go ahead with it."

73 Lorwin and Wubnig, *Labor Relations Boards,* pp. 79–82; Roosevelt to Johnson, Oct. 19, 1933, Official File 466, Box 2, Franklin D. Roosevelt Library, Hyde Park, New York (Official File will henceforth be designated O.F.).

74 A modified and considerably weaker merit clause was permitted in the code of the chemical manufacturing industry because of the special problems of that industry. *Codes,* VI (Washington, 1934), 399–400.

75 N.A.C.C. General Bulletin No. G-1630, Aug. 10, 1933, Pearson Papers; Lea to Karl Ammerman, Oct. 3, 6, 1933, N.R.A. Box 656; Reeves to Lea, Sept. 30, Oct. 23, 1933, Lea to Ammerman, Oct. 24, 1933, N.R.A. Box 676; Lane to Lea, Oct. 25, 1933, Lea to Reeves, Oct. 3, 1933, Reeves to Lea, Oct. 6, 1933, N.R.A. Box 661.

NOTES TO CHAPTER III

1 For a similar but somewhat fuller account of the events described in this chapter, see Sidney Fine, "The Ford Motor Company and the N.R.A.," *Business History Review,* XXXII (Winter, 1958), 353–85.

2 Henry Ford, in collaboration with Samuel Crowther, *My Life and Work* (Garden City, New York, 1922), p. 36; Nevins and Hill, *Ford,* II, 105–13.

3 The Reminiscences of Mr. Herman L. Moekle, Mar., 1955, II, 148–50, Ford Archives.

4 *Ibid.,* II, 149–51; The Reminiscences of E. G. Liebold, Jan., 1953, p. 1406, *ibid.;* David L. Lewis, "Henry Ford: A Study in Public Relations (1896–1932)" (Ph.D. thesis, University of Michigan, 1959), p. 489.

5 Hugh Johnson correspondence folder, Acc. 52, Box 8, Ford Archives; H. Ford to Charles Edison, Oct. 6, 1933; *ibid.;* drafts of Cameron statements, *ibid.;* Reminiscences of Liebold, p. 1407, *ibid.;* Third Interview with Mr. W. J. Cameron by Owen Bombard on June 9, 1952, p. 149, *ibid.;* Johnson, *Blue Eagle,* pp. 235–36; *Detroit Free Press,* July 16, 1933. Cf. the version of the conference in Bennett, *We Never Called Him Henry,* p. 96; and in Charles E. Sorensen, with Samuel T. Williamson, *My Forty Years with Ford* (New York, 1956), pp. 258–59.

6 Daniels to H. Ford, Aug. 18, 1933, Cameron to Daniels, Aug. 21, 1933, Acc. 285, Box 1550, Ford Archives.

7 Frank Campsall to Augustus L. Richards, Aug. 10, 1933, Acc. 52, Box 8, *ibid.;* Cameron drafts in *ibid.; New York Times,* Aug. 6, 1933.

8 Special Meeting of N.A.C.C. with General Johnson . . . , July 28, 1933, Chapin Papers; Johnson, *Blue Eagle,* pp. 236–37; Ford to Edison, Oct. 6, 1933, Acc. 52, Box 8, Ford Archives.

9 Ford to Edison, Oct. 6, 1933, Acc. 52, Box 8, Ford Archives; Reminiscences of Moekle, II, 150, *ibid.; Detroit News,* June 25, 1933.

10 Reminiscences of Liebold, p. 1406, Ford Archives.

11 File of letters in folder 11, N.R.A. Box 656; Walter C. Wilkinson to Roosevelt, Jan. 9, 1934, N.R.A. Box 660; N.R.A. letters on F.M.C. attitude, Acc. 390, Box 10, Ford Archives; Jerome T. Harriman to Ford Motor Co., Sept. 1, 1933, George Gould to H. Ford, July 19, 1934, Acc. 38, Box 75, *ibid.;* various letters in Acc. 6, Boxes 150 and 166; Acc. 23, Box 12; and Acc. 38, Box 73, *ibid.*

12 *Detroit News,* Aug. 30, 1933; *New York Times,* Sept. 1, 2, 12, 13, 14, 1933.

13 Jordan D. Hill, *Relationship of N.R.A. to Government Contracts and Contracts Involving the Use of Government Funds,* N.R.A. Division of Review, *Work Materials No. 49* (Washington, 1936), pp. 3–4.

14 Statement of E. C. Simons, Feb. 11, 1958, Ford Archives.

15 Proceedings of Meeting No. 12 of the S.I.R.B., Sept. 6, 1933, N.R.A. Box 8463; Johnson to Roper, Sept. 22, 1933, O.F. 466, Box 2, Roosevelt Library; Press Conference No. 64, Oct. 27, 1933, pp. 382–83, *ibid.*

16 *New York Times,* Oct. 26, 31, 1933; *Detroit News,* Nov. 21, 1933; McCarl to Secretary of Agriculture, Nov. 10, 1933, McCarl to Secretary of Commerce, Nov. 10, 1933, Acc. 52, Box 8, Ford Archives.

17 Ammerman to Johnson, Nov. 15, 1933, and attached letter for Rexford G. Tugwell, N.R.A. Box 654. The wages and hours reports of the Ford Motor Co. are in N.R.A. Box 669.

18 Proceedings of Meeting No. 23 of the S.I.R.B., Nov. 13, 1933, N.R.A. Box 8463. Johnson delayed matters for a short time by raising the question as to whether Sabine had violated the code of the motor vehicle retailing trade by offering to sell Fords to the federal government below list price. In his ruling of Nov. 10 McCarl had declared that he did not believe that the provisions of the retail code applied to sales to the federal government. He now indicated that the question of a bidder's violation of the code "is for judicial determination and not for consideration by the purchasing or contracting officer in the awarding of a contract." The relevant article of the retail code was officially stayed on July 31, 1934, with respect to sales to governmental agencies. Johnson to Tugwell, Nov. 15, 1933, N.R.A. Box 3885; Order No. 46–23, July 31, 1934, *ibid.;* Hill, *Relationship of N.R.A. to Government Contracts,* pp. 13–14.

19 *Detroit News,* Dec. 2, 1933, May 6, 1934; Hill, *Relationship of N.R.A. to Government Contracts,* pp. 17–18.

20 Hill, *Relationship of N.R.A. to Government Contracts,* pp. 38–42; *New York Times,* May 18, 20, 25, 1934; *Detroit News,* May 6, 14, 18, 25, 26, 1934.

21 *Detroit News,* June 26, 27, Aug. 6, 1934; H. J. Collins to Administrator, N.R.A., June 11, 1934, Frank Healy to Blackwell Smith, June 25, 1934, Healy to Sol Rosenblatt, Dec. 6, 1934, Administrative Order GC-73, Jan. 16, 1935, N.R.A. Drawer 1798; Healy to Donald Nelson, Nov. 6, 1934, N.R.A. Drawer 642.

22 Healy to George Lynch, Oct. 12, 1934, Healy to S. Clay Williams *et al.,* Jan. 3, 1934 [1935], N.R.A. Drawer 642; Sabine to Williams, Oct. 22, 1934, N.R.A. Box 3; *Detroit News,* Nov. 22, 1934. There is a copy of the alleged Cowling telegram in N.R.A. Box 677.

23 Executive Assistant, Division II to W. A. Harriman, Nov. 26, 1934, N.R.A. Box 34; *Detroit Free Press,* Feb. 20, 26, 1935.

24 William A. Simonds, *Henry Ford* (Indianapolis, 1943), p. 247; F.T.C., *Report on Motor Vehicle Industry,* p. 649; *Ward's 1939 Automotive Year Book,* pp. 42, 46; *New York Times,* Nov. 2, 1934. On the domestic sales of motor vehicles alone, Ford suffered a loss of $8,242,026 in 1933 and a net profit of $13,928,183 in 1934. F.T.C., *Report on Motor Vehicle Industry,* p. 651.

Ford's 1934 comeback was aided by improvements in the Ford V-8, a strong advertising campaign, improved relations with Ford dealers, and the refusal to raise prices in Apr. 1934, when its competitors took this step. See *Motor*, LXIII (Jan., 1935), 134.

[25] Atwell to Roosevelt, Sept. 29, 1933, Roosevelt to Mac, Oct. 3, 1933, O.F. 3217, Roosevelt Library.

[26] Ford to Edison, Oct. 6, 1933, transcript of phone conversation with Edison, [Oct. 7, 1933], Edison to Ford, Oct. 8, 9, 1933, Acc. 52, Box 8, Ford Archives.

[27] Roosevelt to Ford, Nov. 7, 1933, President's Personal File 680, Roosevelt Library (henceforth, President's Personal File will be cited as P.P.F.); *Detroit News*, Nov. 26, 1933. As a builder of the Eagle boats during World War I, Ford had had some contact with Assistant Secretary of the Navy Roosevelt.

[28] Ford to Roosevelt, Jan. 30, 1934, Roosevelt to Ford, Feb. 23, 1934, P.P.F. 680, Roosevelt Library.

[29] Confidential memo for the President from S. T. Early, undated, attached to Roosevelt to Ford, Nov. 8, 1934, *ibid.;* Ford to Roosevelt, Nov. 16, 1934, McIntyre to Ford, Nov. 21, 1934, Acc. 285, Box 1676, Ford Archives; *Detroit News*, Nov. 25, 1934. The notation, "Hold till after Cong. elections. S.E.," appears at the bottom of Early's memo.

[30] The workers' version of the events of Sept. 26 is presented in Thomas J. Dunphy *et al.* to Wagner, Oct. 11, 1933, N.R.A. Drawer 641; transcript of conference in Milton Handler's office, Dec. 4–5, 1933, Case 105, N.L.B. Drawer 17; and Ford Motor Co., Transcript of Hearing Held at Chester, Pa., Mar. 3, 1934, N.R.A. Drawer 642. Harris' version is in Statement Dictated by Mr. A. M. Harris, Mar. 1, 1934, Acc. 52, Box 12, Ford Archives.

[31] Transcript of Handler conference, Dec. 4–5, 1933, pp. 2, 5–6, Case 105, N.L.B. Drawer 17; Transcript of Chester Hearing, Mar. 3, 1934, pp. 9–10, 25–26, 87–88, N.R.A. Drawer 642; memorandum based on information supplied by Michael J. Gandiello, Oct. 16, 1933, N.R.A. Drawer 641.

[32] There is conflicting evidence regarding the intention of the workers on the morning of the twenty-seventh. See Dunphy *et al.* to Wagner, Oct. 11, 1933, N.R.A. Drawer 641; transcript of Handler conference, Dec. 4–5, 1933, p. 6, Case 105, N.L.B. Drawer 17; Transcript of Chester Hearing, Mar. 3, 1934, p. 89, N.R.A. Drawer 642; *Chester Times*, Sept. 26, 1933.

[33] Transcript of Handler conference, Dec. 4–5, 1933, pp. 8–9, Case 105, N.L.B. Drawer 17; Dewey to William M. Leiserson, Sept. 27, 1933, Wagner to H. Ford, Sept. 29, 1933, Liebold to Wagner, Oct. 3, 1933, Leiserson to Liebold, Oct. 5, 1933, N.R.A. Drawer 641.

[34] A. J. Bait to H. C. Doss, Oct. 20, 1933, Acc. 52, Box 8, Ford Archives; Atcheson to Doss, Oct. 26, 1933, Acc. 52, Box 12, *ibid.;* Dunphy *et al.* to Wagner, no date, N.R.A. Drawer 641; undated memorandum dealing with the reopening of the plant, *ibid.; Chester Times*, Oct. 14, 1933; *Philadelphia Inquirer*, Oct. 15, 1933; Lorwin and Wubnig, *Labor Relations Boards*, p. 174. There is a copy in Acc. 52, Box 12, Ford Archives, of the communication sent to the Chester employees, following the shutdown of the plant, terminating their services with the company.

[35] Wagner to Atcheson, Oct. 14, 1933, Ford Motor Co. to Wagner, Oct. 16, 1933, memorandum by Benedict Wolf, Oct. 23, 1933, N.R.A. Drawer 641; Wagner to Ford Motor Co., Oct. 17, 1933, Atcheson to Doss, Oct. 18, 26, 1933, Acc. 52, Box 12, Ford Archives; Meeting of Strikers' Committee and Chester Branch Officials, Oct. 25, 1933, *ibid.*

36 Doss to Atcheson, Nov. 8, 1933, and attached reply to workers' demands, Atcheson to Doss, Nov. 14, 1933, Acc. 52, Box 12, Ford Archives.

37 Transcript of Handler conference, Dec. 4–5, 1933, Case 105, N.L.B. Drawer 17.

38 Memorandum by Handler, Dec. 7, 1933, N.R.A. Drawer 641; Daily Reports of the N.L.B., Dec. 7, 1933, N.L.B. Box 86; #45 to George J. Schmidt (Chester factory service head), Nov. [Dec.?] 7, 1933, Acc. 52, Box 12, Ford Archives. Internal evidence strongly indicates that the latter report, only a typed copy of which is available in the Ford Archives, was actually made on Dec. 7. If this is so, #45 was Ed Hoffman, acting secretary of the Chester local, who later was chairman of the communist-dominated Ford Workers' Protective Association against Discrimination, an organization formed by former Chester employees after the A.F. of L. federal labor union was dissolved.

39 Dunphy to Healy, Feb. 22, 1934, N.R.A. Drawer 641; exchange of correspondence between William H. Davis and G. C. Royall and Ford Motor Co., Feb. 27–Mar. 4, 1934, N.R.A. Drawer 642; Transcript of Chester Hearing, *ibid.;* *Chester Times,* Mar. 5, 1934. The National Compliance Board, consisting of the Compliance Director and a member each from the L.A.B. and the I.A.B., heard cases involving violation of a code.

40 "Payroll Data," attached to typed sheet headed, "March 1st, 1934," Acc. 52, Box 12, Ford Archives. The president of the local still had not been re-employed as late as Feb. 22, 1934. Dunphy to Healy, Feb. 22, 1934, N.R.A. Drawer 641. Two of the members of the employees' committee had worked for the company for over 10 years. Meeting of the Strikers' Committee and Chester Branch Officials, Oct. 25, 1933, Acc. 52, Box 12, Ford Archives.

41 Lorwin and Wubnig, *Labor Relations Boards,* pp. 206–7.

42 As the N.L.B. interpreted it, collective bargaining required both parties to manifest "a will to agree," to "exert every reasonable effort" to conclude an agreement, and to be prepared to enter into a bilateral contract containing the specific terms agreed upon. An employer met the test of "reasonableness" if he did not obstruct the free election of employee representatives, if he met with properly accredited employee representatives, put forward counterproposals, and "allowed for the higgling and haggling usual in labor bargaining." *Ibid.,* pp. 175–85.

43 *Ibid.,* pp. 178, 205, 207.

44 T. M. Manning to E. Ford, Aug. 24, 1933, and enclosed report of Aug. 22 meeting, A. J. Lepine to Manning, Sept. 11, 1933, Acc. 6, Box 154, Ford Archives; reports of strikers' meetings in Acc. 52, Box 12, *ibid.*

45 Stenographic Report of Conference Held at the Office of the Ford Motor Car Co., Edgewater, Oct. 19, 1933, pp. 2–3, Acc. 52, Box 12, *ibid.;* Albert F. Wickens affidavit, undated, N.R.A. Drawer 642. The day of the first meeting the foreman of the export department warned the workers in his charge that those attending would be discharged. William Herford affidavit, Nov. 11, 1933, *ibid.*

46 *New York Times,* Sept. 29, 1933; Brown to Doss, Nov. 21, 1933, Acc. 52, Box 12, Ford Archives; In re: Striking Employees of Edgewater, New Jersey, Plant of Ford Motor Co. Informal Hearing Held before Harry L. Tepper, Nov. 29, 1933, p. 3, N.R.A. Drawer 642.

47 Stenographic Report of Oct. 19 Conference, pp. 24–29, Acc. 52, Box 12, Ford Archives; Ford Conference at [New Jersey] State Headquarters, Oct. 19, 1933, pp. 8–13, N.R.A. Drawer 642.

[48] Transcript of Shorthand Notes of Conference at the Office of the New Jersey Recovery Board, Oct. 18, 1933, pp. 12–13, 18–26, N.R.A. Drawer 642; W. M. L[eiserson] memorandum, Sept. 29, 1933, *ibid.;* J. T. Ingram report, Sept. 29, 1933, Acc. 52, Box 12, Ford Archives; Stenographic Report of Oct. 19 Conference, pp. 11–15, *ibid.; Newark Evening News,* Sept. 29, 1933.

[49] Thomas H. Wright, "Why Ford's Men Strike," *Christian Century,* L (Nov. 29, 1933), 1501–2; conversation of E. Ford and Esslinger, Oct. 9, 1933, Acc. 52, Box 12, Ford Archives.

[50] Memoranda of phone conversations between Colombo and James M. Beck, Oct. 17, 1933, Doss to Brown (dictated by Colombo), Oct. 17, 1933, Acc. 52, Box 12, Ford Archives; *New York Times,* Oct. 19, 1933; Transcript of Oct. 18 Conference, pp. 3–11, 30–50, N.R.A. Drawer 642; Stenographic Report of Oct. 19 Conference, Acc. 52, Box 12, Ford Archives; Ford Conference at State Headquarters, Oct. 19, 1933, p. 17, N.R.A. Drawer 642.

[51] Doss to Brown, Oct. 31, 1933, and attached statement, Acc. 52, Box 12, Ford Archives; typed sheet dated Nov. 1, 1933, *ibid.* The press reported that Senator Wagner regarded the company's reply as evidence that Ford was bargaining collectively with the strikers. *New York Times,* Nov. 3, 1933.

[52] Report of strikers' meeting, Nov. 2, 1933, Acc. 52, Box 12, Ford Archives; *Newark Evening News,* Nov. 2, 3, 1933.

[53] Strike committee to E. Ford, Nov. 9, 1933, E. Ford to Wickens, Nov. 21, 1933, N.R.A. Drawer 642; Brown to Doss, Nov. 21, 1933, Acc. 52, Box 12, Ford Archives. Brown noted that 75 per cent of the strikers lived in Kearny and Bayonne and that it was unlikely that the company would "ever secure the right type of worker as long as we continue to pick men from these communities. We believe by going to the better communities, north and west of the plant, we will secure a much better class of worker. . . ."

[54] Brown to Doss, Nov. 28, 1933, and attached report of Nov. 27 meeting, Acc. 52, Box 12, Ford Archives; Tepper hearing, Nov. 29, 1933, pp. 2, 7–8, 10–11, N.R.A. Drawer 642.

[55] Brown to J. Crawford, Dec. 12, 1933, Acc. 52, Box 12, Ford Archives.

[56] Report of strikers' meetings, Dec. 13, 18, 1933, Doss to Cameron, Jan. 8, 1934, and attached report of strikers' meeting of Jan. 8, 1934, *ibid.;* Green to Johnson, Dec. 21, 1933, and Brief of Facts on Behalf of the Striking Employees of the Edgewater, New Jersey, Plant of the Ford Motor Co., N.R.A. Drawer 642; Wickens to Davis, Jan. 18, 1934, *ibid.; Newark Evening News,* Dec. 18, 19, 1933, Jan. 9, 1934; *New York Times,* Dec. 27, 1933.

[57] Davis to Ford Motor Co., Jan. 17, 1934, Craig to Davis, Feb. 2, 1934, N.R.A. Drawer 642.

[58] Davis to Johnson, Feb. 5, 1934, Davis to Ford Motor Co., Feb. 15, 17, 1934, Craig to Davis, Feb. 2, 20, 1934, *ibid.;* National Compliance Board, Hearing on Ford Motor Co. Strike at Edgewater, Feb. 23, 1934, N.R.A. Box 7264.

[59] National Compliance Board to Johnson, Mar. 15, 1934, N.R.A. Drawer 642.

[60] Johnson to Davis, Mar. 24, 1934, and enclosed memorandum of Michelson, Mar. 19, 1934, *ibid.*

[61] Stephens to Davis, Mar. 16, 1934, *ibid.;* memorandum from J. W. Randal to Johnson *et al.,* Apr. 17, 1934, *ibid.* For the reluctance of the Department of Justice to prosecute Section 7(a) cases, see Francis Biddle, *In Brief Authority* (Garden City, N.Y., 1962), pp. 25–26.

[62] Randal to Davis, Mar. 15, 1934, N.R.A. Drawer 642; memorandum from

Randal to K. Johnston, Apr. 2, 1934, memorandum from Randal to Johnson *et al.*, Apr. 17, 1934, *ibid.*

63 Memorandum from Randal to Johnson *et al.*, Apr. 17, 1934, Smith to A. G. McNight, Apr. 17, 1934, *ibid.*

64 Randal to Pollak, Apr. 23, 1934, Pollak to William G. Rice, Aug. 28, 1934, *ibid.*; Randal, In re: Ford Motor Co., *ibid.*

NOTES TO CHAPTER IV

1 The production figures cited are from *Ward's 1939 Automotive Year Book*, pp. 10–11; profit figures are taken from F.T.C., *Report on Motor Vehicle Industry*, pp. 491, 597, 649, 651, 676, 718, 742, 806. On the operations of the corporations as a whole, G.M. showed a net profit after income taxes of $80,-509,396 in 1933, $99,124,495 in 1934, and $176,696,683 in 1935; Chrysler, a net profit after taxes of $14,896,334 in 1933, $9,871,044 in 1934 and $42,452,818 in 1935; and Ford (including Lincoln), a net loss of $7,888,718 in 1933 and a net profit after taxes of $21,362,118 in 1934 and of $18,573,804 in 1935. *Ibid.*, pp. 431, 557, 649. See also *Tenth Annual Report of Chrysler Corporation, Year Ended Dec. 31, 1934*. For profit figures for the first half of 1935 as compared to the first half of 1934, see *Automotive Industries*, LXXIII (Aug. 3, 1935), 128.

2 I. D. Everitt to Barton W. Murray, Feb. 7, 1935, N.R.A. Box 654; History of the Code of Fair Competition for the Automobile Manufacturing Industry (Dec., 1935), pp. 29–31, N.R.A. Box 7575; Reeves to Everitt, July 20, 1934, N.R.A. Box 7837; Reeves to Ammerman, Dec. 26, 1933, N.R.A. Box 7897. The N.R.A. records reveal only two official code-authority meetings. Exhibit M, Automobile Code History.

3 Of 775 approved basic and supplementary codes in operation in Jan. 1935, only 26 allowed for labor representation on the code authority. Lyon *et al.*, N.R.A., pp. 166, 459.

4 *Ibid.*, pp. 212, 275; Automobile Code History, p. 31; Kenneth Simpson to Johnson, Mar. 5, 1934, Exhibit N, *ibid.*; N.R.A. Release No. 3962, Mar. 22, 1934.

5 Reeves to Ammerman, Nov. 10, 1933, Ammerman to Reeves, Nov. 10, 1933, Pearson to Charles D. Hastings, Nov. 18, 1933, N.R.A. Box 7897; Ammerman to Pearson, Nov. 24, 1933, N.R.A. Box 661.

6 Automobile Code History, p. 42; Pearson to Everitt, Apr. 30, 1935, and attached letter from Reeves to Labor Branch, Compliance Division, May 5, 1934, N.R.A. Box 658; P. Johnson to Brown, Nov. 2, 1933, Chapin Papers.

7 Automobile Code History, p. 44.

8 See N.R.A. Boxes 654 and 655.

9 N.A.C.C. General Bulletin No. G-1648, Oct. 20, 1933, Acc. 203, Box 13, Ford Archives; N.A.C.C. General Bulletin No. G-1656, Nov. 28, 1933, Acc. 52, Box 7, *ibid.*; Cronin to Hudson Motor Car Co., Jan. 5, 1934, Cronin to Chapin, Feb. 15, 1934, Chapin Papers; Minutes of a Special Meeting, N.A.C.C. Committee on Labor Relations, Jan. 25–26, 1934, *ibid.*; F.T.C., *Report on Motor Vehicle Industry*, pp. 83–84. On Jan. 22, 1934, the N.R.A. issued *Bulletin No. 7*, which distinguished between labor complaints, involving the violation of the labor provisions of a code regarding wages, hours, and working conditions, and labor disputes, defined as "a situation where a strike or lockout exists or is threatened—or a complaint which because it primarily involves Section 7(a) of NIRA may lead to a labor dispute." The bulletin recommended that code authorities

set up separate agencies to handle complaints and disputes. These agencies were to have an equal number of employer and employee representatives and were to choose an additional member to serve as chairman. The administration member of the code authority was also to be a member, without a vote but with veto power. Lorwin and Wubnig, *Labor Relations Boards,* pp. 272–76; Lyon *et al., N.R.A.,* pp. 446–48.

10 Exhibit M, Automobile Code History.

11 Minutes of Special Meeting . . . , Jan. 25–26, 1934, Chapin Papers.

12 The five persons recommended were Frederick Haynes; Joseph Moynihan, state circuit court judge in Michigan; Fred W. Castator, a Detroit councilman and a founder of the *Detroit Labor News;* Fred M. Butzel, a Detroit attorney and a former vice-president of the Detroit Board of Commerce; and Dr. Merton S. Rice, a Methodist minister. The sixth person suggested by the Committee on Labor Relations had been John Lodge.

13 Reeves to Ammerman, Jan. 28, 29, 1934, N.R.A. Box 654.

14 Ammerman to E. C. Meyer, Feb. 2, 1934, R. M. Wilmotte to Wilson Compton, Feb. 5, 1934, *ibid.*

15 Reeves to E. Ford, Nov. 29, 1933, Dec. 20, 1933, J. C. Crawford to Reeves, Feb. 22, 1934, Acc. 203, Box 9, Ford Archives; Reeves to various companies, July 24, 1934, Acc. 203, Box 13, *ibid.;* Exhibits O–V, Automobile Code History; Reeves to Everitt, Mar. 23, 1935, N.R.A. Box 656; Reeves to A.M.A. Directors, June 27, 1935, Chapin Papers; A.M.A. Bulletin, Oct. 11, 1935, Pearson Papers. A code authority could not insist that companies covered by the code contribute to code expenses unless the code contained a provision making nonpayment of an equitable share of the costs a code violation and unless the code budget and the basis of assessment of costs had been approved by the N.R.A. These conditions did not obtain in the auto industry. N.A.C.C. General Bulletin No. G-1694, Apr. 18, 1934, Pearson Papers.

16 Cronin to Leo Wolman, Mar. 29, 1934, A.L.B. Drawer 4106.

17 Reeves to Limousine Body Co. *et al.,* Aug. 1, 1933, Pearson Papers; N.A.C.C. Bulletin, Feb. 16, 1934, Acc. 203, Box 3, Ford Archives; Ammerman to Reeves, May 25, 1934, N.R.A. Box 654; Ammerman to R. C. Ayers, Mar. 30, 1936, N.R.A. Box 8310; Automobile Code History, p. 5.

18 The N.A.C.C. maintained that this had been the position of the industry and the N.R.A. when the code had been submitted, and the N.R.A. concurred. Pearson to Everitt, Apr. 30, 1935, citing N.A.C.C. Bulletin, Dec. 4, 1933, N.R.A. Box 658; P. Johnson to George L. Berry, June 4, 1934, N.R.A. Box 654. It might be noted that Delco-Remy and Guide Lamp, although units of the G.M. complex, were subject to the automobile parts code because they manufactured parts and accessories for general sale rather than exclusively for G.M. AC Spark Plug, which was in a comparable position, was subject to the auto code, perhaps because it would otherwise have been the only one of G.M.'s Flint divisions subject to another code.

19 P. Johnson to Brown, Nov. 22, 1933, P. Johnson to Chapin, Nov. 10, 1933, Chapin Papers; N.A.C.C. Bulletin, Nov. 15, 1933, Acc. 52, Box 7, Ford Archives.

20 A.M.A. Bulletins, Dec. 27, 1934, Feb. 15, 1935, Acc. 203, Box 6, Ford Archives. For the commercial body code, see *Codes,* XIII (Washington, 1934), 160–72.

21 House Committee on Labor, *Thirty-Hour Week Bill, Hearings on H.R.*

7202 . . . , 73 Cong., 2 Sess. (Washington, 1934), p. 289; Ammerman to Ayers, Mar. 30, 1936, N.R.A. Box 8310.

22 Reeves to Johnson, Dec. 26, 1933, Ammerman to Johnson, Dec. 28, 1933, N.R.A. Box 654; Ammerman to Lea, Jan. 3, 1934, N.R.A. Box 662; letters to Robert C. Graham *et al.*, Jan. 4, 1934, *ibid.; Codes*, V (Washington, 1934), 670–72.

23 Alvin Brown to Administrator, Dec. 28, 1933, N.R.A. Box 661; *Codes*, V, 670.

24 About 85 per cent of the codes, covering somewhat more than half of the employees in codified industries, called for a 40-hour week; approximately half of the remaining codes stipulated a work week of less than 40 hours, and the other half a work week above 40 hours. Lyon *et al.*, *N.R.A.*, p. 368.

25 *Automotive Industries*, LXX (Jan. 13, 1934), 55; *Detroit News*, Jan. 11, 1934; *New York Times*, Feb. 2, 22, 1934; Collins to Green, Jan. 22, 1934, Collins File.

26 Myrick, Jr., *et al.*, "An Economic Survey of the Automobile Industry," Section Three, p. 52, N.R.A. Box 8309; Max Wollering to Chapin, Aug. 21, 1934, Chapin Papers; Statistics folders, N.R.A. Box 676. Total N.A.C.C. factory employment in Apr. 1934 was 224,970 as compared to 237,655 in Apr. 1929.

27 N.A.C.C. Bulletin, Feb. 27, 1934, Acc. 203, Box 3, Ford Archives; *Detroit News*, Feb. 28, 1934; *United States News*, Mar. 16, 1934, pp. 7, 18.

28 *Automotive Daily News*, Mar. 16, 1934; *New York Times*, Mar. 14, 1934; *Business Week*, Mar. 17, 1934, pp. 9–10; *Michigan Manufacturer and Financial Record*, LIII (Mar. 31, 1934), 5.

29 Reeves to Johnson, Apr. 6, 1934, Ammerman to Lea, Apr. 11, 1934, and attached draft of amendment, N.R.A. Box 654; Reeves to Johnson, Apr. 17, 1934, N.R.A. Box 661; N.A.C.C. General Bulletin No. G-1697, May 14, 1934, Acc. 203, Box 5, Ford Archives.

30 Average hours per week of employees in the 40-hour group were 37.1 in Apr., 31.7 in May, 32.7 in June, 31.1 in July, 28.5 in Aug., and 26.7 in Sept. Myrick, Jr., *et al.*, "Economic Survey," Section Three, p. 52.

31 *Codes*, XXI (Washington, 1935), 204; Myrick, Jr., *et al.*, "Economic Survey," Section Three, p. 52.

32 Lyon *et al.*, *N.R.A.*, pp. 370–74. Of 94 motor vehicle firms studied by the B.L.S. in 1928, 55 paid an overtime rate to all or some of their employees, and 48 paid above the regular rate for Sunday and holiday work. B.L.S., *Bulletin No. 502*, p. 16.

33 N.A.C.C. Bulletins, Dec. 19, 1933, Sept. 22, 1934, Acc. 203, Box 13, Ford Archives; Reeves to Everitt, Apr. 19, 1935, N.R.A. Box 659. In Apr. 1935 the N.R.A. agreed to permit the industry to average the hours for employees in the 40-hour group over the entire period Sept. 5, 1933–June 16, 1935, but the industry was satisfied to have 12 months as its averaging period. See Everitt to Murray, Apr. 29, 1935, N.R.A. Box 659.

34 L.A.B. to Murray, Apr. 9, 1935, N.R.A. Box 656; L.A.B. memorandum for Everitt, May 7, 1935, N.R.A. Box 661. Of the codes permitting averaging, 66 per cent limited the period to 17 weeks or less. Lyon *et al.*, *N.R.A.*, p. 373.

35 Reeves to Ammerman, June 8, 1934, Cronin to Ammerman, July 10, 1934, Haynes to Everitt, July 20, 1934, Cronin to Everitt, Aug. 8, 1934, Everitt to R. M. Gates, Aug. 16, 1934, N.R.A. Box 659; Minutes of Meeting . . . before . . .

Everitt . . . , July 23, 1934, *ibid.;* Keith Carlin interpretation, July 23, 1934, *ibid.;* Everitt to C. E. Adams, Aug. ?, 1934, N.R.A. Box 658. The L.A.B. had reservations about the whole idea and preferred that individual employees who were in trouble should seek an exemption from the N.R.A. Raushenbush to Gates, July 24, 1934, *ibid.*

36 Average hours per week for employees in this group were 32.7 in June, 31.1 in July, 28.5 in Aug., and 26.7 in Sept. Myrick, Jr., *et al.,* "Economic Survey," Section Three, p. 52.

37 N.A.C.C. Bulletin, July 23, 1934, Acc. 203, Box 3, Ford Archives; Ammerman to Leighton H. Peebles, Oct. 3, 1934, N.R.A. Box 7551.

38 See Lyon *et al.,* N.R.A., pp. 381–83.

39 Roberts to Murray, May 17, 1935, Stanley H. Fuld to Everitt, Mar. 22, 1935, A. F. Bassett to Everitt, Apr. 2, 1935, Reeves to Everitt, Apr. 19, 1935, Leon Shiman to Roberts, Mar. 25, 1935, N.R.A. Box 659. Between Sept. 1933 and Aug. 1934 the number of office and salaried employees earning less than $35 ranged from 14,048 in Sept. 1933 to 15,455 in May 1934. Their average weekly hours ranged from 35 to 39. Myrick, Jr., *et al.,* "Economic Survey," Section Three, p. 52.

40 Pearson to Everitt, Apr. 30, 1935, enclosing Reeves to Labor Branch, Compliance Division, May 5, 1934, N.R.A. Box 658; Myrick, Jr., *et al.,* "Economic Survey," Section Three, p. 52.

41 P. Johnson to Lea, Sept. 7, 1933, N.R.A. Box 656; N.A.C.C. General Bulletin No. G-1655, Nov. 24, 1933, Pearson Papers; Pearson to Everitt, Apr. 30, 1935, enclosing Reeves to Labor Branch, Compliance Division, May 5, 1934, N.R.A. Box 658; Roberts to Murray, May 10, 1935, Reeves to Everitt, Apr. 19, 1935, N.R.A. Box 659.

42 R. C. Falting to Green, Jan. 23, 1934, Green to Ammerman, Jan. 29, 1934, Falting to Ammerman, Feb. 13, 1934, James Wilson to McGrady, Mar. 8, 1934, Ammerman to Reeves, Apr. 6, 1934, Cronin to Ammerman, May 6, 1934, N.R.A. Box 661; Matthew Smith to Administrator of Auto Code, May 23, 1934, N.R.A. Box 657; Ammerman to Smith, June 15, 1934, N.R.A. Box 660; S.D.E. to L.A.B., Mar. 7, 1934, William Foster to Smith, Mar. 3, 1934, R. E. Covert to Smith, Mar. 3, 1934, N.R.A. Box 660.

43 For the files on the other four cases, which involved Studebaker, Hupp, the Moller Motor Co., and the Henney Motor Co., see N.R.A. Box 655. Hupp was permitted to work 23 employees in excess of the 42-hour average for a period of almost a month provided it paid them time-and-one-half for the overtime.

44 The elaborate file on the Chrysler New Castle case is in *ibid.*

45 Spurgeon Bell to C. A. Bishop, Aug. 9, 1934, Bell to Leon Henderson, Aug. 29, 1934, N.R.A. Box 676; Myrick, Jr., *et al.,* "Economic Survey," Section Three, pp. 111–13.

46 Ammerman to Johnson, Dec. 5, 1933, McCarty to Pearson, Dec. 13, 1933, Herman L. Weckler to Pearson, Jan. 26, 1934, Weckler to N.A.C.C., Apr. 24, 1934, H. K. Hill to A.M.A., Nov. 7, 1934, N.R.A. Box 7897; B. A. Gramm to Pearson, May 22, 1934, N.R.A. Box 7898.

47 Hearing on Code of Fair Practices and Competition Presented by Automotive Parts and Equipment Manufacturing Industry, Oct. 3, 1933, pp. 9, 31, 47–48, 75–139, N.R.A. Box 7268; Seltzer, Memorandum on Proposed Code for the

Automotive Parts and Equipment Manufacturing Industry, undated, N.R.A. Box 717; Seltzer to L.A.B., Oct. 3, 1933, *ibid.*

48 Wilmotte to Raushenbush, June 18, 1934, N.R.A. Box 687; *Codes,* II (Washington, 1934), 603–8; Hearing on A.P.E.M. Code, Oct. 3, 1933, p. 56, N.R.A. Box 7268.

49 N.A.C.C. Bulletin, Feb. 26, 1934, Acc. 203, Box 3, Ford Archives; *Codes,* IX (Washington, 1934), 635–37; Wilmotte to Raushenbush, June 18, 1934, N.R.A. Box 687; unidentified item in N.R.A. Box 719.

50 *Automotive Industries,* LXX (May 26, 1934), 654; *ibid.,* LXXII (June 1, 1935), 738; *ibid.,* LXXIII (Aug. 3, 1935), 128; *Survey of Current Business,* Dec., 1933, p. 54; *ibid.,* Dec., 1934, p. 55; *ibid.,* Dec., 1935, p. 59; Whitney, *Antitrust Policies,* I, 496–97.

51 C. O. Skinner, "More Work at Higher Wages," *Automotive Industries,* LXXI (Nov. 17, 1934), 613–14; A.P.E.M., Factory Employment, Payrolls, Hours, and Wages, 1933–1935, N.R.A. Box 688.

52 Roy Wise to Johnson, Sept. 21, 1933, Richard Lansburgh to Henderson, Nov. 5, 1934, N.R.A. Box 5370; Hearing on the Special Tool, Die, and Machine Shop Industry, Informal Conference, Oct. 31, 1934, pp. 25–26, 29, N.R.A. Box 3243; S. L. Hudd, Report of a Field Investigation of the Tool and Die Industry in the Detroit Area, Feb. 5, 1935, in Myrick, Jr., *et al.,* "Economic Survey," Section Five, pp. 490, 492.

53 Wise to Johnson, Sept. 21, 1933, N.R.A. Box 5370; Report of R. von Hughn and J. A. Hanley, Nov. 29, 1933, N.R.A. Box 5369; Special Tool, Die, and Machine Shop Industry, Code History, p. 2, N.R.A. Document Series, National Archives.

54 *Codes,* III (Washington, 1934), 191. The minimum wage was set at 40 cents per hour.

55 Report of A. F. Bassett, Nov. 14, 1934, N.R.A. Box 5370; Hudd Report, p. 493.

56 The Detroit tool and die manufacturers had been granted an exception from the 35-hour limitation of the P.R.A. for the period Sept. 13–Nov. 5, 1933. Undated and unaddressed letter written by Franklin S. Pollak, N.R.A. Box 181; Automotive Tool and Die Manufacturers Association to N.R.A., Nov. 6, 1933, *ibid.*

57 Automotive Tool and Die Manufacturers Association to Wise, Sept. 26, 1934, Wise to Dexter A. Tutein, Sept. 28, 1934, N.R.A. Box 5370; Order No. 122-19B, Sept. 29, 1934, N.R.A. Box 5372; Informal Conference, Oct. 31, 1934, N.R.A. Box 3243.

58 Smith to Lloyd Garrison, Oct. 2, 1934, N.R.A. Box 5374; Informal Conference, Oct. 31, 1934, pp. 11–13, 16–17, 42–48, 65–69, 86–87, N.R.A. Box 3243; William E. Chalmers to A. H. Caesar, Nov. 7, 1934, Smith to Gates, Oct. 16, 19, 1934, Albert W. Bechtel to Gates, Oct. 23, 1934, Lansburgh to Henderson, Nov. 5, 1934, N.R.A. Box 5370; Larned to Caesar, Oct. 1, 1934, in Myrick, Jr., *et al.,* "Economic Survey," Section Five, pp. 482–85; Hudd Report, p. 590. According to the 1930 census, there were 16,060 tool makers, die setters, and die sinkers and 2361 millwrights in Detroit. Bureau of the Census, *Fifteenth Census of the United States: 1930, Population,* IV (Washington, 1933), 803.

59 Informal Conference, Oct. 31, 1934, pp. 3–5, 56–57, 59–61, N.R.A. Box 3243; Chalmers to Caesar, Nov. 7, 1934, N.R.A. Box 5370; Hudd Report, pp.

491–92. Matthew Smith reported that wages had formerly been about 15 cents per hour higher in the job shops than in the tool rooms of the main plants, but that the main plants were now paying slightly higher wages than the job shops. Informal Conference, Oct. 31, 1934, pp. 60–61, N.R.A. Box 3243.

60 Informal Conference, Oct. 31, 1934, N.R.A. Box 3243; Bassett Report, Nov. 14, 1934, N.R.A. Box 5370; Lansburgh to Henderson, Nov. 5, 1934, Chalmers to Caesar, Nov. 7, 1934, Caesar to Wise, Dec. 14, 1934, *ibid.;* Wise to Caesar, Feb. 1, 1935, N.R.A. Box 5369; Hudd Report, p. 494; Myrick, Jr., *et al.,* "Economic Survey," Section Five, pp. 472–80.

61 Wise to Caesar, Jan. 3, 1935, N.R.A. Box 5369; Automotive Tool and Die Manufacturers Association to A. Howard Myers, Feb. 25, 1935, N.R.A. Box 5370; F. W. Buck to Tutein, June 20, 1935, N.R.A. Box 5372; Hudd Report, pp. 493–94; Myrick, Jr., *et al.,* "Economic Survey," Section Five, pp. 507–8; Special Tool, Die, and Machine Shop Industry, Code History, pp. 15–16, N.R.A. Document Series.

62 N.I.R.B. to Roosevelt, Jan. 28, 1935, Exhibit J, Automobile Code History; Nelson to Johnston, Mar. 1, 1935, Ammerman to Johnston, June 26, 1935, N.R.A. Box 8375; Ammerman to Johnston, Apr. 10, May 9, 24, June 14, 1935, N.R.A. Box 662. Ammerman proposed that the basic work week should be 40 hours and that employees should be permitted to work not more than 8 additional hours each calendar week for 3 periods (a period was to consist of 4 calendar weeks) a year at the regular rate. Firemen, plant engineers, electricians, and employees engaged in maintenance and repair work might work 44 hours per week, and watchmen 56 hours per week. There was to be no averaging, and the maximum hours for any classification of workers could be exceeded only if an overtime rate was paid.

63 Myrick, Jr., *et al.,* "Economic Survey," Section Three, p. 52; N. A. Tolles and M. W. LaFever, "Wages, Hours, Employment, and Annual Earnings in the Motor Vehicle Industry, 1934," *Monthly Labor Review,* XLII (Mar., 1936), 528–29. The Myrick study figures are derived from the monthly reports filed by firms subject to the code. The Tolles and LaFever figures are estimates of the number employed in automobile and body plants. The two sets of figures are similar but not identical. The average number of factory employees in plants covered by the code was 293,983 between Nov. 1, 1933, and Aug. 1934, and 323,237, an increase of about 10 per cent, between Oct. 1934 and July 1935. "Automobile Industry Factory Labor Conditions," appended to A.M.A. Bulletin, Oct. 14, 1935, Pearson Papers. The number of office and salaried employees during the code period ranged from about 14,000 to about 15,450. Myrick, Jr., *et al.,* "Economic Survey," Section Three, p. 52.

64 Witt Bowden, "Employment, Earnings, Production, and Prices, 1932 to January 1936," *Monthly Labor Review,* XLII (Apr., 1936), 857–58; Tolles and LaFever, "Wages ... in the Motor Vehicle Industry, 1934," p. 529.

65 Bowden, "Employment ... 1932 to January 1936," pp. 857–58; Tolles and LaFever, "Wages ... in the Motor Vehicle Industry, 1934," pp. 529, 535; Bureau of the Census, *Fifteenth Census, Manufactures: 1929,* II, 1220, 1227, 1231. The B.L.S. figures for 1933–35 indicate that employment in automobile and body plants, which corresponds closely to employment in the automobile manufacturing industry as codified, constituted about 75 per cent of the total factory employment in the combined motor vehicle industries during those years. In using the 1929 census of manufactures figures for the combined motor vehicle

industries, I have therefore assumed that 75 per cent of the total factory employment was accounted for by the automobile manufacturing division, as later codified. The re-employment record of the automobile manufacturing industry would appear to be even more impressive if the B.L.S. figures for employment in the motor vehicle industry in 1929 (derived from the monthly "trend of employment" statistics in the *Monthly Labor Review*) were used as the basis for comparison with 1933–35 rather than the slightly higher but more commonly cited census of manufactures figures. See B.L.S., *Employment and Earnings Statistics for the United States, 1909–60, Bulletin No. 1312* (Washington, 1961), p. 30, for figures which indicate a somewhat greater degree of re-employment among production workers in manufacturing as a whole than the figures in the Bowden article do.

66 Statistics folders, N.R.A. Box 676; "Automobile Industry Factory Labor Conditions," Pearson Papers.

67 Friday, "Effect of Limitation of Hours on Employment in the Automobile Industry," May 9, 1935, enclosed with Reeves to Macauley *et al.*, May 9, 1935, Chapin Papers. The factory employment of N.A.C.C. members during the first 6 months of 1934 was 85 per cent of the total for the comparable period in 1929 although production was only 58 per cent as great. Wollering to Chapin, Aug. 21, 1934, *ibid.*

68 Statement of the Code Authority . . . , Mar. 6, 1934, Exhibit BB, Automobile Code History; Reeves to N.I.R.B., Feb. 4, 1935, N.R.A. Box 660; Subcommittee of Senate Committee on Judiciary, *Thirty-Hour Work Week, Hearings on S. 87,* 74 Cong., 1 Sess. (Washington, 1935), pp. 299–302; Macauley to Richberg, Apr. 29, 1935, N.R.A. Box 661; A.M.A. General Bulletin No. G-1745, Apr. 18, 1935, Chapin Papers; Reeves to Pat Harrison, Apr. 17, 1935, in Senate Committee on Finance, *Investigation of National Recovery Administration, Hearings Pursuant to S. Res. 79,* 74 Cong., 1 Sess. (Washington, 1935), pp. 2718–20.

69 About 50 per cent of the codes specified a minimum wage of 40 cents per hour for unskilled production workers, and most of the rest set the figure at between 30–40 cents per hour. Lyon *et al., N.R.A.*, pp. 318–19.

70 Statistics folders, N.R.A. Box 676; wages and hours reports in N.R.A. Boxes 663, 667, 671. Ford did not have to raise the wages of any of its employees because of the code minima.

71 Automobile Code History, pp. 64–65; Reeves to N.I.R.B., Feb. 4, 1935, N.R.A. Box 660; Information on the Automobile Industry from Women's Bureau Agents . . . , Fall, 1933, N.R.A. Box 660; McPherson, *Labor Relations in the Automobile Industry*, pp. 8–9.

72 Corbitt wanted the minimum wage in the South reduced to 30 cents per hour for towns below 250,000 population and to 40 cents for towns above 250,000. Corbitt to Ammerman, Dec. 26, 1933, Ammerman to Corbitt, Feb. 8, 1934, N.R.A. Box 655; Exhibit M, Automobile Code History; Ammerman to Ayers, Mar. 27, 1936, N.R.A. Box 8310; Bell to Henderson, Aug. 31, 1934, N.R.A. Box 676; Statistics folders, *ibid.*

73 Reeves to N.I.R.B., Feb. 4, 1935, N.R.A. Box 660. The differential was 14.57 cents in 1929; 13.37 cents in 1930; 12.3 cents in 1931; 11.15 cents in 1932; 12.07 cents in 1933; and 15 cents in 1934. Roos, *NRA Economic Planning*, p. 183. In Apr. 1934 the hourly rates for male employees in 56 occupational groups in automobile and body plants ranged from 56.4 cents for nonproductive service occupations to $1.06 for bumpers and dingmen. This com-

pared with a range of 44.3 cents to 86 cents in 1932 and 57.2 cents to $1.128 in 1928 in the combined motor vehicle industries. Tolles and LaFever, "Wages ... in the Motor Vehicle Industry, 1934," pp. 548–49; B.L.S., *Bulletin No. 502*, p. 2; "Wages and Hours of Labor in the Motor Vehicle Industry, 1932," *Monthly Labor Review*, XXXVI (June, 1933), 1366. Altogether, 197 of 517 codes analyzed in the Lyon study contained "equitable adjustment" formulas of one kind or another, but only 41 codes called for equitable adjustment without some other safeguard. Lyon *et al.*, *N.R.A.*, pp. 345, 353–55.

74 Bowden, "Employment ... 1932 to January 1936," pp. 857–58; Myrick, Jr., *et al.*, "Economic Survey," Section Three, pp. 43–44; Tolles and LaFever, "Wages ... in the Motor Vehicle Industry, 1934," pp. 529, 534, 535, 537; "Automobile Industry Factory Labor Conditions," Pearson Papers; Bureau of the Census, *Fifteenth Census, Manufactures: 1929*, II, 1220. I have assumed on the basis of 1933–35 B.L.S. figures (see n. 65) that approximately 77 per cent of the average weekly payrolls of wage earners in the combined motor vehicle industries was accounted for by the automobile manufacturing division as defined in the code. Cf. B.L.S., *Bulletin No. 1312*, p. 30, for the average weekly earnings of production workers in manufacturing as a whole.

75 Myrick, Jr., *et al.*, "Economic Survey," Section Three, pp. 43–44, 52; "Automobile Industry Factory Labor Conditions," Pearson Papers; Macauley to Richberg, Apr. 29, 1935, N.R.A. Box 661; Friday, "Effect of Limitation of Hours," Chapin Papers; A.M.A., *Automobile Facts and Figures, 1937*, p. 49.

76 *Survey of Current Business*, Dec., 1933, p. 5; *ibid.*, Dec., 1934, p. 5; *ibid.*, Dec., 1935, p. 5; Tolles and LaFever, "Wages ... in the Motor Vehicle Industry, 1934," pp. 530, 534; Bowden, "Employment ... 1932 to January 1936," pp. 857–58.

77 Athel F. Denham, "Day Rates Supplant Group Bonus," *Automotive Industries*, LXXI (Dec. 8, 1934), 702–3; Frank J. Oliver, "It's 'Hour Rates' in Detroit," *Factory Management and Maintenance*, XCIII (Jan., 1935), 9–10, 40–41; Charles B. Gordy, "Back to Day Rates," *American Machinist*, LXXIX (Feb. 13, 1935), 161–63; *Business Week*, Mar. 30, 1935, pp. 21–22; Z. Clark Dickinson, *Compensating Industrial Effort* (New York, c. 1937), pp. 283–84; McPherson and Lucheck, "Automobiles," p. 612; *Historical Statistics*, p. 600.

78 Reeves to Manufacturers, Jan. 8, 1935, enclosing letter to S. Clay Williams, Exhibit HH, Automobile Code History.

79 *Codes*, II (Washington, 1934), 671–76; A.M.A., *Automobile Facts and Figures, 1936*, p. 89. The code authority functioned as a "Subdivision Authority" under N.A.C.C. supervision.

80 *Automotive Daily News*, Jan. 12, 1935.

81 Myrick, Jr., *et al.*, "Economic Survey," Section One, pp. 26–27, 46–49, 92, 150–51; F.T.C., *Report on Motor Vehicle Industry*, pp. 491, 493, 535, 597, 599, 651, 652. In 1929, sales of replacement parts by automobile manufacturers totaled $346,019,661 whereas parts manufacturers sold replacement parts worth $212,-374,000 to other distributors. Myrick, Jr., *et al.*, "Economic Survey," Section One, p. 92. Ford's net profit on domestic motor vehicle sales from 1933 to 1935 was under $6 million, but it netted over $17 million on domestic sales of parts and accessories. F.T.C., *Report on Motor Vehicle Industry*, p. 651.

82 Ammerman Memorandum, Nov. 9, 1933, in Myrick, Jr., *et al.*, "Economic Survey," Section Five, pp. 278–79; Hearing on Code of Fair Practices and Com-

petition Presented by Wholesale Automotive Trades, Oct. 21, 1933, pp. 61–66, N.R.A. Box 7268; B. W. Ruark to Ammerman, Oct. 26, 1933, Volume A, Code 163, N.R.A. Box 211. There is a copy of the code as presented at the Oct. 21 hearing in N.R.A. Box 5805.

83 "Maintenance of Discount Schedules as Provided in Code Is Essential," Volume A, Code 163, N.R.A. Box 211; Myrick, Jr., *et al.*, "Economic Survey," Section Five, pp. 282–85; Cleveland Automotive Jobbers Association to All Major Manufacturers, Jan. 31, 1934, A. J. Routhier to Johnson, June 4, 1934, G. F. Morrissey to Johnson, June 1, 1934, N.R.A. Box 5805. Wholesalers similarly complained that chain stores and mail order houses, because of their buying power, were able to undersell the retail outlets upon which the wholesalers depended. See, particularly, the Fact-Finding folder in N.R.A. Box 5805.

84 Ammerman Memonandum, Nov. 9, 1933, Ammerman to Simpson, Nov. 12, 1933, in Myrick, Jr., *et al.*, "Economic Survey," Section Five, pp. 278, 285; Ruark to Ammerman, Oct. 26, 1933, N.R.A. Box 211; Industrial Advisor's Report, [Dec. 8, 1933], Volume II, N.R.A. Box 5804.

85 Ammerman Memorandum, Nov. 9, 1933, N.R.A. Box 8310; Ruark to Ammerman, Oct. 26, 1933, N.R.A. Box 211.

86 Hearing on Wholesale Automotive Trades Code, Oct. 21, 1933, p. 65, N.R.A. Box 7268; Sturgis to Macauley *et al.*, Nov. 17, 1933, Chapin Papers; N.A.C.C. Bulletin, Nov. 20, 1933, Acc. 203, Box 13, Ford Archives.

87 Hearing on Wholesale Automotive Trades Code, Oct. 21, 1933, p. 64, N.R.A. Box 7268; Ammerman Memorandum, Nov. 9, 1933, N.R.A. Box 8310.

88 *Codes*, IV (Washington, 1934), 189.

89 N.A.C.C. General Bulletin No. G-1676, Feb. 20, 1934, Pearson Papers; Ammerman to Lewis, Feb. 6, 1934, Lewis to Ammerman, Mar. 8, 1934, Everitt to Lewis, Apr. 27, 1934, N.R.A. Box 5805; Presentation of N.A.C.C., Fact-Finding Committee, Wholesale Automotive Trade, Mar. 6, 1934, *ibid.;* Hearing on Meeting of Fact-Finding Committee, Wholesale Automotive Trade, Mar. 6, 1934, N.R.A. Box 7269. Lewis conceded that "no adequate facts" had been presented by the jobbers to substantiate their charges. He pointed to the Ford Motor Co., which was not represented on the committee, as a "disorganizing element" in the trade and noted as an additional disturbing factor the manufacturers who flooded the market with inferior parts.

90 For the development of N.R.A. policy regarding price fixing, see Schlesinger, Jr., *Coming of the New Deal*, pp. 122–25.

91 Brief for Fact-Finding Committee by Wholesale Automotive Trade Authority, May 16, 1934, N.R.A. Box 8375; Hearing on the Wholesale Automotive Trade, Fact-Finding Committee, May 16, 1934, N.R.A. Box 7269; James E. Hughes to Ammerman, June 22, 1934, Everitt to Frank G. Stewart, July 7, 1934, Satchell to Everitt, July 13, 1934, *ibid.; Motor*, LXII (July, 1934), 54. It has been claimed that the jobbers were unable to present the necessary evidence of unfair practices because they could not subpoena information regarding contracts from dealers, vehicle makers, and parts manufacturers. *Ibid.*, LXI (Apr., 1934), 40, 108.

92 Myrick, Jr., *et al.*, "Economic Survey," Section Five, pp. 239–40; *Codes*, IV, 189.

93 Hearing on Code of Fair Practices and Competition Presented by Motor Vehicle Retailing Trade, Sept. 18, 1933, pp. 98–100, N.R.A. Box 7267; *Motor*,

LX (Dec., 1933), 76; *ibid.,* LXI (May, 1934), 74; Vesper to Ammerman, Apr. 21, 1934, Ammerman to Simpson, May 15, 1934, N.R.A. Box 3885; A. J. Brosseau to P. Johnson, Aug. 29, 1933, N.R.A. Box 3832.

94 *Codes,* I, 568–71. With the approval of his state advisory committee and the manufacturer, a dealer could sell models that were being discontinued at less than list price.

95 See Chapter I.

96 *United States News,* Mar. 16, 1934, p. 61; *Automotive Daily News,* Jan. 14, 1935; *Automotive Industries,* LXXII (Jan. 19, 1935), 68; Roberts, "Automobile Industry Study Codes and Effect," Chapin Papers.

97 O. T. Hamilton to Johnson, July 13, 1933, N.R.A. Box 656; Heimlich to Williams, Nov. 26, 1934, enclosing Heimlich to Roosevelt, Nov. 13, 1934, N.R.A. Box 7682.

98 Everitt to Vesper, July 2, 1934, T. W. Wilson to J. F. Delaney, July 5, 1934, W. F. McAfee to Ammerman, July 13, 1934, N.R.A. Box 3885.

99 N.A.C.C. to Presidents and Sales Managers, Aug. 24, 1934, enclosing Vesper to N.A.C.C., Aug. 22, 1934, Pearson Papers; *Automotive Daily News,* July 14, 21, 1934; *Automotive Industries,* LXXI (July 21, 1934), 61, 66; *ibid.,* LXXI (Sept. 1, 1934), 246.

100 Roos, *NRA Economic Planning,* p. 274; *Automobile Topics,* CXV (Aug. 4, 1934), 120; Report of Meeting of Automotive Sales Research Conference, May 21, 1934, Chapin Papers; Smith, *Marketing of Used Automobiles,* pp. 115–18, 124–25; F.T.C., *Report on Motor Vehicle Industry,* pp. 95–96, 215–26; *Iron Age,* CXXXIV (July 26, 1934), 48.

101 *Motor,* LXI (May, 1934), 37; Sloan to Macauley, July 30, 1934, enclosed with Sloan to Chapin, July 30, 1934, Chapin Papers.

102 *Automotive Industries,* LXXI (Oct. 27, 1934), 487; Sloan to Williams, Nov. 13, 1934, N.R.A. Box 656; Chrysler to Williams, Nov. 12, 1934, N.R.A. Box 660; *Motor,* LXII (Nov., 1934), 39; *ibid.,* LXII (Dec., 1934), 24, 90; *ibid.,* LXIII (Apr., 1935), 40; *Automotive Daily News,* May 11, 1935.

103 *Automotive Daily News,* Sept. 22, 1934, May 11, 1935.

104 The matter might also have been handled by the insertion of an appropriate clause in dealer contracts. This procedure was acceptable to the N.R.A., but the Justice Department might have viewed the situation differently. See Williams to Sloan and Chrysler, Nov. 7, 1934, N.R.A. Box 654; Roberts to C. H. Bliss, Sept. 7, 1934, N.R.A. Box 661; and Automobile Code History, pp. 71–72.

105 Surveys by the N.A.D.A. indicated that 982 dealers lost over $4 million on 283,691 used cars in 1933; in 1934, the only full year the code was in effect, 1058 dealers lost only a little over $1.3 million on 325,364 used cars; and in 1935, a total loss of $4.27 million was sustained by 931 dealers on 331,484 used cars. Smith, *Marketing Used Automobiles,* Appendix B.

106 *Automotive Daily News,* Jan. 14, 1935; *Automotive Industries,* LXIX (Dec. 23, 1933), 766, 771; *Motor,* LXII (Dec., 1934), 36; *Automobile Trade Journal,* L (Apr., 1935), 40–41. The Payton study indicated a reduction of 8.2 per cent on the discount on new cars and accessories and the markup on freight and other items.

107 N.A.C.C. General Bulletin No. G-1652, Nov. 11, 1933, Pearson Papers; Ammerman to Simpson, May 15, 1934, Vesper to Ammerman, Apr. 21, 1934, N.R.A. Box 3885; Myrick, Jr., *et al.,* "Economic Survey," Section Five, pp. 84–86.

108 Vesper to Ammerman, Oct. 27, 1933, Vesper to J. R. Lane, Nov. 27, 1933,

Vesper to Knudsen *et al.*, Nov. 27, 1933, G. E. Dawson to Gentlemen, Nov. 3, 1933, enclosed with Monmouth County Automobile Dealers Association to Johnson, Dec. 15, 1933, N.R.A. Box 3885; N.A.C.C. General Bulletin No. G-1652, Nov. 11, 1933, Pearson Papers.

109 N.A.C.C. General Bulletin No. G-1652, Nov. 11, 1933, Pearson Papers; N.A.C.C. General Bulletins No. G-1662, Jan. 6, 1934, No. G-1665, Jan. 12, 1934, N.R.A. Box 3885; J. O. Munn to State Advisory Committee Chairmen, Jan. 12, 1934, *ibid.* The N.R.A. ruled on Mar. 7, 1934, that dealers could sell parts, accessories, and supplies at less than retail price to private fleet operators and government agencies provided these items were sold for the motor vehicles owned by the purchasers, the purchaser owned or operated a garage or service station to maintain his vehicles, and the items purchased were not installed by the dealer in his own establishment. National Control Committee, M.V.R.T., *Bulletin No. 12*, Apr. 19, 1934, *ibid.*

110 Ammerman to Simpson, May 15, 1934, Ammerman to A. H. Ferrandou, Apr. 7, 1934, Vesper to Ammerman, Apr. 21, 1934 (wire and letter), N.R.A. Box 3885; Myrick, Jr., *et al.*, "Economic Survey," Section Five, pp. 86–87.

111 Ammerman to Elmer Blauvelt, Jan. 18, 1934, Ammerman to Simpson, May 15, 1934, Ammerman to Vesper, June 20, 1934, Delaney to Wilson, July 2, 1934, N.R.A. Box 3885.

112 Vesper to Ammerman, June 28, 1934, Vesper *et al.* to Adams, July 3, 1934, McAfee to Ammerman, July 13, 1934, N.R.A. Box 3885; Hearing on the Motor Vehicle Retailing Industry Preliminary Conference, July 24, 1934, pp. 52–56, 93, N.R.A. Box 3848.

113 *Codes*, XIV (Washington, 1934), 588; McAfee to Ammerman, July 13, 1934, Delaney to Roberts, Jan. 10, 1935, N.R.A. Box 3885; M.V.R.T., *Bulletin No. 35*, Aug. 2, 1934, *ibid.;* Preliminary Conference, July 24, 1934, N.R.A. Box 3848.

114 G.M. late in 1934 established 4 dealer councils to meet with members of the executive committee of the corporation to discuss mutual problems, and it decided in the fall of 1935 to insert a 90-day rather than a 30-day cancellation clause in its 1936 dealer contracts. It might be argued that it was the strengthening of the N.A.D.A., for which the N.I.R.A. was partly responsible, that caused G.M. to take these actions. *Iron Age*, CXXXIV (Dec. 13, 1934), 67; *ibid.*, CXXXV (Jan. 3, 1935), 93; *Motor*, LXIV (Oct., 1935), 52. See *Automobile Trade Journal*, L (June, 1935), 18–19, for dealer demands on the factories at the close of the N.R.A. era.

115 Chambers, "Manufacturer-Dealer Relationships," p. 75; Smith, *Marketing Used Automobiles*, pp. 125–27.

116 Chapin to M. Kerlin, May 10, 1933, Chapin to Franklin W. Hobbs, Oct. 9, 1933, Chapin to Walter S. Case, Nov. 12, 1933, Chapin Papers; *Automotive Industries*, LXVII (June 17, 1933), 733; *Detroit News*, Dec. 31, 1933; *New York Times*, Jan. 7, 9, 10, 13, 1934; Roosevelt to P. Johnson, Jan. 9, 1934, P. Johnson to Early, Jan. 10, 1934, P.P.F. 1204, Roosevelt Library.

117 *Detroit News*, Aug. 19, 20, 1934; *Financial Statement of Chrysler Corporation*, June 30, 1935; Report of the Executive Secretary of the Executive Council, Aug. 25, 1934, O.F. 788, Box 1, Roosevelt Library; Senate Committee on Finance, *Investigation of the N.R.A.*, 74 Cong., 1 Sess., pp. 107–8.

118 In 1933, G.M. was responsible for 43.29 per cent of new passenger-car registrations, Chrysler for 25.81 per cent, and Ford for 20.97 per cent; in 1934,

G.M. accounted for 39.84 per cent of new car registrations, Chrysler for 22.88 per cent, and Ford for 28.20 per cent; the figures for the first 6 months of 1935 are G.M., 34.89 per cent, Chrysler, 23.82 per cent, and Ford, 33.47 per cent. The Big Three were responsible for 79.16 per cent of new truck registrations in 1932; 80.08 per cent in 1933; 85.31 per cent in 1934; and 83.52 per cent in 1935. *Ward's 1939 Automotive Year Book,* pp. 36, 46.

119 *Ibid.,* pp. 36, 42; *Automotive News,* Almanac Issue, Apr. 30, 1956, p. 75.

120 *Detroit News,* Oct. 28, Dec. 7, 1933; *Automotive Industries,* LXX (Jan. 13, 1934), 34, 38, 39; *ibid.,* LXX (Apr. 7, 1934), 437; *ibid.,* LXX (June 9, 1934), 696; *ibid.,* LXX (June 16, 1934), 725; Banner, "Competition in the Automobile Industry," pp. 121–25. At the beginning of the model year, the price of the new Chevrolet standard model was increased from $455 to $495, the Ford standard from $500 to $535, and the Plymouth standard from $465 to $510. In Apr. the price of the Chevrolet standard was advanced to $520 and the Plymouth standard to $545. In June these price increases were rescinded.

121 Unit labor costs for the motor vehicle, bodies, and parts industry were estimated by the B.L.S. at 84.5 (1929 = 100) in 1933, 103 in 1934, and 91.6 in 1935. B.L.S., *Productivity and Unit Labor Cost in Selected Manufacturing Industries, 1919–1940* (Washington, 1942), p. 66.

122 According to the B.L.S., average hourly rates in the parts plants increased 30.6 per cent between Mar. 1933 and May 1935, as compared to a 29 per cent increase in the vehicle and body plants, but average hourly rates in the latter throughout the period were 6–9 cents above hourly rates in the former. Tolles and LaFever, "Wages . . . in the Motor Vehicle Industry, 1934," pp. 530, 537. See p. 115.

123 This analysis is partly based on a survey of the industry made in Feb. 1935 by Pierce Williams, a field representative of the Federal Emergency Relief Administration. Williams to Harry Hopkins, Feb. 27, 1935, N.R.A. Box 662. See also *Iron Age,* CXXXII (Sept. 7, 1933), 43; *ibid.,* CXXXIV (July 12, 1934), 51; and comments by R. G. Gill (president, American Austin Car Co.) in "Breakdown of Mail Received in Re: Automobile Manufacturing Code," N.R.A. Box 654. G.M.'s rate of return on the investment in its motor vehicle divisions was 16.93 per cent in 1933, 16.61 per cent in 1934, and 33.76 per cent in 1935. Its net profit on manufacturing operations was 14.40 per cent in 1933, 11.96 per cent in 1934, and 15.34 per cent in 1935. Chrysler's net profit per dollar of sales was 7.5 cents in 1933, 2.9 cents in 1934, and 9.8 cents in 1935. Its rate of return before income taxes on its motor-vehicle investment was 20.44 per cent in 1933, 12.17 per cent in 1934, and 45.93 per cent in 1935. Ford (and Lincoln) suffered a net loss of 4.31 per cent on manufactured products sold in 1933, but registered a gain of 3.37 per cent in 1934, and of 1.11 per cent in 1935. Ford's rate of return before interest and income taxes on its average investment in the motor-vehicle business was −2.16 per cent in 1933, 4.26 per cent in 1934, and 2.2 per cent in 1935. F.T.C., *Report on Motor Vehicle Industry,* pp. 491, 534, 567, 599, 652, 671.

NOTES TO CHAPTER V

1 Green to Collins, Aug. 28, 1933, Green Letterbooks.

2 A member of the federal labor union in the Fisher Body No. 1 plant in Flint later recalled that A.F. of L. organizers ran the meetings of the local.

Oral History Interview of Bud Simons, Sept. 10, 1960, pp. 10–11, Michigan Historical Collections.

3 Chalmers, "Collective Bargaining," V, 33–34; IX, 10–11; Constitution of the A.F. of L., Articles X, XIII, A.F. of L., *Proceedings, 1934* (Washington, n.d.), xxiv, xxvi; Green to Shipley, Jan. 12, 1934, Shipley to Green, Apr. 29, 1934, A.F. of L. Strike File, Local 18347, A.F. of L.-C.I.O. Archives; Green to J. T. Michael, Feb. 5, 1934, *ibid.*, Local 18785; Green to Philip Johns, Aug. 9, 1934, Green to Shipley, Nov. 26, 1934, Green Letterbooks.

4 Similar arrangements were made in other auto centers like Flint and Cleveland.

5 At the 1933 convention of the A.F. of L. the majority report of the Committee on Resolutions stated that the federal labor unions could be used for the temporary purpose of organizing workers in the mass-production industries when the affiliated internationals gave their consent and also to organize plants in small communities where it was difficult for the affiliated unions to give the question of organization their immediate attention. A minority report by Charles Howard, president of the International Typographical Union, stressed the need for experimentation with new methods of organization in the mass-production industries. Both reports were referred to the Executive Council with instructions for it to call a conference of the international unions to consider the problem. The conference was held on Jan. 24–25, 1934. The conference report recommended that the Executive Council should have "the fullest possible latitude" in granting charters to federal labor unions and where "temporary infraction" of the rights of the affiliated unions occurred, the Executive Council was to "adjust such difficulties in the spirit of taking full advantage of the immediate situation and with the ultimate recognition of the rights of all concerned." A.F. of L., *Proceedings, 1933* (Washington, n.d.), pp. 501–4; Taft, *A.F. of L. from Death of Gompers*, pp. 57–58; Morris, *Conflict within the AFL*, pp. 179–85.

6 Green to Max Hayes, July 28, 1933, Green Letterbooks; Digaetano interview, p. 50, Michigan Historical Collections. See also W. W. Britton to Green, Mar. 28, 1934, Green Letterbooks.

7 Eric Peterson to Wharton, May 23, 1934, Wharton to Green, June 1, 1934, May 13, 1935, Brown to Green and Morrison, July 17, 1934, Green Letterbooks; Brown to Wharton, July 27, 1933, Brown to Collins, Mar. 26, June 22, 1934, Wharton to Green, July 29, Aug. 8, 1933, I.A.M. File, A.F. of L.-C.I.O. Archives.

8 Green to Collins, Oct 18, 31, 1933, July 23, 1934, Green to Wharton, Nov. 14, 1933, Apr. 9, 1935, Green to Organizers, Feb. 19, 1934, Green to Dillon, May 21, 1935, Green Letterbooks; Taft, *A.F. of L. from Death of Gompers*, pp. 59–60.

9 Alexander Marks to Morrison, Aug. 22, 1934, Marks File, A.F. of L.-C.I.O. Archives; Collins to Green, Oct. 14, 28, Nov. 7, 1934, Collins File; Shipley to Green, Apr. 29, 1934, A.F. of L. Strike File, Local 18347; Chalmers, "Collective Bargaining," V, 34–35. Collins hoped that the issue of jurisdiction could be referred to the Executive Council pending the complete organization of the industry.

10 Collins to Morrison, May 26, Aug. 11, 18, 1934, Collins to Green, July 19, 1934, Green to Collins, July 23, 1934, Collins File; "Matters for Consideration of National Council," Homer Martin Papers, Wayne State University Archives; U.A.W. News Letter, Oct. 3, 1934, *ibid.*; Official Proceedings First Session National Council U.A.W., July 9–14, 1934, Brown Collection; The Second Ses-

sion of the National Council of United Automobile Workers Federal Labor Unions, Aug. 28–31, 1934, *ibid.;* Minute Book of U.A.W. Union No. 19324, Aug. 28, Sept. 11, 1934, State Historical Society of Wisconsin, Madison, Wisconsin; Minute Book of U.A.W. Union No. 19660, Dec. 7, 1934, *ibid.;* Minutes of Meetings of F.L.U. No. 18331, Aug. 2, 1934, Wayne State University Archives; A.F. of L., *Proceedings, 1934,* pp. xxiv, 199, 609–10, 612–13. The 1934 A.F. of L. convention referred to the Executive Council a resolution that the A.F. of L. issue out-of-work dues stamps to unemployed union members and that it not require the payment of the per capita tax on these members. *Ibid.,* pp. 201, 612–13.

11 Oral History Interview of Michael J. Manning, July 6, 1960, pp. 45–46, Michigan Historical Collections; Oral History Interview of Paul Miley, July 24, 1961, p. 5, *ibid.;* Beckman interview, p. 9, *ibid.;* Collins to Morrison, Oct. 21, 1933, Feb. 16, 1934, Collins File; *Proceedings of the First Constitutional Convention of the International Union, United Automobile Workers of America, 1935* (Detroit, n.d.), pp. 22–24. See also Oral History Interview of Louis Adkins, Aug. 16, 1961, pp. 5–6, Michigan Historical Collections. The A.F. of L. received $47,000 in per capita taxes from the auto workers during the 6-month period ending July 1, 1935. Green to George F. Addes, July 16, 1935, C.I.O. Historical File, Reel 1, A.F. of L.-C.I.O. Archives. Green reported at the U.A.W. convention in 1936 that the U.A.W. locals had paid per capita taxes of $181,377.33 between July 1, 1933, and Oct. 1, 1935, and that the A.F. of L. had expended $249,481.81 on them during the same period. *Proceedings of the Second Convention of the International Union, United Automobile Workers of America, 1936* (Detroit, n.d.), p. 13. For methods the A.F. of L. might have used to devote more funds to organizing, see Morris, *Conflict within the AFL,* pp. 161–62.

12 Collins to Green, July 22, Aug. 12, 26, Oct. 28, Nov. 7, 1933, Collins to Morrison, Sept. 22, Dec. 9, 1933, Collins File; Oral History Interview of Wyndham Mortimer, June 20, 1960, pp. 2–3, Michigan Historical Collections; Oral History Interview of Lew Michener, June 21, 1960, pp. 1–2, *ibid.;* Chalmers, "Collective Bargaining," V, 23–24. See also Lee H. Geswein to Collins, Aug. 19, 1934, George B. Roberts Papers, Wayne State University Archives. Cf. Oral History Interview of Dick Coleman, June 23, 1960, p. 1, Michigan Historical Collections.

13 *Proceedings of Constitutional Convention, U.A.W., 1935,* pp. 22–24; Manning interview, p. 4, Michigan Historical Collections; Collins to Morrison, June 30, Sept. 16, Nov. 4, 1933, Collins to Green, Aug. 12, Sept. 22, Oct. 14, 1933, Feb. 6, 1934, Collins File; interview with Collins, Feb. 4, 1957; interview with Nicholas Kelley, Feb. 4, 1957; interview with Leo Wolman, Feb. 4, 1957; Chalmers, "Collective Bargaining," VII, 24; *Proceedings of Second Convention, U.A.W., 1936,* p. 57; Marjorie Ruth Clark, "The American Federation of Labor and Organization in the Automobile Industry since the Passage of the National Industrial Recovery Act," *Essays in Social Economics in Honor of Jessica Blanche Peixotto* (Berkeley, 1935), p. 79; Minutes of the Third Meeting of National Council of United Automobile Workers Federal Labor Unions . . . , Feb. 23–Mar. 2, 1935, Labadie Collection.

14 Green to Collins, June 30, 1933, Green Letterbooks; "Cooperative Plan," Case 209, N.L.B. Drawer 35; *Detroit News,* July 29, 1933; Wieck, "Automobile Workers," pp. 33–36, 240–42; Chalmers, "Collective Bargaining," V, 31–32; Collins to Green, Sept. 9, 22, 30, 1933, Jan. 22, Feb. 19, 1934, Collins to Morrison, Sept. 16, 1933, Collins File; *New York Times,* Feb. 2, 1934; A.L.B., Steno-

graphic Report of Hearing, In the Matter of: Fisher Body Corp., May 2, 1934, May 2, 1934, p. 39, Michigan Historical Collections; Cronin to Knudsen, Mar. 14, 1934, G.M., Labor Relations Diary, Appendix Documents to Accompany Section 1, Document No. 28; Dillon to Joseph R. Wood, Apr. 10, 1935, Martin Papers.

15 On this point, see Beckman interview, p. 6, Michigan Historical Collections, and McPherson, *Labor Relations in the Automobile Industry*, pp. 59–60.

16 Collins to Green, June 23, Nov. 4, 1933, Collins File.

17 Lloyd H. Bailer, "Negro Labor in the Automobile Industry" (Ph.D. thesis, University of Michigan, [1943]), pp. 67–69, 174–79, 184, 188–92, 367; Collins to Green, Aug. 12, 26, 1933, *ibid.;* Marks to Morrison, Sept. 9, 1933, Marks to Green, Sept. 26, 1933, Marks File; Chalmers, "Collective Bargaining," V, 26–27. See Joel Seidman *et al.*, "Why Workers Join Unions," *Annals of the American Academy of Political and Social Science*, CCLXXIV (Mar., 1951), 76–77, 83.

18 Bernstein, *Lean Years*, p. 340; Collins to Green, Nov. 18, Dec. 15, 1933, Collins File; Collins interview, Feb. 4, 1957; interview with Richard Frankensteen, Apr. 10, 1957; Chalmers, "Collective Bargaining," V, 24–25.

19 *Detroit Labor News*, June 23, 1933; Collins to Green, July 22, Sept. 9, 1933, Jan. 6, 1934, Collins File; Marks to Morrison, Sept. 9, 16, 1933, Marks File; Dillon to Green, Aug. 18, 1934, Green to Dillon, Aug. 22, 1934, Dillon File, A.F. of L.-C.I.O. Archives; Dillon to Green, Dec. 22, 1934, Smith to Green, Jan. 9, 1935, Green to Smith, Jan. 12, 1935, A.F. of L. Strike File, Local 19059; U.A.W. Weekly News Letter, Aug. 25, 1934, Vertical File, A.F. of L.-C.I.O. Library.

20 Lane, *The Regulation of Businessmen* (New Haven, 1954), pp. 34–35. See also Richard C. Wilcock, "Industrial Management's Policies toward Unionism," Derber and Young, eds., *Labor and the New Deal*, pp. 280, 286.

21 Leiserson to Frances Perkins, Apr. 11, 1934, Roosevelt Library. A copy of this letter was kindly supplied to me by Dr. Herman Kahn.

22 Collins to Green, July 15, Nov. 18, 1933, Jan. 6, 20, 22, Feb. 19, 1934, Collins to Morrison, July 28, Aug. 5, Sept. 16, 28, 1933, Collins File; *Flint Weekly Review*, Oct. 13, 1933; Lano to N.L.B., Dec. 27, 1933, Lano to Wagner, Feb. 22, 1934, Case 209, N.L.B. Drawer 35.

23 Final Report of the Automobile Labor Board [Aug., 1935], pp. 15, 23.

24 W. H. Shoemock to Chapin, Aug. 4, 1933, Chapin Papers; F. J. Hays to Charles Sorensen, July 26, 1934, Acc. 38, Box 112, Ford Archives.

25 Senate Committee on Education and Labor, *Violations of Free Speech and Rights of Labor*, 75 Cong., 2 Sess., Sen. Report No. 46, Part 3 (Washington, 1937), pp. 23, 24 (henceforth cited as La Follette *Report No. 46*).

26 *Ibid.*, pp. 23, 47; Senate Committee on Education and Labor, *Violations of Free Speech and Rights of Labor, Hearings Pursuant to S. Res. 266, 74 Cong....*, 75 Cong., 1 Sess., Part 5 (Washington, 1937), pp. 1621, 1863; Part 6 (Washington, 1937), pp. 1879, 2175, 2177, 2186 (henceforth cited as La Follette *Hearings*).

27 La Follette *Report No. 46*, Part 3, pp. 70–74; La Follette *Hearings*, Part 5, pp. 1511–14, 1521, 1534–39; Part 6, pp. 1906–7, 1911, 1913–15, 1928, 1970–73; Clinch Calkins, *Spy Overhead: The Story of Industrial Espionage* (New York, 1937), pp. 98–103.

28 La Follette *Hearings*, Part 4 (Washington, 1937), pp. 1206–8, 1211–13, 1215, 1219–20. On the interesting activities of John Andrews, a Corporations

Auxiliary Company operative who engaged in espionage in the Dodge plant, see Calkins, *Spy Overhead*, pp. 55–57; and Oral History Interview of Harry Ross, July 10, 1961, p. 9, Michigan Historical Collections.

29 A. J. Lepine to T. M. Manning, Sept. 11, 1933, Acc. 6, Box 154, Ford Archives; Nevins and Hill, *Ford*, II, 211n, 591–92; Sward, *Legend of Henry Ford*, pp. 291–93, 306–8, 338; Raushenbush, *Fordism*, pp. 14–15; Oral History Interview of Martin Jensen, Nov. 1, 1960, p. 9, Michigan Historical Collections. In his memoirs Bennett, no doubt with tongue in cheek, noted that the Ford Motor Co. did not have to engage in labor espionage since employees who wished to remain on good terms with the company would voluntarily report on what transpired at union meetings. "We were good listeners," Bennett observed. *We Never Called Him Henry*, pp. 116–17.

30 La Follette *Hearings*, Part 4, pp. 1363–64; Senate Committee on Education and Labor, *Violations of Free Speech and Rights of Labor*, 76 Cong., 1 Sess., *Sen. Report No. 6*, Part 4 (Washington, 1939), pp. 53–54 (henceforth cited as *La Follette Report No. 6*).

31 La Follette *Hearings*, Part 4, pp. 1239–40; *Detroit News*, Feb. 28, 1934; House Committee on Labor, *Proposed Amendments to the National Labor Relations Act*, 76 Cong., 3 Sess., IX (Washington, 1940), 2295. See also Hattley interview, p. 7, Michigan Historical Collections.

32 G.M., Labor Relations Diary, Section 1, p. 21.

33 Neither the Ford Motor Co. nor Studebaker established company unions in its plants.

34 *Michigan Manufacturer and Financial Record*, LII (Oct. 14, 1933), 8; Norman Beasley, *Knudsen* (New York, 1947), p. 153; G.M., Labor Relations Diary, Section 1, pp. 21–22; Fisher to Employees of Fisher Body Co., Aug. 17, 1933, Case 209, N.L.B. Drawer 35; undated Chrysler letter, A.L.B. Drawer 4004.

35 G.M., Labor Relations Diary, Appendix Document No. 9; Wieck, "Automobile Workers," p. 43; undated Chrysler letter, A.L.B. Drawer 4004; Anthony Lucheck, "Company Unions, F.O.B. Detroit," *Nation*, CXLII (Jan. 15, 1936), 74; Henry A. Campeau to Edmund C. Shields, Mar. 17, 1934, N.R.A. Box 1120.

36 G.M., Labor Relations Diary, Section 1, pp. 22–23; *ibid.*, Appendix Document No. 9; "Percentages of Elections [Hudson] as of Sept. 21, 1933," Chapin Papers; *Michigan Manufacturer and Financial Record*, LII (Oct. 14, 1933), 11; Chalmers, "Collective Bargaining," V, 6, 21–22; Wieck, "Automobile Workers," pp. 44–45; Lucheck, "Company Unions," p. 74; Campeau to Shields, Mar. 14, 15, 17, 1934, N.R.A. Box 1120; affidavit of 20 employees of Fisher Body, Cleveland, Mar. 12, 1934, Case 209, N.L.B. Drawer 35; *The Hudson Industrial Association* (Sept. 11, 1933), *ibid.*; *Articles of Association for Employees' Association and Works Council, Chevrolet Motor Co., ibid.*; A.L.B., Fisher Body Hearing, May 2, 1934, p. 46, Michigan Historical Collections; N.R.A. Release No. 4688, Apr. 30, 1934; Lorwin and Wubnig, *Labor Relations Boards*, pp. 155–56. Twelve of the 13 employee-association representatives of the Fisher Body No. 1 plant in Flint were U.A.W. members. Joseph S. Sherer to N.L.B., Feb. 3, 1934, Case 209, N.L.B. Drawer 35.

37 Final Report of A.L.B., Appendix B.

38 There are copies of the various plans in Case 209, N.L.B. Drawer 35, and in A.L.B. Drawers 4003–4006.

39 Chapin to Megargle, Jan. 19, 1934, Chapin Papers.

40 The N.L.B. condemned the initiation of company-union plans by the em-

ployer and his participation in the affairs of a company union when this interfered with the self-organization of the employees or resulted in employer domination. N.R.A. Release No. 4688, Apr. 30, 1934. See also Lorwin and Wubnig, *Labor Relations Boards,* pp. 142–49.

⁴¹ Wieck, "Automobile Workers," pp. 63, 66; A.L.B., Complaint of Associated Automobile Workers against the Hudson Motor Car Co., Jan. 24, 1935, pp. 3–4, 15–16, Michigan Historical Collections; C. H. Gilman to Wolman, Sept. 10, 1934, A.L.B. Drawer 3990; William McHugh to Collins, Aug. 25, 1934, Dillon to Wolman, Oct. 5, 17, 1934, A.L.B. Drawer 4000; G.M., Labor Relations Diary, Section 1, p. 21. On the development of the local independent union, see Leo Troy, "The Course of Company and Local Independent Unions" (Ph.D. thesis, Columbia University, 1958).

⁴² G.M., Labor Relations Diary, Section 1, pp. 29–30; *Detroit News,* July 29, 1934; Carlton to Lea, Jan. 26, 1934, N.R.A. Box 714.

⁴³ Wieck, "Automobile Workers," pp. 50–51, 63. My italics. Wieck was able to examine the minutes of the meetings of this works council, and he also interviewed three of the employee representatives.

⁴⁴ Fountain, *Union Guy,* p. 43; Wieck, "Automobile Workers," pp. 47, 50, 58; Athel F. Denham, "Do Works Councils Work in the Automobile Industry?" *Automotive Industries,* LXXI (Aug. 18, 1934), 198, 201; Lucheck, "Labor Organizations," p. 71; Lucheck, "Company Unions," pp. 74–75; Poplawski interview, p. 5, Michigan Historical Collections.

⁴⁵ Wieck, "Automobile Workers," p. 58. The reports of the employee associations describe the concessions made by the companies, allegedly at the behest of employee representatives. See, for example, G.M. Truck Employees' Association and Works Council, *A Brief Summary of the Year's Activities,* Aug. 9, 1934; *To All Cadillac Employees,* May 7, 1934; Buick Employees' Association, *Works Council Bulletin,* July, 1934; Fisher Body Employees' Works Conference, Tarrytown, N.Y., for the year 1933–34, *Annual Report of the Representatives;* G.M., Labor Relations Diary, Appendix Document No. 15.

⁴⁶ G.M., Labor Relations Diary, Section 1, pp. 1, 30.

⁴⁷ See the transcripts in the Michigan Historical Collections of A.L.B. conferences with the employee associations or bargaining agencies of the following plants: G.M. Truck (Aug. 21, 1934), Flint Chevrolet (Sept. 5, 1934), Chevrolet Gear and Axle (Sept. 12, 1934), Cleveland Fisher Body (Sept. 12, 1934), Saginaw Chevrolet (Sept. 12, 1934), Chevrolet Forge, Spring and Bumper (Sept. 12, 1934), Chrysler Highland Park (Jan. 29, 1935), and Plymouth (Feb. 7, 1935). On the Hudson Industrial Association, see Lucheck, "Labor Organizations," p. 80.

⁴⁸ Lucheck, "Company Unions," p. 75; G.M., Labor Relations Diary, Section 1, p. 29; Final Report of A.L.B., Appendix B. See below, Chapter X.

⁴⁹ Anderson to Green, Aug. 30, 1933, Collins to Green, Oct. 14, 1933, Jan. 20, 1934, Feb. 6, 1934, Collins to Morrison, Feb. 17, 1934, Collins File; Anderson to Morrison, Sept. 2, 1933, Anderson File, A.F. of L.-C.I.O. Archives; Green to Richard Byrd, Feb. 8, 1934, Green Letterbooks; Senate Committee on Education and Labor, *To Create a National Labor Board, Hearings on S.2926,* 73 Cong., 2 Sess. (Washington, 1934), pp. 69, 80, 88, 93–100, 143–49; N.L.B., Stenographic Report of Hearing, In the Matter of Buick Co. . . . , Mar. 14, 15, 1934, *passim,* N.L.B. Drawer 68; *Detroit News,* Feb. 28, 1934.

⁵⁰ *New York Times,* Mar. 7, 8, 1934. The N.A.C.C. informed Davis that it would bring the complaints in question to the attention of the company unions

so that the plans could be brought in line with the law. *Automotive Industries,* LXX (Mar. 17, 1934), 346.

51 Davis to Shields, Mar. 3, 1934, Arthur Altmeyer to Wolman, Apr. 7, 1934, N.R.A. Box 1060; Campeau to Shields, Mar. 14, 15, 17, 1934, N.R.A. Box 1120; Pollak to Wolman, Dec. 20, 1934, Wolman to Pollak, Jan. 18, 1935, A.L.B. Drawer 4005.

52 For a detailed account of the M.E.S.A. strike, see Sidney Fine, "The Tool and Die Makers Strike," *Michigan History,* XLII (Sept., 1958), 297–323.

53 The Flint M.E.S.A. had but recently cut its hours of work from 45 to 37½ by refusing to work on Saturday.

54 Memorandum of the M.E.S.A. in Relation to the Dispute Involving Tool Makers, Die Makers, and Affiliated Craftsmen of Detroit, Flint, and Pontiac . . . , Oct. 8, 1933, Case 81, N.L.B. Drawer 13; Irving J. Reuter to M.E.S.A., Sept. 11, 1933, Knudsen to N.L.B., Sept. 26, 1933, Exhibits A and B, *ibid.;* N.L.B., Stenographic Report of Hearing, Tool and Die Makers Strike in Detroit Area, Oct. 18, 1933, pp. 7–13, 18–24, N.L.B. Drawer 68; *Tool and Die and Experimental Workers of Cleveland and Toledo* [Sept., 1933], pamphlet in Labadie Collection; Brown, "The MESA," pp. 6–7, undated MS in Brown Collection; Dahlheimer, *History of M.E.S.A.,* p. 4; interview with Chester M. Culver, May 8, 1958.

55 *Detroit News,* Sept. 23, 1933; *Detroit Free Press,* Sept. 23, 25, 26, 1933; Knudsen to N.L.B., Sept. 26, 1933, Case 81, N.L.B. Drawer 13; Anderson to Morrison, Sept. 28, 1933, Collins File. The 1930 census listed Flint as having only 1344 tool makers, die setters, and die sinkers and 343 millwrights. Bureau of the Census, *Fifteenth Census of the U.S.: 1930, Population,* IV, 806.

56 N.L.B., Tool and Die Hearing, pp. 25–26, 34, 66–67, 76–77, N.L.B. Drawer 68; M.E.S.A. Memorandum, Oct. 8, 1933, Case 81, N.L.B. Drawer 13; Charles T. Fisher to Larned, Nov. 2, 1933, Brown Collection; *Detroit News,* Sept. 27, 1933.

57 Chalmers, "Collective Bargaining," IV, 4; *Detroit News,* Sept. 23, 25, 26, 1933; *New York Times,* Sept. 27, 1933; *MESA Voice,* Dec., 1934. Culver claimed that only 1700 M.E.S.A. members voted. The M.E.S.A. refused to count the ballots in his presence. Culver interview; *Detroit Free Press,* Oct. 6, 1933.

58 N.L.B., Tool and Die Hearing, pp. 35, 66, N.L.B. Drawer 68; M.E.S.A. Memorandum, Oct. 8, 1933, Case 81, N.L.B. Drawer 13; *Detroit Free Press,* Oct. 7, 1933; *Detroit News,* Sept. 27, 1933. See Chapter IV, n. 58.

59 *Detroit News,* Sept. 29, 1933. There is a copy of the M.E.S.A. demands in Case 81, N.L.B. Drawer 13.

60 *Business Week,* Oct. 7, 1933, p. 6; Collins to Green, Sept. 30, 1933, Collins File; *Detroit Free Press,* Oct. 3, 6, 1933; *Detroit News,* Oct. 2, 4, 5, 10, Nov. 5, 17, 1933; *Tool and Die and Experimental Workers of Cleveland and Toledo;* copy of book of Chevrolet Motor Co. showing work sent out during the strike, in Brown collection; letters from various job-shop and main-plant employers to individual tool and die makers, in *ibid.;* Culver interview; newspaper clipping attached to Carmody to Leiserson, Oct. 6, 1933, Case 81, N.L.B. Drawer 13; Knudsen, *Supervision's Job in 1934,* pp. 5–6; *Iron Age,* CXXXII (Dec. 14, 1933), 37; *ibid.,* CXXXII (Dec. 28, 1933), 39; *ibid.,* CXXXII (Jan. 11, 1934), 37–38.

61 *Detroit Free Press,* Oct. 5, 6, 7, 11, 1933; *Detroit News,* Oct. 3, 6, 1933; N.L.B., Tool and Die Hearing, p. 66, N.L.B. Drawer 68; Fisher to Larned, Nov. 2,

1933, Brown Collection; Smith to Wagner, Oct. 4, 1933, Ralph Covert to Perkins, Oct. 7, 1933, Case 81, N.L.B. Drawer 13; M.E.S.A. Memorandum, Oct. 8, 1933, *ibid.;* Chalmers, "Collective Bargaining," IV, 4–5, 7; Brown, "The MESA," p. 10; F. Jos. Lamb to Roosevelt, Oct. 17, 1933, N.R.A. Box 5371; Stevenson interview, p. 11, Michigan Historical Collections.

62 The *Detroit News* reported on Oct. 23 that up to that time 35 men had been charged with conspiracy to obstruct persons lawfully pursuing their business, 18 with assault with intent to do great bodily harm, 3 with malicious destruction of property, 1 with felonious assault, 3 with hurling missiles at autos, and 2 with assault and battery.

63 M.E.S.A. to Wagner, Sept. 25, 1933, Wagner to M.E.S.A., Sept. 25, 1933, Case 81, N.L.B. Drawer 13; *Detroit Free Press,* Sept. 24, 1933; *Detroit News,* Sept. 28, 29, 1933; N.L.B., Tool and Die Hearing, p. 24, N.L.B. Drawer 68; *New York Times,* Sept. 29, 30, 1933; The Reminiscences of Mr. Chester M. Culver, 1955, pp. 45–46, Ford Archives; Culver interview.

64 Carmody to Leiserson, Oct. 6, 1933, Carmody to Wagner, Oct. 14, 1933, Case 81, N.L.B. Drawer 13; Leiserson memorandum, Oct. 10, 1933, *ibid.;* M.E.S.A. Memorandum, Oct. 8, 1933, *ibid.;* N.L.B., Tool and Die Hearing, p. 67, N.L.B. Drawer 68; *Detroit News,* Sept. 29, Oct. 7, 1933; *Detroit Free Press,* Sept. 30, 1933; Senate Committee on Education and Labor, *To Create a National Labor Board, Hearings on S.2926,* 73 Cong., 2 Sess. (Washington, 1934), p. 308.

65 Joe Brown, Interview with Jay Griffen, Sept. 26, 1933, Brown Collection.

66 *Detroit News,* Sept. 24, 1933; *Detroit Labor News,* Sept. 29, 1933; Wieck, "Automobile Workers," pp. 33–34.

67 Chalmers, "Collective Bargaining," IV, 5–6; *Daily Worker,* Sept. 28, Oct. 1, 6, 11, 18, 1933, Oct. 26, 1934; *Auto Workers News,* Nov., 1933; A.W.U. handbills in Brown Collection; District Committee, District 7, Communist Party, U.S.A., "Statement of Communist Party on Tool and Diemakers Strike," *ibid.;* Brown, "The MESA," pp. 11–14; *Detroit News,* Oct. 13–17, 1933.

68 *Detroit News,* Oct. 6, 14, 18, 1933; Wagner to Macauley, Oct. 13, 1933, Wagner to C. C. Richard, Oct. 13, 1933, Wagner to Knudsen, Oct. 13, 1933, Macauley to Wagner, Oct. 17, 1933, Knudsen to Wagner, Oct. 15, 1933, Case 81, N.L.B. Drawer 13; Culver interview.

69 N.L.B., Tool and Die Hearing, *passim,* N.L.B. Drawer 68. See also Maurice Sugar, "NRA: The Crooked Referee . . . ," *New Masses,* X (Mar. 27, 1934), 9–12; *Detroit News,* Oct. 16, 21, 1933; and letters of protest by M.E.S.A. members in Case 81, N.L.B. Drawer 13.

70 *Detroit Free Press,* Oct. 22, 27, 1933; *Detroit News,* Oct. 23, 25, 26, 27, 1933; *Industrial Worker,* Oct. 31, 1933; M.E.S.A. to Wagner, Oct. 24, 1933, Covert to Larned, Oct. 30, 1933, Case 81, N.L.B. Drawer 13; Fisher to Larned, Nov. 2, 1933, M.E.S.A. to Larned, Oct. [Nov.] 4, 1933, Brown Collection.

71 The Briggs Vernor Highway plant, the Hudson plant, and the Federal Engineering Co. plant sustained some minor property damage early in the morning of Oct. 28. Brown, "The MESA," pp. 17–18; *Detroit News,* Oct. 28, 1933; *Detroit Free Press,* Oct. 28, 1933.

72 *Detroit Free Press,* Oct. 31, Nov. 1, 1933; *New York Times,* Oct. 31, 1933; Brown, "The MESA," pp. 18–20; *Daily Worker,* Nov. 3, 1933; Smith interview.

73 Larned to Wagner, Oct. 30, Nov. 2, 4, 1933, Larned to Wolf, Nov. 1, 1933, Case 81, N.L.B. Drawer 13; Larned to M.E.S.A. and Motor Metals Manufacturing Co., Nov. 2, 1933, Larned to Ainsworth Manufacturing Co., Nov. 4,

1933, Larned to M.E.S.A. and 29 members of A.T. and D.M.A., Nov. 4, 1933, N.L.B. Drawer 132; Culver to Our Members, Nov. 6, 1933, Chapin Papers; Memorandum of Settlement of Die Makers' Strike by R. D. Chapin, Nov. 7, 1933, *ibid.;* Summary Case Reports on Formal Cases, Detroit R.L.B. Box 280; *Detroit Free Press,* Nov. 3, 1933; Dahlheimer, *History of M.E.S.A.,* p. 13; Brown, "The MESA," pp. 20–23.

74 Chalmers, "Collective Bargaining," IV, 5–7; *MESA Voice,* Dec., 1934; *Business Week,* Nov. 25, 1933, p. 15; Oral History Interview of Joseph Piconke, Apr. 13, 1960, p. 4, Michigan Historical Collections.

75 Smith, "The MESA," MS in Brown Collection; Smith interview; Wieck, "Automobile Workers," p. 80; *The MESA. Why? When? Whither?* [1939]; McCracken interview, pp. 7, 25–26, Michigan Historical Collections; Brown, "The Mechanical [*sic*] Educational Strike and Background," MS in Brown Collection.

76 *Detroit News,* Feb. 25, 1934; Dahlheimer, *History of M.E.S.A.,* pp. 15, 51–58; *The MESA. Why? When? Whither?;* Smith, "Militant Labor in Detroit," *Nation,* CXXXVIII (May 16, 1934), 561–62.

77 Lucheck, "Labor Organizations," p. 57; Chalmers, "Collective Bargaining," IV, 10–12; "The Stability of the MESA," Nov. 4, 1934, Labadie Collection; Smith interview. The M.E.S.A. succeeded for a time in organizing the production workers at the Detroit Stove Co. plant. The local went on strike on Apr. 9, 1934, and suffered a disastrous defeat. Chalmers, "Collective Bargaining," IV, 11; Dahlheimer, *History of M.E.S.A.,* p. 21.

78 Dahlheimer, *History of M.E.S.A.,* p. 28; Chalmers, "Collective Bargaining," IV, 11; *The MESA. Why? When? Whither?;* Minutes (Highlights) of the M.E.S.A. Convention, Jan. 2–5, 1935, Brown Collection.

79 Smith, "Militant Labor in Detroit," p. 562; *Cleveland Plain Dealer,* Jan. 3, 1935; *MESA Voice,* Special Issue [1935].

80 *MESA Voice,* Special Issue; *Automotive Industries,* LXXII (Feb. 9, 1935), 168; *Cleveland Plain Dealer,* Jan. 3, 1935.

81 Sugar to Wolman, Feb. 8, 1934, Smith to Williams, Oct. 26, 1934, N.R.A. Box 660; *MESA Voice,* Nov., 1934.

82 Lucheck, "Labor Organizations," pp. 55–56; Stevenson interview, p. 14, Michigan Historical Collections.

83 *Detroit News,* Apr. 5, 7, 8, 10, 11, 12, 13, 1934; Fred Keightly to Kerwin, C.S. 176–580.

84 Dahlheimer, *History of M.E.S.A.,* pp. 19–22; "The Stability of the MESA," Nov. 4, 1934, Labadie Collection; Smith, "Militant Labor in Detroit," p. 561; Chalmers, "Collective Bargaining," IV, 8–9, *Detroit News,* Apr. 13, 14, 15, 17–21, 27, May 3, 1934; *Detroit Free Press,* Apr. 13, 14, May 4, 5, 1934; *Iron Age,* CXXXIII (Apr. 19, 1934), 44. The minimum M.E.S.A. hourly rates established for the job shops as of May 2, 1934, ranged from 90 cents to $1.15. Card in Brown Collection giving M.E.S.A. hourly rates.

85 Dahlheimer, *History of M.E.S.A.,* pp. 25–26; Smith interview; *Detroit News,* Apr. 26, 30, 1934; *Detroit Free Press,* May 15, 1934; *Daily Worker,* Apr. 18, 21, 27, 30, May 5, 17, 1934; Anderson and Mack, *The Case of the Progressives against Smith's Expulsion and Splitting Drive in the MESA* [1934], Brown Collection; McCracken interview, pp. 9, 13, Michigan Historical Collections.

86 *MESA Voice,* Dec., 1934; Federated Press Central Bureau Sheet, May 2, 1934, Brown Collection; *Cleveland Plain Dealer,* Jan. 3, 1935; Chalmers, "Collective Bargaining," IV, 16; Collins to Green, Apr. 14, 1934, Collins File; *New*

York Post, Oct. 22, 1934; McCracken interview, pp. 11–12, Michigan Historical Collections.

87 Thompson, *I.W.W.,* p. 166; *Industrial Worker,* July 18, 25, Aug. 2, 8, 15, 22, 29, Sept. 19, 26, 1933. There are copies of some of the I.W.W. handbills of the period in the Labadie Collection.

88 Chalmers, "Collective Bargaining," IV, 17–18; Thompson, *I.W.W.,* pp. 166–67; work sheet on Murray Body strike, Brown Collection; Pody interview, pp. 17–20, Michigan Historical Collections; Anderson interview, pp. 20–21, *ibid.*

89 *Industrial Worker,* Oct. 3, 10, 1933; C. W. Avery to N.R.A., Nov. 6, 1933, Case 6, Detroit R.L.B. Box 281; Thompson, *I.W.W.,* pp. 166–67; Chalmers, "Collective Bargaining," IV, 18–19; Pody interview, pp. 22–25, Michigan Historical Collections.

90 *Industrial Worker,* Oct. 10, 17, 24, 31, Nov. 7, 14, 21, 1933; *Detroit News,* Sept. 29, 30, 1933; Chalmers, "Collective Bargaining," IV, 19–20; Thompson, *I.W.W.,* p. 167.

91 *Industrial Worker,* Oct. 10, 31, Nov. 21, 1933; Murray Strike Bulletin, Oct. 2, 1933, Brown Collection; F. W. Thompson to Detroit R.L.B. and Murray Corp., Oct. 30, 1933, Larned to Murray Corp., Nov. 4, 1933, Avery to N.R.A., Nov. 6, 1933, Sherer to Murray Corp., Nov. 9, 1933, Gust Hunt to Detroit R.L.B., Nov. 9, 1933, Case 6, Detroit R.L.B. Box 281.

92 Thompson, *I.W.W.,* pp. 167–68; *Industrial Worker,* Nov. 21, Dec. 12, 1933, Jan. 23, Feb. 13, 20, Mar. 13, Apr. 9, 17, Sept. 15, 1934, May 1, 1935; Chalmers, "Collective Bargaining," IV, 20–21; Anderson interview, p. 23, Michigan Historical Collections.

93 On the transitional nature of communist activity during this period, see Max M. Kampelman, *The Communist Party vs. the C.I.O.* (New York, 1957), pp. 10–12.

94 Wolman, *Ebb and Flow in Trade Unionism,* p. 144; Schmies, "The Open Letter and Our Tasks in the Detroit District," *Communist,* XII (Oct., 1933), 990–93; "Directives on Work within the A.F. of L. and Independent Trade Unions," *ibid.,* XIII (Jan., 1934), 113–14.

95 The *Auto Workers News* and the *Daily Worker* for this period regularly criticized A.F. of L. strike tactics. See also A.W.U. handbills in Brown Collection. The quotation is from J. Wilson and Raymond to Delegates of the National Conference of Federal Auto Locals of the A.F. of L., [June, 1934], Labadie Collection.

96 *Auto Workers News,* Nov., 1933, Mar. 10, June 16, July 21, 1934; *Daily Worker,* Mar. 3, July 6, 1934.

97 *Auto Workers News,* Dec. 16, 30, 1933; *Daily Worker,* Nov. 23, Dec. 2, 14, 15, 18, 1933.

98 *Auto Workers News,* Mar. 24, Apr. 7, 1934; *Daily Worker,* Mar. 10, 19–23, 27, 28, 1934.

99 *Daily Worker,* Mar. 20, June 18, Dec. 25, 1934; Jack Stachel, "Our Trade Union Policy," *Communist,* XIII (Nov., 1934), 1101.

100 "The Structure and Membership of the Communist Party in the Detroit Area," MS in Martin Papers. The A.W.U. had made a determined effort to organize the Ford Motor Co., and yet at the time the union was disbanded, it had only 20 Ford members. Bonosky, *Brother Bill McKie,* p. 106.

101 *Daily Worker,* Dec. 25, 1934; Communist party handbill, [Feb. 25, 1935], Labadie Collection.

NOTES TO CHAPTER VI

1 *Detroit News,* Sept. 15, 16, 17, 19, 1933; Martel to Wagner, Oct. 5, 1933, Collins to Wagner, Oct. 18, 1933, Campbell to Wagner, Oct. 2, 3, 1933, Employers' Association of Detroit to Wagner, Oct. 3, 1933, N.L.B. Drawer 132. For the composition of the board, see *Detroit News,* Sept. 16, 1933.

2 Lorwin and Wubnig, *Labor Relations Boards,* pp. 88, 101; Wagner to Larned, Oct. 20, 1933, N.L.B. Drawer 132. The employer representatives included Frederick Haynes; A.R. Glancy, a former president of the Oakland Motor Car Co.; Chester M. Culver, the manager of the Employers' Association of Detroit; and William J. McAneeny, chairman of the board of Hudson. The union members were Frank Martel and representatives of the Metal Polishers, Electrical Workers, Photo Engravers, and Allied Printing Trades. *Detroit News,* Oct. 29, 193.

3 Collins to Green, Nov. 18, Dec. 16, 1933, Jan. 6, 20, 1934, Feb. 19, 1934, Collins File; Collins to Wagner, Nov. 17, 1933, N.L.B. Drawer 13; Martel *et al.* to Wagner, Jan. 6, Feb. 9, 1934, N.L.B. Drawer 132.

4 Wagner to Siedenburg, Feb. 12, 1934, Larned to Wagner, May 1, 1934, N.L.B. Drawer 132; *Detroit News,* Feb. 13, 1934.

5 Unsigned memorandum, Feb. 1, 1934, Wagner to Smith, Feb. 12, 1934, Wharton to Wagner, Feb. 15, 27, 1934, and similar letters to Wagner from various I.A.M. lodges, Robert Fechner to Wagner, Mar. 10, 1934, N.L.B. to Siedenburg, Mar. 19, 1934, Siedenburg to Jesse I. Miller, Mar. 24, Apr. 9, 1934, Smith to Wagner, May 21, 1934, N.L.B. Drawer 132; Green to Collins, Feb. 16, 1934, Green Letterbooks.

6 A.L.B., Fisher Body Hearing, May 2, 1934, pp. 25–26, Michigan Historical Collections; Weckler to Sherer, Nov. 22, 1933, Jan. 23, 1934, A.L.B. Drawer 4089; Wollering to Detroit Regional Labor Board (R.L.B.), Jan. 4, 1934, Case 34, Detroit R.L.B. Box 281.

7 *Decisions of the N.L.B., Aug. 1933–Mar. 1934,* pp. vi–viii.

8 Collins to Green, Sept. 22, Oct. 14, 28, Nov. 18, 1933, Jan. 6, Feb. 9, 1934, Collins to Morrison, Dec. 9, 1933, Collins File; Wieck, "Automobile Workers," p. 35. Collins reported a total membership of 3000 in Detroit on Sept. 9, 1933. J. F. Anderson reported a paid-up membership in Flint as of November 1 of 5400 and an additional 7472 "members" who had made a partial payment or no payment of dues. Collins to Green, Sept. 9, 1933, Anderson to Morrison, Nov. 12, 19, 1933, Collins File.

9 Collins to Johnson, Nov. 14, 1933, N.R.A. Box 7898; *Detroit Labor News,* Nov. 10, 1933; Green to U.A.W., Dec. 1, 1933, L.A.B. to Johnson, undated, Green to Johnson, Dec. 16, 1933, Green Letterbooks.

10 N.A.C.C. Bulletin, Nov. 8, 1933, Acc. 203, Box 3, Ford Archives; N.A.C.C. Bulletin, Nov. 15, 1933, Acc. 52, Box 7, *ibid.;* Reeves to E. Ford, Dec. 22, 1933, Acc. 203, Box 9, *ibid.;* P. Johnson to Chapin, Nov. 10, 1933, enclosing P. Johnson to Brown, Nov. 2, 1933, Chapin Papers; *Automotive Industries,* LXIX (Dec. 16, 1933), 724; *Detroit News,* Dec. 2, 16, 1933; *New York Times,* Dec. 18, 1933; *Codes,* IV, 641–42.

11 Green to U.A.W., Dec. 23, 1933, Green Letterbooks; Collins to Green, Jan. 6, 22, 1934, Collins File; *New York Times,* Feb. 2, 1934; *Detroit News,* Feb. 28, 1934.

12 Green to U.A.W., Jan. 8, 1934, Green Letterbooks.

13 Chalmers, "Collective Bargaining," V, 39–40; Pilkington to Kerwin, Sept. 18, 1933, C.S. 170-9366; Strickland to N.R.A., Dec. 22, 1933, Chalmers to William M. Leiserson, Sept. 17, 1933, Case 141, N.L.B. Drawer 22; Strickland to Abner E. Larned, Sept. 18, 1933, A.L.B. Drawer 3990; "Notice to Employees," undated, *ibid.; Detroit News,* Sept. 18, 19, 1933. The company contributed $1 to the NIRA Association for every $1 contributed by the employees, up to $5000.

14 There is a copy of the agreement in A.L.B. Drawer 3990.

15 Chalmers to Leiserson, Sept. 20, 1933, Case 141, N.L.B. Drawer 22.

16 *Detroit Labor News,* Sept. 22, 1933. The differences between labor and management at the Bower plant following the strike can be traced in detail in Case 141, N.L.B. Drawer 22, and in Bower folder, A.L.B. 3990. See also A.F. of L. Strike File, Local 18311.

17 Index of Formal Files, Detroit R.L.B. Box 280; Activities of the Detroit R.L.B., Weeks Ending Feb. 24, Mar. 3, 1934, Detroit R.L.B. Box 281; Buick folder, A.L.B. Drawer 3991.

18 Folder # 14, A.L.B. Drawer 4089; Sherer to N.L.B., Feb. 6, 1934, *ibid.;* Folder #12, A.L.B. Drawer 4087; Marvel Carburetor folder, A.L.B. Drawer 4000; Cook to Detroit R.L.B., Jan. 19, 1934, E. F. Fisher to Sherer, Feb. 1, 1934, Sherer to Fisher Body, Feb. 26, 1934, Case 209, N.L.B. Drawer 35.

19 Case 42, Detroit R.L.B. Box 282.

20 Activities of the Detroit R.L.B., Week Ending Mar. 24, 1934, Detroit R.L.B. Box 281; Case 78, Detroit R.L.B. Box 282.

21 Case 34, Detroit R.L.B. Box 281; Activities of the Detroit R.L.B., Weeks Ending Jan. 20, 27, 1934, *ibid.*

22 Collins to Green, Oct. 28, 1933, Collins File; Pilkington to Kerwin, Oct. 26, 1933, C.S. 176-747; A. S. Weaver *et al.* to Larned, Oct. 25, 1933, Weckler to Sherer, Nov. 22, 1933, A. R. Glancy to Weckler, Nov. 29, 1933, Collins to Larned, Jan. 3, 1934, A.L.B. Drawer 4089; M. W. Church to Wagner, Jan. 1, 1934, Case 209, N.L.B. Drawer 35.

23 Collins to Green, Jan. 20, 1934, Collins File; Pilkington to Wagner, Feb. 14, 1934, Chapin to Arthur Greer, Feb. 14, 1934, E. F. Fisher to Sherer, Mar. 7, 1934, Case 209, N.L.B. Drawer 35; Charles D. Hastings to F.L.U. 18698, Jan. 22, 1934, Chapin Papers.

24 Green to U.A.W., Jan. 8, 1934, Cronin to Chapin, Jan. 25, 1934, and enclosed correspondence, Chapin Papers.

25 *Decisions of the N.L.B., Aug. 1933–Mar. 1934,* p. vii.

26 N.R.A. Release No. 3125, Feb. 4, 1934; *New York Times,* Feb. 4, 1934; *Decisions of the N.L.B., Aug. 1933–Mar. 1934,* pp. 64–65. Both Johnson and Richberg professed to believe in majority rule in collective bargaining but contended that Section 7(a) stood in the way of the concept of exclusive representation. Johnson, *Blue Eagle,* pp. 293, 343, 423; Richberg, *Rainbow,* p. 151. In their February 3 interpretation of the President's executive order, Johnson and Richberg specifically stated that an employer could not "maintain satisfactory relations with his employees through unlimited negotiations with an indefinite number of employee representatives expressing every possible variety of opinion."

27 Twentieth Century Fund, *How Collective Bargaining Works, passim;* Lorwin and Wubnig, *Labor Relations Boards,* pp. 3–6, 19, 23–24; Leiserson, "Closed Shop and Open Shop," Edwin R. A. Seligman and Alvin Johnson, eds., *Encyclopaedia of the Social Sciences* (New York, 1930–1935), II, 568–70; Sum-

ner H. Slichter, *Union Policies and Industrial Management* (Washington, 1941), p. 57; Paul Douglas, "Shop Committees: Substitute for, or Supplement to, Trade Unions?" *Journal of Political Economy,* XXIX (Feb., 1921), 91–93; "The Houde Decision," *American Federationist,* XLI (Oct., 1934), 1102; National Industrial Conference Board, *Collective Bargaining through Employee Representation* (New York, 1933), p. 13; National Industrial Conference Board, *Individual and Collective Bargaining under the N.I.R.A.* (New York, 1933), p. 16.

28 Lorwin and Wubnig, *Labor Relations Boards,* pp. 10–13, 19–20; Bureau of Applied Economics, *National War Labor Board Docket* (Washington, 1919), I, Dockets No. 19, 22; II, Docket No. 273.

29 Cook to Wagner, Jan. 19, 1934, Pilkington to Wagner, Feb. 14, 1934, Wolf to Pilkington, Feb. 21, 1934, Pilkington to Wolf, Feb. 28, 1934, Case 209, N.L.B. Drawer 35; Collins to Detroit R.L.B., Feb. 13, 1934, and enclosed resolution, Sherer to N.L.B., Feb. 19, 1934, Detroit R.L.B. Box 280; Buick folder, A.L.B. Drawer 3991; Pontiac Fisher Body folder, A.L.B. Drawer 4103. The first request for an election in the industry came from the Pontiac Chamber of Labor in the G.M. Truck plant. G.M. Truck folder, A.L.B. Drawer 3999.

30 Exhibit A, [Nov. 24, 1933], Case 146, N.L.B. Drawer 23; text of D. S. Harder statement, Sept. 1, 1933, *ibid.;* Preliminary Announcement of the Establishing of a Budd Employee Representative Association . . . (Sept. 5, 1933), *ibid.; Proposed Plan of Employee Representation in Plants of Edward G. Budd Manufacturing Co., Philadelphia Works, ibid.;* Budd to Wagner, Dec. 6, 1933, *ibid.;* Testimony of the Employees of the Budd Co., Dec. 8, 1933, *ibid.;* Memorandum of Paul Zens, Oct. 12, 1933, *ibid.; Mr. Budd's Address to the Representatives,* Nov. 9, 1933, *ibid.;* Budd to John Crawford, Acc. 52, Box 12, Ford Archives; Hearing on Alleged Violation of Section VII of Automobile Manufacturing Industry Code by E. G. Budd Manufacturing Co., Jan. 24, 1934, pp. 78–82, 112–26, 184–86, N.L.B. Drawer 60. The plan was of the usual company-union type in the restrictions it placed on the suffrage and on eligibility for membership on the works council. The management was to appoint five management representatives to negotiate with the employee representatives. The plan could be amended only by the concurrent action of a majority of employee and management representatives. As of Jan. 24, 1934, the only change that had been made in the plan was to permit a representative who became a foreman to continue to serve if he remained in the same district and if this was agreeable to his constituents. *Ibid.,* pp. 127–28.

31 Exhibit A, Case 146, N.L.B. Drawer 23; Budd Hearing, pp. 94–100, N.L.B. Drawer 60; Morrison to Francis Sullivan, Feb. 9, 1934, A.F. of L. Strike File, Local 18763.

32 Exhibit A, Case 146, N.L.B. Drawer 23; Price, Waterhouse and Co. to Budd, Dec. 5, 1933, *ibid.;* Budd to Crawford, Dec. 22, 1933, Acc. 52, Box 12, Ford Archives; Budd Hearing, pp. 73–74, 83–84, 151–53, 191–93, N.L.B. Drawer 60; *Philadelphia Evening Bulletin,* Nov. 14, 15, 1933; *Philadelphia Inquirer,* Nov. 16, 1933; *Philadelphia Public Ledger,* Nov. 16, 1933.

33 Guy Basal *et al.* to Jacob Billikopf, Nov. 14, 1933, Billikopf to Budd, Nov. 15, 1933, Wagner to Philadelphia R.L.B., Nov. 21, 1933 (typist marks indicate that this letter, which was followed almost verbatim in the regional board decision, was written by Handler), Case 146, N.L.B. Drawer 23; In the Matter of Edward G. Budd Manufacturing Co. . . . , Nov. 23, 1933, *ibid.*

34 Budd to Billikopf, Nov. 29, 1933, Wagner to Budd and Basal, Dec. 4, 1933, Budd to Wagner, Dec. 6, 1933, *ibid.;* Testimony of the Employees of the Budd Co., Dec. 8, 1933, *ibid.;* N.R.A. Release No. 2144, Dec. 7, 1933.

35 *Decisions of the N.L.B., Aug. 1933–Mar. 1934,* pp. 58–61.

36 Basal to Wagner, Dec. 16, 1933, Budd to Wagner, Dec. 16, 1933, Case 146, N.L.B. Drawer 23; Budd to Crawford, Dec. 22, 1933, Acc. 52, Box 12, Ford Archives.

37 *Philadelphia Public Ledger,* Dec. 19, 1933; Basal to Wagner, Dec. 22, 1933, Joseph M. Richie to Wagner, Dec. 29, 1933, Case 146, N.L.B. Drawer 23; Budd Hearing, pp. 23–24, 84, 104–10, 157–73, N.L.B. Drawer 60.

38 The National Compliance Board consisted of the National Compliance Director and one member each from the I.A.B. and the L.A.B.

39 N.R.A. Releases No. 2678, Jan. 11, 1934, No. 3472, Feb. 25, 1934; Budd Hearing, N.L.B. Drawer 60; *Philadelphia Public Ledger,* Mar. 9, 1934.

40 *Philadelphia Evening Bulletin,* Feb. 26, 1934.

41 *Ibid.;* Handler to Davis, Feb. 14, 1934, Case 146, N.L.B. Drawer 23; Basal *et al.* to Wagner, Feb. 27, 1934, Robert F. Wagner Papers, Georgetown University; Davis to Budd, Mar. 2, 1934, N.R.A. Box 660.

42 N.R.A. Releases No. 3649, Mar. 5, 1934, No. 3715, Mar. 8, 1934; Richie *et al.* to Johnson, Mar. 6, 1934, N.R.A. Box 660.

43 *Philadelphia Evening Bulletin,* Mar. 9, 10, 1934; Lybrand, Ross Brothers *et al.* to Election Committee of Employees Representative Association, Mar. 10, 1934, A.L.B. Drawer 4003; Budd statement, Mar. 13, 1934, N.R.A. Box 660. The addition of 800 votes to the union total and the subtraction of the same number from the employee-association total would have given the union a victory by the margin of 443 votes.

44 *Philadelphia Evening Bulletin,* Mar. 10, 12, 15, 1934; Johnson to Lea, undated, N.R.A. Box 660; N.R.A. Release No. 3873, Mar. 17, 1934.

45 Richie to Roosevelt, Mar. 19, 1934, Case 146, N.L.B. Drawer 23; *Philadelphia Evening Bulletin,* Mar. 17, 19, 20, 22, 1934.

46 *Philadelphia Evening Bulletin,* Mar. 27, 1934; Jean Smith (secretary of H. S. Drinker) to George Buckley, N.R.A. Box 660.

47 N.R.A. Release No. 4128, Mar. 29, 1934. The agreement concluded with the statement, "The strikers are satisfied with the above and will call the strike off." As posted in the plant, however, the sentence read: "In view of the above, the strikers will call the strike off and discontinue their activities in connection with the Budd plant." The local protested that this was "a deliberate attempt by Budd to continue his union-busting, NRA-double-crossing tactics." *Progressive Labor World* (Philadelphia), Apr. 12, 1934. A year after the strike, almost 500 strikers were still out of work. Wieck, "Automobile Workers," p. 78.

48 Alex J. Ross to Morrison, Dec. 16, 1933, Green to Richie, Dec. 26, 1933, Richie to Green, Dec. 28, 1933, Green to Richie, Jan. 9, 1934, A.F. of L. Strike File, Local 18763; Budd Hearing, p. 155, N.L.B. Drawer 60; A.F. of L., *Proceedings, 1935,* p. 735.

49 N.L.B., Stenographic Report of Hearing, In Re: Houde Engineering Corporation, Feb. 6, 1934, Case 12, N.L.R.B. Drawer 254; *Decisions of the National Labor Board, Part II, April 1934–July 1934* (Washington, 1934), p. 37; "To All Houde Engineering Corporation Employees," undated, Case 12, N.L.R.B. Drawer 158; *Constitution and By-Laws of the Houde Welfare and Athletic As-*

sociation of Employees (Oct. 24, 1933), *ibid.;* Thomas I. Emerson Memorandum on Houde Engineering Case, Nov. 14, 1934, *ibid.*

50 Thomas J. Williams to Kerwin, Nov. 6, 14, 1934, C.S. 176-795; Minutes of a Meeting of the [Buffalo] Regional Labor Board . . . , Dec. 28, 1933, pp. 9–12, 22–24, 52, Case 12, N.L.R.B. Drawer 254; N.L.B., Houde Hearing, pp. 2–11, *ibid.;* Emerson Memorandum, Case 12, N.L.R.B. Drawer 158; Russell S. Eggleston to Green, Jan. 20, 1934, A.F. of L. Strike File, Local 18839. The Buffalo R.L.B. found on Mar. 22, 1935, that Houde had discriminated against the union president, vice-president, recording secretary, and two other union officials either by laying them off or refusing to rehire them. *Central Labor Council Herald* (Buffalo), Mar. 29, 1935.

51 Williams to Kerwin, Nov. 6, 14, 1933, C.S. 176-795; Helen Socha to N.R.A. Compliance Director, Dec. 5, 1933, Shortal to Houde, Dec. 11, 18, 1933, Wolf to Buffalo R.L.B., Jan. 3, 1934, Shortal to Wolf, Jan. 5, 1934, Peo to Shortal, Jan. 6, 1934, Eggleston to Shortal, Jan. 8, 1934, Buffalo R.L.B. to Peo, Jan. 9, 16, 1934, Peo to Buffalo R.L.B., Jan. 13, 20, 1934, Shortal to N.L.B., Feb. 8, 1934, Case 12, N.L.R.B. Drawer 158; Eggleston to Green, Jan. 20, 1934, A.F. of L. Strike File, Local 18839; Minutes of Buffalo R.L.B., Dec. 28, 1933, Case 12, N.L.R.B. Drawer 254. The Buffalo board reached its decision on the basis of a union affidavit previously prepared for Peo that authorized stipulated union officials to negotiate with the company for union members.

52 Socha to Wagner, Jan. 27, 1934, Eggleston to Shortal, Jan. 29, 1934, N.L.B. to Eggleston, Jan. 29, 1934, Shortal to N.L.B., Feb. 2, 1934, Peo to N.L.B., Feb. 3, 1934, Buffalo R.L.B. to N.L.B, Feb. 6, 1934, Case 12, N.L.R.B. Drawer 158; Socha to Green, Jan. 28, 1934, John C. Johnston to Green, Jan. 29, 1934, A.F. of L. Strike File, Local 18839. James A. Emery, the general counsel of the N.A.M., and John C. Gall, the associate counsel, filed a brief on the case with the N.L.B. that supported Houde's position. They argued that the "doctrine of undisclosed principal" could not be applied to labor-management relations under the N.I.R.A. The brief is in *ibid.*

53 N.L.B., Houde Hearing, Case 12, N.L.R.B. Drawer 254; *Decisions of the N.L.B., Aug. 1933–Mar. 1934,* p. 87.

54 *Decisions of the N.L.B., Aug. 1933–Mar. 1934,* pp. 83–84; Lorwin and Wubnig, *Labor Relations Boards,* pp. 185–89.

55 Buffalo R.L.B. to N.L.B., Feb. 25, 1934, Shortal to N.L.B., Feb. 26, 1934, Handler to Shortal, Mar. 8, 1934, Shortal to Houde, Mar. 13, 16, 24, 1934, Peo to Buffalo R.L.B., Mar. 13, 15, 17, 26, 1934, Shortal to Peo, Mar. 14, 28, 1934, Shortal to Socha, Mar. 24, 1934, Case 12, N.L.R.B. Drawer 158; Memorandum by Wolf, Mar. 14, 1934, *ibid.;* Williams to Kerwin, Mar. 20, 1934, C.S. 176-795; Johnston to Green, Apr. 17, 1934, A.F. of L. Strike File, Local 18839.

56 Form signed by Edwin Merkley, Mar. 30, 1934, Case 12, N.L.R.B. Drawer 158; Wolf Memorandum, Apr. 9, 1934, *ibid.;* Regional Labor Board . . . , In the Matter of Houde Engineering Corp. . . . , Apr. 12, 1934, Case 12, N.L.R.B. Drawer 254; Johnston to Green, Apr. 17, 1934, A.F. of L. Strike File, Local 18839.

57 Shipley to Green, Jan. 10, 1934, A.F. of L. Strike File, Local 18347; Shipley to Roosevelt, Jan. 6, 1934, Case 101, Chicago R.L.B. Box 308; N.L.R.B., Stenographic Report of Hearing, In the Matter of Bendix Aviation Corporation, Oct. 11, 1934, pp. 40–43, Cases 390–92, Chicago R.L.B. Box 322; *A Brief Documented History of the Laboring People of Bendix Local No. 9—UAW-CIO*

(n.p., [1953]), pp. 7, 10, 11. The Bendix "Plan of Employee Representation" is given on pp. 44–50 of the N.L.R.B. hearing noted above.

58 The Bendix story is covered in detail in Case 101, Chicago R.L.B. Box 308; A.F. of L. Strike File, Local 18347; and C.S. 176-433.

59 Chalmers, "Collective Bargaining," VIII, 8–9.

60 Ramsey to A. Howard Myers, Feb. 1, 1934, N.L.B. Drawer 121; Ramsey affidavit, Feb. 14, 1934, Case 22, Toledo Sub-R.L.B. Box 277; Nash to Dana, Feb. 5, 1934, Dana to Nash, Feb. 16, 1934, *ibid.;* undated sheet headed "Spicer Mutual Benefit Association," *ibid.; Toledo News-Bee,* Feb. 23, 1934.

61 The union also demanded seniority, equal pay for women for equal work, and call-in pay of two hours. *Toledo News-Bee,* Feb. 26, 1934.

62 Ramsey to Wagner, Feb. 23, 1934, N.L.B. Drawer 121; J. A. Minch, "Notice to all Employees," Feb. 23, 1934, Case 2, Toledo Sub-R.L.B. Box 276; Chalmers, "Collective Bargaining," VIII, 10; *Toledo News-Bee,* Feb. 23, 24, 26, 27, 28, 1934; "How the Auto Parts Plant Strike in Toledo Was Settled by Ramsey," Martin Papers.

63 Electric Auto-Lite earned a profit after income taxes of $684,000 in 1933 and of $1,212,000 in 1934; Spicer lost $131,000 in 1933 and earned $670,000 in 1934; and Bingham and Logan Gear suffered a combined net loss of $15,900 in 1933 and of $92,268 during the first 5 months of 1934. *Automotive Industries,* LXX (May 26, 1934), 654–55; *ibid.,* LXXII (June 1, 1935), 738; Anthony Beran to J. R. Kirk, June 26, 1934, C.S. 176-1292.

64 Nash to Wagner, Feb. 24, 25, 1934, N.L.B. Drawer 121; Nash to Ramsey, Feb. 24, 1934, Case 22, Toledo Sub R.L.B. Box 277; Ramsey to Green, Mar. 1, 1934, A.F. of L. Strike File, Local 18384; Nash to Wagner, Mar. 1, 1934, N.L.B. Drawer 150; G.M., Labor Relations Diary, Appendix Document No. 28; Hugh D. Friel to Kerwin, Mar. 4, 1934, C.S. 176-1292; *Toledo News-Bee,* Feb. 24, 26, 27, 28, Mar. 1, 1934.

65 *Milwaukee Journal,* Nov. 10, 12, 1933; *Milwaukee Leader,* Nov. 10, 1933; Oral History Interview of Paul Russo, Apr. 13, 1960, pp. 4–5, Michigan Historical Collections; Henry Ohl to Wagner, Nov. 17, 1933, N.L.B. Drawer 114; Nash to All Factory Employees, Oct. 26, 1933, Case 29, Chicago R.L.B. Box 304. There is a copy of the company-union plan in *ibid.*

66 Ohl *et al.* to Wagner, Nov. 10, 1933, N.L.B. Drawer 114; John F. Kuehnl to Chicago R.L.B., Nov. 10, 1933, Ohl *et al.* to Nash, undated, Nash to Lapp, undated, Ward Bewley to Lapp, Nov. 18, 1933, Lapp to N.L.B., Nov. 21, 1933, Lapp to Nash, Dec. 20, 1933, H. J. Mellum to Jacobson, Jan. 17, 1934, Case 29, Chicago R.L.B. Box 304; *Milwaukee Journal,* Nov. 10, 17, 21, 1934.

67 The workers, upon their return, complained that they were earning only 48 cents per hour, but a new schedule of rates put into effect early in Dec. and made retroactive to Nov. 22 enabled the men to earn 60–65 cents per hour. W. G. Kult *et al.* to Nash, Nov. 21, 1933, Nash to Lapp, Dec. 19, 1933, Mellum to Jacobson, Jan. 17, 1934, Case 29, Chicago R.L.B. Box 304. The average earned hourly rate at the Kenosha plant for the five weeks ending Dec. 2, 1933, was 57.39 cents, and it was 68.68 cents for the four weeks ending Jan. 27, 1934. N.R.A. Box 673.

68 Kult *et al.* to Nash, Nov. 21, 1933, Kuehnl to Lapp, Nov. 21, 1933, Dec. 4, 22, 1933, Nash to Lapp, Dec. 19, 1933, Nash to Kult *et al.,* Dec. 22, 1933, Kuehnl to Chicago R.L.B., Jan. 2, 1934, Stauder to Lapp, Jan. 2, 1934, Stauder to Jacobson, Jan. 7, 1934, Steffensen to Nash, Jan. 12, 1934, Mellum to Jacobson,

Jan. 17, 1934, Jacobson to Mellum, Jan. 19, 1934, Stauder to Steffensen, undated, Case 29, Chicago R.L.B. Box 304; James Mullenbach Report, Mar. 2, 1934, *ibid.;* Jacobson to Wolf, Mar. 3, 1934, N.L.B. Drawer 114.

69 *Milwaukee Journal,* Nov. 13, 1933.

70 Frank B. Schutz to Green, Jan. 21, 1934, A.F. of L. Strike File, Local 19059; J. T. Michel to Nash, Jan. 29, 1934, A.L.B. Drawer 4001; H. H. Seaman to Employees, Feb. 7, 1934, J. J. Handley to Jacobson, Feb. 15, 1934, Case 132, Chicago R.L.B. Box 310; Mullenbach Report, Mar. 2, 1934, Case 29, Chicago R.L.B. Box 304; F.T.C., *Report on Motor Vehicle Industry,* p. 718; *Ward's 1939 Automotive Year Book,* p. 42. The average hourly wage of Nash's Racine workers in Jan. was 61.38 cents as compared to an industry average for that month of 63.8 cents. N.R.A. Boxes 673, 675; Myrick, Jr., *et al.,* "Economic Survey," Section Three, p. 52, N.R.A. Box 8309.

71 The Seaman offer did not apply to the pattern, tool and die, and engineering departments since they had received a wage increase on Feb. 13, but employees in these departments who had not received a full 10 per cent increase were to be brought up to this level. H. H. Seaman to Schutz *et al.,* Feb. 20, 1934, Case 132, Chicago R.L.B. Box 310.

72 Chicago R.L.B. to H. H. Seaman, Feb. 17, 1934, Seaman to Schutz *et al.,* Feb. 20, 1934, Seaman to Chicago R.L.B., Feb. 23, 1934, *ibid.;* Memorandum of Conference . . . by General Manager Racine Plant, Feb. 22, 1934, Case 29, Chicago R.L.B. Box 304; Notice Posted by P. J. Moohan (Kenosha), Feb. 21, 1934, *ibid.;* Mullenbach Report, Mar. 2, 1934, *ibid.;* Steffensen Report to Jacobson, Feb. 23, 1934, Case 139, Chicago R.L.B. Box 310; George S. Nordstrom to Nash, Feb. 24, 1934, A.L.B. Drawer 4001; N.R.A. Release No. 3777, Mar. 12, 1934; *Milwaukee Journal,* Feb. 21, 25–28, Mar. 1, 5, 13, 14, 21–24, 1934; *New Day* (Racine), Feb. 23, Mar. 2, 1934; Chalmers, "Collective Bargaining," VIII, 18; Wieck, "Automobile Workers," p. 83.

73 The Kenosha local was dissatisfied with the plan of bargaining through departmental committees provided in the agreement concluding the Nov. strike, and it also claimed, correctly in the opinion of a Chicago R.L.B. representative, that the company had refused to bargain with the general committee for the plant as a whole. Mullenbach Report, Mar. 2, 1934, Case 29, Chicago R.L.B. Box 304; Jacobson to Wolf, Mar. 3, 1934, N.L.B. Drawer 114.

74 Jacobson to Wolf, Mar. 3, 1934, N.L.B. Drawer 114; Handley to Chicago R.L.B., Mar. 4, 1934, A.L.B. Drawer 4001; *Milwaukee Journal,* Mar. 10, 1934. For the I.A.M. demands, see Alfred Olson *et al.* to Nash, Mar. 5, 1934, A.L.B. Drawer 4001.

75 *Milwaukee Journal,* Feb. 26, 1934; N.R.A. Release No. 3587, Mar. 2, 1934; Mellum notes on Kenosha conference, Mar. 9, 1934, A.L.B. Drawer 4001.

76 E. H. McCarty to Our Employees, Mar. 16, 1934, enclosing McCarty to Handley, Mar. 16, 1934, Chapin Papers; Seaman to Handley, Mar. 16, 1934, Case 132, Chicago R.L.B. Box 310; L. Bentley *et al.* to Nash Motors and Seaman Body, Mar. 19, 1934, Ohl to Jacobson, Mar. 20, 1934, Case 139, Chicago R.L.B. Box 310; *Milwaukee Journal,* Mar. 21, 1934.

77 George W. Smith, Jr., to George Lehman, Dec. 11, 1933 (two letters), C.S. 170-9554; *Auto Workers News,* Dec. 16, 1933; *Cleveland Plain Dealer,* Dec. 17, 1933.

78 Lehman to Green, Feb. 27, 1934, Green to Lehman, Feb. 27, 1934, A. F. of L. Strike File, Local 18463; Green to U.A.W., Mar. 8, 1934, Green

Letterbooks; *Toledo News-Bee,* Feb. 28, 1934; *Daily Worker,* Mar. 2, 1934; Stolberg, *The Story of the CIO* (New York, 1938), p. 164.

79 For the St. Louis story, see Case 6, St. Louis R.L.B. Box 393; Case 90, N.L.B. Drawer 15; and C.S. 176-818. For the Atlanta details, see Case 53, Atlanta R.L.B. Box 228; and A.L.B. Drawers 3990 and 4102.

80 Collins to Green, Feb. 6, 1934, and enclosed night letter, Collins File; *Detroit Labor News,* Feb. 9, 1934; Chalmers, "Collective Bargaining," V, 43–48; *Detroit News,* Mar. 6, 1934; Minutes of Meetings of Federal Labor Union No. 18331, Feb. 15, Mar. 1, 1934, Wayne State University Archives; Pilkington to Wagner, Feb. 14, 1934, Case 209, N.L.B. Drawer 35; Pilkington to Kerwin, Feb. 27, 1934, C.S. 165-1406; N.L.B. memorandum, [Feb. 28, 1934], N.L.B. Drawer 132.

81 Collins to Morrison, Mar. 3, 1934, Collins File; *Detroit Free Press,* Mar. 5, 6, 1934; Chalmers, "Collective Bargaining," V, 48–49. The locals requested a 20 per cent wage increase, a 30-hour week, time-and-a-half for hours above 8 per day and double time for Saturday, abolition or simplification of the bonus wage system, permission for union representatives to supervise the time study and the computation of the efficiency rating whenever there was a dispute as to the rating or timing of a job, seniority, a government survey of the speed-up, and referral to a board of arbitration of disputes that could not be settled by conference. There is a copy of the demands in the Brown Collection. Hudson was given 72 hours to reply.

82 Collins interview; Chalmers, "Collective Bargaining," V, 43–44, 49. On the strength of union strike sentiment, see "Mr. Dewey's memorandum regarding threatened strike of automotive industries in Michigan," [Mar., 1934], C.S. 176-1339.

83 Collins to Wagner, Mar. 1, 1934, Collins to Roosevelt, Mar. 4, 1934, Wagner to Collins, Mar. 6, 1934, Case 209, N.L.B. Drawer 35; Chalmers, "Collective Bargaining," VI, 1–4; Minutes of Meetings of F.L.U. No. 18331, Mar. 8, 1934, Wayne State University Archives; N.R.A. Releases No. 3644, Mar. 5, 1934, No. 3661, Mar. 6, 1934, No. 3678, Mar. 7, 1934; *Detroit News,* Mar. 6, 7, 8, 1934.

84 *New York Times,* Mar. 14, 1934; *Business Week,* Mar. 17, 1934, pp. 9–10; *Automotive Industries,* LXX (Mar. 17, 1934), 327, 342.

85 *New York Times,* Mar. 15, 1934; N.L.B., Stenographic Report of Hearing, In the Matter of Buick Co. . . . , Mar. 14, 15, 1934, N.L.B. Drawer 68. According to Knudsen's biographer, Knudsen caught "more than a little hell" from General Johnson for the opinions he expressed at the hearing. Norman Beasley, *Knudsen* (New York, 1947), p. 155.

86 Jacobson to Wolf, Mar. 20, 1934, Case 139, Chicago R.L.B. Box 310; Chalmers, "Collective Bargaining," VI, 12; G.M., Labor Relations Diary, Section 1, p. 35; *Detroit News,* Mar. 14, 1934; *Detroit Free Press,* Mar. 17, 1934; *New York Times,* Mar. 17, 1934.

87 Bernstein, *New Deal Collective Bargaining Policy,* pp. 65–66; Senate Committee on Education and Labor, *To Create a National Labor Board,* pp. 1–7.

88 Summary of the Activity of the Operations Committee of the N.A.C.C. in Opposition to the Wagner Bill . . . , [Apr. 19, 1934], Acc. 52, Box 7, Ford Archives. A small part of the sum expended was to combat the Fletcher-Rayburn Securities Exchange Control Bill and the Wagner-Lewis Unemployment Insurance Bill.

89 *Detroit News,* Mar. 16, 1934; *Automotive Daily News,* Mar. 16, 19, 1934; *New York Times,* Mar. 14, 19, 20, 23, 1934; N.A.C.C. Bulletins, Mar. 19, 20, 1934, Acc. 203, Box 3, Ford Archives.

90 Senate Committee on Education and Labor, *To Create a National Labor Board,* pp. 69, 102–6, 143–49; *New York Times,* Mar. 18, 20, 22, 1934; *Detroit News,* Mar. 18, 1934; *New Day* (Racine), Mar. 23, 1934; text of address by Green, Mar. 22, 1934, Chapin Papers.

91 N.A.C.C. Bulletin, Mar. 16, 1934, Acc. 203, Box 3, Ford Archives; Chalmers, "Collective Bargaining," VI, 13–15; *New York Times,* Mar. 14, 18–21, 1934; Collins to Johnson, Mar. 20, 1934, Roosevelt to Collins, Mar. 20, 21, 1934, Collins to Roosevelt, Mar. 20, 1934, O.F.407-B, Box 18, Roosevelt Library; N.A.C.C. to Johnson, Mar. 21, 1934, Chapin Papers; *Detroit Free Press,* Mar. 18, 19, 20, 1934; *Detroit News,* Mar. 19, 20, 1934.

92 *Detroit News,* Mar. 21, 1934; *Detroit Times,* Mar. 21, 1934; *Cleveland Plain Dealer,* Mar. 21, 1934.

93 Collins to Johnson, Mar. 20, 1934, Macauley to Roosevelt, Mar. 21, 1934, O.F.407-B, Box 18, Roosevelt Library; N.A.C.C. to Johnson, Mar. 21, 1934, Chapin Papers; *New York Times,* Mar. 14, 18, 19, 20, 1934.

94 N.A.C.C. to Johnson, Mar. 21, 1934, Chapin Papers; Collins to Johnson, Mar. 20, 1934, O.F.407-B, Box 18, Roosevelt Library.

95 *Iron Age,* CXXXIII (Mar. 22, 1934), 39; *Detroit News,* Mar. 3, 21, 1934; Biddle, *In Brief Authority,* pp. 21–22.

96 *New York Times,* Mar. 23, 1934; *Detroit News,* Mar. 23, 1934. Conciliator James Dewey reported that automobile company executives had told him "very emphatically, they would risk a strike or shut down entirely rather than comply with any rulings from any Governmental Agency which would involve the making or signing of a union agreement." Dewey's memorandum, C.S. 176–1339. Asked at his press conference of Mar. 23 if he was using the Wagner Bill as "a sort of hammer over the heads of industrialists," Roosevelt replied: "I would say that the cupboard door is still closed. We have not made a gesture toward the cupboard." Press Conference No. 108, p. 258, Roosevelt Library.

97 Biddle, *In Brief Authority,* p. 39; *New York Times,* Mar. 19, 1934; Tolles and LaFever, "Wages . . . in the Motor Vehicle Industry, 1934," pp. 529, 535. The paid-up membership figures were supplied to me by the Bookkeeping Department of the old A.F. of L. on Aug. 17, 1955.

98 On the limitations of union membership figures, see Milton Derber, "Growth and Expansion," in Derber and Young, *Labor and the New Deal,* p. 4; and William Paschell, "Limitations of Union Membership Data," *Monthly Labor Review,* LXXVIII (Nov., 1955), 1265–69. Dewey reported that he had been "reliably informed" by union officials that 9200 of 13,000 Flint Chevrolet workers and 10,000 of 14,000 Buick workers were union members, that the two Fisher Body plants in Flint were almost 100 per cent organized, and that 8900 of 10,000 Hudson workers were members. Dewey's memorandum, C.S. 176–1339.

99 Green to Executive Council, Mar. 27, 1934, Green to Matthew Woll, Mar. 30, 1934, Green Letterbooks; Address of Richard Byrd, Jan. 31, 1935, Michigan Historical Collections.

100 Johnson, *Blue Eagle,* p. 343. The course of the negotiations can be followed in the *New York Times,* the *Detroit News,* and the *Detroit Free Press.* See also Report of Delegation of the United Automobile Workers Conference

at Washington and at the White House, [Mar. 22, 1934], Everett E. Francis Papers, Wayne State University Archives.

101 The terms of the settlement and the President's amplifying remarks are reprinted in full in the *New York Times,* Mar. 26, 1934.

102 Chalmers, "Collective Bargaining," VI, 18–19, 25; *New York Times,* Mar. 23, 25, 26, 1934; *Detroit Free Press,* Mar. 26, 1934; George E. Sokolsky, "An Experiment in Labor Democracy," *Atlantic Monthly,* CLVI (July, 1935), 55–56; Records of Federal Labor Union 18386 . . . , Mar. 29, 1934, Wayne State University Archives; *Daily Worker,* Mar. 23, 1934; Macauley to Johnson, Mar. 25, 1934, Chapin Papers.

103 Chalmers, "Collective Bargaining," VI, 26–27; *New York Times,* Mar. 26, 1934.

104 A union member was defined as "a paid-up member in good standing, or anyone legally obligated to pay up." *New York Times,* Mar. 26, 1934.

105 Green to Johnson, Mar. 24, 1934, Green Letterbooks; Macauley to Johnson, Mar. 25, 1934, Chapin Papers; Chalmers, "Collective Bargaining," VI, 28–29; *New York Times,* Mar. 25, 26, 1934. On the question of lists, see the excellent analysis of the settlement by Milton Handler, Notes on the Automobile Settlement, N.R.A. Box 7549.

106 Biddle, *In Brief Authority,* p. 38; *New York Times,* Mar. 26, 1934; Chalmers, "Collective Bargaining," VI, 34; Green to Charlton Ogburn, May 9, 1934, Green Letterbooks; U.A.W. Weekly News Letter, May 25, 1934, Collins File.

107 Press Conference No.130, p. 419, Roosevelt Library.

108 Macauley to Roosevelt, Mar. 21, 1934, O.F.407-B, Box 18, *ibid.;* G.M., Labor Relations Diary, Section 1, p. 36; *New York Times,* Mar. 26, 27, 1934.

109 The principles under which the National War Labor Board operated banned coercion by workers in the exercise of their right to organize. National War Labor Board, *Principles and Rules of Procedure.* See also Handler, Notes on the Automobile Settlement, N.R.A. Box 7549.

110 Macauley to Johnson, Mar. 25, 1934, Chapin Papers; Arthur Greer *et al.* to Roosevelt, Mar. 25, 1934, Case 209, N.L.B. Drawer 35; *New York Times,* Mar. 26, 1934.

111 Donaldson Brown to Lammot duPont, Mar. 29, 1934, G.M., Labor Relations Diary, Appendix Documents to Accompany Section 1; Fisher Body Divisions, G.M., *A Statement of Facts* [Apr., 1934]; typewritten sheets containing remarks of Hudson management to Hudson Industrial Association, Mar. 27, 1934, Chapin Papers.

112 For an A.F. of L. analysis of the gains resulting from the settlement, see "A Brief Analysis of President Roosevelt's Order for the Automobile Industry . . . ," Apr. 8, 1934, Collins File.

113 William Leiserson pointed out that the settlement entirely ignored the persistent charges of the U.A.W. that the automobile companies had violated Section 7(a) and the automobile code. Leiserson to Perkins, Apr. 11, 1934, Roosevelt Library.

114 Green to U.A.W., Mar. 26, 1934, Green to Woll, Mar. 30, 1934, Green Letterbooks; *American Federationist,* XLI (Apr., 1934), 356; *New York Times,* Mar. 26, 27, 1934; *Detroit Free Press,* Mar. 27, 1934; *Detroit Times,* May 1, 1934; *Flint Weekly Review,* Mar. 30, 1934; Harry H. Halsey and Cook to Francis, Mar. 25, 1934, Francis Papers; Minutes of Flint Federated Executive Council, Mar. 25, 1934, *ibid.;* Greer to Roosevelt, May 1, 1934, P.P.F.11-U, Roosevelt Library.

[115] *New York Times*, Mar. 27, 1934; *Iron Age*, CXXXIII (Mar. 29, 1934), 36-D; *ibid.*, CXXXIII (Apr. 5, 1934), 13; "The Magician in the White House," *Nation*, CXXXVIII (Apr. 4, 1934), 374. I am inclined to discount the statement attributed to Roosevelt by Frances Perkins to the effect that he believed that he had handled the negotiations badly. Perkins, *The Roosevelt I Knew* (New York, 1956), pp. 303–4.

[116] *Michigan Manufacturer and Financial Record*, LIII (Mar. 31, 1934), 8; *Business Week*, Mar. 31, 1934, p. 5; *Automotive Industries*, LXX (Mar. 31, 1934), 387–88; Walter C. Teagle to Roosevelt, Mar. 27, 1934, O.F.716, Box 1, Roosevelt Library. See the letters from businessmen in N.R.A. Box 660.

[117] *Detroit News*, Mar. 26, 1934; *Detroit Free Press*, Mar. 28, 1934; Mary Van Kleeck, "The Effect of the N.R.A. on Labor," *Proceedings of the National Conference of Social Work, 1934* (Chicago, 1934), pp. 432–34; *Labor Action*, Apr. 2, 16, 1934; *Workers Age*, Apr. 15, 1934; *New Leader*, Mar. 31, 1934; *Industrial Worker*, Apr. 17, 1934; *New York Times*, Mar. 27, 1934; Smith to Johnson, [Mar. 25, 1934], Case 209, N.L.B. Drawer 35; *Daily Worker*, Mar. 19–27, 1934; *Auto Workers News*, Mar. 24, Apr. 7, 1934; Jeremiah Kelly, "Detroit Cries 'Sell-Out!,'" *New Masses*, XI (Apr. 3, 1934), 11–13; A.W.U. handbills in Brown Collection; "The Automobile Armistice," *New Republic*, LXXVIII (Apr. 4, 1934), 200.

[118] Lorwin and Wubnig, *Labor Relations Boards*, p. 113; Handler, Notes on the Automobile Settlement, N.R.A. Box 7549; *New York Times*, May 14, 1934.

[119] Senate Committee on Education and Labor, *To Create a National Labor Board*, pp. 342, 497–99, 502, 710–15; Cronin to Chapin, June 1, 1934, enclosing confidential statement by Sloan on Wagner Bill, Chapin Papers.

[120] Press Conference No. 114, Apr. 20, 1934, pp. 292–93, Roosevelt Library; *New York Times*, Mar. 27, 28, 1934; Bernstein, *New Deal Collective Bargaining Policy*, pp. 71–74; *Senate Report No. 1184*, 73 Cong., 2 Sess., pp. 3–8.

[121] N.A.C.C. General Bulletin No. G-1705, May 29, 1934, Acc. 203, Box 13, Ford Archives; *New York Times*, June 6, 1934; Chapin to Charles R. Hook, June 15, 1934, Hook to Chapin, June 18, 1934, Chapin Papers.

[122] Bernstein, *New Deal Collective Bargaining Policy*, pp. 76–82; *Decisions of the National Labor Relations Board, July 9, 1934–December 1934* (Washington, 1935), v–ix; Lorwin and Wubnig, *Labor Relations Boards*, pp. 115–16.

[123] *Detroit Free Press*, Apr. 4, 1934; N.R.A. Releases No. 4152, Mar. 31, 1934, No. 6849, July 29, 1934; Lorwin and Wubnig, *Labor Relations Boards*, pp. 275–78; Lyon *et al.*, *N.R.A.*, pp. 448–49. Following the settlement, Donald Richberg proposed amending the Wagner Bill by including a merit clause and a list of unfair employee practices and by providing for the protection of employers from employee coercion. Bernstein, *New Deal Collective Bargaining Policy*, p. 73.

[124] Wieck, "Automobile Workers," p. 95; Sherer to N.L.B., Mar. 9, 1934, Detroit R.L.B. Box 280; *Flint Weekly Review*, Mar. 16, 1934.

NOTES TO CHAPTER VII

[1] [Carter], *New Dealers*, pp. 64–65; *New York Times*, Mar. 28, 1934, Oct. 3, 1961; *Detroit Free Press*, Mar. 28, 30, 1934; *Detroit News*, Mar. 29, 1934; *Automotive Industries*, LXX (Mar. 31, 1934), 422–23; memorandum, carded, Apr. 14, 1934, list of names, Mar. 26, 1934, on Secretary of Labor's stationery, and undated, handwritten memorandum, all in O.F.407-B, Box 18, Roosevelt

Library; Wolman to Roosevelt, Feb. 23, 1934, O.F.716, Box 1, *ibid.;* Perkins to author, Aug., 1957; Wolman interview; Kelley interview; Bernstein, *Lean Years,* p. 493; Josephson, *Sidney Hillman,* p. 375. Among those recommended for the position were Leon Marshall, Father Haas, Alfred E. Smith, Frank P. Walsh, and Edwin E. Witte.

2 *Business Week,* May 5, 1934, p. 11; Report of the A.L.B., Feb., 1935, p. 11; A.L.B., Stenographic Report of Hearing, Conference with Members of the Works Council of the Chevrolet Gear and Axle Plant, Feb. 21, 1935, pp. 44–45, Michigan Historical Collections (there is a complete file of transcripts of A.L.B. hearings in the Michigan Historical Collections and in the N.R.A. Records in the National Archives); A.L.B., Stenographic Report of Hearing, Conference with Members of the Works Councils of Chrysler Corp. . . . , Jan. 10, 1935, pp. 47–48; A.L.B., Stenographic Report of Hearing, Conference with Representatives of the A.F. of L. and Representatives of Affiliated Locals of Flint, Aug. 23, 1934, pp. 96–97; Lorwin and Wubnig, *Labor Relations Boards,* p. 377; Chalmers, "Collective Bargaining," VII, 41, 47.

3 Report of A.L.B., Feb., 1935, pp. 8–9; Final Report of A.L.B., pp. 10–11.

4 *Detroit Free Press,* Mar. 30, 1934; Kelley interview; Frankensteen interview; Mortimer interview, p. 10, Michigan Historical Collections.

5 *Detroit Free Press,* Mar. 27, 1934; *New York Times,* Mar. 28, 1934; *Automotive Industries,* LXX (Mar. 31, 1934), 406; Sokolsky, "Experiment in Labor Democracy," pp. 55–56; A.F. of L., *Proceedings, 1935,* p. 750; Oral History Interview of Everett Francis, Oct. 13, 20, 27, 1961, p. 14, Michigan Historical Collections.

6 Collins to Green, Mar. 31, 1934, Collins File; Wolman interview; Kelley interview; *Detroit News,* Jan. 26, 1935.

7 For an expression of Byrd's views on the labor question, see the stenographic reports of his addresses of Jan. 3, Mar. 3, 23, 31, 1935, in the Michigan Historical Collections; *Michigan Manufacturer and Financial Record,* LV (Apr. 20, 1935), 7–9, 17; and Byrd to James Murr, June 26, 1934, A.L.B. Drawer 3999.

8 *Detroit Free Press,* Mar. 30, 1934; Joseph R. Wood to Brown, June 18, 1935, Brown Collection. Byrd eventually dissented in 3 of the A.L.B.'s 244 decisions.

9 A.L.B. Statement, Dec. 14, 1934, A.L.B. Drawer 4105; *Detroit News,* Apr. 3, 1935; Wolman interview. Kelley later stated that Byrd was advised by the other board members to dissent once or twice in order to show his independence. Kelley interview. When Professor Z. Clark Dickinson joined the board's staff early in 1935, Wolman told him to ignore Byrd. Interview with Dickinson, Dec. 1, 1961.

10 When the board was first established, it gave some thought to using field adjusters of the N.R.A.'s Compliance Division or of employing its own investigators to gather the facts in cases submitted to the board, but neither of these ideas was adopted. *New York Times,* Mar. 31, 1934; Edmund C. Shields to John Swope, Mar. 29, 1934, N.R.A. Box 1120; *Detroit Free Press,* June 21, 1934.

11 A.L.B., Stenographic Report of Hearing, In the Matter of Fisher Body Corp., Dec. 16, 1934, pp. 13–14.

12 Final Report of A.L.B., pp. 2, 10; *Detroit News,* Mar. 29, 1934; *New York Times,* Mar. 30, 1934; "Established Procedure for Handling Claims of Employees of the Automobile Industry," A.L.B. Drawer 4106; Collins to Wolman, July 18, 1934, Wolman to Edwin S. Smith, Nov. 23, 1934, A.L.B. Drawer 4105; A.L.B., Stenographic Report of Hearing, Olds Motor Co., Sept. 19, 1934, p. 9; Lorwin and Wubnig, *Labor Relations Boards,* pp. 124–28.

13 A.L.B., Conference with Members of Works Councils of Chrysler Corp., Jan. 10, 1935, p. 44; Herman K. Brunck, Report to the N.L.R.B. on An Inquiry into Industrial Relations Boards, Feb. 26, 1935, pp. 27, 28, O.F.716, Box 2, Roosevelt Library; Lucheck, "Labor Organizations," pp. 93–94.

14 Of the board's 244 decisions, 171, according to my analysis, were in favor of management, 56 in favor of labor, and 17 cannot be classified as victories for either side. Six of the numbered decisions are not really decisions at all since the matters in dispute had been settled before the board could issue a ruling. For tabulations of the decisions that differ somewhat from mine, see Wieck, "Automobile Workers," p. 207, and Joe Brown, draft of chapter on A.L.B., Aug. 21, 1935, Brown Collection.

15 See, for example, Decisions #1, 12, 24, 27, 34, 100, 171, and 204 (A.L.B. Drawer 4092 for the latter).

16 *New York Times,* Mar. 30, 1934; Wolman to Hale, July 26, 1934, A.L.B. Drawer 3999; Wolman to Waldo Luchsinger, Jr., Dec. 18, 1934, A.L.B. Drawer 3997. The N.L.B. late in Apr. 1934 issued a statement of its principles to its regional boards and to the various industrial-relations boards. N.R.A. Release No. 4688, Apr. 30, 1934.

17 *Codes,* IX (Washington, 1934), 936; C. O. Skinner to Lea, Apr. 23, 1934, N.R.A. Box 688; A.P.E.M., Code Authority Bulletin No. 9, May 2, 1934, N.R.A. Box 681.

18 Sparks-Withington folder, A.L.B. Drawer 4002; Wolman to Smith, Aug. 30, 1934, Skinner to Smith, Sept. 17, 1934, N.L.R.B. Drawer 311; Skinner, "More Work at Higher Wages . . . ," *Automotive Industries,* LXXI (Nov. 17, 1934), 610; Ogburn to Perkins, June 28, 1934, enclosing resolution on automotive parts and equipment plants of U.A.W. conference of June 23–24, 1934, A.L.B. Drawer 4105; Official Proceedings First Session National Council U.A.W. Federal Labor Unions, July 9–14, 1934, Brown Collection; letters dated in July and Aug., 1934, from officers of U.A.W. locals to Roosevelt, N.R.A. Box 688; Marjorie Clark to Everitt, Aug. 20, 1934, N.R.A. Box 719; unsigned memorandum, Aug. 27, 1934, A.L.B. Drawer 3990; Britton to Wagner, May 10, 1934, N.L.B. Drawer 97; Green to J. C. Dysart, Sept. 10, 1934, Roberts Papers.

19 See the Ford file in A.L.B. Drawer 3998.

20 Clark to Johnson, Apr. 23, 25, 1934, Smith to Wolman, Apr. 25, 1934, Clark to Pollak, June 6, 1934, Pollak to Wolman, June 22, July 5, 27, Aug. 9, 14, 22, 1934, Kelley to Wolman, Aug. 7, 1934, Wolman to Pollak, Aug. 9, 1934, Wolf to Wolman, Sept. 14, 1934, Wolman to Cameron, Oct. 29, 1934, Jan. 18, 1935. J. De L[uca] memorandum, Nov. 8, 1934, Biddle to Wolman, Jan. 8, 1935, Clark to Wolman, Jan. 23, 29, 1935, A.L.B. Drawer 3998; Pollak memorandum. Dec. 18, 1934, N.R.A. Drawer 642; McCracken interview, pp. 11–12, Michigan Historical Collections.

21 *Automotive Industries,* LXX (Apr. 14, 1934), 459; A.L.B Statement, Apr. 19, 1934, A.L.B. Drawer 4107; Decision #154.

22 On this point, see Brown to Wolman, May 16, 1934, A.L.B. Drawer 3998.

23 *Detroit Times,* Apr. 16, 1934; *Detroit News,* July 4, 1934.

24 Wolman interview.

25 Report of A.L.B., Feb., 1935, p. 2; *Milwaukee Journal,* Mar. 30–Apr. 3, 5, 1934; *Detroit Free Press,* Mar. 31, Apr. 4, 1934; A.L.B. Statement, Apr. 5, 1934, A.L.B. Drawer 4107; Smith *et al.* to Green, Apr. 8, 1934, Smith File, A.F. of L.-C.I.O. Archives.

26 *Milwaukee Journal,* Apr. 6, 7, 10, 1934; *New Day* (Racine), Apr. 13, 1934.

27 *Milwaukee Journal,* Apr. 7, 8, 1934; *New Day* (Racine), Apr. 13, 1934.

28 *Milwaukee Journal,* Apr. 9, 10, 16, 18, 1934; George W. Blanchard to Roosevelt, Apr. 17, 1934, O.F.407-B, Box 18, Roosevelt Library; Chalmers, "Collective Bargaining," VIII, 19. Nash had suffered a net loss of $123,719.16 in Jan. and Feb. 1934.

29 *Milwaukee Journal,* Apr. 10, 12, 13, 17, 1934; *New Day* (Racine), Apr. 13, 20, 1934; "Working Agreement," undated, A.L.B. Drawer 4002; "Interpretation of the Working Agreement," undated, A.L.B. Drawer 4001; H. H. Seaman to Wolman, Apr. 18, 1934, A.L.B. Drawer 4002. The average hourly earned rate at the Kenosha plant was 75.40 cents for the four weeks ending Apr. 28 as compared to 67.42 cents for the four weeks ending Feb. 24. The Apr. 28 figure compared with a rate of 70.46 cents for the Racine plant and 68.46 cents for Seaman Body. N.R.A. Boxes 673, 675.

30 Wieck, "Automobile Workers," pp. 82, 85–86; Chalmers, "Collective Bargaining," VIII, 19. The three locals claimed in June 1934 that the Nash Lafayette, which was assembled in Racine from Kenosha parts and Seaman bodies, was the only union-built car in the industry. *New Day* (Racine), June 15, 1934. For the later difficulties of the Kenosha and Seaman Body locals, see Locals 18785 and 19059, A. F. of L. Strike File.

31 Chalmers, "Collective Bargaining," VIII, 5–6; *Detroit News,* Apr. 5, 6, 10, 1934; *New York Times,* Apr. 6, 10, 1934; *Daily Worker,* Mar. 23, 24, Apr. 6, 1934.

32 *New York Times,* Apr. 6, 1934; *Detroit News,* Apr. 7, 1934; A.L.B. Statement, Apr. 10, 1934, A.L.B. Drawer 4107.

33 *Detroit News,* Apr. 9, 10, 1934; *Detroit Free Press,* Apr. 10, 11, 1934; *New York Times,* Apr. 9, 10, 1934; A.L.B. Statement, Apr. 10, 1934, A.L.B. Drawer 4107.

34 Chalmers, "Collective Bargaining," VII, 1–2; Wolman interview; *New York Times,* Feb. 10, 1935; *Detroit Free Press,* Mar. 30, 1934.

35 *New York Times,* Apr. 6, 8, 9, 10, 1934; A.L.B., Stenographic Report of Hearing, Fisher Body Corp., Conference on the Election, Dec. 16, 1934, p. 14. The officers of the Flint locals, unlike Collins, wanted discrimination cases taken up first by the A.L.B. "as it was mainly for their sake that the Board was set up by our President." Charles M. Schang to Wagner, June 7, 1934, enclosing resolution adopted May 28 by the Flint Federated Executive Council, N.L.B. Drawer 83.

36 A.L.B. Statement, Apr. 6, 1934, A.L.B. Drawer 4107; *Detroit News,* Mar. 30, 1934; Decision #17; Report of A.L.B., Feb. 1935, p. 2; Final Report of A.L.B., pp. 2–3, 15, 27–28.

37 Chalmers, "Collective Bargaining," VII, 3–4, 44–46. See, for example, "Brief History of the Discrimination Case of Carl Alvin Blackmer," A.L.B. Drawer 3990; "Brief History of the Discrimination Case of Ernest C. Nickel," *ibid.;* and Decisions # 16, 18, 115 (A.L.B. Drawer 4084), and 158.

38 Wolman interview; A.L.B. Statement, Apr. 6, 1934, A.L.B. Drawer 4107; A.L.B., Stenographic Report of Hearing, Fisher Body Co. Plant No. 1, Apr. 17, 1934, pp. 89–90; Final Report of A.L.B., pp. 20–22, 27–28.

39 A.L.B., Fisher Body No. 1 Hearing, Apr. 17, 1934, pp. 89–90; Chalmers, "Collective Bargaining," VII, 9–10; Wolman interview; Lucheck, "Labor Organizations," pp. 93–95; Lorwin and Wubnig, *Labor Relations Boards,* pp. 366–67; G.M., Labor Relations Diary, Section 1, pp. 44–45; Dickinson interview; "Matters for Consideration of National Council," Martin Papers.

40 See, for example, Decisions #4, 38, 53, 59, 63, 68, 72, 73, 82, 87, 101, 103, 107, 125, 157, 209 (A.L.B. Drawer 4099), 236, 238.

41 A.L.B., Fisher Body Hearing, May 2, 1934, pp. 55–56.

42 Decisions #1, 3, 8, 9, 10, 12, 13, 24, 38, 55, 71, 72, 80, 94, 102, 123, 151, 169, 231; Dillon to Wolman, Nov. 2, 1934, A.L.B. Drawer 4087; Chalmers, "Collective Bargaining," VII, 6–7. Cook was fired in Jan. 1934 for what the company claimed was his "continued and inexcusable absence from duty" and for infraction of company rules. Cook alleged that he had been dismissed because he had been unco-operative as a company-union representative. The relevant correspondence is in Case 209, N.L.B. Drawer 35.

43 See Decisions #27 and 171.

44 See, for example, Decisions #7, 19, 35 (A.L.B. Drawer 4098), 42, 46, 52, 133, 134, 140, and 220. See also Final Report of A.L.B., pp. 16–17.

45 For cases in which the A.L.B. made at least some general requirement about the rate of pay of re-employed workers, see Decisions #18, 146, and 148. In cases involving victims of discrimination the N.L.B. and N.L.R.B. normally required that the complainants be reinstated immediately or in 5–14 days to their former or an equally good position with the same seniority and the same rights as they had enjoyed before the layoff or discharge. On occasion, they ordered the payment of back wages or upheld the decisions of regional boards requiring back pay. *Decisions of the N.L.B., Aug. 1933–Mar. 1934*, pp. 14, 32, 81, 91; *Decisions of the National Labor Board, Part II, April 1934–July 1934* (Washington, 1934), pp. 9, 27, 30, 55, 60–61, 66, 77; *Decisions of the N.L.R.B., July 9, 1934–Dec. 1934*, pp. 6–7, 17, 19, 32, 52, 58, 61, 62, 83, 88, 118, 142–43, 149, 163–64, 201, 209; *Decisions of the National Labor Relations Board, II, December 1, 1934–June 16, 1935* (Washington, 1935), 42, 50, 148, 225, 262, 421, 429, 495.

46 See Decisions #18 and 114, and Chalmers, "Collective Bargaining," VII, 5–6.

47 A.L.B., Fisher Body No. 1 Hearing, Apr. 17, 1934, pp. 4–5, 42–43, 74–75, 77–78, 85–87, 90; Decisions #16, 17, 18, 78, 131, 135, 138, 158, 166.

48 A.L.B., Flint Conference, Aug. 23, 1934, pp. 94–95.

49 A.L.B., Fisher Body No. 1 Hearing, Apr. 17, 1934, p. 90; A.L.B., Chrysler Works Councils Hearing, Jan. 10, 1935, pp. 45–47.

50 Kelley interview. See Decisions #22, 51, 70, 75, 88, 103, 132, 173, 214.

51 Notes on Conference Nov. 15, 1934, between the Board and Messrs. C. E. Wilson and H. W. Anderson, A.L.B. Drawer 4105.

52 Wolman, "An Experiment in Automotive Labor Relations," *Automotive Industries*, LXXIII (Sept. 7, 1935), 287–88; A.L.B., Stenographic Report of Hearing, Conference with Members of Works Council of Chevrolet Forge, Spring and Bumper Shop, Jan. 3, 1935, pp. 55–56; A.L.B. Report, Feb. 1935, p. 7.

53 Chalmers, "Collective Bargaining," VII, 6, 10–11; Lorwin and Wubnig, *Labor Relations Boards*, pp. 360–61; Wieck, "Automobile Workers," p. 111; G.M., Labor Relations Diary, Section 1, p. 45; Byrd to Wolman, Nov. 17, 1934, A.L.B. Drawer 4005. Wolman doubted that 500 of the A.L.B. cases involved discrimination. "Experiment in Automotive Labor Relations," p. 288.

54 Byrd to McCarty, May 15, 26, 1934, A.L.B. Drawer 4001; *Detroit News*, May 19, 1934; Chalmers, "Collective Bargaining," VII, 30.

55 A.L.B. Statement on Lay-off and Rehiring, May 18, 1934, A.L.B. Drawer 4106.

56 A.L.B. Statement on Lay-off and Rehiring, Jan. 18, 1935, *ibid.*

57 Final Report of A.L.B., pp. 4–5; *Automotive Industries*, LXXII (June 8,

1935), 762. "What most of the former employees making complaints really want," C. E. Wilson advised Byrd on Dec. 10, 1934, "are their jobs back, and they do not really care whether they get preference over someone else who is more entitled to the work or not, and when the rules and regulations are not such that they get put back to work, they become bitter and make a good many general and wild statements. . . ." A.L.B. Drawer 4001. On employee confusion concerning the meaning of the seniority rules, see, for example, A.L.B., Stenographic Report of Hearing, Plymouth Motor Corp. . . . , Feb. 7, 1935, pp. 45–46, 49–50.

58 Hale to Wolman, July 19, 1934, A.L.B. Drawer 3999; A.L.B., Chevrolet Gear and Axle Conference, Jan. 25, 1935, pp. 61–62; Chalmers, "Collective Bargaining," VII, 33–34; A.L.B., Stenographic Report of Hearing, Conference with the Executive Committee of the Bargaining Agencies of the Chrysler Plants, Mar. 28, 1935, p. 22. For decisions involving Class A workers, see Decisions #45, 50, 120, 127. A.P.E.M. members were advised to lay off Class A employees according to their skill and efficiency and to rehire them after Class B and C workers had been re-employed. A.P.E.M., Code Authority Bulletin No. 13, June 25, 1934, Case 12, N.L.R.B. Drawer 158. According to Matthew Smith, Kelley thought that the elimination of transient workers by the A.L.B. rules would provide job security and would make unionism in the industry unnecessary. Smith interview.

59 Byrd to L. M. Bentley, June 1, 1934, A.L.B. Drawer 4001; Byrd to H. H. Seaman, June 1, 6, 1934, Seaman to Byrd, June 4, 1934, Seaman to Wolman, July 26, 1934, A.L.B. Drawer 4002.

60 Notes on Conference, Nov. 15, 1934, A.L.B. Drawer 4105; Decisions #19, 23, 28, 39, 43, 196; Kelley interview.

61 Notes on Conference, Nov. 15, 1934, A.L.B. Drawer 4105; Detroit Fisher Body folder #1, A.L.B. Drawer 3997; John A. Bailey *et al.* to Wolman, June 4, 1934, A.L.B. Drawer 4106; Luchsinger, Jr., to Byrd, Nov. 28, 1934, Wolman to Luchsinger, Jr., Dec. 18, 1934, A.L.B. Drawer 3997.

62 A.P.E.M., Code Authority Bulletin No. 13, June 25, 1934, Case 12, N.L.R.B. Drawer 158; Hale to Wolman, July 19, 1934, A.L.B. Drawer 3999; Decisions #162, 202 (A.L.B. Drawer 4095), 215; Williams to Seaman, A.L.B. Drawer 4002; A.L.B., Stenographic Report of Hearing, General Conference, Fisher Body Corp. and Chevrolet Division, Kansas City, Jan. 17, 1935, pp. 2–3.

63 A.L.B., Conference with Executive Committee of Bargaining Agencies of Chrysler Plants, Mar. 28, 1935, pp. 23, 26, 33–34; A.L.B., Stenographic Report of Hearing, Conference with Works Council of the Employees Association of Fisher Body Corp., Cleveland, Jan. 4, 1935, p. 15; A.P.E.M., Code Authority Bulletin No. 13, June 25, 1934, Case 12, N.L.R.B. Drawer 158; Hale to Wolman, July 19, 1934, William E. Dowell to Wolman, Oct. 7, 1934, Ross to Wilson, Oct. 31, 1934, Anderson to Ross, Nov. 5, 1934, A.L.B. Drawer 3999; Memorandum of J. DeL[uca], Oct. 10, 1934, *ibid.;* Notes on Conference, Nov. 15, 1934, A.L.B. Drawer 4105; Decision #47. For some decisions involving this problem, see Decisions #176, 177, 181, 184, 188, 227, 243.

64 Hale to Wolman, July 19, 1934, A.L.B. Drawer 3999; "Matters for Consideration of National Council," Martin Papers; Official Proceedings First Session National Council U.A.W., July 9–14, 1934, Brown Collection; A.L.B., Stenographic Report of Hearing, Meeting of the New Bargaining Agency of the Chrysler Kercheval Plant and the Chrysler Jefferson Plant with the A.L.B., Feb. 26,

1935, p. 26; Lucheck, "Labor Organizations," p. 100; U.A.W. Local #18331, Meeting of Nov. 8, 1934, Francis Papers; Wieck, "Automobile Workers," pp. 117–18; Memorandum from Dickinson to A.L.B., Feb. 19, 1935, A.L.B. Drawer 4087; Dillon to Wolman, Oct 17, 1934, A.L.B. Drawer 4084. Wolman recalled that normally about 10 per cent of the workers in a plant were placed in Class D, but the A.F. of L. charged that the percentage sometimes ran as high as 20 or 30. Wolman interview; "Matters for Consideration of National Council," Martin Papers. The Pierce Arrow local and some of the locals in the parts plants were able to arrange for the joint union-management determination of merit. Collective Bargaining Agreements, B.L.S. Records.

65 Decisions #29, 31.

66 Decisions #228, 240.

67 Decisions #174, 185, 207 (A.L.B. Drawer 4100), 211, 222, 244; Hale to Wolman, July 19, 1934, A.L.B. Drawer 3999; Anderson to Byrd, Dec. 12, 1934, A.L.B. Drawer 3997; "Matters for Consideration of National Council," Martin Papers. G.M. treated its various divisions as separate employers. Hale to Wolman, July 19, 1934, A.L.B. Drawer 3999.

68 Wolman to Luchsinger, Jr., Dec. 18, 1934, A.L.B. Drawer 3997; Decision #230, A.L.B. Drawer 4087.

69 For examples of decisions in which the employee was upheld, see Decisions #26, 33, 36, 42, 43, 47, 57, 110, 205 (A.L.B. Drawer 4099), 220, 222, 230 (A.L.B. Drawer 4087).

70 Decision #34; Collins to Wolman, Aug. 10, 1934, A.L.B. Drawer 4089.

71 Williams to H. H. Seaman, Aug. 2, 1934, Seaman to Wolman, Sept. 14, 1934, and attached Memorandum to Govern Layoff and Reemployment, Sept. 13, 1934, A.L.B. Drawer 4002; A.L.B., Stenographic Report of Hearing, International Harvester Co., May 6, 1935, pp. 10–26.

72 Chalmers, "Collective Bargaining," VII, 32; A.L.B. Report, Feb., 1935, p. 8; Final Report of A.L.B., pp. 12, 18, 23; Hale to Wolman, July 19, 1934, A.L.B. Drawer 3999.

73 Chalmers, "Collective Bargaining," VII, 31–32, 34; Lucheck, "Labor Organizations," p. 101; G.M., Labor Relations Diary, Section 1, p. 43; McPherson and Lucheck, "Automobiles," pp. 617–19.

74 Final Report of A.L.B., pp. 14–15; Wolman, "Experiment in Automotive Labor Relations," p. 288; G.M., Labor Relations Diary, Section 1, p. 42. Of eleven unspecified motor-vehicle plants studied by the B.L.S. in 1932, all had central employment offices, and the full power to hire in most of these plants was vested in the employment manager or the personnel director. Discharges, on the other hand, were handled by foremen in 3 plants, employment managers in 6 plants, and by higher officials in 2 plants. "Hiring and Separation Methods in American Factories," *Monthly Labor Review,* XXXV (Nov., 1932), 1006, 1013.

NOTES TO CHAPTER VIII

1 Report of A.L.B., Feb., 1935, p. 10; Hall interview, p. 5, Michigan Historical Collections.

2 Report of A.L.B., Feb., 1935, p. 11; *New York Times,* Feb. 10, 1935; Final Report of A.L.B., pp. 5–7, 8–9.

3 A.L.B., Fisher Body Hearing, May 2, 1934, pp. 128–29; A.L.B., Flint Hearing, Aug. 23, 1934, pp. 45–46, 97; *New York Times,* Feb. 10, 1935.

4 A.L.B., Stenographic Report of Hearing, Conference between . . . A.L.B. and . . . Employee Representation Association . . . of Budd Manufacturing Co., Nov. 28, 1934, p. 4; A.L.B. Statement, Mar. 29, 1934, A.L.B. Drawer 4107; Report of A.L.B., Feb., 1935, p. 2; Final Report of A.L.B., p. 29. The A.L.B. explained in a statement of May 26, 1934, that its no-solicitation rule did not apply to nonworking hours even though the discussion took place on company property. Company property, however, was not "to be used as a place for agitation or mass meetings." A.L.B. Statement, May 26, 1934, A.L.B. Drawer 4107.

5 Collins to Wolman, Mar. 29, 1934, A.L.B. Drawer 4102; Chalmers, "Collective Bargaining," VII, 15–22; *Detroit Free Press,* Mar. 31, Apr. 14, 19, 1934; *New York Times,* Apr. 8, 14, 1934; A.L.B. Statement, Apr. 13, 1934, A.L.B. Drawer 4107. The St. Louis Chevrolet and Fisher Body local presented its list directly to G.M. *New York Times,* Apr. 12, 1934. The following locals submitted lists to the A.L.B.: Fisher Body Nos. 1 and 2 of Flint, Pontiac Fisher Body, Cleveland Fisher Body, Pontiac, G.M. Truck, Janesville Fisher Body, Buick, AC Spark Plug, Flint Chevrolet, Hudson, Kansas City Chevrolet and Fisher Body, Atlanta Chevrolet and Fisher Body, and Jackson Motor Shaft. Calendar of Events, A.L.B. Drawer 4105.

6 *Detroit Free Press,* Apr. 19, 1934; *Automotive Daily News,* May 7, 1934; Lucheck, "Labor Organizations," pp. 103–4; Chalmers, "Collective Bargaining," VII, 14–15; Final Report of A.L.B., p. 25.

7 Wolman to Jackson Motor Shaft Co., May 2, 1934, A.L.B. Drawer 4006; Wolman to Perkins, Dec. 20, 1934, A.L.B. Drawer 3990; House Committee on Labor, *Labor Disputes Act,* p. 245. For evidence that the board completed the verification of the lists submitted to it, see Calendar of Events, A.L.B. Drawer 4105.

8 *Cleveland Plain Dealer,* Apr. 11, 16, 1934; *New York Times,* Apr. 11, 1934; *Detroit News,* Apr. 14, 16, 1934.

9 *Cleveland Plain Dealer,* Apr. 13, 1934; *Detroit News,* Apr. 12, 1934; Wolman to Collins, Apr. 12, 1934, A.L.B. Drawer 3999; undated and unsigned copy of letter to Knudsen to be used by U.A.W. locals seeking conferences with G.M., A.L.B. Drawer 4106.

10 A.L.B. Statement, Apr. 16, 1934, A.L.B. Drawer 4107.

11 *Cleveland Plain Dealer,* Apr. 18, 23, 24, 25, 27, 1934; *New York Times,* Apr. 23, 29, 1934; G.M., Labor Relations Diary, Section 1, pp. 39, 41–42; *ibid.,* Appendix Document No. 25.

12 *Cleveland Plain Dealer,* Apr. 24–27, 30, 1934; *New York Times,* May 1, 1934; *Iron Age,* CXXXIII (Apr. 26, 1934), 40; *ibid.,* CXXXIII (May 3, 1934), 44.

13 Records of F.L.U. 18386, Mar. 29, 1934, Wayne State University Archives.

14 *St. Louis Post-Dispatch,* Apr. 23–26, 1934; A.L.B. Report, Feb., 1935, pp. 5–6; John G. Bostwick to Wolman, Mar. 30, Apr. 5, 9, 13, 16, 1934, Bostwick and Herbert C. Neumann to Wolman, Apr. 19, 1934, A.L.B. Drawer 4101; Wolman statement of telephone conversation with Bostwick, Apr. 19, 1934, *ibid.* Figures later compiled by the A.L.B. give the work force at the two plants just before the strike as 4506 and list the number who worked during the strike as

974. Report on Chevrolet and Fisher at St. Louis and Kansas City as of Aug. 25, 1934, *ibid.*

15 William B. Mahoney to Hugh Frayne, Apr. 25, 1934, Green Letterbooks; Case 544, New York R.L.B. Box 48; F.A.A. to Wagner, Apr. 10, 1934, N.L.B. Drawer 97; Tarrytown folder, A.L.B. Drawer 4002; *New York Times*, Apr. 25, 26, 1934; A.L.B., Fisher Body Hearing, May, 1, 1934, p. 5.

16 Martin to Charles E. Coughlin, Jan. 19, 1935, Martin Papers; Bruce Minton and John Stuart, *Men Who Lead Labor* (New York, 1937), pp. 216–17; W. G. Patterson to E. G. Shaw, Mar. 19, 1934, and attached affidavits, C.S. 176-1338. Shaw, the Chevrolet plant manager, insisted that Martin had simply been laid off in a reduction of force. Exhibit A, Mar. 27, 1934, *ibid.*

17 Patterson to Wolman, Apr. 21, 26, 1934, Martin to Byrd, May 4, 5, 1934, Martin to Wolman, May 10, 1934, A.L.B. Drawer 4000; A.L.B. Statement, Apr. 27, 1934, A.L.B. Drawer 4107; affidavit signed by Martin *et al.*, Apr. 25, 1934, A.L.B. Drawer 4103; Officers of F.A.W. of A. Local No. 2 to A.L.B., Apr. 25, 1934, *ibid.; Kansas City Star*, Apr. 28–May 6, 1934; A. R. Gephart to Aubrey Williams, May 4, 1934, N.L.B. Drawer 102; Martin to Collins, July 24, Aug. 7, 1934, Martin Papers.

18 Collins to A.L.B., Apr. 27, 1934, H. L. Johnsey to Wolman, Apr. 24, 1934, A.L.B. Drawer 3990; Minutes of Meetings of F.L.U. No. 18331, Apr. 12, 26, 1934, Wayne State University Archives; *Flint Weekly Review*, Apr. 13, 26, 1934; *Cleveland Plain Dealer*, Apr. 28, 1934; Chalmers, "Collective Bargaining," VII, 35.

19 The production of cars and trucks in Mar. 1934 (338,434 units) was almost triple the output for Mar. 1933 and was more than 100,000 units above Feb. production. Production in Apr., despite the strikes in Cleveland and elsewhere, increased to 352,975 units. *Ward's 1939 Automotive Year Book*, pp. 10–11.

20 Green to Ogburn, May 9, 1934, Green Letterbooks; *Cleveland Plain Dealer*, Apr. 29, 30, 1934; *New York Times*, Apr. 30, May 1, 1934; *Detroit Free Press*, Apr. 30, May 1, 1934; Chalmers, "Collective Bargaining," VII, 19–20, 36; Wieck, "Automobile Workers," pp. 105–7; G.M., Labor Relations Diary, Appendix Document No. 30; Beckman interview, p. 6, Michigan Historical Collections.

21 A.L.B., Fisher Body Conference, Apr. 30–May 2, 1934, *passim;* A.L.B. Statement, May 3, 1934 (not released), A.L.B. Drawer 4107; Minutes of Meetings of F.L.U. No. 18331, May 3, 1934, Wayne State University Archives; *New York Times*, May 1, 1934.

22 Chalmers, "Collective Bargaining," VII, 21; Wieck, "Automobile Workers," pp. 112–13; *New York Times*, May 12, 1934; *Cleveland Plain Dealer*, May 7–10, 17, 1934. In Cleveland the U.A.W. and M.E.S.A. officers at first refused to sit with the company-union representatives but finally agreed to do so on the condition that the company-union men would not take part in the discussion in which the M.E.S.A. and the U.A.W. representatives were involved. Fisher offered the union time-and-one-half for hours above 9 per day and for work on Sunday and holidays. Piece-work rates were to be investigated by a committee of employer and employee representatives. *Ibid.*, May 8, 10, 17, 1934. Knudsen and Dillon participated in a conference at the Fisher Body plant in Janesville at which the company promised to pay for dead time above one-half hour per day. The Lansing Fisher Body local and the management agreed on some

changes in the group bonus plan used in the plant. U.A.W. News Letter, July 27, 1934, Collins File.

23 Green to Ogburn, May 9, 1934, Green Letterbooks; Notes on Conference, Nov. 15, 1934, A.L.B. Drawer 4105; *New York Times,* Feb. 10, 1935.

24 Bostwick to Wolman, Apr. 29, 1934, Byrd to Bostwick, Apr. 30, 1934, Wood to Wolman, May 1, 1934, Wolman to Bostwick, May 3, 1934, Wood to Roosevelt, Aug. 9, 1934, A.L.B. Drawer 4101; *St. Louis Post-Dispatch,* Apr. 30–May 7, 1934; Minutes of St. Louis R.L.B. Meeting, May 1, 1934, St. Louis R.L.B. Box 393; Knudsen to Wolman, May 2, 1934, A.L.B. Drawer 3994; Agreed Statement by the Board (signed by Byrd), May 6, 1934, *ibid.;* George S. Darner *et al.* to Wolf, Dec. 3, 1934, N.L.B. Drawer 15.

25 Copy of statement by Chalmers, Aug. 3, 1934, A.L.B. Drawer 4101; Wolman to Collins, Aug. 3, 1934, Collins to Wolman, Aug. 3, 1934, *ibid.;* A.L.B., Stenographic Report of Hearing, In the Matter of General Motors Corp., Chevrolet Division . . . , Aug. 28, 1934, pp. 14, 19–27, 42–43.

26 Wolman to Marvin E. Coyle, May 11, 1934, Wolman to E. F. Fisher, May 11, 1934, Wood to Byrd, July 2, 16, 1934, Bostwick to Byrd, June 7, 1934, Meyer L. Lewis to Wolman, July 17, 1934, Wood to V. M. Dirkes, July 18, 1934, Wood to P. E. Baugh, July 18, 1934, Wood to Wolman, May 24, 1934, Lewis to Collins, Aug. 24, 1934, A.L.B. Drawer 4101.

27 Ross to A.L.B., June 22, 1934, Lewis to Collins, Aug. 4, 1934, *ibid.;* Wood to Brown, June 18, 1935, Brown Collection; Wood to Perkins, Aug. 8, 1934, C.S. 176-818; Decisions # 126, 130, 131, 134, 135, 137, 138, 140.

28 Wolman to Knudsen, June 8, 1934, Wolman to Fisher, June 14, 21, 1934, A.L.B. Drawer 4101; Ross memorandum, Aug. 24, 1934, *ibid.;* Report on Chevrolet and Fisher Plants, Aug. 25, 1934, *ibid.;* Wolman to Knudsen, June 21, 1934, A.L.B. Drawer 3994.

29 Wood to A.L.B., June 18, 1934, Executive Board, F.L.U. No. 18386 to Ross, Nov. 23, 1934, Wolman to Wood, Nov. 23, 1934, Ross to various St. Louis Chevrolet and Fisher Body workers, Dec. 31, 1934, Jan. 4, 1935, Ray J. Morrison to A.L.B., Jan. 10, 1935, A.L.B. Drawer 4101.

30 Schilling interview, pp. 13–15, Michigan Historical Collections; Wood to Perkins, Aug. 8, 1934, C.S. 176-818; Martin to Collins, Aug. 9, Nov. 30, 1934, Wood to Dillon, Apr. 6, 1935, Martin to Dillon, May 10, 16, 20, June 1, 1935, Martin Papers; Darner and Wood to Brown, July 19, 1935, Brown Collection.

31 Martin to Collins, July 19, Aug. 7, 1934, draft of letter from Martin to Ogburn, Feb. 14, 1935, Martin Papers; Martin, "The Case against Richard Byrd . . . ," *ibid.;* "Petition for Injunction," [Jan., 1935], *ibid.;* "Kansas City Terms of Settlement—Read over Telephone by Mr. Byrd, May 6 [7?], 1934, 12:30 P.M.," A.L.B. Drawer 4000; *Kansas City Star,* May 7, 8, 9, 12, 1934.

32 Knudsen, perhaps with tongue in cheek, said that the strikers should not be taken back according to their seniority because they had not quit their jobs in that order. Knudsen to Wolman, June 11, 1934, A.L.B. Drawer 4000.

33 Final Agreement between Mr. Knudsen and Majority of Board, May 7, 1934, A.L.B. Drawer 4000; Patterson to Byrd, June 4, 1934, *ibid.; Kansas City Star,* May 12, 1934; "Report of progress made in settlement of the Kansas City Strike," July 19, 1934, Martin Papers; Thomas P. Hyland to Kerwin, June 21, 1934, C.S. 176-1338.

34 Martin to Wolman, May 11, July 21, 1934. Patterson to Wolman, May 28,

1934, Martin to Byrd, June 29, 1934, A.L.B. Drawer 4000; Collins to Wolman, July 26, Aug. 3, 1934, Dowell to Wolman, Oct. 3, 18, Nov. 14, 1934, A.L.B. Drawer 4102; Martin to Collins, July 19, 24, Aug. 9, 1934, Collins to Martin, Sept. 12, 1934, Martin Papers.

35 Wolman to Knudsen, June 8, 1934, A.L.B. Drawer 4101; Knudsen to Wolman, June 11, 1934, A.L.B. Drawer 4000; Wolman to Wilson, Sept. 14, 1934, A.L.B. Drawer 4102; Ross to A.L.B., June 22, 1934, A.L.B. Drawer 4103.

36 Dowell to Byrd, June 2, 1934, A.L.B. Drawer 4000; Martin to Lewis, Aug. 2, 1934, Martin to Collins, Aug. 7, 15, 1934, Martin to Dillon, Jan. 2, 1935, Dillon to Martin, Jan. 7, 1935, Martin to Ogburn, Feb. 14, 1935 (draft), Martin to Earl Pugh and C. W. Metcalf, Feb. 5, 1935, Metcalf to Martin, Feb. 6, 1935, Martin Papers.

37 Collins to Morrison, May 17, 1934, Collins File; *Daily Worker,* May 5, 1934; Wolman to Knudsen, May 11, 1934, Knudsen to Wolman, May 14, 1934, Kleinert to A.L.B., May 11, July 19, 1934, A.L.B. Drawer 4002; *New York Times,* May 12, 1934.

38 Minutes of meetings of F.L.U. No. 18331, May 2, 6, 10, 31, June 7, 1934, Wayne State University Archives; Cook to E. J. Parker, May 9, 1934, Francis Papers; Francis, "History of Local #18331—Fisher No. 1 of Flint, Michigan," [1934], *ibid.;* Dillon to Green, May 5, 1934, Dillon File; Dillon to Green, May 17, 1934, A.F. of L. Strike File, Local 18331; *Detroit News,* May 11–14, 16, 17, 1934; *Detroit Free Press,* May 11, 12, 1934; *New York Times,* May 12, 13, 17, 18, 1934; *Detroit Times,* May 14, 1934; *Automotive Industries,* LXX (May 19, 1934), 610; Chalmers, "Collective Bargaining," VIII, 19–21; Wieck, "Automobile Workers," pp. 114–15; Francis interview, pp. 18–19, Michigan Historical Collections.

39 Charles P. Taft to Martin Egan, June 7, 1934, Case 292, Cleveland R.L.B. Box 262; A. J. Muste, "The Battle of Toledo," *Nation,* CXXXVIII (June 6, 1934), 639. There is a chapter on the Auto-Lite strike in William Haskett, "Ideological Radicals, the American Federation of Labor and Federal Labor Policy in the Strikes of 1934" (Ph.D. thesis, University of California, Los Angeles, 1957).

40 *Toledo News-Bee,* Apr. 11, 12, 13, 1934. The proposed union agreement required the company to hire *union members* through F.L.U. No. 18384 or any other union affiliated with the A.F. of L., but it is possible that the local made a verbal request for the closed shop. The local also asked for straight seniority, 2 hours call-in pay, a 35-hr. week, an overtime rate, and elimination of the bonus system. There is a copy of the union proposals in Case 292, Cleveland R.L.B. Box 262.

41 *Toledo News-Bee,* Mar. 26, 27, Apr. 1, 2, 3, 11, 13, 17, 19, 1934; *New York Times,* May 27, 1934; Bingham Stamping and Tool Co., *A Statement to Our Employees, Customers and Vendors* (May 4, 1934), Case 294, Cleveland R.L.B. Box 262. See Chapter VI, n. 33, for profit and loss figures for the three firms.

42 *Toledo News-Bee,* Apr. 13, 14, 16, 17, 19, 28, May 1, 29, 1934; Bingham, *Statement,* Case 294, Cleveland R.L.B. Box 262.

43 *Toledo News-Bee,* Apr. 17, 18, 1934; *Toledo Blade,* Apr. 18, May 19, 1934. The court apparently regarded the Unemployed Council and the Unemployed League as one and the same.

44 Bernard Karsh and Phillips L. Garman, "The Impact of the Political Left," in Derber and Young, eds., *Labor and the New Deal,* pp. 86–97; *Labor Action,*

June 1, Dec. 1, 1934; *Daily Worker,* Feb. 28, Mar. 1, 2, 1934; Louis Francis Budenz, *This Is My Story* (New York, 1947), p. 97; Chalmers, "Collective Bargaining," VIII, 1–2.

45 *Toledo News-Bee,* Apr. 18, May 28, 31, 1934; *Union Leader* (Toledo), May 25, 1934; Muste, "The Battle of Toledo," *Nation,* CXXXVIII (June 6, 1934), 639. Krieger reported on May 21 that Auto-Lite had advanced $4220 for the deputies and Bingham, $725. *Toledo Blade,* May 21, 1934.

46 *Toledo News-Bee,* Apr. 20, 21, 23–27, 1934; *Detroit News,* Apr. 21, 23, 24, 27, 1934; Tracy, Chapman and Welles to Wolman, May 2, 1934, A.L.B. Drawer 4105.

47 *Toledo News-Bee,* May 5, 7, 8, 1934; Leo A. Powers to Green, May 16, 1934, Coleman Claherty to Green, May 17, 1934, A.F. of L. Strike File, Local 18384.

48 *Toledo News-Bee,* Apr. 28, May 2, 4, 10, 23, 1934; Brach to Morrison, May 4, 1934, Brach to Green, May 23, 1934, Green to Brach, May 17, 28, 1934, Green to Claherty, May 17, 1934, A.F. of L. Strike File, Local 18384.

49 *Toledo News-Bee,* May 3, 7, 11, 14, 15, 16, 18, 1934; *Toledo Blade,* May 14, 1934; Muste, "Battle of Toledo," p. 640; *Labor Action,* June 15, 1934; *Daily Worker,* June 16, 18, 1934; Oral History Interview of James Roland, Sept. 25, 1960, p. 6, Michigan Historical Collections; Budenz, "When You Strike, Strike Hard," *Common Sense,* III (July, 1934), 10.

50 *Toledo News-Bee,* May 11, 19, 23, 1934; *Toledo Blade,* May 19, 1934.

51 Auto-Lite spent approximately $11,000 for gas munitions between Apr. and July 1934 and $13,283.96 for munitions, $757 for espionage, and $50,622.91 for "strike expense" during the year 1934. La Follette *Report No. 6,* Part 3, p. 66; La Follette *Report No. 46,* Part 3, p. 82.

52 Unsigned memorandum, May 24, 1934, N.L.B. Box 102; *Toledo News-Bee,* May 24, 1934; *Union Leader* (Toledo), May 25, June 1, 1934; Wieck, "Automobile Workers," p. 121; *New York Times,* May 24, 1934; *Labor Action,* June 15, 1934.

53 *Toledo News-Bee,* May 24, 28, 1934, June 1, 1934. 30 Guardsmen were assigned to the Bingham plant. Deputy sheriffs protected the Logan Gear plant. *Ibid.,* May 25, 1934.

54 *Ibid.,* May 24, 25, 26, 28, 1934; Wieck, "Automobile Workers," pp. 121–22.

55 *Toledo News-Bee,* May 24, 28, 29, 1934, June 2, 13, 1934; Haskett, "Ideological Radicals," p. 181 n; Communist party handbill for mass meeting, May 31, 1934, Toledo Public Library; communist handbills in Brown Collection; *Daily Worker,* May 25–31, June 2, 16, 18, 1934; A. B. Magil, "A Challenge to a Misleader: An Open Letter on Toledo to A. J. Muste," *New Masses,* XI (June 19, 1934), 13; *Daily Worker,* June 18, 1934; *New York Times,* May 28, 1934; *Detroit News,* May 24, 1934; Budenz, *This Is My Story,* p. 97; *Labor Action,* June 15, 1934; Williamson, "The Lessons of the Toledo Strike," *Communist,* XIII (July, 1934), 639–54.

56 The electrical workers, among other things, were seeking the restoration of two 10 per cent wage cuts that had been put into effect in 1932 and a signed contract. Taft to Perkins, June 9, 1934, Case 292, Cleveland R.L.B. Box 262.

57 *Ibid.; Toledo News-Bee,* May 24, 25, 28, June 1, 1934; *Toledo Blade,* June 1, 1934; B. W[olf] memorandum, May 28, 1934, N.L.B. Drawer 122; *New York Times,* June 1, 1934; *Labor Action,* June 15, 1934.

58 *Toledo News-Bee,* May 17, 24, 25, 1934. Because of the resignation of Chairman Nash, effective May 1, the Toledo Sub-R.L.B. was "practically inac-

tive" during the strike. A new chairman was not appointed until May 28, 1934. *Ibid.,* Apr. 20, May 16, 28, 1934.

[59] Taft to Perkins, June 9, 1934 (this is a detailed day-by-day account of Taft's efforts to end the strike), Case 292, Cleveland R.L.B. Box 262. Lind reported to the N.L.B. that the strikers "with very few exceptions" were not responsible for the violence, and Taft concurred in this judgment. *Ibid.;* Lind to N.L.B., May 26, 1934, N.L.B. Box 102.

[60] Taft to Perkins, June 9, 1934, Case 292, Cleveland R.L.B. Box 262; *Toledo News-Bee,* May 24, 26, 29, 30, 1934; Nelson D. Lyons to Wagner, June 1, 1934, N.L.B. Box 102; B. W[olf] memoranda, May 28, 29, 1934, *ibid.;* Lyons to Roosevelt, June 1, 1934, O.F.407-B, Box 27, Roosevelt Library. Lind placed the number of strikers at 464 out of a total of 1723 workers. Wolf memorandum, May 28, 1934, N.L.B. Box 102.

[61] "May 31, 1934—Miniger," Taft to Egan, June 7, 1934, Taft to Perkins, June 9, 1934, Case 292, Cleveland R.L.B. Box 262; Claherty to Green, May 17, 1934, Green to Claherty, May 25, 1934, Brach to Green, June 5, 1934, Green to Wharton, June 11, 1934, A.F. of L. Strike File, Local 18384; *Toledo News-Bee,* May 31, June 1, 1934.

[62] Taft to Perkins, June 9, 1934, Case 292, Cleveland R.L.B. Box 262; Lind to Miller, June 5, 1934, N.L.B. Drawer 130; *Toledo Blade,* June 2, 1934; *Toledo News-Bee,* June 2, 4, 5, 1934; Chalmers, "Collective Bargaining," VIII, 16; Maurice Goldbloom *et al., Strikes under the New Deal* (New York, n.d.), pp. 43–44; Williamson, "Lessons of the Toledo Strike," pp. 639–54; *Daily Worker,* June 11, 16, 1934.

[63] The Auto-Lite agreement is in Case 292, the Logan Gear agreement in Case 293, and the Bingham agreement in Case 294, Cleveland R.L.B. Box 262. Taft stated that Auto-Lite had been paying its workers less than the code minima but had agreed to reimburse them for their labors of the previous 7 months. Taft to Egan, June 7, 1934, Case No. 292, *ibid.* The wage rates provided in the contracts were to remain in effect for 6 months.

[64] W. H. Schomburg to Floyd Bossler *et al.,* June 4, 1934, Case 294, Cleveland R.L.B. Box 262; Beran to Kirk, June 26, 1934, T. J. Coolidge to Perkins, July 6, 1934, C.S. 176-1292.

[65] Fred Schwake to Green, July 9, 1934, Green to Schwake, July 13, 1934, A.F. of L. Strike File, Local 18384; *Nation,* CXL (Jan. 16, 1935), 77; *ibid.,* CXL (Feb. 13, 1935), 183; *New Militant,* May 4, 25, 1935. The union had $3973 in its treasury on Apr. 1, 1934, and $191.02 on July 1, 1934.

[66] Fisher Body Divisions, *A Statement of Facts;* AC Employees' Association to All AC Employees, Apr. 20, 1934, Brown Collection; broadside of Fisher Body Employees Cooperative Association of Cleveland, May 2, 1934, A.L.B. Drawer 4004; A.L.B., Fisher Body Hearing, May 1, 1934, pp. 84–87, May 2, 1934, pp. 29–30; Pieper to Byrd, May 8, 10, 1934, A.L.B. Drawer 3990; Green to U.A.W., Apr. 23, 1934, Green Letterbooks.

[67] Final Report of A.L.B., p. 49; A.L.B. Statements, May 3, 1934 (not released), May 26, 1934, A.L.B. Drawer 4107; A.L.B., Olds Hearing, Sept 19, 1934, pp. 11–12; Notes on Conference, Nov. 15, 1934, A.L.B. Drawer 4105.

[68] G.M., Labor Relations Diary, Section 1, pp. 25–26.

[69] Harry G. Burk to Hale, May 8, 1934, and attached document dated May 8, 1934, *ibid.,* Appendix Document No. 11; Constitution of Fisher Body Employees Cooperative Association of Cleveland, Ohio, Apr., 1934, *ibid.; Consti-*

tution of Fisher Body Employees' Protective Association, Plant Number One of Flint Michigan (May, 1934), A.L.B. Drawer 4004; *Automotive Industries,* LXX (May 26, 1934), 635.

70 Constitution of Fisher Body Employees Cooperative Association of Cleveland, G.M., Labor Relations Diary, Appendix Document No. 11; *Fisher Body Employees' Protective Association, Plant Number One,* A.L.B. Drawer 4004; *Articles of Association for Oldsmobile Employees' Association* (Sept., 1933; Reprinted Aug. 1, 1934), A.L.B. Drawer 4006; *Constitution of the Ternstedt Employees' Association* (May 15, 1934), Brown Collection; *Automotive Industries,* LXX (May 26, 1934), 635; *ibid.,* LXX (June 16, 1934), 746–48.

71 The Hudson plan no longer provided for joint meetings of employee and management representatives and removed the management from the amendment process. House Committee on Labor, *Labor Disputes Act,* pp. 137–42.

72 A.L.B., Olds Hearing, Sept. 19, 1934, p. 41; Collins to Wolman, Aug. 8, 1934, and enclosed complaint against Fisher Body No. 1, Cook and Halsey to A.L.B., Oct. 24, 1934, A.L.B. Drawer 4102; A.L.B., Flint Hearing, Aug. 23, 1934, pp. 5–8, 9–11, 12–13, 15; *New York Times,* Apr. 14, May 14, 1934; Gilman to Wolman, Sept. 10, 1934, A.L.B. Drawer 3990; Woods to Wolman, Aug. 15, 1934, A.L.B. Drawer 4101; Dillon to A.L.B., July 21, 1934, Collins to Wolman, Aug. 8, 1934, A.L.B. Drawer 3993; Smith to A.L.B., Sept. 18, 1934, Wilson to Williams, Oct. 2, 1934, A.L.B. Drawer 3997; Greer to Byrd, Nov. 28, 1934, Greer to A.L.B., Dec 7, 1934, Jan. 19, 1935, Robert Waldron to A.L.B., Dec. 4, 1934, Waldron to Byrd, Dec. 17, 1934, A.L.B. Drawer 3999; Luchsinger, Jr., to Byrd, June 27, 1934, Dillon to Wolman, Oct. 5, 17, 1934, Anderson to Ross, Oct. 18, 1934, A.L.B. Drawer 4000; Law to A.L.B., Aug. 6, 1934, A.L.B. Drawer 4103; Pollak to Wolman, Dec. 20, 1934, A.L.B. Drawer 4005; Ogburn to Wolman, May 9, 12, 1934, Collins to Wolman, May 23, 1934, A.L.B. Drawer 4105; Ogburn to Perkins, June 28, 1934, enclosing resolution adopted at U.A.W. conference of June 23–24, 1934, *ibid.;* Official Proceedings First Session National Council U.A.W., July 9–14, 1934, Brown Collection.

73 Wolman to Knudsen, June 14, 1934, A.L.B. Drawer 4003; Williams memorandum, July 2, 1934, A.L.B. Drawer 4004; Williams memorandum, July 9, 1934, A.L.B. Drawer 4003; A.L.B. Statement, July 17, 1934, A.L.B. Drawer 4107.

74 Williams to John F. Flynn, Aug. 23, 1934, A.L.B. Drawer 4002; A.L.B., Stenographic Reports of Conferences with Committees of the Employee Associations or Works Councils: G.M. Truck, Aug. 21, 1934, p. 3; Flint Chevrolet, Sept. 5, 1934, pp. 4, 8, 12–15, 23–24; Chevrolet Gear and Axle, Sept. 12, 1934, pp. 6, 10–11, 17, 29; Cleveland Fisher Body, Sept. 12, 1934, pp. 8, 28, 31; Tarrytown Fisher Body, Sept. 12, 1934, pp. 5, 15, 20, 22–24; Saginaw Chevrolet, Sept. 12, 1934, pp. 7, 8, 12, 23–24; Chevrolet Forge, Spring and Bumper, Sept. 12, 1934, pp. 3–4, 11, 14, 23–24, 28; Bay City Chevrolet, Sept. 12, 1934, pp. 4, 12, 15–16; Olds, Sept. 19, 1934, pp. 15, 75–76; Woods to Wolman, Sept. 6, 1934, A.L.B. Drawer 4101; Greer to A.L.B., Aug. 30, 1934, A.L.B. Drawer 3999.

75 Handwritten note, Sept. 10, 1934, A.L.B. Drawer 4004; A.L.B., Bay City Chevrolet Conference, Sept. 12, 1934, pp. 17–18; A.L.B., Olds Hearing, Sept. 19, 1934, pp. 41–42.

76 Collins to Wolman, July 31, Aug. 7, 1934, Ogburn to Wolman, Aug. 9, 1934, A.L.B. Drawer 4004; Sept. 7 draft of order issued Sept. 18, 1934, *ibid.;* A.L.B., Flint Chevrolet Conference, Sept. 5, 1934, p. 8; A.L.B. Statement, Sept. 18, 1934, A.L.B. Drawer 4107. Wolman stated that the board saw little point

in calling in the company unions to "spank" them for their errant behavior since what they did would only be in effect until the soon-to-be held A.L.B. elections. A.L.B., Stenographic Report of Hearing, Complaint of Associated Automobile Workers of America against the Hudson Motor Car Co., Jan. 24, 1935, pp. 27–28.

[77] Greer to Roosevelt, Sept. 19, 1934, Memorandum to Miss J. from Mr. Wyzanski, Oct. 12, 1934, Wolman to Perkins, Jan. 25, 1935, A.L.B. Drawer 4105.

[78] G.M., Labor Relations Diary, Section 1, pp. 48–49; Sloan, Jr., to All Employes in G.M. Factories, Oct. 12, 1934, Brown Collection; *Automotive Industries*, LXXI (Sept. 15, 1934), 322–24, 333.

[79] *Michigan Manufacturer and Financial Record*, LIV (Oct. 27, 1934), 8; *New York Times*, Oct. 16, 1934; *Automotive Industries*, LXXI (Nov. 10, 1934), 570; Dillon to U.A.W., Oct. 20, 1934, Labadie Collection; undated broadside, *ibid.*

[80] Dillon to Sloan, Nov. 6, 1934, O.F. 466, Box 7, Roosevelt Library; *Detroit Labor News*, Nov. 23, 1934; *Automotive Industries*, LXXI (Nov. 10, 1934), 572; *ibid.*, LXXI (Nov. 24, 1934), 630.

[81] G.M., Labor Relations Diary, Section 1, p. 50.

NOTES TO CHAPTER IX

[1] Oral History Interview of Tracy Doll, Apr. 21, 1961, p. 18, Michigan Historical Collections; Monthly Reports of Detroit R.L.B., Apr. 30, 1934, Detroit R.L.B. Box 280; Oral History Interview of Herbert Richardson, July 10, 1960, p. 9, Michigan Historical Collections; Oral History Interview of Ted LaDuke, Aug. 5, 1960, p. 8, *ibid.* See also Miley interview, p. 7, *ibid.;* Palmer interview, p. 6, *ibid.;* Oral History Interview of Al Cook, Aug. 31, 1960, p. 22, *ibid.;* John W. Pickering to Martin, Oct. 4, 1934, Martin Papers; Gladys S. Connor to Perkins and McGrady, June 3, 1934, C.S. 176-737.

[2] The paid-up membership of the U.A.W. federal labor unions was 32,501 in in Mar. 1934 and 18,244 in June 1934. Information supplied by the Bookkeeping Dept. of the old A.F. of L. on Aug. 17, 1955.

[3] Minzey to Dillon, Nov. 17, 1934, A.L.B. Drawer 3990.

[4] *Ibid.; Flint Weekly Review*, Nov. 9, 1934, Mar. 29, 1935; *Detroit Labor News*, Nov. 16, 1934; A.F. of L., *Proceedings, 1934*, p. 107.

[5] Collins to Roosevelt, Apr. 9, 1934, O.F. 407-B, Box 18, Roosevelt Library; Lano to Johnson, Apr. 11, 1934, Case 209, N.L.B. Drawer 35.

[6] "A Brief Analysis of President Roosevelt's Order for the Automobile Industry . . . ," Apr. 8, 1934, Collins File; *Detroit News*, Apr. 16, 17, June 23, 1934; *Detroit Free Press*, Apr. 16, 1934; U.A.W. Weekly News Letter, May 8, 1934, Francis Papers; U.A.W. Weekly News Letter, June 27, 1934, A.F. of L.–C.I.O. Library; *Central Labor Council Herald* (Buffalo), May 25, 1934; Wieck, "Automobile Workers," p. 128; *New York Times*, June 24, 25, 1934.

[7] Records of F.L.U. 18386, Sept. 22, Nov. 1, 1933, Wayne State University Archives; [Code] Submitted by U.A.W.F.L.U. 18386, N.R.A. Box 655; Darner and Neumann to U.A.W., [Nov., 1933], C.S. 176–818.

[8] Records of F.L.U. 18386, Nov. 15, Dec. 6, 1933, Jan. 17, 1934, Wayne State University Archives; Collins and Smith to Green, Dec. 6, 1933, Collins File.

[9] The A.F. of L. Executive Council on May 8 authorized the establishment of a research staff in Detroit to investigate problems affecting automobile labor. *Detroit News*, May 9, 1934. In a letter to Green of June 9, 1934 (Collins File),

Collins reported the presence in Detroit of Marjorie Clark and Florence Thorne to initiate the research work and to put out a weekly news letter.

¹⁰ *Documented History of Bendix Local No. 9*, p. 11; Shipley to Green, Apr. 29, 1934, Green to Shipley, May 4, 1934, A.F. of L. Strike File, Local 18347; Green to Powers, May 28, 1934, *ibid.*, Local 18384.

¹¹ Matthew E. Lee to Cook, May 28, 1934, [Cook] to Collins, June 4, 1934, Francis Papers; *Documented History of Bendix Local No. 9*, pp. 14, 79–83; Minute Book of U.A.W. Union No. 19324, June 5, 1934, State Historical Society of Wisconsin. Collins erroneously thought that the St. Louis local was responsible for the conference. Collins to Morrison, June 2, 1934, Collins File. Shipley later incorrectly dated the conference as having taken place on May 18, 1934. Shipley to John L. Lewis, May 27, 1935, A.F. of L. Strike File, Local 18347.

¹² The Cleveland Fisher Body local at that time was also contacting U.A.W. locals with a view to calling a conference "to take up the subject of an International." John G. Barskites to Dear Sir and Brother, May 24, 1934, Francis Papers. There was also some sentiment for an international, industrial union in the Flint Federated Executive Council. Minutes of the Flint Federated Executive Council, Apr. 28, 1934, *ibid.*

¹³ *Auto Workers News*, Dec. 30, 1933, Mar. 10, June 2, 16, 1934; *Daily Worker*, Dec. 18, 1933, Mar. 3, 20, 1934.

¹⁴ Collins to Green, May 26, 1934, Collins File; Green to Collins, May 26, 1934, Green Letterbooks.

¹⁵ Collins to U.A.W., June 6, 1934, Collins to Morrison, June 19, 1934, and attached documents, Collins File; Collins draft of a proposed "Basis of Representation for a National Council," *ibid.*; Chalmers, "Collective Bargaining," IX, 2–4; Wieck, "Automobile Workers, " pp. 126–27; Clark, "The A.F. of L.," p. 88.

¹⁶ Greer to U.A.W., June 14, 1934, Francis Papers; Summary of Resolutions Filed with Detroit Office of A.F. of L. up to . . . June 22, 1934, Collins File; Collins to Martin, Aug. 14, 1934, Martin to Collins, Aug. 16, 1934, Martin Papers; Martin, "To Whom It May Concern," Aug. 16, 1934, *ibid.*; interview with Tracy M. Doll, Dec. 17, 1957; Doll interview, p. 11, Michigan Historical Collections; *Daily Worker*, June 26, 28, July 17, 1934; *Auto Workers News*, July 21, 1934; Wieck, "Automobile Workers," p. 127; Chalmers, "Collective Bargaining," IX, 12.

¹⁷ Summary of Resolutions, Collins File; *Daily Worker*, June 25, 26, 28, July 17, 1934; *Auto Workers News*, July 21, 1934; *Documented History of Bendix Local No. 9*, pp. 84–87; Manning interview, pp. 12, 14, Michigan Historical Collections. The A.W.U. made its position clear in an open letter to the delegates. See J. Wilson and Raymond to the Delegates of the National Conference, [June 1934], Labadie Collection.

¹⁸ U.A.W. Weekly News Letter, June 27, 1934, A.F. of L.-C.I.O. Library; *Daily Worker*, June 26, 1934; *Auto Workers News*, July 21, 1934; *New York Times*, June 25, 1934.

¹⁹ U.A.W. Weekly News Letter, June 27, 1934, A.F. of L.-C.I.O. Library; Chalmers, "Collective Bargaining," IX, 5–6, 9–11; Morris, *Conflict within the AFL*, p. 189; Brown to Wharton, June 26, 1934, I.A.M. File. Green informed Wharton on July 2, 1934, that he would have "demanded" the business agent's admission had he been aware of the situation. *Ibid.*

²⁰ *Documented History of Bendix Local No. 9*, p. 85; *New York Times*, June 25, 1934; *Daily Worker*, June 25, 28, 1934; *MESA Voice*, July, 1934. For other

resolutions adopted by the conference, see U.A.W. Weekly News Letter, June 27, 1934, A.F. of L.-C.I.O. Library, and Ogburn to Perkins, June 28, 1934, and attached resolutions, A.L.B. Drawer 4105.

[21] *MESA Voice,* July, 1934; Chalmers, "Collective Bargaining," IX, 13–14; *Detroit News,* Aug. 5, 7, 8, 1934; *Detroit Free Press,* Aug. 4, 5, 7, 9, 1934; *New York Times,* Aug. 5, 1934; *Automotive Daily News,* Sept. 8, 1934; Collins to Martin, Aug. 6, 1934, and enclosed newspaper article, Martin Papers; Martin to Collins, Aug. 10, 1934, and attached "Statement," *ibid.;* Wieck, "Automobile Workers," pp. 135–36; *Business Week,* Aug. 18, 1934, p. 16. Collins claimed that the Hudson secession occurred at a snap special meeting of the local at which fewer than 200 unionists were present, but Greer said the matter was decided at a special meeting by a vote of 987 to 5. U.A.W. News Letter, Aug. 14, 1934, A.F. of L.–C.I.O. Library; Greer to Green, July 28, 1934, Green Letterbooks.

[22] Margaret Collingwood Nowak, "The Making of an American: The Story of Stanley Nowak," undated MS, pp. 175–76, Wayne State University Library; Smith interview; Doll interview; J. Raymond Walsh, *C.I.O.: Industrial Unionism in Action* (New York, 1937), p. 110; *New York Times,* Aug. 17, 1934; *Auto Workers News,* Aug. 4, 1934; Lucheck, "Labor Organizations," p. 54; Green to William Ollinger, Aug. 18, 1934, Green Letterbooks; Chalmers, "Collective Bargaining," IX, 14; *Detroit News,* Sept. 9, 1934; *Motor,* LXII (Sept., 1934), 138; *Associated,* I (May 10, 1935), 3; House Committee on Labor, *Labor Disputes Act,* pp. 123–26, 142–44, 260; G.M., Labor Relations Diary, Appendix Document No. 54.

[23] Chalmers, "Collective Bargaining," IX, 15–16; Lucheck, "Labor Organizations," pp. 53–54; *Detroit News,* Sept. 3, 9, 10, Nov. 13, 1934; *Detroit Free Press,* Sept. 11, Nov. 7, 1934; Doll interview; *Automotive Industries,* LXXII (June 15, 1935), 783.

[24] Wieck, "Automobile Workers," p. 137; *Flint Weekly Review,* Sept. 21, Dec 14, 1934; *Automotive Industries,* LXXIII (Oct. 12, 1935), 474. The A.L.B. elections indicated the existence of small A.A.W.A. pockets in the Plymouth plant and the Pontiac and Lansing Fisher Body plants. Final Report of A.L.B., Appendix B.

[25] *Automotive Industries,* LXXII (June 15, 1935), 783. In the A.L.B. elections a total of 6083 voters indicated that their candidates were affiliated with the A.A.W.A. Final Report of A.L.B., Appendix B.

[26] *Detroit News,* Aug. 7, 1934; *Business Week,* Aug. 18, 1934, p. 16; *Detroit Free Press,* Aug. 7, 9, 1934; Collins to Green, June 25, 1934, Green to Collins, June 27, Sept. 24, Oct. 22, 1934 (and enclosed resolution), Collins to Morrison, Aug. 11, 1934, Collins File; Collins to Martin, Oct. 1, 1934, Martin File; Manning interview, p. 25, Michigan Historical Collections.

[27] Pesotta, *Bread upon the Waters* (New York, 1944), p. 228; Dillon to Green, Feb. 13, Oct. 5, 1934, Dillon File; Green to Dillon, Sept. 24, 1934, Green Letterbooks; *Detroit Free Press,* Oct. 6, 1934; Dillon to U.A.W., Oct. 15, 1934, Martin Papers.

[28] Collins to Green, June 25, 1934, Collins File.

[29] Marjorie R. Clark, "Recent History of Labor Organization," *Annals of the American Academy of Political and Social Science,* CLXXXIV (May, 1936), 164; Twentieth Century Fund, *Labor and the Government* (New York, 1935), p. 40. The A.F. of L. had set up 8 national councils by the middle of 1935. Morris, *Conflict within the AFL,* p. 167.

30 Hall to Green, Nov. 15, 1934, Hall to Martin, Nov. 15, 1934, Pieper to National Council, Nov. 21, 1934, Dillon to Martin, Nov. 26, 1934, Martin Papers; Hall interview, p. 9, Michigan Historical Collections. The A.F. of L. spent $6356.65 on organizing work by National Council members. The bulk of this sum went to Martin, Kleinert, Hall, and Pickering. *Proceedings of Constitutional Convention of U.A.W., 1935*, p. 23.

31 Martin to National Council, Dec. 8, 1934, Dillon to National Council, Dec. 11, 1934, Martin Papers.

32 Pieper to Dillon, Apr. 11, 1935, Dillon to Martin, Apr. 19, 1935, Martin to Dillon, Apr. 25, 1935, Martin Papers; Hall interview, p. 4, Michigan Historical Collections. See also Richardson interview, p. 16, *ibid.*, and Shipley to Lewis, May 27, 1935, A.F. of L. Strike File, Local 18347.

33 Woods to Martin, Aug. 8, 18, 1934, Martin to Woods, Aug. 23, 1934, Hall to Martin, Oct. 6, 1934, Dillon to National Council, Oct. 10, 1934, Martin Papers.

34 Manning interview, p. 13, Michigan Historical Collections; Jack Skeels, "The Background of UAW Factionalism," *Labor History*, II (Spring, 1961), 163–64; Hall to Martin, Nov. 5, 14, 1934, Kleinert to Martin, Dec. 11, 1934, Pieper to National Council, Mar. 25, 1935, Martin Papers.

35 *Labor Digest*, Mar. 15, Apr. 5, 1935; Mortimer interview, pp. 1, 6–7, Michigan Historical Collections; Miley interview, p. 16, *ibid.*; Minton and Stuart, *Men Who Lead Labor*, p. 217.

36 "Cleveland Conference for an International Union . . . ," undated, Francis Papers; *Daily Worker*, Aug. 22, 1934; Second Session of National Council, Aug. 28–31, 1934, Brown Collection; "Important Notice to All United Automobile Workers . . . ," undated, Martin Papers; Minutes of F.L.U. No. 18331, Sept. 13, 1934, Wayne State University Archives.

37 *Daily Worker*, Sept. 18, 1934; *Auto Workers News*, Oct., 1934; Dillon to National Council, Oct. 12, 1934, Martin Papers. George Lehman was present at the meeting as an observer, but the delegates refused to seat a group headed by Arthur Greer.

38 *Daily Worker*, Nov. 15, 1934. Al Cook of the U.A.W. was debarred from the meeting.

39 Green to Collins, Dec. 12, 1933, Green to Shipley, Nov. 26, 1934, Green Letterbooks; Green to Powers, May 28, 1934, A.F. of L. Strike File, Local 18384.

40 A.F. of L., *Proceedings, 1934*, pp. 192–93, 200, 214–15, 586–98; Perlman, *The Machinists* (Cambridge, Mass., 1961), p. 84.

41 Call to Conference on Jan. 26, 1935, Labadie Collection; Dillon to U.A.W., Jan. 11, 1935, Dillon File; Miley interview, p. 16, Michigan Historical Collections. Several A.F. of L. officials attempted in vain to persuade the White Motor local to rescind its endorsement of the conference. *Labor Digest*, Mar. 15, 1935; Mortimer interview, pp. 9–12, Michigan Historical Collections.

42 *Daily Worker*, Jan. 30, 1935; *Labor Digest*, Mar. 15, 1935.

43 *Kansas City Star*, May 7, 1934; Martin to Collins, June 29, 1934, Martin Papers.

44 Martin and Dowell to Roosevelt, June 19, 1934, Martin Papers; "The Case against Richard L. Byrd," *ibid.*; Decision #99; Collins to Wolman, Sept. 27, 1934, A.L.B. Drawer 4084.

45 Martin to Collins, June 29, 1934, Martin Papers; Wieck, "Automobile Workers," p. 188; Green to Greer, July 23, 1934, enclosing Byrd letter of June 11, 1934, Green Letterbooks; Collins to Morrison, July 21, 1934, Collins File.

⁴⁶ *Motor,* LXII (Sept. 1934), 72; Green to Greer, July 23, 1934, Green Letterbooks; Green to Perkins, July 26, 31, 1934, I. Lee Quick to Perkins, July 28, 1934, Charles O. Taylor to Perkins, July 31, 1934, A.L.B. Drawer 4105; Byrd to Wolman and Kelley, Feb. 3, 1935, A.L.B. Drawer 4106; G.M., Labor Relations Diary, Appendix Document No. 54; A.L.B., Stenographic Report of Hearing, Hudson Motor Car Co., Matter of Employees Bargaining Agency, Mar. 8, 1935, p. 47; Dowell to Martin, Dec. 12, 1934, Martin Papers; *MESA Voice,* Oct., 1934; *Detroit News,* Jan. 26, 1935.

⁴⁷ Green to Ogburn, June 28, 1934, Green Letterbooks; Official Proceedings First Session National Council U.A.W., July 9–14, 1934, Brown Collection.

⁴⁸ Green to Ogburn, July 23, 1934, Green to Collins, July 24, 1934, Green Letterbooks; National Council *et al.* to Wolman, July 26, 1934, Wolman to Collins, Aug. 7, 1934, A.L.B. Drawer 4105.

NOTES TO CHAPTER X

¹ Green to Roosevelt, Sept. 11, 1934, O.F. 466, Box 7, Roosevelt Library; Lorwin and Wubnig, *Labor Relations Boards,* pp. 336–37.

² Proceedings . . . before Sub-Committee of the Regional Labor Board, Apr. 12, 1934, Case 12, N.L.R.B. Drawer 254; Shortal to N.L.B., Apr. 16, 24, 1934, Case 12, N.L.R.B. Drawer 158.

³ Wagner to F.L.U. No. 18839 and Houde, Apr. 26, 1934, Peo to N.L.B., May 1, 1934, Wolf to Ernest Draper, May 9, 1934, B. W[olf] Memoranda, May 17, 25, 1934, Buffalo R.L.B. to N.L.B., May 28, 1934, N.L.R.B. to F.L.U. No. 18839 and Houde, July 13, 1934, Case 12, N.L.R.B. Drawer 158; Memo to the Board Members by Herzog, July 23, 1934, *ibid.;* N.L.B., Stenographic Report of Hearing, In the Matter of: Houde Engineering Co. . . . , May 3, 1934, Case 12, N.L.R.B. Drawer 254; N.L.R.B., Stenographic Report of Hearing, In the Matter of: Houde Engineering Corp. . . . , July 24, 1934, *ibid.*

⁴ *Decisions of the N.L.R.B., July 9, 1934–Dec.,* 1934, pp. 35–44. The board made it clear that it was not laying down a rule as to what constituted the proper unit that would serve as the basis for representation and that this question would have to be determined according to the circumstances in particular cases.

⁵ H.B. Memorandum to the Board, Oct. 17, 1934—Public Reaction to the Houde Decision, Case 12, N.L.R.B. Drawer 158; Houde to N.L.R.B., Sept. 10, 1934, Houde to Employees, Sept. 10, 1934, *ibid.; Buffalo Evening News,* Sept. 1, 1934.

⁶ *Buffalo Evening News,* Sept. 12, 13, 1934.

⁷ Johnson to Houde, Sept. 14, 1934, Stephens to N.L.R.B., Sept. 27, 1934, and attached Memorandum for the Files, Sept. 25, 1934, Stephens to N.L.R.B., Oct. 30, 1934, and attached Memorandum for the Files, Oct. 30, 1934, N.L.R.B. to F.L.U. No. 18839 and Houde, May 31, 1935, Case 12, N.L.R.B. Drawer 158; N.R.A. Release, Nov. 30, 1934. The course of the legal proceedings can be followed in Case 12, N.L.R.B. Drawer 158, and in the *Buffalo Evening News.*

⁸ Collins to Green, Aug. 15, 1934, Martin Papers; Collins to Green, Aug. 23, 1934, Collins File; Green to Roosevelt, Sept. 11, 12, 1934, and attached resolution adopted by National Council, Aug. 31, 1934, O.F. 466, Box 7, Roosevelt Library.

⁹ Green to Reeves and Macauley, Sept. 13, 14, 1934, Green to Ogburn, Sept. 21, 24, Oct. 8, 1934, Green Letterbooks; McIntyre memorandum for the Presi-

dent, Sept. 13, [1934], Green to Reeves, Jan. 8, 1935, enclosed with Reeves to Roosevelt, Jan. 14, 1935, O.F. 466, Box 7, Roosevelt Library.

10 Wolman interview; A.L.B., Conference with Members of the Works Council of the Hudson Industrial Association, Jan. 24, 1935, p. 3; Final Report of A.L.B., p. 29.

11 Wolman, "Labor Relations in the Automobile Industry," *Nation,* CXL (Mar. 13, 1935), 297.

12 "Substantial number" was defined as more than 75 per cent of the average vote cast in each district of a plant. Ross to A.L.B., Mar. 29, 1935, A.L.B. Drawer 4015.

13 A.L.B. Memorandum, Dec. 7, 1934, A.L.B. Drawer 4019; Ross to A.L.B., Apr. 4, 1935, A.L.B. Drawer 4007.

14 Final Report of A.L.B., pp. 33–42, 47; Wieck, "Automobile Workers," pp. 108, 156.

15 A.L.B., Conference with Members of Works Council of Chevrolet Forge, Spring and Bumper Shop, Jan. 7, 1935, p. 46; A.L.B., Stenographic Report of Hearing, In Re: Chevrolet Co. Gear and Axle Plant, Apr. 24, 1935, pp. 16–17; Lucheck, "Labor Organizations," p. 107; *Automotive Industries,* LXXII (Feb. 2, 1935), 132.

16 Lorwin and Wubnig, *Labor Relations Boards,* pp. 11–13.

17 Leiserson, "Mr. Leiserson's Rebuttal," *Nation,* CXL (Mar. 13, 1935), 300–301; Ogburn to Roosevelt, Feb. 7, 1935, O.F. 466, Box 7, Roosevelt Library; Clark, "A.F. of L.," pp. 90–91. The National Mediation Board interpreted the Railway Labor Act of 1934 as requiring railroad employees in a representation election to select some form of collective representation. *Twenty Years under the Railway Labor Act, Amended and the National Mediation Board, 1934–1954* (Washington, 1955), pp. 17–18.

18 Twentieth Century Fund, *Labor and the Government,* pp. 90, 94–95; Wolman, *Ebb and Flow in Trade Unionism,* pp. 78–83.

19 Byrd thought that the voter should have been given the opportunity in the primary to indicate the organization of his own preference rather than the affiliation of his candidate. Byrd, Memorandum on Employee Elections, undated, A.L.B. Drawer 4106.

20 A.L.B., Chevrolet Forge, Spring and Bumper Conference, Jan. 3, 1935, pp. 8–9; *Automotive Industries,* LXXII (Jan. 5, 1935), 5; Decision #210, A.L.B. Drawer 4091; Ross to H. F. Browne, Feb. 8, 1935, Ross to Felix Belsky, Apr. 10, 1935, A.L.B. Drawer 4106; A.L.B., Conference with Works Council of the Plymouth Motor Corp., Jan. 11, 1935, pp. 24–25. For intelligent criticisms of the A.L.B. plan, see Wieck, "Automobile Workers," pp. 163–68, and Lucheck, "Labor Organizations," pp. 116–21.

21 See, for example, A.L.B., Chevrolet Gear and Axle Hearing, Apr. 24, 1935, pp. 4, 9, 10; and A.L.B., Stenographic Report of Hearing, In Re: Oldsmobile Motor Car Co., Meeting of Bargaining Agency, Mar. 9, 1935, p. 39 *et passim.*

22 Wolman, at a later time, improperly classified all ballots that did not specify a union affiliation as a vote *against* trade unionism. Wolman, "Employee Elections in Industry," *Personnel Journal,* XIV (Jan.–Feb., 1936), 244–45.

23 Final Report of A.L.B., pp. 36–38; Lucheck, "Labor Organizations," pp. 106–7; Sokolsky, "An Experiment in Labor Democracy," *Atlantic Monthly,* CLVI (July, 1935), 57; A.L.B., Chevrolet Forge, Spring and Bumper Conference, Jan. 3, 1935, pp. 17, 46; Bennett to Wolman, Mar. 16, 1935, Bennett to Ross, Apr.

9, 1935, A.L.B. Drawer 4106; *National Municipal Review,* XXIV (Sept., 1935), 491.

²⁴ Anderson to Ross, Feb. 26, 1935, A.L.B. Drawer 4106; J. F. Dunn to Ross, Mar. 13, 1935, A.L.B. Drawer 4105; A.L.B., Chevrolet Gear and Axle Hearing, Apr. 24, 1935, p. 10.

²⁵ Wolman to Perkins, Dec. 20, 1934, A.L.B. Drawer 3990; Detroit District Committee, M.E.S.A., handbill, Dec. 14, 1934, A.L.B. Drawer 4005; House Committee on Labor, *Labor Disputes Act,* pp. 96–100; *Designing Engineer,* I (Feb., 1935), 12–13.

²⁶ In elections of this type as of Mar. 15, 1935, the outside unions had won 67.5 per cent (204,582) of the vote. Twentieth Century Fund, *Labor and the Government,* pp. 90–93.

²⁷ Ogburn to Wolman, Aug. 19, 1934, A.L.B. Drawer 4105; Resolution of Detroit District Council, Dec. 10, 1934, *ibid.;* Green to Dillon, Dec. 8, 1934, Green Letterbooks; Dillon press releases, Dec. 8, 12, 18, 1934, Jan. 26, 1935, Dillon File; *Detroit Labor News,* Feb. 1, 1935; Dillon to Wolman, Jan. 11, 1935, A.L.B. Drawer 4105; Ogburn brief submitted to N.I.R.B., Feb. 5, 1935, N.R.A. Box 658; *American Federationist,* XLII (Mar., 1935), 245–46; A.L.B., Stenographic Report of Hearing, In the Matter of Fisher Body Corp., Conference on the Election, Dec. 16, 1934, pp. 6, 14–15; Ross to George Sokolsky, Mar. 9, 1935, A.L.B. Drawer 4106; interview with Ross, Dec. 2, 1961; *New York Times,* Feb. 12, 1935; Ogburn interview, Feb. 5, 1957; House Committee on Labor, *Labor Disputes Act,* pp. 213–14, 245–46, 253.

²⁸ Pieper to Atlanta R.L.B., Sept. 12, 1934, Herzog to Wolman, Sept. 17, 1934, Wolman to Herzog, Sept. 20, 1934, Stern to Coffee, Sept. 24, 1934, Wolf to Wolman, Oct. 15, 1934, Coffee to N.L.R.B., Jan. 10, 1935, N.L.R.B. to Atlanta R.L.B., Jan. 11, 1935, N.L.B. Drawer 98; Executive Board, F.L.U. No. 18386 to N.L.R.B., Nov. 23, 1934, Darner *et al.* to Wolf, Dec. 3, 1934, N.L.R.B. to F.L.U. No. 18386, Dec. 17, 1934, Case 6, N.L.B. Drawer 15.

²⁹ Report to the President by the N.L.R.B. for the Period Dec. 10, 1934, to Jan. 9, 1935, O.F. 716, Box 2, Roosevelt Library; Brunk, Report to the N.L.R.B. on an Inquiry into Industrial Relations Boards, pp. 2–8, 24–28, *ibid.* The file of memoranda dealing with the release of the report is in *ibid.*

³⁰ Biddle to Roosevelt, Dec. 13, 1934, *ibid.; Detroit News,* Dec. 15, 1934; Biddle to author, Aug. 29, 1957.

³¹ Richberg memorandum to McIntyre, Dec. 13, 1934, O.F. 788, Box 1, Roosevelt Library; Richberg to McIntyre, Jan. 14, 1935, Roosevelt to Biddle, Jan. 22, 1935, O.F. 716, Box 2, *ibid.;* Biddle, *In Brief Authority,* p. 36.

³² Biddle to Roosevelt, Jan. 22, 1935, O.F. 716, Box 2, Roosevelt Library; Biddle, *In Brief Authority,* p. 37. Frances Perkins noted a few days later that the President had talked with the N.L.R.B., and "the situation has now been adjusted." Perkins memorandum to McIntyre, Feb. 4, 1935, *ibid.* In his memoirs, Francis Biddle states that Senator Wagner asked him "to hold the Board together" while the fight went on for the enactment of a new labor relations law. *In Brief Authority,* p. 37.

³³ Green to Reeves, Jan. 8, 1935, enclosed with Reeves to Roosevelt, Jan. 14, 1935, O.F. 466, Box 7, Roosevelt Library; Green to Ogburn, Oct. 8, 1934, Jan. 9, 1935, Green to Perkins, Jan. 12, 1935, Green Letterbooks; Ogburn to Wolman and Kelley, Jan. 28, 1935, A.L.B. Drawer 4105; *Detroit News,* Jan. 25, 1935. In his letter to Roosevelt cited above, Reeves wrote that Green's decision to withdraw

from the settlement proved that the A.F. of L., which represented "only a very small percentage of automobile workers," was "irresponsible." At the same time, Reeves expressed the A.M.A.'s "satisfaction with the fair and statesman-like settlement of the industrial relationship problem of this industry, which you effected last March."

34 Executive Council Minutes, Apr. 30–May 7, 1935, Auto Workers File, 1935–1937, A.F. of L.-C.I.O. Archives; Clark, "A.F. of L.," p. 92.

35 Luchsinger, Jr., to Green, Apr. 6, 1935, Dillon to Green, Apr. 12, 1935, A.F. of L. Strike File, Local 19324; Dillon to Green, Apr. 19, 1935, Dillon File; *Automotive Industries,* LXXII (Apr. 27, 1935), 563.

36 After the general elections, the A.L.B. held 10 district elections to fill vacancies created by the death, resignation, or recall of elected candidates or to break a tie. Final Report of A.L.B., p. 48.

37 Opponents of the A.L.B. elections attributed the high turnout to the solicitation of voters by management and the A.L.B. The A.L.B. contact men for the elections did invite eligible voters to participate, and in a few places, apparently, the production lines were stopped to permit voting. *Flint Weekly Review,* Feb. 8, 1935; *Nation,* CXL (Feb. 27, 1935), 238; Final Report of A.L.B., p. 36; Lucheck, "Labor Organizations," pp. 109, 119–20.

38 Final Report of A.L.B., pp. 43–47, Appendices A, B, C. The Report erroneously gives the membership of the Hudson bargaining agency as 73.

39 For the Hupp strike threat, see *Detroit News,* May 11, 13, 14, 15, 1935, and *Detroit Labor News,* May 17, 1935. For the Toledo Chevrolet strike, see Chapter XII.

40 Final Report of A.L.B., pp. 43–44, Appendix B; *Automotive Industries,* LXXII (Apr. 20, 1935), 528; Jacobs to Wolman, Apr. 26, 1935, A.L.B. Drawer 4105; Ross interview.

41 Final Report of A.L.B., Appendix B; Dunn to Ross, Mar. 13, 1935, A.L.B. Drawer 4105; Martel to Ross, Jan. 21, 29, 1935, A.L.B. Drawer 4004; Green to Ross, Apr. 6, 1935, A.L.B. Drawer 4105; Ross to A.L.B., Apr. 18, 1935, A.L.B. Drawer 4008; A.L.B., Chevrolet Gear and Axle Hearing, Apr. 24, 1935, pp. 2–3, 27–28.

42 *Detroit Free Press,* Mar. 16, 1935, *Detroit News,* Apr. 13, 1935; Final Report of A.L.B., Appendix B.

43 *Detroit Free Press,* Dec. 8, 1934; *Detroit News,* Feb. 1, 1935; Final Report of A.L.B., Appendix B.

44 Riley Etchison to Guide Lamp, Oct. 21, 1933, Burke to Etchison, Oct. 27, 1933, Case 42, N.L.R.B. Drawer 167.

45 Ray Kelsay to G. T. Watson, Feb. 28, Apr. 4, June 6, 26, 1934, Stanley Coulter and Watson to Orville Whittaker, Mar. 14, 1934, Watson to N.L.B., June 19, 1934, Anderson to Watson, June 21, 1934, Anderson to Indianapolis R.L.B., June 28, 1934, *ibid.;* Minutes of Meeting . . . , Apr. 4, 1934, *ibid.;* P. A. Donoghue Report, May 21, 1934, *ibid.;* Indianapolis R.L.B., In the Matter of: The Guide Lamp Corp. and Metal Polishers International Union, July 5, 1934, *ibid.;* N.L.R.B., Stenographic Report of Hearing, In the Matter of: Metal Polishers International Union vs. Guide Lamp Corp., Aug. 13, 1934, pp. 43, 44, *ibid.*

46 N.L.R.B. to Guide Lamp, Aug. 2, 1934, Sept. 20, 1934, W. W. Britton to N.L.R.B., Sept. 14, 1934, Indianapolis R.L.B. to N.L.R.B., Sept. 20, 1934, N.I.R.B. to Guide Lamp, Sept. 29, 1934, Hogan to Compliance Division, Sept. 28, 1934, Case 42, N.L.R.B. Drawer 167; N.L.R.B., Guide Lamp Hearing, Aug.

13, 1934, *passim, ibid.; Decisions of the N.L.R.B., July 9, 1934–Dec. 1934,* p. 48. The N.L.R.B. assumed that the ten departments involved were an appropriate bargaining unit.

⁴⁷ Shipley to Steffensen, Sept. 14, 1934, Case 390-2, Chicago R.L.B. Box 322; N.L.R.B., Stenographic Report of Hearing, In the Matter of Bendix Aviation Corp., Oct. 11, 1934, *passim, ibid.;* In the Matter of U.A.W. F.L.U. No. 18347 and Bendix Products Corp., Nov. 17, 1934, Case 199, N.L.R.B. Drawer 198; Walter J. Buettner to N.L.R.B., Nov. 15, 1934, Wolf to Bendix, Nov. 19, 1934, McCarthy to Wolf, Nov. 27, 1934, *ibid.;* James R. Poland to Green, Nov. 27, 1934, and enclosed "Memorandum of Co. Policy . . . ," Nov. 23, 1934, Ogburn to Shipley, Nov. 28, 1934, A.F. of L. Strike File, Local 18347.

⁴⁸ V. Bendix to N.L.R.B., Dec. 17, 1934, Shipley to N.L.R.B., Dec. 18, 1934, McCarthy to N.L.R.B., Jan. 5, 1935, Shipley to Biddle, Jan. 20, 1935, V. Bendix to Biddle, Jan. 29, 1935, Case 199, N.L.R.B. Drawer 198; *Decisions of the N.L.R.B.,* II, *Dec. 1, 1934–June 16, 1935,* 100–105; V. Bendix to C. E. Sorensen, Feb. 4, 1935, Acc. 38, Box 123, Ford Archives.

⁴⁹ Shipley to Green, Feb. 3, 1935, Green to Shipley, Feb. 17, 1935, A.F. of L. Strike File, Local 18347.

⁵⁰ Ogburn petition to N.L.R.B., Jan. 18, 1935, George M. Kennedy to Detroit R.L.B., Feb. 15, 27, 1935, N.L.R.B. to Kelsey-Hayes, Feb. 26, 1935, Siedenburg to N.L.R.B., Apr. 18, 1935, Case 380, N.L.R.B. Drawer 237; B. W[olf] memorandum, Apr. 19, 1935, *ibid.;* In the Matter of the Petition of U.A.W. F.L.U. No. 18677 for an Election by the Employees of the Kelsey-Hayes Wheel Co., Mar. 9, 1935, *passim,* Case 264, Detroit R.L.B. Box 288; N.L.R.B., Stenographic Report of Hearing, In the Matter of Kelsey-Hayes Wheel Corp., Apr. 3, 1935, *passim,* Case 380, N.L.R.B. Drawer 306; *Decisions of the N.L.R.B.,* II, *Dec. 1, 1934–June 16, 1935,* 327–31.

⁵¹ Cadillac Conference, Jan. 3, 1935, pp. 3–4, 38–40; Chevrolet Forge, Spring and Bumper Conference, Jan. 24, 1935, pp. 2–3, 24–27, 40–41; Chrysler Kercheval Plant and Chrysler Jefferson Plant Conference, Feb. 26, 1935, p. 17. I have taken the liberty of abbreviating the titles of the transcripts of these conferences.

⁵² *Detroit News,* Jan. 4, 1935; Pontiac Fisher Conference, Mar. 8, 1935, pp. 12–13, 37–39; G.M. Truck Conference, Mar. 8, 1935, pp. 20–21; Pontiac Conference, Mar. 8, 1935, pp. 6–8.

⁵³ Cadillac Conference, Jan. 3, 1935, pp. 24–29; Plymouth Conference, Feb. 7, 1935, pp. 6, 20; Bay City Chevrolet Conference, Apr. 16, 1935, p. 29; Packard Conference, Mar. 7, 1935, pp. 14–15; Flint Chevrolet Conference, Apr. 12, 1935, p. 13; AC Spark Plug Conference, Apr. 12, 1935, pp. 11–12; Pontiac Fisher Body Conference, Mar. 8, 1935, pp. 39–44; Saginaw Steering Gear Conference, Apr. 16, 1935, pp. 25–26; Chevrolet Forge, Spring and Bumper Conference, Jan. 24, 1935, pp. 21–24; A.L.B., Complaint of A.A.W.A. against Hudson Motor Car Co., Jan. 24, 1935, pp. 37–42; Wieck, "Automobile Workers," p. 67.

⁵⁴ Cadillac Conference, Jan. 3, 1935, pp. 10–15, 17, 23, 52; A.A.W.A. Complaint Conference, Jan. 24, 1935, pp. 48–49; Hudson Conference, Mar. 8, 1935, pp. 21–22; Chrysler Highland Park Conference, Jan. 29, 1935, pp. 3, 40–44; Plymouth Conference, Feb. 7, 1935, pp. 33–34; Pontiac Fisher Body Conference, Mar. 8, 1935, pp. 24–26; Cleveland Fisher Body Conference, Apr. 26, 1935, pp. 50–53; Chevrolet Forge, Spring and Bumper Conference, Jan. 24, 1935, p. 39;

Dodge Conference, Feb. 14, 1935, pp. 34–35; A.L.B., In Re: Hudson Motor Car Co. Conference with Members of Rules Committee . . . , Apr. 12, 1935, p. 21.

55 Chevrolet Forge, Spring and Bumper Conference, Jan. 24, 1935, p. 42; Oakland Chevrolet Conference, Apr. 25, 1935, pp. 20–22; Cadillac Conference, Jan. 3, 1935, pp. 43–44; Fort Wayne International Harvester Conference, May 7, 1935, pp. 5–11; Olds Conference, Mar. 9, 1935, pp. 31–33, 42.

56 Plymouth Conference, Feb. 7, 1935, pp. 21, 27–29; G.M. Truck Conference, Mar. 8, 1935, pp. 27–29; Hudson Conference, Mar. 8, 1935, p. 16.

57 Cadillac Conference, Jan. 3, 1935, pp. 4–9, 15–16; Saginaw Steering Gear Conference, Apr. 16, 1935, p. 20; Bay City Chevrolet Conference, Apr. 16, 1935, pp. 11, 14, 16; Chrysler Highland Park Conference, Jan. 29, 1935, pp. 14–15, 46–48; Dodge Conference, Feb. 14, 1935, pp. 13–15.

58 Wieck, "Automobile Workers," p. 170.

59 Pontiac Fisher Body Conference, Mar. 8, 1935, pp. 9–10; Graham-Paige Conference, Apr. 2, 1935, pp. 20–21, 22; Flint Chevrolet Conference, Apr. 12, 1935, p. 38; Dodge Conference, Feb. 14, 1935, pp. 3–9; Chrysler Highland Park Conference, Jan. 29, 1935, p. 5; Cadillac Conference, Jan. 3, 1935, pp. 9–10; Chevrolet Forge, Spring and Bumper Conference, Jan. 24, 1935, pp. 8–10, 42–43; Pontiac Conference, Mar. 8, 1935, pp. 20–21.

60 Chrysler Kercheval and Chrysler Jefferson Conference, Feb. 26, 1935, pp. 38–39; A.L.B., Conference with the Executive Committee of the Bargaining Agencies of the Chrysler Plants, Mar. 28, 1935, p. 55.

61 Pontiac Fisher Body Conference, Mar. 8, 1935, pp. 4–5; AC Spark Plug Conference, Apr. 12, 1935, p. 3; Buick Conference, Apr. 12, 1935, p. 5.

62 G.M., Labor Relations Diary, Appendix Document No. 41.

63 "Policy for Works Council and Employees Representatives Meetings," Richard Frankensteen Papers (when I examined the Frankensteen Papers, they were in Mr. Frankensteen's possession, but they are, as of this writing, in the process of being transferred to the Wayne State University Archives); *Automotive Industries*, LXIX (Oct. 21, 1933), 488–89.

64 A.L.B., "Rules and Instructions on Bargaining Agencies," Apr. 12, 1935, A.L.B. Drawer 4106.

65 *Detroit News*, Apr. 14, 1935; Dillon press release, Apr. 23, 1935, Dillon File; Ward Grice to Ross, Apr. 19, 1935, A.L.B. Drawer 4006; McNamara to A.L.B., A.L.B. Drawer 4105.

66 Brunk, Report to N.L.R.B. on Industrial Relations Boards, p. 32, O.F. 716, Box 2, Roosevelt Library.

67 "Articles of Association for Employees' Association and Bargaining Agency" (Chevrolet Commercial Body), A.L.B. Drawer 4003; Byrd to Earl D. Green, May 23, 1935, *ibid.;* "Rules of the Bargaining Agency of the Cadillac Motor Car Co. Factory," *ibid.;* Louis Zettel and Oscar W. Johnson to Byrd, May 20, 1935, A.L.B. Drawer 4004; Byrd, "To Newly Elected Bargaining Agencies," A.L.B. Drawer 4005; William Gavine to Byrd, May 9, 1935, A.L.B. Drawer 4006.

68 "Cadillac Rules," A.L.B. Drawer 4003; "Articles of Association" (Chevrolet Commercial Body), *ibid.;* Zettel and Johnson to Byrd, May 20, 1935, A.L.B. Drawer 4004; Harold Mentzy to A.L.B., May 14, 1935, Byrd to Mentzy, May 16, 1935, *ibid.;* Oakland Chevrolet Conference, Apr. 25, 1935, p. 3; Stenographic Report of Meetings of the Bargaining Agency, Hudson Motors, Mar. 12, 18, Apr. 1, 1935, Tracy M. Doll Papers (in Mr. Doll's possession).

69 "Cadillac Rules," A.L.B. Drawer 4003; "Articles of Association" (Chevrolet Commercial Body), *ibid.;* "Objects and Procedure of Collective Bargaining between Employees, Representatives and Plant Management" (Bay City Chevrolet), *ibid.;* Gavine to Byrd, May 9, 1935, A.L.B. Drawer 4006; Minutes of the Joint Meeting of the Labor Relations Committee and the Employees Representative Committee (Willys-Overland, Los Angeles), Apr. 30, 1935, *ibid.*

70 Jacobs to Wolman, Apr. 26, 1935, A.L.B. Drawer 4105; A.L.B., In Re: Hudson Motor Car Co., Apr. 12, 1935, p. 4; Ross to A.L.B., Apr. 23, 1935, Greer to A.L.B., Apr. 24, May 7, 1935, McNamara to A.L.B., May 20, 1935, Wolman to McNamara, May 24, 1935, A.L.B. Drawer 4006; *Detroit News,* Apr. 24, May 16, 17, 1935.

71 Graham-Paige Conference, Apr. 12, 1935, pp. 16, 19; Minutes of Meeting of Fisher Body Employees' Collective Bargaining Agency of Kansas City, May 16, 1935, A.L.B. Drawer 4004; Hudson Conference, Mar. 8, 1935, pp. 53–54, 56–57; Stenographic Report of Fourth Meeting of the Bargaining Agency, Hudson Motors, Apr. 1, 1935, Doll Papers.

72 A.L.B., Conference with Chrysler Executive Committee, Mar. 28, 1935, pp. 17–20; Greer to A.L.B., Apr. 24, 1935, A.L.B. Drawer 4006; McNamara to A.L.B., Apr. 13, 1935, A.L.B. Drawer 4105. The Dodge management made available to representatives a seniority list of their constituents. Decisions Reached in a Conference Held May 16, 1935 . . . , John Zaremba Papers, Wayne State University Archives.

73 See Chapter XII.

74 The bargaining agency consisted of 27 Hudson Industrial Association representatives, 28 A.A.W.A. representatives, and 17 unaffiliated representatives. In the Chevrolet plant in Indianapolis, the A.F. of L. received 32.6 per cent of the primary vote and the employee association, 32.2 per cent. The employee association received 54 per cent of the vote in the Fort Wayne International Harvester plant and the A.F. of L., 33.6 per cent. The employment in these two plants, however, was well below the employment in the Hudson plant.

75 Hudson Conference, Mar. 8, 1935, pp. 12–13, 22–25, 35–36, 49–70; A.L.B., In Re: Hudson Motor Car Co., Apr. 12, 1935, pp. 14–15; Stenographic Report of Meetings of the Bargaining Agency, Hudson Motors, Mar. 12, 18, 25, Apr. 1, 1935, Doll Papers.

76 Byrd to Thomas H. Latham, Feb. 6, 1935, A.L.B. Drawer 4003.

77 Final Report of A.L.B., Appendices B, C; Frankensteen interview; Dodge Main Plant, Works Council Meeting Minutes, Feb. 19, 1935, Special Meeting-No. 1, Frankensteen Papers. The A.F. of L. was entitled to three members on the Dodge bargaining agency, but the eligible A.F. of L. officials refused to serve.

78 Oral History Interview of Richard Harris, Nov. 16, 1959, p. 5, Michigan Historical Collections; Minutes of the Meeting of Employee Representatives at the Dodge Main Plant, Feb. 19, 1935, Frankensteen Papers. Apparently the company refused to permit the bargaining agency to have outside speakers at meetings held on the premises. See S. L. Hudd, Report of Interview of Mar. 14, 1935, with David Gray and Associates, N.R.A. Box 7682.

79 Campbell to Wolman, Feb. 26, 1935, A.L.B. Drawer 4004.

80 Minutes of meeting of Feb. 26, 1935, Frankensteen Papers; Ross interview, p. 14, Michigan Historical Collections.

81 Minutes of Works Council meeting, Mar. 5, 1935, N.R.A. Box 7682; minutes of meetings of Mar. 9, [12?], 19, 1935, Frankensteen Papers.

82 Campbell and Frankensteen to Chrysler, Mar. 23, 1935, Campbell to A.L.B., Mar. 23, 1935, Frankensteen Papers.

83 Conference in . . . Dodge Main Plant, Mar. 27, 1935, *ibid.*

84 A.L.B., Conference with Chrysler Executive Committee, Mar. 28, 1935, pp. 3–6, 8–17, 37–40, 42–46, 58–59, 70–83, 92.

85 Frankensteen interview; minutes of meetings of Apr. 9, 12, 16, 29, 1935, Frankensteen Papers; A.L.B., In Re: Chrysler Motor Corp., Arbitration between Employees Representatives and the Management, Apr. 23, 1935, pp. 4–6, 54–55, 60–61; Minutes of a Special Meeting at the Dodge Main Plant, Apr. 19, 1935, Frankensteen Papers; "President Frankensteen Appeals for Unity . . . ," [1936], *ibid.*

86 Minutes of Dodge Special Meeting, Apr. 19, 1935, Frankensteen Papers. Frankensteen at this conference referred to the union as "a threat, just a war club."

87 Chrysler Arbitration Conference, Apr. 23, 1935.

88 *Proceedings of Second Convention of U.A.W., 1936,* pp. 140–41; *Automotive Industries,* LXXIII (Oct. 12, 1935), 474; Poplawski interview, May 2, 1960, p. 6, Michigan Historical Collections; Harris interview, p. 18, *ibid.;* text of a speech by Frankensteen, Aug. 31, 1935, Frankensteen Papers; *First Year Book and History of the A.I.W.A.,* [Dec., 1935], *ibid.;* First Annual Convention of Delegates of the A.I.W.A., Oct. 12, 13, 1935, Zaremba Papers.

89 *Detroit News,* Jan. 23, Apr. 28, 1935; *Detroit Free Press,* Jan. 23, Mar. 24, 1935; Address of Richard Byrd, Jan. 31, 1935, Michigan Historical Collections; Wieck, "Automobile Workers," pp. 188, 195; Dodge Conference, Feb. 14, 1935, p. 10; McNamara to James Couzens *et al.,* Apr. 2, 1935, A.L.B. Drawer 4005; McNamara to A.L.B., Apr. 13, 1935, A.L.B. Drawer 4105; *Associated,* I (May 10, 1935), 3.

90 *Detroit News,* Aug. 5, 6, 25, 1935; interview with McNamara, Mar. 6, 1958.

91 Lucheck, "Company Unions, F.O.B. Detroit," *Nation,* CXLII (Jan. 15, 1935), 76–77; Lucheck, "Labor Organizations," p. 137; *Automotive Industries,* LXXIII (Oct. 12, 1935), 474; G.M., Labor Relations Diary, Section 1, p. 52, Section 2, p. 174; La Follette *Hearings,* Part 4, p. 1199. The Dodge bargaining agency functioned at least until Mar. 21, 1937. There are copies of its minutes in the Zaremba Papers.

92 Final Report of A.L.B., pp. 54–55; Wolman, "Experiment in Automotive Labor Relations," p. 344; Lucheck, "Labor Organizations," p. 121; Lucheck, "Company Unions," pp. 75–76; *The National Recovery Administration, Report of the President's Committee of Industrial Analysis* (Feb., 1937), p. 156; McPherson and Lucheck, "Automobiles," p. 582; Greer to A.L.B., Apr. 24, 1935, A.L.B. Drawer 4006; Bay City Chevrolet Conference, p. 17; Minutes of Dodge Special Meeting, Apr. 19, 1935, Frankensteen Papers; McNamara interview.

93 *Detroit Free Press,* June 16, 1935; Wolman interview; Kelley interview; Oral History Interview of Carl Swanson, Aug. 8, 1960, p. 5, Michigan Historical Collections.

94 *Proceedings of Second Convention of U.A.W., 1936,* p. 139.

NOTES TO CHAPTER XI

1 Green to Johnson, July 10, 1934, Green Letterbooks.

2 Green to Collins, July 11, 1934, Green to Perkins, July 12, 1934, *ibid.;*

Raushenbush to Chalmers, June 18, 1934, N.R.A. Box 660; R. M. Gates to Chalmers, Aug. 13, 1934, N.R.A. Box 654; Second Session of National Council, Aug. 28–31, 1934, Brown Collection; Report and Proposals on Code for Automobile Manufacturing Industry by L.A.B., Sept. 10, 1934, N.R.A. Box 657.

3 Green to Johnson, Aug. 11, 1934, N.R.A. Box 654; N.R.A. Notice of Hearing: No. 35-B, Aug. 17, 1934, *ibid.;* N.R.A. Release No. 7319, Aug. 18, 1934; Green to U.A.W., Aug. 28, 1934, Green Letterbooks; Brown to Chapin *et al.*, Aug. 29, 1934, and attached letter to Johnson, T. J. Ross to Chapin, and attached documents, Chapin Papers; *New York Times*, Aug. 26, 1934.

4 Memo by K. Johnston, Aug. 30, [1934], O.F. 466, Box 3, Roosevelt Library; Memo for the President by M. H. M[cIntyre], Aug. 31, [1934], O.F. 466, Box 7, *ibid.; Codes*, XVI (Washington, 1934), 223–24; *Detroit News*, Aug. 31, Sept. 1, 1934; *New York Times*, Sept. 1, 1934.

5 *The Secret Diary of Harold L. Ickes. The First Thousand Days, 1933–1936* (New York, 1953), p. 195.

6 *New York Times*, Oct. 26, Nov. 1, 1934.

7 Chalmers to Gustav Peck, Sept. 10, 1934, N.R.A. Box 654; Memorandum by Chalmers, Sept. 13, 1934, *ibid.;* Report and Proposals on Code by L.A.B., Sept. 10, 1934, N.R.A. Box 657; Memorandum by Gates, Oct. 19, 1934, *ibid.* The minimum wage in the new proposals was set at 70 cents for workers engaged in direct production and 60 cents for all others.

8 L.A.B. to Hillman, Oct., 1934, N.R.A. Box 662.

9 There were 46 guaranteed wage plans in effect in 1933, but they were mainly confined to the consumer nondurable goods industries and to retail and wholesale trade. B.L.S., *Guaranteed Wage Plans in the United States, Bulletin No. 925* (Washington, 1948), p. 7; Don A. Seastone, "The History of Guaranteed Wages and Employment," *Journal of Economic History*, XV (1955), 142.

10 Executive Assistant, Division II to Lynch, Oct. 15, 1934, N.R.A. Box 34; Green to N.I.R.B., Oct. 24, 1934, N.R.A. Box 660; [Sloan, Brown, and Chrysler] memorandum, Nov. 1, 1934, N.R.A. Box 661; N.I.R.B. Minutes, Nov. 1, 1934, N.R.A. Box 8448; Press Conference No. 147, Oct. 3, 1934, pp. 100–101, Roosevelt Library; Report of Delegation of the U.A.W. Conference at . . . the White House, [Mar., 1934], Francis Papers; *New York Times*, Oct. 26, Nov. 3, 1934, Jan. 29, 1935; *Detroit Free Press*, Oct. 26, Nov. 2, 1934. Matthew Josephson states that Hillman suggested the establishment of "a commission of inquiry" in a conference with Roosevelt on Nov. 9. The code, of course, had already been renewed by then. If Hillman did suggest the inquiry, it was when he saw the President on Nov. 2, just prior to Roosevelt's announcement of the code's renewal. Josephson, *Sidney Hillman*, p. 376; *New York Times*, Nov. 3, 1934.

11 *Automotive Daily News*, Nov. 3, 1934; *Business Week*, Nov. 10, 1934, p. 7; *News-Week*, IV (Nov. 10, 1934), 6; *Iron Age*, CXXXIV (Nov. 8, 1934), 74; *Codes*, XVIII (Washington, 1934), 495–96; *New York Times*, Nov. 2, 3, 1934; Roosevelt to Green and Macauley, Nov. 2, 1934, O.F. 466, Box 7, F.D.R. Library. This was the first time that the President had personally announced the extension of a code.

12 Green to Roosevelt, Nov. 10, 1934, Green Letterbooks; *Automotive Daily News*, Nov. 3, 1934; *News-Week*, IV (Nov. 10, 1934), 6; Hall to Martin, Nov. 5, 1934, Martin to Hall, Nov. 9, 23, 1934, Martin Papers.

13 Roosevelt to Green and Macauley, Nov. 2, 1934, O.F. 466, Box 7, Roosevelt Library; N.A.C.C. General Bulletin No. G-1648, Oct. 20, 1933, Acc. 203, Box 13, Ford Archives.

14 Edward J. Stevens, "A Quarter of a Century of Progress in Employment Stabilization in the Automobile Industry" (1947), pp. 20–27. The Packard Plan called for an estimate of the probable annual production of Packard cars one year in advance and the manufacture of $\frac{1}{12}$ of this total each month. Packard dealers stored most of the vehicles, and, in addition, the company erected warehousing facilities in Detroit and leased storage space in New York and Chicago. The company assumed the cost of price reductions required to move dealer surpluses. This factor, plus the high value of a Packard agency, induced the dealers to co-operate. The fact that the Packard design was relatively standardized at the time and that only minor changes were made in the model from year to year were favorable to the success of the plan. *Ibid.*, pp. 24–26.

15 *Ibid.*, pp. 28–29.

16 *Ibid.*, p. 32; Leonard Kuvin, "Effect of N.R.A. on the Physical Volume of Production," *Journal of the American Statistical Association*, XXXI (Mar., 1936), 60; Cronin interview; A.M.A., *Stabilization of Employment in the Automobile Industry* (Feb. 25, 1936); C. Parker Anderson, "Regularization of Employment and Incomes in the Automobile Industry" (1946), MS in Bureau of Industrial Relations Library, University of Michigan; Henderson Report, pp. 8–9.

17 Report of Continuous Employment Committee, Nov. 14, 1933, Bureau of Industrial Relations Library, University of Michigan; Stevens, "Progress in Employment Stabilization," p. 33; Measures to Provide More Stable and Continuous Employment in the Automobile Manufacturing Industry. A Report to the Administrator of the N.R.A., Dec. 1, 1933, by the N.A.C.C., N.R.A. Box 662.

18 Measures to Provide More Stable Employment, pp. 1–3, 6–7, 9, N.R.A. Box 662; Committee Report on Stabilizing Employment, [Dec. 5, 1934], Stephen M. DuBrul Papers (in Mr. DuBrul's possession); A.M.A. General Bulletin No. G-1731, Feb. 1, 1935, Exhibit Y, Auto Code History, N.R.A. Box 7575; "Automotive Industry Preliminary Summary of Findings," N.R.A. Box 662.

19 Analysis of the Factors Involved in Determining the Theoretical Ideal Date for Introducing New Annual Passenger Car Models, [1934?], Bureau of Industrial Relations Library, University of Michigan. DuBrul concluded that on the average, a new model announcement raised sales in the month of the announcement by 43 per cent above the average seasonal trend for that month, and by 37 per cent in the second month after the announcement. By the fourth month after the announcement, the new model appeared to generate no additional sales, and by the month before the announcement of another new model, sales were only two-thirds of the normal seasonal level for that month. *Ibid.*, pp. 1–2.

20 Measures to Provide More Stable Employment, pp. 5, 8–9, N.R.A. Box 662; Theoretical Ideal Date, p. 4, Bureau of Industrial Relations Library, University of Michigan; Stevens, "Progress in Employment Stabilization," pp. 8–13, *ibid.*; Anderson, "Regularization of Employment," pp. 22–30; Herman Feldman, *Stabilizing Jobs and Wages through Better Business Management* (New York, 1940), p. 106.

21 Committee Report on Stabilizing Employment, Dec. 5, 1934, DuBrul Papers; Exhibit Y, Auto Code History, N.R.A. Box 7575. Both Chrysler and Nash built up "banks" of unit parts during the winter of 1934–35 in an effort to provide work during a slack period. Nash estimated that the policy aided about half of its employees. *Automotive Daily News*, Jan. 19, 1935; *Detroit Free Press*, May 2, 1935.

22 Measures to Provide More Stable Employment, pp. 9–11, N.R.A. Box 662.

23 *Ibid.*, pp. 3–5; Henderson Report, p. 21. In the Henderson Report it was

argued that the seasonal adjustment of prices would, on the contrary, tend to freeze prices and competitive relationships since price adjustments would have to be concerted and uniform. *Ibid.*, pp. 19–20. Individual manufacturers, of course, sometimes reduced the prices on old models just before their new models were introduced.

24 Measures to Provide More Stable Employment, p. 3, N.R.A. Box 662; *Detroit News*, May 9, 1934; *Automotive Daily News*, May 12, 1934.

25 *Automotive Industries*, LXXI (Nov. 17, 1934), 598–99; *ibid.*, LXXI (Nov. 24, 1934), 629; *Automotive Daily News*, Nov. 24, 1934; Committee Report on Stabilizing Employment, [Dec. 5, 1934], DuBrul Papers; Exhibit Y, Auto Code History, N.R.A. Box 7575; release from office of F.W.A. Vesper, Dec. 12, 1934, N.R.A. Box 7682.

26 G.M., in Mar. 1940, adopted a separation-allowance plan for its salaried workers. Feldman, *Stabilizing Jobs*, p. 255.

27 A.M.A., *Study of Plans for Providing Security from Unemployment* (Oct., 1934), pp. 12–15, A.M.A. Files; Chalmers to Peck, Jan. 4, 1933 [1934], N.R.A. Box 662.

28 Seltzer to L.A.B., Dec. 22, 1933, N.R.A. Box 657.

29 A plan to hold the principal automobile shows in Nov. 1933 had to be called off because several N.A.C.C. members thought that the work that still had to be done on the new models made this "practically impossible." Lea to Reeves, Sept. 22, 1933, Seltzer to Peck, Jan. 3, 1934, N.R.A. Box 656.

30 The annual layoff rate for all manufacturing in 1934 was 36.26; the annual total separation rate, 49.17; and the annual accession rate, 56.91. Byer and Anker, "A Review of Factory Labor Turn-Over, 1930 to 1936," *Monthly Labor Review*, XLV (July, 1937), 157–58.

31 I am not at liberty to divulge the source of this information or to identify the company.

32 Item dealing with this question in DuBrul Papers; Scoville, *Behavior of the Automobile Industry in Depression*, p. 22.

33 Kuvin, "Effect of N.R.A.," p. 60; Committee Report on Stabilizing Employment, [Dec. 5, 1934], DuBrul Papers. I am not at liberty to identify the source of the quotation.

34 Exhibit Y, Auto Code History, N.R.A. Box 7575.

35 *Ibid.*; Stevens, "Progress in Employment Stabilization," pp. 35–36.

36 Dillon to Roosevelt, Nov. 6, 1934, Arthur J. Altmeyer to McIntyre, Nov. 20, 1934, Roosevelt to Williams, Nov. 21, 1934 (italics added), O.F. 466, Box 7, Roosevelt Library.

37 Schlesinger, Jr., *Coming of the New Deal*, pp. 158–59; Joseph Alsop and Robert Kintner, *Men around the President* (New York, 1939), pp. 98–100; *Detroit News*, Dec. 13, 1934; A.M.A. General Bulletin No. G-1725, Dec. 3, 1934, Acc. 203, Box 6, Ford Archives.

38 Memorandum from Henderson to N.I.R.B., Jan. 23, 1935, in Henderson Report; Memorandum from Henderson to N.I.R.B., Feb. 1, 1935, N.R.A. Box 656; *Detroit News*, Dec. 15, 17, 1934.

39 Dillon to National Council, Dec. 8, 1934, Dillon to U.A.W., Dec. 11, 1934, Dillon File; Dillon to Henderson, N.R.A. Box 661; Green to Dillon, Dec. 14, 1934, Green to Spencer Cope, Dec. 27, 1934, Green Letterbooks; questionnaires sent to M.E.S.A. locals in Detroit, Brown Collection; Henderson Report, Exhibit 18; William E. Dennison to Roosevelt, Feb. 6, 1935, O.F. 102-A-B-C, Box 2,

Roosevelt Library; Hearing on Regularizing Employment and Otherwise Improving the Conditions of Labor in the Automobile Industry, Detroit, Dec. 15, 16, 1934, *passim,* N.R.A. Box 7265; *Detroit Labor News,* Dec. 7, 1934; *Detroit Free Press,* Nov. 25, Dec. 5, 1934.

40 A.M.A. Bulletin, Dec. 12, 1934, Acc. 203, Box 6, Ford Archives; J. C[rawford] to N.R.A., Dec. 12, 1934, Acc. 203, Box 9, *ibid.;* Lepine to Henderson, Dec. 18, 1934, N.R.A. Box 656; Brown to Henderson, Dec. 28, 1934, N.R.A. Box 661; Reeves to Henderson, Jan. 5, 1935, N.R.A. Box 677; Reeves to Henderson, Jan. 10, 1935, N.R.A. Box 7674; DuBrul interview, Apr. 9, 1957; Cronin interview; Lansburgh to Henderson, Jan. 4, 1935, N.R.A. Box 7682; "Contacts with Automobile Manufacturers . . . ," undated, Henderson Papers, Roosevelt Library.

41 Memorandum from Richberg to McIntyre, Dec. 6, 1934, O.F. 466, Box 10, Roosevelt Library; [Henderson], "Dec. 8, 1934," Henderson Papers.

42 Hearing on Regularizing Employment, Detroit, Dec. 15, 16, 1934, N.R.A. Box 7265; *Detroit Free Press,* Dec. 16, 1934. The Flint hearings of Dec. 17–18 were jointly conducted by Weiss and Kelly. There are transcripts of all the hearings in N.R.A. Boxes 7265 and 7266.

43 Weiss to Henderson, Jan. 7, 1935, N.R.A. Box 7281; Kelly to Henderson, undated, N.R.A. Box 7682.

44 *Ibid.;* Green to Henderson, Jan. 14, 1935, and attached Memorandum on Conditions in the Automobile Industry as They Affect Employment, N.R.A. Box 660; Hearing on Regularizing Employment, Detroit, Dec. 15, 16, 1934, pp. 108, 205, 237; Flint, Dec. 17, 18, 1934, p. 93; St. Louis, Dec. 28, 29, 1934, p. 332; South Bend, Jan. 2, 3, 1935, pp. 14, 114, N.R.A. Boxes 7265, 7266. The industry's rebuttal of these charges is contained in Analysis and Comments on 'Preliminary Report . . . ,' Feb. 23, 1935, Pearson Papers.

45 Weiss to Henderson, Jan. 7, 1935, N.R.A. Box 7281; Kelly to Henderson, undated, N.R.A. Box 7682.

46 For this material, see N.R.A. Boxes 7674 and 7682.

47 Henderson to Roosevelt, Jan. 23, 1935, O.F. 466, Box 7, Roosevelt Library; Memorandum from Henderson to N.I.R.B., Jan. 23, 1935, in Henderson Report; *ibid.,* Summary, p. 10. The report consisted of a summary of 12 pages, a main body of 74 pages, and 32 exhibits.

48 Henderson Report, *passim.* The report did not consider the merits of a modern-sounding suggestion, contained in a tentative outline for the study, that each company should place "a substantial amount" in a fund in addition to the wages paid to the workers during the months of peak production, with the money to be used for payments to the workers during the period of their layoff. H.B.D., Tentative Outline for Study of Regularization of Employment and Earnings in Automobile and Automobile Parts Industries, Dec. 6, 1934, N.R.A. Box 7682.

49 *New York Times,* Feb. 8, 9, 1935; Cronin to Chapin, Feb. 15, 1935 (two letters), Chapin Papers.

50 P. Johnson to Williams, Feb. 19, 1935, Exhibit K, Auto Code History, N.R.A. Box 7575.

51 Cameron, "Three Questions," in *A Series of Talks Given on the Ford Sunday Evening Hour by W. J. Cameron, 1934–1936* (Dearborn, 1936), pp. 80–82.

52 Analysis and Comments on 'Preliminary Report . . . ,' Feb. 23, 1935, Pearson Papers; Cronin to All Cos. Subject to Automobile Manufacturing Code, Mar. 4, 1935, Acc. 203, Box 6, Ford Archives; A.M.A. General Bulletin No. G-1744, Apr. 12, 1935, *ibid.* The Feb. 23 report did serve as the basis for a public state-

ment by Knudsen that was highly critical of the Henderson Report. *Detroit Free Press,* Feb. 24, 1934.

⁵³ Ogburn to Henderson, Feb. 8, 1935, Henderson Papers; Memorandum from Peck to W. Averell Harriman, Feb. 8, 1935, N.R.A. Box 662. I am not at liberty to divulge the name of the automobile company staff member.

⁵⁴ During the 1920's the employment of the unskilled and semiskilled in the automobile industry increased by 39 per cent, but the number of employees over 45 years of age increased by 51.3 per cent and the proportion of such employees by 8.8 per cent. The A.M.A. pointed out that if the automobile industry had followed the pattern of other manufacturing industries—there was normally a reduction in the proportion of employees over 45 in industries that were growing rapidly—the number of employees in the industry over 45 should have increased by only 28.5 per cent and the proportion of such employees should have decreased by 7.1 per cent. Data for two companies (G.M. and Chrysler?) that accounted for 63 per cent of the industry's employment in 1934 indicated that the percentage of employees of Co. A aged 40 or over increased from 26.6 on Oct. 1, 1930, to 31.3 on Jan. 1, 1933, and of Co. B from 30.3 to 33.9 for the same dates. A.M.A., Analysis of Factory Employee Age as Related to Industry Growth, Aug., 1935, N.R.A. Box 661; Analysis and Comments on 'Preliminary Report...,' Feb. 23, 1935, Pearson Papers. It does not appear that automobile companies in the 1930's made it a practice to discharge older employees, but job applicants over 40 years of age may have been at a disadvantage as compared to younger workers when hiring was underway. For examples of errors in the report with regard to workers displaced by technological improvements, see *ibid.*, and *Detroit Free Press,* Feb. 24, 1935.

⁵⁵ *Historical Statistics,* pp. 600–601. The industry pointed out that it required more man hours of labor to build a Chevrolet in 1935 than in 1929 and that the total hours of labor per average low-priced car in the body plants in 1935 were in excess of the 1929 figure, but since the 1935 car and the 1935 body were not strictly comparable to their 1929 counterparts, the figures cited by the industry do not in themselves indicate a decline in productivity per man hour. Spurgeon Bell did, however, conclude that productivity per man hour in the industry was less in 1934 than in 1933. Analysis and Comments on 'Preliminary Report...,' Feb. 23, 1935, Pearson Papers; *Detroit Free Press,* Feb. 24, 1935; Bell, *Productivity, Wages, and National Income,* p. 289.

⁵⁶ Analysis and Comments on 'Preliminary Report...,' Feb. 23, 1935, Pearson Papers; Memorandum from Peck to Harriman, Feb. 8, 1935, N.R.A. Box 662.

⁵⁷ Clark, "The A.F. of L.," p. 90; Green to Roosevelt, Jan. 17, 1935, O.F. 466, Box 7, Roosevelt Library.

⁵⁸ *New York Times,* Jan. 22, 24, 25, 30, 1935; *Detroit News,* Jan. 25, 1935; Ogburn to Roosevelt, Jan. 28, 1935, O.F. 466, Box 7, Roosevelt Library; Proposed Labor Provisions for Automobile Manufacturing Industry, Jan. 21, 1935, N.R.A. Box 658; Brief Supporting Labor Proposals for Revision of Code for Automobile Manufacturing Industry Submitted by: William Green..., *ibid.* The L.A.B. was willing to settle for somewhat less favorable code terms than are indicated above. W. E. C[halmers], "Confidential-Hillman, Jan. 16, 1934 [1935]," N.R.A. Box 658.

⁵⁹ N.I.R.B. Memorandum, Jan. 24, 1935, N.R.A. Box 662.

⁶⁰ N.I.R.B. to Roosevelt, Jan. 28, 1935, Exhibit J, Auto Code History, N.R.A. Box 7575.

61 Memorandum for Richberg by Roosevelt, Jan. 15, 1935, O.F. 466, Box 7, Roosevelt Library; *New York Times,* Jan. 20, 1935; *Detroit News,* Feb. 1, 1935; Richberg to George Berry, Jan. 9, 1935, Richberg Papers, Library of Congress. Francis Biddle has stated in his memoirs that he did not regard the influence of Richberg on the President as "healthy." *In Brief Authority,* p. 35.

62 Berry to Richberg, Jan. 21, 1935, Richberg Papers; Berry to Roosevelt, Jan. 29, 1935, O.F. 466, Box 7, Roosevelt Library.

63 Wolman interview; *New York Times,* Jan. 31, 1935; Final Report of A.L.B., Appendices A and B. The membership figures for Jan. 1935 were made available to me by the Bookkeeping Dept. of the old A.F. of L. on Aug. 17, 1955. There were approximately 426,000 workers in the main and parts plants in Jan. 1935. Tolles and LaFever, "Wages ... in the Motor Vehicle Industry, 1934," *Monthly Labor Review,* XLII (Mar., 1936), 529, 535.

64 *New York Times,* Feb. 1, 7, 1935; *Detroit News,* Jan. 31, Feb. 1, 1935; N.I.R.B. Minutes, Feb. 11, 1935, N.R.A. Box 8448; Raymond Gram Swing, "The White House Breaks with Labor," *Nation,* CXL (Feb. 13, 1935), 181; Swing, "Pursuing a Prevarication," *ibid.,* CXL (Feb. 27, 1935), 241; *Codes,* XXI (Washington, 1935), 203. The N.I.R.B. reportedly voted 3-2 against extension of the code, but W. Averell Harriman, the N.R.A. administrative officer, later stated that the N.I.R.B. was behind Roosevelt "to a man" in his decision to extend the code. *New York Times,* Feb. 9, 1935.

65 *New York Times,* Feb. 1, 1935; *Detroit News,* Feb. 1, 1935; *Codes,* XXII, 204; interview with Alfred Reeves, Feb. 6, 1957; P. Johnson interview.

66 *Codes,* XXI, 204; *Detroit News,* Feb. 1, 1935; Myrick, Jr., *et al.,* "Economic Survey," Section Three, p. 52, N.R.A. Box 8309; Donaldson Brown to author, Sept. 19, 1957; *New York Times,* Feb. 4, 1935.

67 *Codes,* XXI, 204; Memoranda from Richberg to McIntyre, Feb. 2, 1935, O.F. 466, Box 7, Roosevelt Library; Roosevelt to Ogburn, Feb. 4, 1935, *ibid.* The President himself had referred to the settlement on Mar. 27, 1934, as simply an "informal agreement." Press Conference No. 109, p. 5, Roosevelt Library. The counsel of Section II of the N.R.A. held that the N.I.R.A. authorized the President to enter into agreements with employer and employee representatives and that the settlement was a tripartite agreement that one party could not terminate without the consent of the other two. Analysis by Angus Roy Shannon of the President's Settlement, Mar. 21, 1935, N.R.A. Box 658.

68 Strictly speaking, the President had not promised to discuss the code with the A. F. of L. before renewal. In his letter to Green of Nov. 2, he had stated that he would discuss the impending Henderson inquiry with the A.F. of L., and in his letter to Williams of Nov. 21, he had said that the interested parties should be given an opportunity to review the Henderson Report before action was taken on it. These promises, neither of which was kept, fell short of a commitment to consult on the code itself.

69 *New York Times,* Feb. 1–5, 1935; Subcommittee of Senate Committee on Judiciary, *Thirty-Hour Work Week, Hearings on S. 87,* 76 Cong., 1 Sess. (Washington, 1935), p. 27; *News-Week,* V (Feb. 9, 1935), 10; *Flint Weekly Review,* Feb. 8, 1935; telegrams from U.A.W. federal labor unions to Roosevelt, N.R.A. Box 661. Richberg, in defense of his action, declared that the A.F. of L. had indicated its position in the Henderson hearings and, at all events, could not claim to represent the mass of the auto workers. The code provisions regarding regularization and an overtime rate, he noted, benefited labor, and so there was

no reason to suppose that had the A.F. of L. been consulted, it would have opposed these terms. As for the A.L.B., its elections, Richberg insisted, were showing whom the workers wished to represent them. *New York Times,* Feb. 4, 1935; *Detroit Free Press,* Feb. 4, 1935.

[70] Press Conference No. 180, Feb. 1, 1935, pp. 82–83, 90, Roosevelt Library.

[71] *Daily Worker,* Feb. 4, 5, 7, 8, 1935; Communist party handbill, C.S. 182-106; Memorandum by Matthew Smith and Maurice Sugar, Feb. 1, 1935, Brown Collection.

[72] Pickering to Martin, Feb. 1, 1935, Martin Papers. See also *Racine Day,* Feb. 15, 1935.

[73] *New York Times,* Jan. 31, Feb. 1, 3, 5, 1935; *Nation,* CXL (Feb. 20, 1935), 208–9. Similar views were expressed in the *New Republic,* LXXXII (Feb. 13, 1935), 19; *News-Week,* IV (Feb. 16, 1935), 10; and *Business Week,* Feb. 9, 1935, p. 5.

[74] Memo for McIntyre by K, Feb. 6, 1935, O.F. 142, Box 1, Roosevelt Library; Berry to McIntyre, Feb. 11, 1935, *ibid.*

[75] Green to Roosevelt, Feb. 11, 1935, *ibid.; New York Times,* Feb. 12, 1935; *Detroit Free Press,* Feb. 12, 1935; Frey Reminiscences, p. 560, Oral History Research Office, Columbia University.

[76] Press Conference No. 182, Feb. 8, 1935, p. 100, Roosevelt Library.

NOTES TO CHAPTER XII

[1] Bernstein, *New Deal Collective Bargaining Policy,* pp. 89–99, 112.

[2] Ogburn, . . . Amalgamated Association of Street and Electric Railway Employees of America . . . vs. Twin City Rapid Transit Co. . . . , Brief for Complainants, Case 246, N.L.B. Drawer 41; Ogburn, Reply Brief for Complainants . . . , *ibid.;* Ogburn, Brief in Behalf of U.A.W. F.L.U. No. 18347 . . . , [May, 1935], A.F. of L. Strike File, Local 18347; Matthew Woll, *Labor, Industry and Government* (New York, 1935), pp 82–83.

[3] Senate Committee on Education and Labor, *National Labor Relations Board, Hearings on S. 1958,* 74 Cong., 1 Sess. (Washington, 1935), pp. 43–44, 81, 117, 120, 127, 151, 162–63, 181–82; House Committee on Labor, *Labor Disputes Act,* pp. 205–6, 244–56. See Sumner H. Slichter, "The Government and Collective Bargaining," *Annals of the American Academy of Political and Social Science,* CLXXVIII (Mar., 1935), 113; R. W. Fleming, "The Significance of the Wagner Act," in Derber and Young, eds., *Labor and the New Deal,* p. 145; and D. O. Bowman, *Public Control of Labor Relations* (New York, 1942), p. 157. In France, Val R. Lorwin has pointed out, "Exclusive representation by the majority union . . . would violate the real scruples of a minority's political and religious beliefs," but in the U.S., where unions are "job oriented and not essentially political or religious in attachment. . . . it has been possible to sacrifice the rights of dissenters to effective collective bargaining." "Reflections on the History of the French and American Labor Movements," *Journal of Economic History,* XVII (Mar., 1957), 38.

[4] Senate Committee on Education and Labor, *N.L.R.B.,* pp. 607–13; Reeves to Roosevelt, Apr. 5, 1935, O.F. 102-A (1935), Roosevelt Library; *New York Times,* Apr. 10, 1935; Chapin to Couzens, May 15, 1935, Chapin Papers; A.M.A., *A Menace to the Automobile Business and to All Industry and Trade* (New York, 1935). For the arguments for and against the Wagner Bill, see Bernstein, *New*

Deal Collective Bargaining Policy, pp. 100–109; and Fine, "Government and Labor Relations during the New Deal," *Current History,* LVII (Sept., 1959), 143.

⁵ Reeves to Roosevelt, Apr. 5, 1935, O.F. 102-A (1935), Roosevelt Library; A.M.A. General Bulletins No. G-1742, Apr. 5, 1935, No. G-1751, May 20, 1935, Acc. 203, Box 6, Ford Archives; Chapin to Henry Ittleson, May 10, 1935, Reeves to A.M.A. Members, May 6, 1935 (and enclosures), C. A. Oostdyk to Chapin, May 13, 1935, Chapin to Reeves, May 17, 1935, Reeves to Chapin, May 22, 1935, and attached copies of letters from Reeves to Couzens and Vandenberg, Chapin Papers; "Suggested points to be made . . . ," [May 16[?], 1935], *ibid.;* Bernstein, *New Deal Collective Bargaining Policy,* p. 116.

⁶ *Senate Report No. 573,* 74 Cong., 1 Sess., p. 13; *House Report No. 1147,* 74 Cong., 1 Sess., pp. 20–22; Bernstein, *New Deal Collective Bargaining Policy,* pp. 118, 126–27.

⁷ [Chalmers], "Strike Plans. Sept. 1, 1934," Brown Collection; Dillon to U.A.W., Nov. 8, 1934, Dillon to National Council, Nov. 8, 1934, Green to Dillon, Nov. 12, 1934, Martin Papers; Dillon to Green, Nov. 13, 1934, Green to Dillon, Nov. 20, 1934, Dillon File.

⁸ Dillon to U.A.W., Jan. 30, 1935, Dillon File; N.R.A. Release No. 9878, Jan. 30, 1935; copy of remarks by Dillon, attached to Chalmers to H. L. Brunson, Feb. 8, 1934 [1935], N.R.A. Box 658; *Detroit Labor News,* Feb. 8, 1935. Dillon was provided with an opportunity to apply his policy of militancy on Jan. 31 when 46 wet sanders, who quickly joined the A.F. of L., walked out of the Lansing Fisher Body plant in protest against an alleged speed-up and after having failed to secure a wage increase. The management refused to rehire the strikers, but the federal labor union in the plant, although threatening to strike in support of the sanders, took no more drastic action than to request the aid of a Department of Labor conciliator. The strike soon came to an unsuccessful close. *Detroit News,* Jan. 31, Feb. 1, 3, 5, 7, 8, 11, 1935; Pilkington to Kerwin, Feb. 23, 1935, C.S. 182-199. Two hundred maintenance men, who were members of F.L.U. No. 18276, walked out of the Murray Body plant in Detroit on Jan. 31 after failing to secure a wage increase, but the strike collapsed the next day. Pilkington to Kerwin, Feb. 23, 1935, C.S. 182-198.

⁹ *New York Times,* Feb. 18, 1935; Dillon press release, Feb. 20, 1935, Dillon File; *Detroit Labor News,* Feb. 22, Mar. 1, 1935; *Detroit News,* Feb. 23, 1935.

¹⁰ Minutes of Third Meeting of National Council . . . , Feb. 23–Mar. 2, 1935, Labadie Collection; Dillon press release, Feb. 26, 1935.

¹¹ Green to Reeves, Feb. 27, 1935, Green Letterbooks; Reeves to Green, Mar. 7, 1935, N.R.A. Box 661.

¹² *New York Times,* Mar. 9, 10, 1935; Dillon press release, Mar. 9, 1935, Dillon File; *Detroit Labor News,* Mar. 15, 1935; Green to Chapin (and identical letters to other automobile manufacturers), Mar. 18, 1935, John T. Smith to Green, Apr. 17, 1935, Green Letterbooks.

¹³ *New York Times,* Apr. 10, 1935; *Daily Worker,* Jan. 30, Feb. 25, Mar. 1, 4, 5, 12, 1935; *Labor Digest,* Mar. 15, Apr. 5, 1935; Spisak to Green, Feb. 27, 1935, A.F. of L. Strike File, Local 18614; Minutes of F.L.U. No. 18331, Mar. 14, 1935, Francis Papers; *New Militant,* Feb. 9, 16, 1935.

¹⁴ Dillon to National Council, Mar. 5, 1935, Martin Papers; Dillon to Roosevelt, Mar. 25, 1935, Dillon File; *Detroit News,* Aug. 1, 1935.

¹⁵ On the factional fight, see *Detroit News,* Apr. 1, 4, 1935. The principal

cause for the strike was the company's institution of a group bonus wage plan without consulting the workers. The strike settlement provided that the company, within 30 days, would work out a wage payment plan satisfactory to the workers, that 5 unionists who had been discharged would be rehired, and that management would "recognize and negotiate in a practical way" with the union's bargaining committee. *Detroit News*, Apr. 5, 7, 9, 10, 12, 1935; Dillon press release, Apr. 9, 1935, Labadie Collection; *Detroit Labor News*, Apr. 12, 1935; Dillon to Green, Apr. 11, 12, 1935, A.F. of L. Strike File, Local 18698; "Facts Concerning the Strike of Hupmobile Workers," handbill in Brown Collection.

16 Wood to Dillon, Apr. 6, 1935, Dillon to Wood, Apr. 10, 1935, Martin Papers.

17 Green to Shipley, Feb. 7, 1935, A.F. of L. Strike File, Local 18347; Executive Council Minutes, Apr. 30–May 7, 1935, Auto Workers File, 1935–1937, A.F. of L.-C.I.O. Archives; *Automotive Industries*, LXXII (Mar. 9, 1935), 337, 344; *Iron Age*, CXXXV (Mar. 7, 1935), 37.

18 The Studebaker local was, at the time, discussing with the management an agreement that included a clause forbidding a strike or a lockout while the agreement was in effect. The local thought that the company would sign the agreement if it could be given assurances that it would be excepted from any general automobile strike that might be called. Green informed the local that the A.F. of L. treated agreements as sacred and inviolate, and he asked Dillon to aid the local in negotiating the contract. Alton A. Green to W. Green, Mar. 5, 1935, W. Green to A. Green, Mar. 6, 1935, Dillon to W. Green, A.F. of L. Strike File, Local 18310. Dillon advised the Columbus Auto Parts local to disregard the instructions for a strike vote since it had a signed agreement with the management. Dillon to W. H. Wilson, Mar. 8, 1935, Roberts Papers. Dillon later indicated that Nash and Studebaker would not be affected by the strike vote. *New York Times*, Apr. 10, 1935.

19 Madden to Green, Mar. 2, 1935, A.F. of L. Strike File, Local 18785; Martin to Dillon, Feb. 9, Mar. 28, 1935, Dillon to Martin, Apr. 19, 1935, Martin Papers; Dewey and Chappell to the Secretary [Perkins], Jan. 19, 1935, C.S. 182-106. The total paid-up membership of the Flint U.A.W. locals as of Oct. 24, 1934, was 528. Dillon to Cook, Nov. 13, 1934, and attached "Membership Statement," Oct, 24, 1934, Francis Papers.

20 Kleinert to Martin, Dec. 11, 1934, Pieper to Martin, Mar. 19, Apr. 12, 1935, Pieper to National Council, Mar. 25, 1935, Pieper to Dillon, Apr. 11, 1935, Martin Papers.

21 Pieper thought that the Janesville, Norwood, Kansas City, St. Louis, and Atlanta plants could be closed.

22 Martin to Dillon, May 16, 1935, Martin Papers. For a detailed account of the Toledo strike, see Sidney Fine, "The Toledo Chevrolet Strike of 1935," *Ohio Historical Quarterly*, LXVII (Oct., 1958), 326–56.

23 Chalmers' analysis of the Toledo strike, Apr. 24, 1935, MS in Brown Collection; *Toledo News-Bee*, Apr. 23, 1935; Dillon to Green, June 11, 1935, A.F. of L. Strike File, Local 18384; Williams to Kerwin, Apr. 27, 1935, C.S. 182-370. The chairman of the strike committee did not recall having received any advice from Dillon prior to the calling of the strike. Oral History Interview of James Roland, Sept. 25, 1960, pp. 13–14, Michigan Historical Collections.

24 Muste's Workers Party of the United States claimed its men held 7 of 12 union positions. *New Militant*, May 25, 1935. The Workers party had been

formed by a merger of Muste's old American Workers party and the Trotskyite Communist League of America.

25 Chalmers, "Collective Bargaining," XII, 3–4; *Toledo Blade*, Apr. 26, 1935; *New Militant*, Apr. 13, 1935; Oral History Interview of Joseph B. Ditzel, Sept. 25, 1960, p. 2, Michigan Historical Collections. The average hourly wage of Toledo Chevrolet employees in Apr. 1935 was 69.6 cents as compared to a national average for the industry of 72.8 cents. *Toledo Blade*, Apr. 19, 1935; Myrick, Jr., *et al.*, "Economic Survey of the Automobile Industry" (1936), Section Three, p. 52, N.R.A. Box 8309. For membership in the local and in the Chevrolet plant, see George Addes to Green, Aug. 6, 1935, C.I.O. Historical File, Reel 1, A.F. of L.-C.I.O. Archives.

26 A. J. Muste, *The Automobile Industry and Organized Labor* (Baltimore, [1936]), pp 40–41; Chalmers' analysis, Apr. 24, 1935, Brown Collection; Chalmers, "Collective Bargaining," XII, 3; Final Report of A.L.B., Appendices A, B; *Toledo Blade*, Apr. 10, 1935. In the nominating election, 508 voters expressed no affiliation for their candidate, and 101 voters designated their candidate as affiliated with the company union. The company union did not receive enough votes in the primary, according to A.L.B. rules, to entitle it to representation on the bargaining agency.

27 *Toledo Blade*, Apr. 16, 19, 20, 1935; Chalmers, "Collective Bargaining," XII, 6; Chalmers' analysis, May 16, 1935, Brown Collection.

28 *Toledo News-Bee*, Apr. 22, 1935. The union's demands and the company's counterproposals are given in full in *Automotive Industries*, LXXII (May 4, 1935), 613–14. See also G.M., Labor Relations Diary, Section 1, pp. 55–56; Chalmers, "Collective Bargaining," XII, 7–8; and *Toledo Blade*, Apr. 9, 1935. The union requested a minimum wage of 70 cents per hour and a minimum increase of 5 cents per hour for each employee. The company, pointing out that the minimum wage requested represented a 40 per cent increase, offered a blanket 5 per cent increase.

29 *Toledo News-Bee*, Apr. 22, 29, 1935; *Toledo Blade*, Apr. 22, 1935; *Union Leader* (Toledo), Apr. 26, 1935; Chalmers' analysis, Apr. 24, 1935, Brown Collection; Chalmers, "Collective Bargaining," XII, 5; G.M., Labor Relations Diary, Section 1, p. 55; Roland interview, p. 13, Michigan Historical Collections.

30 *Toledo Blade*, Apr. 23, 1935; *Toledo News-Bee*, Apr. 23, 1935; Chalmers, "Collective Bargaining," XII, 8–9; G.M., Labor Relations Diary, Section 1, p. 56.

31 *Toledo Blade*, Apr. 23, 24, 26, 1935; *Toledo News-Bee*, Apr. 23, 26, 1935; *Strike Truth*, Apr. 26, 1935; Williams to Kerwin, Apr. 30, 1935, C.S. 182-370.

32 La Follette *Hearings*, Part 5, pp. 1511–14, 1518–22; Part 6, pp. 1914–15, 1970–73, 2073–75; La Follette *Report No. 46*, Part 3, pp. 71–73; La Follette *Report No. 6*, Part 3, p. 73.

33 The executive shop committee was transformed into a strike committee once the strike was under way.

34 Roland was discharged on Mar. 28, 1934, allegedly for poor workmanship and for leaving his job without permission. He set up a one-man picket line in protest and was eventually given another job in the plant after the A.L.B. had converted his discharge into a disciplinary layoff. Decision #22; *New Militant*, June 1, 1935.

35 *New Militant*, Apr. 27, May 4, 11, 1935; *Detroit News*, May 12, 1935; J. A. Wilson to Green, May 13, 1935, A.F. of L. Strike File, Local 18384; Chal-

mers' analysis, May 16, 1935, Brown Collection; Kampelman, *Communist Party vs. C.I.O.,* p. 64; *Daily Worker,* Apr. 25, 29, May 4, 11, 1935; Communist and Workers party handbills in the Brown Collection. Publication of the strike committee's organ, *Strike Truth,* was halted after the first issue because some strike committee members thought it "too communistic," but the union voted to resume its publication, and a second issue appeared. *Toledo Blade,* May 1, 1935. The associate editor of the first issue was Art Preis, the secretary of the Toledo branch of the Workers party.

36 *Toledo Blade,* May 2, 1935; Alfred Hirsch, "Why They Lost in Toledo," *New Masses,* XV (May 28, 1935), 13; Williams to Kerwin, Apr. 30, 1935, C.S. 182-370.

37 *Strike Truth,* Apr. 26, 1935; *Toledo Blade,* Apr. 26, 29, 30, 1935; *New York Times,* Apr. 30, 1935. For the Workers party and communist line on this issue, see *New Militant,* May 4, 11, 1935; *Daily Worker,* May 4, 11, 1935; and handbills of both organizations in the Brown Collection. The Workers party picketed the G.M. building in New York on May 6. *New Militant,* May 11, 1935.

38 *Toledo News-Bee,* Apr. 29, 30, 1935; *Toledo Blade,* Apr. 30, May 1, 2, 1935; *Daily Worker,* May 3, 1935; *Union Leader* (Toledo), May 3, 1935; Williams to Kerwin, Apr. 30, 1935, C.S. 182-370; *Cleveland Plain Dealer,* May 1, 1935; *United Auto Worker,* May, 1935; Cora Gentle to President F.L.U. 18762, Apr. 26, 1935, Pieper to Martin, May 1, 1935, Martin Papers; Gilman to Green, May 1, 1935, A.F. of L. Strike File, Local 18488. There is a copy of the Norwood demands in the Labadie Collection.

39 Martin advised Dillon that there was sentiment for a strike in both Kansas City and St. Louis and that the G.M. plants there could be closed but that there would be no strike unless Dillon ordered it. Martin to Dillon, Apr. 25, 1935. The Toledo local failed to prevent G.M. from reopening its Muncie Products Division plant on May 7 to manufacture Chevrolet transmissions. The plant, which was producing a small quantity of transmissions by the time the strike ended, had too limited a capacity, however, to offset the loss of the transmissions normally produced in Toledo. *Detroit Free Press,* May 7, 1935; Chalmers, "Collective Bargaining," XII, 12.

40 Williams to Kerwin, May 22, 1935, C.S. 182-370.

41 Roland interview, p. 15, Michigan Historical Collections; *Toledo News-Bee,* May 1, 1935; *Toledo Blade,* May 11, 1935; *Detroit News,* May 9, 11, 12, 1935; *Daily Worker,* May 9, 11, 13, 1935; Minutes of F.L.U. No. 18331, May 9, 16, 1935, Francis Papers; Chalmers analysis, May 16, 1935, Brown Collection.

42 *Flint Weekly Review,* May 3, 10, 1935; Swanson interview, pp. 7-8, Michigan Historical Collections; Memorandum of Meeting of the Executive Board of Buick F.L.U. No. 18512 with Management of Buick Car Co., Apr. 30, 1935, Brown Collection; typewritten memorandum, May 1, 1935, *ibid.;* Chalmers, "Collective Bargaining," XII, 14-15; *Toledo Blade,* Apr. 29, May 1, 2, 1935; *Detroit Free Press,* May 2, 14, 1935; *Detroit News,* May 12, 1935; *Toledo News-Bee,* May 14, 1935; Dillon to Green, June 11, 1935, A.F. of L. Strike File, Local 18384. The *Flint Weekly Review* of May 17, 1935, reported the May 13 meeting as packed with "reds" from Toledo, Detroit, and Flint. For details of the Buick story, see Fine, "Toledo Chevrolet Strike of 1935," pp. 337–39.

43 *Toledo News-Bee,* Apr. 23, 25, 1935; *Toledo Blade,* Apr. 23, 24, 26, 1935; *Toledo Morning Times,* Apr. 24, 1935; *New York Times,* Apr. 25, 1935. It is difficult to accept Chalmers' statement that Dillon advised against Department of Labor intervention in the strike.

44 Address by Dillon . . . , Apr. 26, 1935, A.F. of L. Strike File, Local 18384; *Toledo News-Bee*, Apr. 27, 29, 1935; *Toledo Blade*, Apr. 29, 1935.

45 On these efforts, see Fine, "Toledo Chevrolet Strike of 1935," pp. 341–43.

46 A.L.B., In Re: Chevrolet Motor Co., Apr. 29, 1935; *Toledo Blade*, May 1, 4, 6, 1935; *Toledo News-Bee*, May 1, 6, 1935; *New York Times*, May 5, 6, 1935; *Detroit Free Press*, May 6, 1935; Williams to Kerwin, May 22, 1935, C.S. 182-370.

47 *Toledo Blade*, May 4, 1935; *Toledo News-Bee*, May 7, 1935; *Strike Truth*, May 7, 1935.

48 Dillon to U.A.W., May 17, 1935, Dillon File; Dillon to Green, June 11, 1935, A.F. of L. Strike File, Local 18384; Chalmers, "Collective Bargaining," XII, 18–19, 40; Chalmers' analysis, May 16, 1935, Brown Collection; *Toledo Blade*, May 6, 1935; Williams to Kerwin, May 22, 1935, C.S. 182-370.

49 Ogburn to Dillon, May 5, 7, 9, 1935, Dillon to Ogburn, May 7, 1935, Green to Ogburn, May 9, 1935, A.F. of L. Strike File, Local 18384.

50 *Toledo News-Bee*, May 7, 1935; Williams to Kerwin, May 22, 1935, C.S. 182-370.

51 *Toledo News-Bee*, May 9, 10, 1935; *Toledo Morning Times*, May 10, 1935; Dillon to Green, May 9, 1935, A.F. of L. Strike File, Local 18384; Dillon to U.A.W., May 17, 1935, Dillon File.

52 During the negotiations, Roland frequently consulted with Muste, who occupied a room on the same floor of the hotel in which the negotiations were being conducted. *Detroit News*, May 13, 1935.

53 Ogburn to Green, May 5, 8, 1935, A.F. of L. Strike File, Local 18384; *Toledo Blade*, May 4, 1935; *New York Times*, May 4, 1935.

54 Chalmers, "Collective Bargaining," XII, 23–25; Chalmers' analysis, May 16, 1935, Brown Collection; G.M., Labor Relations Diary, Appendix Document No. 49. During the course of the strike negotiations, Knudsen had told McGrady that he would make a gentlemen's agreement to deal exclusively with the U.A.W. bargaining committee but that this was "to be treated in strict confidence." Memorandum to Mr. Green from Mr. McGrady from Detroit, May 3, 1935, A.F. of L. Strike File, Local 18384.

55 *Toledo Morning Times*, May 11, 1935; *New York Times*, May 13, 1935.

56 There is a copy of the final agreement in *Automotive Industries*, LXXII (May 18, 1935), 656. The company granted the workers 1-hour call-in pay (they had asked for 2 hours) and time-and-a-half for work on 6 legal holidays (the union had asked for double time for work on Sunday and 7 legal holidays).

57 Chalmers, "Collective Bargaining," XII, 26–28; Chalmers' analysis, May 16, 18, 1935, Brown Collection; Wilson to Green, May 13, 1935, A.F. of L. Strike File, Local 18384; *New Militant*, June 3, 1935; Ditzel interview, p. 5, Michigan Historical Collections. The *Toledo Blade* reported in a front-page editorial on May 11, 1935, that it understood the plant would be closed permanently if an amicable settlement could not be arranged.

58 My account of the May 13 meeting is based on the following: *Toledo News-Bee*, May 14, 1935; *Toledo Blade*, May 14, 1935; *Detroit Labor News*, May 17, 1935; Muste, *Automobile Industry and Organized Labor*, p. 47; Chalmers' analysis, May 18, 1935, Brown Collection; Chalmers, "Collective Bargaining," XII, 29–33; Dillon to U.A.W., May 17, 1935, Dillon File; *New Militant*, June 3, 1935; and Roland interview, p. 16, Michigan Historical Collections.

59 Five of the committee members urged rejection of the settlement. Two members indicated the settlement had some good points, but they did not urge its approval.

60 *Toledo News-Bee,* May 14, 1935; *Detroit Free Press,* May 15, 1935.

61 *Toledo Blade,* May 15, 1935; *New York Times,* May 16, 1935; *Flint Weekly Review,* May 17, 1935; *Detroit News,* May 21, 1935.

62 *American Federationist,* XLII (June, 1935), 588; Dillon to Green, May 17, 1935, A.F. of L. Strike File, Local 18384.

63 *New Militant,* May 18, June 3, 1935; *Union Leader* (Toledo), May 17, 1935; Ditzel interview, p. 5, Michigan Historical Collections; *Daily Worker,* May 14, 15, 16, 1935; Martin to Dillon, May 27, 1935, Martin Papers; Wood to Joe Brown, June 18, 1935, Brown Collection.

64 Reeves to Richberg, May 16, 1935, N.R.A. Box 660; A.M.A. General Bulletin No. G-1750, May 14, 1935, Acc. 203, Box 6, Ford Archives; *Business Week,* May 18, 1935, p. 9; *Iron Age,* CXXXV (May 23, 1935), 41.

65 *New Militant,* May 18, 1935.

66 Chalmers' analysis, May 16, 1935, Brown Collection; *Automotive Industries,* LXXII (June 1, 1935), 721; *American Federationist,* XLII (June, 1935), 591; G.M., Labor Relations Diary, Appendix Document No. 49; P. Johnson Memorandum for A.M.A. Executive Committee, May 18, 1935, Chapin Papers.

67 A second strike had broken out at the Norwood Chevrolet plant when foremen refused admission to the plant to workers wearing union buttons. This problem was disposed of in the Dillon-G.M. talks. *Detroit News,* May 27, 1935.

68 Dillon to Green, May 17, 23, 31, June 10, 1935, Dillon File; *Proceedings of First Constitutional Convention of U.A.W., 1935,* p. 29.

69 *Toledo Blade,* Nov. 18, 25, Dec. 16, 1935; H. S. Grant, "General Motors Strikes Back," *Nation,* CXLI (Dec. 25, 1935), 743–44; Roland to All Members and Officers, Nov. 27, 1935, Francis Papers; La Follette *Hearings,* Part 7 (Washington, 1937), p. 2316; G.M., Labor Relations Diary, Appendix Document No. 49; Ditzel interview, p. 8, Michigan Historical Collections; Williams to Kerwin, Apr. 27, 1935, C.S. 182-370.

70 Dillon to Green, May 14, June 11, 1935, William K. Siefke to Green, May 24, 1935, Green to Siefke, June 19, 1935, A.F. of L. Strike File, Local 18384; Martin to Dillon, May 27, 1935, Martin Papers; Chalmers' analysis, May 16, 1935, Brown Collection; Wieck, "Automobile Workers," p. 231; Muste, "Toledo Thriller," *Nation,* CXL (May 29, 1935), 632; Ditzel interview, pp. 6–7, Michigan Historical Collections; Roland interview, p. 17, *ibid.* Dillon reported to Green in the letter of June 11 cited above that Addes had informed him that not more than 60 people were present at the meeting at which the resolution attacking him was passed.

71 Dillon to National Council, Jan. 17, 1935, Manning, Woods, and Kleinert to Executive Council, Feb. 1, 1935, Martin Papers; Dillon to National Council, Jan. 24, 1935, Labadie Collection; Dillon press release, Jan. 25, 1935, Dillon File; Manning interview, p. 44, Michigan Historical Collections. Dillon had recommended to the National Council members that they elect a 3-man committee to represent them at the Executive Council session and to report back to the National Council.

72 Extract from Executive Council Minutes, Jan. 29–Feb. 14, 1935, Auto Workers File, 1935–1937; Taft, *A.F. of L. from Death of Gompers,* pp. 104–7; Walter Galenson, *The CIO Challenge to the AFL* (Cambridge, Mass., 1960), pp. 124–25.

73 Executive Council Minutes, Apr. 30–May 7, 1935, Auto Workers File, 1935–1937.

74 Minutes of Third Meeting of National Council, Feb. 23–Mar. 2, 1935, Labadie Collection; *Labor Digest,* Apr. 5, 1935.

75 Dillon to Green, Apr. 4, 1935, Green to Dillon, Apr. 8, 1935, Dillon File; Green to Dillon, Dec. 28, 1934, Green Letterbooks.

76 Hall to Martin, May 25, 1935, Woods to National Council, May 23, 1935, Martin Papers. See also *United Auto Worker,* May, 1935.

77 Shipley to Lewis, May 27, 1935, A.F. of L. Strike File, Local 18347.

78 Executive Council Minutes, Apr. 30–May 7, 1935, Auto Workers File, 1935–1937; *Detroit Labor News,* May 10, 1935; Dillon to Green, May 14, 1935, A.F. of L. Strike File, Local 18384; Green to Dillon, May 14, 1935, Green Letterbooks; Dillon press release, June 18, 1935, Brown Collection; Dillon to National Council, June 18, 1935, Martin Papers. Only 28 of the 107 locals to which the questionnaire was sent responded, but, according to an A.F. of L. count that appears to have been inaccurate, these locals represented 16,143 of the 35,228 paid-up U.A.W. members. The reporting locals indicated that over 98 per cent of their members favored the international. Green to U.A.W., June 19, 1935, C.I.O. Historical File, Reel 1; "Automobile," July 12, 1935, *ibid.* There is a more accurate count of paid-up membership at this time in Green to Addes, July 16, 1935, *ibid.*

79 Green to Addes, July 16, 1935, C.I.O. Historical File, Reel 1; Tolles and La Fever, "Wages . . . in the Motor Vehicle Industry, 1934," *Monthly Labor Review,* XLII (Mar., 1936), 529, 535.

80 Green to Addes, July 16, 1935, C.I.O. Historical File, Reel 1.

81 *Proceedings of First Constitutional Convention, U.A.W., 1935,* p. 29. The White Motor local, after a peaceful strike of May 21–27, 1935, negotiated an agreement with the company providing, among other things, for time-and-one-half for hours above 8 per day and for work on Saturday afternoon and for double time on Sunday and holidays; but the union, after examining the company's books, did not insist on a general wage increase. *Cleveland Plain Dealer,* May 21–25, 28, 29, 1935; Memorandum of Negotiations between the White Motor Co., and . . . U.A.W. F.L.U. No. 18463, May 27, 1935, A.F. of L. Strike File, Local 18463.

82 Hearing on Regularizing Employment, Milwaukee, Dec. 30–31, 1934, pp. 95–96, N.R.A. Box 7266; *Racine Day,* Aug. 30, 1935; A. Green to W. Green, Mar. 6, 1935, A.F. of L. Strike File, Local 18310; *Automotive Industries,* LXXIII (July 13, 1935), 39; Frederick A. Harbison and Robert Dubin, *Patterns of Union-Management Relations: United Automobile Workers (CIO). General Motors. Studebaker* (Chicago, 1947), pp. 103–5, 115, 205; Oral History Interview of John Bartee, Apr. 30, 1961, p. 4, Michigan Historical Collections. On Hupp, see n. 15 above. On Pierce Arrow, see P. Johnson Memorandum for A.M.A. Executive Committee, May 18, 1935, Chapin Papers.

83 There are copies of the U.A.W. agreements in Collective Bargaining Agreements, B.L.S. Records. See also *American Federationist,* XLII (May, 1935), 501–10; and *ibid.,* XLII (June, 1935), 615–18. According to A.F. of L. organizer George B. Roberts, the only reason that the president of the Columbus Auto Parts Co. did not agree to a union shop in the signed contract that he had negotiated with the federal labor union in his plant was his fear of the "pressure that might be brought to bear from the larger manufacturers" if he did so. "As soon as there is some law to force the larger manufacturers to deal openly with a union organization," Roberts reported, "he will be one of the first to have a 100% Agreement." Roberts to Dillon, June 24, 1935, Roberts Papers.

84 Wieck, "Automobile Workers," p. 244.

NOTES TO CHAPTER XIII

1 *New York Times,* May 28, 29, 1935; *Detroit Free Press,* May 29, 30, 1935; *Detroit News,* June 6, 1935; G.M., Labor Relations Diary, Section 1, p. 64; Macauley to Chapin, June 13, 1935, and enclosed Packard statement of June 12, 1935, Chapin Papers.

2 *Automotive Industries,* LXXII (June 1, 1935), 717, 741; *New York Times,* July 27, Dec. 8, 1935; B.L.S., *Bulletin No. 706,* p. 15; McPherson and Lucheck, "Automobiles," pp. 609–10.

3 A.M.A. Release, Oct. 14, 1935, Pearson Papers.

4 A.M.A., "Progress in Stabilizing Factory Employment Auto, Body, and Parts Industry," Dec. 1, 1936, Bureau of Industrial Relations Library, University of Michigan; A.M.A., *Automobile Facts and Figures, 1937,* pp. 48–49; Byer and Anker, "A Review of Factory Labor Turn-Over, 1930 to 1936," *Monthly Labor Review* (July, 1937), 157–58. The number of steady workers and the annual wage figures for 1935–36 are those given in the *Facts and Figures* volume rather than the lower figures cited in the A.M.A. report of Dec. 1, 1936, cited above. About 27 per cent of the year's total output was produced in the last quarter of 1935 as compared to about 15 per cent in previous years. More workers were employed in the automobile and parts industries in Nov. and Dec. 1935 than in the last two months of any previous year. In the automobile industry alone, an estimated 72,000 more workers were employed during the last quarter of 1935 than would have been employed had the rate of increase in employment for the first 9 months of 1935 as compared to the first 9 months of 1934 simply been maintained. A.M.A., *Stabilization of Employment in the Automobile Industry.*

5 Anderson, "Regularization of Employment in the Automobile Industry," pp. 49–50, 91. Cf. Feldman, *Stabilizing Jobs,* p. 85. See also Stevens, "Progress in Employment Stabilization," pp. 40–47.

6 Reeves to A.M.A. Executive Committee, Sept. 19, 1935, Marshall to Reeves, Sept. 25, Oct. 4, 1935, Reeves to Marshall, Sept. 30, 1935, Chapin Papers; undated report to A.M.A. Executive Committee by James Cope, *ibid.;* Friday folder, N.R.A. Box 7673; Myrick to Marshall, Mar. 13, 16, 1936, N.R.A. Box 8310; Myrick to M. D. Vincent, Sept. 17, 1935, N.R.A. Box 7671.

7 Reeves to Chapin, Sept. 26, 1935, and enclosed draft of letter to Marshall, Chapin Papers; J. Edward Ely to W. J. Maguire, Sept. 17, 1935, N.R.A. Box 662.

8 Homer L. Calkin *et al.,* compilers, *Preliminary Inventory of the Records of the National Recovery Administration* (Washington, 1952), pp. 4–5; Berry to Reeves, Oct. 9, 23, Nov. 9, 1935, Reeves to Presidents, Oct. 14, Nov. 12, 1935, Jan. 3, 1936, Reeves to Berry, Oct. 11, Nov. 6, 1935, Jan. 2, 1936, Reeves to Macauley *et al.,* Oct. 25, 1935, Berry to A.M.A., Dec. 23, 1935, Cronin to Chapin, Dec. 30, 1935, and attached copy of message from Reeves, Chapin Papers; Memorandum to Executive Committee from P. Johnson, Oct. 14, 1935, *ibid.;* Ellis W. Hawley, "The New Deal and the Problem of Monopoly, 1934–1938: A Study in Economic Schizophrenia" (Ph.D. thesis, University of Wisconsin, 1958), pp. 353–60.

9 *Detroit Free Press,* June 15, 1935; Cronin to Chapin, Nov. 23, 1935, and enclosed Memorandum on National Labor Relations Act, Chapin Papers. Cronin

informed Chapin that the memorandum appeared "to be in line with the position of other member companies in this area."

[10] A.M.A. Memorandum, July 17, 1935, Pearson Papers; Final Report of A.L.B., pp. 14–15.

[11] Clark, "The A.F. of L.," p. 85; undated account by Joe Brown, Brown Collection; Hall interview, p. 7, Michigan Historical Collections.

[12] A.L.B., Chrysler Conference, Jan. 10, 1935, p. 44.

[13] *Detroit News*, June 16, 1935.

[14] *Ibid.;* Ernest K. Lindley, *Half Way with Roosevelt* (New York, 1936), p. 174; Lorwin and Wubnig, *Labor Relations Boards*, p. 377.

[15] My account of the convention is based on the following: *Proceedings of Constitutional Convention, U.A.W., 1935, passim;* Edward Levinson, *Labor on the March* (New York, 1938), pp. 88–93; *Detroit News*, Aug. 26–31, 1935; and Joe Brown's notes on the convention, Brown Collection.

[16] "Automobile Workers Unions Affiliated with the A.F. of L., Aug. 23, 1935," C.I.O. Historical File, Reel 1.

[17] Just before the convention, on Aug. 25, Green wrote President Wharton of the I.A.M.: "I know I am going to be confronted with some problems that will be difficult to solve, but I will endeavor to meet them in such a way as to protect the interests of your International Union as well as all other organizations affiliated with the American Federation of Labor." Green Letterbooks.

[18] Pickering to Green, July 1, 1935, Richardson to Green, July 29, 1935, and attached resolution of Flint Federated Executive Council, C.I.O. Historical File, Reel 1; Pickering to Martin, July 6, 1935, Martin to Ramsey, July 4, 1935, Martin to Dillon, July 9, 1935, Martin Papers; *Proceedings of Constitutional Convention, U.A.W., 1935*, pp. 6–7. Italics added.

[19] A.F. of L., *Proceedings, 1935*, p. 285; Bartee interview, p. 7, Michigan Historical Collections. Cf. Mortimer interview, p. 16, *ibid.;* and *New Militant*, Aug. 31, 1935.

[20] F. J. Michel, the recording secretary of the Racine Nash local, was added to the General Executive Board after the adjournment of the convention. Dillon to G.E.B., Nov. 4, 1935, Martin Papers.

[21] The other 3 delegates were L. R. Richardson of the Studebaker local, Thomas L. Hoskins of the Norwood local, and John North of the Hayes Body local.

[22] Mortimer interview, pp. 17–18, Michigan Historical Collections.

[23] A.F. of L., *Proceedings, 1935*, pp. 283–85, 521–24, 574–75, 730–50, 825.

[24] Martin to Green, Sept. 4, 1935, Martin Papers; Records of Federal Labor Union 18386, Oct. 15, 1935, Wayne State University Archives.

[25] Green to Dillon, Sept. 25, 1935, C.I.O. Historical File, Reel 1; Dillon to G.E.B., Oct. 1, Nov. 4, 1935, Jan. 18, 1936, Martin Papers; *Union Leader* (Toledo), Feb. 21, 1936; *Toledo Blade*, Feb. 17, 1936.

[26] Dillon to G.E.B., Nov. 4, Dec. 5, 7, 31, 1935, Feb. 4, 1936, Martin Papers.

[27] On the Motor Products strike, see C.S. 182-928; Joe Brown, "Summary of the Motor Products Strike . . . ," [1936], Brown Collection; Dahlheimer, *History of M.E.S.A.*, pp. 30–36; *Detroit Labor News;* and *Detroit News*. The U.A.W. local joined the strike on Dec. 20, despite Dillon's statement of withdrawal.

[28] See the Motor Products strike bulletins in C.S. 182-928. The contemplated merger of the independents into the Industrial, Automobile, and Metal Workers Union died a-borning. See Dahlheimer, *History of M.E.S.A.*, pp. 33–36.

[29] See, for example, Dillon to G.E.B., Dec. 31, 1935, enclosing resolution of White Motor local, Dillon to G.E.B., Jan. 6, 1936, enclosing resolution of Pontiac Local 73, and Martin to Dowell, Feb. 12, 1936, Martin Papers.

[30] Martin to Green, Nov. 18, 1935, Martin to Hart, Nov. 22, 1935, Martin to Dowell, Nov. 20, 1935, Jan. 13, 1936, Martin Papers; Mortimer interview, p. 22, Michigan Historical Collections; *Union Leader* (Toledo), Jan. 31, 1936; Skeels, "The Background of U.A.W. Factionalism," *Labor History* (Spring, 1961), 168–69.

[31] John Bartee to Martin, Jan. 15, 1936, Woods to Martin, Feb. 2, 1936, Martin Papers.

[32] Galenson, *CIO Challenge to AFL*, p. 130; Morris, *Conflict within AFL*, p. 221; Report of Homer Martin ... Oct. 1, 1935–Apr. 1, 1936, Martin Papers.

[33] Martin to Hillman, Feb. 10, 1936, Martin to Garst, Feb. 12, 1936, Martin Papers.

[34] Martin to Mortimer, Feb. 10, 1936, Martin to Hillman, Feb. 10, 1936, Martin to Garst, Feb. 12, 1936, Martin to Dowell, Feb. 12, 1936, Martin to Al Davis, Feb. 12, 1936, *ibid.;* Dillon to G.E.B., Feb. 17, 1936, Auto Workers File, 1935–1937; *Union Leader* (Toledo), Feb. 14, 21, 1936.

[35] Dillon to G.E.B., Feb. 17, 1936 (several communications of this date), Auto Workers File, 1935–1937; Richardson interview, p. 10, Michigan Historical Collections; *Toledo Blade,* Feb. 12, 1936. On Martin's talents as a speaker, see also Ditzel interview, p. 10, Michigan Historical Collections; Mortimer interview, pp. 24–25, *ibid.;* and Coleman interview, p. 6, *ibid.*

[36] Skeels, "Background of U.A.W. Factionalism," pp. 170–71; Martin to Dowell, Mar. 18, 1936, Martin Papers; *Union Leader* (Toledo), Mar. 20, Apr. 24, 1936; *New Militant,* May 9, 1936.

[37] Oral History Interview of Carl Haessler, Nov. 27, 1959–Oct. 24, 1960, p. 4, Michigan Historical Collections; Blackwood, "United Automobile Workers," pp. 49, 52; Galenson, *CIO Challenge to AFL,* pp. 130–32; Levinson, *Labor on the March,* p. 147; *Proceedings of Second Convention, U.A.W., 1936,* pp. 11, 22, 71–77, 96–97, 137–38, 135–43, 159–60, *et passim.*

[38] *United Automobile Worker,* May 1936.

[39] Galenson, *CIO Challenge to AFL,* pp. 132–33; Dahlheimer, *History of M.E.S.A.,* pp. 36–37.

[40] Frey to W. A. Appleton, Sept. 9, 1935, Frey Papers, Library of Congress.

[41] Samuel Romer, "That Automobile Strike," *Nation,* CXL (Feb. 6, 1935), 162; testimony of R. J. Thomas, in House Committee on Labor, *Proposed Amendments to the National Labor Relations Act,* IX, 2295.

[42] Broadus Mitchell, "Gears Clash in Detroit," *New Republic,* LXXXII (Mar. 20, 1935), 148.

[43] Myrick, Jr., to Henderson, Oct. 17, 1934, N.R.A. Box 7682. See also Roberts to Myrick, Jr., Oct. 9, 1935, N.R.A. Box 7673.

[44] Miley interview, p. 4, Michigan Historical Collections; *Proceedings of Second Convention, U.A.W., 1936,* p. 12. See also Bartee interview, p. 2, Michigan Historical Collections.

[45] Chalmers, "Collective Bargaining," Table of Contents, p. 9; *Automotive Industries,* LXXII (Jan. 12, 1935), 51; *Detroit Free Press,* Feb. 18, 1935; Cronin interview; Harbison and Dubin, *Patterns of Union-Management Relations,* p. 23.

[46] "Success Story," *Fortune,* XII (Dec., 1935), 124.

[47] Schlesinger, Jr., *Coming of the New Deal,* p. 175.

BIBLIOGRAPHICAL NOTE

No attempt has been made in the pages that follow to list all the works that have already been mentioned in the footnotes. Comment has been reserved for the published and unpublished materials that were of particular value and interest for this subject.

Manuscript Sources

The single most important manuscript source for this study was the Records of the National Recovery Administration (Record Group 9) in the National Archives in Washington, D.C. The task of locating materials relevant to the automobile and related codes in this enormous record group, which occupies six thousand cubic feet of space, has been greatly facilitated by the publication of the excellent Homer L. Calkin *et al.*, compilers, *Preliminary Inventory of the Records of the National Recovery Administration* (Washington, 1952). The complete records of the Automobile Labor Board are included within the N.R.A. record group, but Hugh S. Johnson's personal papers are in private hands, and I was unable to obtain permission to examine them.

The National Archives also contains the complete records (Record Group 25) of the National Labor Board, the first National Labor Relations Board, and the various regional boards of the two organizations. The present N.L.R.B. granted me permission to examine the informal as well as the formal files of cases involving the automobile manufacturing and automobile parts industries. In addition to the case files of the labor boards, there are many items of importance to this study in the general correspondence files of the two agencies. The Records of the Conciliation Service, which have been transferred recently to the National Archives, contain a great deal of valuable material pertaining to automobile strikes and to threatened work stoppages in the industry. The Federal Mediation and Conciliation Service permitted me to examine the relevant case files before the records (Record Group 280) were removed to their present location. These records may not be cited without the consent of the Federal Mediation and Conciliation Service. There are copies of the agreements negotiated by U.A.W. federal labor unions in the Bureau of Labor Statistics Records (Record Group 257) in the National Archives.

Several of the Official Files and the President's Personal Files in the Franklin D. Roosevelt Library in Hyde Park, New York, contain material on the automobile code and automobile labor. The President commented on problems of the automobile code in several of his press conferences, the complete transcripts of which are available in the Roosevelt Library. There is a folder of documents pertaining to the N.R.A.'s investigation of the automobile manufacturing industry in 1934–35 in the Leon Henderson Papers, which are also at Hyde Park. The

Louis McHenry Howe Papers and the two boxes of Frances Perkins Papers for this period, located in the Roosevelt Library, do not have any significant material relevant to the subject of this study.

No items bearing directly on the automobile code are included in the James Couzens Papers or the Donald R. Richberg Papers in the Library of Congress. There are a few interesting observations on the N.R.A. in the John P. Frey Papers, also in the Library of Congress. A cursory examination of the Robert F. Wagner Papers at Georgetown University did not turn up any significant new information pertaining to automobile labor during the N.R.A. period.

There is a considerable amount of data available on microfilm in the A.F. of L.-C.I.O. building in Washington relative to the efforts of the Federation to organize the automobile workers after 1933. The principal filmed collections are the William Green Letterbooks, which contain mostly outgoing letters, the strike files of A.F. of L. federal labor unions, a C.I.O. Historical File, an International Association of Machinists file, and an Auto Workers File. Of unusual importance for this study were the reports of A.F. of L. organizers in the automobile industry and especially of William Collins and Francis Dillon. Unfortunately, these records were not filmed, and they have since been destroyed. I was not permitted to examine the minutes of A.F. of L. Executive Council meetings, but extracts from some of these minutes are contained in the files noted above.

The Homer Martin Papers in the Wayne State University Archives in Detroit constitute one of the most important collections extant on the automobile unionism of the New Deal era. The collection sheds a great deal of light on the operations of the National Council of the United Automobile Workers and also on the opposition to Francis Dillon following the creation of the international union in August 1935. There is an abundance of material pertaining to the Mechanics Educational Society of America, the Auto Workers Union, the Industrial Workers of the World, the U.A.W., and the various automobile strikes of the period in the Joe Brown Collection in the Wayne Archives. There is some correspondence in the Collection, but it is primarily made up of newspaper clippings, handbills, broadsides, pamphlets, and the personal observations of Joe Brown and others. The Everett Francis Papers in the Wayne Archives are primarily concerned with the Flint Fisher Body No. 1 local, of which Francis was the recording secretary. The minutes of the meetings of this local for the N.R.A. period and also of the St. Louis Chevrolet and Fisher Body local are also available at Wayne. Other Wayne collections that proved useful were the George B. Roberts Papers, which provide some information on the Columbus Auto Parts local, and the John Zaremba Papers, which include a set of minutes of the Dodge bargaining agency. The Richard Frankensteen Papers not only contain minutes of some of the regular meetings of the Dodge bargaining agency but also of the off-the-premises meetings that led to the establishment of the Automotive Industrial Workers' Association. I examined the Frankensteen Papers while they were in Mr. Frankensteen's possession; they are now in the process of being transferred to the Wayne Archives.

Tracy Doll made the minutes of the Hudson bargaining agency available to me. The minute books of the Janesville Chevrolet and Fisher Body locals, which I examined on film, are located in the Wisconsin State Historical Society in Madison. The Joseph A. Labadie Collection of the General Library of the University of Michigan has a few items relating to automobile unionism during the N.R.A. period.

Of the manuscript collections that reveal automobile management's reaction to the N.R.A. the most important are the Ford Motor Company Archives in Dearborn, Michigan, and the Roy D. Chapin Papers in the Michigan Historical Collections in Ann Arbor, Michigan. The Ford Archives contain a mass of information pertaining to Ford and the N.R.A. and also, because the Lincoln Motor Company was a member of the Automobile Manufacturers Association (formerly the National Automobile Chamber of Commerce), a considerable amount of data emanating from the A.M.A. as well. The Chapin Papers include a great deal of information on the history of the automobile code from its drafting to its demise and also on the Hudson Motor Car Company, of which Chapin was president. Oscar P. Pearson, who was the manager of the A.M.A.'s statistical department, permitted me to examine the valuable papers in his possession pertaining to the automobile code, and Stephen M. DuBrul of G.M. made available to me a few items dealing with the stabilization of automobile employment. There are copies of several of the A.M.A. reports on this latter subject in the Bureau of Industrial Relations Library of the University of Michigan, which also has copies of most of the A.L.B.'s decisions and of its final report. I was denied access to the A.M.A. records for this period, but the Association did permit me to examine a file of its general bulletins and also made some other items available to me. It would seem that much of what is probably contained in the A.M.A. files is duplicated in the Chapin Papers, the Pearson Papers, the Ford Archives, and the N.R.A. records.

Interviews

The following persons permitted me to interview them with regard to the subject of this study: William Collins, William J. Cronin, Chester M. Culver, Z. Clark Dickinson, Tracy Doll, Stephen M. DuBrul, Richard Frankensteen, Pyke Johnson, Nicholas Kelley, Patrick V. McNamara, Charlton Ogburn, Oscar P. Pearson, Alfred Reeves, Francis Ross, Matthew Smith, and Leo Wolman. In addition, Donaldson Brown, Frances Perkins, Francis Biddle, Donald R. Richberg, and Lawrence H. Seltzer replied to my questions by letter. My knowledge of the development of the U.A.W. has been greatly enhanced by the oral history interviews resulting from the U.A.W. Oral History Project of the Institute of Labor and Industrial Relations of the University of Michigan and Wayne State University. Typewritten transcripts of ninety-four interviews were available at the time of this writing in both the Michigan Historical Collections and the Wayne State University Archives. Oral history reminiscences of William J. Cameron, W. C. Cowling, Chester M. Culver, E. G. Liebold, and Herman L. Moekle in the Ford Archives, and of John P. Frey, John O'Hare, and Rexford G. Tugwell in the Oral History Research Office of Columbia University also contain material relevant to this study.

Newspapers and Periodicals

A considerable number of labor periodicals deal with the development of unionism in the automobile industry after the enactment of the N.I.R.A. For the U.A.W., the principal labor papers consulted were the *Detroit Labor News, Flint Weekly Review, Union Leader* (Toledo), *New Day* (Racine) (the paper became the *Racine Day* in August 1934), *Central Labor Council Herald* (Buffalo), *Cleveland Citizen, Progressive Labor World* (Philadelphia), and *United Automobile Worker.* The *MESA Voice, Auto Workers News, Industrial Worker, Associated,* and *Designing Engineer* were the official organs of the M.E.S.A., the A.W.U., the I.W.W., the Hudson local of the Associated Automobile Workers of America, and the Society of Designing Engineers respectively. The interest of the communists in automobile labor can be gleaned from the *Daily Worker* and the *Communist* as well as from the *Auto Workers News,* and the activities of the Musteites in the industry are commented upon in *Labor Action* and its successor, the *New Militant.*

The most important periodical source for the behavior of the automobile manufacturers during the N.I.R.A. era is *Automotive Industries.* The *Automotive Daily News* and *Motor,* although primarily concerned with the automobile dealer, also contain a good deal of information on the automobile manufacturing industry. The management point of view is also reflected in *Michigan Manufacturer and Financial Record, Iron Age,* and *Business Week.* Of the general magazines of news and opinion, the *New Republic* and the *Nation* paid the most attention to the automobile code.

I examined the *Detroit News,* the *Detroit Free Press,* and the *New York Times* for the entire period that the N.I.R.A. was in effect. In addition, I perused the daily newspapers of the cities in which automobile strikes occurred for the period of the work stoppage. Of these newspapers, the *Toledo News-Bee, Toledo Blade,* and *Milwaukee Journal* had the fullest coverage of strike developments.

Published Government Documents

All of the N.R.A. codes and supplements and all code amendments are given in full in National Recovery Administration, *Codes of Fair Competition,* 23 vols. (Washington, 1933–35). The decisions of the N.L.B. and N.L.R.B. in automotive and other cases are available in *Decisions of the National Labor Board,* 2 parts (Washington, 1934), and *Decisions of the National Labor Relations Board,* 2 vols. (Washington, 1935). Alfred P. Sloan, Jr., presented the views of the automobile manufacturers on the relationship of government to the economy just prior to the enactment of the N.I.R.A. in House Committee on Labor, *Thirty-Hour Week Bill, Hearings on S. 158 . . . ,* 73 Cong., 1 Sess. (Washington, 1933). The industry indicated its continuing opposition to the thirty-hour week in Subcommittee of Senate Committee on the Judiciary, *Thirty-Hour Work Week, Hearings on S. 87,* 74 Cong., 1 Sess. (Washington, 1935). The A.M.A.'s verdict on its experience under the Blue Eagle is given in Senate Committee on Finance, *Investigation of the National Recovery Administration, Hearings Pursuant to S. Res. 79,* 74 Cong., 1 Sess. (Washington, 1935).

The views of automobile management and automobile labor on the state of employer-employee relations in the industry can be gleaned from testimony presented in Senate Committee on Education and Labor, *To Create a National Labor Board, Hearings on S. 2926,* 73 Cong., 2 Sess. (Washington, 1934); Senate Committee on Education and Labor, *National Labor Relations Board, Hearings on S. 1958,* 74 Cong., 1 Sess. (Washington, 1935); and House Committee on Labor, *Labor Disputes Act, Hearings on H.R. 6288,* 74 Cong., 1 Sess. (Washington, 1935). The subject of labor espionage in the automobile industry following the enactment of the N.I.R.A. is explored in Subcommittee of the Senate Committee on Education and Labor, *Violations of Free Speech and Rights of Labor, Hearings Pursuant to S. Res. 266 . . .* , 75 Cong., 1 Sess., Parts 3–7 (Washington, 1937); Senate Committee on Education and Labor, *Violations of Free Speech and Rights of Labor,* 75 Cong., 1–3 Sess., *Senate Report No. 46* (Washington, 1937); and Senate Committee on Education and Labor, *Violations of Free Speech and Rights of Labor,* 76 Cong., 1 Sess., *Senate Report No. 6* (Washington, 1939).

National Recovery Administration, *Bulletins Nos. 1, 2,* and *3* (Washington, 1933), were the initial statements of the N.R.A. on the manner in which the N.I.R.A. was to be implemented. The problem of the award of government contracts to firms that refused to sign or to comply with their industry's code is treated in Jordan D. Hill, *Relationship of NRA to Government Contracts and Contracts Involving the Use of Government Funds,* N.R.A. Division of Review, *Work Materials No. 49* (Washington, 1936). The findings of the Henderson inquiry are presented in N.R.A. Research and Planning Division, Preliminary Report on Study of Regularization of Employment and Improvement of Labor Conditions in the Automobile Industry (Mimeographed; Washington, Jan. 23, 1935). The activities of the A.L.B. are summarized in Report of the Automobile Labor Board (Feb., 1935) and Final Report of the Automobile Labor Board Appointed by the President of the United States under the Terms of the Auto Labor Settlement of March 25, 1934 (Mimeographed; [Aug., 1935]).

The economic characteristics of the industry, a history of many of its concerns, and valuable statistical information, particularly on corporation profits, are given in Federal Trade Commission, *Report on Motor Vehicle Industry,* 76 Cong., 1 Sess., *House Document No. 468* (Washington, 1939). The N.R.A. is analyzed in *The National Recovery Administration, Report of the President's Committee of Industrial Analysis* (Washington, 1937).

Statistics

The wages and hours reports required of the automobile companies by the automobile code, which are available in the Records of the N.R.A. in the National Archives, are conveniently summarized in George Myrick, Jr., *et al.,* "An Economic Survey of the Automobile Industry" (1936), Section Three, p. 52, N.R.A. Box 8309. There is additional statistical information bearing on the automobile manufacturing industry in N.R.A. Boxes 655 and 676. The annual volumes of *Automobile Facts and Figures* (the exact titles vary), published by the A.M.A., and the issues of *Automotive Industries* contain a wealth of statistical data on the automobile industry in all its aspects. I have relied primarily on *Ward's 1939 Automotive Year Book* and the Henderson Report for figures on the share of the market of passenger cars and trucks held by the various automobile companies.

Among the many Bureau of Labor Statistics *Bulletins* and articles in the *Monthly Labor Review* of value to this study, the most important were: B.L.S., *Handbook of Labor Statistics* (1936 edition), *Bulletin No. 616* (Washington, 1936); B.L.S., *Wage Structure of the Motor Vehicle Industry, Bulletin No. 706* (Washington, 1942); N. A. Tolles and M. W. LaFever, "Wages, Hours, Employment, and Annual Earnings in the Motor Vehicle Industry, 1934," *Monthly Labor Review,* XLII (Mar., 1936), 521–53; and Herman B. Byer and John Anker, "A Review of Factory Labor Turn-Over, 1930 to 1936," *Monthly Labor Review,* XLV (July, 1937), 154–75. Productivity and unit labor cost figures for the combined motor vehicle industries are presented in B.L.S., *Productivity and Unit Labor Cost in Selected Manufacturing Industries, 1919–1940* (Washington, 1942).

The ethnic composition of the labor force in the combined motor vehicle industries and its occupational and geographical distribution at the beginning of the depression are given in U.S. Department of Commerce, Bureau of the Census, *Fifteenth Census of the United States, Manufactures: 1929*, 3 vols. (Washington, 1933), and *Fifteenth Census of the United States: 1930, Population*, Vols. III–V (Washington, 1932–33). The *Biennial Census of Manufactures* volumes provide figures on employment, value of the product, value added by manufacture, number of establishments, and aggregate wages and salaries for the motor vehicle and bodies and parts industries. The cost-of-living figures compiled by the National Industrial Conference Board are given in the monthly volumes for the N.R.A. era of the U.S. Department of Commerce, Bureau of Foreign and Domestic Commerce, *Survey of Current Business*. Some of the statistical information elsewhere available is conveniently summarized in Bureau of the Census, *Historical Statistics of the United States Colonial Times to 1957* (Washington, 1960).

Miscellaneous Published Sources

Few studies of significance have been published on the N.R.A. itself or on any of the codes. Although it was completed before the N.I.R.A. was declared unconstitutional, Leverett S. Lyon *et al.*, *The National Recovery Administration* (Washington, 1935), remains the best analysis of the N.R.A. and serves as a convenient point of reference for any study of the statute's ramifications. It tends to view the N.R.A. from the outside rather than the inside, however, and makes no attempt to evaluate its impact on individual industries. It should be supplemented by Charles Frederick Roos, *NRA Economic Planning* (Bloomington, Ind., 1937). There is a penetrating and sympathetic analysis of the N.R.A. which points the way to a necessary re-evaluation of the agency in Arthur M. Schlesinger, Jr., *The Age of Roosevelt: The Coming of the New Deal* (Boston, 1959). There are some references to the automobile code in Hugh S. Johnson, *The Blue Eagle from Egg to Earth* (New York, 1935), but Donald R. Richberg does not touch on the subject directly in *The Rainbow* (Garden City, New York, 1936), or *My Hero: The Indiscreet Memoirs of an Eventful but Unheroic Life* (New York, 1954). The President's relationship to the automobile code is analyzed in Sidney Fine, "President Roosevelt and the Automobile Code," *Mississippi Valley Historical Review*, XLV (June, 1958), 23–50. In his autobiography, *In Brief Authority* (Garden City, New York, 1962), Francis Biddle provides an interesting account of his service on the N.L.R.B. and makes some shrewd comments about President Roosevelt's views on the labor problem. The definitive study of the legislation of the New Deal pertaining to collective bargaining is Irving Bernstein, *The New Deal Collective Bargaining Policy* (Berkeley, 1950). Lewis L. Lorwin and Arthur Wubnig, *Labor Relations Boards: The Regulation of Collective Bargaining under the National Industrial Recovery Act* (Washington, 1935), although it was completed before the N.I.R.A. expired, is the best treatment of the labor boards spawned by Section 7(a) and Public Resolution 44.

The definitive history of the automobile industry in the first half of the twentieth century remains to be written, but there is much useful information in

Lawrence H. Seltzer, *A Financial History of the Automobile Industry* (Boston, 1928); Ralph C. Epstein, *The Automobile Industry* (Chicago, 1928); and John B. Rae, *American Automobile Manufacturers. The First Forty Years* (Philadelphia, 1959). In addition to these volumes and to the F.T.C. *Report on the Motor Vehicle Industry* noted above, there are satisfactory accounts of the economic structure of the industry in Simon N. Whitney, *Antitrust Policies: American Experience in Twenty Industries*, Vol. I (New York, 1958), and Donald A. Moore, "The Automobile Industry," in Walter Adams, ed., *The Structure of American Industry* (Revised ed.; New York, 1954). The history of the Ford Motor Company to 1933 has been competently and interestingly covered in Allan Nevins and Frank Ernest Hill, *Ford. The Times, the Man, the Company* (New York, 1954), and Nevins and Hill, *Ford. Expansion and Challenge, 1915–1933* (New York, 1957). The subject of Ford and the N.R.A. is examined in Sidney Fine, "The Ford Motor Company and the N.R.A.," *Business History Review*, XXXII (Winter, 1958), 353–85. The co-operative relationships among the automobile manufacturers during the code era are analyzed in W. Ellison Chalmers, "The Automobile Industry," in George Galloway *et al.*, *Industrial Planning under Codes* (New York, 1935). Theodore H. Smith, *The Marketing of Used Automobiles* (Columbus, Ohio, 1941), is a satisfactory discussion of the principal problem of the industry in the 1930's as the automobile dealers saw it.

There is a superb account of the American worker in the 1920's and in the Hoover era in Irving Bernstein, *The Lean Years: A History of the American Worker, 1920–1933* (Boston, 1960). The automobile workers in particular in the predepression era are treated in Robert W. Dunn, *Labor and Automobiles* (New York, 1929), but the pronounced left-wing bias of the author lessens the reliability of his work. Although primarily nonhistorical in character, William H. McPherson, *Labor Relations in the Automobile Industry* (Washington, 1940), sheds light on collective-bargaining issues in the industry following the establishment of the international union. More historical background is provided in McPherson and Anthony Lucheck, "Automobiles," in Twentieth Century Fund, *How Collective Bargaining Works* (New York, 1942).

The nature of industrial relations in the automobile industry between 1933 and 1935 is explored in the following articles by Sidney Fine: "The Origins of the United Automobile Workers, 1933–1935," *Journal of Economic History*, XVIII (Sept., 1958), 249–82; "The Toledo Chevrolet Strike of 1935," *Ohio Historical Quarterly*, LXVII (Oct., 1958), 326–56; and "Proportional Representation of Workers in the Auto Industry, 1934–1935," *Industrial and Labor Relations Review*, XII (Jan., 1959), 182–205. The A.F. of L. in the post-Gompers era is uncritically described in Philip Taft, *The A.F. of L. from the Death of Gompers* (New York, 1959). Professor Taft is one of the few persons who has been permitted to examine the minutes of the A.F. of L.'s Executive Council, and this has enhanced the value of his study. There is a more critical and analytical account of the A.F. of L. in the 1920's and 1930's in James O. Morris, *Conflict within the AFL: A Study of Craft versus Industrial Unionism, 1901–1938* (Ithaca, 1958). Edward Levinson's *Labor on the March* (New York, 1938), is an account of labor developments from 1933 to 1938 from a C.I.O. point of view. The chapter on the automobile industry in Walter Galenson's fine volume, *The CIO Challenge to the AFL* (Cambridge, Mass., 1960), is mainly concerned with the U.A.W. after the establishment of the international union, but it has some comments on earlier events as well. Like Taft, Galenson was permitted to examine the minutes of the A.F. of L. Executive Council. There are several chapters of interest in Milton Derber and Edwin Young, eds., *Labor and the New Deal* (Madison, 1957); the most valuable for this study were Bernard Karsh and Phillips L. Garman, "The Impact of the Political Left," and Richard C. Wilcock, "Industrial Management's Policies toward Unionism."

One of the best published accounts of the A.F. of L.'s efforts to organize the auto workers is Marjorie Ruth Clark, "The American Federation of Labor and Organization in the Automobile Industry since the Passage of the National Industrial Recovery Act," in *Essays in Social Economics in Honor of Jessica Blanche Peixotto* (Berkeley, 1935). The discussion at A.F. of L. conventions both before and after 1933 of the problem of organizing the automobile workers may be followed in the published *Proceedings* of these conventions. The *Proceedings of the First Constitutional Convention of the International Union, United Automobile Workers of America, 1935* (Detroit, n.d.), contains an account by Francis Dillon of his stewardship as the A.F. of L.'s national representative in the automobile industry. There is also some material of value for the 1933–1935 period in *Proceedings of the Second Convention of the International Union, United Automobile Workers of America, 1936* (Detroit, n.d.). A. J. Muste's *The Automobile Industry and Organized Labor* (Baltimore, [1936]), emphasizes developments in Toledo in which the Musteites played a part.

The only published history of the M.E.S.A. is Harry Dahlheimer, *A History of the Mechanics Educational Society of America in Detroit from Its Inception in 1933 through 1937* (Detroit, 1951). It is based on material in the Brown Collection and on newspaper sources. The M.E.S.A. strike of 1933 is treated in detail in Sidney Fine, "The Tool and Die Makers Strike of 1933," *Michigan History*, XLII (Sept., 1958), 297–323. Fred Thompson, *The I.W.W. Its First Fifty Years (1905–1955)* (Chicago, 1955), contains a Wobbly version of the activities of the I.W.W. in the automobile industry between 1933 and 1935. The author was the chairman of the I.W.W.'s General Executive Board and the editor of the *Industrial Worker*. Anthony Lucheck's "Company Unions, F.O.B. Detroit," *Nation*, CXLII (Jan. 15, 1936), 74–77, is an excellent short analysis of the automobile company unions and the A.L.B. bargaining agencies.

Miscellaneous Unpublished Material

There are three good unpublished accounts of automobile unionism in the N.R.A. period. The best of these, and one of the most understanding studies available of industrial relations in the automobile industry between 1933 and 1935, is W. Ellison Chalmers, "Collective Bargaining in the Automobile Industry" [1935], a copy of which is in the Littauer Industrial Relations Library of Harvard University. Chalmers was intimately connected with the events he described since he served as an assistant to both Collins and Dillon and was engaged by the Labor Advisory Board to study the automobile code with a view to its amendment. Unfortunately, he completed only eight of the seventeen chapters that he had originally projected. Edward A. Wieck, "The Automobile Workers under the NRA" (Aug., 1935), and Anthony Lucheck, "Labor Organizations in the Automobile Industry" [1936], include information on organizational efforts in the automobile industry that is nowhere else available. Both authors relied on interviews and documentary sources in the composition of their accounts. The Wieck manuscript is in the possession of Mrs. Edward A. Wieck, the Lucheck manuscript in Mr. Lucheck's possession. There are chapters on the threatened automobile strike of March 1934 and on the Electric Auto-Lite strike in William Haskett, "Ideological Radicals, the American Federation of Labor and Federal Labor Policy in the Strikes of 1934" (Ph.D. thesis, University of California, Los Angeles, 1957). George D. Blackwood, "The United Automobile Workers of America, 1935–51" (Ph.D. thesis, University of Chicago, 1951), has a brief account of events before 1935. The distinction between the company union and the local independent union is developed in an historical context in Leo Troy, "The Course of Company and Local Independent Unions" (Ph.D. thesis, Columbia University, 1958). Lloyd H. Bailer, "Negro Labor in the Automobile Industry" (Ph.D. thesis, University of Michigan, [1943]), explains why the Negro automobile worker was unresponsive to the appeals of A.F. of L. organizers.

Significant economic aspects of the automobile industry are capably dealt with in Paul H. Banner, "Competition in the Automobile Industry" (Ph.D. thesis, Harvard University, 1953), and George F. Chambers, "Manufacturer-Dealer Relationships in the Automobile Industry" (Ph.D. thesis, University of Buffalo, 1958). The efforts of the automobile manufacturers to stabilize automobile employment are considered from an A.M.A. point of view in Edward J. Stevens, "A Quarter of a Century of Progress in Employment Stabilization in the Automobile Industry" (1947). The same subject is explored in C. Parker Anderson, "Regularization of Employment and Incomes in the Automobile Industry" (1946). There are copies of both studies in the Bureau of Industrial Relations Library of the University of Michigan. There is some material on the conferences called by George L. Berry in Ellis Wayne Hawley, "The New Deal and the Problem of Monopoly, 1934–1938: A Study in Economic Schizophrenia" (Ph.D. thesis, University of Wisconsin, 1958).

William E. Leuchtenburg, *Franklin D. Roosevelt and the New Deal, 1932–1940* (New York, 1963), and Allan Nevins and Frank Ernest Hill, *Ford. Decline and Rebirth, 1933–1962* (New York, 1963), appeared after my manuscript had been sent to the printer.

INDEX

(The superior figures indicate notes on the pages specified.)